FIFTY YEARS OF NEW JAPAN

VOLUME II

FIFTY YEARS OF NEW JAPAN

(KAIKOKU GOJŪNEN SHI)

COMPILED BY

COUNT SHIGÉNOBU ŌKUMA

LATE PRIME MINISTER AND MINISTER FOR FOREIGN AFFAIRS

ENGLISH VERSION

EDITED BY

MARCUS B. HUISH

VOLUME II

SECOND EDITION

LONDON

SMITH, ELDER, & CO., 15 WATERLOO PLACE, S.W.

1910

KRAUS REPRINT CO.
New York
1970

LC 10-35331

CONTENTS

OF

THE SECOND VOLUME

APPENDICES

PAGE

FIFTY YEARS OF NEW JAPAN

I

THE JAPANESE LANGUAGE

Katsuji Fujioka, Assistant-Professor, Tōkyō
Imperial University

Its Origin

The pride which a man takes in his mother tongue is confined neither to race nor to country, and the Japanese language, like others, has been lauded to Heaven by its devoted students, who assert its divine origin and its superiority over every other in the world. But this very reverence has unfortunately impeded scientific inquiry, for we could not, holding these views, study impartially the relations between our native tongue and other languages.

But the advent of the Méiji era saw the necessity for such a research, especially as we were impelled thereto by the efforts of foreign inquirers ; so at last, in 1886, a course of comparative philology was provided in the Imperial University, which contributed not a little to the study of our mother tongue.

Foreigners had, before this, not been idle in their researches. In 1820 Klaproth assigned the Japanese language to the wide family of Ural-Altaic tongues. In 1857 Boller published the same opinion, and, considering that our language bore a close resemblance to the North Samojedic language, gave some concrete examples—a view which found many advocates. Among these, Gabelentz dwelt on the resemblance between Japanese and Manchurian, while Aston scientifically compared the languages of Japan and Korea, and made public the result of his study. Recently

Klaproth and Boller— Ural-Altaic family— North Samojedic family. Aston and Gabelentz.

(February 1906) a Russian savant, by name Pozdneyeff delivered a lecture in the Peers' Club in Tōkyō on the kinship of our language and that of Mongolia, and explained how exactly alike were the post-positions of the two languages. All these views threw some light on the genealogy of our mother tongue. Though Lowell published his ' A Comparison of the Japanese and Burmese Languages ' in 1891, while others assigned the parentage of the Japanese language to the Indo-Germanic family, at present the advocates of the Ural-Altaic theory are gaining ground.

Lowell's views and the advocates of the Indo-Germanic family.

Nothing can as yet be said to have been satisfactorily proved, for many scholars still take divergent views, and the origin of our mother tongue must consequently be said to be an unknown quantity, although the probabilities point to the ultimate adoption of the Ural-Altaic theory.

I.—From Prehistoric Periods to the End of the Héian Court

As it is impossible to ascertain the primitive form of our mother tongue without touching on its origin or genealogy, which is, at best, uncertain and obscure in the present stage of investigation, we must here rest content with enumerating the different views in regard to the kinship or relation that may exist between our tongue and the Korean, Chinese, and Ainu as well as the Sanskrit languages. We shall also consider how our language, since it became an independent one, has come under the influences of others, and what were the stages of its internal development, &c. It has always to be remembered that intercourse with China had a most remarkable effect upon the Japanese tongue. Chinese characters and Chinese books were freely introduced into Japan, syllabaries of the two kinds, *kata-kana* and *hira-kana*, were framed after ideographs, and Chinese words became mixed with the native vocabulary by thousands.

Relationship with other tongues.

There are not many scholars as yet who are bold enough to affirm that any original similarity or kinship existed between Japanese and Korean, but this view is rapidly gaining ground in learned circles, and we cannot but pay respect, as the pioneer

Relationship with Korean.

of the theory, to Mr. Aston, whose essay, entitled 'A Comparative Study of the Japanese and Korean Languages,' appeared in 1879 in the *Journal of the Royal Asiatic Society*. That our philologists are inclining to this theory is due to his indirect influence. Moreover, the kinship of the two nations is being proved in many other respects also—such as history, legislation, customs, &c.

But we cannot find in these two languages any such root similarities as show themselves, for instance, in those of the Indo-Germanic family. This lends doubt as to the original oneness. Moreover, when we realize that even the advocates of the theory that the two are branches of one and the same tongue cannot explain why there should exist such a wide chasm between them, we cannot but be cautious in accepting the theory.

The original similarity true or false.

If we examine this doubtful point by the light of history, we find that in 463 A.D. the Government appointed interpreters for purposes of intercourse with Korea. In 680 A.D. an envoy from Shiragi in Korea visited the Court and brought with him three students of languages. In 761 A.D., as there were many Korean emigrants from Shiragi who settled and became naturalized in Japan, the Government ordered that twenty youths from the localities where the Koreans had settled should study their language. In 813 A.D. the tongue of the Shiragi folk was taught in Tsushima. This shows that many centuries ago these supposed two branches of one family were so distinct that it was impossible for persons using their speech to understand one another. To prove their original sameness we must go to prehistoric periods, where no clue is available to guide us, and all efforts are likely to end in vain.

Certain it is, however, that intercourse between the two peoples began in the mythical age. Ancient chronicles state that Susanō-no-Mikoto often travelled to Korea. The 'Record of Japan' ('*Nihon Shoki*') affirms that in the eleventh year of the Emperor Sujin's reign (87 B.C.) 'many foreigners became naturalized'; and in 86 B.C. 'foreigners [1] came with interpreters, while naturalization went on everywhere.' In 33 B.C. the

Intercourse between Korea and Japan.

---

[1] The late Professor Mayori Kurokawa understands by 'foreigners' the Koreans.

' Record ' says that the Kingdom of Mimana sent Sona-Kashichi as envoy to pay homage to the Emperor of Japan. These references show that the two nations were associated from olden times, and later history indicates that this friendship was maintained. Hence, if the two tongues were not one in their origin, they must have become considerably intermixed.

The existence or non-existence of letters in the mythical age.

Had we any letters or characters before the introduction of the square Chinese ideographs ? This question as to the existence of ' letters of the mythical age ' has been widely discussed and has some connection with the question of Korean characters. The letters which scholars regard as belonging to the mythical age were various in kind, but are nevertheless adduced to prove the hypothesis. The so-called *Abiru-moji*, which according to the *Nichibunden* consisted of forty-seven letters, are very much like the *Ommun* or Korean popular letters. Hence some scholars affirm that the Koreans imitated our letters and framed the *Ommun*, while others maintain an exactly opposite opinion, and declare that the advocates of the mythical age theory have robbed the Koreans of their invention of letters and based a false hypothesis on the theft. Then there is a set of characters called ' letters of the *Hi-jin*,' namely, the people of the two provinces of Hizén and Higo, and these characters are indicated as showing that the above two hypotheses furnish no satisfactory proof as to the existence of primitive Japanese letters. There was also another set of letters called ' the letters of the *Satsu-jin*,' or the people of Satsuma. But we cannot now ascertain even their forms, and so cannot possibly call them ' mythical characters.'

No characters in the mythical age.

In fine, these hypotheses are not of much value from a scientific point of view to prove the existence of primitive writing. We can only say that there may have been in use characters which had been coined from the Korean letters, and that even these were confined to the use of some districts only. Those who advocated the hypothesis of mythical letters were scholars of the Ashikaga period and after. In their narrow minds it seemed a shame that we should have had no original writing of our own, and they tried to produce specimens of the supposed primitive characters.

We are thus obliged to deny the existence of the old letters, and to say that, if there were any characters in use, they lacked the characteristics of a *national* alphabet.

It is hardly necessary to affirm here that there is nothing in common between the Japanese and Chinese languages. Sounds, forms, constructions, roots of words, order of words, &c., are all different, so that it is altogether useless to discuss their kinship. Yet some maintain an opposite view, alleging that the languages of Japan, Korea, Manchuria, and China were originally one and the same, but gradually became separated, and for proof they point to the fact that many root-words are similar. They maintain that the Japanese, Koreans, and Manchurians continued to lead nomadic lives long after the Chinese had advanced to the agricultural stage, and that the former, roaming as they did, necessarily changed the construction of sentences as well as the forms and order of words, while the Chinese naturally kept their tongue in its pure primitive state.

Comparative study of the Japanese and Chinese languages.

Edkins was the originator of this theory. His work, entitled ' On the Old Japanese Vocabulary,' [1] discusses the point at much length, but the examples which he furnishes to prove his theory are not convincing. For instance, our word for ' to skin ' or ' to strip off ' is *hagu*, and the Chinese use *pak* with the same meaning. We call a horse *uma*, and the Chinese say *mā*, &c. From this resemblance it might be inferred by hasty investigators that the two languages had come down from one and the same forefather, but we must bear in mind that the close intercourse and friendship between the two nations must have caused an interchange of many words and expressions. As we freely imported Chinese civilization and learning, so it was quite natural, nay inevitable, that we should have adopted an abundance of Chinese words and phrases. Hence the existence of a few similar words in the two tongues can hardly prove the validity of the Edkin theory, and we cannot possibly endorse his arguments.

In 215 A.D. a Korean prince, by the name of Achiki, visited the Imperial Court, and in the following year Wani, a Korean envoy, came to pay homage, bringing with him the Confucian ' Analects ' and the '*Senjimon*' ('One Thousand Character

Introduction of Chinese characters.

[1] *Journal of the Royal Asiatic Society of Great Britain and Ireland.*

Composition'). It is said that this was the beginning of the importation of Chinese characters into our country, but actual intercourse between the two nations had originated at a much earlier period. Relations with Korea are indicated by the tours of Susanō-no-Mikoto, and history tells us that many Japanese went to the over-sea kingdom in 20 B.C. Nobutomo Ban asserts, in his '*Dokushi Sétsujutsu*,' that Amé-no-Hihoko, a naturalized Korean prince, first introduced the Chinese characters in the reign of the Emperor Kōréi (290–215 B.C.). If we cannot agree with him, we can at least affirm that the Chinese characters had already been introduced in the reign of the Emperor Sujin (97–30 B.C.). So far as we can see, there is no necessary connection whatever between the introduction of the ' Analects ' and that of ideographs; and although history says nothing about the latter, it is more reasonable to hold that letters had been imported before Wani paid homage to the Imperial Court.

The question of pronunciation. We may assume, however, that our people began to read Chinese books systematically after that prince came to the Japanese Court, and the question naturally arises, What kind of pronunciation did we adopt ? Was it the *Han* pronunciation or that called *Wu* ? We read that Kudara (in Korea) sent Dan-Yōji, ' Doctor of the Five Classics,' to our Court in 513 A.D., and that in 516 A.D. it was requested that he should be replaced by Kō-Ammo, another 'Doctor of the Five Classics.' From this we infer that the pronunciation must have been a Korean modification or corruption, not a pure Chinese one. But Korea had introduced the Chinese characters with the doctrine of Buddhism from Southern China in the time of Chienwen and Hsianwu, Emperors of the East Tsin dynasty. Hence it is reasonable to conclude that the first pronunciation which we learned was Koreanized *Wu* sounds. Hakuséki Arai maintains, however, that we must have been taught first the *Han* pronunciation at the time when Wani came to us, while the *Wu* sounds were afterwards introduced, accompanying the Buddhist religion. Norinaga Motoori, on the other hand, asserts that the *Han* sounds did not come into vogue until the time of the Emperor Kimméi (540–71 A.D.). The authors of the '*Wakun-no-shiori*,' the '*Shōkōhatsu*,' and other works all agree in bringing down the introduction of the *Han* sounds to a much later date, namely, the time when our Government dispatched envoys to the Court of Sui (607 A.D.), as the then reigning dynasty of China was called. The '*Sanon Séigi*' brings it down still further, and affirms that there existed only *Wu* sounds in Japan until the time of the Empress Gwammyō (708–14 A.D.). It also states that no *Han* sounds were heard in our country before the reign of Kwammai (782–805 A.D.). Although scholars thus held different views as to the date of the introduction of the *Han* sounds, yet they all appear to be agreed that these sounds came later to our country than the *Wu* sounds.

Although the *Wu* sounds were the first to prevail, yet our pronunciation seems to have been by no means the same everywhere. According to the period when a teacher arrived, and the country from whence he came, as well as the pupils' ability to catch pronunciation, many varieties of sound were naturally produced. This explains why we occasionally find inconsistency of sounds in the '*Kojiki*' (712 A.D.), although the *Wu* sounds are used almost throughout the book. The '*Nihongi*' (720 A.D.) uses both sounds, while the '*Manyōshū*,' being a compilation of the writings of different ages, seems to have used both methods of pronunciation indiscriminately, regardless even of either hard or soft sounds. We also find in the '*Wamyōshō*,' the '*Shinsén Jikyō*,' and some other works a mixture of different sounds. This is the reason why some scholars believe that we had formerly some specially ancient sounds, as well as the so-called '*Koma* sounds,' in addition to the two principal *Han* and *Wu* pronunciations.

Other sounds besides *Han* and *Wu*.

In studying the pronunciation of Chinese letters and words, we corrupted it not a little, whether it were the *Han* sounds or the *Wu* sounds. But it is a remarkable fact that we still observed the old distinctions which go by the name of the 'modifications of three sounds' (labial, dental, and guttural). These distinctions were, however, passing away towards the end of the Héian Court. If one compares the method of transcribing our sounds by means of Chinese characters, as found in the '*Wamyōshō*,' the '*Manyōshū*,' &c., which appeared before this age, with that found in the '*Ruijū Myōgishō*,'

Modifications of three sounds.

the '*Iroha Jiruishō*,' &c., we find some evidence to prove what has been above stated.

Kana.   Let us next glance at the development of our *kana* syllabary. When the Chinese ideograph entered our country, we learned how to express our ideas with letters which conveyed the same meaning to the two nations, without regard to any difference in other linguistic respects, and at the same time we also used these characters merely as symbols for our own sounds. This latter method was in reality equivalent to the *Lito* of Korea in origin and use, and we find it generally used in our old works like the '*Kojiki*' and the '*Manyōshū*,' whence these symbols came to be called the *Manyō-kana*. They are sometimes designated as the *mana* (true letters), inasmuch as they retain the true forms of real Chinese characters. But the more we used these cumbersome symbols the more we realized their complexity and practical inconvenience. This gradually led to the invention of our two forms of *kana*, the *hira-kana* and the *kata-kana*. The former are abbreviations, or cursive forms of the original square characters, while the latter are nothing but parts of these characters, and are consequently called *kata-kana*, or the 'fragmentary syllabary.'

The hira-kana.   The *hira-kana*, known by other designations such as *sō-kana* (cursive-syllabary), *iroha-kana* (mother-syllabary), or *onna-kana* (women-syllabary), are no doubt simplified forms in cursive style of the square characters. Although tradition ascribes the honour of their invention to Kōbō-Daishi (the great Buddhist Kūkai), yet that is an error due to the fact of his skilful penmanship. There had been very many forms of that kind of *kana*, and even to this day we often meet with various *kana* letters in old documents, which goes to prove that the *hira-kana* was not the invention of any one individual. The law of natural selection had been busy here, and only those forms fittest to survive were allowed to live and take the commonest fixed shapes.

The kata-kana.   The *kata-kana*, or *yamato-kana* (Japanese *kana*), are, as stated above, nothing but the 'radicals' of the square characters, and the honour of invention is ascribed to Kibi-no-Mabi. There is, however, no historical basis to this popular belief. Here again the survival of the fittest must have taken place, and

eventually the present table of *kata-kana* came into existence.
Different forms of *kata-kana*, which we often find in old documents, bear witness against the hypothesis that any single
person was the designer.

When the Chinese characters began to be widely used in
our country, we also began to coin ideographs analogous to
them. These are called the *Yamato* (Japanese) letters, and
of course they cannot be found in any Chinese dictionary.

Sanskrit, which is a branch of the Indo-Germanic family, Sanskrit.
can have no original connection whatever with our language
if it belongs to the Ural-Altaic family. This fact is acknowledged by all. Therefore, if we find words in our language
which bear some resemblance to Sanskrit, they must be solely
a result of later intercourse, when Hindoos, or Chinese who had
some knowledge of Hindoo learning, visited our country, or else
when our countrymen met Hindoos in China or elsewhere.
This is especially seen to be the case when we realize that these
Hindoo-like words came into vogue from the time of the Nara
Court, when Buddhism controlled the country, and, moreover,
history offers no evidence of the two languages having anything
in common. Some Sanskrit words, doubtless, were introduced
into our language after the time of the Nara Court, yet most
of them, coming with the Buddhist Sutras, which had been
transliterated into Chinese, and being read in our own way or
much corrupted, now present forms quite different from their
originals. Nevertheless, the influence of Sanskrit on our
vocabulary and phraseology was great.

Our table of *Gojū-on* (the fifty sounds) was no doubt formed Dēvanā-
after the pattern of the Dēvanāgarī. It is true that some claim gari.
the table to be a pure Japanese invention, and it is also true
that there has been more than one system of arranging sounds.
Yet what we have at present was doubtless arranged after the
Sanskrit model. We cannot, however, determine exactly when
this table was formed. Some say that it must have been after
the Genkéi era (877–84 A.D.), while others believe that it came
into existence after the two forms of our *kana* had become fixed.

In a book said to be part of the '*Zaitōki*' ('Records of Sojourn
in China') we find Kōbō, the learned teacher, explaining the
pronunciation of Sanskrit by means of Japanese sounds ; and

we also know that Jikaku Daishi (another great priest) learned Sanskrit from Tsunrä of Tang at first, and studied subsequently under Ratnacandramati from Southern India, and acquired great skill in its pronunciation.   In the Genkéi period a priest called Annen wrote eight volumes of ' *Shittanzō* ' (' Sanskrit Grammar '). From these we may reasonably infer that the study of Sanskrit was very popular among the priestly class in the ninth century, and the table of fifty sounds must have been constructed at that period.

Relation to the Ainu dialect.

The root relations of the Ainu and Japanese languages have often been discussed, but as yet, unfortunately, no satisfactory conclusion has been reached.   Mr. Batchelor, following the views held by Professor Chamberlain, asserts that there is no radical or original relationship between the two tongues, and yet recognizes the uniformity of roots, and produces examples in support of that view.   Some of these, however, are far from convincing, while others must be looked upon as Japanese words introduced into the Ainu language.

Mutual adoption of words.

History tells us that the Ainu tribe lived in the main island before the Japanese came to the country, and subsequently various relations sprang up between the two.   From this we can easily infer that there must have been mutual adoption of words into their respective languages.   Many words standing for notions relating to civilization were given by us, while some of our names of plants and minerals, as well as geographical terms, belonged to the Ainu vocabulary.   About the Ainu geographical names Chamberlain made careful investigations. He even showed the rules governing the transition of sounds between the two tongues, and, explaining many geographical names by reference to Ainu words, sought to prove that the Ainu tribe had once spread through the middle districts and Kyūshū.   But it seems to me that Chamberlain goes too far. When this view appeared Dr. Yonékichi Miyaké took pains to refute it in detail satisfactorily.

Internal changes of the language.

We have now treated the original relations of our language with others, and also the influence which the latter exercised on the former.   We have now to discuss the phenomena of words appearing in old books, together with the history of philological progress before our tongue took definite form, as well as the later fact of internal change and development. It is not possible to state these changes and improvements without referring to the influence of other languages, but let us for the moment dispense with the idea of foreign influence as much as possible in order to explain the internal alterations.

The ' *Kojiki*,' the ' *Nihongi*,' the ' *Manyōshū*,' the ' *Norito*,' the ' *Semmyō*,' the ' *Shinsén Jikyō*,' and the ' *Wamyō Ruimushō*,' all serve as important materials for investigating changes of words in different periods. The forms which were in vogue before the era of the Nara Court, that is to say, in the primitive ages, we have no means of ascertaining, except by the study of songs which remain in the two first-named old records. We shall, for the sake of convenience, treat these prehistoric words from three points of view : namely, phonology, parts of speech, and syntax.

As regards sounds, conflicting opinions among scholars make us hesitate to believe anything. We become still more sceptical when we find that the table of fifty sounds, once so widely credited, is now generally believed not to contain all the sounds of the time when it first came into use. With regard to vowels, can we be certain that there existed no other vowels except the five ? Were there no long vowels or nasal vowels ? What about the history of diphthongs ? Again, as to consonants, was the old sound *shi* or *si* ? Did the sounds *ti* and *tu* exist before our present *chi* and *tsu* ? Had we formerly the sounds *yi, ye, wi,* and *wu* ? How should we regard ' the *p*-sounds theory,' which maintains that the *h* sound of to-day came from ancient *p* ? These topics have frequently been discussed by foreigners and Japanese, but with no satisfactory result. We must still hesitate to endorse the opinion of the old scholars who deny the existence of the sonants, palatalization, labialization, and gemination in times past. But on scientific grounds we can found a few facts to show that in Japanese no two different consonants can be combined in one syllable ; that no word can end in a consonant; that very few words begin with sonants or a liquid *r* ; that in general the soft sounds were developed later than the hard sounds, and so forth.

We cannot clearly decipher the history of our parts of

Phonology.

speech. There are several opinions. For instance, some believe those empty words called *tenioha* to have come from full words such as nouns ; some declare adjectives and verbs to have but one and the same origin ; and some hold that the verbs which belong to other classes must be reduced back to the first conjugation, namely, to that of the four orders ; while others maintain the dualistic theory of ' the four-order conjugation ' plus ' the lower two-order conjugation ' ; and yet others try to prove monism by taking ' the irregular conjugation of the *na* column' as most primitive. Thus, though some opinions are plausible, few are yet in agreement on the subject.

The Japanese themselves did not originally distinguish the parts of speech as they now exist. That we have eight, nine, or ten parts of speech is really owing to the influence of foreign grammar. But in the old prayers and Imperial messages we find *tenioha* (particles) and inflections of adjectives and verbs, as well as auxiliaries, written in a much smaller hand and a little to the right—which fact no doubt shows a distinction between full words and empty words. Some years later we find the *tenioha* discussed in the ' *Étsumokushō* ' by Fujiwara-no-Mototoshi, in the ' *Yakumo Mishō* ' by Juntokuin, in the ' *Tenioha Taigaishō* ' by Fujiwara-no-Téika, &c. But what they call *tenioha* include words which should be classed as auxiliaries, and yet are counted as post-positions (i.e. *tenioha* in the strict sense of the term), showing how imperfect was the

former idea relating to the distinction of parts of speech. The substantive comes first, the predicate follows, and, if an object is used, it stands before the verb which governs it. The modifiers precede the modified, while empty words always follow full words. Nominatives are very often omitted. Sex is never attributed to inanimate objects. Conjunctions are but few in number, and not much used, while the *tenioha* and terminal inflections of auxiliaries serve as connectives. Accordingly a sentence may be strung out to an almost infinite length. These are the characteristics of our tongue.

The *tenioha*, which served as case-endings of substantives, were frequently dropped before the time of the Nara Court. In this period the *kakari-musubi* (concord between inflected terminals and preceding particles) was not so strictly observed as in the Héian period. The '*Kotoba-no-Tamanoo*,' vol. vii, gives several examples of irregular conclusive forms and treats them as the old fashion belonging to the primitive age. From this we may safely infer that these technicalities of concord were developed in the era of the Héian Court.

But the most remarkable words of that period are the so-called *makura-kotoba*, i.e. ' pillow words.' For instance, *hisakata no* in the phrase *hisakata no sora* (the everlasting heaven, or, as some suggest, the sunshine-direction sky), *tori ga naku* in *tori ga naku Azuma* (the east where the cock crows), and *ashi ga chiru* in *ashi ga chiru Naniwa* (Naniwa where the reeds fall), are pillow words. As to the origin of these words there are two hypotheses : one maintains that they are simply ornaments invented for the sake of harmony and rhyme, while the other holds that they were at first useful adjuncts to distinguish words having the same or similar sounds but different senses, though they had come to be mere euphemistical additions in the time of the Nara Court. Be that as it may, they are undoubtedly a unique production of that age, and a peculiar phenomenon in our tongue. They are now used in verse only.

II.—The Periods of the Kamakura and Ashikaga Reigns

The periods that followed the enlightened age of the Héian Court were full of disturbances and wars, and consequently literature declined, orthography was corrupted, the written style became confused with the Chinese classical style, and even common speech began to be altered, thus giving rise to the dissimilar dialects of the western and eastern capitals. As to foreign tongues, we imported what are called the ' Tang sounds ' with the Zen sect of Buddhism. The study of Chinese phonetics also began at this period. These are almost the only facts in this age worth mentioning.

The original form of our language is seen in old prayers and Imperial commands. Ever since the time of the importation of Buddhism, Chinese classics had flourished. The seventeen articles of Prince Shōtoku's Constitution and the laws of

Blending of the Japanese and Chinese classics.

the Taika era were written in classical Chinese style. The Emperors Saga and Nimmyō were so absorbed in the study of that literature that they even edited collections of home-made Chinese poems. In the meantime the native literature showed wonderful development. Such masterpieces as the '*Takétori Monogatari*,' the '*Utsubo Monogatari*,' and the '*Genji Monogatari*' appeared. But even these original works were under the influence of the Chinese classics. Nor are the Imperial commands, which serve as a model of the old native style, entirely free from a tint of the Celestial Empire. But when Emperor Uda abolished the practice of sending a special envoy to China (called *Kentōshi*), Chinese literature began to decline in Japan, and during the period of the Kamakura Government both literatures lost their special characteristics and became blended into a mixed style. The '*Gempéi-séisuiki*' and the '*Taihéiki*,' for instance, are written in what we call the complex style of Japanese and Chinese classics.

We may, however, notice in this period changes of idiom and the ascendancy of the eastern dialect, which now began to be used in legal and political documents as well as in literature.

Mixing of the two dialects.

We shall here say nothing about the language used in the mythical age, but the dialect used in the time of the Nara and Héian Courts was that of the Kinai (Kyōto, Ōsaka, and their neighbourhood). It was considered the standard, and our literature was built upon this base, all other dialects being looked down on as vulgar and unrefined. The '*Manyōshū*' and the '*Kokinshū*' (905 A.D.) bear testimony to this fact. In these we find a set of songs written in other dialects and classed under the name of '*Azuma Uta*,' or ' Songs of the East,' contempt for these strange dialects being thus indicated. It is true that this ' standard speech ' continued to be one of the greatest and most influential forms in our language, yet the eastern dialect began to acquire value in proportion to the rise of the two houses of Minamoto and Taira and the establishment of the Kamakura Government. That the standard dialect was thus influenced is seen from history. The '*Taihéiki*' states that *samurai* from Kamakura came to Kyōto in numbers; they ridiculed the words employed by the Court nobles, and the latter began to use the eastern dialect. In short, a special

dialect was formed out of the two, and we can see it in the
works of the priests at Kamakura, which were published
between 1394 and 1477, and in other volumes, such as the
'*Mikawa Monogatari*,' the '*Shaséki Shū*,' the '*Kyōgén Ki*,'
and the ' *Setsuyō Shū*.'

We often find Tang sounds side by side with *Han* and *Wu* *Tang
sounds. This is a form of Chinese pronunciation which came sounds.*
to our country with the Zen sect of Buddhism. At that time
we already had what were called Sung sounds, but these very
probably were only another name for the same thing. China
was then under the Sung dynasty, and our national intercourse with her was close. In 1171 Kakua, a famous priest,
came back from China, and in 1191 Yéisai, another priest
of renown, returned home, bringing back with them the
Tang sounds. In 1306 the ' *Shūbun Inryaku* ' (' Collection
of Sounds '), a work by Kokwan-Zenji (a priest), taught the
Tang sounds by means of *kana*, and all later works of a
similar character pursued the same method. In the Muromachi
era the priests of Kyōto were addicted to poetry and the
tea ceremony, and flattered the Shōgun assiduously, while,
at the same time, their influence among the people was also
great. Hence the Tang sounds, which these parasites greatly
valued, began to be mixed with the every-day language of the
ordinary people and obtained firm root in our mother tongue.

A book of Chinese phonetics was first introduced in the *Chinese
reign of the Emperor Kaméyama, but Kūkai, the renowned phonetics.*
priest, had previously discussed the matter. He went to
China in the reign of Te Tsung of the Tang dynasty, and
having mastered the phonetics, came home and published the
' *Bunkyō Hifuron*,' which treated of the ' four tones ' of
Chinese characters. Henceforth this study was carried on in
our country, but it attracted little notice. In the era of Bunyéi
(1264–74) a priest of the Tengyōin at Nara found at the
bottom of a chest an old volume, which was none other than
a phonetic text, but no one could comprehend what it was about,
except a priest called Shimpan, who understood the Sanskrit
phonology, and he gave translation marks to the book and
edited it. A little later (in 1306) Kokwan Zenji (a priest)
published the ' *Kōyéki Sanjūin* ' and explained the rules for

pronunciation. In the Kyōroku era (1528–31) Kiyowara-no-Nobukata reprinted and published the book of Shimpan. It gave much impulse to Chinese phonetics, and several editions of the work were called for (1772–80), but most of them, except the ' Kyōroku ' and 'Éiroku ' editions, were hasty, and consequently worthless, reproductions.

Sanskrit.   The classics of the old Hindoos were introduced to us through the Chinese ; and, at the time of the South and North dynasties, a priest called Dōgén published his 'Hattenjōshō,' which explained the declension of nouns. Besides this, we have Yūkwai's (1345–1416) 'Shittangakki Kikigaki,' and Chōkaku's (1346–1410) 'Shittan Ketchakushō,' &c. Thenceforth the study of Sanskrit flourished.

III.—THE TOYOTOMI AND TOKUGAWA PERIODS

The western and eastern dialects.   From the time when the Ashikaga Shōgunate came into power the influence of the eastern dialect (Yédo dialect) had been gradually increasing, till the Tokugawa Government brought it to a state of paramount importance. As the literary language the western dialect (Ōsaka dialect) had held almost the sole monopoly, but during the Genroku and the Kyōho eras (1688–1735) the eastern dialect entered the domain of *belles lettres*, and thereafter continuously imparted lustre to our literature.

Portu-guese.   About this time Japan came under the influence of European languages. The Portuguese were the first to open up trade with us, and as the civilizations of the two countries were of different types, we naturally lacked many words which they possessed. This led to the adoption of Portuguese, and we find many names of articles of every-day use and technical terms relating to Christianity which were taken from their language. So, too, Portuguese missionaries studied our tongue and wrote many dictionaries and works on grammar. Some Christian books were rendered into Japanese and written with Roman characters. Several fragments of these old documents still remain, and are invaluable as furnishing a clue to the study of the ancient forms of our language—at least so far as concerned the dialects that prevailed in Nagasaki and its neighbourhood. Sir Ernest Satow's ' The Jesuit Mission Press in Japan,' which was nothing less than a large collection of occasional reports dispatched by the missionaries to their mother country between 1591 and 1610, is also very valuable for its scientific research.

As we added many Portuguese words to our vocabulary in **Spanish.** the course of this intercourse, we also adopted not a few Spanish words on account of their association with the Far East. As early as 1610 the Spaniards edited at Manila a Japanese and Spanish dictionary and some other similar works.

The Dutch tongue gave us a key to the rich secret **Dutch.** vault of Western science. In 1720 the Shōgun Yoshimuné granted permission to study foreign books of science, though the Government at that time professed the exclusion policy and put everything foreign under the ban. The fact was that the Shōgun highly admired the Dutch for their knowledge of astronomy. This led to a luxuriant growth of foreign science and literature in the native soil of Japan, and not only European technical terms but also numerous words of common use crept into our vocabulary. Many works on the Japanese language and its grammar were also printed in Dutch.

English, by lending us some of its valuable stores, gave to **English.** our tongue a finishing touch, especially as we came into con-tact with the material civilizations of both hemispheres. In 1862 we had an English-Japanese dictionary, and a few years later (1865) we had the same kind of work, popularly known as the ' Satsuma Edition.' These were the pioneers of the English language, destined to flourish throughout the empire in subsequent decades.

Although French men-of-war came with the British vessels **French.** to the Loochoo Isles in the Kōka era (1846) to seek for commercial relations, and although mutual intercourse has continued from then up to the present time, their language has done nothing more than give us a few words, such as ' chapeau,' ' champagne,' &c.

Our intercourse with the Russians is of remote origin. At **Russian.** Nagasaki and Matsumayé several students devoted themselves to the study of that language, yet it had no influence whatever on our tongue.

German.

    Dr. Siebold, a German who came to Japan in 1823 as a Dutch officer, contributed not a little to our knowledge of natural history and medicine. But at that time we were busily learning the medical art and science of the Dutch, so the immediate influence of Siebold's native tongue was virtually confined to inducing students of Dutch to study a new European language. But anyone who knows how profoundly German terms entered into our medical world, to the exclusion of the Dutch as well as other languages at large, will scarcely deny that events have crowned the patient endeavours of that old physician. The German tongue, however, did not do much to improve our common speech.

Chinese, Sanskrit, and Korean.

    The national relations between Japan and China were very close, and thus modern Chinese words came with imported goods, and even to this day we find many words of the Celestial Empire incorporated in the dialects of Kyūshū and its neighbourhood. In the scientific world the science of Chinese phonetics flourished, and inspired many works in that line. But it is to be regretted that the bad effects of that teaching were also remarkable. For instance, their rules for reducing sounds (*hansétsu-hō*) were much abused and corrupted. In the meantime the study of Sanskrit showed great improvement and progress, so that pupils were able to comprehend its minute details. As to the Korean language, it made no impression on our mother tongue, though some useful dictionaries by Koreans appeared during this period.

IV.—THE MÉIJI ERA

The Tōkyō dialect.

    The Yédo dialect which flourished under the Tokugawa Shōgunate is now the dialect of the Imperial metropolis. The dialects of all parts of the empire grafted upon this form of speech now constitute the Tōkyō dialect, which is steadily spreading throughout the land with the increase of organs of communication and with the growing perfection of educational equipment. Thus the criterion by which our language is measured may properly be sought in the dialect of the metropolis.

    The seeds of Western civilization sown during previous eras

began to bear fruit with the Restoration, and our modern language of the Méiji era has become exceedingly rich. We adopted technical terms from the respective countries which contributed to our knowledge of their particular sciences. Many common words also became naturalized, and the syntax of our day is very different from what it was formerly. Among foreign languages English has exerted the greatest influence upon our tongue. Hundreds of English words are intermingled with our daily vocabulary. Not a few signboards and trademarks are written in English. There is hardly anybody in Japan who does not know the Arabian figures.

The modern importation of European languages.

But what is still more remarkable is that we translate with the Japanized Chinese many foreign terms thus imported, and thus there have arisen new idiomatic phrases. Although Japanese native learning flourished at one time, yet our senior scholars were almost entirely votaries of the Chinese classics. Hence the introduction of foreign words and the coining of new phrases were inevitably effected by translating after the Chinese mode. In the meantime the art of printing has made wonderful progress, so that these new words and phrases appearing in print circulate throughout the empire. These are the causes of the inevitable result now seen. And strange to say, these very words and phrases thus made ready for use have been reimported into China since the China-Japan War.

Japanese-Chinese terms.

The compositions of the present day reflect the digested, refined thoughts of European civilization, but as we needed a wider vocabulary to meet all the varied phases of new thoughts and sentiments, we were necessarily driven to have recourse to our old source of words—the Chinese language. The *kusazōshi* (popular novels) of the Tokugawa period were written entirely with the *hira-kana*, while novels of the present day are written in *kana* and square letters having the *kana* in small type by their side to show their pronunciation. This is due to the fact that the Chinese characters cannot be dispensed with, though they are very difficult for the common people to master.

Modern compositions.

This difficulty was so apparent that Baron Mayéjima, in 1867, addressed to the Shōgunate a memoir on the improvement of the national script, in which he discussed the advantages of abolishing Chinese characters altogether. This caused much

Various views as to the improvement of the letters in use.

discussion, and various opinions prevailed as to the advisability of abolition, although no one doubted the hardship of learning them. In 1883 the Kana Society, which advocated the use of *kana* to the exclusion of all Chinese characters, came into existence, and in the next year the Roman Letters Society arose, the cry against the use of the Chinese letters then becoming loud and vehement. But soon a reaction set in, and opinions opposed to the disuse of the Chinese characters were formulated. After the China-Japan War the discussion on this subject again arose. In 1899 the Imperial Educational Society established a department for the improvement of the national characters under its control, and in 1900 the Department of Education appointed a Committee for Investigating the Method of Spelling Words with Roman Letters. An official limit was also fixed to the number of Chinese characters taught in elementary schools after 1901. The Higher Council of Education then passed a resolution to strike out Chinese compositions from the text-books of middle schools. These are doubtless reflections of the growing objection to the use of the cumbersome ideographs of the Orient. It is not at all to be wondered at that knowledge of the Chinese classics is now declining among the mass of the people.

The *kana*.   The *kata-kana* has been used up to this time conjointly with the square characters in the official gazette and other public documents. In the daily papers and magazines it was used at one time, but now only foreign words are spelt with it. The forms of the *hira-kana* were for a long time various, but this syllabary has now been made uniform by an instruction of the Department of Education issued in 1900.

The rules for using *kana*.   The rules for using *kana* had, as already mentioned, become loose and confused since the end of the Héian Court, but during the Tokugawa reign native learning flourished, and with its revival the old rules were resuscitated in their original form. This is the so-called 'historical orthography.' Although the Department of Education adopted it at the beginning of the new educational *régime*, yet the mass of the people seldom observed it carefully, and consequently the authorities abolished the *jion-kana-zukai*, or rules for writing the sounds attached to Chinese characters, and substituted the new system in the school text-books. With regard to the improvement of the *kokugo-kana-zukai*, or of the system of spelling native words with *kana*, there has been a sharp struggle during the past few years between men who insist on keeping the historical forms and men who advocate the adoption of phonetic spelling throughout.

In letters we still use the old epistolary style, in which Styles. almost every sentence ends with an auxiliary *sōrō*. In public documents we retain a free Sinico-Japanese style. Nor do we yet wholly give up the native classical style of the ladies in the Héian Court, while also a mixed style, classical and common, is beginning to flourish. But a disposition for the unification of the oral and the written styles is tolerably strong, and ever since 1887, when the idea of having pure original letters of our own, and spelling words with them, became prevalent, the above disposition has been encouraged and has borne some fruit.

In short, this era has very many forms and varieties of Conclu-characters, words, and sentences which cannot easily be sion. assimilated into one ; and yet the advancement of science and literature, combined with the progress of the community at large, is doing not a little towards unification. In 1902 a Committee for Research into the Japanese Language was instituted, and in accordance with the views of the Tōkyō Academy submitted to the Minister of Education in 1879, this Committee has been working in the line of investigating dialects, fixing a standard language, and making necessary improvements in the use of Chinese characters, as well as compiling a lexicon of the national tongue. In short, the Committee seeks to solve all questions relating to the subject. We hope their efforts will soon be crowned with success.

JAPANESE RELIGIOUS BELIEFS: *SHINTŌ*— THE *KAMI*

Professor Kunitaké Kumé

Meaning
of *Shintō*. *SHINTŌ*, the doctrine of the *kami*, has naturally undergone modifications as it has passed down the ages. Even the name '*Shintō*' was not given to it until the introduction of foreign religions. Turning over the pages of ancient history, the word occurs for the first time in the following passage in the ' *Nihon Shoki* ' (' Annals of Japan,' compiled in 720 A.D.) : ' The Emperor Yōméi (586 A.D.) believed both in Buddhism and *Shintō*.' Here *Shintō* means the indigenous cult, as distinguished from Buddhism and Confucianism. Under a mystical symbol in the ' Yi-King,' the Chinese ' Book of Changes,' Confucius remarks that *Shintō* (i.e. divine way of Heaven) arranges the four seasons : ' The sages of yore, therefore,' says he, ' taught people according to the divine way (*shintō*), and there was peace on earth.' As this symbol is said to stand for the looking up towards heaven from below, the word ' *shintō*,' as used here, may be taken in a sense more or less connected with our signification. *Shintō* in this primitive sense is, therefore, not peculiar to Japan. ' Buddhism is a *Shintō*,' says Chisung, a Chinese monk, ' a *Shintō* with a deeper conviction.' Following the same logic, Christianity may be considered a monotheistic *Shintō*. *Shintō* is everywhere in the world, for all religions are *Shintō*.

Kami Nagara.   Our native faith, before it was christened *Shintō*, seems for centuries to have gone by the archaic name ' *Kami Nagara*,' an adjective or adverb meaning ' of the very *kami* ' (of the *kami* as such). The ' *Nihon Shoki*,' alluding to the phrase

22

' *kami nagara mo waga miko* ' (our son *kami nagara*) in the edict of the Emperor Kōtōku (645 A.D.), explains it with these words : ' *Kami Nagara* is an unconscious observance of the doctrines of *Shintō*, because *Shintō*, with or without a name, existed from time immemorial.' It is not an easy thing to render a Japanese word into Chinese, English, or any other language ; for instance, the original meaning of *nagara* is, according to Lu-Tien's Dictionary, ' to be and not to be at the same time,' being composed of *naku* (not to be) and *aru* (to be). Thence it has come to mean ' like,' ' on,' ' in,' ' by,' ' as soon as,' &c. ' *Kami nagara mo waga miko* ' is similar in structure to ' *hana nagara mo fubuki* ' (*hana* meaning here ' falling blossoms,' and *fubuki*, ' flying snow-flakes '). In ancient times there was no *Shintō* as a systematic religion, but it existed as an implicit faith of the people from time immemorial. To this primeval cult have the modern Shintōists—I should say the Neo-Shintōists, who made their first appearance in the seventeenth century—made extraneous additions. ' From the Emperor's coronation ceremony to the trifle of giving an order or doing anything,' says Shigétō Tani, for example, ' the dictates of *Shintō* must be strictly observed, for *Shintō* has existed from time immemorial.' But the modified *Shintō* is no longer *Kami Nagara*, no longer an unconscious observance, but a conscious effort to place *Shintō* on the same level with Buddhism and Confucianism—an effort that could scarcely have been approved or even dreamed of by the compilers of the ' *Nihon Shoki*.'

Discrimination is indispensable for a student of history. To view an ancient faith from the modern standpoint is a serious mistake too often made. Readers are requested to lay aside their preconceptions, if they have any, before examining the general outlines of *Shintō*, which I shall now endeavour to trace.

' *Kami* ' is a comprehensive term applicable to anything high or above oneself, such, for example, as ' a deity,' ' an emperor,' ' a feudal chief,' ' an elevated place,' or ' hair on the head.' As the very focus of *Shintō* is thus a vague and indefinite term applied alike to gods and heroes, or to natural phenomena, *Shintō* naturally offers no direct opposition

The word kami.

to other religions. The Emperor is conceived as a living *kami*, under whom lies a gradation of *kami* and *shimo*, namely the higher and the lower, the elder and the younger, the father and the son, the protector and the protected, down to the lowest peasantry in their weather-beaten huts. What, then, is the greatest *kami* revered by the Shintōists ? It is the very *Ruler of the Universe*. When a Japanese is tempted to commit a sin or a folly, his conscience whispers to him, ' *kami* sees all,' for the high *kami* is thought to be omniscient.

Genea-logy of the *kami*. The ' *Kojiki* ' (' Records of Ancient Events,' compiled 711–12 A.D.) and the ' *Nihon Shoki* ' (720 A.D.) are the two oldest historic works upon which all other histories of ancient Japan are based. These two derived some of their material from the still older ' *Téiō Kéifu* ' (' Genealogy of Emperors '). Attempts have been made to construct a systematic creed of *Shintō* upon the basis of the time-honoured myths recorded in the two books, but it is in vain to try to organize a system out of a primitive *kami-nagara* faith.

The ' *Kojiki* ' opens with the cosmogony of the world as follows : ' In the beginning of heaven and earth there came into existence, in the midst of high heaven, a *kami* whose name was Amé-no-Minakanushi-no-Kami. Next arose two *kami*, Taka - Mimusubi - no - Kami and Kami - Mimusubi - no - Kami. These three *kami* were self-begotten, single and invisible. The world was young, like a drop of oil floating on the surface **The *kami* of heaven and the *kami* of earth.** of the water. And things thereon sprouted upward like the shoots of the *ashi* (reed), from the midst of which emanated another *kami*, Umashi-Ashikabi-Hikoji-no-Kami. Next came Amé-no-Tokotachi-no-Kami or Kuni-no-Tokotachi-no-Kami. These *kami* were also self-begotten, single and invisible.' From Amé-no-Minakanushi descended the Emperors and the Imperial family, including the house of Idzumo ; and from the two Mimusubi sprang the noble families. The *kami* of heaven (chieftains of pure blood) and the *kami* of earth (chieftains of mixed blood) were, too, descended from them.

Children of the *kami*. Amé-no-Minakanushi is the founder of the Imperial dynasty. The midst of the High Heaven (*Takama-no-Hara*) is the metropolis of the country. The two Mimusubi are the Logos of Amé-no-Minakanushi, and hence, in the narrower sense, stand for marriage. Through marriage with the line of Amé-no-Minakanushi they became ancestors on the maternal side of the Emperors and the Princes Imperial. They are for this reason sometimes called the *mioya-kami* (ancestral *kami*). The lesser chieftains were together spoken of as the eight myriad *kami*, and, being the sons of other *kami*, were also called *mikoto* (noble sons) or *hiko* (sons of *hi*, the sun, fire, spirit) and *himé* (daughters of the sun, fire, or spirit). The eight myriad *kami* held an occasional assembly on the banks of the River of Peace. From the beginning of the heaven and the earth Japan was thus a large family, with the Emperor as the family head. No hedge was set up between ruler and ruled, and no castes or family names existed, for all people were alike the sons of *kami* under the Imperial patriarchism. ' Our sons *kami nagara* ' they were called by the Emperor Kōtōku in his edict of 647. Later on, the *Kwō-bétsu* (families descended from Emperors) and the *Shin-bétsu* (families descended from *kami*) were distinguished. Further, when their sons and their sons' sons greatly multiplied, they were divided into the various family orders of the *Omi*, the *Muraji*, and others. The Emperor now assumed the title of *Tennō* (Heavenly Emperor), and the sons of *Kami Nagara* became his subjects.

Umashi-Ashikabi-Hikoji-no-Kami is not mentioned in the *Umashi.* Genealogy of the Emperors. Apparently he is another manifestation of the omnipotent reproductive power. When the earth was young and soft and unstable, and had not yet been firmly fixed by Kuni-no-Tokotachi, sweet things sprouted upward like the shoots of the reed. The ancient Japanese had a fancy for the word *umashi* (sweet), after the name of the above-mentioned *kami*.

In all other religions, prayers are offered for benefits from the deities, but the sons of *Kami Nagara* seldom pray for a benefit. Indeed, no word exclusively meaning ' benefit ' is found in our ancient vocabulary, the word ' sweetness ' being used for it. There is another word, *saga*, which is often trans- *Saga.* lated a ' benefit,' ' luck,' or ' happiness,' but its real meaning was ' nature '—' naturalness.' A thing of *saga* is one under the control of the natural laws. ' There is no *saga* ! ' was a remark uttered when a difficulty arose for which there was no natural remedy. Izanagi-no-Kami, when he met an under-world army sent against him, exclaimed: 'Oh, there is no *saga*!' and went to Kyūshū in order to cleanse his body. 'Obey nature, enjoy sweetness,' is the plain commandment of the primitive *Shintō*.

Genealogy of the Imperial ancestors.

From Kuni-Tokotachi-no-Kami the genealogy runs as follows :

> Kuni-no-Satsuchi-no-Kami
> Toyo-Kumo-no-no-Kami
> ⎰Uhijini-no-Kami
> ⎱Suhijini-no-Kami
> ⎰Ō-Toji-no-Kami
> ⎱Ō-Tomabé-no-Kami
> ⎰Omotaru-no-Kami
> ⎱Kashikoné-no-Kami
> ⎰Izanagi-no-Kami
> ⎱Izanami-no-Kami
> Amatérasu-Ō-Mikami
> Tsukiyomi-no-Mikoto
> Susanō-no-Mikoto.

Among the last three were divided their father's dominions, the heaven, the dark world, and the hoary sea. This and other things recorded remind us of the myths of the ancient Greeks. Some writers even go so far as to assume a genetic connection between the Japanese and the Hellenic mythologies—a conclusion too hasty for the historical student. Perhaps from the cradle of the primitive human stock sprang forth brother tribes, of genesis and traditions considerably similar. One of these hypothetical tribes may have settled on the shores of the Ægean Sea, while another, proceeding eastward, may have finally dwelt upon the idyllic isles of the Rising Sun.

Shintō ceremonies.

The two pre-eminent as well as characteristic *Shintō* ceremonies are the *harai* (blowing off) and the *misogi* (washing off) : purifications by means respectively of wind and of water. The origin of these ceremonies can be traced back to the beginning of our ethnic traditions. Izanagi, going round the eight islands that constituted Japan, is said to have remarked :

' The land to which I have given birth is full of the mist of the morning.' And he breathed a breath, whereupon there arose a *kami* of the wind, called *Shinatobé* (*shina* suggesting ' order '), who blew off the mist towards the sea.   Hence the phrase, ' to blow off in *shinato's* winds.'   The *misogi* or the water-purification is more important than the *harai*, wind-purification. As before mentioned, when Izanagi made a precipitate retreat from the under-world army of Izanami, he went directly to a river in Kyūshū to cleanse himself from the contamination. *Shintō* mentions no sin, but defilement.   Death and blood are considered especially defiling.   If a man touches an unholy thing he is defiled, and, to be restored to his former purity, he must resort either to the *harai* or the *misogi*, according to the established rituals.   As the *kami* is all-wise and all-seeing, the purification should be thorough : one should be cleansed body and soul, to the very bottom of one's heart.   This is the true meaning of Japanese purification.   Hence the hymn :

Purification.

> Pure be heaven.
> Pure be earth.
> Pure be within, without,
> And the six roots ;

the six roots signifying the five sense-organs and the heart, the organ of feeling.

Half a century ago Commodore Perry of the United States brought to Japan a work on universal geography, which at once became a favourite subject of study for our students. In this book the Japanese were described as a people cleanly in habits.   Ill-informed readers fancied that the phrase meant only bodily cleanliness, and that only in comparison with other races.   By and by, as Japan was opened to foreigners, and hordes of filthy Koreans and still filthier Chinese visited the land, our countrymen came to realize the phrase in its intended sense.   This good habit was largely due to *Shintō*, which has instilled an idea of cleanliness into the very life and thought of the entire Japanese nation.   Nevertheless, the Chinese and the Koreans had a *Shintō* of their own, developed by their ancient sages.   Their *Shintō*, however, has failed to produce a like result upon those races.   A Chinese acquaintance of the writer accounted for the fact as follows : ' On the continent,'

Idea of cleanliness.

said he, ' all is vast and discordant, while Japan is purity itself. Silver waves and snowy breakers encircle the island empire. The atmosphere is pure, the wind is refreshing. A clear sky hangs above the beautiful land. Crystal streams murmur down the green hillsides.   Born and brought up under the influence of such surroundings, one cannot but be sensitive to the slightest defilement.' The argument seems cogent. It was not *Shintō* alone that made us a cleanliness-loving people, but rather Japan's pure air and clear waters may be said to have given rise to her blowing and washing ceremonies, and made *Shintō* a cleanliness-loving religion. True, purification and ablution are more or less common to all religions.   The Chinese Confucianist, for example, washes his body and dons a clean garment in his worship of Heaven. He does not take a daily bath, however, as does every Japanese. The ' *kami* abhorreth uncleanness ' is a thought largely, if not exclusively, characteristic of the Japanese, for the dusty wind of Peking can scarcely blow off, or the yellow waters of the Hwang Ho wash off, impurity. Hardly more satisfying either is Buddhist incense or Hebrew anointment.

Sacrifice.   Sacrifice was offered from the earliest times, though without the exalted meaning attached to the Christian rite.   When Susanō committed offences against the laws of Heaven, the assembly of the *kami* imposed on him the sacrifice of his finger-nails and toe-nails, the latter to appease the wrath and the former to solicit a favour of Amatérasu, his elder sister. This is the origin of the *ashibarai* and the *yoshibarai*, two forms of expiatory ceremonies. The custom of imposing a sacrifice, often carried to absurd excess, became so prevalent among the common people that, until as late as the seventh century, landlords on the highways freely imposed money-sacrifices on defiled travellers.

Prayers.   *Shintō* prayers are chanted in beautiful, highly poetical liturgies called the *norito*, which form a branch of our classic literature.   The chanting of a *norito* is called ' *hosaki* ' or ' *hoki* ' (to bless), for it has more the sense of a benediction than of a supplication. The Coronation Liturgy chanted by the chief priest is called *Amatsu-Yogoto* (heavenly blessing). Some other liturgies are called the *koto-agé* (*hoki* in loud voice). There is an ancient song, 'A Japanese never cries '—meaning, never cries to the *kami*. Instances, however, of simple exclamation are not rare in Japanese records. Izanagi, standing by the River Odo in Kyūshū when washing his body, exclaimed in verse :

> The upper ford is too rapid,
> The lower ford is too slow,
> Nor too rapid nor too slow
> Is the middle ford.

Prince Yamatotaké, pushing his conquests to the strand of the Sea of Sagami, exclaimed : ' I shall jump over this narrow ditch ! ' Notwithstanding, to utter cries to the *kami* in case of a danger that one must brave, or a distress that one must endure, is regarded as unbecoming a true son of the Land of the Rising Sun, though the *koto-agé* or cry as a special form of liturgy is preserved in the house of Nakatomi, the chief priest.

Ukéhi is an oath-taking in its proper sense. When Susanō, ruler of the sea, went up to heaven riding on a whirlwind, mountains and waters loudly resounded, and the earth quaked. ' What meanest thou ? ' said Amatérasu, armed with a bow and arrows. ' Art thou come to lay thy hand on my throne ? ' ' Nay, sister,' the tempest-god replied, ' I come to see thee.' He made an *ukéhi* and gave up his sword, taking in exchange her necklace of curved jewels, washed it, bit and blew it off to the winds, and from it sprang five gods, whereby his innocence was proved. This is deemed the origin of *ukéhi*. On some occasions, however, the word is applied to a blessing, as an antonym of *noroi* (a curse). When the chief of Ada gave his two daughters Tokiwa and Sakuhana in marriage to the grandson of Amatérasu, he made the following *ukéhi* :

> Health be thine, as the Eternal Rock, Tokiwa,
> That weathers the snows and the winds.
> And Glory be thine, as the glory
> Of the bloom of the Blooming-Flower, Sakuhana.

An *ukéhi*, even if a curse, was sung in verse.

Thus far I have briefly noted the *Shintō* rites performed by ancient emperors and local chiefs. As to the modes of

Marginal note: Oath-taking.

Mutual
under-
standing
between
the
Emperor
and his
subjects.

popular worship, they are not mentioned in any of our early
histories. Perhaps the people seldom ' cried ' (koto-agé).
Even in later times, when Buddhism was widespread among
all classes, and prayers on a grand scale were offered to the
Buddha, these were generally public prayers for the peace,
good crops, health, longevity, and prosperity of the whole
nation. Private prayers for private purposes were rarely made
by the people. To this day devotees of Shintō pray only for
the Emperor's welfare, not for their own, and the Emperor
offers his daily prayer for the welfare of his subjects. He is
regarded as a living kami, loved and revered by the nation
above all things on earth, and himself loving and protecting the
nation, who are deemed sons of Kami Nagara and are entrusted
to his care by the kami. This mutual understanding obtains
between every individual Japanese and the Emperor. The
Sovereign studies our needs and feels our sorrows. What more
have we, then, to ask from the kami directly ? Thus Shintō
(doctrine of the kami) is kundō (doctrine of the Emperor), for
Shintōism is Mikadoism ; ' the kami's will is the Emperor's
will ' is a maxim inscribed on the heart of every Japanese.
Herein one may see the fountain-head of our patriotic spirit,
whose marvellous activity has served to raise Japan in these
fifty years to the level of the first-rate Powers of the world.
In this consideration, again, is shown the fact that Shintō is not
a religion in the same sense that Confucianism or Buddhism is.

In our language the word matsurigoto (governance) is
derived from the word matsuri (rituals). Governmental
and ritualistic affairs, however, were not entirely undiffer-
entiated even in the days of the kami. After a prolonged
struggle between the kami of heaven and those of earth,
the leader of the latter, Ōkuninushi of Izumo, gave up
his ' visible supremacy' to the Imperial son of Amatérasu,
and kept to himself an ' invisible supremacy ' in the field
of religion. Whether this ' invisible supremacy,' too, was
given up in course of time is unknown. Be that as it
may, it is evident that the government of the first historical
Emperor, Jimmu, of the sixth generation from Amatérasu, was
a theocratic one. In his bed-chamber, ' under the same roof
and on the same floor with himself,' he kept the three Holy

Relics (insignia) of the great ancestress, namely a mirror, a sword, and curved jewels. His two ministers, Ama-no-Tanéko-no-Mikoto and Amatomi-no-Mikoto, forefathers of the Naka-tomi and Imibé families respectively, supervised the rituals as well as the affairs of State : ' The Emperor was the patriarch. The palace was the synagogue. Materials for votive offerings were stored in the Imperial storehouse called the Sacred Tower, for things Imperial and things sacred were one and the same ' (from an Imibé's ' *Kogoshūi* '). Such was the government of our early Emperors. The local governors, derived from families which had once been of the *kami* of heaven and now were of faithful *kami* of earth, ruled their provinces in a similar way. Their administrative quarters were called heaven-temples and earth-temples. In the reign of the tenth Emperor, Sujin, two of the Relics, i.e. the mirror and the sword, were consecrated in a particular shrine in Kasanui ; and in the next reign, of the Emperor Suinin, they were removed further to the Great Shrine of Isé, erected for the purpose. From this time onward a gradual differentiation of *kami* and men, of religion and government, of emperor and subject, was at work. Even then, however, the keepers of the larger shrines called themselves *mikoto* or *hiko*, and the chief priests of the nation ranked above the Ministers of State. The chief priests were also the State-diviners, divination being performed by means of oracles and scapulimancy. Sortilege and astrology were introduced from Korea in much later times.

Shintō votives include, besides the products of the soil and the sea, *futotamagushi*, which is an evergreen tree (*sakaki*) uprooted. The upper branches are decked with blue and white strips of silk and cotton, and to the lower branches are hung a mirror, a sword, and a string of curved jewels. The mirror is the emblem of wisdom, the sword of courage, the curved jewels of love. The three Holy Relics referred to above were orginally used for the same purpose. Lord Chikafusa Kita-bataké lays undue importance on the Relics when he calls them the Divine Regalia of the Throne, for the use of the three things was not restricted to the Emperors. Local chiefs set up their own evergreens, and hung their own mirrors, swords, and beads. When the Emperor Chūai went to Kyūshū,

Shintō votives.

the governor of Ito decorated a ship with evergreens, jewels,
mirrors, and swords, and welcoming the Emperor off the island
of Hiko, said : ' My august lord, mayest thou reign in peace
like the smooth roundings of the jewels.   Like the bright
mirror, mayest thou see all things in thy dominion, and slay
thine enemies on the edge of the sword.'   The sword is the
spirit of the Japanese.   Our country's old name is ' Hosohoko-
Chitaru-no-Kuni ' (' land where the slender blade is sufficient
in all things ').   Sword in hand, with the *kami* overhead,
our forefathers subjugated the savage aborigines.   Sword
in hand, with the *kami* overhead, we defeated our invaders
and enemies.   Those, it may be noted, who charge the Japanese
with bloodthirstiness are ignorant that blood and death
are especially abhorred by the *kami*.   The Japanese fight
when they must, and fight always with clean hands.

Palaces
and
temples.

The Kashiwabara Palace of the Emperor Jimmu is described,
in primitive exaggerated language, as having massive pillars
raised on the bottommost rocks, and lofty cross-beams exalted
unto the width of the high heaven.'   In the ancient style of
building, the cross-beams project crosswise along the gable
angle, and are sometimes called ' wind-beaters.'   The Great
Shrine of Isé is rebuilt every twentieth year, exactly as palaces
were built two thousand years ago, with pillars of unpainted
wood and lofty cross-beams to a roof of thatch, cleanly in
every way and extremely simple.   On a grander scale was built
the Hisumi Palace of Ōkuninushi.   When he graciously
resigned his ' visible supremacy,' Taka-Mimusubi took com-
passion on him, and built for him a palace ' of tall, massive
pillars and wide, thick planks, bound together with mulberry-
bark cords, each a thousand fathoms long and made into one
hundred and eighty knots.'   This, perhaps, was the masterpiece of our ancient architecture.   Tourists through Western
Japan may visit the monument, now better known by the name
of the Grand Temple of Izumo.   The sites and names of
ancient temples are sources of intense interest to the historian,
as those temples were so many stations, political and military,
of ancient Japan.   The High Spirit Temples and the Divine
Spirit Temples mark the immigration of the two Mimusubi.
The Kashima, Katori, and Awa temples indicate colonies of

the Court nobles of the Emperor Jimmu. The *hiko* and *himé* temples along the coast of Échizén and Noto suggest outposts built by seafaring *kami* of old in seaports of commercial importance.

Apart from those politico-military temples, we should not forget that there were also shrines built purely for religious purposes. For such purposes, however, especially in earlier times, even a shrine was sometimes altogether dispensed with, the ground being simply marked off with a *himorogi* (holy hedge) and a *iwasaka* (stone wall). Ōkuninushi enshrined the Spirit of Happiness and the Spirit of Terror on Mount Mimoro, and erected a *kannami* (holy railing), otherwise called a *shiki* (cliff-castle), in the district, thenceforward called Shiki Gōri (cliff-castle district). A stone wall, a *kannami*, and a cliff-castle are not different from each other in any substantial way. The Emperor Jimmu marked out a spirit hillock on Mount Tomi, and a village below received the name of Shiki Mura (cliff-castle village). Spirit hillocks and shrines, with the one notable exception of the Great Shrine of Isé, were enclosed in those days within holy hedges and stone walls. A poet in the ' *Manyōshū*,' or ' Ten Thousand Leaves of Poetry ' (762 A.D.), sings :

> Would that the *kannami's* holy hedge protected man's heart from evil temptations.

Mount Kannami, as a local name, remains to this day in several parts of the country. It is invariably a hillock at the end of a mountain range, overlooking a fertile valley, where one might imagine a *kami* descending from heaven, ' cleaving with might heaven's manifold clouds.' Discoveries have been made recently of gigantic stone circles on Mount Rai, Mount Kōra, and in the districts of Yamato and Honami. Mount Rai, with its precipitous side studded with innumerable caves called ' The Devil's Dens,' rises in the mountain ranges of Chikuzén and Hizén. On its southern slope, commanding a view of the plain of Saga, stand Mount Kannami and a stone circle, which latter, in all probability, is the stone wall erected by the governor of Ito. The stone circle of Mount Kōra is the burial-place of *Kōra Tamataré,* the famous ancient armour ;

The shiki.

The kannami.

and those of Yamato and Honami are the cliff-castles of the governors of Yamato and Fumi respectively. They are remains of the ancient shrines set up by the *kami* of earth, and are interesting as the largest megalithic monuments of Japan, bearing some resemblance to the Druidical circles of England and Britany, though the difference is wide.

History of *Shintō*.

Wafted on the general current of emigration, *Shintō* found its way with our forefathers into Japan. A people highly imaginative, the invaders imbibed the pure air, the clear waters, and the sweetness of the blossoms of the promised land, developed beautiful myths, and carried the idea of cleanliness to a high degree of perfection. As time went on, and the nation emerged into the light of history and civilization, the effects of Chinese influence, imported mainly through Korea, were remarkable. By the Emperor Sujin and his successor the Holy Relics were removed from the Imperial bed-chamber to the Great Shrine of Isé, and the religious element of government was distinguished from the political, in conformity with the Chinese system. The ruler became more separated than before from the ruled. People assumed family names after the Chinese fashion. The Chinese method of writing and Chinese arts and science were introduced, along with the Chinese Shamanism (called *Onyō dō*), a cross between Taoism and Woohanism, loaded with a thousand superstitions of astrology, geomancy, incantations, and the like. Nor were the *Shintō* priests slow in adopting the newly imported crafts. The more they were overshadowed by the Buddhists and lost hold on the Government, the more they struggled to gain a hold on man by playing upon his fears and fancies. With divinations (*saniwa*), ordeals (*kugatachi*), and other demonological arts, the *Shintō* priests contrived to influence the Emperors and exercise an immense spiritual power over the nation. This state of things was a degradation rather than an improvement. Erelong, however, great tides of Confucianism and Buddhism overwhelmed the country like ocean waves. After terrible struggles between the three systems of teaching, especially between *Shintō* and Buddhism, a peace was finally established, whereby the sphere was virtually divided among the three. *Shintō* received the dominion of the public ceremonies, Buddhism of religion, and Confucianism of ethics. *Shintō*, polished from the rust of the preceding ages, shone once more in the pure lustre of the faith of *Kami-Nagara*, and the *Shintō* arch-priest, the *Jingi-kwan*, ranked above the Ministers of State, ' because,' said Lord Kitabataké later, ' Japan is the Holy Land.'

The chief ceremonies supervised by the *Jingi-kwan* were : in summer and winter, the semi-annual *Misogi* (great lustrations) ; in spring, the *Toshigoi* (prayer for a fruitful year) ; in autumn, the *Niinamé* (offering of the first rice) ; and, after a coronation, the *Daijōé* (grand offering of rice). The *Niinamé* was first practised by Amatérasu, who planted a field with rice for that purpose. The origin of the *Toshigoi* is not certain, though probably as old. Offering of the first rice naturally prevails among the Eastern nations, with whom rice is the staple food. So the Chinese worship Sheo, the god of the soil, and Chie, the inventor of agriculture. The Koreans also at a great festival offer rice to Heaven. Tourists through Japan will find in every village special shrines called *ujigami* (family god) or *ubusuna* (tutelary gods), while the villagers call themselves *ujiko* (family's sons). A part of a rice-field is consecrated to the shrine and tilled by the ' family's sons ' or parishioners. When the good autumn comes to reward their honest labour with golden harvest, they gather the products, brew *saké* (rice wine), make *mochi* (rice cake), and offer them to the family god. From the straw they twist the *shiménawa* (sacred ropes) to hang around the family shrine. The festival lasts three days. They eat the rice cakes and drink the rice wine, and indulge in a thousand pastimes in their own manner. Guests are invited—uncles, aunts, married daughters, and little lads. All the villagers become brethren. A group of such villages makes a province, and the aggregate of the provinces makes Japan. Japan is a large family—a home of sweetness, harmony, and love. Love ties our hearts to that of the Emperor. He is our father of fathers. He calls us *ōmitakara* (precious things), as we are his precious things entrusted to his care by the *kami*. ' I am rich, if my people are rich,' is the motto of the Japanese Emperor.

The knowledge of the *kami* is the fountain of all virtues.

Chief cere-monies.

D 2

Fountain
of all
virtues.

A Japanese, however ignorant, is proud of having an Emperor descended from a high ancestress. In his opinion the Emperor is everything, superior even to the local *kami*. There is a proverb, 'The Emperor is ten times good, whereas the *kami* is nine times good.' There is a play of words in this saying. 'Nine times good,' or, in Japanese, *kuzén*, is similar in sound to *kusén*, or an Imperial ordinance by which honorific titles are conferred on the local shrines in order to fix their precedence in the pantheon of *Shintō*. The same titles are conferred on the provincial governors, who pay homage to the Emperor, as the local family gods pay homage to Amatérasu, his ancestress. These local shrines are units of the present *Shintō* system.

Character-
istics of
Japan.

Thus far I have briefly described how *Shintō* went on through centuries of vicissitudes and modifications. The Japanese mind, like Japanese scenery, is characteristically clear, cheerful, and open—open to receive anything and stamp it with the national genius. Bigotry and prejudice are little known where a *sakura* (cherry) blooms. Observe, for instance, the attitude *Shintō* has assumed towards religions brought from other lands. First, when Chinese Shamanism appeared upon the scene, it was made a tool of by the *Shintō* priests, and then it gave way to Confucianism, without carrying its superstitions even so far as in the country whence it came. To Confucianism Japan is indebted for refinements in her political systems and Court etiquette. Virtually, however, it was absorbed into the native Imperialism, and the filial piety of China has given place to the loyalty of Japan. Last of all came Buddhism with its subtle and profound doctrines. These again were never really popular until a syncretic form of Japanese Buddhism was developed. In the present state of things, the Japanese revere the *kami* side by side with the Buddha, and are not very particular as to which is which. If Confucianism, Buddhism, sciences, arts, and philosophy have done great things for Japan, Japan's remarkable power of absorbing, digesting, and assimilating these heterogeneous elements should not be lost sight of. The Continental civilization, grafted on the vigorous stock of the native *sakura*, has bloomed forth in profuse splendour, to the glory of the nation and the admiration of the world.

From the salutary moral effects that *Shintō* has produced *Shintō morals—Makoto.*
upon the Japanese, foreigners may infer that it must possess
an excellent code of morals. There is no greater error. Strange
as it may seem, our ancient vocabulary is void of ethical
terms, except one solitary word, *makoto*—Truth. ' Be true,'
was the sum of *Shintō* morals. *Dōtoku*, virtue ; *jin*, humanity ;
gi, justice ; *kō*, filial piety ; *téi*, brotherly love ; *chū*, faithfulness ; *shin*, honesty—all these are foreign importations and
of Chinese origin. A Japanese of the masses, even in these
days, has little fancy for the high-sounding names, ' humanity,'
' justice,' and so forth. Precepts are taught by words, but the
precept of all precepts, the foundation of moral teachings,
the ultimate end of *Shintō* purifications by wind and by water,
can be implied in that one word—*makoto*. Once Emperor
Wu-Ti of China asked a philosopher what were the principal
things in government, when the philosopher's laconic answer
was : ' Government is not words, but actions.' I do not know
whether it is so or not in political matters, but assuredly the
intrinsic value of moral teachings lies not in words but in
actions. Eloquence is nothing before the *kami*.

> The *kami* blesseth,
> Not him who prayeth,
> But him whose heart strayeth
> Not from the way of *makoto*.

This aphorism is due to the famous poet-patriot Michizané
Sugawara, deified as *Temmangū*.

Chinese is a language peculiarly rich in ethical terms. By *Chinese ethical terms.*
combining the root-ideographs, we can make a great number
of such terms. For example, ' inner ' and ' heart ' put together
is ' faithful ' ; ' man ' and ' words ' constitute the character
standing for ' honesty.' ' Be faithful and honest,' says Confucius, ' to your neighbours. With honesty, faithfulness,
sincerity, and modesty ye can go to the end of the world.' The
great sage lavishes his synonyms apparently for euphony's
sake. Moreover, he applies the same word ' faithfulness,'
sometimes to friendship, sometimes to modesty, sometimes to
loyalty, and sometimes to honesty, so that the delicate shades
of language are blent and blurred, until we are at a loss to

understand their exact meaning.   A thousand words that cannot be understood are not worth a single clear word.

Makoto a grand edifice of the True Religion.

That one word, *makoto*, is the foundation of all Japanese morals, a foundation on which is to be raised a grand edifice of the True Religion.   Confucianism and Buddhism made their advent to meet that craving.   Buddhism is a great religion, with its vast literature and profound philosophy, easy to believe in, but difficult to comprehend.   Only the rich and the noble have had leisure to give themselves up to its study.   The *samurai* class were wont to temper their mettle by contemplation, following the doctrine of the Dhyana or Zen sect.   But the working majority who earn their daily bread, drifting in the wide ocean of Eternity, can only do their best to attain Buddhahood by repeating Buddha's name or the name of the holy scriptures.   Emperor Hanazono himself, a great scholar of Buddhism, complained of his inability to penetrate into the five phases and the three mysteries of Buddhist theology, or into the Dhyanaic contemplation, so that he could not but resort to the sacred formulae.   Theology is for the learned, contemplation for the gifted, and the sacred formulae for the pious.   But a man must first of all be true—true to himself, true to the Emperor, true to the faith he professes.   That one word *makoto* is the foundation of Japanese morals, religion, and government, truthfulness towards the *kami* and the Emperor having developed ultimately that matchless moral standard *Bushidō*.

Confucianism, Buddhism, and Shintō.

Confucianism and Buddhism, with all their fine maxims and profound philosophy, could not ' protect man's heart from evil's temptation ' and keep it from ' straying out of the way of *makoto*.'   No one but the *kami* can say that this or that religion is true or false.   But as an historian, and in history's light, I can safely say that Buddhism, in spite of its former grandeur, is now practically a mere Coliseum.   The philosophical part of Confucianism as expounded by Chu-Hi, who drew largely from Buddhism, is little more than a shallow imitation of Dhyanism.   The Buddhists, Confucianists, and Shintōists—Neo-Shintōists, in particular—have been raising whirlwinds of controversy, ethical, theological, and metaphysical, till one is heartily tired of lending an ear to them.   Is

there no other religion ? Is there no religion more effective
and more inspiring, establishing a true kingdom of heaven on
the *terra firma* of *makoto* ?

Christianity first entered Japan in the last half of the *Christian-*
sixteenth century, when Nobunaga Oda, the leading feudal *ity.*
lord and an avowed enemy of Buddhism, invited Jesuit missionaries to Kyōto, the ecclesiastical centre of Japan. These holy
fathers, to his surprise, burned temples, destroyed sacred
mirrors, desecrated cemeteries, and, in these and other ways,
shook Japan's moral structure to its foundation. Such an
open outrage was intolerable to the Japanese, and the fathers
were expelled the country. From this time onward Christianity—*Kirishitan*, as it was called—became another name
for witchcraft and bigotry. Electricity, steam-engines,
cannon, chemicals, and all things European were alike hated
as things *Kirishitan*. Our country lay in perfect seclusion for
more than two hundred years. At last, after 1853, increasing
knowledge of the world gradually opened our eyes to the
dazzling spectacle of Western civilization. Christianity, far
from being mere magic, was now explained as a great religion
—the religion of love to nations of all quarters and men of all
races. When the first Japanese ambassador, Prince Iwakura,
went round the world, I had the honour of travelling with him.
At New York I was introduced to the Young Men's Christian
Association and the Bible Society, and there, for the first time
in my life, I witnessed the marvellous influence of Christianity
upon the social and home life of the Americans. I was so
impressed that I wrote home a long letter to the following
effect : ' Reverence is the mother of industry and of peace.
Like oxygen, it kindles fire and supports life, bringing everywhere light, warmth, and comfort. Man cannot do without
it for a moment. Christianity has many absurdities. Some
religions are more philosophical, others more poetical. But in
point of moral impressions and indefatigable faith, undaunted
by dangers and unshaken by adversities, what other religion
can cope with it ? ' Meanwhile, American and European
missionary bodies were not slow in promulgating their faith
on Japanese soil. Things that were seemingly ' absurd ' were
given noble significance, or explained on a philosophical basis.

The ' moral impressions,' on the other hand, seem to have lost something of their value in the minds of thinking Japanese. If Christ is divine, propagandists of his teachings are men, and, being men, have often given way to human weaknesses. All the same, the essence of Christianity has been silently gaining ground in nooks and corners of every Japanese heart. And this is just what we wanted most. Rites and rituals are mere outward forms. A register of the converts is one thing and the Kingdom of Heaven is another. The Japanese, who for two hundred years have disliked the phantoms of *Kirishitan*, are now admiring its reality, for the teachings of Christ, polished of their historical rust of nineteen hundred years, are nothing else than glorious manifestations of that *makoto* long cherished by the sons of the *kami's* Land.

Japan, the Land of the *kami*.
Japan has been called the *kami's* Land from time immemorial. When Empress Jingō invaded Korea, a king of the peninsula exclaimed : ' Woe to Korea ! Gods sail upon us from the Holy Land, for I have long heard there is a Holy Land in the eastern seas, called Japan, ruled by a divine king called Tennō.' At another time King Shiao-ku of Pih-tse, hearing that there was a Noble Land in the eastern seas, sent an ambassador to it by way of the Kingdom of Cho-chunn. And the King of Cho-chunn said : ' The Noble Land lies where the sun rises : only I have never been there.' People on the Asiatic coasts all identify Japan with the Isles of the Blest in their myths, and some Chinese have even come hither in search of nectar. To say that Japan is the Holy Land given birth to by Izanagi and Izanami, and that our Emperor is the descendant of the *kami*, may sound strange and ridiculous to an Occidental ear ; but to a genuine Japanese it is neither ridiculous nor strange. Japan is the Land of *kami*. The *kami* is conceived as the Supreme Lord of the Universe. All religions are *Shintō*. Religions, whatsoever they be, are welcome to the Holy Land, and no religion that cannot enter it deserves the name.

Sages and the *kami*.
In the Constitution of the Japanese Empire the Emperor stands *shinséi*, or ' divine and wise.' It is not meant that he has anything in common with the ' sage ' kings of China who headed rebellions and usurped the throne. The primitive Chinese were a patriarchal tribe, as all primitive nations are,

but, in course of time, an ambitious usurper would rise—a wise king, as he loved to be called. His descendants would inherit the land, but their declining morality would enfeeble themselves and their people.   Then the priesthood would take up the people's cause, claiming the supremacy of the spiritual kingdom over the temporal, while the king, on his part, would put forth a counter-theory of the divine right of kings.   Compare this cycle of revolutions with the state of things in Japan, the *kami's* Land, and its unbroken line of successive rulers from Amatérasu to the present Emperor, and from him on for ever.   Japan's Emperor is not a usurper's son.   He claims no divine right : the conception of ' right ' finds no place between him and us.   He is our father. The father grudges not his life for the sake of his children, and the children grudge not their lives for the sake of their father.

We must thank the *kami* for the prosperity of our Imperial household.   We must also thank the *kami* for the steady development of our country, especially in these fifty years.   We must thank the *kami* for the sweet works of *Shintō*, that has infused a clean conscience and *makoto* into the life and thought of the Japanese, and laid the foundation of our nationality, *tokiwa kakiwa*, firm and immutable.

' Superstitions ! ' a scientist may say ; ' Heathen ! ' a Christian might call us.   But no one except the *kami* can tell that this or that religion is ' heathen.'   As for science, what does it know ?   Did not Newton say that he was like a little child playing on the seashore, while a boundless ocean of Truth lay undiscovered before him ?

Superstition.

One word more.   Is mankind the happier with religions, or without them ?   In what religion, then, do I believe ?   I cannot answer that question directly.   I turn to the *Shintō* priest in case of public festivals, while the Buddhist priest is my ministrant for funeral services.   I regulate my conduct according to Confucian maxims and Christian morals.   I care little for external forms, and doubt whether there are any essential differences, in the *kami's* eyes, between any of the religions of the civilized world.

My religion.

Being a student of history, I am studying the wisdom of the *kami* through its manifestations in history.

JAPANESE RELIGIOUS BELIEFS : CONFUCIANISM

Professor Tétsujirō Inouyé, D.Litt. (Japan)

Confucianism originated, as its name indicates, in the teachings of Confucius, and ever since its foundation it has been looked up to as the guide of every-day life by the people of the Oriental nations, and has exercised a powerful influence over their minds for more than 2300 years. Regarded from its outward form, it appears to be a religion, but, while religion deals mostly with spiritual conceptions, Confucianism concerns itself principally with secular morality, and, unlike religion, is free from ritual observances and superstitious notions. In this respect Confucianism is rightly regarded as a moral system, clearly distinguished from religion.

Confucianism was first introduced into Japan in the sixteenth year of the reign of the Emperor Ōjin, or 285 A.D. according to the ordinary table of historical dates, but probably some 120 years later.

It met with no opposition, and in this respect, too, it differed from both Buddhism and Christianity, which were strongly resisted at their introduction, resulting in each case in much bloodshed. This indicates that its teachings were from the first in harmony with the innate character of the Japanese.

The history of Confucianism in Japan may be divided into four periods :

I. The first, extending over some 1000 years, from *circ.* 400 to 1298 A.D.

II. The second, extending over 303 years, from the arrival of Néi-issan, a Chinese priest, in 1299 to 1602.

III. The third, extending over about 265 years under the Tokugawa Government, i.e. from 1603 to 1867.

IV. The fourth period, since the Restoration in the first year of the Meiji era (1868).

Of these periods, the third was the most propitious to Confucianism, the fourth being only an after-glow. It is for this reason that we shall consider the third period at some length, only briefly treating the others, although, since Confucianism has been indisputably the most powerful source of influence in modelling our national character, we must make a special study of all the stages of its development, if we want to know where the fountain-head of the stream of our civilization lies.

THE FIRST PERIOD (CIRC. 400–1298 A.D.)

In the reign of the Emperor Ōjin, the King of Kudara, the ancient name of a principality of Korea, sent one Achiki as envoy to the Japanese Court. This man, who was well versed in the Chinese classics, recommended to the Emperor a compatriot, Wani by name, as far more learned than himself. At his suggestion the Emperor sent for Wani, who came in the year following and offered to the Throne the 'Rango' ('Analects') and the 'Senjimon' ('Thousand Ideographs'), which he had brought with him from his native country. The Crown Prince, Uji-no-Wakairatsuko, studied under him, and in the course of time mastered these Chinese classical books. This was the beginning of Confucianism in Japan. *[margin: Introduction of Confucianism.]*

In the reign of the Emperor Tenchi (662–71 A.D.) a university was founded in Kyōto, and in that of the Emperor Mommu (697–707 A.D.) a statute was promulgated which provided for the establishment of a Central University in Kyōto and provincial schools in the provinces. In the Central University the offices of *Hakasé* (Professors) and *Jokyō* (Assistant-Professors) were instituted, and in the provincial schools those of *Hakasé* (Professors) and *Ishi* (Physicians). The text-books appointed to be used in these institutions were the ' *Chü-Yih*,' the ' *Shêng-Shü*,' the ' *Chü-Li*,' the ' *Yih-Li*,' the ' *Li-King*,' the ' *Shi-King*,' the ' *Chun-Chu*,' Tsao's commentary on ' *Chun-Chu*,' the ' *Hsiao-King*,' and the ' *Lun-Yü*.' Of these the first eight were to be studied separately, while the last *[margin: Establishment of the Central University and provincial schools.]*

two were to be taken up with others. For the purpose of teaching these books, standard works of annotation were prescribed.

Confucianism in the Héian period. In the Héian epoch (784–1184 A.D.) scholars appeared in unbroken succession who lectured on the Confucian classics or wrote Chinese prose and verse. Learning flourished to such an extent as to suggest a comparison with the brilliancy of the Augustan age. But the scholars of those days confined their studies to the annotations and commentaries of the Han and Tang ages, and they forgot the spirit whilst studying the letter. As is well known to students of Chinese literature, these annotations and commentaries invariably aim at elucidating passages in the Confucian classics from a philological point of view, showing no trace, however slight, of profound philosophical reasoning. Consequently they are entirely destitute of practical use. Inasmuch, therefore, as these formed the foundation upon which scholars of the time based their studies, it is no wonder that they also should have remained slavish copyists of ancient commentators and mechanically pursued their course along settled lines, making no new and original essays. In this respect the Confucianism of the period may be said to have been mere formalism.

Michizané Sugawara. In the long list of distinguished names connected with the Confucianism of this period, that of Michizané Sugawara stands out by far the most prominently. But even he did not make Confucianism his life study, as did the Confucianists of the third period. A follower of Confucius on the one hand, he was a worshipper of Buddha on the other, and, as a result, the moral principles of loyalty and filial piety, and the religious doctrines of renunciation and *Nirvana*, occupied their places in his mind without the least conflict or unity—thus evidencing that in those days even a man of his scholarship, not to speak of other men of lesser learning, did not venture to found views of life and of the world exclusively upon the basis of Confucianism.

Decline of Confucianism. In the sixth year of the Kwampéi era (894 A.D.) Michizané was appointed Imperial envoy to the Chinese Court and Ki-no-Haséo vice-envoy. At that time China was ruled by Chao-tsung, the last Emperor of the Tang dynasty, whose reign was marked by a series of civil wars, and revolution appeared to be impending. Informed of this state of affairs in

China, Michizané saw the uselessness of sending an envoy thither, and notified this to the Emperor, who accepted his suggestion. In consequence official intercourse with China came to an end, and a great check was given to the influx of Chinese civilization. In addition to this, the banishment of Michizané to Kyūshū, on account of an accusation brought against him by his opponents, served to accelerate the decline of literature in the Héian epoch ; and in the general decadence of learning, Confucianism could not but share a tendency which was intensified in the Kamakura epoch. But at the moment when such an unhappy condition reached its lowest depth, germs of a reactionary movement were, as we shall now show, fast fermenting.

The Second Period (1299–1602)

After Japan's Imperial envoy had ceased to be sent to China at the suggestion of Michizané Sugawara, official communication between Japan and China was entirely suspended for a long period of time, although private intercourse of a kind was still maintained. In the Kamakura epoch, however, a change came about, for intercourse between Buddhist priests of both countries had begun to be carried on to a considerable extent, and this ultimately served to restore the old relations between Chinese and Japanese culture, until, at the beginning of the thirteenth century, the Sung school of learning was introduced into our country. It is not known who was the first to introduce this branch of Confucian culture, but there is little doubt that such a person as Ni-Ishan, a Chinese priest who came to Japan in the first year of the Shōan era (1299), had much to do with the propagation of the doctrine. He numbered among his pupils such men as Kokwan, Chūgan, Musō, &c. Kokwan opposed the principles laid down by the Ch'ing brothers and by Chutsze, and Chūgan also questioned the theories formulated by Chang and Ch'ing. Musō refrained from commenting on the Ch'ing brothers and Chutsze, but his pupil, Gidō, pointed out the superiority of the Sung school to the system of the Han and Tang ages. Besides these priest-scholars, Genné, a contemporary of Kokwan, taught the

Influence of the Sung school of learning.

Sung school of learning in the city of Kyōto. Some authorities say that he was a brother of Kokwan, and if we can trust this statement, we may well conclude that he must have studied this system of learning under the guidance of the latter. Later on, such master-minds as Giyō, Ishō, Kéian, Nampo, and others studied the Sung school and handed it down to posterity, thus laying the foundation of the prosperity of learning under the Tokugawa *régime*.

Origin and nature of the Sung learning.

We stay here for a moment to notice some characteristic traits of the Sung school of learning. This branch of Confucianism is a system of thought founded by the Ch'ing brothers and Chutsze and other scholars of the Sung dynasty. It is elaborated on the dualistic basis of *ri* and *ki* (the former indicating the naturally existent idealistic principle and the latter the material principle). In this respect its scope of study is far removed from that of the original Confucianism. To seek an explanation of what conspired to call forth this new movement we must look to history. During the Sui and Tang dynasties, Buddhism predominated throughout the Chinese Empire, and eventually almost stifled Confucianism. But the latter, being a profound system of ethical thought, indigenous to the Chinese soil, could not long remain passive under the sway of a foreign religion. Something had to be done to restore it to its former position of influence. Among a great many Confucianists of the Sung dynasty, Chutsze (1130–1200), above all, grasped the spirit of Buddhism, and, using it as the framework, clothed it with the flesh and blood of Confucianism, and thus evolved the theory of the dualism of *ri* and *ki* above referred to. It was largely due to his strenuous efforts that vitality was restored once again to decadent Confucianism. The system of learning which flourished in the Han and Tang dynasties occupied itself in expounding passages in the Confucian classics by means of annotations and commentaries, chiefly from an etymological and philological point of view, and thus naturally was barren of practical interest and utterly devoid of fresh vigour. The Sung school of learning, on the other hand, did not attach much moment to minor details of etymological study, but attempted to grasp directly the true spirit of Confucianism as reflected in the learner's own mind. In order to know the mental attitudes of the ancient sages, therefore, it was deemed unessential to have recourse to far-fetched explanations of the etymology of their sayings, the theory being that the subject-matters were discoverable near at hand in the mind of every learner. In short, the Sung school of learning was a new form of the exposition of Confucianism with some admixture of Buddhist elements. Compared with the original form of Confucianism, it differed in many respects, and marked great progress in profundity of reasoning. This Sung school of learning, introduced into Japan in the period we are now considering, stood out in remarkable contrast to the system of the Han and Tang ages, prevalent in the preceding period : it brought vitality to the Confucianism of the day, and qualified it to be taken for a standard of moral conduct.

It was solely through Buddhist priests that the Sung school of learning was introduced in the second and handed down to the following period. Throughout the second period Japan was still under the sway of the ' Dark Age ' and lay in a welter of confusion. Warlike pursuits prevailing everywhere, to the exclusion of everything else, the light of learning would have failed permanently but for the tender care of the priests, who, as a rule, stood aloof from and above the influence of the rise and fall of principalities. Above all, the ' five Buddhist monasteries ' (*Go-zan*) rendered great service in this direction. As for the Sung school of learning, it was almost monopolized by the priests of the Zen sect. But while priests of this sect studied the Sung school, they did not attempt to propagate it, the fact being that although the Sung school adopted much of Buddhistic thought, it carried on a strong crusade against Buddhism as a moral standard. It would have been, therefore, a great contradiction for professed Buddhists to acknowledge faith in the Sung school. Hence they did not, or could not, venture to advocate it, whilst some, including Kokwan and Chūgan, even condemned it openly. Such priests as Giyō, Ishō, Kéian, and Nampo did not go so far as that, and sometimes, indeed, spoke in favour of it, but even they were not bold enough to abandon their offices in the Buddhist ministry to advocate the Sung philosophy. All things considered, we may

Position of Buddhist priests in learning.

conclude that in the second period Confucianism, receiving a stimulus from the introduction of the Sung system, was steadily preparing for future progress. Only the time was not yet fully mature, and it continued still in a dormant stage.

THE THIRD PERIOD (1603–1867)

Revival of learning.

When Iyéyasu Tokugawa subjugated all the militant generals of the time and established his government upon the basis of feudalism, an end was put to the long-continued series of disturbances, and peace was restored to a suffering nation. Learning, long forgotten by the majority of the people, now began to find favour once again in the eyes of an increasing number of patrons, and with it Confucianism came to assume a position of prime importance as an educational system. The Sung school of learning, which in the preceding period had been studied by Buddhist priests co-ordinately with their own religious subjects, now began to assert its independence, and to be invested with a significance hitherto unknown. Previously, though there had been a number of Buddhist priests who took delight in studying the Sung school of learning, none of them had ventured to give up their religious profession in order to advocate it. Now, however, this state of things was greatly modified, and towards the close of the second period and at the beginning of the third, we see priests voluntarily abandoning their offices in the Buddhist ministry and adopting Confucianism as the true canon of ' secular morality.'

Foremost among this group of men was Séikwa Fujiwara, the pioneer of Confucianism in the Tokugawa age, and once a priest in the Buddhist temple, Shōkokuji. So, too, Jichū Tani, the founder of the Southern school (*Nangaku*), who had been at one time in the service of another Buddhist temple called Shinjōji, in Kōchi. So also it was with Ansai Yamazaki, one of Jichū's best pupils, who advocated the Chutsze school in Kyōto. He came from the temple Myōshinji, where he had passed his early life. Consequently, Buddhism began to decline in proportion as Confucianism became more and more influential. This was only a natural tendency of the time, when culture was liberated from all forms of old religious superstitions and came into direct contact with 'secular morality.' Thus a new epoch in the history of thought was brought about.

As has already been said, the first man to leave the Buddhist ministry and become a scholar of Confucianism was Séikwa Fujiwara (1561–1619). He started a school in Kyōto and taught the philosophy of Chutsze, and thus became, indisputably, the pioneer at this period of this field of the revival of learning. Of him we may say that, although his scope of study was wide, his research was not extensive, and he produced very few masterpieces in either prose or verse, although the greatness of his contributions to the literary world can be seen from the following three points of view :

In the first place, he was the earliest advocate of the Chutsze school, which became the most influential branch of learning throughout the Tokugawa age. If his researches lacked thoroughness, the courage with which he opened this new field deserves commendation. Moreover, the Chutsze school, which he promoted, was neither narrow nor exclusive, but wide and comprehensive, in its basis and structure ; for he was magnanimous enough to admit, in the scope of his studies, the principle laid down by Luh-Siangshan and that by Wang-Yangming. Although Séikwa gave up his belief in Buddhism because he thought it an inhumane religion, yet he admitted that it agreed with Confucianism in so far as the process of philosophical reasoning was concerned. Hence it may be said that his liberal mind harmonized not only the doctrines of Chutsze and Luh-Siangshan, but also the teachings of Buddha and Confucius.

Secondly, he applied *watén* (indications with the *kana* by means of which written Chinese can be read in the same way as Japanese) to the 'Four Books' and the 'Five Classics,' the chief Confucian Classics, for the benefit of the reading public. The *watén* method of reading written Chinese, however, was not his invention. Before his time Giyō had already applied it to the ' *Shi-King*,' and later it was improved by Kéian and Nampo respectively, and then handed down to Séikwa.

Thirdly, a man of sterling character and magnanimous disposition, he succeeded as an educationalist, turning out from his school many excellent pupils, of whom Razan and Sékigo may especially be noted.

Razan
Hayashi.

Razan Hayashi (1583–1657) was not only the most brilliant of all the pupils of Séikwa, but also a genius, hardly equalled by any of his contemporaries. Being in the service of the Tokugawa Shōgunate from the time of the first Shōgun, Iyéyasu, to that of the fourth Shōgun, Iyétsuna, he took an active part in the work of framing laws and regulations, and preparing official documents. Erudite, widely informed, highly talented as a prose writer, he adhered to the Chutsze school more pronouncedly than his master, but, unlike the latter, he lacked toleration towards schools other than that to which he belonged, and made wholesale attacks on the teachings of Luh-Siangshan, Wang-Yangming, Taoism, Buddhism, and Christianity. *Shintō*, alone, he not only did not oppose, but tried to bring into harmony with Confucianism. He wrote more than 150 sets of books ; but so far as ethical theories were concerned, he did nothing more than faithfully copy Chutsze. Thus, although he did not give the world any original ideas, there were among his descendants many great scholars who carried on his office of Government educationalist for many generations. For over two hundred and sixty-five years his family continued to be the centre of the educational system of the whole country. Not to speak of their undisputed influence and well-deserved reputation, the Chutsze school, advocated by them, became the foundation of the educational system of the Tokugawa Government, and had much to do with the development of the national character.

Junan
Kinoshita.

Sékigo Matsunaga was another eminent pupil of Séikwa ; and among the pupils of Sékigo the best known was Junan Kinoshita (1621–98). A talented writer in prose and verse, he was even more distinguished for his upright character. Though not an able theorist, he was a moralist in every sense of the word. Instead of attempting to formulate elaborate principles or abstruse systems, he directly exemplified his moral ideas by his daily conduct. He had an unusually large number of pupils whom he spiritually inspired, and among these were many famous scholars. Struck with this assemblage of brilliant pupils, Shishin Usami, who once visited the school, spoke of it as a ' garden full of many-coloured peach and plum blossoms.' He was undoubtedly the most influential education-alist of his age.

In the long list of Junan's great pupils, Hakuséki Arai (1657–1725) easily occupies the foremost rank. To a power-ful character he added profound scholarly attainments. From his youth his aspirations knew no bounds. He used to say: ' If I, being born a man, cannot become a feudal prince in my lifetime, I would fain become the King of Hell after my death.' A feudal prince, indeed, he could not become, but he rose to a height of literary pre-eminence attained by no one else in his time. He was not a moral philosopher, but well versed in history, archæology, and other subjects, and a highly gifted writer of prose and verse: he also took the lead in the study of European learning in the Tokugawa age. He wrote perhaps more books than any other scholar of that era, leaving behind him more than 160 sets of volumes.

Hakuséki Arai.

Side by side with Hakuséki, Kyūsō Muro (1658–1743) was one of Junan's eminent pupils. Like his master, he was a moralist, proficient in Confucian learning and a good prose writer. It was not by Hakuséki, but by Kyūsō, that Junan's method of training pupils in practical morality was preserved. In the closing years of his life he contracted a chronic disease, and was confined to his residence at Surugadai in Yédo, but the undaunted scholar still continued to lecture on moral philosophy to his pupils, whom he trusted to transmit his teachings to posterity. At this time Sorai had begun to advocate the Classical school of learning in Yédo, and supported by such master-minds as Shuntai Dazai, Nankaku Hattori, and Shūnan Yamagata, his theory had awakened keen interest among the scholars of the day, and begun to permeate the country far and wide. But the modest Kyūsō did not attempt a contest with the leaders of the new movement, but quietly and humbly went on preaching his own principles. With Sorai on the one hand and Tōgai Itō on the other, both opposed to his theory, he upheld his position persistently. It was thanks to his noble efforts, in spite of the rapidity with which the Classical school

Kyūsō Muro.

gained ground among the scholars of the time, that the Chutsze system of ethics was preserved and handed down to the present time.

Tékisai Naka-mura.

Besides Junan and Kyūsō, Tékisai Nakamura (1629–1702) and Ékkén Kaibara were widely known as great scholars of the Chutsze school. The former, a contemporary of Jinsai Itō, a leading scholar of the Classical school in Kyōto, set up a school in the same city, and there taught the Chutsze system. This relation of Tékisai to Jinsai bore some similarity to that of Kyūsō to Sorai in Yédo. He wrote many books, of which the most remarkable was the ' *Himé Kagami* ' ('Lives of Vir-tuous Women ')—remarkable when we consider that the spirit of the age was not favourable to female education.

Ékkén Kaibara.

Ékkén (1630–1714), Kyūsō's senior by some years, was a man of great and many-sided talents, who wrote, to expound his principles, such books as the ' *Taigiroku* ' (' Great Doubts '), the ' *Shinshiroku* ' ('Meditations'), the ' *Jigoshū* ' (' Essays'), &c. He also compiled many other books on morals for the young and the comparatively uneducated. As these latter were written in a very easy and simple style, so as to be intelligible even to the mass of the people, they were extremely far-reach-ing in influence, and did much to raise the moral standard of the general public. He did not set up a school of his own and had comparatively few pupils, but his great merit lay in diffusing moral education among young folks by his popular works, and in this respect he was hardly equalled, certainly not surpassed, by any of his contemporaries. He initiated a theoretical study of education, elucidating its aim, method, process, scope, &c., and on this account he was not only a great educator, but a pioneer in the field of pedagogical studies. According to him, the aim of education, in the ultimate analysis, is the perfection of moral character.

Revival of the Chutsze school.

In the period between the latter part of the seventeenth century and the beginning of the eighteenth (the Genroku and Kyōho eras), besides the Classical school, which, advocated by Jinsai, Sorai, and their followers, had by this time become very influential, the *Setchū* (Eclectic) school was fast gaining popu-larity. On the other hand, the Chutsze school suffered gradual eclipse, and towards the end of the eighteenth century (the Anyéi

and Temméi eras) it was in a state of decline.   To ameliorate
this condition, a law was passed in the Kwanséi era (end of the
eighteenth century) strictly prohibiting the *Igaku*, or heterodox
schools, as all schools other than the Chutsze, which was the
only *Séigaku* or recognized standard of the educational system,
were called.   This act of legislation was quickly followed by
the revival of the Chutsze throughout the country, and around
the Hayashi family, which was still its centre, there arose a
constellation of scholars, among whom Ritsuzan Shibano (1734–
1807), Jishū Bitō (1745–1813), Séiri Koga (1750–1817) were
especially illustrious.   These pundits adhered to the principles
laid down by Junan and Kyūsō, and endeavoured to give a
uniformity of system to the country's education.

The example set by the Shōgunate of making the Chutsze
school the recognized standard of education, to the exclusion of
all other schools, was soon followed by several local clan
governments ; radical educational reform was thus conducted throughout the empire, and all other educational
systems came to be considered as obstacles, especially in the
eyes of office-seekers, and grew less and less potential.   But
whatever may have been the minor advantages attending this
prohibition of ' heterodox schools ' of learning, a consequential
evil arose out of it, namely, that it checked the channels for
new and original ideas, and imposed rigid restrictions upon
freedom of thought.

But fortunately a champion, Issai Satō (1772–1859), ap-   Issai Satō.
peared in the arena, who, combining the two systems of
Chutsze and Luh-Siangshang, returned to the magnanimous
attitude of Séikwa Fujiwara and influenced many young men
of the day.   He was disparagingly spoken of by some as a
' worshipper of Chutsze openly, and an adherent of Wang-
Yangming secretly,' but it cannot be disputed that he played a
great part in training many highly gifted pupils.

A little later than Issai, Sanyō Rai (1780–1832) became   Sanyō
famous for his scholarly attainments.   He was a son of Shunsui,   Rai.
and studied for some time under Jishū Bitō.   Both his father
and his master were advocates of the Chutsze philosophy, so
he also may be properly classed under that head, and this is
confirmed by a statement in the story of his life written by one

of his pupils named Égi. But he was no doctrinaire, and,
besides, he on occasions expressed sympathy with Wang-
Yangming rather than with Chutsze. In a word, he devoted
his rare talent and unrivalled energy to the study of history,
tempered with political and economic views, and his highly
patriotic utterances greatly inspired the Royalists of the latter
days of the Tokugawa Shōgunate. The doctrines of the
Chutsze school, as expounded by Séikwa Fujiwara and handed
down by his followers, were couched in very moderate terms ;
but another branch of the same school, far more extreme and

The Southern school.
which called itself the *Nangaku* (Southern school), made its
appearance in Tosa Province in the seventeenth century,
being first advocated by Baikén, then by Jichū Tani, and

Ansai Yama-zaki.
finally by Ansai Yamazaki (1618–82), who taught in Kyōto.
Ansai apparently refrained from attempting to formulate
original theories ; but, making a text-book with such passages
from Chutsze's works as constituted the most essential elements
of his ethical principles, he endeavoured to exemplify these
teachings in the practice of his daily life. For this reason his
precepts, like religious doctrines, were strongly formulated, to
the exclusion of all other systems of thought. He maintained
that man ought to elevate his inner soul with reverence and
regulate his outer conduct with righteousness. In view of its
strict doctrine, his school is naturally open to the charge of
being narrow and exclusive. In his closing years he tried to
reconcile *Shintō* with Confucianism, and his principles thereby
lost much of their consistency and clearness, but it must be
noted to his credit that by so doing he aroused self-respect in
the nation.

After his death his school divided into four main branches,
upheld respectively by Kéisai Asami (1652–1711), Naokata
Satō (1650–1719), Shōsai Miyaké (1662–1741), and Isai Tamaki
(— –1736). Of these, that advanced by Isai Tamaki belonged to *Shintō*, the other three to the Chutsze school. There
were also among Ansai's pupils some who were entirely independent of any of the branches, and under this head came
Sōkén Yonékawa, Raisai Fujii, and Shinzan Tani.

Ansai's system exercised a far-reaching influence on the
trend of contemporary thought, and such well-known Royalists

as Kéisai Asami, Shikibu Takénouchi, Daini Yamagata, and others were all turned out from his school.   It also had a great bearing on the Mito system of learning.

For the purpose of compiling a complete history of Japan, Mitsukuni Tokugawa invited a number of distinguished scholars to his feudal town Mito, and these formed themselves into the Mito school.   This school did not definitely profess to adopt the Chutsze system, but, as a matter of fact, those who took part in the compilation of the history, with few exceptions, advocated it.   Among them especially Sempō Kuriyama (1671–1706) and Kwanran Miyaké (1675–1712) had come from the Ansai school.   Suikén Tachihara (1744–1823) alone belonged to the Classical school, but such influential persons as Yūkoku Fujita (1774–1826), Tōko Fujita (1806–55), and Séishisai Aizawa (1782–1863) adhered to the Chutsze system, and it was these men that enthusiastically asserted the nobility of our national character and tried to awaken the national conscience. *The Mito school.*

In enumerating the systems of Confucian teaching in the third period, we must mention, besides the Chutsze school, the Wang-Yangming school, the Classical school, the Eclectic school, &c.   The Wang-Yangming school was so named because it originated in the philosophy founded by Wang-Yangming (1472–1528), a scholar in the Ming dynasty of China.   In Japan, Séikwa Fujiwara had already paid much attention to Wang-Yangming's theory of the *Ryōchi*;[1] nevertheless, as has been already stated, he adhered chiefly to Chutsze.   The first veritable advocate of the Wang-Yangming school in this period was undoubtedly Tōju Nakaé (1608-78).   Starting in early life as an adherent of the Chutsze school, he afterwards became an advocate of the Wang-Yangming, and in his later years enthusiastically advanced its theory of the *Ryōchi*.   He maintained that the *Ryōchi* not only formed an essential factor in the original nature of an individual, but also a real entity in the universe.   In this he agreed with the philosophy of the Vedanta school ; but, after all, his paramount merit lay in the practical rather than in the theoretical side of his doctrine. A man of superb character, he did not preach what he could *Wang-Yangming school.*

[1] This term has a sense similar to ' conscience,' but is of wider and deeper import.

not practise, for every word that he uttered was based on his own experience. Well might his contemporaries call him 'Ōmi Séijin,' or 'The Sage of Ōmi Province.'

Banzan Kuma-zawa. Of Tōju's pupils the most distinguished was Banzan Kumazawa (1619–91). There was a marked difference in personality between Tōju and Banzan. Upright and sincere, the former was an ideal moral teacher, while the latter was a man of genius, gifted with a fine quality of statesmanship. He occupied an important position in the service of the Lord of Bizén, and his rare administrative ability was the wonder and admiration of the age. But as his learning had been acquired in the school of Tōju, it may fairly be said that the latter's theories found their application in the former's states-manship. Thus it is true, from one aspect, that, but for Banzan, Tōju would never have risen to such prominence in public estimation ; but it is also true, from another aspect, that nothing save Tōju's personal influence could have modelled Banzan's great statesmanship. These two famous men, de-pendent upon each other, combined their efforts to consolidate the foundation of the Wang-Yangming school in this country.

Later conditions of the Wang-Yangming school. Many scholars, such as Shōan Miyé, Sékian Miyaké, Shissai Miwa, Yūkin Kawada, Tōri Nakané, &c., advocated the Wang-Yangming philosophy, but, nevertheless, it gradually lost in-fluence and was finally cast into the shade by the Chutsze and the Classical schools. Issai Satō put his faith in the Wang-Yangming, but lacked the courage to advocate it openly and pretended to hold to the Chutsze school. As for Chūsai Ōshio (1794–1837), although he was bold enough to profess publicly his adherence to the Wang-Yangming school, it is a matter for regret that he incurred the suspicion of the Shōgun for political reasons and met with a tragic and premature death.

The Wang-Yangming school and the new civi-lization. Finally, it must be noted here that the Wang-Yangming school exercised great influence over the minds of many patriots who played important parts in the formation of New Japan, and thus accelerated the introduction of the new civilization. Shōnan Yokoi (1809–69), Shōzan Sakuma (1811–64), Yasuomi Maki (1812–64), Senan Kasuga (1812–78), Takamori Saigō (1826–77)—all these reformers either

belonged to the school or came under its influence. As this
school makes the law of the *Ryōchi* its fundamental principle, it
urges men to put into action whatever their conscience judges
to be good and right. One disadvantage of such a system is
that it often tends to give excessive weight to subjective judgment and disregards the environment in which a man is placed,
but its extremely practical spirit necessarily deserves high
commendation.

Besides the Chutsze school and the Wang-Yangming, there
arose in the second half of the seventeenth century another
system, calling itself the *Kogaku-ha* or Classical school. It
boldly denounced the Sung school of learning as defiling the
pure and genuine system of Confucius by introducing certain
Buddhist and other elements, and proclaimed the establishment of a direct connection with the original Confucianism.
The founders of this system were Sokō Yamaga (1622–85)
and Jinsai Itō (1627-1705). Both these men had pursued at
first the Chutsze school, and it was a striking coincidence that
they framed this new system independently of each other in
the same year, namely 1662, although it was the former that
first wrote on the Classical school.

The Classical school.

Sokō published his work ' *Séikyō Yōroku* ' (' Compendium
of Confucianism ') in three parts in the year 1666. A book of
small dimensions, the author in it strongly opposed the Sung
school of learning, and went so far as to declare that ' the true
teachings of Confucianism totally decayed during the Sung
dynasty.' This brought upon him the indignation of the
Shōgunate, who banished him to Akō in Harima Province. Ten
years later he was recalled from exile, and returned to Yédo,
where he passed eleven quiet but discontented years in his
residence in the Asakusa district. He wrote a number of
books, one of which, the ' *Séikyō Yōroku*,' was confiscated by
the Shōgunate, and its blocks were destroyed ; but the others
have been preserved, thanks to the efforts of his pupils, who
copied them all. In revolt against the scholars of the Sung
school, who unduly emphasized the principle of *ri* (reason), he
advanced the importance of *jin* (benevolence or charity),
declaring that benevolence and righteousness constitute the
essential principle of the teachings of the ancient sages. In

this respect he may be said to have pursued the same course as Jinsai Itō, who regarded the virtues of benevolence and righteousness as the ' way ' of life. In his work ' Séigakuhen ' (' Exposition of Confucianism '), Sokō strove to evolve a system of his own, but after all he rendered greater service to his country as an advocate of the *Bushidō* than as a moral philosopher. Besides being himself a strict observer of the disciplinary code of the *Bushidō*, he wrote a number of books on the subject, as the ' *Bukyō Shōgaku* ' (' Introduction to the *Bushidō* Culture '), the ' *Gorui* ' (' Random Thoughts '), and the ' *Haisho Zampitsu* ' (' An Exile's Autobiography '), and expounded the central principles of the *Bushidō*, giving it an educational character. The famous vendetta of the forty-seven *rōnin* was an outcome of his influence. He had many followers in succeeding ages, and by them the *Bushidō* has been handed down onwards to to-day. His adopted son, Takatsuné, and his grandson, Kōdō Tsugaru, also wrote works on the *Bushidō* ; and Yūzan Daidōji, one of his pupils, also excelled in knowledge of the *Bushidō*, judging from the quality of his work the ' *Budō Shoshin-shū* ' (' Elementary Book of the *Bushidō* Culture '). Shōin Yoshida, a patriot who lived shortly before the Restoration, was greatly inspired by Sokō, as evidenced by his work the ' *Bukyō Kōroku* ' (' Lectures on the *Bushidō* Culture').

The *Bushidō*, a kind of moral discipline peculiar to our people, has been handed down from time immemorial, and in the Kamakura age it was developed and embodied in a set of precepts, but it remained for the genius of Sokō to form it into a system connected with Military Science, *Shintō*, Confucianism, and Buddhism, he himself standing out prominent as an embodiment of the *Bushidō* spirit.

Jinsai Itō.   As has already been noted, Jinsai began to advocate the Classical school at the same moment as Sokō ; but they worked independently of each other, the one in Kyōto and the other in Yédo. Opposed to the negative attitude of the scholars of the Sung school, he assumed a positive attitude, declaring that the aim of life was to perfect one's personality by active development of individuality. This theory of his aims at the same ideal as Green's theory of self-realization. Again, adopting Mencius' doctrine, he regarded *jin-gi* (benevolence and righteousness) as the fundamental principles of human relations.   In this his teaching bore a great resemblance to Schopenhauer's theory of ' Menschenliebe ' and ' Gerechtigkeit ' or Spencer's interpretation of ' Justice ' and ' Beneficence.'   To go further in preaching the importance of benevolence, he manifested the same spirit as that which characterizes the thirteenth chapter of St. Paul's First Epistle to the Corinthians. Unlike the scholars of the Sung school, who urged men to return to nature, his attitude was extremely positive and progressive.   He thought it better to strive for a development of one's natural capacities than to guard oneself over-cautiously against committing minor blunders.   His noble character and profound scholarship enabled him to preach practical morality in highly inspiring terms.   But being the founder of a new school, he had not sufficient time to perfect it, and it was left for his son Tōgai to put the finishing touches to his theory.

Tōgai (1670–1736) was a man of rare sincerity and faith-fulness, and although he was somewhat lacking in insight and originality, he was exactly fitted for the work of perfecting his father's system.   Besides arranging and publishing Jinsai's manuscripts, he wrote a number of books himself, informed with his father's principles.   Though very modest and humble in disposition, his sense of filial piety was so strong as to make him call himself ' a man of filial piety.'   Obedient to his father in every way, his heart rebelled against the idea of altering even a word uttered by him.   In these circumstances his life-work did not go beyond the continuation of the task initiated by Jinsai.   He thus established the famous Horikawa school of thought.   Tōgai Itō.

Another champion of the Classical school, Sorai Mononobé by name, but generally called ' Bussorai ' (1666–1728), appeared in the arena under the stimulus of Jinsai.   But in time he took a direction quite opposite to the latter.   Beginning his career as an adherent of the Chutsze school, he became a supporter of the Classical school at the age of forty-nine, and wrote many books, such as the ' *Bendō* ' (' Explanation of the True Principles '), the ' *Benméi* ' (' Explanation of the Technical Terms of Confucianism '), the ' *Gakusoku* ' (' Rules for Classical Learning '), setting forth his original views on many points.   Sorai Mono-nobé.

Although Jinsai and Sorai alike belonged to the Classical school, there was a great difference between the theories of the two. Sorai maintained that in pursuing classical learning, one must have a thorough knowledge of the etymology of ancient writings, which, according to him, was the only highway leading to the desired goal. Accordingly, he explored the Confucian classics from a philological point of view and made a special study of ancient etymology. It is for this reason that his system is often called *Kobunjigaku* (Ancient Etymology school). Jinsai urged men to follow the steps of the ancient sages in character-building ; whereas Sorai argued that it was not given to the average man to attain the perfection of the ancient sages, and he ought to be content with accomplishment in a single department of learning. Again, Jinsai regarded the law of benevolence and righteousness as the fundamental principles of life, whereas Sorai contended that the regulation of social relations in accordance with the rules of manners and ceremonies was of paramount importance. He thus stood on a utilitarian basis. Previously to this Sokō Yamaga had already taken up a utilitarian position, but he had not been able to form it into a theory. So it was through Sorai that Utilitarianism was first advocated as an influential system. Furthermore, while Jinsai thought that moral principles came by nature, Sorai maintained that these had been framed by the ancient sages.

In many respects Sorai's theory greatly resembled that of Hobbes. For instance, he declared that right and wrong were determined only in the sight of the law of the State ; that, as man's true nature was self-interest, and, if let alone, would work rueful havoc in society, the task of establishing laws to regulate the populace must be performed by the arbitrary will of a despotic monarch.

Finally, unlike Jinsai, who worshipped Mencius, Sorai adored Siuntsze, and formulated the theory of the immutability of personality, based upon the latter's doctrines. In this he expressed the same idea as Schopenhauer, who held that man's personality is permanent and remains unchanged by any circumstances in his life.

In a word, though both Jinsai and Sorai advocated the

Classical school, they disagreed in many points of their theories. But the difference between them was not so great as that between Sorai and the adherents of the Sung school. Indeed, Sorai had almost nothing in common with the latter, so far as the theoretical side of their studies was concerned. Disregarding speculative researches, he charmed the reading public by his thoroughgoing etymological interpretation of the classics as well as by his rich and elegant diction.

Among many brilliant pupils of Sorai, Shuntai Dazai (1680– 1747) stood out in special prominence for his theoretical study. In some respects he pushed to the extreme his master's theory. As is well known to students of Chinese culture, the teachings of Confucius were interpreted from two main points of view by Mencius and Siuntsze respectively. Mencius drew suggestions from the law of sincerity of Tszesz, Confucius' grandson, and placed great stress upon conscience, making the nobility of man's inner virtue the starting-point of his doctrines. Siuntsze, on the other hand, greatly emphasized the importance of external expressions of reverence and held that man should be regulated from without. While the former took the autonomic position, the latter adhered to the heteronomic. It has been stated elsewhere that Jinsai adopted Mencius' system. Sorai, on the other hand, enlarged upon Siuntsze's doctrine, and his theory was followed by Shuntai. Indeed, the last named went so far in advancing the heteronomic law as to declare that, whatever depraved thoughts a man might harbour in his mind, he was virtuous as long as he could restrain their issue in deference to the rules of manners. He also esteemed man's original nature, and in this respect was in agreement with Nietzscheism and the Naturalism of to-day.

Shuntai Dazai.

Besides the Chutsze school, the Wang-Yangming school, and the Classical school, which we have considered in the preceding paragraphs, there were the *Setchū Gakuha* (Eclectic school), the *Kōshō Gakuha* (Philological and Historical school), and the *Dokuritsu Gakuha* (Independent school). The first of these, i.e. the Eclectic school, professed not to attach itself to any special academy, but to aim at establishing a perfect system, comprising the theories of all schools. Its attitude was strictly impartial, but as it lacked a solid basis, it failed to become an

The Eclectic school.

influential system, and most of its advocates gradually went over to the Philological and Historical school. Among the scholars of the Eclectic school, such persons as Héishū Ki (1728–1801) rendered meritorious service to the advancement of moral ideas.

The Philological and Historical school.

The Philological and Historical school aimed at making inquiries into classical writings and drawing conclusions from facts. The method adopted by it was somewhat scientific, yet after all it may be classed properly as the Classical school in the broad sense.

The Independent school.

Strictly speaking, there could exist no such thing as an Independent school, for all branches of Confucianism are based upon the teachings of that great sage. But for convenience' sake, scholars who could not be classed in any of the above-mentioned schools were put under this head. Of these we must mention Baién Miura (1723–89) and Sontoku Ninomiya (1787–1856) as representatives.

Baién Miura.

The first named mainly engaged in philosophical researches and evolved a system of Cosmology entirely his own, which he called *Jōrigaku*, or the Science of Reason. His theory is set forth in his works, the '*Gengo*' ('Mysterious Words'), the '*Kango*' ('Bold Words'), and the '*Zéigo*' ('Superfluous Words').

Sontoku Ninomiya.

Sontoku Ninomiya strongly advocated agricultural morality. Though on the whole he agreed with Utilitarianism, he esteemed 'motives' also. In other words, he held that motives transcended utility. By his conduct in practical life he showed how far the 'motives' of Idealism and the 'results' of Utilitarianism could be harmonized. His thoughts owed much to *Shintō* and Buddhism, but in the final analysis their fountain-head was to be sought in Confucianism.

Confucianists and the new civilization.

That the majority of those who participated in the making of New Japan, towards the end of the third period, consisted of Confucianists is an undeniable fact. For example, such enthusiastic patriots as Tōko Fujita, Shōnan Yokoi, Shōzan Sakuma, Shōin Yoshida, Sanai Hashimoto, &c., were at the same time ardent Confucianists. Of all the branches of Confucianism, the Chutsze school and the Wang-Yangming school produced most pioneers of the new era. Again, comparing these two schools, we note that the latter especially turned out many great men in proportion to the small number of its supporters.

It may be added that the readiness with which our people grasped and adopted the newly introduced Western civilization was in the main due to the mental training that they had received from the study of Confucianism throughout the Tokugawa age.

THE FOURTH PERIOD (SUBSEQUENT TO THE RESTORATION OF 1868)

The Confucianism of the Méiji era is nothing but a continuation of that of the preceding period. It has no specially characteristic features of its own. It is to be noticed, however, that in consequence of the introduction of Western civilization which revolutionized every phase of our country's social relations, Confucianism has undergone a great decline. To-day its eminent representatives are gradually lessening, and even those who remain no longer wield any considerable influence as in the past. It is true that various schools of Confucianism which arose one after another in the Tokugawa age have not yet altogether passed out of being, but their condition is such that their existence is scarcely recognized in learned circles. It is also true that there will always be some scholars who study Confucianism by modern methods, yet it can be said with safety that the glorious era of the cult, when it influenced the popular minds like a religion side by side with *Shintō* and Buddhism, will never return.

But it must not be supposed for a moment that Confucianism has perished in every sense of the word. On the contrary, its spirit not only remains deeply impressed on the minds of the mass of the people, but it also constitutes the backbone of the national education of the new era. All its essential teachings are present in the existing educational system, though its name is no more observable. As the educational ethics of the present day is founded on a scientific basis, its system and contents are far more perfect and complicated than those of Confucianism ; but, in the last resort, one agrees with the other in making the highest good the ultimate goal of human activities, in regarding the perfection of personality as the aim of action, in attaching special importance to motives rather than to results when judging of the right and wrong of an action. Further, the central term *jin* (benevolence) in Confucianism expresses the same idea as the word ' humanity,' which is to-day the goal of mankind. Herein Confucianism transcends all religions. And the moral education of our era, though it is not to be identified with Confucianism, has this in common with the latter, namely, that it stands aloof from and is above religion in the popular sense of the term, and enjoys freedom from any form of superstition. It therefore moves in perfect harmony with the principles of modern science. The doctrine that moral education must be backed by some historical religion has been shattered entirely by recent experiments. In Europe, France separated education from religion in 1881, and the example was soon followed by Italy. We have reason to believe that some day all other civilized countries will take the same step. But in our country this has been done ever since the Restoration in 1868. Not only that, even in the Tokugawa epoch the same system was in force to some extent. It was, indeed, the experiments made in that period that paved the way for the general acceptance, in the present era, of this form of education. The example of giving moral education without the aid of any historical religion was set by Confucianism. The present system of moral culture in Japan is founded upon this basis, only clothed in a more progressive form. It directly points to the goal of mankind, the universal and eternal principle of humanity, apart from any religious dogma. For this reason we conclude that, though the framework of Confucianism has already decayed, its soul, still living as before and forming the essential part of present-day education, will continue to exist in a new garb for long ages to come.

IV

JAPANESE RELIGIOUS BELIEFS : BUDDHISM

Professor J. Takakusu, D.Litt. (Japan), D.Phil., M.A.

Various religious systems have had their origin in India, but almost all of them were based on nationalistic or racial lines. Buddhism alone is distinguished as cosmic in character, as the first to break through the bonds of nationalism to become a universal religion and a great missionary movement, unobstructed by barriers of race. This caused it to spread not only throughout India, but over more than half the then known world. *Buddhism a universal religion.*

During the reign of King Asoka (*circ.* 250 B.C.), its missionary field is said to have extended to Bactria and other Greek settlements in the North, Greece, Egypt, Macedonia and Syria in the West, Ceylon in the South, and the Malay Peninsula in the East, until in 67 A.D. it finally reached China. Thence it spread to Korea, and in the year 552 A.D. the sacred books of Buddhism were brought to Japan. Introduced at an opportune moment, Buddhism was welcomed by all classes, and the majority of the people soon became its adherents. It is needless to say how powerful was its influence over the formation of beliefs and moral principles ; and this influence extended to politics, education, literature, industry, and art—in fact, there was nothing that was not impregnated with Buddhism, or influenced by its priests. In other words, the ancient civilization of Japan owed its rise to Buddhism. There is one strange fact concerned with the introduction of the religion into Japan which is worthy of notice—namely, that, whilst on the Continent the original spirit of Buddhism was forgotten, and its adherents clung to a corrupt form, as soon as it was brought into Japan it underwent a refining process. The corrupt forms were *Spread of Buddhism.*

Buddhism
Japanized.

rejected, and only that which seemed to the Japanese pure
and good was retained, to be remodelled, as it were, and formed
into the Buddhism of Japan. It was not, therefore, a mere
transplanting of the Buddhism of India, China, Annam, or
of Korea, but a new and distinct form of religion. It was
through this that Japan happily escaped from being poisoned
by the unhealthy forms prevalent on the Continent.

Buddhism in Japan before the Restoration

Introduc-
tion of
Buddh-
ism.

There is no means of ascertaining the exact date of the
introduction of Buddhism into Japan; but, as it was in the
thirteenth year of the reign of the Emperor Kimméi (552 A.D.)
that the King of Kudara (Pekche, a province of ancient Korea)
presented the Japanese Court with an image of Buddha and
the sacred books, which act was followed by the coming of
Buddhist priests and nuns, engravers of images, and temple-
builders, it may be presumed that this was the date of its
formal entry.

Prince
Shōtoku.

In the reign of the Empress Suiko (593–628 A.D.), the Prince
Imperial Shōtoku, who had control of the Government and was
an earnest adherent of Buddhism, endeavoured to propagate the
doctrines of Buddha—first laying down the constitution of the
country in seventeen articles, which established the hierarchical
form of government and made Buddhism its foundation.
For those who desired to study and live up to the precepts
of the Enlightened One, the Prince established monasteries,
and, in addition, founded a free hospital and dispensary for the
poor, and a home for widows and orphans. His philanthropic
and educational enterprises caused Buddhism to flourish for
a time; but, although it thus prospered during his regency, no
sectarian division had yet appeared, nor was it until after the
death of the Prince in 621 A.D. that it began to be divided into
various sects.

Rise of
sects.

Three years after the Prince's decease, Ékwan came from
Koma (Kōryō, another province of ancient Korea), and,
expounding the Three Treaties, founded the 'Three Sāstras'
or 'Sanron' sect, which was the beginning of sectarianism in
Japan.

In the ninth year of the reign of the Emperor Kōtoku (653 A.D.), the priest Dōshō, who had been in China studying the doctrine of Vijñaña-mātra (Idealism) under Hiuen-tsang, returned to Japan and established the ' Hossō ' sect (Dharma-Iakshana), of which the immediate consequence was the dispatch to China of many students, who brought back not only Buddhism, but the civilization of the golden age of the Tang dynasty.

Students sent to China.

In 735 A.D., during the reign of the Emperor Shōmu, Dōsén, a Chinese priest, and Bodhisena, an Indian Priest, came over bringing with them the Avatamsaka-Sutra, and later the priest Shinshō came from Shiragi (Simra, yet another province of ancient Korea) to give lectures on these sacred books, and lay the first foundations of the ' Kégon ' (Avatamsaka) sect in Japan.

In the Nara period (710–94 A.D.), Buddhism was at its height during the reign of the above-mentioned Emperor Shōmu (724–48 A.D.), and this was the time when the large temples were built, and the great image of Buddha set up. It was also an epoch of great activity in philanthropic effort of various kinds, all of which works of charity centred in the Dowager Empress Kōmyō, who, it is said, from her religious and charitable spirit, even condescended to tend the lepers in the medical baths with her own hands.

Nara period.

In the sixth year of the reign of the Empress Kōkén (754 A.D.), the Chinese priest, Kanjin, visited Japan and propagated the Vinaya (Discipline), thus forming the Vinaya or ' Ritsu ' sect.

The four sects above mentioned—namely, the Sanron, the Hossō, the Kégon, and the Ritsu, and two subordinate ones, the Kusha and Jōjitsu—were called the six sects of the Nara period. Among them the most flourishing were the Sanron and the Hossō.

These six sects, however, having been founded soon after the introduction of Buddhism, were simply transplanted forms of the religion as it then existed in China, and were not well adapted to the condition of the Japanese nation. Accordingly, a new Buddhism, which would admit the national gods as incarnate forms of Buddhas, was preached at the time, but although every effort was made to bring about the change, nothing which could be called a distinct Japanese Buddhism appeared until Saichō (Dengyō) and Kūkai (Kōbō) founded the 'Tendai' and 'Shingon' sects respectively.

Corruption of priests. As has already been stated, the Buddhism of the Nara period—that is, some two hundred years after the faith had been first brought into Japan—was at its height during the reign of the Emperor Shōmu ; but as a reaction against the prosperity it then enjoyed, corruption soon began to creep into the system. The Buddhism of the Court became merely the performance of religious rites and ceremonies, and the chief aim of the priest was the acquisition of Court favour. As in all other hierarchical forms of government, the corruption spread to political circles and society at large, so that the whole administrative organization was degraded and thrown into a disorderly and lawless condition. Lamenting such a deplorable condition of things, Saichō and Kūkai endeavoured to **Two reformers.** establish a new Buddhism, and as, just at that time, the Emperor Kwammu was reorganizing his government and removing his palace to Héian (Kyōto), the reformation of religion commenced at the same time as the political house-cleaning.

Two new sects. In the twenty-third year of the Emperor's reign (804 A.D.), Saichō and Kūkai, most favoured and trusted subjects, went to China. The former returned the next year (805 A.D.) and established the 'Tendai' sect, while the latter came back in 806 A.D. to found the 'Shingon' sect, and these are called the two sects of the Héian (Kyōto) period. It is true both sects were brought from China, but their doctrines were greatly modified to suit the Japanese, and, in order to adapt Buddhism to the new country, Saichō and Kūkai freely admitted all the existing gods of Japan as incarnate forms of one or other of the Buddhas, and treated them as such.

Influence of the two sects. Almost all the principal *Shintō* shrines had some Buddhist priests attached to them, to whom the performance of half of the religious rites was entrusted. Thus the Japanized Buddhism appeared in contrast with the six sects of the old capital, while the six old sects, on the other hand—awakened by the new movement—revived and showed fresh activity. Notwithstanding this, for four hundred years onward—from the reign of Kwammu (782 A.D.) to the founding of the Shōgunate by Yoritomo at Kamakura in 1192—the Tendai and the Shingon sects exercised the greatest influence.

At first they sent out educated and learned missionaries to propagate their doctrines; but towards the end of the Héian period, even Japanese Buddhism showed a tendency to decline and lose its true spirit. Coupled with this the dignitaries of the capital adopted riotous ways of living; while in the provinces the rich followed their example, and thus the general moral standards and laws again fell into disrepute. Politicians also tried to take advantage of religion, and Buddhists of politics; whilst the priests gradually became arrogant and lawless in character, so much so that it was beyond the power even of the Emperor to control them. Thus the country was thrown into general confusion and disorder, and once more the need was felt for a new school to give religion fresh life and power. *Degradation of priests.*

To meet this urgency Ryōnin started the ' Yuzū Nembutsu ' sect, Hōnén the ' Jōdo,' Ippén the ' Ji,' Shinran the ' Shin,' Éisai and Dōgén the ' Zen,' and Nichirén the Hokké or 'Nichirén,' each of which made its appearance during the period extending from the latter part of the Héian to the middle of the Kamakura era. All of them, save the Zen, formulated their doctrines so as to be easily understood, and thus to attract the masses, while the Zen sect succeeded in gaining a powerful hold over the beliefs of the military class in the belligerent era. *Reformation.*

The Shin sect, which, by considering missionaries and priests as secular, and permitting them to marry and eat meat, was successful in reaching even the lowest section of the people, and the Hokké sect, which mingled the power and will of Mahomet with the spirit of Sākyamūni, and had a potent influence generally, were the two sects most modified to suit the Japanese spirit, so much so that, compared with Continental Buddhism, hardly any similarity can be found between them. *The Shin and the Hokké sects.*

During the four hundred years that separated the Kamakura period from that of Tokugawa, the sects which did the most effective work were the Jōdo, Zen, Shin, and Hokké; for the influence of the Yuzū Nembutsu and Ji sects were confined to a certain time and locality. The Zen sect deserves special mention *Summarized description of different sects.*

for having produced many eminent priests during the long wars of the periods of the Hojō and the Ashikaga (1299–1573 A.D.). Finding many adherents among the military classes, it contributed not a little to the formation of *Bushidō*, the doctrine of knightly behaviour.

Prohibition of Christianity.

As for the remaining sects, they accomplished nothing worthy of note; for although nominally existent, they had actually ceased to be so. When Iyéyasu Tokugawa, after bringing order out of the chaos then existing in the country, became Shōgun, he found that the Roman Catholics, who came to Japan about 1542, were secretly plotting. Seeing that they were endangering the country, he adopted the policy of closing it against foreign intrusion, and strictly forbade the propagation of Christianity or belief in it. At the same time, he lent support to the Buddhists, and gave the priests authority to take a census, whereby, under the name of ' An inquiry into religious belief,' everybody was forced to adhere to one or other of the sects of Buddhism. From this time onwards the whole nation became professedly Buddhist, and its priests secured special powers, and a position of influence in society.

Abuse of privileges by priests.

But abuse of their privileges made them arrogant and purely ritualistic, until they finally departed altogether from the true spirit of the Buddhist mission, and it may be said with truth that, during the two hundred and sixty years or more of the Tokugawa dynasty, Buddhism merely sustained an existence of form without spirit.

Summary.

The above is a short history of Buddhism in Japan from the time it was first brought into the country down to the Restoration, and it may be divided into three periods : the first, from the time it was primarily transmitted from China down to the Buddhism of the Nara period ; the second, from the generation of Nara Buddhism down to the time when Saichō (Dengyō) and Kūkai (Kōbō) founded new schools of Buddhism, or the Héian period ; and the third, from the fall of Héian Buddhism, and the formation of the Jōdo, Shin, Zen, and Hokké sects to supersede it, down to the Restoration.

Glancing over these different epochs in the history of Buddhism, a marked development is evident in each period. The second was a great improvement on the first, for it effected large modifications in its doctrines to adapt them to the Japanese, while in the third these were even more striking.

Thus Buddhism in Japan has never remained inactive or become effete, but reaction has followed reaction, and reformation reformation—a constant refining and remodelling going on to meet the needs of the people. Comparing this with the Buddhism of China—which once corrupted remained so, even to the extent of endangering the country—it may be said that Japanese Buddhism is in thorough accordance with the spirit of its great founder.

It has been demonstrated by history that the Japanese have the peculiar power of carefully analysing anything they import and remodelling it to suit their conception of its ideals, and upon this faculty the development of their religious beliefs has been based.

INFLUENCE OF BUDDHISM ON JAPANESE CIVILIZATION

The laws of good government, education as a system, arts and sciences, agriculture and industry, all these were introduced into this country from China and Korea by the priests who came here temporarily or permanently, and by the Japanese priests who went to those countries to study and investigate religion. When Dōshō, the founder of the Hossō sect, came back, he, for the first time in Japan, caused wells to be dug by the wayside, bridges to be built, ferry-boats to be placed at the river crossings, and drains to be cut in the streets. His disciple Gyōgi, travelling throughout the country, opened paths over the mountains, excavated canals and repaired the roads ; whilst Fushō, also a priest of Nara, planted trees by the wayside to shade travellers—in fact, from the efforts of the propagandists the work of opening up the mountainous districts and cultivating the fields received a new impetus. Among the various industries introduced into Japan by the religious fervour which helped to improve art and science the following may be mentioned : the carving of images, building of temples, painting, and the manufacture of tiles, concrete, lacquered and earthern wares, woven goods, embroideries, paper, ink, and dyeing materials.

It was also through the Buddhists that calendars, music,

Buddh-istic by products.

and useful plants were brought into the country, and by means of their philanthropic work medical art was improved, schools and orphan asylums built, and hot springs discovered. In addition, the Buddhists supplied profound metaphysical thought to the people, who had up to this time rested content with simple mythological legends which inculcated only purity and righteousness and the worship of nature and ancestors.

In the literature of Japan there are marked traces of the influence of Buddhism and its tenets. The arrangement of the fifty sounds of the *kata-kana*, or square characters, was based upon Sanskrit, and that of the forty-seven sounds of the *hira-kana*, or curved characters, was made from a poem embodying the Buddhist doctrines ; neither is there a single classical production that does not take its tone from Buddhism. The works of the two greatest women-writers of the Héian period—the *Genji Monogatari*' of Murasaki-Shikibu, and the ' *Makura-no-Sōshi*' of Séi-Shōnagon, for example—are plainly coloured with Buddhism. Moreover, the poems of various styles take their key-note from it, and express its views.

In the Kamakura period, when the country was torn by war and disorder, it was the priests alone who preserved literature and were versed in it. The so-called literature of the ' Five Monasteries' of Kyōto and the study of classical Chinese were left to the priests, and the first primary school in Japan had its origin in the temple schools called ' *térakoya.*' Outside the realm of literature, also, traces of Buddhist influence can be found in music and song, both classical and popular ; even military science was influenced more or less directly, and, as has already been said, ' *Bushidō*,' or the doctrine of knightly behaviour, was largely affected by the teaching of the Zen sect.

From this array of facts we can safely conclude that the civilization peculiar to Japan and existing before the Restoration undoubtedly had its source in Buddhism.

THE INFLUENCE OF OCCIDENTAL CIVILIZATION ON BUDDHISM AFTER THE RESTORATION

The history of Japanese Buddhism in pre-Restoration times is divided into three periods. It has now entered a fourth, and it remains to be seen whether in this period also, Buddhism will,

as it did during the preceding three, continue to progress with
the tide of advancement, controlling the hearts of the people
and supplying the urgent demand for a new form of religion.
One thing, however, is certain, that Buddhism, awakened by
the marvellous advance of New Japan, is undergoing, at present,
gradual but decided reformation.

During the Tokugawa period Buddhism enjoyed special A blow to
Court favour, but this was far from being the case at the time Buddhism.
of the Restoration. The peculiar privileges granted to the
Buddhist temples were then taken away, and all the honours
and titlés conferred on the priests cancelled. Hitherto, the
followers of Confucianism and *Shintō* always looked upon
Buddhism with envy, on account of the subordinate position
they themselves had to occupy ; so, taking this opportunity,
they raised the cry, ' Down with Buddhism ! ' and made every
effort to substitute *Shintō* as the national religion.

On all sides the Buddhists experienced violent opposition,
but the blow fell upon the priests alone, for the minds of the
people had been so deeply affected that they were quite un-
disturbed, and the majority remained true to the faith. The
priests themselves, instead of bowing to the storm, were
aroused to new activity, and after several reactions had ensued
within six or seven years after the Restoration, they once more
showed a progressive tendency.

The characteristically broad-minded nature of the Japanese, Influence
the new knowledge brought back by the priests who went to of Chris-
Europe and America, and the methods and attitude taken by the tianity.
Christians in their missionary work, gave the Buddhists new
incentives for the improvement of their organization, doctrines,
and philanthropic work.

The Buddhists of old, both on the Continent and in Japan, Propaga-
had made the whole world their mission-field, and zealously and tion of
earnestly propagated Buddhism abroad. When the science of abroad.
navigation was in its infancy, it was the priests who dared to
cross the ocean to Korea or China, and some even attempted
to penetrate to India regardless of the dangers and difficulties
of the journey.   This zeal and ardour were, it is true, somewhat
weakened when the exclusive policy of the Tokugawa dynasty
was enforced ; but after the Restoration the spirit revived, and

the Shin, Jōdo, Hokké, and Zen sects sent missionaries to China, Korea, Siberia, the Malay Peninsula, and various Oriental ports, and even as far as Hawaii and several States along the Pacific coast of the United States.

Activities of the Buddhists.

Quite recently, too, priests have been making an attempt to reach the heart of Tibet and Central Asia : these adventurous undertakings being simply a revival of the spirit of the old Buddhists, influenced indirectly by the new power from the Occident. With regard to prison-preaching, we find—with the exception of one or two gaols, where the *Shintō* priests or Christian ministers are preaching—that the work is in the hands of the Buddhists, who carry it on after the best methods known in the West, and thus render great service to the country by their efforts among the prisoners. At the present time Buddhist services are conducted in the Army, at factories, and among the poor ; while associations of young men, women, and children are growing up everywhere. When we observe the orphan asylums, deaf-and-dumb schools, charity hospitals, prisoners'-aid societies, and free lodging-houses established by the Buddhists, their social and philanthropic influence becomes increasingly manifest.

New fields for Buddhism.

Temperance and reformatory societies have also been organized ; whilst another evidence of the Christian influence upon Buddhism is shown in the establishment of sectarian schools of various kinds, and especially in an eagerness to start schools for girls and women—a point to which hitherto small

Education for the Buddhist priest.

attention has been paid. A great change is further to be noted in their missionary schools, where they now teach various branches of science and philosophy side by side with their own doctrines. The simplification of the art of printing has of course greatly assisted them in their work, and a marvellous

Buddhistic publications.

increase in the number of pamphlets published and distributed by them is to be noticed—almost one-half of the magazines published in the empire being Buddhist in tone. Influenced by the scientific methods of investigation prevalent in the Occident, Japanese students have begun to handle Buddhism historically, and to submit it to free and open discussion ; a certain body of young Buddhists even considering it to be the only way to find the truth.

All this shows that the opposition which the Buddhists encountered in the early days of the Restoration only served to rouse them to fresh activity, and that during the last fifty years they have been making slow and steady progress until at last, in the open field of competition, and under the protection of the constitution which grants to the people freedom of belief, they have restored their religion to its ancient position of influence.   But, although this is so, its present condition is not one with which to rest contented.   The old religion cannot satisfy thirsty souls, and this generation requires of the Buddhists not only new activities in their religion, but constantly renewed activity.

The question whether Buddhism, in a new form, will arise and be welcomed by an ever-advancing people whose souls still call for the truth, is yet unsolved.   But one thing is certain : whilst the Buddhism of the Continent is dead, the Buddhism of Japan still lives, though somewhat weakened, and if this ancient religion is to come forth into the arena of the twentieth century with fresh vigour and activity, and preach new glad-tidings to the world, it will not be the Buddhism of India, but that of Japan, that will bring this about.

JAPANESE RELIGIOUS BELIEFS : CHRISTIANITY

Yōichi Honda, Bishop of the Japanese Methodist Church, and Yakichi Yamaji

THE history of Christianity in Japan must be divided into two periods : the earlier, that of the Roman Catholic Mission, and the later, that of the Protestant and other Missions. The history of the first named does not come directly within the scope of our survey, but we cannot pass it by without noting how the Japanese were reverently impressed by the noble examples of perseverance shown by the foreign missionaries of the day under the severest persecution, and by the unflinching spirit of martyrdom exhibited for the cause of their faith by the native Christians of the time, who are reported to have numbered no less than 280,000.

The religious condition about the time of the Méiji Restoration. The policy adopted by the Tokugawa Government ended in enervating the spiritual activities of the Japanese people. Buddhism was treated and protected as if it were the only national religion in the days of the Shōgunate. Priests took no active steps in proselytizing work, and yet the people had to enrol themselves as their followers, in order to prove themselves unconnected with the so-called ' evil heresy of Christianity.' But such official favour caused the priests to lose their missionary zeal, and the people to lose earnestness for studying the rationale of religion, which was thus reduced to a matter of mere ceremonial. Meanwhile the onward progress of Western civilization was breaking down the barriers of old Japan and preparing the way for the Méiji Restoration.

The policy of the Shōgunate, which fettered freedom of thought among the people, had reduced their faith to a merely nominal attribute, so that they were at once dazzled by the glamour of Western civilization, which found them lacking in normal mental reservations. They did not know how to deal with foreign civilization, and so, at first, accepted anything presented in its charming name, supposing that a new Japan could thus be formed. The Government authorities of the day were as credulous about radical progress. They thought there was nothing better to be done at the moment than to transplant Western civilization into Japan, the best thing for her being to make herself exactly like Western countries. Such being her conviction, Japan suddenly abandoned her old life and hastened to adapt herself to the new conditions.

Christianity had been so long under the ban of the Government and the people, that it raised its head with great caution when the ban was removed. The earliest endeavours were naturally made by foreign missionaries and the teachers engaged in English schools in different parts of the country, amongst whom may be named the Revs. G. F. Verbeck, D.D., David Thompson, D.D., and E. P. Veeder, D.D., of the *Kaiséi Gakkō* (Government College) of Tōkyō; W. S. Clark, LL.D., of the *Nōgakkō* (Agricultural College) of Sapporo; the Rev. S. R. Brown, D.D., of the *Shūbunkan* School at Yokohama; Captain Janes, of the *Éigakkō* (English School) at Kumamoto; John Ing, of the *Tōōgijuku* School at Hirosaki; W. E. Griffis, D.D., of the Fukui School; and the Rev. George Cochran, of Mr. Kéiu Nakamura's *Dōninsha* School, Tōkyō. The first church of native Christians was founded at Yokohama, where Japanese students of the English tongue congregated in those days. The Rev. James Ballagh and other reverend gentlemen of the Dutch Reformed Church resided there as missionaries, and a number of young men who made a study of Christianity under the first-named American missionary, decided at last to be themselves baptized. This was the foundation of the Presbyterian Church of Japan, the *Nihon Kirisuto Kyōkwai*.

English schools.

Before we proceed to give an account of the infancy of the first Christian Church in Japan, we must refer to the Christian disorders at Nagasaki, which proved a serious difficulty to the Government authorities at the time of the Méiji Restoration. These arose in this way:

The Christian disorders at Nagasaki.

In spite of the Shōgunate's strict prohibitions, there were undoubtedly a number of people at or near that city who secretly believed in Roman Catholicism as a family tradition, and some of these living in the village of Urakami presented themselves suddenly in the Roman Catholic church of the Foreign Concession, Nagasaki, on March 17, 1865. Upon this reaching the ears of the Buddhist priests they at once made a complaint to the governor of the city; but before any steps could be taken the Shōgunate Government was overthrown and the Imperial *régime* set up.

Resuscitation of Christianity.

The Christian faith had prevailed so extensively in olden times in Japan that even the power of the Tokugawa Shōgunate had been ineffectual to sweep away the faith and to blot out its traces altogether. And consequently some secretly practising Christians were found at Kyōto in 1829, and even more in Kyūshū, the ancient stronghold of the Christians. It was, therefore, only probable that a number of people at and near Nagasaki, who had secretly preserved their inheritance of Christian doctrines and ritual through many generations, should become bold enough to confess their faith and to surprise the Governor of Nagasaki by their numbers. The new Government, which had taken the place of the Shōgunate, was obliged to deal with these ' heathens ' who thus defied the long-standing prohibition, and consequently the authorities posted

Placards against Christianity.

up, in different parts of the country, placards saying: ' The evil religion of *Kirishitan* is strictly prohibited as heretofore.' This epithet ' evil ' applied to the Christian religion was at once disapproved of by the representatives of foreign Powers residing in the country, and it was consequently erased, the authorities altering the notification as follows :

' 1. Prohibitions relative to the religion of *Kirishitan* shall be strictly observed as heretofore.

' 2. Evil religion is strictly forbidden.'

The milder policy of the Government.

But this was an alteration in the letter only. The Government still held fast to the anti-Christian policy, and at the time of the demonstration by the Urakami Christians, Noboru Watanabé, a *samurai* of the Ōmura clan, was dispatched to

Nagasaki to arrest the Christians and to enforce the prohibition there. Soon afterwards, Kido, a State Councillor (*Sanyo*), was sent to the same city. His orders were to place those thus arrested as Christians, more than 3700 in all, in the charge of different fiefs, so as to compel them to abandon the objectionable faith. But the order was useless, for, regardless of punishment, none obeyed the admonition thus given. Moreover, strong objection to the step was raised by the French minister of the time. Upon this the Government authorities, who had been so eager to exterminate Christianity, changed their policy and the Christian prisoners were allowed to return to their homes, and a certain sum of money was given to them for the purpose of restoring their houses and farms. This happened in 1870. Thus the Government abandoned its hostile attitude towards Christians and adopted a tolerant policy within three years of its accession to power.

The foreign missionaries, who had been waiting for an opportunity to extend their work in Japan, considered this to be an opportune moment to urge forward their work. Count Ōkuma, who was engaged at that time in the ungrateful task, as an official of the Government, of dealing with the Christians, has told his experience of those days : ' We were confident that these people would no more oppose an authoritative command than would a young girl of sixteen. But contrary to our expectation and unlike the usual docility of their nature, they held fast to their religion. When threatened with punishment, these " audacious rascals," not afraid of the Government, became all the more resolute. Thus I found that religious belief is not to be dominated by political orders.' Even a young girl was not afraid of the angry reproofs of Government officials in solemn conclave, nor hesitated to sacrifice her own life rather than forsake her religion—a fact which testifies strongly to the moral worth of the Japanese people. The foreign missionaries may well have looked upon these incidents with satisfaction. Assured that their time had come at last, they devoted themselves to their work with the greatest zeal ; while many young men who frequented the missionaries houses for the study of English were becoming imbued with the spirit of reformation, the *Zeitgeist* of those days. They saw

Perseverance of Christians.

that everything old in society was being swept away. They found new ideas boldly advocated by the leaders of society. They failed to reap satisfaction from the old faiths, and so they confessed their belief in the new : in other words, they were caught in the nets set by the foreign fishermen. Thus arose at Yokohama the first Christian Church in Japan. Besides all this, Prince Iwakura, Premier of Japan at that time, touring Europe, encountered strong disapproval on the part of Western public opinion against the anti-Christian measures of his Government, and telegraphed home to his Cabinet to withdraw the placards posted against Christianity.

The first Church.

The first Christian Church thus founded on the seashore, within the limits of the Foreign Concession at Yokohama, on March 10, 1872, consisted originally of eleven members. The group of students who joined this Church are now old in years, and have become elders of the Church, but in those days they were young and full of energy. Their youthful blood was stirred by the spirit of reform, and they advanced boldly into the spiritual battle-field. Most of them could understand but little English, nor could they master the contents of theological books; yet no sooner did they read such Chinese works as 'Tien-tao Tso-yüen' ('God, the Fundamental Source of the Universe') than they felt that they had come into contact with a new teaching. In listening to the foreign missionaries' sermons, zealous in spirit but awkwardly expressed in the Japanese language, they felt as if something precious but before unknown was being expounded to them. They considered themselves to have tasted a faith much sweeter than all the forms of older faiths extant in Japan, and they now enlisted willingly in the cause of the new creed.

Kéiu Naka-mura.

The young proselytes found in Masanao Kéiu Nakamura, a profound Chinese scholar in the direct service of the Shōgunate, a champion fully sympathetic with their cause. He had resided in England prior to the downfall of the Shōgunate, and had seen how her civilization was based upon religion. During twenty years of labour he had studied the doctrines of human nature and the heavenly way, taught in the Chinese classics. He saw that these doctrines were manifest in Christianity, and he agreed that the teaching of Confucius was not antiquated, but that Christianity, as then prevailing in the Western world, was no less than a higher and greater Confucianism. After his return to Japan, necessitated by the fall of the Shōgunate which he served, he did not hesitate to show his sympathy with Christianity, and Christianized Confucianism—or, in other words, Christian ideas as explained in terms of Confucianism— became the basic principles of his arguments. In the year that the Yokohama Church was founded he penned ' A Foreigner's Epistle to His Majesty the Emperor of Japan,' which he published anonymously in a periodical entitled 'Shimbun Zasshi' (The News Journal). In this he advocated Christianity as the spiritual foundation of civilization, and as such not merely to be admitted to Japan, but also to be encouraged in any country where Western culture and institutions were already adopted.

Such was the beginning of a movement which has spread. The small Christian Church began its activities despite all manner of persecution, for many of the younger members of the Church were expelled from the families into which they had been adopted, simply because they believed in this ' evil' religion. Others were ostracized by their earlier teachers from the same cause. But they did not give in, and Christianity soon became a subject of popular discussion. *Persecution.*

A book entitled ' Benmō' (' Exposure of Falsehood '), by Sokkén Yasui, the greatest Confucian scholar of the age, appeared as a challenge to the active progress of the new religion. It was the first voice of scholarly disapproval which Christianity encountered at the time of its transplantation into Japan, and it was also the most sensible criticism of the new faith by the adherents of the older Japan. One cannot but regard with admiration the writer's attitude as a debater in reading through his fifth volume, which contains the climax of his arguments. His essay was a masterpiece, rare at a time when the level of men's knowledge was not high. His criticism of the Bible was acute enough to make the Christians reflect upon their own beliefs. But the young men of that age, hungering after a new principle, were not inclined to listen to arguments of the old school, especially as, at this moment, Jō Niishima, who had graduated at the Amherst College in the *' Benmō,' by Sokkén Yasui.* *Jō Niishima.*

United States, returned as a Congregational missionary and commenced work. (See also *post*, p. 151.)

A social contrast.

We now witnessed a remarkable social contrast. On the one hand, the young statesmen of new Japan at the height of their success were intoxicated with the delicious wine of vainglory.[1] On the other, we find a set of young men praying in their inner chambers with the determination to become mission workers, who had not where to lay their heads. Those of the former category, who had accomplished so much in the recent Restoration, performed doubtless a great work in the history of Japan, but they had already finished their part and were entering upon a state of satiety. One cannot but be struck with the contrast, as strong as that between a vernal scene of flowers about to fade away, and a winter field, desolate, yet promising the return of a new spring.

Moral reaction.

Such a social contrast was mainly due to the law of reaction. Its operation constituted the most salient fact in the oath taken at Hanaoka-yama, Kumamoto. This incident occurred a little more than a year after the return of Jō Niishima, and in its significance the little Church in Japan saw an auspicious prospect opening up before her.

The oath at Hana-oka Hill.

Like several other great fiefs in Japan, that of Kumamoto had invited and engaged a foreigner, Captain Janes, an American layman recommended by Dr. Verbeck, as teacher in the *Han-Gakkō* (the Clan School). This school kept up the teaching of young men of the *samurai* class in that province, even after the clan system had been abolished through the Méiji Restoration. Like most of the foreigners engaged in the different clan schools at that time, this American captain taught his pupils not only English, but also Christianity, and many were so influenced, that one day, in the summer of 1876, they gathered together upon Hanaoka-yama, a hill near Kumamoto, and there took an oath to devote themselves to the work of the spiritual reformation of Japan. Their position is thus described by the Rev. Hiromichi Kozaki, one of their number:

Kozaki's narrative.

' How I became a Christian is an old story with me. I was

[1] Ryūhoku Narushima refers to this when he describes how the public morality of Tōkyō had deteriorated from the purer standard of the older Yédo to the wanton and licentious self-indulgence of the leading statesmen of the most powerful fiefs, which had done much to overthrow the feudal *régime*.

one of some sixty pupils in Captain Janes's school; but, as I had been born and brought up in the family of a Confucian scholar, I did not look at the Christian books for a long time. But my friends in school insisted that I should read them as being good for purposes of reference, and at last I was persuaded to do so. I passed through many doubts and struggles before I discovered in them certainties upon which I could rest assured; but since then my faith in the one God has remained unchanged, as the true way, the right and immovable ground of our religion. Some time later on, those of us who had the same principles met together and bound ourselves under an oath. We swore one with another: " If we engage in politics or military affairs, we may probably attain to positions of eminence, yet these will be quite unimportant in their nature when regarded as life-work, and besides there are many who engage in such pursuits. Had we not therefore better devote ourselves to what others cannot so easily do, and let the sphere of our life-work be the spiritual one ? Thus we will turn the human mind from superstitions, and recall it to the true and right way. We are ready to face whatever hardships and difficulties may overtake us." Such was our entrance upon a religious life, which, when it became known outside our own circle, surprised our parents and others very much, for naturally nothing had been farther from their intention, in putting us to study in the school, than that we would turn ourselves into Christian bonzes. Moreover they thought that such a course was inexcusable, and wanting in loyalty and patriotism. It was in consequence of this that the school was closed and everybody was sent home to his parents. As for me, my father was already dead, and although my mother, of course, was very anxious about my case, I explained to her that I had done nothing wrong, and that I was going to do good hereafter, about which she need not trouble herself at all. She understood me fairly well, and I had not much difficulty in behaving just as I thought best. But some of us had terrible difficulties. The mother of another of us, Yokoi, was about to kill herself, because her son had turned out such a heretic while belonging to the family of a Confucian scholar. She held herself responsible for the event, and unpardonable in the sight of her family ancestors, her feudal lord, and her dead husband. Yokoi had an uncle, another Chinese scholar, who tried to win him back with earnest remonstrances, but he remained inflexibly resolute, and was finally cut off from all intercourse with his relatives. The father of Yoshida, one of the party, even went so far as to unsheathe his sword before his son as if to behead him. But the young Yoshida offered his neck, saying that he esteemed the Way more than his life. His father, who had used this threat only to win back the young man, instead of cutting him down, called him a great fool and kicked him out of the house.'

As a general rule, the young men of Kyūshū were anxious to become either Government officials or politicians, and cared for little else as their life-work; but an exception was witnessed in this ' Kumamoto Band,' who determined to devote themselves to the work of the spiritual regeneration of Japan.

Reaction against Europeanization. At this time there had already appeared a current of sentiment inauspicious to the prospects of the young Christian Church; it was to be found in the reaction against extreme Europeanization. In the first years of Méiji, most of the progressives were indiscriminate imitators of things Western. But such a phenomenon was not to last long, for as more was learnt of the West, they found that its civilization had a long history of its own, and they began to see the impossibility of making Japan Occidental all at once. Signs of this reaction could be seen on all sides in society, but the most remarkable case was that of Yukichi Fukuzawa, who advocated the preservation of the best features of Japanese customs.

Attacking the policy of radical Europeanization adopted by the Government, he openly blamed the cosmopolitan principle of human brotherhood as the root of this rash movement.

Sarcasms of Fukuzawa. Naturally enough he turned his satirical pen against the Christians. This he did in his magazine ' Katéi Sōdan.' His essay was short, but his sarcasm was keen. To begin with, he stated that there were some Christian evangelists who, when they travelled abroad, depended with unblushing effrontery upon charitable persons with whom they had no relationship whatever. These he called 'educated mendicants.' He ridiculed their anxiety about the spiritual condition of the Japanese people and their perplexity about the superstitions of their fellow-countrymen, while all the time they were unable to earn their own living. Further, he rallied them on playing the *rôle* of paid conductors to Paradise and of professional agents for traders in morals. In conclusion, he declared that, however noble the ideal of the universal brotherhood of men might be, it is no more than the golden world of an idle dream, and that the Japanese people should, as their first duty, endeavour to secure the highest independence and fullest autonomy of their nation.

But the human mind cannot be satisfied with mere worldly principles and purely materialistic morality. Religion has a basis in the human mind much deeper than was understood by this 'sage of Mita,' and it claims from mankind a piety far higher than his attitude towards nature, and this claim it was that turned a body of the Japanese young men not to Yukichi Fukuzawa, but rather to Jō Niishima. When the civil war broke out in Kyūshū, such reactionary tendencies, engulfed in a greater social agitation, disappeared for a time. *The claim of the human mind.*

With the close of that disturbance, the rivalries of the feudal clans were once for all obliterated from the Japanese mind, and an age of philosophical discussion and political science set in. In this new arena, four theories strove in succession for mastery over the Japanese mind, namely : *The age of philosophical discussion and political science.*

1. French Republicanism, represented by French scholars.

2. English Empiricism and Utilitarianism, represented by Fukuzawa's school *Kéiō Gijuku.*

3. Conservative Reaction, represented by the Educational Department of the Government.

4. The Evolution Theory and Agnosticism, represented by the Tōkyō University.

The band of French scholars devoted themselves to inspiring society with the idea of natural rights; but they did little more than make a straightforward declaration of their creed —that law is the product of popular likes and dislikes. To the people only just awakening to politics, the simplicity of these arguments made them easy to comprehend, and the *Jiyūtō*, or Liberal party which represented the political views of the French school, consequently advanced up to a certain point with ever-widening influence, owing to the simple ideas about human rights which formed their platform.

The English empiricists.

But among seekers after the new learning of the West there were many who looked indifferently upon such ideas as natural rights. They were the men of the *Kéiō Gijuku*, who represented English empiricism and utilitarianism, with others belonging to the same phase of thought. They may be named, for convenience' sake, the English empiricists. Following Hume, Buckle, Mill, Bentham, and Gibbon, they advocated empiricism in science, utilitarianism in politics, and scepticism in religion. Readers must, however, not overlook circumstances which evoked a distinct current of conservative tendency, although French republicanism and English empiricism appeared to divide the whole of the mental life of the Japanese people into two camps.

Christians and those advocating the natural rights of the people.

Between such conflicting currents of thought, Japanese Christians had to pass through diverse experiences. They were sometimes regarded as siding with those who advocated the natural rights of the people, and it is no wonder, and quite easy to understand, that some of them had to espouse the cause of pure rationalism and democratic principles. Christianity is always in intimate relationship with the mental life of the West, and pure rationalism and democratic principles were nothing but products of the latter. This was one of the factors that created a union between Christians and the disciples of natural rights. Again, some of the leaders of the Christian Church—such as Niishima—breathed the air of freedom while abroad, and became hearty believers in democratic principles; and, further, a majority of the foreign missionaries also grew up in the same atmosphere. This, again, was a reason for close relationship between the Christians and the Liberals.

The main cause of their friendly relation.

But these were subordinate causes only, for the main ground must be sought in the necessity which obliged the Government of the day to join with the reactionary Conservatives and to flatter them. It had no reason to regard

Christianity itself as an enemy, but the official policy, which fostered reactionary conservatism more and more, led some of the Conservatives to confound Christians with political lecturers on pure rationalism and democratic principles. Even some of those who well understood the distinction between politics and religion, applied the epithet ' Christian ' to their political opponents for the purpose of slandering them. This situation drove the Christians to side with the popular party and to promote a sympathy between them. This it was that caused the friendly relations between the Christians and the Liberal party. Taisuké Itagaki, leader of the *Jiyūtō*, denounced the three religions of *Shintō*, Confucianism, and Buddhism as detrimental to the national progress of Japan, and openly asserted his sympathy with Christianity in the city of Kōfu in March, 1882. This illustrates how a section of the *Jiyūtō* members, who had originally represented the idea of natural rights only, tried to lend a helping hand to the Christians in those days.

But the Christians' great enemy was neither the reaction to Confucianism nor that to Buddhism. For although these reactionaries did not like Christians, they stood up with them against the sceptical and libertine disposition of the age. It was rather the English empiricists that the Christians challenged at that time as cpen antagonists in the arena of theory. Meanwhile, the Tōkyō University, which had long been rallying its forces, suddenly commenced activities and advocated the evolution theory and agnosticism. This aroused a new sensation in the spiritual life of the people, and impressed the Christians with the sense that a new antagonist had entered the field. *Antagonists of Christians.*

In short, the mental life of the people at this time was in a state of chaos—without unity, without order, and without a goal. Native ideas fought against imported ideas. One form of imported ideas fought with another. These different forms of sentiment rivalled each other, and the whole field of moral activity presented the semblance of anarchy. At this juncture we find the Christians admirably officered in their strenuous combat. At Kyōto the *Dōshisha* school of Niishima received into its bosom, and was much strengthened by, the young men *Brave fighting of Christians.*

of the 'Kumamoto Band' who had taken their oath at Hanaoka-yama ; while their seniors had already betaken themselves to different parts of the country, where they occupied the first line in the evangelical battle. In Tōkyō the learned members of the Christian Church assisted by publishing a magazine, called ' Rikugō Zasshi,' in 1887. The Church was thus equipped with able organs for the spiritual conquest of the country.

The 'Rikugō Zasshi.'

The Dōshisha and the other missionary schools also improved their organization step by step, and did their best to train up champions to devote themselves to spiritual warfare, while the 'Rikugō Zasshi' entered more and more eagerly into a struggle : first with sceptics, empiricists as well as utilitarians, and then with the University thinkers. This magazine was a rarity in the literature of the day, and we cannot but admire the heroism with which it fought the University men, in spite of its insignificant equipment. In the first place, the editors insisted that the evolution theory does not always command absolute authority. In this line Dr. H. P. Faulds, founder of the Tsukiji Hospital, was a fair antagonist of Professor E. S. Morse. The former, presenting himself wherever the latter lectured, argued against the evolution theory as by no means wholly proven. But other Christians found the drift of the theory to be irresistible, and changed their logic, claiming theism to be consistent with evolution, and asserting that it could best account for the design of nature arranged by the great Divine wisdom. They said that the Copernican demonstration, the Baconian philosophy, and modern scientific researches once appeared likely to undermine the beliefs of the Christian Church, and at first she greatly feared such a result ; but they had ultimately proved themselves to be the best agents for purging the essence of the Christian faith from all forms of superstition, and were in effect offerings to the glory of God. The position of the evolution theory was considered by these Christians to have a similar mission toward the Christian Church of the day. In their eyes the evolution theory did not in any way conflict with the Christian faith, and agnostics, in their real nature, tended to return to the true source of the universe by way of reaction from empiricism. Agnosticism, indeed, was another illustration of the human mind groping for God.

Christians and the evolution theory.

With such views these thoughtful Christians continued to oppose the atheistic conclusions drawn from the evolution theory, and thus the Christian Church of the day advanced with slow, yet steady, steps, whilst the comparatively stagnant state of the political world since 1884 has been a circumstance not unfavourable to the Church's progress.

We must not overlook the work of female education as one of the achievements of the Christian Church, and especially of the foreign missionaries in Japan. The Méiji Government paid some little attention to the question from the first, but the people, who by tradition and custom had become timid and conservative about the education of women, were indisposed to give them a higher education. In spite of this, the missionaries from the first advocated the rights and duties of women, and the importance of their education, and in pursuance of this gathered together girl students in schools specially founded with a view to this end. *Female education.*

The problem of Treaty revision from the Restoration onwards was a harassing matter for our statesmen. Especially did it attract public attention in the late 'eighties, when popular excitement concerning it reached a climax consequent upon the anticipated adoption in 1887 of the Inouyé Draft, compiled by the statesman of that name. Viewed simply as a political question, Treaty revision had nothing to do with Japanese Christianity, but in order to secure the smooth passage of this revised draft, the Government did everything possible to clothe the people with the garments of Western civilization. Laws were adopted which were drawn up in foreign style, the teaching of foreign languages was encouraged in the schools, and means of facilitating free intercourse between foreigners and natives were eagerly resorted to. Such a policy served undoubtedly to promote the social tendency called Europeanization. *Treaty revision.*

Outside the circle of Government officials, there were also many who affected the Western style of education, and earnestly advocated the necessity of Europeanizing Japan. The number of Japanese travelling abroad increased, and many of the leading statesmen, soldiers, scholars, and other influential men started to make the tour of the world. Societies were organized *European ization.*

for the improvement of the Japanese drama, and of the writing and spelling, including the adoption of Roman letters in place of ideographs.   Various other improvements were adopted in connection with the arts, literature, and mode of living.   The climax was reached in a doctrine propounding that Japanese should marry foreign women in order to effect an improvement of the race.   All these things were done for the purpose of converting Japan both externally and internally so that she might become a member of the coterie of Western nations.

Ascendency of Christianity.
It is no wonder that such changes in social environments gave an impetus to the study of the English language and tended to increase the number of students both male and female in mission schools, and added to the influence of the Christian Church.   Some even of the University professors who had advocated Spencerism and had passed acrimonious criticisms against Christianity, now changed their arguments and displayed their goodwill towards it.   The authorities of the Foreign Department of the Japanese Government respectfully invited the leading native ministers of the Christian Church to their residences, and, like Moses upon Pisgah, these saw the land of promise extending below them.   Impelled by this current, many young men flocked to the Church, and Christian lectures and meetings commanded greater audiences than those held by party politicians.   ' Let us establish Christ's Kingdom in Japan, for the fields are white and the harvest-time has come.'   This was the sentiment indulged in by all Christians, for they were favourites of fortune, living under the charm of great hope.

But the attempted treaty revision proved a failure, and the policy of turning the country into a fancy-dress ball of Europeanization was buried amidst the sneers and jeers of the people.   Fortunately, however, the Western tastes and learning which had been cultivated side by side with the prosecution of this policy did not suffer through its failure.

Dōshisha University.
At this juncture Dr. Niishima entered upon his enterprise of founding the *Dōshisha* University.   This was the boldest project undertaken by a Japanese Christian.   Up to this time the three centres of culture occupying the whole field of

Japanese education had been : first, the Tōkyō University, in cluding the other Government schools under the auspices of the Educational Department; secondly, Count Ōkuma's *Semmon Gakkō*; and thirdly, Mr. Yukichi Fukuzawa's *Kéiō Gijuku*. The Christians were surrounded by these forces, and had only mission-schools in different parts of the country, and their influence was too insignificant to make them a match for their opponents. They therefore proposed to take a daring leap and establish a centre for Christian education in Japan. Dr. Niishima took the deepest interest in the spiritual education of Japan. His educational principle was to make men live ' a still higher and nobler life.' With this principle he conceived the idea of founding the *Dōshisha* University. Proceeding once more, in 1885, to America, he appealed to all well-wishers and friends for contributions to the funds, and upon his return to Japan he published, in 1888, a plea for the establishment of the *Dōshisha* University, removing to Tōkyō for a time to avail himself of every possible means for the accomplishment of his purpose. But to our infinite regret he died in the midst of his endeavours, whilst all his efforts failed to satisfy his own aspirations.

The progress of the Christian Church in Japan, which had hitherto made rapid strides, appears to have called a halt about the time when the movement for the *Dōshisha* University was inaugurated, and, in fact, may be said to have taken very slow steps since then. This was due, on the one hand, to external pressure coming from the conservative reaction, and, on the other, to internal laxity resulting from theological controversies. *Progress of Christianity retarded.*

Christian theology in Japan was in its very infancy up to 1884–85. But such among the Church members as were accustomed to read new foreign books began about this time to turn their attention to the so-called new theology and to grope after the new ideas destined to change the very basis of Christian doctrines. Fumio Yano, for instance, advocated in the ' *Hōchi Shimbun*' (a daily paper) that the doctrine of Unitarianism should be adopted in Japan. The Rev. Dr. W. Spinner was sent out by the General Evangelical Protestant Mission Society of the Tubingen school, the Rev. Arthur May *Theological controversies.*

Knapp, of the American Unitarian Association, came over in
the spring of 1887, and Mr. Otto Schmiedel, of the above-named
German Mission, arrived in the autumn of the same year. The
next year Mr. Knapp gave lectures upon the doctrines held
by his society, and, on the other hand, a ' General Evangelical
Church ' was formed by a number of the Japanese Christians
under Dr. Spinner. The year 1890 saw a magazine called *The
Unitarian* started as an organ for propagating Unitarianism,
and another called the '*Shinri*' (*Truth*) as an organ for propagating the higher criticism of the Tübingen school. A
third factor was furnished when the Rev. George L. Perin
arrived in the country as a missionary of the Universalist
Mission. Of these theological schools, that advocated by the
General Evangelical Church as representing the Tübingen
school was of such weight as to shake the Japanese Church to
its very basis; for investigation of the Old and New Testa-
ments, based upon scientific and historical criticism, was the
weapon wielded by this school. In meeting philosophers'
objections to their doctrines, Christian scholars had been
accustomed to defend Christ as a historical person, the Bible
as a book historically authentic, and Christianity as a product
of historical facts beyond and above the scope of discussion.
But the Tübingen school attempted to apply the method of
scientific research to the problem of the historical value of
Christianity. This was the sharpest blow struck at the core
of the question. The Christian scholars of Japan could not
but be alarmed at such a powerful and radical criticism. They
had hitherto been blind to the recent progress of religious
thought and had believed solely in what foreign missionaries
adhering to orthodox doctrines told them. Moreover, strange
to say, voices calling for a new theology began to be heard
from within the Church, almost contemporaneously with the
coming of this novel theory. In the July number of the
Rikugō Zasshi, 1889, the Rev. H. Kozaki discussed the problem
of biblical inspiration. Against the doctrine of the infallibility
of the Bible as an inspired book written by the saints, which
had been upheld so long by the orthodox Church, he argued
that the term ' inspiration ' could only mean the Divine influence given to its writers. The Rev. M. Masahisa Uémura,

who returned in 1890 from his foreign travels, advocated the necessity of revising the Creed. Likewise, Mr. Yokoi, who returned to Japan about that time from a Western tour, pleaded also for progressive views. Some doubted the doctrine of the Trinity, others objected to that of Redemption, and still others jeered at the dogma of the Immaculate Conception. The *Rikugō Zasshi*, which had been looked upon by the Japanese public as the sole organ of the Christian Church in the country, became a devoted mouthpiece of the new theology, and appeared to have fallen entirely into the hands of the progressists. Of course, such views of the new theology were not formidable to the future prospects of the Church, for, although the theological field in Japan was much distracted by them, that was by no means a singular phenomenon in the history of the Church which had often been assaulted by terrible outbursts of criticism and scepticism. But just as commonplace persons cannot comprehend the lives of heroes, those who have not religious life experience in themselves cannot prosecute the religious study of Christianity. The insight of those who advocated the new theology was not deep enough in this respect, for they made historical and scientific study their alpha and omega. Nevertheless it is to be regretted that faith became colder from that time onwards among Japanese Church members. The more intellectual class valued less and less the creed of the Church to which they belonged, and the progress of the Church during the period that has elapsed since then has presented hardly any feature worthy of note.

We must diverge a moment here in order to describe the struggle of the Christian Church with the conservative reaction which occurred contemporaneously with the theological controversy above mentioned. The mental life of Japanese society, which had been busily engaged in importing Western civilization, and had consequently been quite favourably disposed towards Christianity, now suffered a serious reaction. National culture as opposed to cosmopolitan culture had manifested itself several years previously, when Count Inouyé's draft of the revised treaty failed to be passed, and had gradually converted a large class of men to its views. The so-called

The conservative reaction.

German ideas began, from about 1884, to spread among
University professors and Government officials. If the *laisser-
faire* principle and cosmopolitanism of the Manchester school
could be called ' English ideas,' the characteristics of the
German ideas may be said to consist in laying greater importance on administrative institutions and legislatures as well as
on national spirit. In the next year, that is in 1885, Viscount
Arinori Mori became Minister of Education in the Itō Cabinet.
As an earnest advocate of national education, he believed in
the theory that pupils should be educated for the benefit of
the State, and that schools should bring up young men for the
sake of the country. In an age when liberty, cosmopolitan
civilization, and the thoughts of Mill and Spencer, as well
as the doctrines of Christianity were advocated, and when
the State was regarded as one of the necessary evils, he devoted
himself in his capacity of Minister of Education to manufacturing faithful subjects of the State, and he regarded military
education as the best means to that end. The steps he took
for these purposes were simply an earnest of the approach
of the national reaction. But he was not yet powerful
enough to divert the great current of the still prevailing
Europeanization. In the meantime, Count Inouyé's device
of treaty revision met with failure. Antipathy to Europeanism
showed itself openly for the first time, and nationalism saturated
the mental life of the people. It was the Christian Church
that suffered most from this change.

The so-
called
*lèse-
majesté.*
The balance of thought, which had long been weighed down
by the liberal and cosmopolitan principle, began now to sway
in the other direction. Whenever a current of new ideas
bursts out suddenly, its fresh force is apt to produce a certain
measure of unnecessary sacrifice. Details of the Uchimura case
are still fresh in the memory of the public. A professor in the
First Higher School, Tōkyō, he conscientiously hesitated to
bow before the picture of His Majesty, since, in the religious
sense of the word, he regarded ' bowing' as equivalent to
' worship.' This occurred on the Imperial Birthday in
1890. It brought down upon him the ignominious charge
of *lèse-majesté*, and he was exiled for ever from the
educational field. The public, which had long looked

upon the attitude of Christians with a suspicious eye, were startled by this decided step on his part, and were led to apply to Christians the calumnious epithets of 'disloyal' and 'anti-patriotic.' Another case similar to this occurred at Kumamoto in January, 1892. Mr. Téijirō Okumura, a teacher in the Kumamoto *Éigakkō* (English School), spoke about the philanthropic principle at the inauguration of a new president of his school, and said that there is no distinction of nationalities in the eyes of philanthropists. The conservatives in the district, shocked at this declaration, denounced him clamorously. Mr. (now Baron) Masanao Matsudaira, Governor of the Prefecture, enjoined the authorities of the school to dismiss him. This may be called the second Uchimura case. Thenceforth the waves of nationalistic reaction increased in volume and came dashing against the bulwarks of the Christian Church, threatening to sweep this so-called 'heathenism' altogether from the country. This spirit of the age found expression most clearly in an essay ' On the Conflict between Religion and Education,' published by Dr. Tétsujirō Inouyé in 1893. The points of his argument were nothing more than that (1) the educational principles of Japan must be based upon the Imperial Rescript relative to Education ; (2) the principle of the Educational Rescript is that of nationalism and of faithfulness to one's parents as well as to the Emperor, while Christianity is cosmopolitan in principle, and devoid of nationalism. He contended that, because Christianity advocates equal love to all, it does not make for attachment to one's own country, and because it places the heavenly Father and Jesus Christ above one's Sovereign and parents, it is contradictory to the principle of faithfulness to these latter. (3) Lastly, he pointed to the con- flict thus arising as inevitable, according to his view, between Christianity and education. *Dr. Inouyé's attack.*

It was but reasonable that Christians should not maintain silence towards Dr. Inouyé's essay. *The Christian Young Men*, the organ of the Young Men's Christian Association, set up the defence that the bases of education and religion are entirely different from each other, one being national and the other universal, and hence that it is quite illogical to talk *Christian vindi- cations.*

of a conflict between the two. Christian thinkers of all denominations joined in the discussion. The most striking vindication was offered by Mr. Gorō Takahashi. The 'Kokumin-no-Tomo' (Nation's Friend), in which this learned writer published his essay, was the most influential among contemporary periodicals, and consequently his thesis acquired additional publicity. But whilst Christians thus did their best to defend their own faith, the general opinion in educational circles sided wholly with Dr. Inouyé. The conception that education should stand upon nationalism, and that Christianity is contradictory to the spirit of the Educational Rescript, was accepted among them, as if it were an indisputable proposition.

General inactivity of the Church.

Partly owing to theological controversies within, and partly owing to objections from the educationalists without, the Christian Church of Japan now sank into a state of inactivity. From 1892 onwards, its progress was not marked by any salient feature. In fact Japanese Christendom has presented deplorable signs on all sides during the last sixteen years, the most noteworthy of them all being that a number of the so-called Christian leaders have gradually cooled in their affections towards the Church. Some who were once renowned captains of the Church retired from its work quite early and placed themselves in business circles. Others drifted into politics, no one knows when. Yet again, others, young and accomplished, representing progressive Christianity, withdrew from their churches. Some of these did not hesitate to say that they could find better means of improving their spiritual nature by reading such writers as Emerson or Carlyle at home than by attending church. Not a few of the theological students, educated in mission-schools of different denominations, fell away. Christian educationalists felt a constantly increasing want of able pupils in their schools.

Representative Christians leaving the Church.

The causes.

How was it that the Japanese Christian Church, which for a time had the brightest prospects before it, was thus reduced to a state of dull inactivity? It is by no means a complete explanation to ascribe it solely to theological controversy, opposition on the part of the educationalists, and unfitness of foreign missionaries for the circumstances and conditions of Japan. There were two still greater factors. They were nothing less than a rise in the standard of the people's manner of living, and the general trend of Western Christendom. Wealth and the scale of living of the Japanese nation has altered to an extent almost unequalled in the whole world.

For instance : the commercial and industrial classes of Japan, which had been so long subordinated to the *samurai* class, occupied now a position which enabled them to rule and control politicians. Their status of former days was radically changed. The business world was now in a position to attract men of talent into its circle, paying them comparatively high salaries. Formerly, young men who were not inclined to politics betook themselves to literature, and those disinclined to the latter devoted themselves to religious work. But a change has come. The business world invited youths into its vast and fruitful arena. 'Behold, the fields are white and the harvest truly is plenteous, but the labourers are few.' These words described the actual state of the business world of Japan rather than that of her spiritual world at this time. For those who engaged in work of the Church, it was inevitable that they should labour hard on a thankless task and be content to lead a life of privation. On the other hand, here was another world beckoning to their activities and holding out to them the promise of greater remuneration and of quicker promotion. It was but natural that the talented men of the rising generation throughout the country should betake themselves, not to the Church, but to the commercial world. For these reasons we consider that the improved scale of living was the first cause of the temporary inactivity of Japanese Christendom.

The first cause.

It is a most noteworthy fact in the mental life of modern Japan that the spiritual distance between herself and other parts of the world has been shortened simultaneously with the advance of civilization, as well as with the development of means of communication throughout the country. This fact caused the Japanese Church to stand upon the same level of theological thought as Western Churches. Now, it is an undeniable feature of the Occidental Church that she passed through a stage of transition in the latter half of the nineteenth century. In some parts of her field we may find sparks of revival or currents of old-fashioned faith, resulting from

The second cause.

devotion to classical study, and maintained above the drift of the age. But the evident trend of Western Christendom is towards a universal decrease of church attendance, of Bible reading, and of belief in the doctrine of the Trinity, as well as of faith in what were regarded by the older theologians as the fundamental principles of Christianity, such as the Immaculate Conception, Miracles, the Resurrection, and the Ascension. Such being the situation abroad, it was not to be expected that the Japanese Church alone should maintain its old status. Thus we find the second cause of the general inactivity of the Japanese Church in the trend of Western Christendom.

The future of the Church.

Is there no future before the Christian Church in Japan ? We cannot be so pessimistic as to answer in the affirmative, for the condition of Japanese spiritual life for the last few years indicates a revival of the call for a religion.

The result of nationalist education.

The principle of the so-called nationalist education did not incite any objection so far as concerned its aim of bringing up good citizens. Yet the means adopted for that purpose were too mechanical to give free and full play to the instincts of students. Although apparently successful in persecuting the Christians, who were still few in number and weak in influence, the system could not satisfy the claims of the students who came to its schools. One and the same principle was applied to every school in the country, under the belief that success could thus be attained in bringing up men of loyalty and patriotism, which was the ideal of education. This proved, however, to be a mere dream. The attitude of Japanese youths towards the mechanical process of loyal and patriotic education was quite serious at first. But when the process was dinned into their ears perpetually, it ultimately evoked distaste. They could not bear to be crammed with a superficial principle, whether it was a reasonable one or not, and those of stronger character revolted at last. It was expected by the advocates of nationalist education that men of loyalty and patriotism would thus be educated. But, on the contrary, there appeared, among those thus taught, cases of extreme individualism, engrossed in the pursuit of self-indulgence much more than in the problem of public welfare. Stars and violets, the emblems of love, became the theme of conversation and verse most popular among them. The problem of politics and diplomacy, which had attracted them with greater force, lost their charms. The advocates of nationalist education were thus driven to appreciate the bankruptcy of their own principle, and though they would not confess it, they changed their old policy of expelling the Christian religion from the school precincts, and began even to some extent to welcome its teachers.

We have already referred to the decrease of talented youths devoting themselves to religious work as a result of the people's improved scale of living, which drove them one after another into the business world. But every social tendency has its own limit beyond which it will not pass. Japanese youths, who had been eager to pursue self-indulgence on the material side of their life, began now to suspect that their hopes would be in vain in the present state of society. They found that the rich class alone partook of the ever-increasing sum of national wealth, inasmuch as the present distribution of capital rested upon the principles of individualism and liberalism. Socialism and state socialism, which had so long been a feature of Western ideas, were in this way permitted to knock at the doors of the Japanese Empire. This is a sign by no means to be overlooked in looking at the future prospect of the Christian Church. Not only so, but there are some young men who, having noticed the impossibility of acquiring their material objects in the present social system, have turned back again to the religious world and engaged in evangelical work, though of course talented youths, who had once flown off to the industrial world, could not find their attachment to their old nests of the more spiritual nature renewed. This is another reason for our being optimistic as regards the future of the Christian Church. *Reaction against the materialistic tendency.*

The international status of Japan has undergone most striking and radical changes in the last ten years. She has now taken rank with the great Powers of the world. She has acquired the right and responsibility of speaking on all questions of international relationship. In other words, Japan has placed herself now among the masters who rule over the world's affairs. She has been hitherto in a hermitage, absorbed in maintaining her own independence as the Flowery Island of the Far East. But now she has turned herself into a Power, *Changes in international relations.*

H 2

acting as one of the arbitrators in the diplomatic court of the nations. In the course of such a transition, it is inevitable that remarkable modifications should come in the popular sentiments of the nation. Henceforward, in the affairs of the world, Japan has to stand upon religious and philosophical ideas with which all Western nations can sympathize. This situation, then, must serve to turn the Japanese mind once more to a re-examination of Christianity, which has so long been the ruling faith of civilized nations.

For these reasons we firmly believe that the day will come to the Christian Church in Japan when she will resume her activity, reinvigorated with fresh power.

PHILANTHROPY IN JAPAN

THE LATE TAIZŌ MIYOSHI, MEMBER OF THE
HOUSE OF PEERS

THE relation of the Emperor to the Japanese nation being **Bene-**
similar to that of a father to his family, the benevolent deeds **volence**
that the head of the Imperial House has done from generation **Imperial**
to generation for the benefit of his people are far too numerous **family.**
to be tabulated. But we may cite an instance or two out of
innumerable generous acts : the Emperor Suinin in 2 B.C. substituted for the ancient practice of *junshi*,[1] the burial of an
earthen image ; again the Emperor Nintoku (316 A.D.), observing from the scanty smoke that wreathed above the people's
houses how poor and wretched they were, exempted the nation
from taxes, and condemned himself to live in a ruined palace,
remarking that the poverty of his subjects was his own ;
and the Emperor Daigo (in the tenth century) stripped himself
of his garments one winter evening in order to experience
what some of his subjects might be suffering from cold and
starvation at that moment. A *gisō*, or charity granary,
was provided against times of scarcity as early as the days
of the Taihō statutes, promulgated in 702 A.D. ; and in times
of famine, taxes were wholly or partly remitted, rice was
given out, and provisions, clothing, and medicine were granted
to the helpless, sick, and disabled. The Imperial House has
always willed that it should participate in the pleasure and
pain, the joy and sorrow, of its subjects.

The principles of benevolent administration inculcated

---

[1] Its origin is not certain, but its motive was to follow one's lord, in whose
service one had been, to the land of the dead.

Influence
of Buddh-
ism.

by Confucianism were well adapted to the national character
of the Japanese, and were much followed in practice, as were
those of philanthropy as taught by Buddhism. The Tennōji
Temple at Naniwa (now Ōsaka), erected by Prince Shōtoku
in 593 A.D., consisted of the ' *Kéidénin*,' the main temple of
worship ; the ' *Hidénin*,' an asylum for orphans, helpless
persons, &c. ; the ' *Ryōbyōin*,' or hospital ; and the ' *Séyakuin*,' a dispensary for the poor who could not afford to pay
for medicine. Later a ' *Séyakuin*,' or dispensary, and a
' *Hidénin*,' asylum for the poor, were established at Nara
in 730 A.D., by contributions from the officials serving the
Empress Kōmyō and the Fujiwara family. We learn from
contemporary official documents, which were issued to urge
on the superintendents of the institutes, that the above institutions were established in both wards of the capital, even
as late as in the Héian era, to give help to foundlings and
destitute patients. When Hidéyoshi came into power, in the
last years of the sixteenth century, he organized a new
' *Séyakuin*,' in the south portion of the Imperial Palace.
Thither sick people were invited and received free treatment
and medicine.

Philan-
thropic
work
of the
priest-
hood.

Philanthropists in religious circles were never wanting in
olden times. Many noble priests, from Dōshō (*ob.* 699 A.D.)
and Gyōgi (*ob.* 749 A.D.) downwards, are still looked up to
for their virtues as benefactors of the people. At the end
of the thirteenth century a great priest appeared in the
person of Ninshō to embellish the history of Buddhism.
He built bath-houses, hospitals, and asylums for the poor
and helpless, and visited these institutions every day to
comfort the sufferers. Afterwards he lived in the Tennōji
Temple, where he founded a ' *Hidénin*,' and gave help to no
less than 57,200 persons : he even built hospitals for sick
horses. He received the title of ' Iō-Nyorai,' or ' Buddha, the
King of Physicians.'

Bene-
volence of
generals.

The Ōnin war of the Ashikaga dynasty in the latter half
of the fifteenth century converted Japan into one vast battle-
field ; but, dark as was the age in matters of letters and religion,
the moral sense, inherent in the character of the nation, never
failed to manifest itself. Thus the belligerent chiefs and

generals, after every great battle, summoned Buddhist priests to perform memorial services over the killed not only of their own followers, but of the enemy. Their chivalry, paying the highest deference to the dictates of honour, knew no partiality towards friend or foe. The orphans of the enemy, who had fallen for the sake of his lord, were cared for, and warriors were constantly instructed that the implacable enemy of yesterday should be treated as a friend after his death.

When the Tokugawa Shōgunate of Yédo restored peace, and literature was revived in the middle of the seventeenth century, philanthropic work underwent gradual development. The Shōgun Tsunayoshi established a '*Jusan-in*,' or employment asylum for the protection of criminals in gaol and wandering tramps, on Ishikawajima, a delta at the mouth of the River Sumida, in 1682. These were given employment and taught moral lessons, so that they could be released and re-establish themselves in business if their friends or relatives would look after them. There was also a *tamari* (place of detention) in the prison, where sick convicts who had committed minor offences, vagabonds, and homeless outcasts were taken in and cared for. Philanthropic work of the Shōgunate.

The eighth Shōgun, Yoshimuné, took a special interest in pauper-relief, and followed the advice of Shōsén Ogawa, a physician of Yédo, and founded a ' *Yōjōsho*,' or pauper's sanitorium, at Koishikawa in 1722, which supplied free medical treatment and beds to the sick and helpless people in Yédo. He also commanded the medical officials to compile a handbook of domestic medicines and distribute it among the people.

In the great famine which visited Yédo in 1791, Lord Sadanobu Matsudaira, Counsellor to the Shōgun Iyénari, established a thorough system of relief for the poor, and after five years' careful examination of the yearly municipal expenditure, ascertained the average which should be made the standard for taxation, and by economizing expenditures and saving the surplus, he not only reduced the outlay but was able to amass a reserve. He also encouraged co-operation between the Government and the people for the protection and relief of the helpless, orphans, foundlings, and maimed ;

he built fifty-three public granaries in Yédo and its neighbourhood, and stored tens of thousands of *koku* of rice, to be given to needy people in case of famine or other emergency.

In accordance with the old system of the *gisō*, or charity granary, every clan laid by a certain amount of the harvest each season, sold it to the needy at a low rate in ordinary years, and gave it freely in years of scarcity. During the great famine of 1783–84 Shigékata Hosokawa, lord of Kumamoto, and Harunori Uyésugi, lord of Yonezawa, who had always taken the greatest interest in the civil administration of their respective fiefs, not only had provisions already prepared against such an emergency, but exerted themselves to the utmost in the cause of the poor, so that no case of starvation was reported in either of the fiefs. Sadanobu Matsudaira started public works in his fief Shirakawa, giving employment to the poor; and when he found that women outnumbered men, and that the death-rate of children was excessive, he opened his treasury ungrudgingly for the support of the aged and the protection of infants, so that in a few years the population of his fief considerably increased. Grants were also made to the mother of triplets for hiring wet-nurses. These charitable deeds were performed in almost every clan, being considered to be in accordance with the precepts that had been followed of old by the Imperial family.

Early in the Tokugawa rule, an autonomic body—namely, the 'goningumi,' or guild of five men—was established in every town and village. It was an altruistic institution, its chief object being mutual assistance for the improvement of agriculture, postal delivery, religious belief, morality, finance, and charity and relief work. The guilds so formed maintained themselves without help from the Government. If a foundling or a sick traveller was found, or if a calamity occurred in a guild, the members had to co-operate in making the necessary provision, the cost of which was defrayed by the authorities. The 'goningumi' was composed of every five houses in a town or village, and the head of one of the houses was the elder, or, as he was called, the 'kumi-gashira' or 'kumi-oya. He had to see that the members helped and encouraged one another and participated in one another's sufferings and joys, and he was responsible to the high officials for everything, great and small, that happened in the guild. This association was first organized 1200 years ago, when the Yōrō statutes came into force (718 A.D.), and it was subsequently established in every place however remote.   (See also vol. i. p. 321.)

From 1769–1810 the country's resources were as yet so little developed that many of the poor could not bring up their own children. This did not escape the notice of Naoatsu Takegaki, who was a *Daikan*, or local governor, of the Shōgunate. Grieved at such a state of affairs, he gave all his fortune for the benefit of poor children and exerted himself to the utmost in their behalf, so that he succoured no fewer than 3200 children during twenty years of his service in the Government. Shirobéi Suzuki of Kanuma, Shimotsuké, was of the same mind, employing his spare moments in visiting child-bearing women, giving them money after delivery, to provide for the infants, thus saving the lives of over 500 children. Noble deeds of this kind were practised everywhere throughout the country.

Protection of children.

The weak and the maimed had been under the special protection of the law for generations, but no law was in existence for the protection of the blind. Nearly a thousand years ago the custom arose of the blind shaving their heads as *Mékura-bōshi* or blind priests, and following the professions of music, shampooing, and acupuncture. They were later put under the charge of a family of Court nobles called Kuga, and some of them even received the priestly titles of 'Kengyō' or 'Kōtō,' being treated differently from ordinary people. Under the Tokugawa dynasty, blind men were permitted by law to charge higher interest on loans of money than that which was fixed by the Government. So, too, upon the completion of a building, at weddings and funerals, or on any other special occasion, the corporations of the blind often received gifts from the house concerned, although, in spite of this sympathy, nobody appears to have troubled himself about the question of protecting them. This seeming indifference is accounted for by the fact that, although no system of protection was superficially visible, such a system had long been in unostentatious operation.

Protection of the blind.

Shin-én
Satō.

The country produced many great philanthropists during the two centuries and a half that it enjoyed peace under the Tokugawas. Among them were Shin-én Satō (1769–1850) and Sontoku Ninomiya (1787–1856). The former devoted himself to relieve famine and poverty, and earnestly preached the doctrine of agrarian administration among the feudatories.

Sontoku
Nino-
miya.

The latter taught, with his practical example of frugality and virtuous conduct, that good government and the protection of the poor must be founded on ethical training. Guilds under the name of 'Hōtokusha,' first organized through his influence, are still found in several parts of the country and are doing good work in the way of self-government in villages. One such was the 'Hōtokusha,' which was first

The
'Hōto-
kusha.'

organized in Odawara, Sagami, the birthplace of Sontoku, by Yoshimichi Yasui, one of his followers, in order to propagate his teachings after his death. Following this step, cognate associations bearing the same title were established in several districts, and there are now 208 'Hōtokusha' and 425 branch associations in twenty-one prefectures. The organization of the 'Hōtokusha' resembles that of a trade union, with an addition of religious teaching, called the Hōtokukyō, or the gospel of requiting grace. Its principal teachings are to requite the four graces—Heaven, Country, Sovereign, and Parents—by good and righteous conduct, and to follow in practice the three great principles of assiduity, frugality, and humanity. It regards faithful labour as a token of gratitude for heavenly gifts, and as a man's obligation towards Heaven, and in consequence it emphatically condemns its neglect or misuse, and urges the employment of Heaven's gifts economically, and the spending one half of one's earnings only on one's support, and the saving of the other half. It warns people against selfishness in the enjoyment of heavenly benefits, and insists that they should be shared with neighbours. Thus the 'Hōtokusha' has given great encouragement to the work of education, of production, and of charity. Prominent among the acts of relief are the rebuilding of decaying villages, the planting of forests, the reclaiming of lands, and assistance to the poor. It does not believe in indiscriminate charity nor bestows free material gifts on sufferers, its chief method of relief being to provide employment for them and to instruct them in faithfulness and assiduity of labour.

The ' *Kan-onkō*,' or gratitude guild, is another association similar to the ' *Hōtokusha*.' It had its origin in Akita pre-fecture, where the first of these institutions was started by Sukenari Nawa, an official-merchant in the clan government of Akita in 1829. When the clans were abolished at the Restoration, the funds of this guild, which by that time were large, were, by mistake, confiscated by the Government; but over 54,700 *yen* were returned. In 1881 Sukétomi Nawa, grandson of Sukénari, was received in audience by the Emperor during His Majesty's tour to the north-east, and received a grant for the preservation of the guild. This association, which has given aid to over 2,500,000 persons during its life of more than sixty years, has now under its protection over 300 persons of all conditions, to whom gifts of rice and medicine are made. Three months is the maximum period of relief, and after the expiration of that time no aid is given without due investigation, for which purpose special inquiries are prescribed. *The 'Kan-on-kō.'*

In 1868, when the administrative authority, which had been in the sole possession of military chiefs for seven hundred years, was restored to the Emperor, the despised appellations of *éta*, or ' pariah,' which had long been applied to a class of people supposed to be below the human level, and of *hinin* (lit. an in-human being), applied to beggars, were removed, whilst the name of *daimyō*, and the titles of others, who had long enjoyed the possession of large territories and had exercised wide authority, were abolished, and the *samurai*, stripped of the special privileges long attaching to their order, were brought down to the level of the common people, the ancient caste system being thus entirely removed. Almost every system and institution being thus subjected to radical change, the old-time practices of philanthropy shared in the general confusion, and the poor were consequently much neglected.

It was at this time that Christianity found its way into the country. It breathed new life and activity into the declining relief work, and gave a great impetus to Buddhism, so that the people began to feel the necessity of co-operating in the social *Influence of Chris-tianity.*

Phil-
anthropic
work
since the
Restora-
tion.

work of religious bodies. Many philanthropic works, public
as well as private, have made remarkable progress since
the Restoration. The most important of these are the
following :

The
Tōkyō
City
Asylum
for the
Poor.

The Tōkyō City Asylum for the Poor was organized by
the Tōkyō Prefecture in 1872 to shelter beggars and outcasts
and to give them employment. Its origin is traceable back
some 150 years, and at the Restoration it had acquired considerable funds. These were now allocated to the assistance
of the city's needy ones, and as a first step 140 poor men and
women were housed in the mansion of the former lord of
Kaga, now the site of the Tōkyō Imperial University. The
asylum was also supported out of the local taxes ; but when
the city regulations came into force it passed, and has ever since
remained, under the superintendence of the Tōkyō municipality. Its funds, including annual gifts that Her Majesty the
Empress has been pleased to grant since 1885, as well as contributions from many other benevolent supporters, have reached
the sum of 397,800 *yen*, and it has given aid to no fewer than
18,880 persons since its foundation. To-day, there are over
a thousand invalids under its protection, and it is the largest
and most complete work of philanthropy in this country.
The Director of the Asylum is Baron Éiichi Shibusawa, one
of the greatest financiers in our country, through whose
influence and strenuous efforts it has reached its present
prosperous condition.

The
Tōkyō
Charity
Hospital.

The Tōkyō Charity Hospital was established in 1882
with the object of giving free medical treatment to the poor.
Dr. Kanéhiro Takagi, Naval Surgeon-in-Chief, is its head.
It is supported by contributions from the Imperial family and
other well-wishers. Since its foundation it has taken more
than 7000 patients into its wards, and treated over 70,000
out-patients as well as some 170,000 one-day patients. Having
a fund of some 250,000 *yen*, it is one of the best supported
charity hospitals in Japan.

The
Tōkyō
Sugamo
Hospital.

The Tōkyō Sugamo Hospital is an asylum for lunatics,
established in 1879, under the supervision of the Tōkyō
Prefecture. In addition to lunatics, who are able to pay their
own expenses, the hospital takes in poor people, and insane

strangers who may be picked up in the streets, and treats
them free. It has now some 300 in hospital, and Dr. Shūzō
Kuré, Professor of the Tōkyō Imperial University, is its
superintendent.

The hospitals and asylums for lepers in Japan have, for
the most part, been founded and managed by foreign missionaries. The first of the kind was the ' *Kamiyama Fukuséi* '
Byōin, started at Hakone by a French Catholic Father, and
it has taken in about a hundred lepers. The ' *Ihaien* ' at
Meguro, Tōkyō, founded by an American lady missionary,
Miss Youngman, in 1894, has some fifty patients under its
protection. The ' *Kwaishun Byōin* ' at Kumamoto, started
by two English lady missionaries, Miss Riddell and Miss Knott,
in 1895, has also some fifty lepers ; while the ' *Tairōin*,' which
a French Father missionary and a Sister organized in the
same city in 1897, has about thirty patients. These lepers'
asylums, though supported chiefly by the missionaries in
charge and their foreign friends, are receiving no little help
from Japanese. Hospitals for lepers.

The Kyōto City School for the Blind and Dumb, which
receives those from the western half of Japan, was the first
institution of its kind. Its organization was started by Mr.
Dembéi Kumagai, who was the chief official of a ward in
Kyōto, about 1875, and Mr. Tashiro Furukawa took charge of
its educational work : the Kyōto Prefecture enlarged it in
1878 and made it a public institution. Kyōto City School for Blind and Dumb.

At about the same time another similar institution was
organized in Tōkyō—namely, the Tōkyō School for the Blind
and Dumb. At first it was called the ' *Rakuzén Kai* ' Society,
and was projected and supported by some sympathizers, both
native and foreign. Later, the Educational Department took
it under its direct superintendence, and Mr. Shimpachi Konishi
is now the Director. Tōkyō School for the Blind and Dumb.

The first private orphanage to be established in Japan was
the ' *Fukudenkai*,' organized by some Buddhists in 1879 ;
it has a fund of 20,000 *yen*, and supports some hundred orphans. The 'Fukuden-kai' Orphanage.

The Okayama Orphanage, founded by Mr. Jūji Ishii, a
Christian, through the influence of the late George Müller of
the Orphan House, Bristol, England, who visited Japan in Okayama Orphanage.

1885, is the best organized one to be found in this country. During the Russo-Japanese War and the famine of the north-eastern provinces it opened its doors to receive hundreds of fatherless and helpless children. These two orphanages receive an annual contribution from the Imperial household.

'Takinogawa' Orphanage.

The *'Takinogawa Gakuén'* was organized to receive girls, made orphans by the great earthquake of Mino and Owari in 1891. Its founder was Mr. Ryōichi Ishii, a Christian educator, and it is the only institution in Japan devoted to the education of the weak-minded. There are also in Ōsaka the ' *Hakuai Sha* ' (a Christian institution) and the ' *Hanaifushoku Kwai*.'

The *'Hakuai Sha'* and the *'Hanaifushoku Kwai.'*

The former is under the superintendence of Mr. Jitsŭnosuke Kobashi, and the latter, started by Mr. Toshirō Kashima, has Mr. Michio Doi as its Honorary President. Both are asylums for orphans, foundlings, and poor children, who are instructed in industrial pursuits. They are well organized, and have so far done very good work.

Tōkyō Reformatory.

The Tōkyō Reformatory is a *Shintō* institution established for the correction of bad children, with Mr. S. Takasé as its Director. The Home School, in Tōkyō, is a Christian in-

The Home School.

stitution of the same kind. Its director is Mr. Kōsuké Toméoka, a former chaplain of prisons. It has a training department for those who desire to devote their lives to philanthropic work.

The Reformatory Department, or the ' *I-no-Kashira* ' School, belonging to the Tōkyō City Asylum for the Poor, lately founded, is also for the correction of bad children.

Hara's Prison-Gate Rescue Home.

The most remarkable rescue home for released prisoners is the Ex-Convict's Home under the superintendence of Mr. Tanéaki Hara, Tōkyō, a former chaplain of prisons. When a general amnesty and special commutation were granted to prisoners at the death of her late Majesty the Empress-Dowager in 1897, Mr. Hara induced influential people to provide means of assisting the freed prisoners and thus organized this Home which has since been greatly extended by means of Imperial donations and other contributions.

System of the rescue of the poor,

Lastly as to the poor laws. The only laws, that have been enacted since the Restoration for the benefit of the poor, are the Relief Regulations, the Regulations for the Protection of Sick Travellers, the Relief Fund Regulations, and the Reformatory Regulations.   On account of the Relief Regulations aids were given, according to the last returns, to 2446 maimed, 3843 aged, 5805 sick and weak, and 2009 young and feeble—14,103 persons in all ; and the money paid on their account was 177,000 *yen*.

The law allows seven *to* (10 *to* = 1 *koku*) of rice a year to the protector of a foundling for bringing it up, although the gift covers only a part of the real expense : there are now some 2000 children thus protected at an expense of 15,827 *yen*.

The Relief Fund Regulations were founded on the old system of the charity granary, and the relief funds of the prefectures have reached 30,000,000 *yen* in round figures. No payment is made from these funds except in great and pressing emergencies, the chief aim being to support sufferers temporarily till they can obtain work.

The Government attaches greater importance to the prevention of poverty than to its succour, lest relief should enfeeble the spirit of independence and self-support, thus producing lazy, inactive people.   Hence strictly negative methods of relief have been officially adopted.   The Imperial Family, on the contrary, has shown its benevolence everywhere, and in every national calamity, or on the occasion of any other unusual occurrence, the Imperial Household is always the first to bestow gifts on the sufferers, besides, as already stated, giving annual contributions to charity works of every kind.   When His Majesty the Emperor was in mourning for Her Majesty the Empress-Dowager Éishō, he was pleased to give the considerable sum of 380,000 *yen* towards works of local relief and charity.   The local governments raised public and private contributions to add to the Imperial gifts and this fund is now over a million *yen*.   Our relief and charity works have thus good prospects.

Whilst on one hand the Imperial family shows such love towards the nation the people, on the other, inspired by the Imperial benevolence, follow the example set by their Sovereign, and immediately take steps for the relief of sufferers by any disaster or misfortune.   During the Russo-Japanese

War, it was remarkable how the Government and the public extended their benevolent hands to relieve the helpless families, widows, and orphans of our soldiers.

Statistics.

Table of philanthropical and relief establishments (from the returns of the Home Department).

Number of charitable institutions in Japan   ..   273

Classified according to religion :

Forms of Religion.						Number of Institutions.
Shintō	..	..	..	..	..	1
Buddhist	..	..	..	..	..	83
Christian	..	..	..	..	..	25
Non-religious	..	..	..	..	..	115
Uncertain	..	..	..	..	..	49

According to the varieties of charity work, they are :

	Single.	Having more than one Establishment.
Relief of the poor	74	18
Education of orphans and foundlings ..	64	13
Education of poor children	20	—
Free medical treatment	30	11
Reformatories for bad children	5	7
Prison-gate relief	26	11
Feeding of the aged	6	1
Giving employment to the poor ..	8	1
Miscellaneous (relief of soldiers, education of blind and dumb, charity fund)	10	7
Total	243	69

VII

CULTURE AND EDUCATION IN OLD JAPAN

Count Shigénobu Ōkuma

I.—Education in the Remote Past

Any traces of education, which may have existed in pre- Ancestor Worship. historic times, are naturally to be gathered rather by inference than aught else. Probably the first may be seen in the old cult of Ancestor Worship, in which ancestors were deified as foster-gods or guardian deities (*ubusuna-gami* or *uji-gami*: literally, 'gods of the birthplaces'). To them poems and songs were recited, and it is probable that the first instances of education consisted in teaching these to the younger genera- tion. A similar instance occurs in Roman history where, when there were neither schools nor teachers, children were taught a spirit of patriotism by reciting 'the twelve tables' and by hearing their mother's tales concerning the valiant deeds of their forbears.

All the ancient legends which were put into concrete form in The '*Kojiki*' and '*Nihon Shoki*.' the '*Kojiki*' and '*Nihon Shoki*,' written in the eighth century, must also have been learnt by countless generations. These books show what a wide influence they exercised on the moral culture of the people and on the spirit of nationalism and fidelity to the Throne.

II.—Education in Early Historic Times

It was only when freer and more frequent intercourse with Introduc- tion of Confu- cianism. the main Continent was possible that knowledge and education of any worth came to be established. This in the first instance appears to have come to Japan through the ports of Kudara.

For we read that in the reign of the Emperor Ōjin (284 A.D.) a learned man named Achiki came thence and was nominated historiographer to the Imperial Court, and from the same country also came an eminent scholar, Wani, who was familiar with the Chinese classics. The Emperor ordered the latter to start a school and to give the young prince, Waka-Iratsuko, lessons in the Chinese language and literature.

Wani brought with him two noted Chinese classics, the Confucian ' Analects ' (' *Lunyu*,' in ten volumes) and the 'Thousand Character Essay' ('*Ts'ien Tsu Wen*,' in one volume), and presented them to the Emperor as aids to general education. The Crown Prince continued his studies under Wani for some years, and became a very learned man, so that when an ambassador from Koma (Northern Korea) came with tribute to Japan, the Prince detected disrespectful words in the address presented to the Emperor and caused it to be rejected.

Its influence.

The good fruits of the importation of Chinese books and ideographs showed themselves in the promotion of foreign intercourse, in the development and improvement of national history, caligraphy, mathematics, and industry, and in the inculcation of moral virtues—such as fidelity, filial piety, humanity, and righteousness—in the minds of the people.

Reconciliation of *Shintō*, Confucianism, and Buddhism.

Henceforward the wind of admiration for Continental literature blew in every direction, and the waves of civilized knowledge continued to flow in unceasingly. The Continental countries were already converted to Buddhism, and that religion, after spreading over the Peninsula of Korea, permeated the country of ancestor worship. It was in the reign of the Emperor Kimméi (552 A.D.) that an image of Buddha, presented to that Sovereign by the Kingdom of Kudara, was entrusted to the Minister (*Daijin*) Soga, and that the diffusion of the new religion by erecting temples in the capital was publicly sanctioned. In course of time it spread in every direction and caused a great revolution in the thoughts of the people. What *Shintō* and Confucianism had hitherto taught concerned only ideas of the present world, but thenceforth the people were to be instructed in the retribution theory of the three worlds of human existence. Thus they came to understand the principle of performing good and virtuous deeds in the present, in order to atone for sinful acts in the past, and in order to produce good effects in the future. Buddhism was adopted as the national religion, and the temples Hōkōji and Horyūgakumonji were established for its propagation.

Prince Shōtoku, who acted as Regent in the reign of the Emperor Suiko (593 A.D.), furthered education by promulgating codes, by importing Chinese learning, history, laws, almanacs, divination, incantation, and various other arts and sciences. Moreover, to give further encouragement to the study of Confucianism and Buddhism, Ono-no-Imoko and other students were sent to China, then under the Sui dynasty. Students and priests were also sent, and thus contact with the Continent became more and more frequent. Takamuku-no-Kuromasa and Shōan Minabuchi, who were accompanied to China by Ambassador Fei, of that country, came back to Japan after thirty-three years' absence, and a priest, Bin, after twenty-five years. They brought home with them the Sui system of religion and learning, thus opening a new era in which the previously prevailing system was destined to undergo reform. In the first year of the reign of the Emperor Kōtoku (645 A.D.) the Minister of the Right (*Udaijin*), Soga-no-Ishikawamaro, submitted to the Emperor his opinion that Government measures should only be discussed after all the deities, heavenly and earthly, had been duly worshipped. Thus he effected a reform in the system of government, and by harmonizing the three creeds of *Shintō*, Confucianism, and Buddhism he succeeded in associating administration with religion and learning.

III.—EDUCATION UNDER THE IMPERIAL RÉGIME

The advance of civilization and the growth of the family system in the country brought about the necessity for reform in the old administration. The study of Chinese literature had begun with the Emperor Ōjin's appointment of Wani and Achiki to the positions of *Hakasé* and adviser; yet, as a result, the two families of *Bun* (*littérateurs*) and *Shi* (historiographers) were the sole administrators of Government measures. In the beginning of the reign of the Emperor Kéitai (513 A.D.) a

Promulgation of laws and ordinances.

number of the *Gokyō Hakasé* (*Hakasé* of the Five Classics) were appointed in addition to the above, with a view to conducting investigations in the three paths of literature, history, and law. Further, it being considered essential that the standard of religion and administration should be adopted from Continental methods, persons aspiring to be Government officers were compelled to study Chinese learning.

So, too, upon the adoption of Buddhist principles, students and priests were sent to China, where they were required to investigate her literature and institutions. By these means, and in conformity with the tendency of the times at home and abroad, the well-known administrative reforms known as the Taikwa Reformation were carried out. According to these, official regulations were fixed, and a local administrative system was, by way of trial, enforced in Kinai (the capital and its surrounding provinces), with the object of making preparation for the promulgation of laws and ordinances. A further aim of this reform was to consolidate and distinguish families which had increased during successive generations, by creating certain grades among them and by causing them to undertake the administrative business of the central and local government offices. But as a certain restriction was put upon official appointments, persons below the second grade were not permitted to enjoy freedom in politics and learning. After the lapse of twenty years a body of laws and ordinances, entitled ' *Ōmi Ritsuryō,*' was promulgated and published, but these afterwards underwent many changes. Finally, in the reign of the Emperor Mommu, a code of laws and ordinances known as ' *Taihō Ritsu* ' and ' *Taihō Ryō* ' was enacted. Although, in all this legislation, there are not found any provisions directly relating to the interests of the masses, yet the compilation of such laws and ordinances finds a parallel only in the work of Justinian the Great, and they certainly rendered great service in the future of Japan.

According to the educational system of this period, affairs relating to the University and National Schools were under the control of the Ceremonial Department of the Imperial Court, and no special administrative organ for educational affairs existed. Schools were for the education of the upper class only, and their chief object was to prepare men to become officials. In after years, illustrious families of the upper classes gradually commenced to establish private schools of their own. The following diagram shows the system of education in those days : ◁ System of education.

Government institutions.	Kyōto.	Daigaku (University).	Classics. History and Composition. Laws. Arithmetic. Pronunciation of Chinese Language. Caligraphy.
		Semmon-Gakujo (Institute of Special Knowledge).	
		Tenyaku-Ryō (Medicinal Department).	Medicine by male practitioners. Medicine by female practitioners. Acupuncture. Massage. Divination. Pharmaceutics.
		Gagaku-Ryō (Musical Department).	Japanese Music. Chinese Music. Kudara Music (Korean). Koma Music (Korean). Shiragi Music ,, Pantomime.
		Onyō-Ryō (Department of Divination).	Divination. Almanac compilation. Astrology.
	National Schools in localities.		
Private institutions.	Schools for noble families.	Kōbun-in (for the Waké family). Kangakuin (for the Fujiwara family). Junnain (for the Minamoto family). Sōgakuin ,, ,, ,, Gakkan-in (for the Tachibana family).	
	Schools for common people.	Sōgéishuchiin.	

University students in those days were selected from among talented youths of from thirteen to sixteen years of age, belonging to families of not less than the fifth grade of rank or to those of the East and West Boards of Historiographers, the number admitted being about four hundred. The official faculty of the University consisted of professors of classics, ◁ University and National School.

literature, and history, called *Hakasé*, and masters of various arts, called *Shi*.

National Schools were founded in every province, being placed under the control of local governors. These schools were designed for the education of the children of the governors, and the teachers were called *Kuni-Hakasé* (*Hakasé* of National Learning). The school age of the children was the same as in the University, and the number of students for each school varied according to the size of the district, ranging from twenty to fifty. Thus the total throughout the empire was some three thousand. According to the methods of discipline pursued in the University and in the National Schools, it is to be observed that the order of seating the students was arranged in strict conformity with their ages, and that the relation between teacher and student was maintained in a very rigid manner. As the Chinese classics and history were the principal subjects of study in the University, and as Confucianism was adopted as the proper school of learning, the rite called *Sékitén*, or Festival of Confucius, was performed with great reverence twice a year—in spring and autumn. As to the special treatment of University students, the Government granted them their expenses for food and clothing and also allowed them the use of books gratis.[1] Regulations relating to examinations for degrees and appointment to Government offices were very strict, and students were specially prepared for official careers, their course of study being regulated accordingly, appointments being given to them after graduating.

Private seminaries.

On the other hand, from the period of the Kyōto Court (794 A.D.) there was a noticeable growth of private seminaries, having their origin in the desire of illustrious families to maintain and develop their influence by educating their children. The first institution of this kind was *Kōbunin*. It was located to the south of the University, and was founded by Waké-no-Hiroyo, who thus carried out a project of his father, Waké-no-Kiyomaro. To this school he contributed books numbering many thousand volumes, and lands measuring forty *chō* (100 acres). Subsequently, the *Kwangakuin* of the

---

[1] The books in those days were all in manuscript and were very deficient, the art of printing being unknown.

Fujiwara family, the *Junnain* and the *Sogakuin* of the Mina-moto family, and the *Gakkwanin* of the Tachibana family were established in succession. But to all these schools the members of these families alone were admitted, and the only school that gave instruction to all classes was the *Sōgeishuchiin*, founded by the great priest Kūkai, and this was the pioneer of common education in Japan. The establishment of this school dated from 828 A.D., under the reign of the Emperor Junna. Its chief object was to inculcate the teachings of Buddhism, but Confucianism was also taught.

IV.—CULTURE AND LEARNING DURING THE PERIOD OF THE IMPERIAL RÉGIME

Although the field of education in those days was occupied mainly with the learning of the Tang dynasty and partly by the principles of Buddhism, yet the environment of original Japanese ideas had never been dispersed by these influences. In the early days of Buddhism in Japan the Emperor Bitatsu did not entertain any belief in it, but favoured the study of literature and history—that is, what was called *kidén-gaku*. The Emperor Yōméi, however, believed in Buddhism, and paid great reverence to *Shinto* also. His crown prince, Shōtoku Taishi, was the one who reconciled the three principles of *Shintō*, Confucianism, and Buddhism. *(Japanese ideas and Chinese knowledge.)*

The studies arranged in the University of this period, and which received prominent attention, were Chinese history and the classics. Men possessing a thorough knowledge of the classics as well as of history, and competent to display their acquisitions in their own writings were called *literati*, and were entitled to belong to the *Kansai* (talents of China) category. In this way a great impulse was given to the practice of composition. Such a tendency continued up to the time of the Nara Court, and produced women even who could read Chinese; the ideal being that Japanese verses and songs should be written with Chinese characters, and composed so as to apparently follow Chinese syntax; but owing to the different phraseology of the two languages, this intention proved fruitless. From the time of the Kyōto Court, however, *(Advancement in literature.)*

an endeavour was made to simplify the complex forms of Chinese characters borrowed for phonetic purposes, by means of syllabaries called *hira-kana* and *kata-kana*.[1] Thenceforward the use of these mediums for writing Japanese developed largely, the *Kana* compositions being first adopted by the Imperial harem of the Empress and Court ladies, where a number of noted female writers appeared. All these changes in literature and learning occurred during the tenth century.

In the reign of the Empress Ichijō (early eleventh century) the Empress Akiko gathered around her as ladies-in-waiting a number of talented women like Murasaki-Shikibu, Akazomé Émon, Izumi Shikibu, Isé-no-Ōsuké, &c., who excelled in verses and composition. Murasaki-Shikibu composed the ' *Genji Monogatari*,' and Akazomé Émon the ' *Éiga Monogatari*.' The others also were authoresses. Men and women of the upper class in those days were of necessity admirers of elegant and refined manners in every-day life, and consequently the culture of arts—such as caligraphy, painting, Chinese verses and composition, Japanese poems, music, songs, dancing, &c.— made considerable progress.

V.—THE KAMAKURA AND ASHIKAGA PERIODS

Diffusion of education.

From the foregoing it will be seen that the literary training of Court society was reaching a high level; for the majority of the nobility devoted their lives to study, and left to the military class not only martial, but civil matters. This had the result of attracting those warriors residing in the provinces to Kyōto, strengthening their unions against each other, and, in order to secure their own position and honour, encouraging the members of their families and their subordinates to render service to the State. They also imbued them with the spirit of fearlessness and indifference to death and trained them in martial exercises. This tendency had the further effect of converting the provincial districts into fields of martial exercises, where the so-called *Wakon*, or soul of Japan, was fostered and developed. Military magnates took with them to the capital their youths and subordinates thus educated and trained, in order to

---

[1] See p. 8 *ante.*

discharge the duties imposed upon them by the nobles. It was only natural that, while sojourning there, these provincials absorbed the elements of literature as pursued by the Court nobles, and developed their education. Thus literature became gradually diffused throughout the whole country, notwithstanding a general decline of education in National Schools.

From the twelfth century onwards political strife had existed between the two illustrious families of Minamoto and Taira, and this ultimately resulted in the fall of the latter family and the establishment at Kamakura of the Shōgunate by Yoritomo, chieftain of the Minamoto clan. About the same time a doctrine of the Zen or Dhyana creed, called *Shin-in* (Mental Impression), was preached by the priests belonging to that sect and began to gain vogue. It gradually took possession of the field and exerted wide influence, becoming an inspiring force in every town and village, and an essential factor in the moral training of military men. It also caused a sudden change in Buddhism, and gave no small impulse to the development of *Bushidō*, or the cult of the 'way of the warrior.' From the beginning of the Kamakura Shōgunate simple manners were much appreciated, and, as a consequence, the system of education and the rites of Confucian worship degenerated into mere formalities. Literary pursuits were monopolized by the Court nobles, military men being wholly absorbed in feats of arms and horsemanship. It is related that when a rescript was given by the retired Emperor Shirakawa to Yasutoki Hōjō at the time of the Jōkyū disturbance, only one out of five thousand warriors could read the document. But subsequently, when Imperial princes became Shōguns, a number of Court nobles came down to Kamakura in their suite, and as these nobles encouraged the study of laws and literature, military men began to attach importance to literary pursuits. *Decline of learning.*

The Kanazawa Library was established by Akitoki Hōjō at Shōmyōji (a Buddhist temple) in the latter part of the Kamakura period (about 1270). It contained almost all the Japanese and Chinese works that could then be found in the world. Each volume of the Chinese classical books was stamped in black '*Kanazawa Bunko*,' and each of the *Kanazawa Library.*

Buddhist books bore the same impression in vermilion. The volumes were shown to any person of any grade who wished to read and study them.

In those days priests alone pursued literature as a profession, and they were driven to it from the necessity of reading canonical books. Thus the five principal monasteries of Kyōto and those of Kamakura were the centre not only of the Zen teaching, but also of literature. The noted books published in and after the Kamakura period were almost entirely written by priests, and general education may be said to have been only kept alive by the existence of monasteries, where the children of military men received instruction. School age usually extended from about ten to fifteen or sixteen years, and the scholars *Térako.* were called *térako* (literally, 'monastery children'). Their principal course of study was penmanship, but lessons in reading, spelling, and etiquette were also given. The curriculum, however imperfect, comprised various branches of knowledge, which were imparted by the simplest methods, and were no small assistance to the development of common sense which was derived from this system of education.

Ashikaga After the great disturbance of the Southern and Northern *Gakkō.* Courts the time was not favourable to the organization of formal institutions of education, and during the Ashikaga period there was, in addition to the Kanazawa Library, only one school, called *Ashikaga Gakkō*, in the Province of Shimotsuké. The date of its establishment is unknown; but in 1439 it was reorganized by Norizané Uyésugi, the buildings being repaired, and an area of rice-fields being assigned for its maintenance, together with a valuable collection of Japanese and Chinese works of every description. The functions of teaching were entrusted to the hands of Buddhist priests, and it attained to a flourishing condition, notwithstanding the great disorder that prevailed throughout the country. In the period of the Tokugawa Shōgunate repairs of the buildings were effected, and the institute continued until within a few years of the Méiji era.

Bushidō. In order to understand the condition of Japanese education from this time onwards it is necessary to explain the system of *Bushidō*, just as it is necessary to consider the system of chivalry in order to comprehend the condition

of European education during the Middle Ages.   After the
inauguration of the family system, some of the families in
local districts of necessity split up as their members increased
with years, and though they received, at the time of the
Taikwa Reform, certain allotments of rice-fields for their
maintenance, still it was inevitable that they should undergo
vicissitudes.   Among them were some who, on account of
the popularity they enjoyed in their districts, became subordinate officers of the provincial governors (*Kokushi* and
Gunshi) and grew to be renowned.   But they did not lose
the instincts transmitted to them by heredity from ancient
times, for they always aimed at good manners, a stalwart
physique, and a spirit of loyalty and devotion.   It was their
habit to render service to the Court and in military affairs,
their special pursuits being archery and horsemanship, which
originated in their service as guards at the Imperial Court,
where they learned the value of discipline.   To develop their
military *morale* they were subjected to ordinances laid down
by the chieftains of the great families to which they were
attached.

The two illustrious families of Minamoto and Taira, which
sprang from the Imperial family, resided in their respective
provinces and there consolidated the strength of their subordinate families as above mentioned.   Whilst they undertook
the responsibility of guarding the Emperor at Kyōto, they
struggled with each other for military ascendancy.   In the
sequel, the Taira family, which had originally displaced
the Fujiwara from political supremacy, was overthrown by
Minamoto-no-Yoritomo, who succeeded in gathering to his
standard all military men throughout the eight eastern
provinces and finally obtained military control of the whole
country.   He established himself as Shōgun at Kamakura and
encouraged the spirit of militarism.

At that time the contrast between Kamakura and Kyōto
was great.   In the former refinement was esteemed much
as it used to be in Athens, whereas in the latter people used
to tell their sons, when going to the battle-field : ' Receive
arrows on your forehead, but never in your back '—an
utterance of the same spirit as shown in the Spartan motto :

'If not victorious, return on a shield.' Yoritomo exhorted his subordinates in the following terms :

> 'Respect the Deities, esteem Buddha, and raise the fame of your family.'
> 'Train yourself in martial exercises.'
> 'Eschew everything vulgar and indecent.'
> 'Abhor timid or effeminate deeds.'
> 'Practise plainness and economy.'
> 'Strive for the favour of your lord.'
> 'Keep your promises.'
> 'Be faithful unto death.'
> 'Fear not a powerful enemy.'
> 'Disdain not a weak enemy.'

By these simple precepts he inculcated among his subordinates habits of frugality and chivalry.   Other great families throughout the land also endeavoured to attain fame and prosperity by encouraging the military valour of their retainers, and the result was that, when the Mongols invaded Japan on the crest of a wave of conquest that had swept over the whole of China, our trained soldiery threw themselves on the invaders and absolutely annihilated them.   Thenceforth the moral culture of the *Bushi*, or military men, was carried out by inculcating the principle of subordinating life to duty and physical culture, and by training in martial exercises—such as archery, horsemanship, swordsmanship, and the use of the spear.   Ranking as the head of the four classes (*Shi*, *Nō*, *Kō*, and *Shō*: military men, farmers, artisans, and merchants), *Bushi* always maintained their honorary position, considering themselves the protectors of the country for the sake of the Sovereign, bearing the responsibility of quelling disturbance and restoring peace, regarding their two swords as the palaces of their souls, esteeming propriety and a sense of shame as the essentials of morality, and regarding them as dearer than life itself.   When Kenshin Uyésugi enacted his criminal laws, he put the confiscation of a *Bushi's* swords at the head of all punishments, loss of life being one degree less severe.   It is not surprising that what the *Bushi* shunned more than death was cowardice.   This spirit spreading throughout the whole country finally inspired

Hidéyoshi's expedition to Korea, which, after trampling down the whole of the eight provinces of Korea, caused the Ming Sovereign himself to tremble.

This invasion not only spread the fame of Japan's military valour over the Asiatic Continent, but brought withal a knowledge of books and literature, as well as various improvements in arts and industries. It was at this time that the importation of movable types assisted greatly in developing printing, which produced no small effect on the diffusion of culture and learning, and caused a revival of literature and arts.

VI.—EDUCATION UNDER THE TOKUGAWA SHŌGUNATE

The warlike disposition of Hidéyoshi, the pacification of his own country, and his invasion of Korea, left him but little time to direct matters of interior administration. These were perforce left to his successor, Iyéyasu Tokugawa, who took a deep interest in the causes and effects of tranquillity and disturbances—ancient and modern—and, when establishing the Shōgunate at Yédo, devised various executive measures which were put into practice under the third Shōgun, Iyémitsu.

Iyéyasu, though born in a time of great disorder, was both a student and a bibliophile, and much of the material for the administrative system, which he built up, was derived from old volumes and manuscripts.

Encouragement of learning by Iyéyasu.

Immediately upon his elevation to the Shōgunate he devoted much time and effort to the printing and publishing of a number of Japanese and Chinese works. In his so-called ' Legacy,' or ' Testament,' it is stated that the culture and learning of Japan being behind those of other countries, schools should be established in the interests of the country's reputation, and that, since from his youth to the assumption of the Shōgunate, what he had always held most sacred was neither money nor jewels, but excellence of moral character, his descendants should carry out his intention by always observing the golden rule which says : ' Human happiness may naturally be found in learning, and should be sought therein.' These sayings clearly indicate the springs of Iyéyasu's conduct throughout life. The measures he adopted for the encouragement of culture and learning were four—namely, investigation of old books and documents, employment of learned men, establishment of schools, and publication of books. The founding of the *Daigaku-Shōhéikō* (University of Chinese Classics) and the compilation of the '*Honchō Tsugan*' ('Classical History of Japan') in a later generation were but in pursuance of the ideas of Iyéyasu.

Tsuna-
yoshi.

There still existed at this time certain families of scholars patronized by the Imperial Court, and none but Buddhist priests were allowed to publicly engage in education. But in the days of the fifth Shōgun, Tsunayoshi, Nobuatsu Hayashi, a grandson of Nobukatsu Hayashi, was appointed by the Shōgunate to be University Superintendent, and the study of literature was greatly encouraged. By his order portable copies of the Four Chinese Classics were prepared for the sake of convenience, and were commonly called '*Denchū-bon*' (books for use in the palace). During the thirty years of his tenure of office he paid special attention to learning, and used often to visit the residence of *daimyō*, where he himself read books to the *daimyō* and his household. As a consequence, all the *daimyō*, as well as their vassals, engaged in a rivalry of learning. Thus national literature, Buddhist learning, medical science, &c., attained high degrees of development, while men of letters or learned scientists came to the front in rapid succession.

Yoshi-
muné.

The apogee of culture was probably reached in the time of the eighth Shōgun, Yoshimuné, who was the wisest ruler of the Middle Age. He was acute enough to employ all the talents in the service of the Government, and thus achieved signal success. During his rule of twenty-nine years he paid special attention to matters of education, as may be inferred from his ordering the compilation of books on geography, the establishment of an astronomical observatory and the rescission of the prohibition against the importation of foreign books, and other cognate measures. The following incidents show his care for social education:

He ordered Kyūsō Muro (a learned scholar) to compile the '*Rikuyu-Éngi Taii*' ('Outline of the Principles of Six Kinds of Instruction'), the '*Gojō Wakai*' ('Japanese Commentary on the Five Moral Virtues '), and the ' *Gorin Wakai* ' (' Japanese Commentary on the Five Moral Relations '). These he caused to be given to teachers of penmanship at Yédo as copybooks for children ; whilst he also granted money for the copying of the legal ordinances of the time. He allowed a private school to be established at Fukagawa (Yédo) and prohibited immoral publications, or indecent performances at theatres.

The eleventh Shōgun, Iyénari, founded the *Wagaku Kōdansho* (Institution for Lectures of the Japanese Classics), and the twelfth Shōgun, Iyéyoshi, held teachers of caligraphy responsible for correcting the evil customs of the people, inculcating loyalty and filial piety, and giving assistance to the administration. For these purposes he ordered them to adopt as copy-books the legal ordinances of the era, the ' *Jitsugokyō* ' (' Scripture of Truth '), the '*Daigaku*' (' Greater Learning '), the ' *Shōgaku* ' ('Lesser Learning'), the '*Onna Imagawa*' (' Women's Ethics '), the ' *Onna Kōkyō* ' (' Women's Filial Piety '). All this indicates how much special attention was paid by every Shōgun to matters of education.

The institutions for education existing during the period now under review were as follows : *Shōhéikō* (University for Chinese Classical Learning), *Wagaku Kōdansho* (Institute for Japanese Classical Learning), and *Kaiséijo* (Institute of Western Knowledge), under the control of the Shōgunate ; the clan schools under the great fiefs ; private boarding-schools where Chinese literature was taught ; and *terakoya* where elementary subjects were taught to children. All these were established in accordance with the requirements of the time. The *Shōhéikō*, which may be regarded as corresponding to the University of the Imperial *régime*, was an institution where the Shōgun's retainers were instructed in Chinese classical learning. At the time of its first opening there was an attendance of more than three hundred students, and the curriculum consisted of : (1) Chinese classics—expository lectures being given on the Four Books and Five Classics according to the principles of the Cheng-Chu school. (2) Chinese history, in which investigations were made according to the standard of the chronological records of Chu and the *Tsugan Komoku*. (3) Japanese

Institutions for education.

history, including the subjects of *Rikkokushi* (History of
Six Countries), *Honchō Tsugan* (Japanese classical history),
and the Tokugawa's records. (4) The laws—comprising the
Chinese laws of the Tang, Ming, and T'sing dynasties, together
with Japanese laws, ordinances, and precedents, &c. (5) Prose
and poetry. In short, the chief object of instruction was to
encourage the *samurai's* fidelity by inculcating the legal
principles of the Ming dynasty and the philosophical truths of
the Sung dynasty. Hence, more attention was paid to Chinese
instruction than to Japanese learning; but inasmuch as Iyéyasu
devoted no small pains to investigating old books and documents and encouraged historical research, the importance of
studying Japanese native books was generally felt.

'History of Great Japan.' Mitsukuni, lord of Mito, commenced at this time the
compilation of the '*Dai-Nihon-Shi*' ('History of Great Japan');
in the interests of his ancestors, and for the sake of Japanese
literature, he entrusted the compilation of a commentary on
the '*Manyōshū*' ('Collection of a Myriad Leaves') to Chōryū
Shimokōbe, who was followed by the priest Kéichū in the task
of preparing the book under the title of '*Manyō Daishōki*.'
Moreover, Mitsukuni ordered the compilation of the 'Code of
Ceremonial Regulations in the Imperial Court' ('*Réigi Ruitén*').
In the time of Yoshimuné investigations were made into facts
concerning the antecedents of the military class, and the
ancient record of the Ninagawa and Isé families was thus brought
to light. A work in forty-eight volumes, namely, the '*Kojikidén*'
('Commentary on the Record of Ancient Matters'), was at this
time brought out by Norinaga Motoori as the result of thirty-
five years' labour. He it was who, by denouncing the principles
of Confucianism and Buddhism, attracted the eyes and ears
of the learned. There was also a blind man by the name of
Hokiichi Hanawa, noted for a splendid memory and for great
learning orally acquired. At his request the Shōgunate established the *Wagaku Kōdansho* (Institute for Japanese Classical
Learning) in 1793. He compiled 1300 volumes of the '*Gunsho
Ruijū*' ('Classified Collection of Japanese Classics'). At that
time there were several schools of learning having as their aim
the renouncement of the fundamental doctrines of Chinese
classical erudition (the Cheng-Chu school); but the Shōgun did

his best to check the propagation of these principles as false doctrine, and to encourage the cause of classical learning: to this end he employed Kunihiko Shiba and Boku Koga as professors of the *Shōhéikō*, and selected so large a number of talented men from various provinces for admission that the accommodation for students had to be rearranged.   But his efforts were in vain, for new Western ideas also flowed in through the study of Dutch, which then prevailed.

The Japanese people, endowed with a progressive spirit, had long felt dissatisfied with their own and Chinese learning.   In the early days of Iyéyasu the foreign countries that held commercial supremacy in the East were Portugal, Spain, and Holland.   He, as is well known, adopted the open-door policy and allowed England as well as the three just named to trade with Japan; but detecting the scheming and aggressive aims of the Christian missionaries, he was forced to change his policy and adopt that of seclusion.   This policy, however, was opposed to the natural temper of the people in general, and so we find in the time of the sixth Shōgun, Iyénobu, a learned man, Hakuséki Arai, opening a way for the investigation of Western arts and sciences by compiling books known as '*Séiyō Kibun*' and '*Sairan Igén*' (both relating to things Western), with the aid of certain Roman Catholic missionaries through the intervention of the Dutch.

Dutch learning.

The Shōgun Yoshimuné, struck with the profound knowledge possessed by the Dutch concerning astronomy and geography, and with the clearness of the illustrations in their books on these sciences, ordered his retainer Bunzo Aoki to study Dutch works.   In proportion as Aoki's researches progressed the importance of medical science was felt more and more by him and others.   At last, in 1862, the *Kaiséijo* (Institute of Western Knowledge) was established under the Shōgun Iyénari in place of the old institute of medical investigation which had previously existed, the accommodation for students being greatly enlarged at the same time.   The course of study was at first Dutch learning only, but gradually English, French, German, and Russian were added to the curriculum, and books relating to geography, medical science, physics, chemistry, natural history, and military science were also read

This Institute of Western Knowledge was the precursor of the present Tōkyō Imperial University.

Han or fief schools.

Under the various fiefs, great and small, *Han* or clan schools had for a long while previously been established for the education of the fief's retainers, and the number of these schools gradually increased. The subjects of study taught in them were almost the same as in the *Shōhéikō*—Chinese learning, as a matter of course, being the principal. No school fee or other charges were exacted from the students, and practical military art was taught by specialists at their residences. As regards general education, it is to be noted that children of from seven or eight years of age to fifteen attended school from their own homes, and that, when above that age, they became boarders. The method of instruction consisted in reading, reviewing, hearing teachers' expositions of the meaning of books, the students explaining them in turn, composing poetry and prose at certain intervals of time, writing compositions on given subjects, and so forth. Examinations were conducted monthly by teachers, and in the spring and autumn by high officials of the fief governments. The object of these examinations was merely to signify approval of students who showed ability and to censure those whose attainments were inferior. The number of these *Han* schools towards the end of the Tokugawa dynasty aggregated over two hundred and forty. Among them the most noted were the *Méirindō* of Nagoya, the *Zōshikwan* of Kagoshima, the *Kōjōkwan* of Yonézawa, and the *Kōdōkwan* of Mito.

Private boarding-schools.

As to private boarding-schools for Chinese learning, there were two kinds—namely, schools taught by persons officially attached to the Shōgunate, or to a *Han* government, and schools taught by a private individual. Among the latter the most noted was a private boarding-school in Kyōto, known as the *Horikawa Gakkō*, where a learned scholar, Jinsai Itō, gave instruction. He maintained this school for more than forty years, and educated over three thousand pupils. He insisted that indifference to criticism, impartiality, and self-control should be considered as of the first importance in learning, and that much talking should be condemned as an evil habit. The learning of this period had for its chief object moral education.

The subjects taught in the *Terakoya* to the children of the common people were reading, letter-writing, arithmetic, etiquette, and caligraphy, which was the principal course. The readers in use were the '*Sanjikyō*' ('Three Metres Precepts') the '*Jitsugokyo*' ('Scripture of Truth'), the '*Shōbai Ōrai*' ('Commercial Letters'), &c., but the lessons differed according to the different callings of the children, with a view to practical application in daily life. Thus the method of teaching, though not complete in the true sense, could not be called inadequate for purposes of ordinary business. The school age of children was from seven or eight years to twelve or thirteen. At the time of entering school the children were taken to the teacher's house accompanied by their elders. Kneeling before the teacher and requesting to be taken under his care, they made oral promise to the effect that they would submit to punishment of any sort, in case they committed a fault. The relation of teacher and pupils thus established was to be regarded as that of master and servant, or of father and son. Consequently, the pupils respected their teachers as if they were their own parents, and the teachers, in turn, brought them up as if they were their own children. The teachers were mostly persons with good reputation, living in the same locality with the children, and so familiar with the household customs of every family that they could subject the children to strict discipline according to their characters. Moreover, as they were much respected and trusted by the parents and brethren of the children, they gave instruction to these persons also, according to circumstances.

The educationists of the present era, though they have introduced Western principles of intellectual education and methods of teaching, still keep in their memory the methods of discipline that prevailed in former generations.

Intellectual education in those days was far from perfect; but as the principle that 'everyone should attend diligently to his own occupation and serve his country' became the golden rule to be observed by every class, whether high or low, the new method of teaching was easily assimilated by all, and its general diffusion soon showed its effect on society.

Physical education was conducted by military drill and arts

Marginal notes: Relation of teachers and pupils. Spiritual education.

K 2

Physical
education.

adapted to warfare, but during the early era of the Tokugawa Shōgunate, when peace began to reign after so long a war, many of the courses—archery and horsemanship, for instance —became mere formalities. Subsequently, archery in the style of Héki and his pupil Yoshida, and horsemanship after the methods of Ōtsubo and Hachijō, came into fashion, but gunnery fell into disuse. As to swordsmanship, the *Yagyū* style widely prevailed, Munélosh Yagyū becoming instructor of the Shōguns Hidétada and Iyémitsu, to whom he imparted his art of *Shinkagé*. About the same time Musashi Miyamoto invented the two-sworded style, which was popularized by his pupil, Aoki. Again, Chōisai Iishino invented the art of using sword and spear at the same time. He claimed divine inspiration by the gods ' Kashima ' and ' Katori,' and called his method *Shindō*. His pupil Ichiu Morooka invented another style of fencing called *Mijin*. The priest Inyéi of Nara inaugurated the *Hōzōin* style by using a sickle-spear, and Ōshima invented the *Tanéda* style. *Jūjutsu* had its origin in the art of boxing taught by a Chinese of the Ming dynasty, and there were two styles subsequently developed by a priest, Séigō, and by Shishin Sékiguchi. Another art, called ' Binding,' was practised in the three styles of *Takénouchi*, *Mujinsai*, and *Imagawa*. All these arts were taught to the *Bushi*, who used to practise them at places of exercise called *Dōjō*, while at the same time they educated their moral and nervous strength in accordance with the principles of the Zen teaching and of mental philosophy. When they found themselves master of their arts they used to travel on foot throughout the country, and in order to exercise and test their courage they would spend nights in deep valleys or dense forests. Competition in accomplishments often led to deadly duels, and the winners in these combats were readily engaged by *daimyō* to teach their retainers. *Bushi* who could not master one of these arts were struck off the military roll. Owing to long prevalence of peace and prosperity the custom of duels ceased, and though the *Mushashugyō* (knight-errantry, or practice of visiting every place of the country to seek adventures) still prevailed, it was pursued in only a formal manner, and degenerated into a display of ability in sham-fighting. Nevertheless, under the various *daimyō* there were still some experts who devised new styles. In a word, the habit of inuring the body and mind to exposure to cold and heat was counted as evidence of the strength of any clan where such a habit prevailed, and served also for the maintenance of its supremacy, while stimulating the fashion of despising cowardice and feebleness.

But the fashions of later times were antagonistic to the practice of these virtues ; for military men who had been accustomed to court hardship now lapsed into votaries of luxury. On the other hand, though social order relaxed and *Bushidō* waned, a certain reactionary movement took place among the people. This was called *Jinkyō* (spirit of knightly commoner). It would seem that in Japan, when *Bushidō* declines *Jinkyō* flourishes. The rise of this latter spirit was not without cause ; for the people, ever since the era of Ōnin, had watched the perpetual struggle for supremacy among military men, and had become imbued with the spirit it displayed. Moreover, at the moment when the spirit of *Bushidō* commenced to wane, that of *Wakon* (spirit of Japan), which had remained latent, began to manifest itself in the form of *Jinkyō*. No sooner did this latter make its appearance than its influence spread in all directions, and its effect upon society was manifested not only in the full development of popular literature, but also in the realm of popular amusements. Public recitals of martial deeds inspired lofty ideas in the souls of ignorant people, whilst musical recitations appealed to their heart. In this way national education received a great impetus from *Jinkyō* ; and artistic and poetical ideas, which are the natural characteristics of our people, were greatly developed even among the lower classes. This is evidenced in the songs and poems written on tablets which are still dedicated to temples or shrines in rural districts, and in their love of flowers which they use constantly to decorate the front of their shops or their court-yards. In other words, it may be said that the nation became accustomed to imbibing drops from the vase filled with the fine liquor of civilization, brewed during past ages by the upper classes, and that they were thus prepared to ultimately welcome the new and joyous era of Méiji civilization.

EDUCATIONALISTS OF THE PAST, AND THEIR SHARE IN THE MODERNIZATION OF JAPAN

Professor Kazutami Ukita, D.C.L. (Japan)

Educational elements in Japanese civilization.

THAT the advancement of our country in civilization during the last fifty years has been primarily, if not entirely, due to education is a fact recognized both at home and abroad. But it is a great mistake if, as is often the case, this is set down to such educational enterprises as date no farther back than half a century. Nor are those foreigners right who, seeing that the Government as early as 1872 instituted a national educational system embracing a university, middle and primary schools, think that the present state of our civilization has been secured solely through its efforts. Such views may lead them to look upon us as an extraordinary kind of people, who, having passed, as it were in a night, from an uncivilized to a civilized state, cannot be judged by the ordinary laws of human experience, and to consequently regard our civilization as only skin-deep and unstable. The slightest survey of our past should dispel such hasty conclusions. For the genesis of what has led to such surprising results is to be sought far back in our history, and certainly not so late as in the last fifty years ; nor have they been attained through governmental undertakings only, but to a great extent through private and individual efforts.

Influence of philosophy and religion.

Just as the European mind in medieval ages was trained by the theology and philosophy of the period, which, though astonishingly imperfect by the side of modern science, ultimately paved the way for the age of the Renaissance, and thus contributed much to modern civilization. so the Japanese mind had been cultivated and developed by the literature, philosophy, and religion of China and India long before coming into contact with things Occidental.   The philosophies and religions of China and India, however, could only be of use up to a certain point, for though but little inferior to those of medieval Europe, they were checked in their subsequent development, lacking, as they did, the scientific treatment which the Greeks left to the Europeans.   Again, had the Japanese been like the Hindoos and Chinese, who, taking pride in their own civilizations, clung to them with the obstinacy of bigoted conservatism and refused to imbibe foreign influence, their fate might have been no better than their neighbours'. But by a fortunate fate they were islanders accustomed to change, and they did not think it degrading to receive the influence of other countries.   Nay, further than that, they always welcomed foreign civilization with an open mind, and were not slow to seize what good things they found in it and to assimilate them with their own.   This, then, is what differentiates the Japanese from their Asiatic brethren in spite of their great indebtedness to the latter, and this it is that has ultimately led them to their present condition of advancement.

Assimilating powers of the Japanese.

Again, the immediate causes that worked out this advance are to be sought not merely in governmental efforts, but rather in the educational enterprises of private individuals who led the people in the right way.

Modern European civilization is the result of multitudinous causes working for centuries past, but it is since the days of enlightenment and the Liberal movement in the eighteenth century that we find in it that marked progress which has given it its essentially modern character.   It is strange that that century was also a significant one for our country—in that she then first began to shake off her long dreams of seclusion and develop a tendency to welcome Western civilization.   Since 1639, for political reasons, the Tokugawa Government had put Christianity under a ban, closed Japanese ports to all European vessels except those of the Dutch, and prohibited the people even to read Western books.   So, though there were some native interpreters in Nagasaki who spoke Dutch,

Starting-point of modern Japan.

they could not read Dutch books ; and though there were Japanese surgeons who belonged to the so-called Dutch school, they did not learn what scanty art they possessed from foreign books, but only through observation or hearsay.   At the
Study of Dutch books. time, however, of the eighth Shōgun, Yoshimuné (1713–44), Zenzaburō Nishi, Kōsaku Yoshio, and others, all inter-preters in Nagasaki, feeling it a disgrace not to be able to read a word of the Dutch they professed to speak, petitioned the Government to allow them to read Dutch books and to study the written language.   The Shōgun Yoshimuné being a wise prince did not hesitate to grant the petitioners their request. Upon this, Nishi and others borrowed dictionaries from a Dutchman and copied three of them—earnest efforts which moved the foreigner to present Nishi with the lexicons.   Nishi afterwards tried to compile a small dictionary for the use of his countrymen by translating from the Dutch originals, but death overtook him before he was half through his task. Yoshio, however, became proficient in surgery by reading Blenck's work, and taught it to over six hundred students.

Bunzō Aoki.   At this time there was one Bunzō Aoki who was allowed specially to use the Government library on account of his fondness for learning.   In 1739 he was appointed one of the official lecturers on Chinese classics, and as in this capacity he referred from time to time to the advisability of using Dutch books, the Shōgun Yoshimuné ordered that he and Genjō Noro, a physician, should be allowed to read them. On this the two men did their best to learn something of the language under a Dutch captain whenever he came to Yédo, or from his interpreter.   But as this happened only once a year, and as the European language is written from left to right and not up and down as is ours, the construction also being much distorted from a Japanese point of view, they were overcome by difficulties, and their study of several years amounted to but little.   At last, in 1744, Aoki was sent to Nagasaki, and with the help of such men as Nishi and Yoshio, came for the first time to understand something of elementary Dutch.   He stayed there for several years, and returned to Yédo after learning about four hundred of the most common words, with their etymology, pronunciation, and derivation.   By this time the Shōgun Yoshimuné was dead, and things were not as favourable as in former days. Moreover, on account of the want of teachers, as well as of books, he could not pursue his study further, and was only able to write an ' Elementary Dutch Word-Book ' and a ' Dutch-Japanese Conversation Book.'   Meanwhile Noro, the physician, produced a translation of a treatise on botany, which was the first book in Japanese on Western science.

In Japan, from olden times, medical science was in great repute—being called the art of benevolence—and a skilled physician was considered equal in merit to a good statesman. Hence, under the Tokugawa Government and in all the clans appertaining to it, clever physicians were sure of a good practice, the outcome being the creation in Japan, before the Restoration, of a class advanced in thought and fitted to understand the spirit of Western science and its methods. Social position of Japanese physicians.

On the medical staff of the Nakatsu clan in Buzén there was a physician by the name of Ryōtaku Maéno (pseudonym, Rankwa,[1] 1723–1803).   An orphan from his boyhood, he was brought up at the hands of his uncle, Zentaku Miyata, of the Yodo clan, a learned man, and moreover one who took peculiar views of everything.   In educating his nephew he constantly advised him to study whatever was little cared for at the time, and thus, guarding against its being entirely neglected, to hand it to posterity with added improvements of his own. His view was that if one took up a study which was pursued universally, the chances were that one had to lag behind others all through life without any opportunity of making a name.   The best plan, therefore, was to strike out in a new direction, to originate at least one thing, and thus to endeavour to lead the world—in a word, to specialize.   The boy bore his uncle's precepts in mind and grew to be a gifted and strong-willed man, but as a physician, serving the lord of his clan, he stayed in Yédo.   One day a friend, on visiting him, showed him a volume of a Dutch work which he had brought, asking if he could read it.   Maéno did not answer.   But from that moment he made up his mind to study Dutch and to put into practice what he had been taught by his uncle ; Ryōtaku Maéno.

---

[1] ' Rankwa ' literally means ' Hollandization.'

and though then in his fortieth year, he went to Bunzō Aoki to be instructed in the language. Aoki admired his spirit and gladly taught him all the words he knew, as well as the contents of his own ' Elementary Dutch Word-Book.' But this being insufficient, the following year (1770), when he went down to Nakatsu with his lord, Okudaira, he asked permission to visit Nagasaki and to stay there for a hundred days. Receiving this he went thither, and, associating with Kōsaku Yoshio and other interpreters, added over two hundred words to his vocabulary of five hundred which he had learned from Aoki, and returned to Yédo, taking with him some anatomical charts by a Dutchman.

Gempaku-Sugita.

About this time, Gempaku Sugita (1733–1817), physician to Lord Sakai of the Obama clan, Wakasa, being born in a house of hereditary surgeons of the so-called Dutch school, was endeavouring to improve his professional knowledge. It happened about 1767 that Kōsaku Yoshio, then noted for his surgical ability, came up to Yédo with a Dutch doctor, and Sugita availed himself of this opportunity to call at their lodging and learn their methods. He watched the operations done by the Dutchman, and was much struck by his skill. One day Yoshio showed a valuable book of his to Sugita, saying that it was a treatise on surgery by Lorenz Heister, imported only a year before. Sugita could not read a word of it, but finding it marvellously thorough and unlike any work in Japanese or in Chinese, he determined at least to copy its illustrations ; so, borrowing it, he worked at copying until far into the night, and so finished it while Yoshio was still in the city. Sugita had now to wait for some years to see another Dutch book, but in 1771 he came across two. Still unable to read, but thinking that the anatomical pictures of the human body contained in one of them, though very different from what he knew, must have been drawn from life, he wanted to purchase them for his library, but he was too poor, and was only enabled to do so through the kindness of his lord.

Value of Western science recognized.

The time now seemed to have at last arrived for Western science to take root in Japan. In March of the same year, just after the above books came into Sugita's possession, he learned that the dissection of an executed criminal was to take place at Kotsukappara.   Thinking this a rare chance of comparing the anatomical pictures in his newly bought Dutch book with the real objects, he was overjoyed, and informed those specially interested among his friends.   Sugita knew Maéno only slightly, the latter being his senior by ten years; but, thinking it improper to leave any enthusiastic student of medicine uninformed, he sent a special messenger and asked Maéno to meet them the following day.   Next morning, when they all assembled at the appointed place, they had their first surprise in the form of two books which Sugita and Maéno brought, and which proved to be imprints of the ' Tafel Anatomia.'   They proceeded to the scene of the dissection, and as they compared the real body with the Dutch drawings, they were surprised to find that, unlike what Chinese books taught, it exactly resembled them.   The dissection of a human body had been in the past attempted seven or eight times by official surgeons; but as the internal organs were not at all like those described in the old Chinese books, which were firmly believed to be true, they were always assailed with doubts, and could only console themselves, it is said, with the idea that the people of the Celestial Kingdom must be organically different from others !

On the way home, the three men, Ryōtaku Maéno, Gempaku Sugita, and Junan Nakagawa, talked together over the wonderful revelation afforded by the day's operation.   It was a shame, they thought, that they, serving as physicians to their respective lords, were ignorant of these things, and it behoved them to ascertain, even rudimentally, what was the structure of the human body, and to base their art on that knowledge.   Sugita then observed : ' If we could only translate this " Tafel Anatomia," how much benefit would that bring to our art, making clear to us every part of the human body !   Would that I could read it ! '   ' To read Dutch,' said Maéno, ' is my long-cherished desire.   But to my great regret I have no good friends to study with.   I went to Nagasaki some years ago and learned something of it, so, if you desire, we will read together with what little knowledge I have as a basis.'   The other two were delighted, and promised to do their best if he would help them.

Maéno, Sugita, and Nakagawa.

The 4th of March 1771 was the day on which New Japan was born. As long as our race endures, the resolution of these men should be remembered with gratitude. How difficult, however, their undertaking was may be gathered from a book called the ' Beginnings of Dutch Study in Japan,' which may be said to be the autobiography of Gempaku Sugita. One passage runs thus : ' When we gathered together the following day at Maéno's house and faced the " Tafel Anatomia," we felt as if we had launched on a wide sea in a rudderless boat. We were at a loss how to steer our course, and remained dumfounded. The difficulty was enormous. For instance, in reading such an easy sentence as " The eyebrow is the arch of hair over the eye," a long spring day's labour barely enabled us to understand even a word of the line. One day, as we read about the nose, we came to a full stop where the word " ver-heffend " occurred. There was no complete " woordenboek " then ; we had only a small one which Maéno had brought from Nagasaki. Consulting it, we found as explanation that when a branch of a tree is cut, the wood will *verheffend* at the place, and that when a garden is swept, the dust will gather and *verheffend*. So we tried to guess what the word meant. It occurred to me that when a branch of a tree is cut, the wood will rise at the place after a while, and that when the dust is swept, it will rise, too. Now as the nose is a prominent feature of the face, it might be said to *verheffend*, or rise from the face. The other two approved my interpretation, and so we settled its meaning. I was as pleased at my success as if I had found a gem of the first water. We believed, however, in the saying, ' To do belongs to man, to accomplish, to Heaven,' and we met regularly, and assiduously faced our task. Light is sure to come to those that seek it, and after a year or so had passed we greatly increased our vocabulary, and naturally came to know something of Western life also. We acquired ease in reading, and could translate more than ten lines a day where the matter was not too difficult. Of course we never lost a chance of asking the help of the Dutch interpreters when they came to Yédo every spring. We had dissections, too, once in a while, and often cut up animals to compare them with our text. Thus two or three years were spent. We had come gradually to taste the sweets of the study, so that the regular days for meeting were awaited with as much eagerness and impatience as a child feels on the approach of a festival day.'

In this way, with Ryōtaku Maéno as a leader, Gempaku Sugita, Junan Nakagawa, and those who joined them later, all co-operated in translating the ' Tafel Anatomia.' Sugita especially took pains to put down what he had read immediately, and improving the style of translation rewrote the whole eleven times in the course of four years and finished at last the publication of the ' New Treatise on Anatomy.' ' New Treatise on Anatomy.'

This was in 1774, and these men now became a centre for the study of the Dutch language. Ryōtaku Maéno and Gempaku Sugita especially taught it to many students, and assiduously endeavoured to popularize it. Maéno thoroughly understood the language at last, and could read any Dutch book ; so availing himself of this knowledge, he determined to study the history and life of Western countries, and devoted his whole time to the task, leading a recluse's life on the pretext of being an invalid. He was reported to his lord, Okudaira, for neglect of his official duty as a physician, but Okudaira replied that to attend to the sick was a duty, and to endeavour to benefit the world as did Maéno was also a duty. Crowned with success.

Another young Japanese, Gentaku Ōtsuki, was, through the help of Sugita and the support of the lord of Fukuchiyama, Tamba, who took special interest in the study of the Dutch language, able to visit Nagasaki, and through a certain interpreter improved his knowledge of the language so that he was able to publish two volumes of the ' First Book in Dutch ' (1788). It appeared at an opportune moment and encouraged many to begin its study. Gentaku Ōtsuki.

Foreign nations now urged Japan to open her ports. In 1804 a Russian envoy came to Nagasaki and asked permission to trade. Three years later two Russian vessels came and pillaged the island of Yézo. The following year an English ship entered Nagasaki harbour in despite of prohibition. The Tokugawa Government wanting to know somewhat about these foreign countries, ordered Ōtsuki to collect information from Dutch sources, and the result was the publication of Translation Bureau.

two books, ' *Hokuhén Tanji* ' (' Things Northern ') and ' *Bashin Hikō* ' (' Private Opinions ').   In 1811 the Government established a Translation Bureau in the Astronomical Observatory and deputed Ōtsuki to translate Dutch books, this being the first time that the Government appointed a scholar of Occidental learning as an official.

Genshin
Udagawa.

Another man of note at this time was Genshin Udagawa. He had been a pupil at one time or another of Ōtsuki, Miné, and Katsuragawa.   Diligent and hard-working, he translated several books on anatomy, forming them into thirty volumes of ' Western Medical Science.'   Later he abridged them, giving prominence to the more important portions under the title of ' Handbook of Medical Science,' with plates printed from copper engravings—a work which was eagerly welcomed by students.   He was afterwards appointed an official in the Observatory and engaged in the translation of Dutch books. The ' Handbook ' did more than any other work of the time to arouse interest in the study of Dutch.

Shindō
Tsuboi

Genshin Udagawa had under him several promising pupils, among them being Shindō Tsuboi (1795–1848), who was especially famous as an educator.   He was born at Ikéda, Mino, lost his father at ten, and was brought up by his elder brother, Priest Jōkai, doing menial work in return.   Through his brother's advice, however, he took to study, and came up to Yédo in the fourteenth year of his age.   Being poor, he supported himself as a shampooer, but at twenty-two was induced to become a physician of the Occidental school through reading the ' Handbook of Medical Science ' translated by Udagawa.   After many years of penury, Udagawa, struck with his zeal, took him into his house in 1819, and being now provided with food and clothing, Tsuboi could at last concentrate his mind on study.   He ultimately set up at Fukagawa through the help of Udagawa, and started with one assistant, but his fame soon spread, especially as he was so generous that he supplied gratis to the poor not only medicine, but also rice, salt, and fuel ; nor did he charge anything to literary men or artists.   The lord of Chōshu hearing of this appointed him as his private physician.

Tsuboi died in 1848 at the age of fifty-four, just five years

before the coming of Commodore Perry to Japan. His pupils His successor and eminent pupils.
numbered over 2000, and his pupil and son-in-law, Hōshū
Tsuboi, had among his followers Baron Keisuké Ōtori, Baron
Hiroyuki Katō (ex-President of the Imperial University of
Tōkyō), and others.

The progress we have noted in medical science and in the Prosperity of Dutch learning.
study of Dutch was all made anterior to 1853, when Commodore
Perry's expedition took place, and from it we may deduce
how internal preparation for the opening of the country had
been going on.

Besides the main stream of Western learning we have
traced thus far, there were many minor ones ; for instance, in
1826 Rinsō Aochi wrote 'Aerial Phenomena,' and started the
study of physics ; in 1839 Yōan Udagawa (adopted son of
Genshin Udagawa) opened the way to chemical study by
writing 'Elementary Chemistry' ; in 1847 Saburō Fujii wrote
the first book on the study of English ; and about 1850 Éishun
Murakami studied French by himself, and taught it. These
were all results of individual aspiration and exertion, for the
Government was usually on the side of the Conservatives. Governmental attitude towards the new movement.
For instance, so late as 1848 it prohibited the study of Dutch
medical science, except surgery, on the pretext of constitutional
differences between natives and foreigners, and checked the
publication of medical books to protect the old Chinese school
of physicians. Although the Yédo Government and the lords
of clans were somewhat lax in enforcing these prohibitions,
anyone who, embracing new ideas, discussed the topics of
the day or inquired into the national policy, was punished
mercilessly.

Shihéi Hayashi, of the Sendai clan, a contemporary of Maéno Shihéi Hayashi.
and Sugita, learning about the colonization policy of Western
nations through Dutchmen at Nagasaki, and finding national
defence to be a matter of great importance, wrote two books,
'Kaikoku Héidan' ('The Defence of the Sea-girt Empire') and
'Sangoku Tsūran ('General Conditions of Three Foreign
Countries'). His warning, however, was misunderstood, and
the Government, thinking that he was agitating men's minds
uselessly with a false alarm, confiscated the books and ordered
their author to be confined in his brother Kazén's house.

Chōéi
Takano
and
Kwazan
Watan-
abé.

Another patriot, Chōéi Takano, of the Mizusawa clan, in consequence of the action of the Government in refusing permission to an English vessel to trade, and desiring to rouse the people from their dreams of seclusion, wrote ' *Yumé-Monogatari* ' (' Dream Tales ') ; whilst his friend, Kwazan Watanabé, of the Tahara clan, wrote ' *Ketsuzetsu Shōsetsu* ' (' A Jay Story '), ' *Shinki Ron* ' (' Present Adjustments '), and ' *Banron Shiki* ' (' Some Private Opinions on Foreign Matters '). The Government, enraged at their presumption in discussing national questions, imprisoned Takano for life and sentenced Watanabé to death. The capital punishment, however, was remitted, and after two years Watanabé was sent back to his province to be confined for life, but he put an end to himself (1841). Takano escaped from the prison when it was on fire, and coming back to Yédo and assuming a different name, worked on translation. But he also committed suicide (1850) when about to be rearrested.

Rise of
private
schools
teaching
Western
learning.

By this time there were in the country a good many Dutch scholars, some of whom opened private schools and taught the new learning of the West. Rintarō Katsu (afterwards Count Awa Katsu), who rendered great service to the country at the Restoration, was one : he opened a private school in 1850 with Kōji Sugi as principal, and taught Dutch and Western military drill. The well-known Ryūma Sakamoto and Tétsunosuké Tomita were among his students. Again, Séikéi Sugita, grandson of Gempaku, who had studied Dutch under Shindō Tsuboi, became a distinguished scholar, and was a translator at the Observatory from 1840. In 1854 he resigned that post and applied himself mainly to translating a treatise on gunnery, which resulted in the publication of eight volumes on ' Elementary Gunnery.' The year after the Government had decided to open the country it established the *Bansho Shirabé-dokoro*, or ' Institute for the Study of Foreign Books,' and appointed Séikéi Sugita and Gempo Mitsukuri as its professors. Séikéi Sugita could also read German and Russian, and had his own private school. Ryōtéi Shingū, of Kyōto, was another of these educators ; on his return from Nagasaki, desirous of encouraging the study of Western medical science, he started a school called the Junséi Shoin, expending about 10,000 *ryō* out of his own purse. He died in 1854, at the age of sixty-eight.

Whilst the greatest Dutch scholar in Yédo at this time was Séikéi Sugita, there was another in Ōsaka who was his equal, if not his superior. This was Kōan Ogata. Ogata belonged to the Ashimori clan, Bitchū. Being of delicate constitution, he gave up military pursuits and determined to learn medicine, and at the age of fifteen he came to Ōsaka and studied science under Tenyū Naka. Five years later he went to Yédo and studied Dutch under Shindō Tsuboi, but was so poor that he worked for over a year at teaching before entering Tsuboi's school, and that not sufficing he supported himself by making artificial eyes. Subsequently he went to Nagasaki, completed his study under a Dutch physician, and, in 1838, established himself at Ōsaka. He was very popular and soon acquired a large practice, and in the same year he opened a private school called the *Tékitékisai Juku*, which was quickly crowded.

Ogata was the author of a ' Treatise on Diseases ' and many other books, but he is to be remembered chiefly for his peculiar fitness as an educator. During twenty-four years subsequent to the opening of his school until its close in 1862, he educated over 3000 students. Among those who studied under him, and who afterwards strove to introduce new civilization for the making of New Japan, we may mention Masujirō Ōmura, Sanai Hashimoto, Yukichi Fukuzawa, Sensai Nagayo, Kéisuké Ōtori, Yoshitada Hanabusa, Tsunétami Sano, Kensai Ikéda, and Shūhéi Mitsukuri.

In 1857 some eighty physicians of the Dutch school practising in Yédo united in establishing a place for vaccination, which they used as their meeting-house. Three years later it was made a Government institution, and was changed, the next year, into a place for teaching the Western science of medicine under the name of ' Western Medical Institute.' Ogata was invited from Ōsaka to act as its head, and thus medical education passed into the hands of the Government. Ogata died in 1863, at the age of fifty-four. His hospital at Ōsaka, managed by his sons, is still flourishing.

In the small town of Sakura, near Yédo, another school of Dutch scholars appeared, Taizén Satō being its originator. Especially skilled in surgery, he was in 1844 invited by Lord

Kōan Ogata.

Ogata as an educator.

Western Medical Institute.

Taizén Satō.

Hotta, of the Sakura clan, to Sakura, where he established the first private hospital in Japan, called *Juntendō* Hospital, and so numerous were those seeking his treatment that the place was always crowded. He also organized a private school, and gathered many students. He adopted one of the most talented among his pupils, Shōchū Yamaguchi, as his successor, making his own sons heirs to other families. The late Baron Jun Matsumoto, once Army Surgeon-General, and Count Tadasu Hayashi, ex-Minister for Foreign Affairs, are sons of Taizén Satō.

Shōchū
Satō.

Shōchū Satō was born in Shimōsa in 1827. One day, while he was studying medicine under Buntaku Andō in Yédo, a man with a deep wound received in a quarrel was carried in during Andō's absence to be treated. Shōchū, though a lad of only sixteen, took a needle and thread from a seamstress, and calmly closed the cut with some twenty stitches. Andō on returning home saw the result, and exclaimed : ' He is a born surgeon ; he should seek a better master than I.' To his great joy, the boy was sent to Taizén Satō, who taught him Dutch surgery and took him to Sakura, where he was made to conduct operations in his master's stead. In 1860 he went to Nagasaki and studied under Dr. Pompé, and so assiduously did he apply himself that he won the admiration of Pompé, who not only taught him all that he knew, but also often entrusted him with important surgical operations. On his return after three years, he received a present of Stromeyer's 'Surgery,' which he found so useful that he translated it; he also erected a hospital and a medical school at Sakura which attracted many students. The Yédo Government tried to secure his services, but he would not accept the offer ; at the time of the Restoration (1868), however, he was in the field with the Commander-in-chief of the Imperial Army, and when the Government opened a university in Tōkyō the same year, he was given the degree of *Daihakasé*, and was made, in 1869, head of the Medical College. Subsequently he became Chief Court Surgeon as well, and waited on the Emperor. In 1873 he resigned both posts on account of ill health, and started a private hospital called *Juntendō* at Yushima, Tōkyō. He died in 1882, and was succeeded by his nephew, Dr. Susumu

Satō (now Army Surgeon-General and Baron), who had completed his medical studies in Berlin and Vienna, and who made the *Juntendō* Hospital as influential as the University Hospital, Tōkyō. Shōchū's adopted son, Shunkai, manages the work at Sakura, and the Satōs are flourishing in both places.

Tōkai Hayashi, son-in-law of Taizen Satō and adopted father to his youngest son, Tadasu, was another man of note. He was born at Kokura, Buzen, in 1812, and was first a friend of Satō, subsequently became his pupil, and then married his daughter. After Satō went to Sakura, he remained in Tōkyō, practised medicine and had a private school. He had travelled and studied at Kyōto, Ōsaka, Yédo, and Nagasaki, and had earned his livelihood by translating a Dutch book on Pharmacology, making thirty copies of it by himself, and selling them at three *ryō* a copy. Not until the age of thirty-one was he able to establish himself in Yédo. His translation of 'Pharmacology' was much in vogue, and was copied by many; but it contained numerous errors due to both the translator and transcriber, so having revised and amplified it, he applied to the Medical Institute for permission to publish it, but was refused after waiting for three years. Not until 1850, when serving under the lord of Kokura, was he granted permission. In 1860 he became head of the Ninomaru Pharmacy in Yédo, and then attendant physician to the Shōgun Yoshinobu, and after the Restoration went down to Shizuoka with the ex-Shōgun's son Iyesato (now President of the House of Lords), and later became sub-Director of the hospital at Numazu (1869). The following year he was appointed Director of the Ōsaka Medical School. Subsequently he became sub-Chief of Court Physicians, and waited on the Dowager Empress. He died in 1895, at the age of eighty-three.

The conclusion of treaties with five Western nations in 1858 was taken by the bigoted portion of the people as a weak surrender on the part of the Tokugawa Government to the threats of foreigners. Cries of denunciation filled the air, and men who sided with the open-door policy were in danger of being assassinated: in fact that great statesman, Lord Ii (Kamonno-Kami), who advocated the policy and signed the treaties

Tōkai Hayashi.

Yukichi Fukuzawa.

for Japan, fell a victim in 1860, as did the noted scholar, Shōzan Sakuma, also an advocate of liberal intercourse. In such dangerous times there was, however, one man who stood bravely by himself, not desisting from inculcating the principle of Western civilization, and who finally became one of the greatest educators in modern Japan and a man of wide social influence. He was the late Yukichi Fukuzawa. Born at Nakatsu, in Buzén, in 1835, disliking the constraint of the feudal system and wanting to find some way to a life of independence, he went first to Nagasaki to study Dutch, and ultimately came up to Ōsaka in 1855 to enter Ogata's school.

A poor student.

How hard he studied in the school may be seen by the way he, as well as others, laboured at copying. The library of Ogata's school contained two important books on medicine and physics; but as there was not more than one copy of each, a student had to copy any part if he wanted it for his exclusive use. One day, however, a valuable book was shown to Fukuzawa by his master, who had borrowed it from the lord of Chikuzén, then staying in Ōsaka. It was a Dutch translation on physics, based on Faraday's theory of electricity, and it had cost the lord about eighty *ryō*. Fukuzawa of course wanted to copy it; but as the sojourn of the lord in Ōsaka did not extend to more than three days and the book had to be returned in that time, he could not possibly hope to do so by himself. So, getting the help of two or three of his friends, he tried to copy at least the most important portion of it. As they could not unbind the volume and divide the labour, as was usually done with Japanese books, they so arranged that one of them should write while another dictated, the rest being ready to take the place of whoever tired. In this way the work was accomplished in three days' and two nights' uninterrupted toil.

Fukuzawa takes up English study.

When he had finished his education, Fukuzawa was invited by Lord Okudaira of Nakatsu, and, coming up to Yédo, taught Dutch (1858). The next year, as the treaties with the five Western nations were put into force and the port of Yokohama was opened to trade, he went there and, finding the need of English for intercourse with foreign firms, made up his mind to set about the task of learning it. Thus far the only foreign language in vogue was Dutch, and that was studied mostly by students of medicine, a man like Fukuzawa, who pursued it for its own sake, being rare; but he now turned to English with equal zeal, encountering great difficulties, for there was no teacher of English in Yédo.   But finding Takichirō Moriyama, an interpreter of Nagasaki, staying there for a while, he walked over ten miles daily to study with him, but all to little purpose. So he began to work by himself with the help of a Dutch-English dictionary and a Dutch-English conversation book, and was at last able to read fairly well.   In 1860 he visited America in the suite of Envoy Kimura, and, two years later, went to Europe with another envoy; and as the result of these visits he published his observations, entitled ' Séiyō Jijō ' (1866), and made known to his countrymen the real state of Western civilization and the condition of the world.

Fukuzawa's private school, called the *Kéiō Gijuku*, is the oldest of the modern schools in Japan.   In 1860 the *Bansho Shirabé-dokoro* (Institute for the Study of Foreign Books) of the Yédo Government added to its curriculum courses in English, French, German, and Russian, besides Dutch, and also established a class in chemistry; in 1862 it changed its name into *Yōsho Shirabédokoro*, and subsequently to *Kaiséijo* and enlarging its scope, sent students to England to study; but it was completely broken up, as were many private schools, during the war of the Restoration (1868–69), and this was the greatest disaster to letters that had befallen Yédo for two hundred and fifty years.   The *Kéiō Gijuku* is, therefore, the only school that has existed from before the Restoration, or that was not closed in that time of general disturbance.   The name was taken from the era of Kéiō, but it was really opened seven years prior to that (1858).   Only Dutch was taught at first, but from about 1862 English was added, and taught after Fukuzawa's method. At first there were some hundred students, and these were reduced to eighteen during the war of the Restoration.   But Fukuzawa never lost heart.   It is said that he was reading with his students a new book on political economy by Wayland on the day when the battle was being fought close by at Uyéno (now Uyéno Park) on the 23rd of June, 1868.   He was

Kéiō Gijuku.

indifferent to the political questions of the day, but believed in Western learning and in his students, saying that as long as his school existed Japan was entitled to the name of a civilized nation.

Fukuzawa had two aims in life—to educate young men through his school, and to guide society through his writings. For three-and-forty years from the time he first came up to Yédo in 1858, until his death in 1901, he led the nation with pen and tongue, and sought no other fame than that of an educator. The Japanese as a rule think it a great honour to be in Government service; but excepting that he was once a translator to the Tokugawa Government, Fukuzawa kept himself aloof from an official career, in spite of his great influence both in Government circles and among the public.

His literary works.

His writings are voluminous. Counting only those that have been collected in 'Fukuzawa's Complete Works' as deserving preservation, they amount to fifty books, all written in a simple style easily read by anybody. One is worthy of special mention—namely, '*Gakumon-no-Susumé*,' or 'Inducement to Study,' in small volumes, seventeen in all, published from time to time from 1871 onwards. Over 3,400,000 copies of it are said to have been sold. The opening sentence is remarkable : ' Heaven does not create men over men or men under men '; which shows how he endeavoured to inculcate the doctrines of the equality of men and of their worth.

His influence in political and commercial circles.

Formerly, public speaking—as such—was not practised in Japan: we only having story-telling, musical recitations, old-fashioned Buddhist preaching, and later, new-fashioned Christian missionary preaching. Fukuzawa was the first to start public speaking in Japan under the term *enzétsu* (which means, ' delivery '), and he built a hall for that purpose at his own expense in 1874. His activity did not end there, for from 1882 onwards he published a daily paper called the ' *Jiji* ' (*Times*), which eventually became one of the most influential organs in the Far East. So though Fukuzawa was never invested with official power, he had three great organs—a school, a newspaper, and books; and his influence was far above that of any ordinary statesman in Japan. His school opened its university department in 1890, embracing the colleges of literature, political economy, law, and politics, and became the first private university in Japan.   The school has educated over 20,000 students ; and many graduates now occupy important positions in society as high officials, as members of the Diet, or as directors of private firms.   As the result of his encouraging the spirit of independence, most of his pupils sought a career in business, and thus their influence did much for the progress in commerce and industry of modern Japan.

Fukuzawa died on the 3rd of February, 1901.   The House *His death.* of Representatives passed unanimously a resolution that it sincerely condoled the death of this great man, who had early stood for the opening of the country and had devoted his life to the cause of education.   Twenty thousand people took part in his funeral, displaying their heartfelt grief.   A year before his death, the Court sent him a gift of 50,000 *yen* for his educational service.[1]

The *Kéiō Gijuku* is still flourishing.   Besides a university, it comprises a preparatory department, middle, grammar, and business night-schools, and has over 2500 students.

Thus we see that the new learning of the West first made its appearance a hundred and fifty years ago in the form of *Begin-* medical science.   It was soon followed by physics, chemistry, *nings of ethical* pharmacology, mathematics, and astronomy, to which list *and* military science was added after 1848, and later, history, *spiritual education.* political economy, and law.   It was, however, not until 1868, when Fukuzawa secured Wayland's 'Ethics,' that the moral ideas of the West were first introduced, and it was mainly through the hands of Kéiu Nakamura, as we shall see, that these were diffused, for people at first had eyes only for the material side of Western civilization, and were mostly strangers to the beauty of its spiritual side ;   neither could many be found to give education on this new basis.   Jō Niishima, however, who ranked only second to Fukuzawa as an educator, *Jō* was one of these few.   Born at Annaka, Kōtsuké, he went to *Niishima.* America, in spite of the prohibition, in 1864, at the age of twenty-one, working his passage as a sailor in an American

[1] For his Biography, see *Japan Soc. Trans.*, vol. v. p. 280.

merchantman. Its owner was Alpheus Hardy, of Boston, who, taking great interest in the young man, remained ever afterwards a warm supporter of his work. In 1871, on the occasion of a tour made by Ambassador Iwakura through Europe and America, Niishima followed the suite as interpreter, inspected schools of note in America, and visited England, Scotland, France, Switzerland, Holland, Denmark, Germany, and Russia, afterwards going back to America to finish his education. He had had old *samurai* training while in Japan, and now, thoroughly imbued with the spirit of New England Puritanism, he came back to his native land towards the end of 1874 with the sole desire of establishing a private Christian school and educating his countrymen in the spiritual essence of Western civilization. The following year he started the *Dōshisha* English School in Kyōto. A fortunate occurrence attended the opening. For some time back an American gentleman, by name Captain Janes, had been teaching in the English School of the Kumamoto clan. He was a devoted Christian, and through his personal influence a body of young Christians rose among the students. The school, however, was closed in 1876, and these young men entered the *Dōshisha* and eventually formed the basis of its future success. It had at first a boys' English college and a theological seminary, but soon it added a girls' and a nurses' school.

The *Dōshisha* English School.

Niishima's educational work.

Fukuzawa taught mainly the secular knowledge of the West and encouraged the spirit of independence and self-respect, but Niishima put more stress on spiritual training, and, believing that men do not live by bread alone, placed education on a Christian basis. He wanted his countrymen to know, not only about the steam engine and electricity, but also about the spirit and faith of Luther and Knox, and above all, about their source of life—the Bible. He was, so to speak, a baptized *samurai*, and, limited as his influence was compared with that of Fukuzawa, it reached far deeper. Though he had the backing of a missionary society for his work, still his success must be sought in the trust people had in his personal character. In 1889 he published his appeal to establish a private university, whereupon, in spite of the fact that it would be a Christian institution, many of his countrymen responded, and contributed to the amount of tens of thousands, while Mr. J. N. Harris gave 100,000 dollars for the erection of a science school. To the great regret of all, Niishima died the following year, and the *Dōshisha* was shorn of much of its strength, but its schools still remain as a great monument to the founder's personality. The graduates now number more than a thousand, part dedicating their lives to the spread of Christianity, and part engaging in all kinds of work—political, literary, educational, and commercial. Niishima believed not only in Christian education, but in its compatibility with the spirit of free investigation. He took as his motto : ' Liberal education and free Church.' He also, like Fukuzawa, was never in Government service, and was proud to call himself Jō Niishima, a commoner of Kyōto. (See also *ante*, p. 81.)

Among the private schools in Japan at the present time, the Waséda University, with Count Ōkuma as President, may be said to be the most flourishing. It was at first called the *Tōkyō Semmon Gakkō* (Tōkyō College), and was started by Count Ōkuma and his friends in 1882. The Count, a member of the Saga clan, studied Dutch early, and going to Nagasaki before the Restoration, learned English from Dr. Guido F. Verbeck. For his service to the country at the time of the Restoration he was made vice-Minister of State for Foreign Affairs and of Finance, at the age of thirty-one, in 1868, and from 1873 to 1880 he held the portfolio of Finance during the difficult transitional period from the feudal to the constitutional form of government. The following year he resigned the ministerial position, and espousing the popular cause, formed, on the one hand, a strong political party as a preparation for the opening of the Diet, and, on the other, established a private school where young men were to be educated in the duties of a citizen. Thus he became leader of the Progressist party and the founder of the *Tōkyō Semmon Gakkō*.

[Marginal note: Count Ōkuma and the Waséda University.]

The Count's opinion was that, in order to be imbued with a spirit of independence and self-government, we must first inaugurate independence of learning, and that, to this end, a large private school independent of any official restraint, where the student should be left free to choose whatever course of study he likes, was necessary. The late Azusa Ono was of

[Marginal note: Count Ōkuma's plea for the independence of learning.]

the same opinion, and co-operated in starting the *Tōkyō Semmon Gakkō*. Hitherto colleges in Japan had mostly used foreign books as text-books, which made it a *sine qua non* that one must first be versed in some foreign language in order to receive higher education. But Sanayé Takata and others, who managed Count Ōkuma's school, conceived that the study of a foreign tongue was necessary only to enlarge the fields of reference, and that instruction itself should be given principally in Japanese and by Japanese books. The Count put the same view in another way. 'The learning and education of one country should not rely solely on the system of another country. Unless they are rooted in the character of the people, they cannot be said to be independent.' And for these reasons the *Tōkyō Semmon Gakkō* stood for independence of learning, which fact was enough to explain its success.

Waséda University.
It had, at first, courses in politics, political economy, and law, to which were added courses in literature in 1889, and teachers' courses in 1899. In 1902 it was reorganized and styled the Waséda University, with departments of politics, law, and literature, to which a department of commerce was added in 1903. It is now under the presidency of Count Ōkuma and the directorship of Dr. Sanaé Takata, and has over 6000 students. What has contributed most to its great success is the personality of the Count himself.

Three Professors of Waséda University.
Next to the founder, the men to whom the success of the University is attributable are three of its professors—Sanaé Takata, Taméyuki Amano, and Yūzō Tsubouchi—who have been connected with it for the past twenty-five years. Takata as a young politician and able school administrator, Amano as an authority in political economy, and Tsubouchi as the pioneer of the new school of literature, are widely known in Japan. While the services of even one of them would be a material gain to any educational institution, the united effort of the three has been undeniably a great factor in the success of the University.

Demand for private schools.
The Government, since the Restoration, has encouraged all kinds and grades of education, but the accommodation in Government institutions is never sufficient to meet the public

demand, and so from time to time private schools, with special purposes, have risen and supplied the need. Viscount Mori, once Minister of Education, laid in 1874 the basis of the Tōkyō Higher Commercial School, which was later converted into a Government institution.

Hidétoshi Murakami, who taught French as early as 1853, opened a French school called the *Tatsuridō*, which was continued till 1877 ; Shimpachi Séki had an English school, called the *Kyōritsu Gakusha*, from 1870 to 1883 ; and Kéiwu Nakamura established the *Dōninsha* to teach Chinese and English in 1873, which lasted until 1885. All these establishments gave education on a higher grade to those who, for one reason or other, did not enter Government schools. *Three important private language institutions.*

Murakami was decorated by the French Government in 1885 for his endeavour to start the study of French in Japan. He died five years later aged eighty, and received a message of condolence from the Imperial Court ' for his great service done to the educational cause by opening a way to French study, by giving instruction under difficulties with laudable zeal, and by writing or translating books of merit.' *Hidétoshi Murakami.*

Séki was a man who bravely advocated the policy of opening the country amidst the clamour of anti-foreign opinions in the latter part of the fifties. As a student of English he was the one who early found the uselessness, from a practical point of view, of the so-called *hensoku* or ' wrong method ' in studying language, which was pursued at the Institute for the Study of Foreign Books of the Tokugawa Government. Wanting to acquire ability to converse directly with foreigners, he first studied in 1860 under Manjirō Nakahama, who had been abroad, and also learned grammar from Kichijūrō Nishi. Then going to Yokohama to further his knowledge, he became servant to a foreigner. In 1861 he was appointed official interpreter, and went to America in the suite of a Japanese envoy. In 1868 he became interpreter in the American Legation, and three years later established a private school, the *Kyōritsu Gakusha*, to teach English. It had at one time nearly a thousand students. In 1872 he was appointed Chief of the Translation Bureau in the Department of Finance, and also taught in the special school attached to it. Among *Shimpachi Séki.*

the more noted men who were once his pupils we may mention Ukichi Taguchi, Saburō Shimada, and Denzaburō Hatano.

Kéiwu Naka-mura.

Nakamura, born at Yédo in 1831, was already a considerable scholar in Japanese and Chinese classics when, in 1847, he became a pupil of the noted Dutch scholar, Hoshū Katsuragawa. He, however, gave up Dutch for English later, and studying hard, was said to have copied out an English dictionary. He served in the Tokugawa Government as an official Chinese scholar, went to Europe in 1866, and, returning in 1868, stayed at Shizuoka with the Shōgun Yoshinobu. While he was there he translated the American Constitution, George Washington's ' Farewell Address,' and Mill's ' On Liberty,' and wrote anonymously an article on Christianity. In 1872 he came up to Tōkyō and was employed in Government service. Relinquishing the caste of *samurai* and becoming a commoner, he established a private school called the *Dōninsha* in 1873, which was soon crowded with students aware of his fame. Two years later he opened a girls' department and encouraged women's education. In the same year he was entrusted with the first directorship of the Tōkyō Girls' Normal School and founded a kindergarten. In 1877 he was made professor in the Imperial University, and in 1890 he was elected a member of the House of Peers, and died the following year at the age of sixty, being honoured with a special Imperial message of condolence.

An inter-preter of Western ethical ideas for Orientals.

He was a man of fine literary taste, of sound scholarship, and of classic mood. Warm in friendship and happy in doing good, he made no enemy and led a pure life, revering Heaven and loving men. His translations of Smiles's ' Self-Help' and ' Character' had a greater influence over young men in the early 'seventies than any other book of the day. A devout Confucian scholar himself, he was also an admirer of Christian faith and morality, and was most fitted to interpret Western ethics to Orientals. That our country has made such progress in the new civilization is due to the efforts of such a gentle yet progressive reformer as well as to those of aggressive reformers like Fukuzawa and Niishima. Nakamura's school, while it lasted, was one of the three greatest private institutions in

Tōkyō, the other two being the *Keiō Gijuku* and the *Kyōritsu Gakusha*.

Makoto Kondō was born in Yédo (1830), and belonged to the clan of Toba, in the province of Shima. He studied first Dutch, then English, and finally German, and was an expert in surveying. From 1862, for more than twenty years he was employed as naval teacher, first by the Tokugawa and then by the Imperial Government. In 1869 he established a private school named *Kōgyokujuku*, and trained many young men for naval services. He has turned out of this private institution nearly six hundred naval officers, among whom may be counted Kamimura and several other vice- and rear-admirals. He died in 1886, at the age of fifty-six. *Makoto Kondō.*

There are two more educators in their special fields to be mentioned. Sen Tsuda is known as the first student of agriculture according to Western methods. He founded in 1875 the *Gakunōsha*, and through a private agricultural school and the magazine *Agriculturist*, strove to introduce improvements in farming. Kōji Sugi was the first to start the study of statistics in Japan. From 1868 to 1870 he was at work on a census privately in Shizuoka Prefecture, and in 1879, under the instruction of the Government, he compiled a complete series of statistics of the population of Kai Province. In 1883 he opened a private school of statistics and tried to popularize the science. *Sen Tsuda the first agricultural educator.* *Kōji Sugi the first instructor in statistics.*

The place of the private educational enterprises sketched above in our educational field will be now clear; they were complementary to, but in many cases they led, governmental enterprises. While the orderly and systematized Government institutions have done so much to diffuse education and new knowledge, the private institutions have had the merit of turning out men of exceptional gifts. We have already had occasion to refer to this fact; but to add one or two more instances: the private village school (*Shōka Sonjuku*) of Shōin Yoshida, who was sentenced to death in 1859 for an attempted revolution against the Yédo Government, produced such great statesmen of the Restoration as Princes Itō and Yamagata. Again, the private school established in Kagoshima by Takamori Saigō, who resigned his post as Minister of State *Contribution of private schools to national enlightenment.*

in 1873 together with Taisuké Itagaki (Count Itagaki) and others on the rejection of their Korean expedition project by their colleagues, produced several who took the lead in the Civil War of 1877.   Itagaki also established the *Risshisha*, out of which grew the first political party in Japan, called the ' *Jiyūtō* ' (Liberals).

Means of
social
education.
To complete our survey, let us now turn to some private efforts aiming at social education.   The first was the publication of a magazine as early as 1873 called the ' *Meiroku Zasshi*,' by such men as Yukichi Fukuzawa, Shūhei Mitsukuri, Sen Tsuda, Baron Tsuda, Shū Nishi, Baron Hiroyuki Katō, Kōji Sugi, and Viscount Mori.   It had for its object the discussion of any timely topics.   The next grew out of the meeting of Japanese students studying in London in 1873, and was called the ' *Kyōson Dōshū* ' (Fraternity).   After their return home they built a hall in 1877, where they met twice a month and debated political and social matters, and also published a magazine called the '*Kyōson Zasshi*' to diffuse advanced ideas.   The next year they held their first annual meeting at the lecture hall of the Imperial University, and gave public speeches and invited several hundred noted citizens to a banquet at the Shōheikwan, Yushima.   After this, public speaking became a main feature of the association, and they held regular monthly meetings.   While arousing public interest at home on all important questions, they also made it a point to represent Japan and the Japanese abroad, and in 1881, seeing the necessity of the revision of the treaties with foreign nations, they wrote an essay showing the progress Japan had made, claiming that she was worthy of being ranked with Occidental States, and translating it into English and French, circulated it among distinguished men of the West.   Those who were promoters and secretaries of the association were Azusa Ono, Tatsui Baba, Kojirō Iwasaki; and those who took part in the public speaking were Dairoku Kikuchi, Kentarō Kanéko, Inajirō Tajiri,[1] Taizō Miyoshi, Kazuo Hatoyama, Mokurai Shimaji, and Séiran Ōuchi.[2]   The association in this

---

[1] Kikuchi, Kanéko, and Tajiri are now peers, and were once ministers of State.

[2] Shimaji and Ōuchi are well-known Buddhists.

form lasted till 1880, when it was, in consequence of the promulgation of the Law of Public Meetings, changed into a social club.

In concluding, let me enumerate some of the more con- Some important private colleges. spicuous institutions out of the thirty-five private colleges now existing in Japan, together with the number of their students, to show what importance they are assuming in supplying the national need.

Of the Waséda University and the *Kéiō Gijuku* University we have spoken at length. The first of five great private schools primarily for the study of law in the order of their importance is the Méiji University. Erected in 1880 by Tatsuo Kishimoto, Kōzō Miyagi, and Misao Yashiro, it had 3549 students in 1905, most of whom were law students. The graduates were then 3832. The *Hōgaku-in* University, established in 1885 by Nobushigé Hozumi, Gijin Okuda, Rokui-chirō Masujima, Kenkichi Okayama, and others, has now some 1600 students and 3500 graduates. The Hōséi University, established in 1879 by Masakuni Satta and others, had 2105 students and 1219 graduates in 1905. The Nippon University, established in 1892 by the late Count Akiyoshi Yamada and others, had then 2500 students and 1700 graduates. The *Senshū Gakkō*, established in 1880 by Mr. (now Viscount) Inajirō Tajiri, Mr. (now Baron) Tanétarō Megata, Nagatané Sōma, and the late Jūkaku Komai, has some 600 students and 1000 graduates.

As to language schools, the *Kokumin Éigaku-kai*, estab-lished in 1888 by Yaichirō Isobé, has 1400 students and 1600 graduates. The *Séisoku Éigo Gakkō*, established in 1896 by Hidésaburō Saitō, had 4200 students and 800 graduates in 1905. These two are the principal private schools for teaching English. The *Doitsu Kyōkwai Gakkō* for teaching German, established in 1877 by the late Viscount Yajirō Shina-gawa, had 712 students with 167 graduates in the German course, and 746 graduates in the secondary course. And the *Gyōséi Gakkō*, established in 1888, and changed to a middle school in 1899, by Hidéyuki Matsuoka, Genzō Akiyama, and others, for teaching French, had 330 students and 50 graduates in 1905.

For girls' higher education only one school may be mentioned besides the mission schools and Government schools. This is the *Nippon Joshi Daigakkō* or Women's University, originated by Jinzō Narusé.

Conclusion.

Such is, then, a brief survey of the private educational enterprises in Japan and of the great part they have played in modernizing the country. It is, of course, a mere sketch, and I regret very much not to have been able to give an expansive account of all the enterprises and the men concerned in them. Nor have I touched upon the great educational services done by Christian missionaries, but that is because the topic will receive separate treatment by an abler hand than mine.

NATIONAL EDUCATION IN THE MÉIJI ERA

Marquis Kimmochi Saionji, late Prime Minister and Minister of Education

It is almost unnecessary to state that since the Restoration of 1868 Japan has made rapid progress in educational work. But during the forty odd years since that event took place there have been so many revolutionary changes and variations in the educational *rôle*, that I now propose to show how education itself has advanced, until it has at last attained to its present condition of prosperity.

Immediately upon the Restoration, His Imperial Majesty, followed by his Court nobles and barons, proceeded to the Shishindén Palace to worship the gods who reign over heaven and earth, and he there took an oath to promote the welfare of the nation. This consisted of five articles,[1] in which were clearly set out the principles of national education. The fourth said : ' We shall abolish old irreverent customs and walk in the great and just ways of Heaven '; and the fifth : ' We shall seek knowledge in the four quarters of the globe.' The foundations of our national education were firmly fixed from that moment.

Education in the first years of Méiji.

In the first year of Méiji (1868) the two institutions of the *Kōgaku* and the *Kangaku* were organized in Kyōto as a preparatory step towards establishing a university on the following lines : ' The learning of China and Europe should serve as the two wheels for the carriage of the old doctrines of the land. The *Kōgaku*, or learning of Japan, and the *Kangaku*, or learning of China, should not be disfigured by useless controversies, nor should they

[1] See Vol. I, p. 141.

become partial or prejudiced towards each other.' In the following year a university was founded at Shōhéizaka for the purpose of superintending educational affairs throughout the whole country, and this, in two years' time, assumed the name of *Mombushō*, or Department of Education. Takatō Ōki and Shimpéi Etō were appointed Minister and Vice-Minister of Education respectively, and Fujimaro Tanaka, Third Minister, was dispatched to Europe and America in the capacity of Commissioner of Educational Affairs, to study how education was conducted on those continents.

Educational system.

In 1872 an Educational Law was issued, and the foundation of compulsory education was laid. The instruction promulgated by the Government stated that all people, high or low, and of both sexes, should receive education, so that there should not be found one family in the whole empire, nor one member of a family, ignorant and illiterate. The instruction stated also that higher education should be left to the more gifted, but that parents are responsible for giving elementary education to their children—boys as well as girls. These provisions clearly indicate the spirit in which the educational laws were started in Japan. In the same year the whole country was divided into eight *Daigaku* districts (reduced to seven in the following year), each with a University (*Daigakkō*). Each of these districts was subdivided into thirty-two *Chūgaku* districts, each with a Secondary School (*Chūgakkō*). A *Chūgaku* district consisted of 210 *Shōgaku* districts, each with an Elementary School (*Shōgakkō*). Thus throughout the country there were to be eight universities, 256 secondary schools, and 53,760 elementary schools : the ratio being an elementary school for every 600 inhabitants. In the next year revisions and additions were made in the Educational Law, and regulations were framed for Industrial schools providing courses of Mineralogy, Engineering, Agriculture, and Commerce. That technical education, whose full import was realized only twenty years later, should have been conceived and planned by the Government at such an early date, and that over fifty thousand elementary schools should have been started, though there had not previously been a single school of an elementary type in the country, are suggestive facts showing plainly how earnest the Government was at that time in matters of education. In so doing they assimilated much of the French system.

In 1872 normal schools were founded by the Educational Department, and Mr. Scott, an American, was employed as a teacher to give lectures on the method of teaching in elementary schools. In Ōsaka, Sendai, Nagoya, Niigata, Hiroshima, Nagasaki, and other principal cities, the Government founded normal schools under its own direct control, for the purpose of setting an example to other localities ; but as all the cities and prefectures soon began to compete in establishing normal schools, the Government, about 1877, closed all the directly controlled schools, with the exception of those in Tōkyō, and entrusted the training and education of elementary school teachers to local authorities.

Normal schools.

In 1877 the Medical and the *Kaiséi* Schools were combined under the name of the Tōkyō University, so that higher phases of science and literature might be studied. It then consisted of four colleges, namely, Law, Science, Literature, and Medicine, and as such was the predecessor of the present Imperial University of Tōkyō.

The University.

When Mr. Fujimaro Tanaka returned from Europe and America he published a work, ' *Rijikōtéi*,' on the educational systems of all the countries which he had visited. He also translated into Japanese the American School Laws, in which the educational system of every state of that republic is treated of. He further translated many books on education and pedagogy written by Americans. The system was also indebted to Dr. David Murray, an American scholar, who served the Educational Department as adviser, and also to students who had studied in the United States, and for these reasons it resembles in many respects that of our trans-Pacific neighbours.

American influence.

The Educational Law being still inadequate, it was supplemented by an Imperial ordinance issued in 1879, by which the basis of national education was fixed by localities, local governors being empowered to enact all regulations for public schools, subject to the sanction of the Minister of State for Education. The consequence of the Government virtually giving up the direct control of educational affairs was that for a time a tendency to decline showed itself in education. This

Imperial Ordinance relating to Education.

M

resulted in a revision of the ordinance being effected in 1880. By this revision the Government resumed control over educational affairs and enacted new regulations for elementary schools, which were vigorously enforced. In the meantime, many English books, written by Spencer, Bain, and other great scholars, were extensively read in the country, and the excellence of the English educational system was fully discussed and advocated by students who had returned from England.

The principles of freedom and popular rights which agitated society at that time culminated in the birth of political parties ; memorials were addressed to the Government urging the establishment of a Parliament, and these resulted in an Imperial rescript relating to the formation of a Diet being issued in 1881. It was soon found that teachers were mixing themselves up with political affairs, and consequently Mr. Fukuoka, Minister of Education at that time, issued ' Disciplinary Regulations for Elementary School Teachers ' (1881), prohibiting them from meddling with either politics or religion. Later on he summoned the school inspectors of all the prefectures and gave instructions to them on the national educational policy, laying stress upon moral education as follows :

' A school teacher should not rest content with a mere knowledge of text-books on morals. What is essential for him is a character upright, lovable, and respectable, combined with varied experiences and ability adequate to control children. Hence men of wide information and sound morals, who have untainted honour and popularity, should be selected as teachers, so that pupils may learn more and more to be quiet and orderly and to pay respect to others. The teaching of morality should be based upon the native doctrine of the Empire, and on the principle of Confucianism.'

After the Restoration, Western civilization was imported on a large scale by all ranks of the people. So blindly did men follow everything foreign, that whatever was old, whatever had been handed down from their fathers, was rejected. And as in science and art the superiority of the Occident was especially apparent, the blind followers of the West were in such a hurry to drink of this new Pierian spring that some of them went the length of despising morality as a silly fancy of bygone times. This mania for foreign ideas prevailed for some fifteen years after the Restoration. A natural reaction, and the awakening of the nation to a consciousness of having blundered, caused Confucianism, which, with its morality, had been humbled to the dust, to again find exponents. In 1882 a course of Japanese classics was provided in the University, the object being to study and investigate the institutions and literature of our own country. This was prompted by an apprehension that our ancient learning might be wholly sacrificed on the Occidental altar. Elementary schools were formerly supported, partly by local taxes, and partly by the Government; but in 1881 this Government aid was discontinued, and the schools were maintained by means of local taxes. In August 1885 revisions were introduced in the Ordinance relating to Education, and all elementary schools founded by the prefectures, cities, and villages were permitted to charge tuition fees, in view of the prevailing financial stringency which obliged the local authorities to be rigidly economical in their expenditure. For children whose parents or guardians could not afford to pay any tuition fees simple courses were provided, and they were taught in separate buildings, or at least in separate class-rooms. If, however, their number was small, they were taught gratis with their more well-to-do comrades, and attended the same classes. *Revisions of 1885, and new ordinances of 1886.*

In December of the same year the Cabinet was organized for the first time. Viscount Arinori Mori, being appointed Minister of Education, began at once to realize his cherished ideas relating to education. In 1886 the Ordinance relating to Education was replaced by three new ordinances relating to elementary schools, normal schools, and universities, while general rules for all schools were fixed, and our educational system was at last settled upon a sound basis.

According to the Ordinance relating to Elementary Schools, the school age of a child was to last eight years—from six to fourteen—and parents or guardians were under obligation to make their children receive general education. Elementary schools were of two grades, primary and higher, and the course in both extended over four years, although, to suit the conditions *Elementary school education and higher education.*

of certain localities, courses of three years were allowed.
A secondary school, an institution to impart essential knowledge to persons desirous of pursuing a business or occupation,
and also to those who wished to enter the higher grade schools,
was also added. This was also divided into two grades, higher
and ordinary. The whole country was then partitioned into five
districts, each with a higher middle school in it, and these were
of two kinds, namely, those whose expenses were entirely borne
by the National Treasury, and those partly supported out of
local taxes. The aim of these institutions consisted chiefly in
giving instruction essential to students desirous of entering
the University. Three departments, Legal, Medical, and
Technical, were soon after added to the higher schools, some
having all these, others one or two only. Ordinary middle
schools were established in every prefecture, and their courses
ran over five years instead of six, as had been originally fixed.

The normal school.

Normal schools to train teachers were of two kinds, higher
and ordinary, and every prefecture had to establish at least one.

Imperial University and the University Hall.

The Tōkyō University, combined with the Technological
University founded by the Public Works Department, is now
the Imperial University. It consists of five colleges, Law,
Medicine, Engineering, Literature, and Science, besides a
University Hall provided for the benefit of graduates who
desire to pursue their studies and investigations in greater
detail. To these were added in 1890 the Tōkyō School of
Agriculture and Forestry, which had been under the charge of
the Department of Agriculture and Commerce.

Government School Inspectors.

To superintend educational work throughout the country
School Inspectors were appointed by the Department of
Education.

German school of education.

Viscount Mori, when Minister of Education, added the
English language to the curriculum of elementary schools,
especially putting stress upon the pronunciation. He invited
Herr Hausknecht from Germany to give courses of lectures on
pedagogy in the Imperial University. It was this that caused
Germanism to become prevalent through the empire, and
as it accorded with our conservatism, it grew so popular that

Conservatism.

the German style was adopted in everything, and helped to
reinforce Japanese conservatism.

The appointment of Viscount Akimasa Yoshikawa as Minister of Education in 1890 was marked by the issue of an Imperial Rescript on Education, in which the principles of education and the basis of moral teaching were laid down. The Ordinance relating to Elementary Schools was also revised, so that elementary education might be carried on in harmony with the system of self-government recently granted to prefectures and municipalities. It was based on a thorough investigation of the educational system of Germany, and was doubtless an improvement. It maintained that the chief aim of elementary schools was to establish a basis of moral and national education, and to give general knowledge and accomplishments essential to life, having in view, among other things, the physical development of the rising generation. The courses of study extended over three or four years in ordinary elementary schools, while those in higher elementary schools were two, three, or four years. District inspectors were appointed to superintend educational work in districts. A law relating to the pensions for retired teachers and for families of deceased teachers in city, town, and village elementary schools was also enacted.

Imperial Rescript on Education.

Regulations relating to the Methods of Instruction in Elementary Schools were issued in 1891. The first article ran as follows : ' In education the greatest attention should be paid to moral culture. Hence, whatever is found, in any course of study, relating to moral or national education should be taught with care and assiduity. All teaching being based upon matters essential to life, lessons should be so taught that they may all be turned to practical uses.' Thus it was made clear that the aim of elementary school education consisted not merely in developing intellect, but also in forming character.

Regulations of elementary schools.

When Viscount Inouyé was appointed Minister of Education in 1893, he maintained the necessity of encouraging the study of national literature, and he applied himself most earnestly to starting industrial education. As a first step towards this end he enacted regulations for technical schools, and earnestly urged their establishment. Through him the Institute for the Training of Technical School Teachers was founded, the National Treasury paying 150,000 *yen* each year

Inouyé's administration.

for its support—a sum which was increased to 366,000 *yen* in 1907. Under such encouragement and patronage technical education made remarkable progress. In 1894 an Ordinance relating to Higher Schools (or National Colleges) was issued, and the higher middle schools, which had hitherto been merely a preparatory department of the Imperial University, were remodelled as higher schools, while the special departments of Law, Engineering, and Medicine were provided, besides preparatory courses for pupils who wished to enter the University. Though the organization of the higher schools has gradually relapsed to its previous condition, technical education has continued to prosper.

Educational administration since 1894.

In October 1894, when I was appointed Minister of Education, high schools for girls were coming rapidly into existence in every prefecture, owing to an increasing number of girl graduates of elementary schools who desired to receive higher grades of education. But there was as yet no regulation relating to them, and so, in 1895, Regulations for High Schools for Girls were issued. Subsequently a Board of Medical Councillors on School Hygiene was instituted for the purpose of investigating sanitary affairs, and an Imperial Ordinance relating to Additional Salaries for Teachers in City, Town, or Village Elementary Schools was issued. The frequent changes of the Cabinet since 1896 have resulted in the chair of Minister of Education being occupied by many different persons, yet the fundamental principles of educational administration have remained one and the same, to the great advantage of education throughout the empire.

Among the chief events which occurred in the years 1896–98 may be mentioned the following : The establishment of a High Council of Education as the paramount authority in matters of educational administration, subject only to that of the Minister ; the enactment of regulations relating to the salaries of city, town, or village elementary school teachers, local authorities being required to pay such salaries in the ratio of the number of teachers employed ; the reappointment of Government inspectors of education, whose office had been abolished in 1893 ; the appointment of local inspectors of education so as to perfect the organ for educational inspection ;

the issue of an Ordinance relating to Normal School Education, replacing the old ordinance (which had been proclaimed in 1886) ; the founding of the Imperial University of Kyōto, which started a new College of Science and Engineering ; the appointment of school physicians in public and private schools to look after the health of the pupils.

In 1899, Count Sukéki Kabayama being Minister of Education, the Ordinance relating to Secondary Schools was revised. Such schools being institutions where higher grades of general education essential for men are given, each prefecture was required to establish at least one secondary school. The Regulations relating to the High Schools for Girls were replaced by a new Ordinance, which defined such schools as institutions where higher grades of general education essential for women are provided, and each prefecture was ordered to found at least one high school for girls. A part of the indemnity paid by China was set aside as a fund for general education, and an Ordinance relating to Private Schools was promulgated, these being put under the control of the Department of Education.

In 1900 the Ordinance relating to Elementary Schools was revised, and regulations for carrying it out were enacted. The number of Chinese characters to be used in elementary schools was limited, and the form of the *kana* syllabary, as well as its spelling, were settled, so that the burden of school children might be lightened. In the following year detailed rules for carrying out the Ordinances relating to Secondary Schools and High Schools for Girls, as well as the Regulations relating to Schools of Marine Products, were issued. Summer Institutes were organized for the benefit of instructors engaged in secondary education. In 1902 the Hiroshima Higher Normal School was established in Hiroshima, and Special Institutes for Training Secondary School Teachers were also organized in order to supply vacancies in secondary schools. Secondary education was rapidly advancing, and public and private secondary schools, as well as high schools for girls, were being established in numbers, while miscellaneous schools also increased rapidly. Secondary schools and high schools for girls, which had been 81 and 13 respectively in 1894, increased to 215 and 69 in 1901.

Administration of 1899.

The administrations of 1900 and 1901.

Ordinance relating to Special Schools.

In 1903 an Ordinance relating to Special Schools was issued, and Regulations relating to Public and Private Special Schools were enacted. These special schools had hitherto been under the General Regulations relating to Miscellaneous Schools, but graduates of secondary schools who wished to receive a higher grade of education had rapidly increased in number, and the Department thought it advisable to control special schools by means of particular rules.

Private schools.

Education in our country has doubtless made rapid progress under the protection of the Government, but we must not forget that private schools have contributed much to its development. Most conspicuous of these private schools were the *Kéiō Gijuku* of Fukuzawa, the *Dōninsha* of Dr. Nakamura, the *Kōgyokusha* of Kondō, the *Senshū Gakkō*, the Méiji Law School (now the Méiji University), the School of English Laws (now the Central University), the Waséda Special School (now the Waséda University), the *Wa-Futsu* Law School (now the Hōséi University), the School of Science, and the *Dōshisha* in Kyōto. With the promulgation of the ordinance all these schools, except the *Dōninsha*, which was abolished in 1882 or 1883, were reorganized so as to possess the system of universities, and are in a most prosperous condition.

Text-books.

In 1903 portions of the Ordinance relating to Elementary Schools were revised, and the inspection system of text-books for use in elementary schools was replaced by the so-called ' National Sanction System.' When the administration of elementary schools commenced, the Department compiled all text-books and distributed them throughout the empire, there being then few books suitable for use as such. But later, many text-books having been published in rapid succession by private firms or individuals, the Government allowed schools to choose their text-books from among these compilations. In 1886 readers and histories for the use of elementary schools were edited by the Department, but these soon ceased to be used extensively, whilst text-books published by private firms or individuals were heartily welcomed throughout the whole country. In 1900 and 1901 the old system of sanctioning the works of private persons and using them as text-books became irksome, and, public opinion being against it, the Diet presented a memorial to the Government to have the Inspection System abolished and the text-books compiled at the national charge. In 1902 we had a ' text-book scandal,' which led in the next year to the adoption of the National Sanction System.

Japan had at this time the misfortune to enter upon a war with Russia. Nevertheless, His Majesty the Emperor gave us his august command : ' Though the nation is in a state of war, education shall by no means be neglected. All educators shall do their duty with zeal and assiduity.' So well did educators obey the spirit of this gracious rescript, that the influence of the great war was scarcely felt in the field of national enterprise. On the contrary, all the schools which had been planned came into existence and prospered. In 1907 some revisions were introduced into the Ordinance relating to Elementary Schools, the term of compulsory education being prolonged from four years to six on the one hand, while, on the other, the treatment of elementary school teachers was improved and their pensions increased. The Normal School Regulations were enacted in the same year, and a short course of one year was provided for graduates of secondary schools and high schools for girls, so that they might obtain the teacher's certificate for the elementary school education.

Besides the Imperial University of Tōkyō, the Imperial University of Kyōto was developed in 1899 by the addition of the two Colleges of Law and Medicine, and as a branch institution the Fukuoka Medical College was established in Fukuoka in 1903, and a College of Literature was opened at the same University in 1906. In the same year the Imperial University of the North-East was founded, and the Sapporo Agricultural School, established by the Colonization Department in 1872, and transferred in 1893 to the control of the Department of Education, after having been under the Department of Agriculture and Commerce and also under the *Hokkaido-Chō*, has now become one of its colleges. As to the Imperial University of Kyūshū, its basis is already created, a new College of Engineering (soon to be established) and the Fukuoka Medical College being its foundations. Thus we shall have four universities in the near future.

Expansion of the Imperial University.

Since the Restoration Japan has made rapid progress
in many ways, and this is not less apparent in the realm of
education than in other directions ; and since there is constant
growth in this line, one may safely take an optimistic view
of our education in the future.

Statistics.   The expansion of the national education may best be
gauged by the following statistics :

School Attendances

	1903.	1907.
Children of school age	7,416,930	8,183,413
Under school age (6 years) ..	1,006,720	1,158,483
	6,410,210	7,024,930
Children at school	5,976,124	6,841,083
	93 per cent.	97 per cent.

Schools, Number of Teachers and Pupils, 1907

	Number of Schools.	Number of Teachers.	Number of Pupils.
Elementary Schools	27,125	122,038	5,713,664
Blind and Dumb Schools ..	38	208	4,034
Normal Schools	69	1,176	19,359
Higher Normal Schools (for Men)	2	122	975
Higher Normal Schools (for Women)	1	45	365
Temporary Training Schools	4	15	87
Secondary Schools	285	5,462	111,436
Girls' High Schools	132	2,011	40,272
High Schools (University Schools)	7	291	4,888
Imperial Universities	3	503	7,370
Professional Schools	53	1,745	26,318
Industrial Schools	5,284	5,738	250,090
Training School for Industrial Teachers..	3	—	173
Various Other Schools ..	2,173	7,705	150,668
Total	35,179	147,059	6,329,699

NOTE

The following statement concerning Japanese education, which it will be seen points to certain forthcoming changes in the system now in vogue, and to the reasons therefor, has been very recently (July 1909) transmitted to the Western Press :

A new system of education for Japan has been prepared under the superintendence of Mr. Komatsubara, the Minister of Education, and it will shortly be submitted to the consideration of the High Council of Education.

It seems to be the general opinion throughout the country that Japan cannot successfully compete with Occidentals as long as she retains her present system of education. The main reason is that education takes too long in Japan. According to the present system a boy enters a primary school, where he spends five years, and then goes on to a high school for three years, graduating at a university after a three or four years' course, according to subjects. If no time at all were wasted, students would graduate at one of the Imperial universities at the age of twenty-three or twenty-four. But, owing to the insufficiency of the high schools and the difficulty of passing the competitive entrance examination held each year, added to the difficulty of passing through the high schools in less than four or five years, the number of students who reach the age of thirty by the time they have finished their university course is very large. The shortening of the course must lead to the lessening of the subjects to be studied. Specialization will begin in the secondary schools.

The greatest difficulty of all connected with education in Japan is the extreme complexity of the Japanese language. Japanese students to-day are attempting what is only possible to the strongest and cleverest of them, that is to say, two or three in every hundred. They are trying to learn their own language, which is in reality two languages, blended or confused the one with the other, according to the point of view, while attempting to learn English and German, and in addition studying technical subjects like law, medicine, engineering, or science.

For years past the Department of Education has been again and again entreated to allow either English or German to be dropped according to the subjects studied by high school students, but the reply has always been that the Imperial universities insist on having both languages taught. The Japanese teachers at the high schools have demonstrated that the progress made in either of these foreign languages is miserably slow, owing to the excessive demands made on the students' powers by other subjects.

The result of the present system of education in the case of a large number of students is exhausted physical powers and lack of thorough efficiency in any subject. Many students after graduation at the university find themselves quite unfit to enter upon the duties of life with the energy that is essential to success.

X

COMMERCIAL EDUCATION IN JAPAN

PROFESSORS TAMÉYUKI AMANO, D.C.L. (JAPAN), AND
MASASADA SHIOZAWA, D.PH.

THE marked progress that Japan has made in commercial education in the last few decades is the direct outcome of the growth of national industries and the development of economic ideas during that period. For if we contrast the economic conditions of to-day with those of fifty years ago, we cannot fail to recognize that we have passed at a bound from a stage of development such as prevailed in medieval Europe to the latest modern industrial stage. It becomes, therefore, necessary to survey historically our economic conditions and thoughts, if we want to arrive at a right understanding of the present state of commercial education in Japan.

The origin of Japanese commerce dates back far into the early days of our history. Tradition tells us that in very ancient times fairs were held for the exchange of goods, and when the Emperor Kwammu founded the city of Kyōto as the capital of Japan, in 794 A.D., he divided it into two districts, establishing fifty-one shops in the east and fifty-three in the west district, to facilitate the exchange of goods. At that time Ōsaka, then called Naniwa, was the commercial centre of the country, while Hakata in Kyūshū Island was the chief port for foreign as well as domestic trade. It is needless to say that by this era the use of money as the medium of exchange had become general. Later the political power of the country passed into the hands of the military class, but this did not stifle commerce, for trade with China was maintained to some extent ; and, finally, circumstances led to the opening of commercial intercourse even with Europe, although, of course, this was checked by the seclusion adopted by the Tokugawa Shōgunate in the seventeenth century, which from that time onward concentrated the people's attention solely upon internal business.   When, after two hundred and fifty years of this seclusion, the call of the new civilization came, Japan was only too ready to respond to it, and promptly set about the work of reforming outworn social structures.   Once more society was thrown into confusion, but out of chaos came order, and the foundation of New Japan was laid at this critical moment.   True, the formative process is even now hardly complete, but things are steadily moving towards this goal. Such being the case, it seems fitting that the present survey should begin with the condition of affairs in the Tokugawa *régime*.

Economic condi-tions and commer-cial education in the pre-Restora-tion period.

Space will not allow us to dwell on the economic conditions of the early and middle ages, but we cannot dispense with a description of those of the feudal age, under the Tokugawas, which extended over more than two hundred and fifty years. In this period the so-called 'money economy' was perfected, the requisites for 'town economy' were in existence, and some sign even of the advent of 'national economy' dimly showed itself, although the institution of feudalism was not favourable to its growth.   Clearly defined class distinctions were in force which graded the members of the community into the orders of (1) soldiers, (2) farmers, (3) artisans, and (4) merchants.

Place of commerce in society.

Positions of honour and political power being monopolized by the military class, all industrial pursuits were held in more or less contempt, and commerce especially was despised as an occupation not becoming an honourable citizen.   The moral doctrines of Confucianism and the disciplinary code of the *Bushidō* governed the popular mind, and in consequence the political, military, and literary professions were highly esteemed, while money-making was held in contempt.   We do not wish to assert that Confucianism paid no regard to social and economic prosperity : on the contrary, it is interesting to note that savants often preached that agriculture was the basis of economic well-being.   So, too, social necessities gave rise to a number of more or less complicated problems, and, as a result of the development of the monetary system, such subjects as the currency question and the regulation of prices attracted from time to time the attention of scholars and statesmen, yet in the final analysis contempt for profit-seeking pursuits carried everything before it. Agriculture alone being regarded as the source of general welfare, its encouragement was one of the avowed policies of the feudal age. This was doubtless due in part to the prevalence of the time-honoured doctrine that agriculture is the only truly productive industry ; but it was also the outcome of the fact that rice, the principal product of the fields, formed the medium of exchange side by side with money, so that the income of a feudal lord as well as of his vassals was measured by means of it, and an abundance or scarcity of the crop of rice served as a standard to measure the increase or decrease of national wealth, and had a great bearing on the financial conditions of the nobility.

It will thus be seen that in the early part of this period economic ideas were still in their infancy, and the merchant class was despised everywhere.

The most noticeable phenomenon at the maturity of the feudal system was the growth of cities throughout the empire. The feudal nobles, numbering about three hundred in all, constructed their castles or head-quarters in their respective territories, and their dependants settled around these castles, and thus developed cities. Naturally merchants resorted to such centres, and, on the one hand, supplied the needs of the *daimyō* and their vassals, and, on the other, facilitated the exchange of the goods of the farmers and artisans. By and by these traders increased in importance, and finally formed themselves into an indispensable class in every city throughout the land. *Growth of cities.*

Moreover, owing to the long-continued reign of peace, the standard of living in general was raised to a considerable extent, and this resulted in a bettered condition for every industry. Improvement after improvement was introduced into the production of food-stuffs and clothing materials, and an unusual degree of dexterity was attained in the making of ornamental, artistic, and luxurious articles. Yédo, as *Development of industry and commerce.*

the city of Tōkyō was then called, being the political centre of the feudal system, became also the commercial centre of the country, and business was actively carried on there. Such large cities as Ōsaka and Nagoya followed as important commercial centres. Penetrating into every nook and corner of the empire, the importance of commerce was no longer questioned.

With this development, different systems and institutions relating to business transactions naturally grew out of old-standing customs and usages. The systems of wholesale and retail trade, middlemen and guild organizations were gradually completed.

Influence and position of merchants.

As time went on, merchants came to the front in Yédo and other cities, and exercised no little influence over financial circles. Although feudal lords and vassals apparently despised them, they were in reality dependent upon them for financial support. Not infrequently, under various pretexts, feudal lords levied great impositions upon wealthy merchants, whilst the latter, on the other hand, patronized by feudal lords, enjoyed special privileges. Such being the case, although merchants were nominally classed at the bottom of the social scale, many virtually wielded a by no means insignificant influence.

Nor must we ignore the fact that in this peaceful period the position of the merchant class was far safer and more stable than that of the *samurai*, for, whilst it was not difficult for the merchant to preserve the wealth gotten of his fathers, and to enjoy it peacefully, the feudal tenure of the *samurai* was precarious and subject to the caprice of the *daimyō*. Thus in Yédo and other great cities there were many families of merchants of long standing kept up by inheritance, generation after generation.

Commercial education.

Besides the fact that the field for commercial activities was limited to home trade, the methods of business dealings were for the most part hampered by time-honoured customs. Consequently any sort of advanced knowledge was not regarded as necessary for a merchant, and no special system of commercial education existed. Learning was monopolized by the *samurai* class, and the distinction between learning and commerce was parallel to that between the *samurai* and the merchant. There were, indeed, a considerable number of merchants who, mingling with the *samurai*, pursued their studies in public schools or private institutes, but their so doing was not to acquire commercial knowledge, but to gratify their love of learning. Merchants generally shunned academic pursuits. It is true that in the *térakoya*, or schools for young folks, children of merchants were taken in as pupils, but such institutions were for elementary rather than for commercial education.

Apprenticeship was, in truth, the sole means of commercial education, such as it was. A young man who desired to enter business had to be engaged as an apprentice (*detchi* or *kozō*) in a merchant's family, and only after a long period of strict training in business practices could he set up for himself.

According to the custom of the day, a parent who wanted to make a merchant of his son had to send the latter at the age of ten years or thereabouts to a merchant's family to serve as an apprentice. At first the apprentice was required to do petty work of the simplest character, such as carrying goods and cleaning the shop in obedience to the orders of the master or the clerks, and, as occasion arose, attending upon the master when he went out. At the age of fifteen or sixteen he received a small wage, and, being sometimes called *tédai* (junior clerk), took up more important work and had to see to the proper delivery of goods or the paying and receiving of cash. In some large establishments he even took responsibilities in the matter of the sale and purchase of goods under the superintendence of the master or the *bantō* (senior clerk). The means of support for an apprentice was provided by the master, while the former received no pay except in the form of occasional pocket-money.

Most apprentices were wholly illiterate, and even those who had learned something of penmanship and arithmetic in private schools or under private tutors while in their fathers' houses possessed hardly more than an elementary knowledge of these subjects. So masters generally provided some means for educating them in the evening in letter-writing, arithmetic, and penmanship. The text-books then in use were such as the ' *Shōsoku Ōrai* ' ('Manual of Letter-writing') and the ' *Shōbai*

Ōrai' ('Manual of Commerce'). The former treats of the forms
and technical terms of letter-writing, while the latter describes
all matters concerning business transactions. The contents
were very simple and plain in character, yet they included all
subjects of knowledge necessary for merchants of the day.
Various forms of account-books, the qualities of different
kinds of money, processes of sale and purchase, methods of
transportation and storage, information relating to marine
and agricultural products, food-stuffs, textile fabrics, furniture,
the principal commodities of the time—all these subjects were
described in detail, and, moreover, cautions in handling different
kinds of wares and suggestions as to the duties of merchants
were fully given. Such knowledge was sufficient to meet the
needs of those days.

The term of service for an apprentice was specified by the
contract, but usually extended over four or five years. When
the apprentice had completed this term, he was promoted in
turn to the position of junior and senior clerk. When a senior
clerk had served at his master's shop for a series of years without
any grave fault, he was usually provided with capital by the
master, and thus became an independent master himself. The
capital thus given consisted sometimes of a certain amount
of property, sometimes of a certain number of customers,
the proportion being determined chiefly with reference to his
record of service. When he became an independent merchant,
he had usually to carry on his business under the same commercial name as his master's. This was called 'dividing the
sign.'

Sons of well-to-do merchants were not infrequently sent
to some other merchants' families to serve as apprentices,
and even when staying at their fathers' houses they had to
undergo training in actual business like ordinary apprentices.
Subsequently, when they grew experienced in all branches
of commercial transactions, they succeeded to the business
of their fathers or brothers. This form of commercial training is even to-day observed in some old-fashioned business
establishments.

To sum up what we have stated—in those days the position
of merchants was still low in the social scale, and they

were content with this state of things. It was therefore natural that they should have been, broadly speaking, admittedly unchivalric in character. Having a somewhat low moral standard, they made it their sole aim to accumulate wealth, not questioning the means employed.

The great work of the Restoration, completed in 1868, opened a way for the rise of a new social organization. Many forces in society obstructive to the growth of New Japan were swept away one after another. Above all, the abolition of the feudal system exercised immeasurable influence on the progress of the movement. The old-standing system of social hierarchy was done away with, and the idea of the equality of all men was implanted in the people's minds, slowly yet universally. Many restrictions placed upon trade and commerce were removed, and the principle of industrial freedom established itself firmly. Commercial pursuits gradually began to take their rightful place in society. Of course the influence of deep-rooted customs and prejudices was still palpable, but nevertheless the world movement of modern industry affected to a great extent the whole mechanism of the economic life of the Japanese people.

Development of commerce and commercial education after the Restoration.

Influence of the Restoration.

When the system of political centralization was established shortly after the Restoration, the Government found it to be of prime importance to consolidate the financial basis of the country so as to advance the national welfare, and, inasmuch as the growth of national wealth was reasonably considered to be the foundation of sound finance, the authorities paid special attention to the development of economic resources. As the prosperous condition of Western nations became better known, the desire of the Government to accelerate the progress of industry was intensified. Following their example, it took all possible steps to encourage every branch of industry, and sometimes even went so far as to undertake enterprises on its own account. To give some illustrations : moved by the proposition that the strength of Western nations lay in the increase of wealth by means of commerce, it established the *Tsūshōshi* (Board of Foreign Trade) in 1868, and the *Tsūshō Kaisha* (Trading Company) and the *Kawasé Kaisha* (Exchange Company) in the following year, in order to carry on

Industrial policy of the Government.

foreign trade as an official undertaking. It also took upon itself to a certain extent the management of railways, communications, mining, and several other industries, and thus endeavoured to afford guidance to private enterprises. Some of these works ended in failure, yet the underlying principle was not only justifiable in itself, but also serviceable for educational purposes at such an early stage of our economic reconstruction.

Increase of private undertakings.

At the same time business enterprises of a non-official character greatly increased, and in some cases even high officials of the Government left their positions to become promoters of private commercial or industrial corporations. The most remarkable changes took place during the decade following the year 1868. It was during this period that several new methods of business management were introduced from the West, and the systems of banking, joint-stock companies,

Introduction of Western thought.

&c., were adopted and developed. While necessity prompted the development of new industries, the economic ideas of the West were introduced, and were destined to wholly supplant the old erroneous conceptions of commerce. Some branches of Western learning had long been studied in this country in the days of the Shōguns, but these consisted chiefly of medicine, tactics, &c., and the study of all social sciences, especially of economics, had been left for a later period. Hence it was only in the early part of the Méiji era that the late Yukichi Fukuzawa and others commenced to study political economy, using such books as Wayland's ' Elements of Political Economy.' A little later the works of English classical economists, such as Adam Smith, John Stuart Mill, &c., began to be read among well-educated people, and the economic doctrines of the Manchester school affected to a large extent the public's mode of thinking. The study of economics was also admitted into the university curriculum. The result was that the old fallacy that all lucrative trades and industrial pursuits were contemptible gradually disappeared, and men came to be persuaded that commerce is as potent a factor as anything else in the greatness of a nation.

But the influence of the feudal system still lingered on, and industry and commerce were slow to gain an equal footing with

politics and law, though their value was now recognized, and
the position of merchants still remained low in the social scale.
Nor was any serious attempt made, by the merchants themselves, to elevate their position, old customs and usages being
tenaciously clung to and no trouble being taken to improve
the means of commercial education.   This was chiefly due to
the fact that it was enlightened persons in official or non-
official circles, and not merchants themselves, that were first
awakened to the importance of economic pursuits and the
necessity of advancing commercial education.   Moreover, the
circumstances of the time demanded our earliest attention to
the enactment of new laws and institutions fitted to the altered
conditions of society, and the training of the people to fit them
to these new systems required a long period of experience.

When, however, the great political crisis had been success- Begin-
fully tided over and the work of administrative reform fully nings of
carried out, the attention of the people naturally turned to the mercial
economic side.   educa-
tion.

In 1872 the Government promulgated the National Bank
Act, framed after the model of the American banking system,
and in 1874 it opened an institute (*Kwaikéi Kōshūsho*), to train
students in book-keeping and accountantship, on the premises of
the Paper Money Issuing Bureau in the Treasury Department,
the idea being to train men for banking business and book-
keeping, the necessity of which was then keenly felt.   The
service of an English banker was procured as instructor.   This
institute was continued till 1879, and, though it was conducted
on a comparatively small scale, we must look upon it as the
first endeavour to educate bankers.

The first private school established expressly for tuition in
commerce was the *Shōhō Kōshūsho* (Commercial Training
School), founded in August 1875, in Owarichō, Tōkyō, by
the late Viscount Arinori Mori at his own expense.   At
that time, when people's minds were still engrossed with
political problems and little or no attention was paid to commerce, this man, with keen foresight, did not fail to discern
the movement of the undercurrent of society.   His institution
was the basis upon which the present Tōkyō Higher Commercial School was founded some years later.   In November of

the same year Mori was appointed Minister to China, and the
management of the school fell to the care of the Tōkyō Chamber
of Commerce, a body organized by leading merchants of that
city, and again, in 1876, its charge was transferred from the
Chamber to the Tōkyō Prefectural Government. At the same
time its location was removed to Kobikichō, and the late Jirō
Yano was appointed principal. His excellent executive ability
gave new life to the school.

Admission to the school was allowed to young men above
fifteen years of age who had some knowledge of the English
language. The course of study extended over three years,
during which period lessons in commerce were given with
foreign text-books, along with book-keeping and the principles of economics. But the importance of advanced
commercial education seems not to have been even then fully
appreciated by the general public, for in July 1881 the
Tōkyō Prefectural Assembly passed a resolution to cease
defraying from the Prefectural Treasury the expenses of the
maintenance of the school, under the pretext that all expenses
relating to commercial education should be borne by the
National Treasury. This was a deadly blow to the school,
which was obliged to suspend its educational work for a time,
until, thanks to the united efforts of the members of the staff
of the institution, a subsidy from the Agricultural and Commercial Department was secured, and the school was reopened
later in the year. The amount of the subsidy, however, was
not sufficient to cover expenses, so the deficit had to be made
good by contributions from citizens of Tōkyō interested in the
advancement of commercial education.

Although society was still comparatively indifferent to
higher commercial education, the rapid progress our industries
were making caused many merchants to see the necessity
of educating their children. To meet this demand, private
commercial schools of lower grade were established one after
another with the object of training children of merchants
in elementary arithmetic, reading, &c. These institutions
numbered six in all up to 1877. In the same year the Tōkyō
Prefectural Government established the Commercial Evening
School, with a view to remedying the defects of these imperfect

private schools and imparting more systematic knowledge to those who engaged in actual business and had no time for study during the day.   The school was divided into two departments: one for adults and the other for minors.   The course of study in both departments covered a year, during which period, besides lessons in reading and arithmetic, the elementary geography of Japan and of the world and commercial terms and phrases were taught.   The experiment made by this school being satisfactory, in 1879 the Prefectural Government decided to extend the system, and under the general head of *Shomin Gakkō* (Popular Schools) established one school in each district of the city of Tōkyō with a view to diffusing elementary commercial knowledge.   About the same time, in the provinces also there were founded a number of elementary commercial schools with one or two years' courses.   The curriculums of these schools consisted of reading, arithmetic, geography, commercial terms and phrases, &c., of a little higher grade than those in the *Shomin Gakkō*.   But, after all, the chief aim of these institutions was rather to give elementary education to those who were not in a position to obtain regular school education than to promote commercial education, and they were far from being able to meet the growing demands of the industrial society of the day. It was chiefly for this reason that the system of commercial education of a secondary grade adopted by the *Tōkyō Shōhō Kōshūsho* (Tōkyō Commercial Training School), already referred to, was copied by the then rising commercial schools, at first in Kōbé and Kanagawa in 1878, and then in many other places throughout the country.   Most of these latter were named after the *Shōhō Kōshūsho* (Commercial Training School), and as a rule taught such subjects as economics, commercial geography, commercial law, &c.   The course of study generally extended over two or three years, and admission was allowed to graduates of primary schools or those of equal standing.   These schools surpassed in every way the above-mentioned elementary commercial institutions, and served as the foundation of the present system of secondary grade commercial education.

Further, the extension of banking business consequent on the promulgation of the National Bank Act in 1872, together

with the growth of company enterprises, necessitated more than
ever the study of Western methods of book-keeping.   In this
line also the example shown by the Government in opening a
training school of book-keeping and banking business in 1874,
as we have already stated, soon found followers among the
people, for from 1877 private schools for teaching book-keeping
were established in rapid succession, in order to prepare young
men for employment in banks or other business corporations,
and their number increased considerably from 1881.   In these
institutions the so-called ' short course ' method was adopted ;
for, as a rule, the whole course of study was gone through in a
period ranging from two months to half a year.   Imperfect
in many ways, they nevertheless deserve mention as having
met the urgent need of the time.   From the fact that these
institutions were steadily on the increase, we also see evidence
of the change then taking place in the commercial condition
of our country.

Advance
of
economic
condi-
tions,

After the Restoration our commerce was no longer shut up
in the former small circle, but began to participate directly
in the world movement.   In addition to this, the Government,
animated by a desire to augment our national wealth and power
by developing various public resources, took every step to
encourage private enterprise.   The result was a flourishing
condition of different industrial schemes based on entirely up-
to-date systems.   The mechanism of commerce now became
so much more complicated that, for its successful working,
there were needed legions of fresh hands trained in the latest
methods.   In reality, too, it was under the direction of those
who had received more or less new education, and not by old-
fashioned merchants, that the responsibilities of banks or other
company organizations on any large scale, which then arose
in rapid succession, were always taken up.   And it was a
happy sign of the times that these new leaders of industry
possessed a considerable degree of self-respect and contributed
much, consciously or unconsciously, to the enhancement of
the position of commerce in society.

But, for these new tendencies, a large amount of credit must
be given to the development of economic ideas due to the
growth of the study of political economy.   After that study

was started among a certain circle of scholars in the early period of the Méiji era, as has already been stated, there appeared gradually a number of scholars and writers who endeavoured to direct public attention to the discussion of economic subjects. Of course in those days the situation of the country caused politics to be most to the fore in society, but at the same time economics, being a product of actual necessity, soon became widely diffused amongst the people. At first the economic thought of the English classical school was mainly to the front, to be later followed by the German school of economics, and both combined their forces to convince the public that the development of ' national economy ' is a paramount factor of the advance of a nation.

Thus commercial education progressed step by step, even whilst the general public was still comparatively indifferent to it. The growth of the Tōkyō Commercial Training School may be rightly considered as evidence of this tendency. In 1884 this institution was placed under the direct jurisdiction of the Agricultural and Commercial Department, changing at the same time its name to the ' Tōkyō Commercial School.' This was the first instance of the Imperial Government undertaking the direct control of a commercial school. The same year Regulations for Commercial Schools were promulgated with a view to supervising commercial education. Its general status was still very low, and the curricula of the schools very irregular and imperfect; in fact, the Tōkyō Commercial School was distinguished from its kindred institutions by the high level of its standard and the systematic methods of its teaching, being by far the best school of the kind. In 1885 it was transferred from the direct control of the Agricultural and Commercial Department to that of the Educational Department. After that many changes were made in the rules and curriculum, but almost in every case the whole course of study remained fixed at five years. In 1887, for instance, the rules of the school were fundamentally recast, the standard of instruction was raised, and the school's name was once more changed to the ' Tōkyō Higher Commercial School.' It has since made marked progress.

A further step was taken for the extension of commercial

The Tōkyō Higher Commercial School.

Commer-
cial edu-
cation of
lower
grade.
education in November 1893, when Viscount K. Inouyé, then Minister of Education, issued Regulations for the *Jitsugyō Hoshū Gakkō* (Industrial Supplementary Schools), with a view to extending commercial education of lower grade. The system of these supplementary schools was originally intended to promote the development of various branches of industry. It divided the schools into four kinds, viz. technical, agricultural, marine products, and commercial. Those employed, or about to be employed, in actual business might be admitted to the school. The standard of instruction was to be determined according to circumstances, but it was required that it should not be below that of graduates of the lower grade primary schools. The choice of subjects to be taught was made to suit the needs of the place where each school was situated.

Encour-
agement
by the
Govern-
ment.
The Government gave instructions to each prefectural governor to encourage the establishment of industrial supplementary schools, a policy which proved conducive to the extension of industrial education in general and commercial education in particular. Their establishment followed rapidly, and whilst in 1894 they numbered only 9 throughout the country, in 1904 they were as many as 124.

The Government went so far by way of encouragement as to grant subsidies from the National Treasury, and to this end in 1894 a resolution was passed for appropriating annually the sum of 150,000 *yen,* upon which vote the system was carried into effect from the following year.[1] The schools entitled to receive a subsidy were limited to (1) industrial schools established in accordance with the rules of organization approved by the Minister of Education, and whose standard was not lower than that of the second-year class of secondary schools, or the highest class of the higher grade primary schools ; (2) elementary commercial schools whose standard was not lower than that of graduates of lower grade primary schools ; and (3) the above-described industrial supplementary schools. The method of granting, and the amount of, the subsidy were in each case to be fixed with the approval of the Minister of Education, and the term of the grant was five years.

[1] The amount of the subsidy varies from year to year : in 1905 it was 279,590 *yen.*

In the decade immediately following the year 1884, when the Government issued the General Rules for Commercial Schools, the educational systems adopted in different schools were still irregular and lacked uniformity, so that Government supervision proved very difficult, and the necessity of formulating a general system became urgent. Therefore, in January 1899, the Industrial School Ordinance and the Regulations for Commercial Schools were promulgated. According to the latter, ordinary commercial schools are divided into two classes. The course of study must extend over at least three years in the first, three years or less in the second class, and admission is to be allowed in schools belonging to the first class to graduates of the higher grade primary schools or those of equal standing, and in schools belonging to the second class to graduates of lower grade primary schools or those of equal standing. Many schools were established in accordance with the provisions of these Regulations throughout the country, and their number rose from twenty-eight in 1899 to seventy in 1906. *Improvements in educational system.*

In 1902 the Government revised the Regulations for Industrial Supplementary Schools in order to cause elementary industrial education to keep pace with the fast-progressing industrial education of secondary grade. They have now to be provided by the local self-governing bodies of cities, towns, and villages; but for convenience' sake they may also be attached to local industrial schools of secondary grade, to serve as models for other similar institutions. This policy of official encouragement, combined with many other forces in society, has greatly accelerated the progress of various branches of industrial education, which is now prevalent all over the country.

The growth of commerce and industry that set in after the Chino-Japanese War depended much upon highly educated business men, and hence the necessity of extending higher commercial education was felt even more keenly than it had ever been. Candidates for admission to the Tōkyō Higher Commercial School, where alone advanced commercial education up to quite recently could be given, constantly increased in number, and at last exceeded 1000 a year; but owing to the *Progress of higher commercial education.*

limited accommodation of the school, only about fifteen per cent. of that number could be taken in. To remedy this defect, the Government established in April 1901 another higher commercial school in Kōbé, and at the same time the Ōsaka Municipal Commercial School recast its curriculum and changed its name to the ' Ōsaka Higher Commercial School.' Again, the Government reorganized the Yamaguchi High School in February 1905, and converted it into a higher commercial school, and in March of the same year established the Nagasaki Higher Commercial School.

Admission to the higher commercial schools is allowed to graduates of secondary schools or those of equal standing. The term of study extends over four years, to wit, one year for the preparatory course and three years for the principal course. All the higher commercial schools, except that of Ōsaka, which is under the control of the municipality, are placed under the direct jurisdiction of the Minister of Education. Though the schools have increased in number, they are yet incapable of accommodating even one-half of the candidates, whose number has been the increase for some years past. The proportion of applicants for admission and those admitted in 1905 was 1656 to 394 in the Tōkyō Higher Commercial School, 578 to 124 in the Kōbé Higher Commercial School, 437 to 113 in the Nagasaki Higher Commercial School, and 250 to 101 in the Yamaguchi Higher Commercial School.

Demand for commercial colleges.

Seeing this tendency of things, there arose many advocates for the establishment of commercial colleges, whose pleadings resulted in the matter being seriously taken up. The Tōkyō Higher Commercial School, for instance, attempted to materialize the proposition, but its efforts brought forth no fruit on account of many obstructions. It thereupon started a post-graduate course of two years, giving to post-graduates the degree of *Shōgyō Gakushi* or ' Bachelor of Commerce,' and it has thus become a commercial university in substance though not in name. In 1907 a petition for establishing commercial universities was introduced into the Imperial Diet, and was passed, and the public is now anxiously waiting to see it put into practice.

The Waséda University, prompted by a desire to meet the urgent demand for the establishment of commercial universities, also decided in 1903 to open a Commercial Department, the *Commer-cial De-partment in Waséda University.* term of study being fixed at over four years and a half, to wit, one year and a half for the preparatory course and three years for the main course. When the time arrived for the opening of the Department, 773 students were admitted at once, and in the following year as many as 1301. And now each year a far greater number of students are admitted to this Department than to any other, which shows that the importance of higher commercial education has of late been greatly appreciated, and that a majority of the talented young men of the nation are entering the industrial sphere. The example set by Waséda University has since been followed by many other private universities, and we cannot but surmise that the time for the foundation of Government commercial universities is not far off.

The present prosperous condition of commercial education *Conclusion.* is attributable to the material growth of New Japan. It indicates, on the one hand, that the old pernicious idea of commerce being a despicable occupation has entirely disappeared, and that consequently the position of merchants in society has been greatly raised; and, on the other, that owing to the recent rapid progress of our industry, well-educated business men are in ever-increasing demand. True, in a large number of old-fashioned commercial establishments the out-of-date system of apprenticeship is still tenaciously adhered to, but in banks and other corporate establishments, and in many progressive private firms, graduates of all sorts of commercial schools are engaged to a greater extent every year. Formerly it was held that no advanced education was needed for a merchant, but to-day stern reality shows that the management of any large-scale enterprise must be undertaken only by the highly educated. Finally, it is evident that, though until recently most of the talented youth of the country sought places in official circles, now even those who have made a special study of politics and law not infrequently choose to enter the commercial world, and hence that the present prosperity of commercial education is in no way a mere accidental occurrence.

THE EDUCATION OF JAPANESE WOMEN

Jinzō Narusé, President of the Nippon Women's University

Conspicuous as has been the progress attained in the diverse spheres of national activity since the opening of the country to Western intercourse fifty years ago, the course of events attending women's education has been no less remarkable. The advance in this respect has been so thorough that it now presents an aspect of having undergone entire renovation.

Before a tree blooms into beautiful blossoms and luxuriant foliage, it requires long years of struggling growth and careful cultivation. So it has been with the education of women, which has its own history dating to a remote past. In order to fully understand and appreciate the subject in its present phase, we must of necessity look backwards, and so I devote the first part of the present essay to a general survey of the changing phases of the world of women in Old Japan and of the ideas which governed the progress of their education.

I. Women of Old Japan

Women's education in the Tokugawa period.

From olden times Japan has always possessed more or less machinery for the education of women, with home as its working centre. Compared with the part education played in the life of men, it did not receive, however, as much or as early attention as it should have done. Nevertheless, as far back as the beginning of the seventeenth century, the days when the country was entering a period of renaissance in art and literature under the peaceful administration of the Tokugawa

Shōgunate, thinkers were directing their minds to the subject.
And there appeared, as representing Confucian doctrines,
' Shikigenshō,' by Razan Hayashi, and the ' Mōanjō,' by
Shozō Suzuki, which treated of the theme from the Buddhist
point of view.　But it was Tōju Nakaé (1608–78) who
first promulgated the idea that education was necessary for
them.　A noted Chinese classicist of the Wang-Yangming
school first published ' Harukazé,' and then ' Kagamigusa,'
in which he endeavoured to embody precepts especially fitting,
as he judged, to women.　In his opinion it was not enough
for women merely to cultivate poetic fancies : they should
apply themselves to studies that trained their minds, and
he urged them to qualify themselves for managing households
by developing such virtues as gentleness, obedience, charity,
honesty, &c.　Nakaé's foremost disciple, Banzan Kumazawa
(1616–97), followed him with ' Joshikun ' and ' Joshikun
Wakumon.'　In these treatises Kumazawa went a step further
than his master, and taught that women must not stop at
being merely guided by the principles of gentle obedience,
charity, honesty, &c., but that they should learn to exercise
their minds, seek knowledge of teachers, and study some of
the Chinese classics, so as to become accomplished in the
Confucian moral teachings.　In short, while giving the highest
place to the cultivation of virtues, he also urged them to be
mindful of their intellectual development.　But it remained for
Ékkén Kaibara (1630–1714) to enter more elaborately into
the subject of women, and establish a new school of teaching.
Kaibara was, indeed, a luminant of the first magnitude in
the firmament of education in modern times : he gave thought
to many points which had not occurred to his predecessors.
At the time when neither Nakaé nor Kumazawa had said
much beyond the cultivation of virtues, Kaibara stood forth
and declared that ignorance or undeveloped intellectuality was
at the bottom of women's many shortcomings, and that,
therefore, they should receive an education which would
develop their intellectual powers.　In his day mathematics
and household economy were debased branches of knowledge
in the eyes of scholars ; but he taught that women should
learn both, and explained his methods not in an abstract way,

but by giving rules and precepts in a detailed and practical fashion. To outline his teaching : Up to the age of seven, girls were to be instructed in the same way as, and together with, boys; but beyond that age they were to be segregated. Thence onward, they were to be taught reading and writing principally through the medium of *kana* characters, while they were also to learn to make supplementary use of Chinese ideographs. They were to commit to memory ancient poems of a classical type, and then to become acquainted with primary Chinese classics, and also to read treatises on women by orthodox scholars. Above the age of ten they were not to be allowed to go about outside their homes, where they were principally to be taught the arts of sewing, weaving, and counting, at the same time that their attention was directed to the mysteries of household economics. As they grew up they were to be warned against all vulgar and obscene literature and songs, care being taken to bring them up so that they should not be lacking in the four cardinal attributes of women, namely womanly virtues, womanly address, womanly deportment, and womanly service ; thus, when the day came for their marriage, they would not be found defective in everything that made for true womanhood. It was in his ' *Wazoku Dōjikun* ' that he laid down these views of his in detail.

Some of Kaibara's admirers of a later generation compiled a concise summary of this work and published it under the name of Kaibara's ' *Onna Daigaku* ' (' Greater Learning for Women '), which, happening to suit the social condition of the day, became at once a work of authority and fame. Afterwards there appeared ' *Jogakuhan*,' by Gempo Ōé, and other works for women's edification by other authors ; but these were nearly all of them productions inspired by the ' *Onna Daigaku*.' In fact, it was this work that for generations supplied matter for reading and calligraphic exercises at the *térakoya* schools, where children of the lower classes received their education. It became a custom, too, for the families of the upper classes throughout the country to have a copy of ' *Onna Daigaku* ' as a household work for the instruction of their daughters. Thus for a long time the book was looked up to as an embodiment of ideals for women, this state of things continuing well into the days of the present post-Restoration era. It is not too much to say that the female ethics of the Tokugawa period were largely governed by the teaching of this book. Consisting of nineteen paragraphs or tenets, its pervading spirit is to tie women down to a life of reverence and obedience. It goes no further than giving rules for the behaviour of women, in accordance with the four feminine principles formulated in the Chinese classic on etiquette already referred to, namely womanly virtues, womanly address, womanly deportment, and womanly service. On the question of conjugality, it advocates the old Chinese doctrine of 'seven grounds for divorce,' and denounces remarrying on the part of women. Preaching throughout a rigorous differentiation of duties and conduct between man and woman, the book is a faithful exponent of the Confucian teaching on the relations of the sexes.

In 1725 another popular book for the instruction of women, under the title of ' Onna Shōgaku ' (' Smaller Learning for Women '), came to be circulated. Practically identical with the ' Onna Daigaku ' in the main drift of thought, it taught that ' Unto a woman her husband shall be her heaven, and the relations of husband and wife shall be like those of a lord and his subject.'

Among the contemporaries of Kaibara were Tekisai Nakamura and Raisai Fujii, who each published a work on women's instruction ; but their books were little more than a re-hash of the Confucian teaching, and could not lay claim to any advanced ideas on the education of the sex. Even the famous Lord of Shirakawa, better known by the name of Rakuō, who lived between 1758 and 1829, and wrote ' Naniwaé ' at the request of his bride, as well as, later, his celebrated ' Rakuō Kanna Hikki,' did not attempt much more than to popularize Confucian ideals, although his books were not lacking in passages and precepts of practical usefulness. In his inner heart he seems to have entertained an idea that woman would be better off without any learning. At all events, to him the noblest thing in women was to be by all means affectionate, gentle in heart, conciliatory and obedient in disposition. It will thus be seen that, while this statesman writer paid zealous attention to the cause of male education, he left nothing behind him worthy of special consideration in that of female, except that he followed the old beaten track of Confucianism. Before the Tokugawa *régime* came to an end there appeared other writers with various publications for the guidance of women ; but the remark just made is equally applicable to them all, and so long as women remained under the yoke of the teaching of this school, there was no chance for them to drink fully of the joys of a freely developed mind.

Women in olden times.

Looking back to the days of yore, however, it is seen that the causes which led to bodily inactivity and loss of energetic spirit among our grandmothers were not the growth of a single generation. In early antiquity the country was free from the evils of masculine superiority, for the history of those days records innumerable examples which go to prove that women had a voice in politics, took part in warlike affairs, and held their own on an equality with men in the conduct of social business in general. For instance, in the sixth century we have Ōbako (wife of Mitsugi-no-Ikina), who, facing death in distant Korea, put men to shame by her display of an indomitable spirit of loyalty and unconquerable fortitude. Another example is that of Kamitsukéno-Katana's wife, who, by her exhortation and assistance, enabled her husband to defeat and subjugate the rebellious Yézo tribe. Later, as Buddhism began to get a stronger foothold in the country, its doctrine that woman is a creature of sin, treacherous and cruel in nature, produced among the sex a tendency to self-effacement. Nevertheless, in the eighth century the Imperial Throne was successively occupied by empresses, and, with the spirit of activity predominant in Court circles, ladies of strong mind wielded no little influence in society. There appeared women of such power that they even took an active part in affairs of State, as in the cases of Waké-no-Hōkinni, who, in conjunction with her brother Kiyomaro, repressed the notorious priest Yugé-no-Dōkyō, an Imperial favourite, and of Kibi-no-Yuri, who, in co-operation with Kibi-Daijin, brought the Emperor Kōnin to the Throne. Coming down to the tenth century, a decided change overtook the world of women. They lost their mental and moral vigour. Literature became a fashion among them, and they thought of, and aimed at, nothing but how to appear delicately graceful and languidly gentle. The effete disposition thus bred among one-half of the population grew into a cloud that veiled much demoralization, and women became such coy and timid creatures that they were too shy to look into the faces of male members even of their own family. With the coming of the twelfth century, when the military class rose to power, women's career took another turn, an extreme doctrine of female chastity being the feature of life chiefly forced on them. The result was the almost absolute segregation of the sexes, women being taught only to be retiring and self-effacing. For instance, in the Kamakura days, one constant thought hammered into women's heads was, that they should be unceasing in their prayers and devotional practices after Buddhistic fashion, and take the veil if uneasy in mind. In some cases they were even taught not to emerge from the inner refuge of their homes after the age of ten. The tendency thus outlined gained, instead of lost, force as generations passed on, and the truth of this will be found more than verified by reference to the clan constitutions of feudal barons, who flourished in the sixteenth century. Whether we look at the ' Family Rules ' of Shingén Takéda of Kai, or the ' One Hundred Articles ' of Motochika Chōsokabé of Tosa, the pervading idea is the same. Or shall we glance at an epistle sent to Ujiyasu Hōjō's daughter by Genan, a member of the Odawara Hōjō ? They all utter warnings against admitting into the female quarters any manner of men, including even relatives, to say nothing of priests, merchants, and performers of all kinds. On the other hand, they also forbid outings for women. Such was the general custom of the age, evolved from the growing influences of Buddhism. On the revival, however, of Confucian learning under the Tokugawa Shōgunate, most of the Chinese classicists of the day directed their attack against the evil of allowing women to give themselves up to spiritual observances, and made endeavours to take them out of the Buddhist atmosphere and free them from its enervating influence. Unfortunately, these scholars had their own weakness, and under them women, freed from

In the Kama-kura days.

In the sixteenth century.

In the Tokugawa régime.

Buddhistic thraldom, were to be subject to the severity of the Confucian doctrine as to the relations of the sexes. It was not yet given to women to see the world for themselves and broaden their views. In these circumstances it was unavoidable that the tide should continue to rise still higher in favour of the idea of masculine superiority.

Striking features in the Héian epoch.   Thus surveyed, it will be noticed that the Confucian school held a preponderating sway over the education of women in modern times in Japan. It must not be forgotten, however, that other schools continued also to have exponents and adherents. One of these is a current of thought rather than system that dates back to the Héian epoch, extending from the latter part of the tenth to the early decades of the eleventh century, when the civilization of the country centred in Kyōto. That period had social manifestations of its own, and thus a great impetus was given to the cause of women's education. The circumstances were these : in those days the Fujiwara family were at the zenith of their greatness, it being from among their princesses that the Court chose empresses and Imperial consorts. The Fujiwara vied with each other in giving the best possible education to their daughters, so that the latter might not be found unworthy of elevation when a call came from the Court. Consequently, each princess required a large staff of lady teachers to attend her, and on her entry into the Court these followed her thither to become Court ladies. As may be imagined, the literary and intellectual attainments of these ladies told largely on the popularity and influence of the princess whom they served, and, in turn, on the power of the princess's parental family. Thus there arose a demand for women of high qualifications, and they were forthcoming. This was more especially the case in the early part of the eleventh century, under the reign of the Emperor Ichijō. At that time Fujiwara-no Michitaka's daughter, Sadako, was a sharer of the Throne, and his brother Michinaga's daughter, Akiko (known as Jōtōmon-in), was also in the Court as Princess of the Middle Palace. The Empress and the Princess each had under her a train of women of high accomplishments. Seishōnagon headed the list of fair scholars who surrounded Princess Akiko. She it was who achieved

lasting fame by writing ' *Makura-no-Sōshi*,' which is as remarkable for the vivacity and strength of the authoress's mind
as for the elegance and terseness of its style. The Empress's side
had its representative in Murasaki-Shikibu, who left behind
her the renowned ' *Genji Monogatari*,' which made her name
immortal.[1] She was a virtuous woman of austere type, chaste
in heart and pure in conduct, but withal gentle and obedient as
a wife. Her ' *Genji Monogatari* ' is a voluminous work of fifty-
four books, essentially a serial fiction, abounding incidentally in
faithful pictures of social conditions in the high spheres of the
day. It is not necessarily designed to be instructive. Nevertheless it is a work of genius, possessing the rare merit of being
charmingly beautiful in style, with interest unflaggingly sustained throughout. Moreover, the loftiness of the authoress's
character helped to attract the attention of after ages. For
these reasons the ' *Genji Monogatari* ' came to be regarded,
alike by male and female students of national literature, as a
model *par excellence* of style and diction in prose and poetical
compositions. Some of its admirers went even so far as to
attempt, not without success, to found a system of education
for women on the ideals exemplified in the characters of the
' *Monogatari*.' It is this particular school which, retaining
some followers till this day, must not be left out of count in
studying the history of women's education in Japan. For be it
remembered, that, in spite of the fact that woman's ideal
throughout the rest of the Héian days was to be graceful in
appearance, tender in heart, and gentle in movement, and that
from Kamakura days onward, when the wave of military
ascendancy swept over the country, society entered a new
phase, the aristocrats rallying round Kyōto, the seat of the
Imperial Court, still adhered to a line of education governed
by the ' *Ménoto-no-Fumi*,'
reputed to have been penned by Nun Abutsu, of ' *Chikubashō* '
by Naganori, or of an epistolary homily written by Kanéra
Ichijō for the wife of the Shōgun Yoshimasa, will more than
bear out the above statement ; and this in its turn shows that
there had arisen, and continued to grow, a tendency among

The
' *Makura-
no-Sōshi* '
and
' *Genji
Monoga-
tari*.'

---

[1] The *Monogatari* has been translated in part into English by Suyématz
Kenchio (now Baron Suyématsu). London: Trübner. 1882.

women of the higher class to look back to Murasaki-Shikibu as their ideal of womanhood, and to the characters of the ' Genji Monogatari ' as specimens of men and women moving in model society. In the renaissance days under the Tokugawa *régime*, many scholars of the Chinese school, headed by Ékkén Kaibara, and followed by Gempo Ōé, Ayatari Ōkino, and so on, determined as they were to subserve everything to the Confucian teaching, strongly resented the wide popularity enjoyed by the ' Genji Monogatari.' They considered the work low in moral tone and totally unfit for their daughters' perusal. On the other hand, there were other Chinese classicists of note, who, while upholding the Confucian doctrines, did not hesitate to commend the ' Monogatari.' One of these was Banzan Kumazawa, who likened the book to the ' Shi-king ' of China, as a correct record of manners and customs and of ceremonials and amusements in the olden times, and defended Murasaki-Shikibu as one who, for the instruction of posterity, gave the result of her study of the problems of humanity by portraying, alike, good and bad characters. Also ' Honchō Téijo Kagami ' (' Japanese Mirror of Chastity'), published in the Genroku era, characterizes the ' Genji Monogatari ' as a work unsurpassed in richness of information about old official ceremonies and etiquette on the one hand, and in being the acme of elegant diction and graceful manner on the other. Of the characters in the ' Monogatari,' Murasaki-no-Ué and Akashi-no-Kata were pointed out as ideal models for women. ' Honchō Téijo Kagami ' consists of thirteen volumes, dealing with everything pertaining to the good-breeding of women, including the questions of how a woman should look after her appearance, what things she should have about her, how she should be disposed in mind and heart, and so on. Its directions extend to the minutest matters, and the different characters in the ' Monogatari ' are brought in to illustrate each of these points. There were other writers who, if not so enthusiastic in their support, were far from wholly rejecting the ' Monogatari.' Among the works of this class of authors, mention may be made of ' Onna Mampō Misao Kagami ' by Raisai Fujii, and ' Yamato Jokun ' by Izawa. These argued that the ' Monogatari ' would constitute a worthy mirror for women's behaviour when judiciously sifted of some of its features. To generalize, scholars and teachers who took a favourable view of Murasaki-Shikibu's monumental work were those who not only wanted it to be widely read as a help to the intellectual development of women, but also endeavoured to make it a foundation on which to build up the moral virtues of women. These men have had successors in their ideas and efforts down to recent times, and it may be added that, in the households of the Tokugawa Shōguns and other aristocrats of the land, the ' Monogatari ' continued to be given a very high place among books to be studied by women. Thus it is not without reason that the disposition to be subdued but cheerful, and chaste but gentle and graceful, has grown to be a characteristic of a section of our women. It is worth while, therefore, to note that the perpetuation of this tendency has been the ideal of a certain school of educationists.

Another school that next calls for attention is that which *Téijodō.* would attach greatest importance to *Téijodō,* which, for lack of an adequate equivalent in English, may be described as womanhood of the Spartan type. In reaction from the laxity that crept into the relations of the sexes in the Héian days, *Bushidō,* which, towards the close of that epoch and the beginning of the Kamakura period, had grown into a code of principles for men of the military class, came to be adopted also for the guidance of women under the modified name of *Téijodō.* *Téijodō* demands that, once married, a woman must under no circumstance whatever entertain any frivolous thought, and that her mind shall in this respect be ' rigorous as the winter's frost,' with a determination even to sacrifice life in order to preserve honour and constancy. This doctrine is set down in the famous ' *Jikkunshō,*' which first saw the light in 1252 and is known as the pioneer book of women's instruction in this country. Since then books upholding this line of teaching have never ceased to appear. Indeed, in the ascendant days of the military class, the *samurai's* wife was taught how to conduct herself in the face of emergencies and to keep always active in her mind the strong and indomitable spirit of maintaining at all cost the strictest chastity. Hence in *samurai* families a method of practical education was always held in the highest esteem, and their women were veritable counterparts of Spartan wives and daughters. Nor are instances wanting to show how faithfully this doctrine was adhered to in the actual happenings of life. There is Késa-Gozén, who killed herself to remain true to her husband ; there is the wife of Katsuyori Takéda, who by her own hand shared death with her husband rather than be taken captive ; there is the consort of Katsuiyé Shibata, who after his death followed him by committing suicide. Cases of this kind are indeed too numerous to be cited, and they were all the result of practical education. That this school held its own throughout the Tokugawa period is seen from the circumstance that its ideals are elaborated in all books of any consequence that appeared from time to time for the instruction of women. Sokō Yamaga (1622–85), a great reviver of *Bushidō* in modern times, says in his advice to women : ' The wife of the *samurai* has a duty of great moment to properly manage household affairs in place of her husband. The vicissitudes of life must not influence her conjugal devotion. Nor shall she change her mind in presence of questions of life or death. She shall be possessed of the spirit of constancy and fortitude so as to be ever ready to combat against intruders or face death before an enemy. Thus it results that women must not be educated to be effeminate or languid.' Coming nearer down to our own days, Shōin Yoshida (1831–59), who had some of the chief actors in the drama of the Restoration for his disciples, also followed a similar line of teaching in his ' *Jokai*,' or ' Women's Guidance.' So also such books as ' *Honchō Rétsujo Den* ' (Lives of Japanese women of the most rigorous principles), ' *Honchō Onna Kagami* ' (' Japanese Women's Mirror '), and a host of others were published for popular reading, all exhorting women to constancy and inflexibility. And the period under review produced not a small number of women who may be regarded as the personification of such teaching. Among these the most noted were the wives of Kazutoyo Yamanouchi, Tadaoki Hosokawa, and Shigénari Kimura. This school was certainly different from the Confucian, which lays greatest stress on reverence and obedience, or from the advocates of the ' *Genji Monogatari*,' who look up to gracefulness and gentleness as their ideals, and it should be given consideration of its own in studying the development of female education in Japan.

II.—INFLUENCE OF WESTERN CIVILIZATION

Regarding the different lines of thought on the education of women summarized in the preceding section, it may be said that they represent the theories of thinkers and scholars rather than principles which have been acted upon to a complete extent.   Even in cases where practice has actually followed precept, it cannot be said that the results fully realized the ideals.   For instance, the strict principle, borrowed from China, about the segregation of the sexes after the age of seven, received rigid observance only in a limited section of the community : in others it failed to be followed even in public places of education.   Again, the Chinese classicists were persistent in their advocacy of the doctrine of ' seven grounds for divorce ' ; but in practice this code found few followers.   On the other hand, in the face of the demand for graceful effeminacy, there appeared women who outdid men in masculine qualities.   It goes without saying that the different schools each exerted its influence in its own way according to the condition of society in the various ages.   But it would appear that each being burdened with often impracticable principles, the persons to be educated were not able to wholly conform with the models set before them.   Further, as each school held up a banner of its own ideals, nothing like unity in systems of education could be attained.

In the midst of this confusion there appeared a new streak of light on the horizon of women's world.   In 1549 a Jesuit missionary, Francis Xavier, arrived in Kyūshū and began to preach Christianity.   Thereafter Jesuit propagandists actively engaged in the work of evangelization, until their missionaries gained access to many parts of the interior of the country.   The result was the introduction of a new civilization, and this turn of affairs could not but have an effect in awakening women to a sense of their social position.   From that time

Stimulus of Western civilization.

onward there grew up a new tendency among a section of
our women to be active in mind and body. A glance over
the ' *Séikyōshi* ' (' History of Western Religion '), which is
regarded as an accurate record of the events of those days, will
bear out the statement just made, the conduct of the Japanese
women who find a place in the book being particularly remarkable in this respect. The period of this new impulse did not
last long, however, for the Jesuit missionaries and Japanese
Catholics were swept away from the country after a short
period. The new light was thus extinguished by a blow of
the political hand, but it is recognizable that the undercurrent
of thought set in motion by it while it burned, continued to
grow as a latent force. In the meantime, the trend of affairs
within and without the country shaped the course of events,
so that, as early as the beginning of the nineteenth century,
the exclusionists had to give way before those who desired to
adopt ideas from abroad, and from the last half of that century
our daughters developed a tendency to regard as a moral
duty the pursuit of a regular course of education. It was then
that a new day with promising prospects opened on the cause
of female education. Everything Western was now being
fast introduced into the country, and as a new period dawned
upon our sons in the matter of education, the circumstance
could not but be a turning-point in the education of daughters

Girls'
schools
estab-
lished by
the old
clans.

also. So it was. Many clans began to establish girls' schools,
in order that their education should be conducted there instead
of at home. Between 1870–72 such schools were opened by
the clans of Izushi, Toyooka, Matsué, Iwakuni, Nagoya, Fuku-
yama, and others, and their curricula were a compromise of
old and new ideas. Ante-dating the new system of national
education adopted by the Government, these girls' schools were
imperfect in many respects ; and being still influenced by old
prejudices, their doors were not opened to the daughters of all,
but only to those of the privileged class. With the enforcement
of the new system of education, these had all to be closed
after a short existence. But the important service they
rendered to the country must not be forgotten ; for none of
them were started without their founders being prompted by
an idea that their daughters, in order to grow up to be good

wives and noble mothers, should have proper training, and they all endeavoured to widen the sphere of female knowledge. Brief as their life was, these schools possessed the honour of being, and the right to be remembered as, pioneers in ushering in an epoch of great innovation in the education of women. Side by side with this fact, note should be taken of the con- spicuous part played directly and indirectly by Protestant missionaries and their wives in popularizing their ideas of female education and elaborating equipment for the purpose. To give examples, there are, in the first place, Ferris's Anglo- Japanese Girls' School and the *Kyōritsu Jogakkō* of Yokohama ; the *Joshi Gakuin*, the *Aoyama Jogakuin*, and the *Rikkyō Jogakkō* of Tōkyō ; the *Dōshisha Jogakkō* of Kyōto ; the *Jogakuin* of Kōbé ; the *Baikwa Jogakkō* of Ōsaka—all of which are well known and prospering to this day.   In writing a history of female education in the Méiji era, these institutions should be credited with having proved powerful agents for disseminating new Western knowledge and the English lan- guage among the daughters of the land.   Besides these, there were individuals who, independently of religious connections, devoted themselves to the cause of education for women. Among these mention should be first made of the late Dr. Mannén Matsumoto of Chichibu, who, early in the Méiji era, came up to Tōkyō and opened a girls' school of his own, the students of which were the earliest to gain admittance to the Government Female Normal School, and were destined to be the pioneer women-teachers of the daughters of New Japan.

[margin: Christian mission schools for women.]

[margin: Private girls' schools.]

III.—Promulgation of the New System of Education

As related in the last section, a new day dawned on the education of women immediately upon the Restoration. But the innovation did not extend over the country as a whole, and the benefits derivable from it were confined to a limited class of society.   Furthermore, though started more or less simultaneously in different parts of the country, the attempts quite lacked unity of views among those who promoted them.   This state of things changed, however, after the year 1872, when a new system of education was promulgated throughout the country. Since then considerable progress has been made in perfecting the work, and to-day the ideas governing its advance are rapidly consolidating. We certainly owe much to Western civilization for founding this system and adopting these ideas, but once introduced they have followed lines of development peculiar to Japan, and before proceeding to describe the present position of things, it is proper to trace the course along which the different departments of the system have progressed.

(a) *Education of the Aristocracy*

That there should be no class differentiation, but that equality throughout should be the guiding principle of education, is theoretically as true in the case of female as in that of male education. But where a community is actually divided into distinct classes, it is convenient that each should possess a more or less modified system to suit its own needs. With the exception of the Peeresses' School in Russia, the education of higher-class women in all civilized countries in modern times has been carried on at home, not in institutions especially established for the purpose. But in this country we have the Girls' Department of the Peers' School. Its origin may be traced to the need, consequent on the new order of things brought about by the Restoration, to emancipate the daughters of aristocratic families from the thraldom of narrow ideas and cramped intellect, and to instil into their minds the light and power of new knowledge, so that they might be regenerated as wives and mothers, broadened in view, made healthy in body and active in spirit. It was judged that the best means to attain this end was to educate women in school, and hence the establishment of the Peeresses' School. On the 14th of September 1871 the Emperor issued a rescript to the nobles of the land encouraging foreign travel, and in a passage which occurred therein referring to women's education, His Majesty said :

Imperial rescript.

' We still lack an established system of education for women in this country, and they are generally deficient in the power of judging and understanding things. How children grow up depends on how their mothers bring them up, and this is a matter of supreme importance. It is commendable that those who go abroad from now onward should take with them their wives and daughters or their sisters. These would then see for themselves how in the lands they visit women receive their education, and would also learn the way to bring up their children.'

Thus urged, the demand for women's education continued to grow, and in 1877 a girls' department was opened in the Peers' School for the daughters of aristocratic families, and curriculums of primary and secondary grade education were provided for them. The decade or so that followed was remarkable for the rush made for new knowledge in all spheres of society ; in short, Western civilization flowed in with the irresistibility of a rising tide, bringing with it the good and the bad promiscuously. That was in the days when the national system of education had not yet been placed on a firm foundation. Whereas the policy of the Government and of the different schools themselves was to attach the greatest importance to the moral side of education as well as to the physical, the general tendency was all in the direction of intellectual development, for, as a result of a mental habit of long growth, scholars and students generally were averse to building up their physique.

The Peeresses' School.

In 1885, by order of the Empress, the Peeresses' School was established, and was made an institution independent of the Peers' School. It was divided into primary and secondary grade departments, each having a six years' course, and its doors were thrown open, not only to the daughters of peers, but also to those of all families having eligible qualifications. In 1907 the institution was again made a department of the Peers' School, and it remains the only institution of the kind that has grown and is growing under Imperial patronage. It has succeeded in restoring moral culture to the place of highest importance in the students' minds, and also in creating among them a deep interest in physical deportment. Besides the two courses already mentioned, the school now contains a seminary where students may pursue higher branches of art and learning, and this new departure is giving good results. The advent and growth of this institution may, indeed, be regarded as opening a new epoch in the education of the daughters of our upper classes.

(b) Primary and Secondary Grade Education for Women in General

The system of education for women in general, irrespective of their social position, has also attained a considerable degree of completeness in its organization and equipment since the Restoration. Not that the country possessed no educational machinery prior to that event. The higher classes had means to provide for the education of their children at home ; but this could not be so with the lower classes, and it was necessary that there should be some machinery to meet the want. The institutions that arose out of this need were the *térakoya* and the *shingakusha*. The former was, so to speak, a by-product of Buddhism. The propagation of Buddhism in this country had one deplorable result, namely, the lowering of the social status of women. On the other hand, it directed their minds towards charitable endeavours, and the parish temples set up in ancient times served as centres of popular education in their day. Coming down to the warlike period of military ascendancy, it fell to scholastic priests to keep burning the light of learning and carry on the work of education, such as it was, for the people. The services thus rendered to the cause of education by Buddhism deserve recognition. One of these was the establishment of the *térakoya*. It originated in using temples as schools, with priests for teachers. Latterly it ceased to be an institution run by Buddhist priests only. *Shintō* priests, unattached *samurai*, doctors, village elders, even women were now at liberty to open a *térakoya*, which thus developed into a secular school. It took in as pupils the children of both sexes of the common people between the ages of seven and fifteen. As a general rule the boys and girls were not allowed to sit together while at lessons in *térakoya*, each sex being grouped by itself.

The
térakoya.

They were, nevertheless, taught in common in the same hall, and it will be seen that the Chinese doctrine about the segregation of the sexes at the age of seven was set at defiance. As to the method of teaching, it was of the single-class system, one master teaching every subject to every pupil, although of different attainments. The system was, naturally, defective in many points; but, despite all imperfections, the gradation and correlation of the different subjects taught were fairly maintained, and the results were generally excellent. In the case of girls, as in that of boys, penmanship was given the first place of importance as a compulsory subject of study. Girls were especially taught to write in *kana*, and were then given lessons in easy reading and arithmetic, and also sewing. As for *iké-bana* (decorative arranging of cut plants) and *cha-no-yu* (tea ceremony), these were taught only to girls who desired to be so instructed. In penmanship, calligraphic excellence was not the only aim. Copy-books were not mere collections of detached words and phrases, but were in reality elementary text-books of different branches of knowledge. Hence, as girls advanced in their penmanship course, they were at the same time taught morals, composition, reading, history, geography, and so on, this ingenious method being even availed of to give instructions in housekeeping and business economics. Of these text-book copy-books, those most generally in use were ' *Onna Imagawa* ' (which imparted rudiments of general knowledge), ' *Onna Daigaku* ' (already referred to), ' *Onna Kinshin Ōrai* ' (which taught women how to behave), ' *Onna Téikin Ōrai* ' (a sort of treasury of home ethics for women), ' *Onna Kōkyō* ' (which taught a daughter's duties towards her superiors), ' *Jokai* ' (see Section I), &c. The art of counting, which had no place in the curriculum for the upper classes, was taught rudimentarily at *térakoya*, and its knowledge was very useful to children of business people, more especially to the housewives of the middle and lower classes. Then, almost parental as were the relations between the master and his pupils, those between the children's elder relatives and the master were always most cordial, and this circumstance greatly facilitated the work of the *térakoya*. As such the *térakoya* was an organ well fitted for keeping up the standard of morals among the common people.

Standing somewhat higher than the *térakoya* in the scale of learning imparted were institutions known by the name of *shijuku*, a term almost out of use now, but very popular up to thirty or forty years ago. Some *shijuku* took in both boys and girls, giving them a common course of teaching. So far as can be definitely ascertained, the *shijuku* and the *térakoya*, found scattered throughout the country between the closing days of the Tokugawa *régime* and the early days of the Méiji era, numbered altogether about 17,000. In these schools girls were generally outnumbered by boys, the former's total number not coming up to one-half of that of the latter.

An institution of an associative nature rather than of school organization, and therefore somewhat different to those hitherto described, was the *shingakusha*. Literally, *shingaku* means 'heart science,' and *sha*, 'house' or 'society.' The *shingaku* aimed at making individuals perceive, understand, and act up to his or her heart's quality as stamped by nature, and it came to form a subject of popular study in the beginning of the eighteenth century. This cult, for such it really was, was started by a man named Baigwan Ishida (1685-1744), who aspired to create a new moral force for the guidance and spiritual conversion of business circles, especially the sons and daughters of tradespeople. Its growth was comparatively rapid, and in 1782 Toan Téjima, a prominent disciple of Ishida, opened in Kyōto a *shingakusha* under the name of *Gorakusha*; and nine years later, in 1791, Téjima's best pupil, Dōji Nakazawa, founded the *Sanzénsha* in Yédo (Tōkyō). These two establishments became radiating centres whence the cult spread its teaching throughout Western and Eastern Japan. The devices followed for mastering the 'science' were various; but preaching occupied the largest part of the cult's activity, and it bore a close relation to the education of women. This preaching was addressed both to men and women, and here, too, a system of co-education of the sexes was followed. Men and women sat in one and the same hall, except that they were grouped by themselves according to sexes. In the congregation were children of tender age, illiterates side by side with

The shinga-kusha.

those possessing a fair education, and they all listened to the 'moral talk' which, given in easy, every-day diction, taught how to become enlightened in heart, and inspired action in good causes. Among the leaders of the cult was a nun, Jion, who stood high among the disciples of its founder, Ishida. She did good work in preaching the imperativeness of giving proper education to those who are burdened with the momentous duty of bringing up children. Téjima devoted himself principally to explaining the rules of etiquette and personal behaviour required of women, and also those pertaining to the relations of husband and wife, not in a cut-and-dry style of preaching, but in a manner entertaining and appealing to the understanding of his hearers. Nakazawa was a master-hand at inventing parables, and being, besides, gifted with the art of making a happy choice of easy expressions, his 'talks' on womanly virtues were always powerful in their effect. The part thus played by the cult in the moral culture of women, who form an important section of the community, was not inconsiderable. It is true that the 'scientists' followed in the main the Confucian doctrines of 'three cases of obedience' and 'seven causes for divorce'; but those whom they chiefly tried to reach being of the uneducated class, their instruction well fitted the needs of their audiences. At one time the cult possessed about two hundred 'schools' distributed in different parts of the country, and it is indisputable that the corrective influence they exerted on the morals of the female community at large was not insignificant.

Thus the *térakoya, shijuku,* and *shingakusha* were institutions imparting primary and middle grade education to the children of the middle and lower classes in modern times, before the reorganized national system was established. Moreover, in most cases, where families could afford it, daughters were further instructed at home in the arts of sewing, weaving, spinning, cooking, playing the *samisén* (a popular string instrument), and even dancing, according to the direction of their parents' tastes. In some instances, too, a course in these acquirements, or some of them, was the only training required of girls. Thus the education of our daughters in those days was anything but perfect. But it should be remembered that about the time that the country was opened for Western intercourse—that is fifty years ago, more or less—a tendency had grown among the daughters of the common class to desire education of their own accord, and to consider it fortunate if they were able to continue for long their attendance at the *térakoya*. Then, as stated above, so soon as the doors had been opened for the inflow of the Western civilization, the more foreseeing of the prefectural governors, formerly *daimyō*, untied their purse-strings and set the example of establishing girls' schools. Nevertheless, the fact remained that the education of women in general was left in a state of neglect as compared with that of the male sex, and the matter attracted the Emperor's attention. Therefore His Majesty, in a rescript proclaiming the new system of education, condemned the old practice of leaving the question of women's education out of State consideration, and this admonition became the corner-stone, as it were, on which was built the great structure we see to-day. In 1872 the new system was put in force. Since then the primary school regulations have undergone various changes, but they remain the same in their essential features. Under the system now in operation, both boys and girls of all classes must enter school at the age of six. The elementary primary course is finished in four years, and the higher primary course in four years, or the latter may be discontinued after two years. Girls who have finished the second-year course of the higher primary education are allowed to enter the girls' high school. Boys and girls are taught either separately or together in classes, according as local conditions require. The compulsory period of education for both sexes has hitherto been four years ; but as the result of a recent enactment this is now extended to six years. As for the number of girls attending the primary schools, it is yearly increasing. According to official returns for 1905, out of 100 school-age girls 93·34 were attending schools. The ratio is somewhat low in comparison with that of boys, the figure for the latter being 97·72 out of every 100 ; but the showing is steadily improving.

The secondary education. Turning to the secondary education of women, the Government established the *Tōkyō Jogakkō* (Tōkyō Girls' School) in 1872, and provided lessons in national literature, English,

The primary-grade education.

manual arts, &c. It had a preparatory department which admitted girls of an age above eight and below sixteen. The school was closed in 1877. In the same year that saw the opening of the *Tōkyō Jogakkō*, the Government inaugurated another girls' school in Kyōto under the name of *Éi-Jogakkō*— English Girls' School (the present First Girls' High School of Kyōto). In 1882 a new department, named Girls' High School, was added to the Tōkyō Women's Normal School, with the object of giving girls a general education of high grade, having for its principal aim the inculcation of moral and ethical principles and the sending forth of accomplished young women of good character. About the same time girls' institutions of a similar nature were established in a few other prefectures ; but up to the end of 1885 their total did not exceed nine. In 1886 the Middle School Ordinance was put in force, and the Girls' High Schools came to be classed as secondary institutions where a general education of high grade, thought necessary for girls, was to be imparted. With the promulgation of the Girls' High School Ordinance in 1899, it became compulsory for every prefecture throughout the empire to possess one or more schools of this class within its bounds. Among non-official girls' schools, the *Atomi Jogakkō*, founded in 1875 and conducted by Mrs. Kwakéi Atomi, was the first of the kind established. About the year 1887 such institutions largely increased in number. In 1905 the total number of government and private girls' schools stood at 100, with 31,574 students. Still, compared with those for male, whose figures stood at 271 schools and 104,551 students, the ratio was but one to three. Seeing that the population of the country is divided nearly equally between the two sexes, it is evident that there is room for a much greater development and amplification of accommodation for women's education.

IV.—TECHNICAL EDUCATION

The primary and secondary schools now in existence may be regarded as fairly completing the system whereby our daughters are given opportunities to build up their character, cultivate virtue, and prepare themselves for becoming useful

Technical education in old days.

members of society, worthy wives and good mothers. But it
is indispensable, also, that there be institutions where some
of them may learn special branches of art, or professions, so
that when need arises they may be able to earn their own living.
But in this country a system of education having this object
in view is of comparatively recent development. It is a mistake, however, to suppose that no thought was ever given in
earlier days to education of this kind. Women, it is true, were
not admitted into State universities and provincial colleges,
where Chinese classics and literature were mainly taught, but for
some branches of art and science special seats of learning were
at one time attached to one or another department of the
Government, and their doors were open to women, eligibility
being confined to specified subjects of study. For instance,
in the *Jibushō* of the *Dajōkan* there was a Bureau of Music,
conducted by four Master Singers, who had thirty male singers
and one hundred female singers studying under them. These
women singers, after their graduation, were called to service
and kept permanently in the Ladies' Quarter of the Imperial
Court. Similarly, the Imperial Ladies' Quarter had lady
weavers and seamstresses occupying three graduated positions.
In the households of Princes of the Blood and of distinguished families of high lineage, wet nurses held a high
position, being closely interested in the education of the
noble children they fostered. In the field of surgery, a
midwifery office formed part of the Medical Bureau and the
profession was confined to women, thirty students, ranging
in age between fifteen and twenty-five, being taught from
time to time under official instruction. These women,
when sufficiently qualified, were given positions in the
Imperial Household. There also existed in the Court seven
medical posts held by women. History also records instances
of women who followed massage as their profession. In
all the foregoing cases, however, the training was discontinued on account of its non-success. Thereafter, until recent
times, no further official endeavour was made to provide
technical education for women, but those who wanted to learn
any art or science had to seek masters for themselves. In rare
instances some succeeded in leading an independent life by

means of the profession thus acquired.   In consequence, however, of the great strides made in the field of education in later days, a demand arose for the technical training of women in lines which befitted their nature.   The first response to this demand was the establishment of a special school wherein to instruct women for the profession of teaching.   In 1874 the Tōkyō Women's Normal School was opened as a Government institution, and in the following year the Empress gave it a sum of 5000 *yen*, showing thereby how deeply interested Her Majesty was in encouraging female education.   Since then female normal schools have sprung up in many prefectures under official control.   In 1886, in consequence of the operation of the Normal School Ordinance, these establishments were divided into two classes, namely Higher Normal and Ordinary Normal schools.   The Ordinary and Higher Normal schools were places where women were taught to become respectively primary teachers and normal and secondary school teachers.   There are two Women's Higher Normal schools in existence at present, one in Tōkyō, another in Nara.   These institutions consist of three departments, Literature, Science, and Arts, each course covering four years.   The Women's Ordinary Normal schools have undergone more or less changes in organization ; but for the present they form a female department of Ordinary Normal schools, and are found established in all the prefectures.   According to official statistics for 1905, 980 women were engaged in secondary grade teaching, and 22,268 were teaching in primary schools.   Besides, 835 matrons were conducting 313 kindergartens in different towns of the country.   To name private institutions, the graduates of which are entitled to receive a licence for secondary grade teaching in English, there are the *Joshi Éigakujuku* and the *Aoyama Jogakuin*. In the practice of medicine, the Home Office made a beginning in 1884 by permitting women to take part in the Doctors' Diploma Examination, carried out annually by the Department.   This departure furnished an opportunity for such women of note as Ginko Ogino and Zuiko Takahashi to engage actively in the work of promoting this line of education among their sex.   A private enterprise named the *Tōkyō Joi Gakkō* (Tōkyō Women's Medical School), which started in a very small

Technical education in recent times.

way, is now training several hundreds of women for the profession. Moreover, there are now women's departments both in the *Nippon Igakkō* and the *Tōkyō Igakkō* (*igakkō* means ' school of medicine'). Lady doctors are but of very recent creation, yet throughout the country there are already more than 130. As for the training of midwives and nurses, there are, to begin with, the Japan Red Cross Society, the *Tōkyō Jikéi Byōin*, and numerous other hospitals both in Tōkyō and the provinces, which show good results in turning out well-qualified women. The number of licensed midwives and nurses pursuing their vocations in the country is too numerous to be easily ascertained.

It may be observed here that. gentle and obedient as are our women in ordinary circumstances, they seem to possess a latent indomitable spirit of fortitude and courage, a product of long historical association and traditional training. Once roused into activity, they show themselves capable of behaviour which is little short of marvellous ; this was evidenced over and over again by the calm and cheerful way in which our women nurses went about their business at the front with absolutely no fear of death, often falling in the discharge of their duties, in both the China-Japan and Russo-Japan campaigns.

As regards commercial education for women, a way has now been opened by the establishment of the *Joshi Shōgyō Gakkō* (Women's Commercial School) by Dr. Kenzō Wadagaki, graduates from which school are being favourably received by the business community.

Art education in Old Japan.

In other branches of technical education, such as music, fine arts, and various manual arts, Old Japan possessed no special machinery. But, as these formed part of the accomplishments necessary for women as worthy wives and good mothers, means were always provided for girls to obtain personal instruction from different specialists. In these circumstances there were women who achieved renown by devoting themselves to special lines of art handed down in their families. Going back to a remote past, we have Princess Tachibana, wife of Prince Shōtoku, who won undying fame by embroidering the holy *mandara* scarf. In the Héian days it is well known that the women of the time were in general highly accomplished

in music and painting. To mention some special cases : there
was Chiyo Tosa, who, in pursuit of her father Mitsunobu's
profession, earned a reputation which still exists, whilst in
music the name of Ôtsū Ono has come down to us. The
other arts that inseparably enter into the lives of accomplished women, as they have always done from ancient times,
are sewing, *hana-musubi* (knot-shaping), *iké-bana* (decorative
cut-plants arranging), *cha-no-yu* (tea ceremonial), *kōgi* (incense burning), and the ceremonies and etiquettes pertaining
to the tender sex. Such arts are still cultivated as of old,
some of them on account of their usefulness, and others because
of the beauty, gracefulness, or the elevating effect of the actions
involved. There have been cases of women who learned and
pursued these accomplishments, or some of them, as a means
of subsistence ; but, generally speaking, they were cultivated
in the spirit already pointed out. To-day the arts of music,
painting,   sewing,   embroidery,   knitting,   artificial-flower
making, photography, and so on, are taught in schools. It
should be observed, however, that the attention paid to them
by our daughters is of the same type as that transmitted from
their mothers of yore, being studied, primarily, as part of their
general accomplishments, the idea of employing them as a
means of livelihood being of secondary consideration. The
present Government Academy of Music was organized as
such in 1887, its prototype being the *Ongaku Torishirabéjo*
(Bureau for Investigating Music), established in 1879. The
courses of study in this school are divided into three, viz. the
vocal course, the instrumental course, and the chorus-singing
course. The school possesses, also, a normal department, where
students are trained to become, in the case of women, teachers
of music in primary schools and in female schools. As for
technical schools of other kinds for women, there are the
Tōkyō Saihō Jogakkō (Tōkyō Women's Sewing and Tailoring
School), the *Joshi Bijutsu Gakkō* (Women's Fine Arts School), the
Kyōritsu Joshi Shokugyō Gakkō (Associated Women's Technical School), the *Tōkyō Gigéi Gakkō* (Tōkyō School of Arts),
the *Joshi Kōgéi Gakkō* (Women's Industrial Arts School), and
the *Shashin Gakkō Joshibu* (Women's Department of the
School of Photography).

V.--HIGHER EDUCATION OF WOMEN

Female
scholars
since the
Tokugawa
days.

With the recent rise of the tide of female technical education, a need began to be felt for higher education. Looking back to the past, it was only in a limited section of society that girls were enabled to enjoy the light of the best education. In the modern days of the Tokugawa Shōgunate learning in general was in a high state of advance and prosperity, but for all that, women's world as a whole remained practically unaffected, and such of the sex as did follow high courses of study were practically women brought up in the homes of strict Confucianists, or those who were compelled by circumstances to devote themselves to scholarly attainments. But, judging from the records left behind by those women who, by reason of their position or otherwise, went through what may be termed a higher education, it is evident that they were the better for their attainments, and many of them rendered good service to society. Thus, in the Genroku era, when scholarly pursuits were in the ascendant, we have Tokén, the wife of Ékkén Kaibara, who was noted for proficiency in the Chinese classics, general literature, and penmanship. Another was En (1660–1725), daughter of the classicist Kenzan Nonaka, whose extensive learning and sturdy moral character enabled her to carry on her father's work. She published the ' Oboroyo-no-Tsuki,' a book of no ordinary literary merit. Tsū Inouyé (1660–1730), who mastered the Chinese classics under her father, excelled in poetical composition. To name others, there were Taira-no-Akiko, a mathematician ; Shūshiki Kikugotéi, an epigrammatist ; Réi Arakida, a lady historian of great authority ; and Tsukuba Toki, Yonoko Udono, and Shizuko Yumiya, a celebrated trio who studied under Kamo-no-Mabuchi, a profound scholar of national classics. Coming nearer to our own days, we find Kōran Yanagawa and the Baroness Nakashima, the first known as a poetess and painter as well as for her high womanly virtues, and the second for wielding no little influence as a lady politician and poet. The names of many others could be cited if necessary in this connection, but it will suffice to say that they were women who either belonged to a special class or grew up in exceptional circumstances. No road had yet been provided for giving to women at large access to higher education—a fact doubtless attributable to the prevailing conditions of society. But comparatively few as are these exceptional cases, they justify the conclusion that women are not intellectually unfit to study the higher branches of learning and advanced sciences, and also that feminine virtues do not suffer by the acquisition of profound knowledge. At the same time, it hardly needs to be pointed out that the so-called higher education, as obtained in days gone by, was trammelled by moral doctrines of one kind or another and was defective in many respects. Especially true is this statement as regards the question of physical culture. In some cases young women were taught the art of using the halberd, or of archery, a legacy of warlike days ; but neither art was ever included in the regular course of study or training at any stage of female education.

In view of the all-sided advance the country had attained since the Restoration, it was intolerable that our daughters alone should, in the above important respect, remain subject to the same disadvantages that surrounded their forebears. It was their due that they should have provided for them machinery whereby they might complete their education by attaining to the full development of their intellectual, moral, and physical faculties, and emerge into the world ready to discharge their heavenly ordained duties as women as well as members of society. It was this necessity that called our Nippon Women's University into existence. The Women's Higher Normal and Technical schools, of which a general description has already been given, may be regarded as institutions furnishing ' higher education.' But they cannot be said to go far enough. In Europe and America the doors of colleges and special classes are now generally open to women as freely as to men ; in this country the matter has not yet advanced to this stage. In principle there should be no objection to admitting female in common with male students into our Imperial universities. But how or when this should be done is a question that can be decided only after careful consideration as to the history of women's education in this country and the past and present conditions of society. Sudden

The
Nippon
Women's
University.

and blindly radical changes never bring good results in educational systems. Not that we should ever forget to atone for our own shortcomings by adopting the good points of others ; but there are European and American principles and methods of education which cannot be transplanted intact into our soil. Our system of education has its own history of development, and what suits us must be an arrangement not only meeting the requirements of our women, but also one in consonance with our form of government, and in harmony with our social conditions. We believe all these points have been most carefully considered in planning the organization of the Nippon Women's University. Respecting the higher education for women that obtains in Europe and America, it may be said to be built on the principles of equality of the sexes and equal education for men and women. To say nothing of the universities where the sexes are taught in common, even a purely female college differs from a man's college only in that its students are all girls : otherwise the two are exactly alike in all that pertains to the curricula of teaching. This is quite different from the case of the Nippon Women's University, where the courses of study and their choice are so arranged as to be in full accord with the political and social conditions of the country, as well as with the peculiar characteristics of our women. How far this statement is verifiable will be seen from the fact that in the educational circles of Europe and America this University is regarded as a new experiment worthy of respectful watching. Promoted by the enthusiastic support of a large number of influential persons, the Nippon Women's University was opened in April 1901. In September of the same year it had the honour of being granted a sum of money by the Empress. It consists of the University proper and affiliated or attached schools, the two divisions making an integral whole. The University courses are those of Household Management, Literature, Pedagogy, Physical Sciences, Physical Education, Music, and Fine Arts. Each course is finished in three years, and a post-graduate course [1] of three years, more or less, is provided.

[1] At present this post-graduate course alone corresponds in standard to men's university education in Japan.

The attached schools are denominated Kindergarten, Primary School, and Girls' High School, which together constitute the General Education Department. Another affiliated department is the Special Department, where courses of industrial arts and commercial education are given. Beginning with the Kindergarten and ending with the University courses, the teaching is carried on in accordance with the all-pervading principle and policy of consistent and continuous co-ordination. Out of the seven University courses provided in the curriculum, the first four only, namely those of Household Management, Literature, Pedagogy, and Physical Sciences, are now open. The others will follow later on. The standard of work done and of lessons given in these various departments is, in each case, regulated by the main object of keeping in close touch with the requirements of the time, so as to be always consonant with the progress of society.

It is not its system and organization alone that the Nippon Women's University regards as its special feature : its claim extends equally to methods of teaching and training. Space does not permit us to dwell at length on the experiences and guiding ideas of its authorities ; but the gist of what is being actually done is as follows : Viewed from the standpoint of the individual, the ideal goal of the University is the realization of self, the full development of the natural gifts of the individual, the fulfilment of heaven's ordained duties. From the political and national point of view, it is the realization of the idea of State and country. From the standpoint of the human community, it is the realization of the idea of society. And from the standpoint of mankind, it is the realization of the idea of humanity. If we regard it from woman's point of view, it is a means of realizing womanhood. Finally, from the home point of view, it is the realization of the ideal of home. Using the word ' realization ' in the sense of the full development of all good qualities and powers and their practical application, the University devotes a large part of its efforts to realizing home, since it is judged that the national trend of affairs makes this line of endeavour very important. The institution is only about ten years old, but it now possesses a total endowment fund amounting to nearly 500,000 *yen*, and is educating 1300 students under a teaching staff of over eighty.

VI.—IDEALS OF FEMALE EDUCATION

In view of the comparative neglect in which the education of women was left in the past, there is no gainsaying that the advance made in this department of social endeavour within a brief period of less than half a century is very striking. It should be remembered, however, that, although the machinery of education was developed to a tolerable degree of completeness not long after the opening of the country to Western intercourse, there continued to be a wide discrepancy in the theories and ideals of education. It is true also that, in modern times, several schools were established to diversify the education of women. But it remains undisputed that the Confucian doctrines were the most widely propagated and exerted a controlling influence. They were those embodied in the ' *Onna Daigaku,*' to which reference has been made more than once, and they live to-day in the vague and almost crude notions involved in what is called *kenbo ryōsai* (wise mother and excellent wife). In 1899 the late Mr. Fukuzawa published a criticism on the ' *Onna Daigaku,*' and almost simultaneously his ' *Shin Onna Daigaku* ' ('Women's New Great Learning'). In the former the author exposed the inconsistencies of the ' *Onna Daigaku* ' and denounced its teachings as behind the times. In his own ' *Shin Onna Daigaku* ' Mr. Fukuzawa gave free expression to his ideas about women and their bringing-up, grouping these ideas into twenty-three rules or tenets. Regarded by itself to-day, there is nothing extreme about the book as a whole, but read side by side with the old ' *Onna Daigaku* ' Mr. Fukuzawa's production was destruction itself. He urged the widening of opportunities for the coming together of men and women ; separate living and households for parents and their married children ; no interference by relatives-in-law in the affairs of a wife ; equality of husband and wife ; the sanctioning of second marriages for women, and so on. Mr. Fukuzawa seems to have based his teaching for women on the theory of marriage as a contract, and to have consequently regarded the equality of husband and wife as

Mr. Fukuzawa's ideas of female education.

their right. It is doubtful, however, whether his views are all
that can be desired theoretically or practically. For it is highly
problematical whether, in the present social condition of our
country, his teaching about setting up an independent household by married people could be carried into practice with
salutary results. It is incontestable, however, that his ' *Shin
Onna Daigaku* ' has had no inconsiderable effect in elevating
the position of women and forcing men to reflect on their
conduct in the relations of the sexes. Nevertheless, the most
that can be said is that his teaching went no further than
replacing the old notions with new ideas as to regulating the
relations of parents and children and husband and wife.
But there are numerous other questions and problems affecting
women's education. Of these the most prominent is in connection with the endeavours of Christian missionaries who are
striving to convert our daughters to their ideals of Christian
womanhood. In these ideals are included faith in God, and
many other points of excellence. But their propagators
are generally not sufficiently well informed as to the actual
condition of affairs in this country, so that they often fall
into the error of trying to make European or American
women of our daughters, and their educational efforts tend to
produce undiscriminating Westernization, which our society does
not want. It is a matter for congratulation, however, that
the Christian schools in the country have of late begun to show
signs of more or less coming into harmony with our national
circumstances. After all, however, they cannot escape being
regarded as a method of education that begins at the wrong end,
for a system of education that suits one country cannot be
built on the history and customs of another, but must have
for its foundation the actual surrounding conditions of society.

Regarding the higher education of women, opinions have
been advanced before now urging its needlessness. It has been
argued that women are by nature not gifted with sufficient
intellectual power to profit by a higher education. Some have
even gone so far as to contend that women, in a struggle to cope
with what is beyond their mental capacities, would only con-
sume their mind and body in vain efforts, and would, further,
injure their feminine virtues. Nor is it entirely without reason

Christian mission-aries' views on our women's education.

that these views have been advocated.   At one time, when the
inrush of Western ideas assumed the character of an inundation,
a sudden effort was made to force upon women the study of
difficult subjects and profound branches of science, practically
no thought being given to their mental experience in the past.
The results were not satisfactory.   A reaction followed in the
form of anti-higher-education views, and for a time these were
powerful enough to influence public opinion.   But judging in
the light of how our women fared with such higher education as
did exist for them, and also in view of information obtainable
from Europe and America, there is nothing to be feared as to
the future.   In any case, the general social tendency in this
country is all in the direction of a higher education for women.
But whether in the field of general education or of higher
education, the crying need is the creation of women favourably
developed in mind and body, possessing a noble character
and reasonably independent views.   They should be equally
well developed in mind, heart, and body, so that they may
better be able to discharge their natural duties as wives and
mothers.   If possible, they should be equipped with accomplishments which, if need be, will give them an independent living.
Further, as members of society they should strive to bring out
in full the special qualities of their sex, and be even possessed of
a noble aspiration to contribute towards the progress of the
country and take part in the general effort to elevate humanity
to a higher plane of enlightenment.   In these circumstances
our women are called upon to come forward with firm resolution
and burning enthusiasm such as shall sustain them in the
great work confronting them.

Our re-
sponsi-
bility.

Since the beginning of our history it has been the lot of
our daughters to feed on and digest imported civilizations, all
the time building up characteristics peculiar to themselves.
Latterly they have been drinking freely at the fount of Western
civilization, and, under the guidance of the new light illuminat-
ing their ancestral qualities, many of them are now engaged
in the work of educating their sisters of far Siam and Tibet,
and also of China, some at the behest of the royalties of those
countries.   On the other hand, the numbers of women, young
and grown up, coming to these shores from the countries of

the Asiatic continent and islands in search of education are yearly and monthly increasing. It is as though the day is at hand for our daughters to become the rallying point for their sisters of the whole Orient, and as such to take an active part on the world's stage. That they owe not a little to Western civilization in gaining such a position is admitted ; but when we reflect that the result is not less due to the tremendous power of advance and development which has always lain dormant in our women, the consciousness cannot but be most gratifying to us all. This thought also awakens in us a growing sense of the greatness of the responsibility that falls on the shoulders of those engaged in the work of educating our daughters. A question arises : ' What is it that we must never for a moment lose sight of as we strive to give a sound education to our daughters on the lines above indicated, and what is it that we should always endeavour to make our pupils and students remember and obey ? ' It is the Imperial Rescript on Education issued in 1890. No less important is it to bear in mind the unvarying and deep interest which Her Majesty the Empress has always taken in the education of our daughters. Thus encouraged and privileged, it behoves them to vow to render their share of service to the State, to the country, and to the cause of humanity generally.

XII

THE INTRODUCTION OF WESTERN PHILOSOPHY

Yūjirō Miyaké, D.Litt. (Japan)

No student of the history of Japan can fail to recognize that she has consistently progressed throughout the whole of her national career, and has done so whilst almost every other country of the so-called Orient—for instance, Korea, China, India, and Persia—has retrograded from a glorious past. Is the reason for this her geographical position? It is often so stated with much plausibility. Japan is an island empire and has a most extensive coast-line compared with her superficial area, and her fertile arable districts are divided into numerous sections by mountain ranges, the whole topographical aspect presenting a striking contrast to the insipid monotony of neighbouring continents. These peculiarities resemble in many respects those of the Greece of ancient history and the Great Britain of to-day. Undoubtedly this insular condition has been of the greatest advantage to Japan's homogeneity as a nation, whilst the mountainous nature of the country has bred a spirit of independence in different localities, and its various subdivisions have prevented the country from drifting into monotonous somnolence. So, too, with regard to her national thought: freedom of expression, combined with intercourse of ideas, has given it full scope for healthy development—a fact which also calls for special attention.

Unique geographical position of Japan.

Although the system of government in Old Japan was, in form, a despotic autocracy, tyranny did not exist, and of despotism few examples can be cited. There have been strong-handed rulers, but they have never been tyrants. Tyranny

Japan's government a lenient one.

226

was impossible, it would seem, even had the rulers been inclined towards it. Moreover, it is extremely rare to find, in the past, political power used for repressing freedom of thought. Not only with regard to the national thought, but also in the case of ideas introduced from abroad, free expression was allowed so far as it did not interfere with the peace of the State. Although there have been many bitter political struggles in the course of Japan's history, the progress of thought seldom suffered from them, and, even in the midst of internal strife, free intercourse of ideas was permitted. I need not here cite examples, for they will be found scattered over the pages of previous writers in the realms of politics, religion, and philosophy.

Freedom of thought.

Not only were the counsels of wise men considered and respected by the nation at large, but the rulers of different clans vied with each other in their eagerness to take into their service *literati* of fame and profound learning, and the centres of erudition and culture gravitated to localities where the greatest number were domiciled, nor were any artificial barriers placed in the path of learning. Those bent on study, either classical or theological, were allowed perfect freedom to go anywhere and at any time. Though the *Séido* was established in Yédo by the Shōgun's Government as the central seat of education, students flocked to any locality where a noted literate lived, either to Kyōto, or the capital of a fief, and instances were not rare of students from the northernmost province of Ōshū migrating to the southern island of Kyūshū. Among Buddhist priests it was an important part of their theological studies to travel the country in order to cultivate their mind and intellect, and there were not a few whose footsteps can be traced in every part of the empire. Among the Zen sect there was a curious custom of catechism, in which, if a head priest of a temple was worsted by his adversary—an itinerant priest in most cases—he was under the obligation of resigning his position in favour of his rival. Such a usage induced many an ambitious Zen priest to pay controversial visits to the temples throughout the country, and there are not wanting instances in which poor itinerant priests rose to fame by a single success.

Freedom of learning.

The state of learning in olden times has a certain analogy

with that of the German Confederation, the different states
of which, though politically rivals, keep an open door for
Confu-
cianism in
China.
students at their universities. Whilst in Japan both Confucian
ethics and Buddhist doctrine flourished, the reverse was the
case in the countries of their origin. It is difficult to say with
any degree of definiteness at what period the Confucian teaching reached its zenith in China, or to ascertain the extent to
which Confucian teaching morally affected Chinese society.
But it is certain that oftentimes its flourishing condition
was due to a mere whim of the Sovereign, and that its study
by such an one was accompanied by weakness in other directions, and in later times its retention by the State was mainly
due to its serving as a medium of examination for official
appointment.

Confu-
cianism
and
Buddhism
in Japan.
With regard to Buddhism, it had been declining for a long
period in its country of origin, India, before its arrival in Japan.
After its introduction into China, although its doctrines
flourished at one period with great splendour, it sank into
insignificance or degenerated into superstition with the lapse
of time, and there is hardly any pure Buddhism in China at the
present day. On the contrary, in Japan, although Confucianism and Buddhism, both of foreign origin and taught
by foreigners, occupied for a number of years a somewhat
inferior position, they ultimately came to be assimilated and
digested by the whole nation, who not only succeeded in
absorbing all the knowledge possessed by the expounders of
the two creeds, but even excelled, in many respects, the
countries in which they originated.

Assimilat-
ing power
of the
people.
That extensive abuses sprang up in connection with the
Confucian and the Buddhist doctrines can hardly be denied,
in view of the crowd of unworthy *literati* and Buddhist priests
whose names are on record. At the same time it is beyond
doubt that there were many men who earnestly applied themselves to master the real essence of the doctrine, regardless
of outside formalities, and who succeeded in their attempts.
Neither Confucianism nor Buddhism has ever reached its
zenith, for there is still a wide field left for further development.
But what was possible to be assimilated appears to have been
taken in, and if there is room for any unfavourable criticism

it must be attributed to lack of materials rather than to want of power of absorption on the part of the Japanese.

It is not, therefore, to be wondered at that Japan has been able to assimilate the learning of the West in a space of little more than half a century, when the profound previous culture it has had is taken into consideration.

Though surprised at the outset the Japanese quickly prepared themselves to supply what they lacked by appropriating the arts and sciences in which foreign nations excelled. At first subjects having direct concern with externals—namely, the welfare of the State and of the body—were naturally most paid attention to, and consequently military and medical sciences were first introduced. Politics and law followed, while physics and chemistry came in the train of medicine—sure tokens that the nation had rehabilitated its internal affairs. *Order of the importation of Western learning.*

The introduction of philosophical study into Japan might have taken place sooner if its condition had been more advanced in the United States, from which we first received it. But that nation being essentially practical, and the study of philosophy being there allied with religion, the incoming of philosophical ideas to our country was necessarily delayed. Among American philosophical books which were first introduced into Japan was ' Ethics ' by Professor Francis Wayland, the much-respected President of Brown University. His works were widely read by Japanese students just before and after the Restoration, and his ' Ethics ' and ' Political Economy ' were highly recommended at the time, both in America and Japan. *Philosophical study.* *Ethics.*

The first lectures on logic were given by Professor James Summers in the class-rooms of the *Kaiséi Gakkō* (afterwards the Tōkyō University) in 1873, the text-books used being Fowler's ' Deductive Logic ' and Mill's ' Logic.' In the following year Professor Syle lectured on psychology under the name of philosophy, using Hopkins's ' Study of Man ' and Haven's ' Mental Philosophy ' as text-books. Guizot's ' History of Civilization ' was used as the text-book of history, and was popularly used in such schools as the *Kéiō Gijuku* as a text-book of translation for the highest class, until it came *Logic.* *Psychology.* *History.*

about 1876–77 to be superseded in favour of Buckle's work, the civilization of Japan being made the theme of a special treatise at the time.   When the late Professor Toyama came back from the Michigan University, in 1876, he was appointed a professor in the *Kaiséi Gakkō*, and afterwards Professor of

Sociology.   Literature in the Tōkyō University.   During his connection with the University he gave lectures mostly based on Jevons's 'Logic,' Bain's 'Psychology,' Spencer's 'Biology,' 'Psychology,' and 'Sociology,' and John Fiske's 'Cosmic Philosophy'; he was also greatly instrumental in introducing the Spencerian doctrines among the student class.   About the same time Bentham's

Utilitar-   'Utilitarianism' began to be popularly read, the late Count
ianism.   Mutsu translating it into Japanese under the title of '*Rigaku Séiso*' during his imprisonment for a political offence.   There were other scholars who translated Montesquieu's 'Esprit des Lois' from the English version, and there was also a body of students, known as the pure French school, who concentrated their attention on the propagation of Rousseau's opinions. But by far the greatest impression produced upon the thinking

Darwinian   public of Japan was the advent of Professor E. S. Morse, who
theory.   spared no pains to introduce the theories advanced by Darwin and Huxley.   The Darwinian theory of man's descent from a monkey was in itself sufficient to surprise the Japanese students, and Professor Morse's eloquent discourses, accompanied by skilful figures on the black-board not only made a great impression on students, but also had a great influence on the public.   Together with Darwin's 'Descent of Man,' Spencer's theory of evolution naturally became very popular, and his principles of sociology appear to have been employed to interpret all social phenomena.   The late Professor Fenollosa, who came to Japan from Harvard University, gave lectures, together with Professor Morse.   His lectures on religion were,

Spen-   however, based on Spencer's 'Sociology.'   In short, Spencer
cerian   was supreme at the time, and Mr. Fukuzawa's '*Jiji Shōgen*,'
doctrine.   or 'Random Thoughts of the Time,' largely based on Galton's theory of heredity, is nothing but a reflection of the ideas in vogue at the epoch.   At this juncture Dr. Joseph Cook, visiting Tōkyō on his trip round the world, gave several lectures antagonistic to Professor Morse, and attacked Darwinism and the

Spencerian doctrines in the hope of undermining their influence. Owing, however, to the wide circulation of the Spencerian doctrine, the public had reached such a stage as to be competent to criticize his theories instead of blindly following them, and so Dr. Cook's lectures, though admired for their eloquence, were not convincing.

There was, at this era, another under-current at work. Professor Cooper had been, for some time, giving lectures on Kant's 'Critic,' and Professor Fenollosa commenced to lecture about 1880 on the history of philosophy from Descartes to Hegel, using Schwegler's work for reference on the subject. Bowen's 'Modern Philosophy' was also introduced, and was much read by students, who were able to follow the lectures by its aid. Fenollosa lectured also on Hegel's 'Logic' by Wallace. This was the turning-point of Japanese thinkers towards German philosophy. While Professor Toyama still remained an exponent of Spencer, and defended his 'First Principles,' the students who read Kant's 'Critic' and Hegel's 'Dialectics' grew dissatisfied with his idea of the unknowable. On metaphysical theories they gradually became estranged from the Spencerian and came to appreciate the post-Kantian and Hegelian doctrines. Professor Fenollosa's discourses, lacking in subtlety and exactness, gave an impression akin to that produced by scratching one's feet outside one's shoes, yet his eloquence had no small influence upon students. In one sense his attitude indicated the tendency of American learning at that time, for German philosophy was beginning to find its way into America, and lectures on the subject were heartily welcomed in the class-rooms of her universities. Fenollosa probably came to our country with the view of introducing the new tendency of thought which he had himself felt at home. Being impressed with the subtlety of Hegel's system, he was so much occupied in introducing it that he had not time to criticize it.

German philosophy.

In 1885 Dr. George W. Knox (at present professor in the Union Theological Seminary of New York) was invited to lecture at the Tōkyō University. He was followed by Professor Busse (at present professor at the Koenigsberg University). Both these inclined to the doctrines of Lotze, who at once began to attract many Japanese admirers, some of the

Other foreign professors in the University.

missionaries even sharing the inclination.   This fact shows that Japanese scholars had now come to give precedence to German philosophy.   But a change took place when Dr. Tetsujirō Inouyé (at present professor at the Imperial University in Tōkyō) came back from his studies in Germany in 1890, and rather undervalued Lotze, going to the length of declaring that it was doubtful whether Lotze clearly understood what he wrote about.   Professor Busse was followed by Professor Koeber, who still occupies the chair at the Imperial University of Tōkyō and who is regarded as a man well qualified to interpret German philosophy.   He is much esteemed by students on account of his high personal qualities.   He apparently belongs to no particular school, but appears to be intent upon the eclectic study of all philosophers, choosing those that are best worth studying.   Nevertheless his views give more or less the impression of a decided hue of Schopenhauer.   But whatever may be the popularity of a professor in the class-room, students nowadays are fully awake to the general tendency of Occidental philosophy.

About the year 1898 the name of the late Professor Paulsen of Berlin University, following that of Professor Wundt, came to the front in Japan, being regarded as a great authority on the subject of philosophy, and his opinions bearing on the main features were largely quoted.   The 'History of Philosophy,' by Professor Windelband of Strassburg University, and the 'Elements of Philosophy,' by Professor Kuelpe of Würzburg University, are also much used for reference.   Green, fitly known as the Hegel of England, is now attracting the general attention of thinkers, his theory on the realization of self being regarded as a valuable key to ethical interpretation, and he is an instance of the fact that, although the study of philosophy in our country appears to be entirely Germanized, yet, as a matter of fact, German philosophy is made intelligible to our students rather in its Anglo-Saxonized form than in its original state.

Anglo-Saxonized German philosophy.

At this juncture a fact which caused commotion among the thinking public was the introduction of Nietzsche.   He has been much criticized in his own country, but has largely held the attention of thinkers in Japan, although his bold opinions

Nietzsche-ism.

appear only to have satisfied the curiosity of a certain set, and, generally speaking, Green and Paulsen are still the most extensively followed.

Since 1906 a Faculty of Literature has been established at the Kyōto Imperial University, the philosophical section being under Professor Kuwaki and Assistant-Professor Tomonaga.

In 1884 the professors and students of philosophy at the Tōkyō University inaugurated a philosophical association in co-operation with other persons interested in philosophy, which issues a monthly magazine on matters connected with philosophy. The publication has reached a little more than two hundred numbers, and, though it cannot be considered a very important organ, it must not be ignored. *Philosophical association.*

Works on philosophy published in Japanese are increasing year by year, and it is now possible to become acquainted with the general principles of philosophy without the aid of the works of foreign writers. In psychology, Haven was translated into Japanese at an early date, and from 1877 onwards Bain was popularly studied, with Carpenter's and Maudsley's works for reference. In and after 1883 Sully was widely read. Professor Wundt's name was as comparatively unknown in Japan as in his native country for a long time. *Philosophical books in Japanese.*

The new psychology was introduced into Japan for the first time when Professor Motora (at present professor at the Imperial University in Tōkyō) returned from Johns Hopkins University and began to lecture on psycho-physics. From this time forward, psychological investigation became experimental, the attempt being to measure and explain all mental phenomena by means of instruments, statistics, and numerical calculations. That psychological investigation must be based upon experiment has now become an established principle, the merit of which must chiefly be attributed to Wundt. There are, however, few who have attempted the translation of his works, though he is considered a great authority on the subject in Japan. Being too voluminous for ordinary text-books, they have not been translated into Japanese except in detached portions. A work like that of Hoeffding is more popular, having been translated into Japanese for the use of students. Although the study of psychology in Japan appears *New psychology.*

to have entirely fallen under the supremacy of the Germans, the lectures of such men as Professor Ladd of Yale University, who visited Japan for the purpose, have also made their influence felt. As to Professor William James of Harvard University, not only have his works been translated into Japanese, but he is considered in some respects to be superior even to Wundt, so that at least in the category of names Germany has not had a monopoly.

There are at present many scholars who carry on original investigations, as Professor Motora and Dr. Fukurai, the latter of whom is making special researches into hypnotism. At the Kyōto Imperial University Professor M. Matsumoto is in charge of the same subject, an experimental laboratory having been established.

Ethics.   In the department of ethics the works of Wayland, Hopkins, Janet, Sidgwick, Muirhead, Green, and Paulsen are much used, Professor Nakashima being in charge of the faculty at the Tōkyō Imperial University, and Assistant-Professor Tomoéda at the Kyōto Imperial University.   There are various associations for the advancement of moral education, the *Nippon Kōdōkwai* (Japanese Association for the Propagation of Morals), founded by the late Dr. Nishimura in 1876, being still existent. For the investigation of practical problems the *Téiyū Rinrikwai* is considered more important.

Sociology.   The study of sociology in Japan traces its origin to the works of Guizot, Buckle (' History of Civilization '), and Carey ('Political Economy '); while, at one period, Spencer's 'Principles of Sociology' was most widely read, Dr. Nagao Ariga publishing his ' Social Evolution ' in Japanese. From about 1887 Ward's ' Dynamic Sociology ' has been a favourite study. After him Gumplowicz and Giddings were held in high esteem among students of sociology, the latter's work having been translated into Japanese. At present Professor Takébé occupies the chair at the Tōkyō Imperial University, and is engaged in inaugurating a new departure.

Comparative religion.   With regard to the study of comparative religion, Professor Max Müller's works have been assiduously studied by a certain set of scholars, for the reason that Dr. Nanjō and Kasahara studied Sanskrit under him and subsequently served as assistants for a certain number of years. A chair of Comparative Religion has lately been created in the Tōkyō Imperial University : it is occupied by Professor Anézaki, who claims to have succeeded in discovering the connecting link between Christianity and Buddhism. The Max Müller Library now in our possession will be of great advantage to students of Sanskrit as well as to those of comparative religion. At the Kyōto Imperial University Professor B. Matsumoto, of the Faculty of Literature, holds the chair of Hindu Philosophy.

As to æsthetics, Williams's and Hartmann's works have been translated into Japanese, while the works of Bosanquet are also widely read. At present Professor Ōtsuka holds the chair at the Tōkyō Imperial University, and as a chair has also been created at the Kyōto Imperial University, a special professor is expected to be appointed there also. *Æsthetics.*

To sum up : Western philosophy first came into Japan through England and America. German philosophy, which influenced the Anglo-Saxon philosophy, began to assume ascendancy in Japan about 1880, and since 1887 it has enjoyed absolute predominance, but its influence is limited mainly to scholars and students, and there is some difficulty in saying to what extent it has affected the popular mind. Though not strictly belonging to the province of pure philosophy, the theory of evolution advanced by Darwin and Spencer has exercised a far-reaching influence upon the ideas of ordinary thinking men. Readers of their works have decreased in number, yet the theory itself still retains a strong hold upon the popular mind. Haeckel's works have also been widely read, and his ' Riddle of the Universe ' has been translated into Japanese. Dr. Baron Katō, formerly President of the Tōkyō University, though originally an exponent of the German school, has entirely discarded German philosophy and is attempting to interpret all phenomena, both natural and human, in accordance with the Darwinian theory of selection. It is somewhat strange, however, that with regard to politics his views are thoroughly German, for he rejects the idea of liberty as formulated by the English school of Spencer. *A general statement.*

Whether Spencer's theory of liberty or his theory on

Followers of Spencer.

evolution has had the greater influence upon the popular mind it is hard to tell. The Liberal party in Japan, which, at the time of its formation, adopted the principles of liberty advanced at the time of American Independence and the French Revolution, gradually came to modify their views, and adopted, to a great extent, the opinions of Spencer as their political platform: even a man like Count Itagaki, the founder of the Liberal party, being among the strong advocates of the English philosopher's opinions. At about the time of the promulgation of the Constitution, when political views were not so simple as formerly, the people who inclined toward the Liberal party still relied upon Spencer, and the importance with which

Laband and Bornhak.

he was regarded by the public may well be likened to the weight attached to the theories of Laband and Bornhak by a certain section of Japanese officialdom.

The people in general are, however, perfectly satisfied with the verdict of common sense, under whose guidance they make no grievous mistakes, leaving the study and investigation of philosophical subjects to specialists. With regard to the basis of ethics, it may be safely affirmed that ethical opinions are, on the whole, very moderate. Extreme opinions advanced at times are limited to a minority of prejudiced elders or inexperienced youths, no radical views worthy of name having yet taken deep root in the minds of the people.

The works which were chiefly instrumental in disseminating the philosophical ideas of the West most widely and in the simplest manner among the young men of Japan were evidently

Carlyle and Emerson.

those of Carlyle and Emerson, especially the latter. Though showing a tinge of German ideas, they were largely circulated in company with the general diffusion of the English language. There are among the Unitarians many who have adopted Emerson's works as their standard, and the so-called rejuvenated Buddhism, though partaking, to a greater or less extent, of the theories of Hegel, may well be replaced by the opinions propounded by Emerson.

In all matters pertaining to science and philosophy Germany long held the supremacy here as elsewhere, but of late signs of anti-German reaction are to be noted in Japan. The fact that

Demolin's 'Anglo-Saxon Superiority,' introduced into Japan some years ago, has enjoyed so much popularity here may be taken as a sure indication of the change, the book having been translated and widely read by the Japanese. Although it is customary, even at present, to send students to Germany in large numbers, they do not commit themselves to German ideas to the extent they did formerly. While filled with admiration at the state of learning in Germany, people feel that something is lacking, something higher and purer than the German intellect can give, and even in matters relating to scientific opinion the Germans are not blindly followed. 'Anglo-Saxon Superiority.'

Up to the present, Germany, with great show of reason, has been looked upon as a leading factor in philosophy. It is, however, doubtful whether she will be able to retain her exalted position.

In company with the immense progressive strides that different branches of science have made in Germany, philosophy may also be stimulated to a certain extent. Yet it is open to doubt whether the so-called pure German philosophy has not been checked in its growth. Kuno Fischer, a great authority on the history of philosophy, especially the modern, has not initiated a single original opinion of his own, though he has so thoroughly analysed the opinions of other great philosophers and expounded points which the authors themselves did not think of. This may be taken as an evidence of the check experienced in the growth of pure German philosophy. It is a question how it will be developed hereafter, and though the theories of Schopenhauer and Hegel are imposing as systems of philosophy, it is hard to tell how they will be developed hereafter. Even a man like Lotze, acknowledged as the greatest philosopher after Hegel, has had such an end. Studying the 'Critic' of Kant, he inaugurated his theory of epistemology as a rejuvenated Kantian school, and, although he succeeded in treating the subject more in detail, it is doubtful whether he could reconstruct that branch of mental science known from old as philosophy. Philosophers from ancient days have striven to grasp a solution of the problem of the universe, and epistemology, though it may be able to furnish a partial solution and may well be placed on the Future of German philosophy.

same standing as Ethics or Æsthetics, can hardly be said to embrace the whole domain of philosophy. If the works of such men as Schopenhauer and Hegel are to be taken as the standard of pure German philosophy, we need not go to Germany alone, for there are many works in Hindoo philosophy which treat of similar subjects. Though Hindoo philosophy falls far behind German in minuteness of analysis, the former excels in many points of organization. The 'Zend-Avesta' of Schopenhauer and the 'Zarathustra' of Nietzsche may be outcomes of the influence of Oriental philosophy. It is most probable that by scrutinizing the bulky literature of Hindoo philosophy the greater part of the so-called pure German philosophy may be obtained. The difference between the Oriental philosophy based on the Hindoo, and the Occidental based on the German, lies in the amount of scientific experiment. Eliminate experimental investigation and there is not much difference left between the Oriental and the Occidental systems. The characteristics of Occidental philosophy become more prominent in proportion to the amount of scientific investigation contained, and it is the English school of experimentalists that has succeeded in enhancing this characteristic of Occidental philosophy. The 'Critic' of Kant is the product of such influence. The epistemology, acknowledged as consisting of pure investigation without any assumptions, may be considered, from surrounding circumstances, as an approach to scientific investigation. The term 'scientific investigation' is somewhat vague in its significance, and the system being as yet in the first stage of development, whether it will be firmly established or not must be decided by actual proofs rather than by words. There are many assumptions as yet; but to reject assumptions merely as such may be likened to a pigeon which flies off in search of a vacuum, being afraid of the atmospheric resistance.

In Germany great progress has been made in all branches of learning, and she excels England, in certain respects, in scientific investigation. In the realms of psychology and biology the same is the case, and what was once acknowledged as the English characteristic is to be found in a greater degree in Germany at present. Such a tendency may, however, have the effect

Hindoo philosophy. (marginal note)

of removing the German philosophy farther from its original course. Although German philosophy may make continued progress, it will be in a direction entirely different from what was known as the German school. It is a matter of the past to view philosophy and the history of philosophy as synonymous. In what other branches of learning is such an anomaly now seen ? Students of natural philosophy would ridicule the idea of confounding natural philosophy with its history. The two terms may, it is true, be synonymous to a certain extent, but it must be deemed an utter fallacy to confound them *in toto*.

In the new development of German philosophy recourse is had to the aid of science. Although Hartmann bases his opinions chiefly on Schopenhauer, his principal merit lies in his having accumulated a great number of scientific facts. Lotze being a profound physiologist, his theories bearing on physiology are most worthy of attention, while Wundt was also a learned physiologist, and his chief merit lies in his having explained the psychical action by means of physiology. Haeckel was a pure biologist, and all of them have proved their powers by means of science. But the question arises, Are these methods sufficient to satisfy the wants of philosophy, and may they not be due to failure in applying science rather than to want of metaphysical investigation ? To whatever extent the problem of the relation of mind to body may be solved by means of physiology, and the relation of human species in the world of living organisms by means of biology, these are nothing but mere spots on the earth, and may be said to have little effect in solving the problem of the almost infinite universe. Recourse must be had to such branches of science as kinetic astronomy, physical astronomy, and many others. The progress of philosophy ought to go hand in hand with that of science, although there are many matters which cannot be covered by scientific investigation only, and must be accomplished by recourse to the philosophy of the old school. The epistemological problems must certainly be organized according to the epistemology of the present day, but, at the same time, they must have the aid of every other branch of science for their solution, otherwise philosophy will remain a merely tentative solution of the universe. Only Spencer and Hegel have succeeded in some

Value of modern German philosophy.

measure in accumulating scientific facts of all descriptions and solving problems not possible by means of Oriental philosophy alone. The future development of philosophy depends upon the practical use to which scientific investigations are put.

Oriental philoso- phy.

Confucianism and Buddhism are studied under the de- signation of Oriental philosophy in Japan; and although the methods of investigation employed by old Confucian *literati* and Buddhist priests were very imperfect, yet they suc- ceeded in solving many problems, and those prominent among them appear to have been able to master recesses of philosophy more profound even than the German philosophy. Viscount Kunitaké Watanabé, formerly Minister of Finance, is of opinion that all philosophical ideas of the West are trace- able in the doctrines of the Zen sect of Buddhists—a view worthy of serious consideration.

If Germany may be taken as the leader of philosophy, Japan has no reason to despair of equalling or even excelling her. The reason why the works of such men as Hegel and Schopenhauer are not regarded with much surprise here is because similar ideas were already extant. What is wanting in Oriental philosophy is scientific investigation, and on that account it has fallen below Western philosophy. If progress is made in scientific investigation in Japan there should be no difficulty in rivalling Germany. Germany may well be proud of her splendid systems of philosophy, which are still pursued with assiduity. However, just as Rome, with her monuments of ancient civilization still extant, such as the Coliseum and the marble baths of Caracalla, experiences not a little difficulty in developing herself into the capital of renovated Italy, so must Germany, with her splendid and various systems of philosophy, experience the same difficulty, at the present moment, in realizing her hopes of new development. In Japan there is no system of philosophy worthy of the name, and nothing to prevent a creation of a new one, notwithstanding the fact that she has had such a lengthy training. If Japan only succeeds in assimilating the scientific knowledge of the world there is nothing whatever to prevent her from becoming foremost in philosophy among the countries of the earth. She

Prospect of Japanese philoso- phy.

has been, up to the present, entirely occupied in assimilating the vast array of scientific knowledge of other countries, and only time will prove to what extent she can succeed in the domain of philosophy.   The problem in Japan is not one of the past half-century, but one of the next cycle.

XIII

MATHEMATICO-PHYSICAL SCIENCE IN JAPAN

Professor Jōji Sakurai, Tōkyō Imperial University,
D.Sc. (Japan), LL.D.

Forty years only have elapsed since Western science was transplanted into this country; yet, owing in a measure to the fertility of the soil, it has grown with such rapidity and to such an extent that every branch of it would require one specialist, at least, to furnish an account of its development with anything like completeness. The number and variety of important papers issued in the *Memoirs of the Science Department*, the *Journal of the College of Science*, the *Bulletin of the College of Agriculture*, and other publications of the Tōkyō Imperial University; the Publications and Reports of the Earthquake Investigation Committee, the Journals and Proceedings of the several learned societies, and even the recently started *Bulletin of the College of Science and Engineering*, Kyōto Imperial University, bear witness to the correctness of this statement.

For the purpose of the present work, however, it has been considered to be both unnecessary and undesirable to enter into voluminous details, but to divide the subject broadly into Mathematico-Physical Science and Natural Science, and it is with the former of these that the writer has now to deal, Professor Mitsukuri taking charge in the following paper of the latter. In spite of this limitation the writer is perfectly aware of the great difficulty of his task, and would not have undertaken it had he not been convinced of the importance of placing on record the development of science in this country, and had he not been assured by his friends and colleagues of assistance in their own special departments.

It has been freely asserted that the rapid progress of modern science in Japan is mainly due to the pre-existence of circumstances favourable to its healthy growth.   One of these circumstances is the high degree of culture attained during the past, and especially during the period of seclusion.   For so early as the eighth century, in the reign of the Emperor Mommu, regulations were promulgated providing for the organization of a university in the capital, with a local school in each of the provinces.   Many important private schools also sprang up in various parts of the country, and all these institutions, which attracted a large number of students, contributed in no small degree to the general promotion of learning.   But a long period of political disturbance, during which education was thrust into the background, soon followed, and it was not until the beginning of the seventeenth century, when Iyéyasu, the first and greatest of the Tokugawa Shōguns, established the seat of government at Yédo, that peace was restored, and with it educational activity.   Successive Shōguns promoted the cause of education, and under their patronage, during a long period of tranquillity, extending for over two centuries and a half, it attained a high degree of development throughout the country.

Culture in the Feudal Age.

A central and highest seat of learning, the celebrated *Shōhéikō*, was established at Yédo, to which scholars were invited from every quarter, and the attendance of students was much encouraged by liberal endowments.   Each *daimyate* had high schools, founded by the feudal lord for the education of his retainers' children.   Although higher education was in these times essentially classical and, as a rule, restricted to the upper classes, and therefore cannot be said to have been either general in its scope or universal in its extent, the degree of development attained was a fair one, and not only were large numbers of valuable works of art and literature produced, but philosophical and literary inquiry also attained a considerable degree of activity.   It was this culture which enabled the Japanese people to qualify themselves for the study of Western science and for the assimilation of Western ideas and institutions.

Tokugawa era.

Another circumstance which has contributed more directly

R 2

True cause of the rapid development.

to the rapid development of Western science in Japan is the strong aspiration for its study which manifested itself from an early period. The Portuguese and the Spanish, during the first half of the sixteenth century, were the first to bring some of their arts to Japan, but they were destined to be entirely replaced by the Dutch, who began to trade with us somewhat later. Religious reasons, which have been spoken of in an earlier chapter (Vol. I, p. 17), led the Tokugawa Government, in 1638, to adopt a policy of seclusion and to expel all foreigners from the country, except the Dutch, who alone were allowed to pay occasional visits to our shores, and it was through them that the arts and sciences of the West were gradually introduced. Surgery and medicine particularly took root in the land, for foreign arts of healing were regarded as miraculous. But study was carried on under almost insuperable difficulties, on account of the existence of the law prohibiting the importation of all European books,[1] and of the difficulty of reading them. Besides, anti-foreign feelings were both strong and general.

Dutch learning.

In spite of these difficulties, which, in not a few cases, even cost students their lives, the scholars of Dutch made greater and greater exertions to improve themselves and to propagate Western ideas, and the lives of these men afford us noble examples of endurance and self-denial. This spirit and this craving for the knowledge of the West have thus been inherited through ages, and it was, therefore, only natural that, when once the door of Japan was opened and Western science was introduced into our system of education, its study and cultivation should have been prosecuted with zeal and success.

Opening of the country to Western learning.

It cannot, either, be doubted that the general diffusion of the English language has made access to the field of knowledge incomparably easier, and the zeal and energy with which the American and European professors early engaged in our educational work taught us to study science for its own sake. Last, and by no means least, the facilities invariably afforded by foreign universities to Japanese students, who have thus been enabled to gather the best fruit of their studies and bring

[1] Exceptions were made by the eighth Shōgun, Yoshimuné, in the case of non-religious books.

it back with them, have contributed to the rapid and healthy development of science in this country.

Not only is science now taught and cultivated in the Imperial Universities, but it also forms an important portion of the subjects in the High Schools, the Technical High Schools, the Higher Normal Schools, the Higher Commercial Schools, the Higher Agricultural Schools, and Special Medical Schools—all of which are provided with properly equipped chemical and physical laboratories for giving more or less extended practical instruction to students, and important scientific work has been done in some, at least, of these institutions. From an educational point of view, it may be worth adding that scientific subjects enter largely into the curriculum of study of all the secondary schools, whether public or private, and that the number of these secondary schools where provisions are made for giving practical exercises in simple chemical and physical experiments to the boys and girls is more and more increasing.

Institutions for the study of modern sciences.

While thus busily engaged in the scientific education of her sons, Japan has always shown herself ready and willing to associate with other nations in any important scientific undertaking, as may be seen from the fact that, besides sending delegates to almost all the International Scientific Congresses, she is represented on the International Seismological Committee, the International Geodetic Association, and the International Catalogue of Scientific Literature, the number of ' slips ' sent to the Central Bureau in London in connection with the last-mentioned work, during the four years 1901–4, amounting to 3600. The above facts, taken in conjunction with another— namely, that Japan was a feudal country less than fifty years ago, will give an idea of the rapidity and extent of the development of science in this country.

Connection with international scientific associations.

The Tōkyō Imperial University has been the centre of this development, and what follows here is essentially a sketch of the scientific work of this institution, with a short historical introduction in each case ; the particular subjects to be treated in this chapter being Mathematics, Astronomy, Physics, and Chemistry, together with Seismology and Meteorology. Although neither seismology nor meteorology forms a special

Tōkyō University.

course of study in the University, both have attained a comparatively high state of development in recent years, and one of them, moreover, is a peculiarly Japanese science.

MATHEMATICS

Mathe-
matics in
Japan. Mathematics has a special claim to be first considered in any history of Science in Japan, for it was the only one to be developed to any considerable extent during the period of seclusion, through the foundation of a school for the special purpose of its study. Séki, born in 1642, the same year as Newton, and a man of exceptional mathematical ability and originality, was its founder, and it is worthy of remark that neither the mathematics of this school had a foreign origin nor did its later development receive any assistance from external sources. True, in very old days something of Chinese mathematics found its way into Japan, and, after the introduction of the abacus by Mōri at the end of the sixteenth century, it made certain advances, but, apparently, not beyond the simplest rudiments of algebra and geometry. Again, Hayashi is stated to have learned and taught something of Western mathematics during the first half of the seventeenth century, but no traces of this appear to have been left. Be that as it may, the mathematics cultivated by Séki and his school was, in many respects, much unlike that of the West, and there seems to be not the least doubt that it had a purely Japanese origin.

Japan's
history of
mathe-
matics. Mr. Endō, to his great credit, compiled some years ago a complete history of old Japanese mathematics, retaining its peculiar nomenclature and notation; while Baron Kikuchi and Professor Fujisawa have both done valuable services in this Old
mathe-
matics
explained. connection : the former, in a series of papers published in the Proceedings of the Tōkyō Mathematico-Physical Society, has explained, in the clear and intelligent language of modern mathematics, several of the methods of the old Japanese mathematicians, with their mysterious and clumsy operations wrapped in obscure phraseology ; the latter, in an admirable paper read at the Second International Congress of Mathematics held in Paris in 1900, has given a concise account of the work of Séki and some of his disciples. To these three authors the writer is under a deep obligation for important information, but more especially to Professor Fujisawa, upon whose paper the following condensed account of the work of Séki and his school is very largely based.

In reducing every mathematical operation to writing, Séki. instead of dealing with the bamboo-rods which were in vogue up to his time, Séki was enabled to introduce an improved notation, which led him to numerous important discoveries in algebra, accompanied by a sudden expansion of its domain. Among his discoveries may be mentioned the calculus of finite differences; some ideas of limits, infinites, and infinitesimals; the theory—most probably algebraical—of maxima and minima; summation of a certain class of series; the so-called principle of the circle, including some methods of rectification, quadrature and cubature of curves and surfaces.

'The so-called *Principle of the Circle*, which in the absence of any suitable name, is translated from the original, seems to be the climax of Séki's discoveries, and is held by men of the old school to be comparable with the discovery of the infinitesimal calculus by Newton and Leibnitz. It appears to consist in an ingenious application of the idea of limits and the summation of infinite series to problems which nowadays belong to the geometrical application of the integral calculus. My opinion is that the so-called "principle of the circle" is a name given to the aggregate of various methods of rectification, quadrature and cubature of curves and surfaces without the formal use of differential and integral calculus, very much like the methods which were in vogue prior to the times of Bernoulli and Euler, such as those to be found in the work of Wallis. No doubt this name was given to the method because the latter was first found in connection with the rectification of the circle' (Fujisawa).

According to the usage of those times, most of Séki's important discoveries were, during his lifetime, kept secret among a select few of his immediate disciples, of whom Araki and Takebé were the best known, and were only published in a fragmentary form after his death.

The 'principle of the circle' appears to have always been a Ajima. favourite subject of study with Séki's school, and its most successful applications are, perhaps, due to Ajima, who, during the latter half of the eighteenth century, further advanced the mathematics of the old school. Instead of occupying himself with finding the entire periphery and the entire area of a circle, as had been the aim of his predecessors, he showed how the area of any sector may first be found and then the length of any arc of a circle, and he was led to formulate a complete theory of integration based upon the summation of infinite series. A complete theory of spherical trigonometry is also to be attributed to him. Wada—another mathematician of this school—whose work was done mostly in the early part of the last century, published, among other things, an improved method of finding the length of a circular arc, which was so far developed that it did not essentially differ from the modern method.

Wada.

The above brief account will show that mathematics under a peculiar form was developed to a considerable extent during the period of seclusion, and yet this mathematics is now entirely obsolete. The reason is not difficult to find. Not only was its language utterly obscure, but its methods were, as a rule, of a most haphazard nature, as may be exemplified from this—that it took Iwata, one of the latest and most typical of the old Japanese mathematicians, nearly two years of arduous labour to solve a certain theorem, and fifty-two sheets of paper to give its solution, and yet, as Professor Kikuchi observes, ' if he had known the modern methods the solution could have been set down in a few lines.' Moreover, controversies and even petty jealousies between various sub-schools, which came to be established among these mathematicians in later years, were rife, and problem challenges were their frequent occupation, they keeping their discoveries secret for the purpose. Such mathematics and such a spirit were both wholly incompatible with the new light which Japan was about to see. With her opening to the West, and her subsequent Restoration, and the promulgation of a code of education, the mathematics of the old school was entirely put out of sight, and, in its stead, a mathematics ' which has no schools, and whose universal language is intelligible to all civilized nations,' was systematically introduced.

Old mathematics now entirely obsolete.

It is true that, some years before the Restoration, elements of Western mathematics were already known, and, in 1863, they were, for the first time, taught at the *Kaiséijo* by the late Baron Kanda. So, too, some European works on elementary mathematics were translated by Yanagawa and others, but it was only after the Restoration that systematic study began. Even for some years afterwards mathematics was not separated from other branches of science, but was either included in the course of Engineering, as at the *Kaiséi Gakkō* and the old Engineering College, or studied together with Physics and Astronomy, as was the case in the earlier days of the Tōkyō University. But even in this form it made great advances.

It was during this period that Dr. (now Baron) Kikuchi, after having studied mathematics for some years at Cambridge, where he greatly distinguished himself, returned home and was appointed the first Japanese Professor of Mathematics in the Tōkyō University, just then reorganized. During a long and unbroken service of twenty-one years, from his first appointment as Professor of Mathematics in 1877 down to 1898, when he assumed the Presidency of the Tōkyō Imperial University, Dr. Kikuchi greatly advanced the position of this branch of science in Japan, not only by his personal teaching, but also by promoting and encouraging its study in various ways. It was chiefly through his efforts that a special course in Mathematics was, for the first time, estab- lished in 1881. In the founding of the Tōkyō Mathematical Society in 1877, and more especially in its reorganization into the present Tōkyō Mathematico-Physical Society seven years later, he was one of the most active promoters. Refer- ence has already been made to a series of interesting papers on the Mathematics of the old Japanese school published by him in the Proceedings of the last-named Society, and these papers throw light into regions previously almost totally dark. His excellent text-books on geometry have done immense service in aiding eager students in their studies, while his popular writings and lectures have invariably had the happy effect of propagating mathematical ideas among the non-mathematical, and of exciting interest in, if not creating a taste for, this abstract science. As Director of the Department (later College) of Science, organizer and President of the Earthquake Investigation Committee, and in various other capacities, he also promoted the study of other branches of science in no small degree.

Dr. Fujisawa.

The appointment of Dr. Fujisawa as Professor of Mathematics, in 1887, to be the colleague of Professor Kikuchi, was marked by further progress in the study of this branch of science. He was one of the three students of the Tōkyō University who first graduated in the course of Physics in 1882, and who were all destined to become men of eminence. Unlike the others, however, he devoted himself afterwards to the special study of mathematics, pursuing it further for some years in Strassburg, and also in Berlin, under the late Professor Kronecker, and, in common with German mathematicians, he laid much stress upon the importance of Higher Analysis. It was he who, in Japan, inaugurated the study of the Theory of Functions, both general and special, and he it was who organized a Mathematical Seminary in the College of Science, which, it need hardly be said, added much to the efficiency of mathematical studies. Besides the paper on the Mathematics of the old Japanese school, already referred to, Professor Fujisawa has made some important contributions to modern mathematics—as have also Professors Takagi and Sakai, both of whom are his colleagues and former pupils—and has published them in the *Journal of the College of Science* and in the Proceedings of the Tōkyō Mathematico-Physical Society, but it is beyond the power of the writer to analyse them, even if the limited scope of this chapter allowed it.

Tōkyō Mathematico-Physical Society.

The Tōkyō Mathematico-Physical Society mentioned above, which, as already incidentally stated, was organized in 1884, counts well over two hundred members. It meets once a month for the reading of papers and their discussion, and its Proceedings contain valuable communications on mathematical, physical, and astronomical subjects.

ASTRONOMY

Old Astronomy.

The history of Astronomy in Old Japan is almost entirely that of almanac compilation. One notable and creditable divergence is, however, to be found in the publication

of a book, entitled 'Rekishō Shinsho' (' New Treatise on
Astronomy '), by Shizuki, at the end of the eighteenth century.
There is nothing very remarkable about the book itself, which
was, for the most part, compiled from a Dutch translation of
John Keill's work, with occasional notes and additions by the
compiler, but it treated of astronomical and physical subjects
which were novel in this country at the time.   But the extraordinary point is, that, in the appendix to the third and last
volume, he published a view of the formation of the Universe,
which was nothing less than the Nebular Hypothesis, and which
covered much the same ground as the view put forward by
Laplace in 1796.   Attention was first called to it by Mr. Kanō
in an article published in the ' Tōyō Gakugéi Zasshi' (Oriental
Journal of Sciences and Arts), xii. 294, to which the reader
must be referred for details.   It is true that there is a good
deal of crudeness in Shizuki's ideas ; but it appears certain
that he came to these ideas quite independently of Western
philosophers, and much credit is due to him for discussing
a subject of such vast theoretical importance at a time when
science was almost wholly unknown, and when astronomy
was synonymous with astrology.

True, distinction was made between astronomers and
astrologers even from the remotest period, but only in name ;
or, rather, if Astrology is the art of telling events, good or
evil, by observing stars, then the astronomers were astrologers
and the astrologers compilers of almanacs.   It would be
quite out of place here to go into the history of almanac
compilation ; suffice it to say that a difference of nearly two
days between actual events and the calendar, which had
been adopted from China more than eight hundred years
previously, and the non-occurrence of eclipses mentioned in the
calendar, led to the abolition of the old and the introduction
of a new calendar—namely, the Téikyō Calendar—in 1685,
under the direction of one Yasui, who was afterwards made
astronomer to the Tokugawa Shōgun.   But this calendar was
again modified before very long upon more attention being
paid to the matter.   Yoshimuné, the eighth Shōgun, took a
special interest in astronomy, and, in 1744, caused an astronomical observatory to be established at Kanda, equipping

Astro-
nomers
and astro-
logers.

Téikyō
Calendar.

Shōgun
Yoshi-
muné.
The first
observa-
tory in
Japan.

it with meridian and other instruments, mostly of his own make. As the Téikyō Calendar already showed some deviation, he invited Nishigawa to introduce necessary corrections, which were further modified on several occasions, until the present solar calendar was adopted in 1872.

The observatory, after a temporary closure, was re-established in 1765 at Ushigomé, and removed to Asakusa seventeen years later. It was in this observatory that, in 1811, a bureau of translation was established, which subsequently became an educational institution and has since grown into a part of the present Imperial University at Tōkyō.

Compilation of almanacs.

After the Restoration, the work of compiling almanacs was placed in charge of the Astronomical Bureau established at Yushima, was afterwards transferred to the Department of Home Affairs, and was ultimately placed in charge of the Tōkyō Imperial University. An astronomical observatory attached to the Navy Department was established at Azabu —the seat of the present Tōkyō Astronomical Observatory— while a University observatory was erected at Hongō for the purpose of giving practical instructions in astronomical observations to a certain section of the students.

Tōkyō Observatory.

The present Tōkyō Astronomical Observatory arose out of the amalgamation of the astronomical section of the Department of Home Affairs and the astronomical observatory of the Navy Department with the University observatory; it has been placed under the control of the University since 1887, with Dr. Térao, Professor of Astronomy in the College of Science, as its Director. Besides being occupied with astronomical observations, the compilation of almanacs, and the instruction of University students, it gives the standard mean time every noon to the Tōkyō Post and Telegraphic Office, whence it is distributed to all telegraphic stations throughout the empire, and also furnishes corrected time by telegraph for the noon signals at Tōkyō, Yokohama, and Kōbé.

Standard mean time of Japan.

The standard mean time of Japan, mentioned above, is that of the 135th meridian, east of Greenwich. The necessity for uniform methods of counting longitude and time was long felt by all civilized nations, and the Washington Prime Meridian Congress of 1884, at which Japan was represented by Professor Kikuchi, rightly decided in favour of Greenwich as the origin from which to count both longitude and time. In choosing the standard mean time of Japan, the fact that it could be easily compared with Greenwich time had to be considered, and, on a representation being made to the Government—chiefly by Professor Kikuchi—the 135th meridian time has been uniformly adopted since January 1, 1887, differing from Greenwich time by exactly nine hours, and not differing from the natural time at any place in the whole of Japan by more than half an hour. The time used in Formosa differs an hour from the above.

Among other kinds of work undertaken in the Tōkyō Astronomical Observatory may be mentioned solar and stellar photography—the latter having led to the discovery of a new asteroid by Professor Hirayama some years ago, named by him ' Tōkyō '—and also the determination of the variation of latitude. The last-named work, to which reference will again be made under Seismology, was begun ten years ago by Dr. Kimura, who is now in charge of the Observatory at Mizusawa, specially established for the purpose by the Imperial Goedetic Commission. It may be mentioned that Mizusawa is one of the four localities officially chosen by the International Goedetic Association, on the parallel of north latitude 39° 8', for studying the movement of the pole. *Solar and stellar photography.* *Determination of the variation of latitude.*

On several occasions astronomical expeditions have been successfully carried out for the observation of total solar eclipses, and the reports of these and other observations are embodied in the ' *Annales de l'Observatoire Astronomique de Tōkyō.*' *Observations of total solar eclipses.*

PHYSICS

Shizuki's book, already referred to under Astronomy, was not merely an astronomical work, it was also a treatise on Physics. The first volume dealt with the rotation and path of planets, their magnitudes, and other astronomical questions; but in the second and third volumes subjects belonging to the proper domain of Physics and Kinematics—such *Oldest book on Physics.*

as air, water, specific gravity, gravitation and various kinds of motion resulting from its action—were dealt with. A corpuscular theory of light was also given. This important work may rightly be regarded as the first of its kind that has appeared in the country, but for some reason or other it seems to have been long forgotten.

Works on Physics in the pre Restoration era.

More recently, but in the pre-Restoration era, works on Physics, also compiled from Dutch sources, were published by Aoji, Hirosé, and Kawamoto, all of whom were more or less engaged in the study of this branch of science ; the last-named being perhaps the first to construct a camera and succeed in taking photographs.

Photography.

Study of Physics in Tōkyō University.

Physics, together with Mathematics, was, however, for the first time systematically studied in the French section of the Tōkyō University, and, although the study was discontinued before long, it contributed much to the subsequent development of science : Professor Terao, Director of the Tōkyō Astronomical Observatory, Dr. Nakamura, Director of the Central Meteorological Observatory, Professors Namba and Miwa, of the Kyōto Imperial University, and others having graduated from this section. Upon the French section being abolished, separate courses in Mathematics, Physics, and Astronomy were established in the Department of Science.

Dr. Yamagawa.

Some years previously, Dr. Yamagawa, on his return from America, was appointed Professor of Physics, which position he held until he succeeded Professor Kikuchi as President of the Imperial University in 1901. In the former capacity he greatly promoted the study of Physics, his constant devotion to the cause of science during a long service of more than a quarter of a century having attracted a large number of eager and gifted students. As the Director of the College of Science he added very largely to its welfare.

Three foreign professors.

The College of Science was fortunate not only in having had such active promoters as Drs. Kikuchi and Yamagawa as its Directors and among its professors, but also in having obtained the services of several eminent men of science from England and America. Professors Ewing, Mendenhall, and Knott all contributed largely to the healthy development of Physics in this country, by actively encouraging original research. It was Professor Ewing more especially who, in Professor Ewing. the early days of the Department of Science, planted deeply the seeds of a scientific spirit, by making the students associate with him in his experimental investigations in Magnetism, and the immense influence which those early investigations had upon its future development may be seen from the fact that, of all subjects, Magnetism is the most actively cultivated in this country. This is, undoubtedly, also partly due to the fact that Professor Knott, who succeeded him, made this particular subject his speciality, but its origin must be traced to the earlier days of Professor Ewing.

The old Engineering College was also fortunate in being Engineering College. able to count among its professors such men of eminence as Professors Ayrton, Perry, and Gray, who by active prosecution and encouragement of research greatly promoted the study of Physics, though this branch of science did not form a special course in this institution, but was taught with the object of qualifying engineers for their profession.

A word of tribute to the memory of two Japanese physicists The late Mr. Ichikawa and Mr. Shida. is fitting in this place. Ichikawa, who studied Physics under the late Professor Balfour Stewart in Manchester, was a man of much originality, and Shida, the earliest and ablest of the pupils of Professor Ayrton, though educated as an electrical engineer, was an enthusiastic physicist : both made several important contributions to Physics, and both seemed destined to share very largely in its future development. Their comparatively early death was a great loss to science.

The more recent development of Physics in this country Professor Tanakadaté. is due essentially to the energy and enthusiasm of Professors Tanakadaté and Nagaoka, both of the College of Science. The former, who was one of the earliest of the pupils of Professor Ewing, and also one of the three graduates of 1882, was sent to Glasgow for the further prosecution of his studies under Sir William Thomson (Lord Kelvin). Full of originality and rich in resource, he has been able to make several contributions not only to Physics, but also to Seismology, the most important of all being, perhaps, those relating to Earth Earth Magnetism. Magnetism. Already, in 1887, he had undertaken a magnetic survey of Japan in conjunction with Professor Knott, and after the great Mino-Owari earthquake of 1891, another survey was conducted by him in that district, in order to investigate whether changes in the magnetic elements of the country had been caused by that great seismic event. The result of the latter survey showed that there has been a most remarkable change in the isomagnetics of the district. With the view of getting more accurate information both as to the normal distribution of magnetic force in the country and the extent and nature of local disturbances, a third survey was conducted during the years 1893–96 under his direction, the report of which has been published as volume xiv of the *Journal of the College of Science*.

Professor Nagaoka.

While Professor Tanakadaté has been more particularly occupied with the practical side of Magnetism, his colleague, Professor Nagaoka, has been employed with its scientific investigation. Already in his student days he was engaged in experiments on the combined effects of torsion and longitudinal stress on the magnetization of nickel, during which he discovered the remarkable and quite novel fact that the polarity of a nickel wire may change sign under certain circumstances. To quote the author's own words : ' For weak stresses, the changes of magnetism came out as was to be expected, but when the load exceeds a certain limit this is no longer the case. The changes of magnetism become gradually altered, and beyond a critical value of the longitudinal stress, one end of the nickel wire acquires the two opposite kinds of magnetism during the torsion and detorsion, notwithstanding the absolute constancy of the magnetizing force both in direction and magnitude.' This important discovery forms the starting-point of his other numerous and brilliant researches on magneto-striction, with which he has enriched the science and upon which he, as the best authority, was asked to write a report and submit it to the International Physical Congress held in Paris in 1900. Professor Nagaoka's scientific activity is, by no means, confined to the single subject of magnetism, important papers on several other subjects having been published by him, including that on the elastic constants of rocks ; researches which have led to the interesting discovery that in some rocks there is a remarkable ' hysteresis ' in the relation of stress to strain.

Important pieces of work have also been done by Professor Tsuruda, Dr. Honda, and others of the Tokyo University, and by Professors Muraoka and Mizuno of the Kyōto University, the latter of whom has made the study of electric waves his speciality, but want of space prevents their being described here. Other professors in the Univer- sities.

Brief reference must, however, be made to the system of Weights and Measures, which was definitely and legally fixed in this country in 1891, Professors Kikuchi and Yama- gawa, among others, having served on the committee. While the popular standards of weights and measures were retained in the form of *kan* and *shaku* respectively, simple and accurate relations were established between these and the standards of the metric system—a *kan* having been defined as fifteen-fourths of a kilogram, and a *shaku* as ten-thirty-thirds of a metre. It is necessary to add that the establishment of this system of weights and measures conferred a great boon upon scientific and non-scientific alike. Weights and Measures.

CHEMISTRY

The appearance in 1839 of ' *Séimi Kaisō* '—a Japanese translation by Yōan Udagawa of William Henry's ' Epitome of Chemistry,' published in 1828, from its Dutch version through a German one—may be rightly regarded as the beginning of the study of Chemistry in this country. Although the book treated merely of elementary facts and views, which could not be regarded as advanced even at the time, great credit is due to Udagawa for having introduced this new branch of science into Japan, at a time too when translation itself presented no few difficulties and when science was generally but little known. Moreover, it was not a mere translation, for he adduced several examples from among facts long known both at home and in China, and supplemented the text with a number of notes giving the results of his own observations and experiments. ' *Séimi Kaisō*.'

It was, doubtless, the appearance of this work that led

Study of
Chemistry
in the
Tokugawa
age. such men as Kawamoto, Katsuragawa, Utsunomiya, and others to the study of Chemistry in the pre-Restoration era, and the Tokugawa Government, recognizing the great importance of this branch of science, established a chemical laboratory at the *Kaiséi-jo*. The laboratory was, however, very poorly equipped, and kitchen utensils had to serve the purposes of eager experimenters. In 1865 Mr. W. K. Gratama of Holland was invited to teach Chemistry at the *Kaiséi-jo* ; but, before his services began to bear fruit, the institution was closed owing to the Restoration.

Professor
Gratama.   Soon after that event, and, in fact, in the same year, the chemical laboratory, somewhat better equipped, was opened at Ōsaka, and Mr. Gratama was at first invited to take charge of it. He was, however, soon succeeded by Dr. H. Ritter, and here, as in the Yédo laboratory, elements of Qualitative Analysis and simple practices in manufacturing processes were taught. This institution was subsequently removed to Tōkyō, but ultimately abolished.

     Meanwhile the *Kaiséi-jo* was revived and the new Code of Education promulgated, with a systematic introduction of Western sciences into the curriculum of study. But it was not till 1874, when a new and well-equipped laboratory was opened Professor
Atkinson. and Mr. R. W. Atkinson was invited from England to assume the duties of a Professor, that the more advanced study of Chemistry as a special branch of science was inaugurated. Professor Atkinson remained until 1881, and during the seven years of his service promoted the study to an extraordinary degree. His duties were onerous, as he had to lecture on Analytical Chemistry, Organic Chemistry, Theoretical Chemistry, Technicological Chemistry, and even Metallurgy, each for several hours a week and to attend constantly to the routine work of the laboratory. But these did not prevent him from undertaking important original researches himself and directing those of the students. The writer, who was one of his first students, recalls with gratitude those early days when he, with constant devotion and untiring energy, taught pupils to tread in the true path of science.

Dr.
Divers.   In the same year as Mr. Atkinson, another English chemist, to whom Japan owes even more, was invited to assume the

Professorship of Chemistry in the old Engineering College.   Dr. S. Divers was most successful as a teacher and most active as an investigator, and his work had a far-reaching influence upon the development of Chemistry in this country.   Whether in the old Engineering College or in the College of Science, to which his services were transferred on the amalgamation of the former institution with the Tōkyō University in 1886, and where he remained until his return to England in 1889, he always taught the prime importance of studying science for its own sake, and was constantly engaged in experimental investigations either by himself or in association with his students, the much-neglected Inorganic Chemistry receiving a particularly large share of his attention.   The number of important papers bearing his name, and published in the *Journal of the College of Science,* alone totals more than fifty.

Going back once more to the early days of the Tōkyō University, mention may be made of the fact that Dr. Matsui, now Director and Professor of Chemistry in the College of Agriculture, returned from America in 1880, after five years' study, and that the duties of Professor Atkinson were, after his leaving Japan in the next year, shared between him and the writer, just then returned from England.   In 1885, distinction was made between Pure and Applied Chemistry, the latter having been transferred from the Department of Science to the newly organized Department of Technology (soon afterwards combined with the old Engineering College to constitute the new College of Engineering), and with it also the services of Professor Matsui. *Pure and Applied Chemistry*

Pure Chemistry alone thus came to be cultivated in the College of Science.   The contributions made by Dr. Divers to the development of Inorganic Chemistry have already been referred to.   On his leaving Japan, he was succeeded by one of his old pupils, Dr. Haga, who likewise is a most enthusiastic and painstaking experimental investigator, and who, either alone or in association with Dr. Divers or his own pupils, has contributed a large number of important papers on complex inorganic compounds containing nitrogen and sulphur. *Inorganic Chemistry*

In Organic Chemistry more or less work has been done in the College of Science and other institutions, Professor Kuhara of *Organic Chemistry*

s 2

the Kyōto Imperial University being one of its most active promoters. The great importance of General Chemistry, or, to use a more widely adopted though unhappily chosen name, **Physical Chemistry** Physical Chemistry, which since 1887 has been developed with great strides in Europe, was early recognized in this country, and, thanks to the labours of Professors Ikéda and Ōsaka, among others—who have made important contributions to this department of Chemistry, and whose excellent text-books, based upon the broader and more general lines of modern development, are extensively read and studied—Physical Chemistry is more widely diffused, if not indeed more deeply rooted, in the general educational system of Japan than, perhaps, in that of any other country.

Technological Chemistry In the earlier days Technological Chemistry formed an essential portion of general chemical education, some of the leading men in this department—for instance, Dr. Takamatsu of the Tōkyō Gas Company, Dr. Takayama of the Government Laboratory, Dr. Nakazawa of the Kyōto Technical High School, Dr. Takaminé of New York, Dr. Shimosé of the Shimosé Powder Factory, and Professor Kawakita of the College of Engineering—being the old pupils of either Mr. Atkinson or Dr. Divers, and these men or their own pupils, have all contributed to the development of chemical industry in this country, either by encouraging the study of its application to industrial arts or by conducting and directing important work. Although the chemical industry of Japan cannot be said to be highly developed as yet, the fact is not discouraging that there are now more than ten sulphuric acid factories, whilst thirty years ago there was only one, and that in other directions either a similar growth has been witnessed or new industries have been started.

Pharmaceutical Chemistry Pharmaceutical Chemistry has also been known from an early date. Indeed it was already taught in the old Medical School in the Tokugawa period, and its study was later promoted by the German and the Dutch chemists engaged in the work of medical education, amongst whom special mention **Dr. Eykmann** may be made of Dr. J. F. Eykmann. But it is since Dr. Nagai **Dr. Nagai.** assumed the Professorship of Pharmacy in the College of Medicine that this branch of Chemistry has been cultivated with great activity. He began his study of Chemistry at Ōsaka in the pre-Restoration era, and afterwards went to Berlin, studying for many years under the late Professor A. W. Hofmann. Like his illustrious master, he is one of the most enthusiastic and successful workers in original research, and has enriched Chemistry in its application to Pharmacy with several contributions. It must not be forgotten that Dr. Tahara and others have also contributed to the development of this branch of Chemistry. The study of Medical Chemistry has been started comparatively recently, but some important work has already been done by Professor Kumagawa and others. *Medical Chemistry*

The College of Agriculture, ever since the days of the Komaba Agricultural College, has been the centre of the development of Agricultural Chemistry. Professor Kinch was the first who devoted himself to the education of agricultural chemists in this country, and, although his service was of comparatively short duration, there is not the least doubt that his labours have borne plentiful fruit, as the subsequent development of this branch of Chemistry shows. Both Dr. O. Kellner and his successor, Dr. O. Loew, have also contributed most abundantly, the work of the latter being confined not alone to Chemistry in its application to practical farming, but extending far and deep into the Chemistry of vegetable physiology. *Agricultural Chemistry* *Professor Kinch.* *Professors Kellner and Loew.*

The different departments of Chemistry are represented in the Tōkyō Chemical Society, founded in 1878. It has served the most useful purpose of bringing chemists of different specialities together for the advancement of their common science. It has nearly five hundred members, and publishes a monthly ' *Journal* ' containing many extracts from papers published in foreign countries. The Society of Chemical Industry, though only started in 1898, has a much greater numerical strength, counting over eight hundred. It also publishes a monthly ' Journal ' devoted to the progress of chemical industry both at home and abroad. *Tōkyō Chemical Society.* *Society of Chemical Industry.*

SEISMOLOGY

No other country in the world probably affords such facilities for the study of earthquakes as Japan, nor is there anywhere else such necessity for their scientific investigation ; *Japan and the study of earthquakes.*

it is therefore only to be expected that it occupies a unique position in the world as regards Seismology. Consequently there is a special chair of Seismology, and an institute attached to it, in the Imperial University of Tōkyō, and also a special committee for the investigation of earthquakes under the direct control of the Minister of Education. Moreover, all the provincial meteorological stations throughout Japan are equipped with instruments for recording and measuring earthquakes, and seismic phenomena are systematically studied.

Baron Kikuchi and Seismology. Baron Kikuchi, who in various capacities has encouraged the study of earthquakes in every possible way, published in 1904 an admirable monograph, entitled ' *Recent Seismological Investigations*,' and with his kind permission the writer has made free use of it in preparing this part of the present chapter.

Professor Milne. It was through the labours of Professors J. Milne, T. Gray, J. A. Ewing, and others, in the 'seventies of the last century, that this new and important branch of science was born in this country. It was more particularly through the exertions of Professor Milne, who, among other things, organized the Seismological Society of Japan in 1880, that interest in this science was stimulated and its systematic study greatly promoted. Professors Ewing and Gray have both done valuable service by devising and improving the means of recording and measuring the intensity of earthquakes, and thus facilitating their scientific study. The *Transactions of the Seismological Society of Japan* (discontinued after 1892) contain valuable communications by them and other scholars on questions relating to earthquakes, during the earlier period.

Professor Sekiya. Among Japanese seismologists the name of the late Professor Sekiya, whose death in 1896 was a great loss to science, must be first mentioned. It was he who, having made this branch of science a special subject of study, first occupied the chair of Seismology on its establishment in the Tōkyō University in 1886, and both in this capacity and, later, in that of a member of the Earthquake Investigation Committee, he contributed largely to the further development of Seismology. His modification of Professor Ewing's Bracket Seismograph, in which the period of swing of the pendulum was made much longer

and which enabled reliable measurements of strong earthquakes to be taken ; his comparison of earthquake motion in
hard ground and in soft soil, in a pit and on the surface ; the
inauguration, at his suggestion, of a system of seismic triangula-
tion for determining the velocity of propagation of earthquake
waves ; the collection and examination of the account of
earthquakes recorded in history from the beginning of the
fifth century down to recent times—a work which involved
much time and labour, but which supplies important data as
to the distribution of earthquakes in respect to time and space
—may, among other things, be mentioned.

The work thus commenced has been taken up and greatly **Professor Ōmori.**
advanced by Professor Ōmori, successor of Professor Sékiya in
the chair of Seismology, and others.   Professor Ōmori's contributions are too numerous even to name ; a mere list of the
titles of papers published in the *Journal of the College of
Science*, the Publications of the Earthquake Investigation
Committee, the Proceedings of the Tōkyō Mathematico-
Physical Society, and other periodicals, would take up several
pages, and a few only of the more important points can be **Ōmori's seismograph.**
brought to light.   In instrumental investigations he has
succeeded in constructing a seismograph, which can be
made to give records not only of ordinary earthquakes, but of
small pulsatory oscillations and of slow changes of level.   Of
these microseismic or insensible motions, the pulsatory oscillations must be distinguished from the others as being not of
earthquake origin, for they are of constant and continuous
occurrence, and it has been observed that earthquakes rarely
occur while pulsatory oscillations are active; whilst on the other
hand, local shocks are often produced when they are in a state
of minimum activity.   The observation of these small pulse-
like oscillations has, on several occasions, enabled Professor
Ōmori to predict the occurrence of an earthquake within some
ten or twelve hours.   Other valuable information has been
obtained by the use of this exceedingly sensitive seismograph.

Mention must here be made of Professor Tanakadaté, who, **Professor Tanaka-daté's seismograph.**
beside those already named as contributors to the instru-
mental investigation of earthquakes, designed both the Parallel-
Motion Seismograph for strong earthquakes, and the Spiral

Seismograph for recording vertical motion, which are now largely in use in this country.

From the statistical study of earthquakes, Professor Ōmori has come to some important conclusions with respect to the mutual relation between destructive earthquakes and the ordinary small shocks, as to the frequency of their occurrence, the relation of annual seismic variation to geographical position, the relation of diurnal variations of seismic frequency to variations of barometric pressure, and time variation of the frequency of after-shocks—the last of which is found to follow a simple law and to be representable by a rectangular hyperbola. In the practical application of seismic experiments to the study of the vibration of walls, railway bridges, bridge piers, &c., and fracturing and overturning of columns, with the view of arriving ultimately at a knowledge as to the best forms of structure to be adopted in an earthquake-country like Japan, Professor Ōmori has been no less active, and both his deflecto-graph and vibration-measurer have done valuable service. It is hardly necessary to remark that in the study of these practical problems, architects and engineers, as well as seismologists, have materially assisted.

Practical application of seismic ex-periences.

Physical investigations, such as the study of earth magnet-ism, variation of latitude, elastic constants of rocks, &c., have in no small degree contributed, and promise to further contribute, to the exact knowledge of seismic phenomena. Reference must be made to the remarkable change of isomagnetics observed by Professor Tanakadaté attending the Mino-Owari earthquake of 1891, as well as to the extensive magnetic survey conducted under his direction. Besides these occasional sur-veys, continuous magnetic observations are being made at five different stations pretty evenly distributed over the whole length of Japan—viz. at Némuro, Sendai, Tōkyō, Kyōto, and Kumamoto—and on several occasions it has been found that magnetic disturbance preceded or accompanied earthquakes. Observations of the variation of latitude, made at the Tōkyō Astronomical Observatory by Dr. Kimura as a part of the work of the Earthquake Investigation Committee, seem to show that all the destructive earthquakes occur either exactly, or almost exactly, when the latitude is at a maximum or

Earth-quakes and earth magnet-ism.

Astro-nomical study of earth-quakes.

a minimum : non-destructive extensive earthquakes also in-dicating a similar relation, though in a less marked degree. Professor Nagaoka's recent work on the determination of the elastic constants of rocks, already referred to, has thrown much valuable light upon the problems relating to the propagation of seismic waves. In addition to these, measurement of gravity and of underground temperature, and study of the change of water-level in wells and of periodic oscillations of the waters of lakes, bays, gulfs, straits, &c., have also elucidated facts of importance and interest.

The geological study of earthquakes has been conducted both by organizing a systematic volcanological survey, under the direction of Professor Kotō, and by making scientific expedi-tions to the scenes of severe earthquakes, volcanic eruptions, subterranean sounds, &c. These surveys and expeditions have already furnished important data, and it appears that all recent earthquakes of an extensive nature owe their origin to mountain-forming agencies, while earthquakes due to volcanic eruptions are confined to a small area. *Geological study of earthquakes.*

The later development of Seismology, of which a very cursory account has been given, is almost entirely the work of the Earthquake Investigation Committee, which was organized in 1892, in consequence of representations to the Government made, immediately after the great earthquake of the previous year, by Baron Kikuchi in the House of Peers and adopted by a large majority. It has two objects in view : to investigate whether there are any means of forecasting earthquakes, and what can be done in the way of reducing their disastrous effects to a minimum. Both the Publica-tions of the Earthquake Investigation Committee in foreign languages and the Report of the same Committee in the Japanese language show that a great deal of important work has already been done in the attainment of these objects ; but that much more yet remains to be accomplished goes without saying. *Earth-quake Investi-gation Com-mittee.*

METEOROLOGY

Meteorology is not studied as a special branch of science, except that there is an optional course of lectures upon it in the College of Science; still this paper will be incomplete without an account, however cursory, of the system of meteorological service now in operation in Japan.

Meteorological observations.

The present organization of meteorological service in this country, which is placed in charge of the Central Meteorological Observatory, under the supervision of the Minister of Education, extends over the whole empire, with the exception of Formosa and the Pescadores—these being under the direct control of the Governor-General of Formosa. It was initiated by an Imperial Ordinance in 1894, according to which the Central Meteorological Observatory was established in Tōkyō, and a number of provincial stations were organized in suitable localities.

First meteorological station.

Its previous history is short. The first of the meteorological stations was established in 1872 at Hakodaté, and, three years later, a meteorological service was inaugurated in the Department of Home Affairs, the service of storm-warning following five years later. In 1882 a system of weather-telegraphy was established and weather-maps were printed, and in June of the next year a weather forecast was, for the first time, exhibited at every police-station in Tōkyō. The work of the Central Meteorological Observatory was finally transferred to the Department of Education in 1895.

Central Meteorological Observatory and its works.

The Central Meteorological Observatory which, under the name of the Tōkyō Meteorological Observatory, was first established in 1875 in the precincts of the Imperial Palace, in connection with the meteorological service inaugurated by the Department of Home Affairs, undertakes :—Discussions and publications of meteorological observations ; prediction of weather ; storm-warning ; telegraphic information of the predicted weather and storms to the subscribers ; verification of meteorological instruments and observations on meteorological, seismic, magnetic, and electrical phenomena. The Observatory is equipped with barometers, thermometers, actinometers, hygrometers, anemometers, pluviometers, sunshine-recorders, seismometers, electrometers, magnometers, instruments for measuring the height and velocity of clouds, and instruments and apparatus for verifying the meteorological instruments.

There are altogether 1348 meteorological stations. Of Meteoro-logical stations. these, seventy are provincial stations; fifteen being those of the first order—equipped with a barometer, thermometer, hygrometer, maximum and minimum thermometers, solar radiation thermometer, terrestrial radiation thermometer, earth thermometer, anemometer, wind-vane, rain-gauge, evapori-meter, sunshine-recorder, and a seismograph for the purpose of hourly observations. Those of the second order are fitted up with barometer, thermometer, hygrometer, maximum and minimum thermometers, anemometer, wind-vane, rain-gauge, and a seismograph for making six observations a day. The duties of these provincial stations are to make meteorological observations at their respective localities, investigate the climatology of the administrative districts of the prefectures concerned, and issue local weather-forecasts according to the predictions issued from the Central Meteorological Observatory. They have also to forward meteorological telegrams, monthly meteorological registers, and annual reports to the Central Meteorological Observatory. Of the remaining number, two (which are equipped as the provincial stations of the first order and situated on islands in the Pacific Ocean), are attached to the Central Meteorological Observatory—their observations and telegraphic information are of great importance to the prediction and investigation of typhoons ; seven are controlled by the Governor-General of Formosa, and sixty-four consist of semaphore stations, lighthouses, private stations, &c., the outfit of which is the same as that of the provincial stations of the second order. The rest, consisting of village offices, district offices, police-stations, schools, &c., are meteorological stations of the third order, and are generally provided with a set of maximum and minimum thermometers, an ordinary ther-mometer, a rain-gauge, and a few other instruments. In these, daily observations are made of temperature, rainfall, the amount of cloud, the direction and force of wind, &c., and they send meteorological registers to the provincial stations to which they belong.

The choice of all the instruments in the provincial and Instru-ments. other stations is entrusted to the Director of the Central Meteorological Observatory. They are minutely examined and compared with the standard instruments of the Central Meteorological Observatory before they are sent to the respective stations, and are set according to the instructions issued from it, which also give the method of observations and their reductions in strict conformity with the decision of the International Meteorological Committee. It may be added that a temporary school, usually with a term of six months, is open in the Central Meteorological Observatory to train the members of the provincial stations in elementary mathematics, physics, meteorology, and seismology, with practical exercise in the use of instruments and the methods of observation.

Weather Prediction.

The service of Weather Prediction depends upon telegraphic information received at the Central Meteorological Observatory three times a day from domestic stations, and twice a day from over twenty foreign stations—Manila, Hong-Kong, Amoy, Shanghai, Tientsin, Vladivostock, Alexandrovski, &c. Besides this regular information the Central Meteorological Observatory also receives special telegrams from domestic stations, reporting the minimum pressure, its time of occurrence, the maximum velocity of the wind and its direction, &c. The data thus obtained are immediately entered on a chart. The changes of pressure and temperature in the preceding twenty-four hours, the variation of pressure in the past eight hours, the departures of pressure from its normal, and the cloud-forms are also charted ; isobars and isotherms are then drawn, and the general weather prediction issued to the stations of the ten meteorological districts into which Japan is divided for the purpose, these stations preparing and issuing predictions for their respective localities. Both general and local weather predictions are for the following twenty-four hours beginning at 6 P.M. for the day of issue. The local forecasts of the provincial stations are immediately distributed over the administrative districts through police-stations, country offices, &c., by means of telephone or telegraph and through newspapers. The service of Storm-Warning is carried on in much the same way, and the provincial meteorological stations, weather-signal stations, and storm-signal stations indicate the predicted weather or storm by hoisting up flags or displaying signals. It may be of interest to add that the successes in

Storm-Warning.

the prognostications of general weather forecasts and storm-warnings, which are verified according to the method usually employed by the meteorological observatories of other countries, are respectively eighty-two per cent. and seventy per cent. as the average of many years' work.

Besides the meteorological service proper, sketched out above, a system of maritime meteorological observation has been organized since 1888, according to which all Japanese ships of over one hundred tons take meteorological observations on board at regular intervals every day, in accordance with certain instructions, and forward the meteorological logs to the Central Meteorological Observatory. Systematic observation of rainfalls, thunderstorms, earthquakes, and even of such matters as the periods of arrival and departure of birds of passage ; the dates of appearance or disappearance of fire-flies, grasshoppers, crickets, and other insects ; the dates of sowing, budding, appearance of ears, flowering, ripening, and fruit-bearing of rice, wheat, cherry-trees, &c., are also carried on both by provincial meteorological stations and by individuals, such as schoolmasters, village and country officials, and volunteer observers, and their reports are sent to the Central Meteorological Observatory either directly or through the provincial stations. *Maritime meteorological observations. Other systematic observations.*

Magnetic observations also form a part of the work of the Central Meteorological Observatory, a separate magnetic observatory being erected in its precincts, where variations of the three elements of terrestrial magnetism are continuously registered, besides their absolute measurements, which are taken once a month. Continuous observations of the variations of magnetic elements are also made at Némuro, Sendai, Kyōto, and Kumamoto, as already mentioned under Seismology, and their daily photographic records dispatched to the Central Meteorological Observatory for comparative study. *Magnetic observations.*

With regard to the verification of meteorological instruments, this is undertaken at the Central Meteorological Observatory whenever a demand is presented, and fixed fees are paid in stamps. The number of instruments of all sorts verified during the year approaches 3000. *Verification of meteorological instruments.*

The publications of the Central Meteorological Observatory

are the *Daily Weather Map*, copies of which are distributed immediately by post to local meteorological stations, public bureaus, newspaper offices, libraries, &c. ; the *Monthly Report*, containing the observations of the provincial stations ; the *Annual Report*, divided into two parts—the first part containing monthly means of the observations of all the stations in Japan, and the second part containing discussions on the meteorology of Japan during the current year. These Reports are in both Japanese and English. In addition to these, the *Monthly Weather Review*, giving a brief *résumé* of current weather, thunderstorms, and earthquakes in the preceding month, is printed exclusively in Japanese, while the *Bulletin of the Central Meteorological Observatory*, containing results of investigations on Meteorology and allied sciences by the officials of the Observatory, is printed in foreign languages, two or three volumes appearing in the year.

The above account, which is based upon a pamphlet, bearing the title *The Organization of Meteorological Service in Japan*, will show that this service, although of recent origin, is in a state of development which compares favourably with that of any other nation. This happy result is chiefly due to the efforts of the Director of the Central Meteorological Observatory, Dr. Nakamura, through whose courtesy the above-mentioned pamphlet has been placed at the disposal of the writer, and to whom the latter's best thanks are due. It must be added that Dr. Wada, who takes charge of the service of weather prediction, has also had a large share in the work.

XIV

NATURAL SCIENCE IN JAPAN

K. Mitsukuri, D.Ph., D.Sc. (Japan), Professor of Zoology, Science College, Imperial University of Tōkyō.

Nothing perhaps illustrates so well the high level of civilization to which Japan of the pre-Restoration period attained, as the fact that such comparatively non-utilitarian departments of human knowledge as Natural Sciences were assiduously cultivated. It would indeed have been strange if a people with such an innate love of nature as the Japanese had not early been attracted by plants, birds, fishes, insects, and minerals. Apart from an æsthetic knowledge of these objects, their systematic study appears to have been begun at an early stage, probably owing to the necessity of having an intimate knowledge of them as *materia medica*. As Count Ōkuma in another chapter of this work (p. 117) has informed us, there was already, in the eighth century of the Christian era, established in Japan an Imperial University with four departments—Ethics, History, Jurisprudence, and Mathematics—and with the prescribed number of four hundred students. There were also at the same time bureaus devoted to Astronomy, Astrology, Calendar Compilation, and Meteorology, and a Medical College with professors of Medicine, Surgery, Acupuncture, Necromancy (the art of healing by charms), and Pharmacology. The last-named branch of study included the collection, cultivation, and investigation of medicinal plants, and thus a considerable amount of botanical knowledge must have been accumulated by that time.

The Natural History studies which thus arose as a handmaiden of medicine seem to have remained in that subordinate

Natural Sciences before the Restoration.

Natural
History
in the
Middle
Ages.

Tokugawa
age.

Natural-
ists in the
Tokugawa
period.

Exhibi-
tions.

Works by
natural-
ists.

position all through the Middle Ages, when fighting was the
occupation of the upper classes and learning was at its lowest
ebb.   It is not surprising, therefore, that there is little worthy
of note during those long years in connection with Natural
Science.   But when Iyéyasu and his successors secured a
peace of two hundred and sixty years, literature, the arts, and
all peaceful industries were developed with remarkable vigour
and rapidity, and the study of Natural History rose to an
importance which claimed the position of an independent
study, although emphasis was always laid on its relation to
Medical Science.   Many scholars, eminent in these subjects,
arose whose names are still household words.   Such are, for
instance, Hakuséki Arai, Jakusui Inao, Gennai Hiraga, Ekken
Kaibara, and Ranzan Ono.   The last-named naturalist
(1727–1809) was so famed for his extensive knowledge that,
we are told, his pupils numbered nearly a thousand.   His
'Honzō Kōmoku Kéimō,' published in 1803 in forty-eight
parts, probably reached the high-water mark of the Natural
History of this period.   The excursions and expeditions undertaken by these men and others with the view of collecting
natural objects, among which plants were especial favourites,
were frequent, and all parts of the country seem to have
been explored in this way.   These tours went under the name
of 'materia medica collecting,' and, to this day, naturalists
in remote parts of the country are often asked if the objects
collected are to be used as medicine, or what medicinal properties they possess.   Naturalists also held frequent meetings,
to which each brought his treasures, and thus extensive
collections were made and exhibited to the public.   Of such
displays the exhibitions given by Gennai Hiraga in Yédo
were perhaps the most famous.   The works written by these
naturalists were also numerous, and covered a wide range
of subjects, many being encyclopædic in their compre-
hensiveness and size.   One of the most extensive extant
in Japanese—'Shobutsu Ruisan,' compiled by Jakusui
Inao under the patronage of the lord of Kaga, consisted
of 1000 parts, and was the outcome of many years' work.
My colleague, Professor Matsumura, in his book on the plant-
names of Japan, gives 306 titles of Japanese works on botanical

subjects compiled previously to 1868. Many of these have beautifully coloured illustrations, which serve their purpose even at the present day, and are of great use in identifying the Japanese names of animals and plants. Several botanical gardens were established during this period, chiefly owing to the necessity of cultivating medicinal plants. Thus the present Botanical Garden of the Imperial University, by no means the first of its kind, was established early in the Tokugawa period—viz., in 1681—and was long renowned as the *Koishikawa O-Yakuén* (Garden of Medicinal Plants in Koishikawa).

Botanical gardens.

In the middle of the eighteenth century, an event took place which was of great significance not only for Natural History studies, but also for the whole field of learning—nay, for the destiny of Japan itself. This was the mastery as we have seen (Vol. II, p. 139) of the Dutch language by a few earnest physicians, Ranka Maéno, Gempaku Sugita, and others. This success, together with the visits of Thunberg (1775) and Siebold (1821), had its effect upon Natural History studies also. The system of Linnæus, especially in regard to plants, seems to have been well grasped, with very little delay. The most noteworthy productions of the new school on Natural History were probably ' *Shokugaku Kéigen* ' (' Elements of Botanical Science '), by Yōan Udagawa, 1835, and ' *Sōmoku Zusétsu* ' (' Icones Plantarum '), by Yokusai Iinuma, 1832—the latter being a standard work even at the present day. It is perhaps a circumstance worthy of record that a work on the use of the microscope was published in 1801.

Physicians and Dutch learning.

Productions of the new school.

Looked at from the standpoint of modern Science, the Natural History of the pre-Restoration period, in spite of the zeal, industry, and erudition of its devotees, cannot be said to have attained a very high degree of cultivation. In its methods it went perhaps little beyond pre-Linnæan days in Europe. The study of natural objects was always pursued, ostensibly with the purpose either of collecting *materia medica*, of discovering things that might be used as food in case of a famine, of identifying Japanese objects with names given in Chinese works on Natural History, like ' *Honzō Kōmoku,*' or of making comments on these works. In some of their highest efforts, it

Pursuit of Natural History in the pre-Restoration period.

is evident that naturalists looked beyond these comparatively barren ends, and investigated animals, plants, and minerals for their own sake and from an innate love of such things. Botany was the most highly developed ; Zoology and Mineralogy lagging sadly behind, and not rising above the plane of elaborate discussions over mythical objects or monsters.

The Restoration and the progress of modern Science.   With the 1868 Restoration came a wholesale reconstruction of all political institutions, and the country underwent, and is still undergoing, a social revolution such as has seldom been witnessed in any part of the world. Along with many other things, the old school of Natural History was swept away as chessmen from the board at the end of a game. So far as Natural Sciences are concerned, there was a complete break-up at this period. From the start the Imperial Government laid great weight on the introduction of modern sciences, until at the present day Natural Sciences may be said to be fairly well established. In helping this development the Imperial University of Tōkyō has played a very active *rôle*, and its history is the history of Science in Japan up to the present day. I will now briefly go over the history of this development, referring separately to each of the Natural Sciences.

ZOOLOGY

Professor Morse.   I take up Zoology first, as I am most familiar with its history and know it mainly at first hand. The modern school of Zoology in Japan dates from the appointment of Professor Edward S. Morse (of Salem, Mass. U.S.A.) to the chair of Zoology at the University of Tōkyō in 1877. This appointment was a most fortunate one, for he had qualities which fitted him to be a pioneer. His indefatigable zeal and genial manners were calculated to rouse enthusiasm among his pupils, and won many friends for the new science among all classes of society ; while his lectures, popular or otherwise, drew attention for the first time to the immense strides which biological sciences under the stimulus of Darwinism were making in the West. With a few students under him he soon had in working order a tolerably good museum—the nucleus of the present

zoological and anthropological collections of the Science
College. Although Professor Morse stayed in Japan only
two years, he accomplished a wonderful amount of work. On
his return to America he was succeeded by Professor C. O.
Whitman, now of the University of Chicago, who introduced for   Professor
the first time modern technical methods. Thus two Americans   Whitman.
stood sponsors to the modern school of Zoology in Japan.

Since 1881, development has been mainly in the hands of   Zoology
our own people. The spirit of earnest study which signalized the   to-day.
Natural History school of the pre-Restoration days is happily
revived, but with higher and wider purposes, and with greater
facilities for successful attainment. Though only some twenty-
five years have passed since the new departure, a vigorous school
has already sprung up, which I may perhaps say, without
appearing immodest, has already made some not insignificant
contributions to Science.

There can be no doubt that the establishment of the marine   Marine
station at Misaki by the Imperial University, in 1887, gave   station of
a great impetus to the study. Situated at the point of the   Misaki.
peninsula jutting out between the Bay of Sagami and the
Bay of Tōkyō, it has access to localities long famous as the
home of remarkable forms of animal life. Along the coast
all sorts of bottoms are found, yielding a rich variety of littoral
forms. The operations, which have the Misaki Laboratory
for their base, are at present confined mostly to the Sagami
Sea. Within this area we may distinguish two parts—one
that is shallower, and the other deeper, than 100 fathoms.
The bottom deepens comparatively slowly down to the 100-
fathom line, although this line is nowhere very far from the
shore, and at some places extremely close. At the 100-fathom
line there is, generally speaking, a very sudden deepening,
and in many places there must be almost perpendicular cliffs,
for two soundings, distant only by a stone's-throw, often give,
one 80–100 fathoms, and the other over 200 fathoms. Towards
the centre of the sea there are 500–600 fathoms, and in one
place 970 fathoms. A very important spot is a shoal known
as the Okinosé, where the shallowest water is only 37 fathoms
deep, and the declivities of this submarine peak form a ground
extremely rich in animal forms. It is evident that volcanic

phenomena have had a great deal to do in forming the peculiarities of the bottom in the Sagami Sea. Faunistically, we
can distinguish the shallower areas above the 100-fathom
line as the home of the sea-lily (*Metacrinus*), and of many
forms of the sea-pen (*Pennatulids*), as well as of a very rich
littoral fauna of tunicates, worms and their allies, molluscs,
cœlenterates, echinoderms, fishes, &c. The cliffs that go down
from the shallower parts into deeper parts are overgrown
with a luxuriant crop of fixed animal life, just as mountain-sides
are covered with plants. In the deeper parts themselves there
are the glass-rope sponges (*Hyalonema*), (sold in abundance
at Énoshima), Venus's Flower Basket (*Euplectella*), and a host
of other glass-sponges, many as delicate in their structure
as the finest lace-work. It is also the home of the frill shark
(*Chlamydoselachus*), of the goblin shark (*Mitsukurina*), and of
the rare mollusc *Pleuretomaria*. The allies of these forms are
known as fossils from the Tertiary and older geological formations; and while all seem to have perished in other parts of
the world, they somehow survive here. It is here, also, that
a gigantic crab (*Macrocheirus*), often 13 feet or more in the
span of its claws, and a hydroid (*Branchiocerianthus*), 7 feet high,
are found, being the largest of their kind in the world. Also
numerous deep-sea fishes, some finding their way through
the dark abyssmal depths by their phosphorescent light-
organs. Recently three new species of *Chimœra* have been
brought up from this part. Nor are the surface-waters backward in richness. This is due to the fact that the great warm
current (the ' Black Current' or ' *Kuro Shiwo* ') sweeps by
not many miles out, and a branch of it often comes into the
harbour of Misaki. Many kinds of *Siphonophora* and *Cteno-
phora*, *Salpa*, *Doliolum*, *Liriope*, *Appendicularia*, *Noctiluca*,
Heteropods, *Pteropods*, and the larvæ of littoral forms—among
which are *Actinotrocha*, *Pilidium*, *Tornaria*—are names that
occur at random, and the list could easily be made much
longer.

In view of the richness of the marine fauna around the
marine station at Misaki, it is natural that many of the investigations carried on by Japanese zoologists are concerned with
marine animals. The results of most of these investigations are

given in the *Journal of the College of Science*, which publication *Journal* was begun by the Tōkyō University in 1887, for the purpose *of the College of* of carrying abroad intelligence of scientific investigations *Science.* conducted in Japan. The Journal has been favourably received in every part of the world where scientific investigations are pursued, and has done much towards showing that sciences are being studied in modern Japan in a sound and thorough-going manner. The twenty volumes of this Journal which have been hitherto published contain, among others, some important zoological contributions, of which I have enumerated certain of the most important in Appendix D (i), at the end of this volume, as showing the scope and trend of the investigations.[1]

More intimately connected with us are some of the recent *Drs.* works of Dr. David Starr Jordan, of Leland Stanford University, *Jordan and Dean.* and Professor Bashford Dean, of Columbia University. These zoologists paid prolonged visits to Japan, and we were glad to be brought into close relations with such distinguished naturalists. The extensive series of articles on Japanese fishes which have been recently published by Dr. Jordan and his assistants are, therefore, of a peculiar interest to us, as are also Dr. Dean's works on Chimæra and Myxinoids.

Memorable also were the visits of the U.S. Fish Commission steamer *Albatross*, with Dr. Alexander Agassiz and his scientific *Professor* staff on board. Mr. A. Owston, of Yokohama, also aided the *Agassiz.* progress of our Science by his enthusiastic investigations of the Sagami Sea in his yacht, *Golden Hind*, and by frequently placing the latter at our disposal.

The Tōkyō Zoological Society, directly descended from *Tōkyō* the Tōkyō Biological Society which Professor Morse helped *Zoological Society.* to establish during his residence in Tōkyō, has been steadily gaining in importance. It has now a membership of three hundred, and has two publications : (1) The *Zoological Magazine* (in Japanese), published monthly, and whose volumes are now in the twenties, is intended chiefly to popularize the science by disseminating sound knowledge of Zoology among teachers and others ; (2) *Annotationes Zoologicæ Japonenses*, published

[1] For further particulars as to the Marine Products of Japan see Vol. I, Chap. xxv, p. 594.

in European languages and intended to contain minor contributions not so formal as those in the Science College Journal.
The magazine is now in its ninth volume.   The Society,
having as yet no quarters of its own, is domiciled temporarily
in the Zoological Institute of the Science College in the Imperial
University.

A list of the principal places in Japan where zoological
studies or investigations are being carried on is given in
Appendix D (ii).

BOTANY

The late
Professor
Yatabé.

The pioneer of Botanical Science in modern Japan was the
late Professor R. Yatabé, a graduate of Cornell University,
U.S.A.   He was appointed to the chair of Botany in the
Tōkyō University in 1876, and immediately began to busy
himself with the study of the flora of Japan.   Every vacation
he fitted out, under the auspices of the University, a collecting
expedition to some favourable localities in our country, and
generally led it himself.   The herbarium in the Botanical
Institute thus soon became the best as regards Japanese flora,
which standard has been easily maintained to the present
day under his successors.   Collecting has also gone on unceasingly, and the field of activities has been extended
within recent years to Loochoo, Formosa, Korea, and

Tōkyō
Botanical
Gardens.

China.   The old Botanic Garden, which, as mentioned before,
was started long ago as a place for cultivating medicinal
plants under the Tokugawa *régime*, and in which the present
Botanical Institute is located, has had constant additions
made and been assiduously improved, as was natural in the
circumstances which allowed free intercourse with foreign
countries.   Recently a branch garden has been established
in Nikkō for the collection and cultivation of Alpine plants.
The staff of the Botanical Institute has had important
accessions from time to time ; in 1886, Professor Matsumura
joined it, and has had charge of the Institute since the retirement of Professor Yatabé ; in 1895, Professor Miyoshi, who
has charge of Plant Physiology ; and, in 1905, Professor Fujii,
who specializes in Morphology.

To Japanese botanists belongs the credit of having made one of the greatest discoveries in Plant Morphology of recent years. In the spring of 1896, Mr. Hirasé, an assistant in the Botanical Institute, found the spermatozoids in the pollentube of *Gingko biloba*; and later in the same year, Professor Ikéno, of the Agricultural College, discovered the spermatozoids in *Cycas revoluta*. The discovery of the spermatozoids among the Gymnosperms has attracted wide attention in the botanical world of every country, and has been called by some high authorities in Europe one of the most remarkable events in Plant Morphology during the latter half of the nineteenth century, bridging, as it does, the interval between the Phænerogams and Cryptogams in the matter of reproduction. *Discoveries in Plant Morphology.*

As in the case of Zoology, a number of botanical papers are found in the *Journal of the College of Science*—the more important of them being enumerated in Appendix D (iii). *Botanical papers.*

The Tōkyō Botanical Society is temporarily domiciled in the Botanical Institute of the University. It is a flourishing society with over three hundred members, and publishes a monthly botanical magazine, whose volumes now number twenty-three, with parts in the Japanese and European languages.

The principal places in Japan where botanical studies are carried on are: the Botanical Institute of the Science College, under Professors Matsumura, Miyoshi, and Fujii; the Botanical Institute of the Agricultural College, under Professors Shirai and Ikéno; the Botanical Laboratory of the Sapporo Agricultural College, under Professor Miyabé. *Botanical institutes.*

GEOLOGY

When the resources of a country are to be developed, it is generally to mineral wealth that people look first, and it is obvious, even to the most obtuse, that the aid of Science must be called in to take the earliest steps in this direction. It was probably in this sense that, in 1862, not long after the opening of Japan to foreign commerce and intercourse.

Blake and Pumpelly. the Tokugawa Government engaged two Americans, W. P. Blake and R. Pumpelly, to investigate the mineral resources of Japan. Very soon after the restoration of the Emperor to full power, and when it had been decided to develop the resources of Hokkaidō as quickly as possible, the department of the Government (the *Kaitakushi*) which had charge of this work engaged an American, B. S. Lyman, to make a geological survey of Hokkaidō. With another American, H. S. Munroe, and many Japanese assistants, Lyman made a survey of the coal-fields and other mineral districts. He was afterwards engaged in the geological survey of other parts of Japan, in which he principally visited oil-fields and other mining districts (1876–79).

Geology in Tōkyō University. In the Tōkyō University the teaching of Geology was at first under the charge of foreign professors, mostly German. These were K. Schenk, H. S. Munroe, E. Naumann, David Brauns, and Karl Gottsche, succeeding one another in the order named. Among the earlier Japanese teachers of the subject were T. Wada and T. Harada. On the return of Gottsche to Germany, B. Kotō, who had been prosecuting his studies in Germany, was appointed to the chair of Geology. He has since been joined by Professor Yokoyama, whose speciality is Palæontology, and Professor Jimbō, who makes Mineralogy his speciality. Professor Kotō has not confined his geological researches to Japan proper alone, but has extended them to Formosa and Korea, in the latter of which countries he spent a large part of two years in laborious and difficult journeys, crossing and recrossing the country in various directions.

Mineralogical and palæontological papers. The principal geological, mineralogical, and palæontological papers in the *Journal of the College of Science* are set out in Appendix D (iv).[1]

First geological examination of the country. The first geological examination of Japan was made by Mr. T. Wada in 1878, under the auspices of the Home Department, the provinces of Kai and Izu being mapped out at the time. At the end of the same year, Dr. Edmund Naumann, then Professor of Geology in the Tōkyō University, advised the

---

[1] For further particulars as to the Minerals of Japan see Vol. I, Chap. xxvi, p. 604 (Mining).

undertaking of a systematic geological survey of the empire and submitted a plan for the same to the Minister of the Home Department. In May, 1879, that plan was adopted and the present Imperial Geological Survey was organized and placed under the direction of Dr. E. Naumann. It was afterwards transferred to the Department of Agriculture and Commerce, and its directorship, since the retirement of Dr. Naumann, has been successively held by Mr. T. Wada and Dr. T. Kochibé, while well-known scientific men like Dr. Fesca, Dr. Korschelt, Dr. T. Harada, and Dr. J. Takayama, have been connected with it in one or another capacity. *Geological Survey.*

Its objects as set forth originally were as follow : *Objects of the survey.*

1. A topographical survey of the whole of Japan (excluding the Hokkaidō) ; the construction of maps and sections showing the relation and distribution of the different formations and illustrating the geological structure of the country.

2. An agronomical survey ; the construction of maps, showing the characters and positions of soils, and an examination of the soils with the view of preserving and improving their fertility ; especially an agronomical survey of those portions of the country not yet under cultivation, but likely to be fit for cultivation ; and an inquiry into the quality, abundance, and accessibility of such mineral fertilizers as may be found.

3. An examination of ores and coals, of deposits of such materials as might prove useful in the arts and manufactures, of building-stones, and materials necessary for other technical purposes.

There are two series of geological maps. At first the country was divided into five reconnaissance divisions, and three more divisions—including Formosa, the Loochoo Islands, and the southern islands of the provinces Ōsumi and Satsuma —have been added since. Each of these reconnaissance divisions was subdivided into smaller divisions, which were to extend over 1 ° of longitude and ½ ° of latitude. The geological maps were to correspond to this method of division. The reconnaissance maps were to be on the scale of 1 : 400,000, and were to represent the general geological features of each reconnaissance division. Five of these, corresponding to the *Geological maps.*

original five reconnaissance divisions, have been published. Maps of the other kind were to be on the scale of 1 : 200,000, corresponding to each of the smaller divisions, and on them geological formations are delineated in different colours, and the localities of materials possessing any economic importance are indicated by conventional signs. Of these detailed maps, sixty-six have been published up to the present, leaving thirty-three more to be finished.

Agro-
nomical
maps.

Of the agronomical work, a survey of forty-one prefectures out of forty-five in Japan has been made, thirty-eight being already finished, and three still in progress. Agronomical maps (scale 1 : 150,000) of thirty-five prefectures had been issued up to 1904.

Besides the regular work, the geological survey of special districts important from the economical point of view—such as coal-fields, oil-fields, various ore-deposits—has also been made.

Geological
survey
of the
Hokkaidō.

A further geological survey [1] of the Hokkaidō was begun in 1888 under the direction of K. Jimbō, as chief geologist, with the object of making a general reconnaissance of the whole of Hokkaidō and explorations of its mineral resources. After Jimbō left the position in 1891, his assistants continued the work till 1896.

Professor
Wada.

In connection with Geology, special mention should be made of Mr. T. Wada's collection of Japanese minerals, which he has spent many years in bringing together, and which is considered the best of its kind in existence. His book on 'Minerals of Japan' (1904) is recognized as the standard work on the subject.

Tōkyō
Geological
Society.

The Tōkyō Geological Society is domiciled in the Geological Institute of the Science College, Imperial University, and publishes a monthly periodical, the *Journal of the Geological Society of Tōkyō*, which is in its sixteenth volume. The Tōkyō Geographical Society is an aristocrat among scientific societies, being the only one that has rooms of its own and is patronized by princes and noblemen. It publishes the *Journal of Geography*, which is now in its twenty-first year.

[1] Previous ones had been made (see Vol. I, p. 609) by Messrs. Blake and Pumpelly, and later by Lyman.

ANTHROPOLOGY AND ARCHÆOLOGY

One of the incidents of Professor Morse's residence in Japan was his discovery and investigation of a prehistoric shell-mound at Ōmori, near Tōkyō. He had often noticed, when travelling by railway, what seemed to be a section of a pre-historic shell-mound near the station of Ōmori, and, going to the spot at an early opportunity, he found his surmises to be correct. He made a thorough study of the mound, and published the results in a Memoir of the Tōkyō University. This event seems to have made a great impression on one who was then a small boy—S. Tsuboi. All through his boyhood, his student days, and as a professor in the Science College, he never swerved from the purpose of making a thorough study of prehistoric remains in Japan, and by his enthusiasm and genius he succeeded in establishing the study of Anthro-pology and Archæology in the University and in forming a band of enthusiastic investigators in these matters in Japan. In 1900, the number of spots from which the remains of the stone age had been collected by Tsuboi and his followers had swelled to the large total of 3468, of which 328 are reported to be shell-heaps, and the map in the Anthropological Institute of the Science College, on which these spots are marked with red points, begins to look like the face of a patient afflicted with measles. The number of interesting facts which these investi-gations have brought out in regard to the prehistoric inhabitants of Japan is very great. Nor are these archæological researches the only directions in which Japanese anthropologists have exerted themselves. They have studied savage and primitive races in Japan and its neighbouring countries. Thus the Ainu of Hokkaidō, the aborigines of Formosa, the Miao-Tze of the Province of Sze-Chwan in China, &c., have in turn been carefully and minutely studied by Professor Koganéi (of the Medical College), Professor Tsuboi, Mr. Torii, and others.

The Tōkyō Anthropological Society, with its journal (now in its twenty-fourth volume), has aided greatly in the prosecution of these studies, and may be said to be a model of an active scientific association.

Marginal notes: Shell-mounds. Anthropology in the Tōkyō University. Professor Tsuboi. Tōkyō Anthropological Society.

In the foregoing pages I have tried to give an idea as to what the status of the Natural History studies was in the Tokugawa days, or at the time when Commodore Perry first came to Japan, and how each of the principal Natural Sciences has started and developed in modern Japan. In each the course is very much alike. At first, European or American experts in a given subject were engaged to teach our people, and as the pupils, by study at home and abroad, came up to the required standard, they were placed at the head of their respective departments. So I hope we shall never forget our indebtedness to foreign teachers, some of whom spent the best years of their life in our country in loving and zealous devotion to their duties, and what can at present be done to show our appreciation in the way of decorations, pensions, monuments, &c., has not been neglected. The names of these men will assuredly not fail to be handed down in our history as those of benefactors of our country.

XV

THE DEVELOPMENT OF MEDICINE IN JAPAN

PROFESSOR TANÉMICHI AOYAMA, M.D. (JAPAN), AND UKABU
FUJIKAWA, M.D.

THE art of medicine being an important factor of civilization,
its development in any country necessarily bears a close relation to its progress in civilization.   But when it is required, as
here, to describe the development of the art as briefly as possible, it becomes necessary to treat it independently, showing
it, as best one can, apart from the other factors of civilization.
To treat of the subject conveniently we propose to divide it
into six periods, namely :

First period—from the prehistoric age to the reign of the
ninth Emperor Kaika (about 100 B.C.), the ' mythical age '
of Japanese medicine.

Second period (about 100 B.C.–600 A.D.)—from the reign
of the Emperor Sujin to the beginning of that of the Empress
Suiko.   It was in this period that Japan conquered Korea and
made her pay annual tribute ; as a consequence of which event,
not only the civilization of Korea found its way into Japan,
but also Confucianism and Buddhism entered through the
same medium, and the medical art of China and India followed
in their wake.

Third Period (about 600 A.D.–1570)—from the reign of
the Empress Suiko to the end of the Ashikaga Shōgunate.   In
this are included the two epochs of Japanese history—the
Nara and Héian—when intercourse with China was extensively
carried on, and when the medical art—first of the Sui
and Tang, and later of the Sung and Ming dynasty—was
introduced.

[margin note: Periods in the development of medicine.*]*

Fourth Period (1570–1750)—comprising the epochs of the supremacy of the Oda and the Toyotomi families and the first half of the Tokogawa Shōgunate. The medical art of Europe was then introduced, and was practised side by side with that adopted from China.

Fifth Period (1750–1870)—from the middle to the end of the Tokugawa Shōgunate. During this period the medical art of the West gradually gained ground. At the same time, however, the art transplanted from China also thrived, so much so that Japanese physicians of that school showed in all branches of their profession a skill much superior to that of their *confrères* on the other side of the sea.

Sixth Period (1870 onwards).

Primitive stage.

The practice of medicine in the earliest times was, all the world over, synonymous with superstition—the art of healing being almost entirely sympathetic or necromantic. Japanese medicine in its infancy was no exception to that rule. Tradition tells that, in the age of demi-gods, Ōnamuchi-no-Mikoto and Sukunahikona-no-Mikoto found methods of healing for men and for domestic animals, and also established the *modus operandi* of charms to exorcise the evil influences of beasts, birds, and insects. Here and there in the oldest historical writings we find it related that a few drugs were used —though in their crude state—with the definite object of healing such and such diseases, and, moreover, that bleeding, and a kind of water cure (by hot springs), were practised as far back as in the mythical age. There being no traces whatever that these methods of treating disease were adopted from foreign countries, we cannot but conclude that Japan had an art of medicine which she could call her own.

Effects of intercourse with Korea.

This primitive art underwent a complete change in the second period immediately after Japan was brought into contact with Korean civilization. In the time of the Emperor Suinin (first century, B.C.), the country of Mimana in Korea was united to Japan's dominion, and this soon led to the introduction of Korean civilization. It is said that a physician from Shiragi, a part of Korea, cured a certain disease in the legs of the Emperor Inkyō (beginning of fifth century), and the more celebrated doctors of the time were all Koreans engaged exclusively by the Court and nobles.

Subsequently, Japan was morally and intellectually affected by the introduction of Confucianism and Buddhism, and the original Japanese medical art, which had been superstitional, became at a bound philosophical and religious. In the first year of the reign of the Empress Suiko (593 A.D.) a Buddhist temple called Shitennōji was established in Naniwa (now Ōsaka), and in connection with it were founded a poor asylum, a free dispensary, and a charity hospital. *Effect of introduction of Confucianism and Buddhism.*

Chinese medicine and pharmacy were introduced into our country *pari passu* with gradually increasing intercourse. In the reign of the Emperor Mommu, a medical school was founded, according to the *Taihōryō*, a code of laws promulgated by the Emperor. There were in it special departments for internal medicine, surgery, pediatrics, acupuncture, shampooing, opthalmology, dental surgery, otology, &c. Among other regulations, the students, who were brought up at State expense, had to study seven years for internal medicine and five for pediatrics or surgery, and had to pass an examination before they were appointed government physicians. Coming to the Héian epoch (794–1191 A.D.) various works on the art and science of medicine were published. ' *Daidōruijūhō*,' and other books of that age, are still extant and enable us to imagine to what a flourishing state medicine attained in those days. *Introduction of Chinese medicine.* *Early books on medicine.*

Though the Chinese continued to be the only school of medicine in Japan until the introduction of the European, yet, during the thousand years of its continuance, it naturally underwent frequent modifications owing to the influence of its surroundings. Notwithstanding this, during the Héian epoch, the medicine of the Tang and of the Sung dynasty reigned supreme; and ' Ping-Yuan Hou-Lung ' and ' Chin-Chin-Fang,' the two great medical works of China at that time, were looked up to as infallible authorities. Flourishing as Buddhism was during the Nara epoch, it had not yet attained the degree of influence that it did in the succeeding Héian epoch, when our doctors came to believe in the doctrine contained in the Buddhist scriptures—namely, that all human sufferings were describable to discord between the four elements (earth, water, *The Héian epoch.* *Influence of Buddhism.*

fire, and air), and their methods of dealing with diseases were consequently materially affected. Under the ever increasing influence of Buddhism they went so far as to try to cure diseases simply by religious rites and supplications.

Influence of philosophical ideas of the Sung dynasty.

In the Kamakura epoch (1192–1332) intercourse with China was held successively with the Sung, Yuan, and Ming dynasties, and was extensively carried on in the succeeding Ashikaga epoch (1336–1573). During that period there prevailed in China a philosophical doctrine which sought to explain all natural phenomena by assuming the existence in the universe of two opposing elements, positive and negative, and this doctrine had great influence in modifying both her science and her art of medicine, which became entirely philosophical. Such were the tenets of the Sung school which, when introduced into Japan, were at once adopted. But as Buddhism still continued to spread and as those that studied medicine were mostly priests, some religious elements naturally entered into their practice. Thus very briefly was our healing art influenced, in the first three periods, by the introduction of Chinese medicine and Chinese and Indian philosophy. We shall now pass on to the Fourth Period and describe the changes brought about by Japan's contact with the civilization of the West.

Effects of intercourse with the West.

For some two thousand years from the beginning of her history Japan had intercourse only with Korea, China, and some other neighbouring countries ; but during the supremacy of the Oda family, the ' Southern Barbarians,' as the Portuguese and Spaniards were called, visited Japan and imported guns, powder, cotton, and tobacco, and taught the doctrine of Christianity. Thus were we first brought into contact with the civilization of Europe, and our medical art influenced by knowledge undreamt of.

First visit of Portuguese navigators.

It was in 1543, about forty years after the discovery of the route round the Cape of Good Hope, that a Portuguese merchant vessel came drifting to the shores of Kyūshū—a most important event in the history of Japan, as being the first appearance of any Europeans in our latitudes.

No sooner had the Portuguese entered into trade relations with Japan than they began to propagate their religion. In

1549 the famous Jesuit, St. Francis Xavier, came over the sea, Jesuit
full of energy for proselytizing work.   To this end he found it mis-
sionaries
expedient to aid the poor and treat their diseases gratuitously. and
In 1556 Sōrin Ōtomo, *daimyō* of Bungo and a Jesuit convert, medicine.
established at Funai a hospital for the indigent, and placed
it under the charge of a Jesuit physician called Lewis de
Almeida, who chiefly treated leprosy.

When Nobunaga Oda practically assumed the government Nobunaga
in the stead of the Ashikaga family, whilst on the one hand he and
Chris-
vigorously persecuted the Buddhist sects of Tendai and Ikkō, tians.
on the other he was well disposed and even generous to the
Christians.   In 1568 he gave them a plot of ground of four
chō square (about ten acres), at the entrance to the Shijō Street
of Kyōto, where they could build a church.   It was called
Nambanji (Church of the *Namban* or Southern Barbarians),
and towards its maintenance he contributed land yielding 500
koku (about 2500 bushels) of rice.   Two priests, who served
the Church, being well versed in the practice of medicine, built
wards on the premises, where poor patients were invited and
treated free of charge, all of course for the purpose of facilitating
evangelical work.   Their petition to plant and cultivate medical
plants was also granted, Nobunaga giving them an area of
fifty *chō* square in Mount Ibuki in the province of Ōmi ; thither
they transplanted three thousand kinds of medical plants, of
which the *artemisia vulgaris*, still used in moxibustion (cauteri-
zation), is said to have been one.

Hidéyoshi Toyotomi, who succeeded the Oda family in Persecu-
1585, became indignant at the intrigues of the priests of the tion of
Jesuits by
Nambanji, and sent a troop of soldiers to surprise the church, Hidé-
and had the priests escorted to Nagasaki, whence they were yoshi.
made to embark for their own country and were ordered never
to return, but their medical art was propagated by some of their
disciples at Ōsaka and Sakai, where it took firm root.   It Medical
was in this way and at this time that the medical art, designated art of the
Namban
as that of the *Namban* school, came to be established. school.

The foreigners who took the place of the Portuguese and
Spaniards in supplying Japan with Occidental civilization Dutch
were the Dutch and the English, whom the Japanese called and
English
‘ Red Hairs.’   The first Englishman that visited this country traders.

was William Adams. He arrived in a Dutch vessel at the shores of the province of Bungo in April 1600. The Dutch had begun to come towards the close of the sixteenth century, but they had no important possessions in the East before the establishment of their East India Company in 1602, nor had they as yet any trade with us worthy of notice. But immediately after the latter event they began to carry on an extensive commerce with Japan, and the English East India Company being established about the same time, there arose a keen competition between the two Companies for commerce with these islands.

Dutch merchants.

Hidéyoshi had been in his grave some time, and the government was now in the hands of Iyéyasu Tokugawa, who gave permission to English and Dutch ships to carry on commerce. But in 1621 the English merchants withdrew, and Dutch ships alone received permits, the licensed port of commerce being removed in 1641 from Hirado to Nagasaki. The Dutch East India Company took care to have always, among other officers, a physician resident at Déshima in Nagasaki for a certain term of years. This was with the object of making the Japanese realize what advantages they could derive from intercourse with foreigners, and of inducing them to open their country to foreign commerce. The most celebrated among these doctors were Armans (beginning of the seventeenth century), Caspar Schambergen (1649–50), Hoffmann (1688), and Engelbert Kaempfer (1691–92). Christianity being put under the ban of the Government, strict orders were given to the Dutch Company not to import books, and the natives were forbidden to read them. But this prohibition did not extend to the study of medicine, and the native ' interpreters ' were allowed free intercourse with the Dutch doctors and permitted to learn their art. This gave rise to the ' *Ollanda*,' or Dutch school of medicine; and there appeared various schools of surgery, namely, the Narabayashi, Yoshida, Kurisaki, Murayama, Katsura, and Caspar, which differed from one another in minor points.

Dutch medicine.

The pathology of Western medicine was founded on the doctrine of Hippocrates and Galen that all bodily sufferings had their source in discord among the four humours, blood, phlegm, yellow bile, and white bile, of which the human body is composed. Thus it will be seen that it differed but little from Chinese pathology, which ascribed all diseases to the discord of gas, blood, and phlegm, and so, in the practice of this art, the European school did not show any conspicuous superiority to the Chinese school. In surgery the works of the celebrated French surgeon, Ambroise Paré, were considered authoritative. It seems that the application of ointments was the chief feature of the European surgery, and it is needless to say how primitive the art was at that time.

After the introduction of European medicine Japan never ceased to hold intercourse of a kind with Europe, which was successively represented by Portugal, Spain, England, and Holland, but she did not derive any important benefit from the other sciences and arts of the West.

The translation in the latter part of the eighteenth century, by a physician of the Chinese school named Ryōtaku Maéno, of an odd volume of a Dutch medical work, and his success, after four years of the hardest application, in giving to the world four volumes of his ' Kaitai Shinso ' (' New Treatise on Anatomy '), has been already told (Vol. II, p. 141). This was the first translation of a European book on medicine ever printed in Japan. *First translation of European book on medicine.*

The reading public quickly acknowledged the superiority of European medicine, for they saw that it was not an outcome of idle speculation, but the result of honest investigations founded on observation and experiment. Those who had the foresight to look into the hopeless future of the Chinese school flocked to Yédo, where Maéno and his collaborator, Sugita, lived, and began to study the Dutch language as well as medicine. In the course of a few years there were translated Dutch books, not only on medicine, but also on astronomy, the industrial arts, &c. This gave rise to what is called the *Ran-gaku,* or ' Dutch Learning,' with the study of medicine as its centre. Medical students now could learn from native teachers and from translated books. But the Dutch learning may more properly be said to have had its beginning earlier than this, for Yoshimuné, the eighth Shōgun, surprised at the fineness and accuracy of pictures in Dutch books, abolished in 1720 the prohibition *Prevalence of the Dutch school of medicine.*

against the import of European books except those relating to Christianity. A Government physician of the name of Genjō Noro was ordered to study the Dutch language, and later, with the rise of the Dutch learning, the interpreters at Nagasaki were allowed to read Dutch books. The English language also began to be studied in 1809, when Motoki, Nishi, Yoshio, Baba, and other Nagasaki interpreters were ordered to make it their special study. In 1847 the '*Eibumpan*' ('English Grammar') was published by Saburō Fujii. The translation of the above-mentioned 'Anatomical Plates,' with explanations, was followed by that of European books on diagnosis, pathology, pharmacology, *materia medica*, internal medicine, surgery, obstetrics, and ophthalmology, together with some physical, chemical, and botanical works. The more important among them were Heister's ' Surgery ' (1792), Gorter's ' Internal Medicine ' (1793), Plenke's ' Ophthalmology ' (1815) and ' Surgery ' (1830), Rosenstein's ' Pediatrica ' (1830), Roose's ' Physiology ' (1832), Richerland's ' Physiology ' (1857), Hufeland's ' Experiences ' (1857), &c. Consequently, about the middle of the last century, the Japanese became more or less acquainted with the general outlines of European medicine.

Study of English.

In addition to this we must mention the names of several Dutch and German doctors, who, residing at the Dutch settlement of Déshima, taught their art to interpreters and others. They were Thunberg (1776–77), von Siebold (1823–29), Mohnike (1848–52), Pompe van Meedervort (1857–60), Baldwin (1861–66), and others.

Eminent foreign teachers of medicine.

Von Siebold deserves special mention, as, immediately after his arrival at Nagasaki in 1823, he began clinical lectures in the houses of the interpreters Yoshio and Narabayashi, opened a school at Narutaki where he taught medicine and botany, and by dint of zeal and perseverance, as well as by the greatness of his character, contributed much towards the advancement of foreign medicine in this country. How energetic he was may be gathered from the fact that, simultaneously with these labours, he busily studied Japan and things Japanese as no ordinary man could. It is true that, before his time, there had been much activity shown in the popularizing of foreign medicine for the space of thirty or forty years after the rise of the Dutch

Von Siebold.

learning, such as the teaching of ophthalmology by Rikkei Sugita, the commencement of the practice of internal medicine by Chōshuku Yoshida, &c., but it was only after von Siebold came and taught that the Japanese learned to operate in ophthalmology and obstetrics, about which they had hitherto had only book knowledge. In this way medicine, from being a mere study of books, passed into a real art in which the hand could execute what the mind dictated. Hence von Siebold the doctor deserves as much renown in Japan as von Siebold the Japanese scholar enjoys in Europe.

Of his pupils, the most famous were Gemboku Itō, Séikai Totsuka, Chōéi Takano, Sanéi Ozéki, Ryōsai Kō, Genséki Habu, Gendō Takénouchi, Kéisuké Itō, &c. Itō, Totsuka, and Takenouchi were afterwards appointed Government physicians, Habu and Kō opened the practice of European ophthalmology, and Takano was involved in politics, all contributing to popularize European medicine. *Siebold's pupils.*

But meanwhile the Chinese school had been making remarkable progress, and had reached such a degree of development that it was now far ahead of the art as practised in the land which had given it birth. It soon came in collision with the new Dutch school, and a petition was presented to the Government by the men of the old school to prohibit the practice of Western medicine. In 1849 this petition resulted in the issue of an order which made it necessary to obtain Government permission to translate Dutch books on medicine. The censorship being placed in the hands of the Government board of medicine, the members of which were mostly doctors of the old school, the publication of European medical books was thus practically prohibited. *Conflict between Western and Chinese schools.*

But shortly after this Commodore Perry visited Japan, and the country fell into a state of unrest. All parties were agreed, however, as to the necessity of strengthening the national defences, and such medical books as treated of gunshot wounds naturally came into urgent demand, ' *Jūsō Sagén* ' (' Treaties on Gunshot Wounds '), a translation by Shunsai Ōtsuki, for instance, being allowed to be printed. It appeared in 1854, and thenceforth the persecution to which the Chinese school had subjected Western medicine gradually lost its *Visit of Commodore Perry.* *Superiority of Western medicine generally acknowledged.*

rigour. Soon after this, an order was even issued to encourage
the study and practice of the Dutch school, and the Government
established two medical schools, one at Yédo and the other
at Nagasaki. Thus, while the political and diplomatic world
of Japan was in the throes of violent commotion caused by
Perry's visit, our medicine was the first to be favourably
influenced by that event.

English
influence.

As already mentioned, Japan's intercourse with Great
Britain in the Fourth Period was of short duration, and English
influence on our medicine was not so great as that of Holland,
Germany, and France. But it would be an injustice to say
that England contributed nothing to our medicine. There are
instances that show how much we owe her. The ' Sankwa
Hatsumō ' (' Elements of Obstetrics '), published in 1795, by
Kakuryō Katakura, a pupil of Génétsu Kagawa, the celebrated
specialist of midwifery, contains pictures of difficult parturitions
taken from an English book, though the name of the book and
of the author are now forgotten. Further, there is in the same
volume a picture of William Smillie's forceps, and the author
recommends the use of an instrument fashioned after this model.
Following this suggestion, Ryutéi Tatsuno soon after invented
an instrument which he christened Hōtōki, and which may be
said to be the first forceps for obstetric operations ever used
in Japan. It will be seen from this that the practice of eminent
English doctors did, through the medium of Dutch physicians,
find its way into Japan's medicine in the Fifth Period of
its history.

Effects of
the inter-
course
with
America.

But it was in the beginning of the Sixth Period, and after
Terry's visit, that English influence materially affected our
medicine. That event led to Japan's intercourse with
America, and medicine shared in the results of the close
contact that ensued with American and English sciences. In
1860 Shūkéi Makiyama, a Government doctor, went to America
on board one of our warships, and about this time medical
books began to be imported from America in large numbers,
while the works (in Chinese) of Hobson, an English doctor,
were reprinted.

In the first year of Méiji, the battles attending the Restoration sharply emphasized the need of military surgery, and an

English doctor, William Willis, was engaged to accompany the Imperial forces to the north-eastern part of the country, where he conferred much benefit on our surgeons by showing them various novel examples of surgical operations. When peace was restored, the Government established a hospital in Tōkyō with the intention of making it the basis of a future medical college, and offered the care of it to the Englishman who had done so much during the war. He complied with the request, and, according to the English system, he set up a medical school attached to the hospital and devoted himself to educating students as well as managing the hospital. It was a great success, containing at one time as many as three hundred patients.

New epoch of medical development.

But two years later the Government changed its original plan, deciding to invite professors of medicine from Germany, and to put the hospital and school under their charge. So William Willis left the capital and was engaged in the medical school at Kagoshima. There he worked till 1877, and a large number of excellent medical men were turned out at his school.

Introduction of German medicine.

In order to carry out its plan of adopting the German system of medical education, the Government, simultaneously with inviting German professors, decided to dispatch students to that country to prosecute the study of medicine. Thirteen were consequently sent, and the next year two German military surgeons, Müller and Hoffmann, arrived, pioneers of many German professors who followed in their wake. The more conspicuous among them were Wernich, Disse, Schulz, Denitz, and especially Baelz and Scriba.

The Various improvements have been introduced into the system of medical education, and it has attained such a degree of perfection that there are at present, besides the Medical College of the Imperial University of Tōkyō, two other Colleges of Medicine at Kyōto and Fukuoka. In all these university colleges the course runs for four years, the professors are all Japanese, and graduates are given the title of *Igakushi*. In addition to the above three colleges there are eight medical schools, five of which are maintained by the Government and three by the prefectures in which they are. The course in these schools runs for four years, and graduates obtain the

Improvements of medical education.

title of *Igaku-Tokugyōshi.* Many graduates from these colleges and schools go abroad, to Germany as a rule, for study, some by Government order and others at their own expense.

Influence of English medicine. Although in 1870 William Willis left the capital, and German professors were invited to teach medicine in their own language, an English doctor, W. Anderson, was engaged in the Naval Medical School, and some graduates from that institution were sent to England and America, so that English influence still continued to make itself felt. Gray's ' Anatomy,' Flint's and Dalton's ' Physiology,' Lindel's, Gross's, and Sane's ' Surgery,' and many other medical works in English were introduced.

Dentistry was introduced by an American, who opened practice at Yokohama about 1872. There are many Japanese who have learned this art in America, and the dentists enjoying the largest practices are all graduates from American schools.

Recent progress of medicine. Limits of space do not allow us to describe in full the marvellous development medicine has made in the last twenty years. Suffice it to say that there is no branch of medicine which has not an association of the fraternity for its special **Medical magazines.** promotion and study, and that there are over fifty medical magazines. Among these last the more important contain extracts from English and German magazines, and one has a special section written in English. The memoirs of the medical colleges of the Imperial universities are written entirely in German, and those of the Military Medical School are written in German and in Japanese.

Number of medical practitioners. According to the latest returns the medical practitioners number over 36,000, of whom 15,000 have studied Chinese or old Dutch medicine, while some 7000 have received the latest medical education in schools and colleges. Graduates from the universities in Europe and America are given licences to practise without examination. Those who have studied in private schools and under individual doctors have to pass an examination, held twice a year (in spring and autumn), before they are allowed to commence practice. There are over 10,000 practitioners of this class.

Conclusion. A nation is no prophet's gourd, the civilization it has attained is the sum-total of all the factors which have contributed to make up the great whole. Moreover, throughout the period of its development each factor has had a history of its own. Our medicine is what it is, because it has maintained a long course of improvement. It was because we had our primitive medicine in the 'Age of the Gods' that medicine could be introduced from Korea. Had not our original medicine and that introduced from Korea made ground, the Chinese and Indian medicines could not have been adopted, and it was again on account of the presence of the last two that the medicine of the West could be introduced and assimilated. Just as Japan, absorbing all the civilization of the world, has succeeded in producing one peculiar to herself and is now at a high point of progress, even so our medicine, absorbing everything excellent in the systems with which it came in contact, has succeeded in assimilating them all, so as to make itself a science and art worthy of this glorious era.

XVI

MEDICINE AND HYGIENE IN JAPAN, AND THEIR INDEBTEDNESS TO ENGLAND AND AMERICA

Professor Hiizu Miyaké, M.D. (Japan)

Following, as this paper does, one which treats of the development of medicine in Japan, it must of necessity travel over some ground that has already been traversed. This will, therefore, be my excuse for omitting all mention of events anterior to fifty years ago, in which English or American surgery and medicine played a part, and commencing my story with the first introduction of Japan to these professions in the countries themselves. This occurred in 1860, when the Shōgunate Government sent their first envoy to America, Shūkéi Makiyama, a physician of the Dutch school, going with him by the *Kanrin Maru*, the first Japanese warship that crossed the Pacific. They arrived at San Francisco, and, while there, directed their attention to the subject of medical progress in America, but only to see how hopelessly behindhand they themselves were; and thus, dumfounded, they returned empty-handed. My father was an acquaintance of Zenshirō Narusé, a member of the party, and through him managed to get some seeds of American medicinal plants. Up to that time all medicinal materials had been brought to this country over tropical seas, and naturally, before arriving, had lost more or less of the active properties that they were stated in Dutch books to possess. Having thus obtained new materials from America, my father had the satisfaction of producing drugs giving proper effects. The Government of the United States, too, kindly presented to our envoy certain books on medical science, which in our eyes to-day

Introduction of American medical herbs.

American medical books.

we find of no special merit, some of them containing certain homeopathic elements such as are seen in the Chinese system. Nevertheless, they were of great value at that time.

In that year, namely 1860, Dr. J. C. Hepburn, the first American medical missionary, who was sent to Japan by the American Dutch Reformed Mission, and the first compiler of a Japanese-English Dictionary, came to Kanagawa, and gave medical attention to the sick of that district, at the same time affording our physicians a chance of studying under him. Later he opened a dispensary at Yokohama, which resulted in an extensive practice. At that time a number of English physicians attached to the British troops happened to be at Yokohama, and they assisted him in his surgical operations. Tanosuké Sawamura, a celebrated actor, suffering from gangrene in one of his legs, underwent an operation at the hands of Dr. Hepburn and the English surgeons. They also procured for him a Selph's artificial leg—a very ingeniously made affair. Some Dutch surgeons in Nagasaki had been reputed for professional skill at a much earlier date, but this being the first instance of so brilliant a success accomplished at a place in close proximity to the capital, the fame of the operators spread through the length and breadth of the land. Shortly afterwards Alexander E. Vedder, naval surgeon on board an American warship, resigned his post and opened practice at Yokohama for foreign residents and seamen. Under him I received instruction and training, and I also studied at Dr. Hepburn's dispensary. He used to tell us that France was taking the lead in medicine, and Germany following in its wake. In spite of this, after the Restoration in 1868, Japan decided to follow Germany in medicine. It was probably due to Dutch physicians at Nagasaki who had spoken in praise of recent progress in German medicine, and opinion in this country was influenced by their words. At this moment there was residing at Nagasaki an American, the Rev. G. F. Verbeck, who afterwards became the teacher of Count Ōkuma and other notabilities. He, too, urged that Japan should learn medicine from Germany, and accordingly our Government expressed to Prussia its desire that she would send us some medical teachers. But as

Dr. Hepburn.

Alexander Vedder.

Dr. Verbeck's advice.

it happened, she was then engaged in war with France, and some two years elapsed before she could comply with our request. Previously to this, during the war of the Restoration, an English physician, Dr. Willis, was in the employ of the Imperial Army, and when the war came to an end he was appointed surgical instructor at the Military Hospital in Tōkyō. He was the first to teach us aseptic treatment, of which we had hitherto no knowledge.

Dr. Willis's service.

Thus it will be seen that, before the German teachers arrived, English surgery had taken root in Japan, and immediately afterwards the English system of internal treatment came into frequent use. As too an American physician, Dr. Henry Hartshorne's work on the ' Theory and Practice of Medicine' was at this time translated into Japanese by Dr. Kōhéi Kuwata, the popularity it gained was a further blow to the Dutch school. In those days intercourse between Germany and Japan was very limited, and few could read German, so that medical instruments, drugs, and books came chiefly from England and America, whose language we well understood, and very seldom, if ever, from Germany. This circumstance doubtless assisted in inducing us to welcome Anglo-American influence in medicine.

English medicine.

To go back for a moment. In 1862, or thereabouts, an English physician named Benjamin Hobson had translated some English medical works into Chinese ; these dealt with surgery, obstetrics, and internal medicine. My father purchased these books from China, and, seeing that they differed greatly from the Dutch system in the treatment of diseases, he reprinted them with certain linguistic alterations. This publication, together with the various influences which came upon us after the Restoration, removed the last trace of Dutch medical influence. And thus, although, as I have said, Germany at the beginning played an important part on the medical stage in Japan, there were nevertheless many who went to England or to America for the prosecution of their studies, a practice which continues up to the present time.

Removal of Dutch medical influence.

In dentistry especially we owe much to America, and many cross the Pacific to qualify themselves in that department.

American dentistry.

The art of nursing the sick having originated with Miss Nightingale, we have naturally looked for instruction to her native land. Nursin of the sick.

Hygiene, I need hardly say, is nothing more than one department of medicine, and is sometimes called Preventive Medicine, since by means of it we ward off illness. This preventive medicine developed first in England, and was then adopted by the Americans, who enforced its rules by the help of administrative means. In the early years of Méiji, when Japanese officials were sent to Europe and America for investigations of all kinds, Dr. Sensai Nagayo was dispatched to America. The main object of his visit was to study the system of medical education, but he soon found that the adoption of administrative measures with a view to promoting public health was of more urgent need than the promotion of medical knowledge itself. To learn this England seemed to him best suited, being the home, as it were, of hygiene, and accordingly he crossed over to England, after a very short stay in America. In England he found that the sanitary system and its practice were all but perfection, and, rather to his disappointment, too good for imitation. Consequently he went to Holland, thinking that in a country where hygiene was carried out on a smaller scale it would be easier to learn, and, after gathering a certain amount of knowledge there, he returned, and tried to apply by degrees to his own country what he had learned beyond the seas. Hygiene. Sanitary system of England.

The first step in improvement was the introduction of a licentiate examination for physicians. The subjects in which the candidates had to be examined were anatomy, physiology, *materia medica*, medicine, surgery, ophthalmology, and obstetrics. At this time, however, there was no book in a concise form which dealt with these subjects for the use of candidates. Consequently when the translation of Dr. Hartshorne's 'Compendium' appeared, it met with enthusiastic welcome from all medical students, and the Government, too called in its aid for examination purposes. Licence examination of physicians.

Shortly after the Restoration English warships began to frequent Japan, and many seamen who came on shore contracted diseases of the worst description. The British Measures for preventing venereal diseases.

Admiralty thereupon made representations to the Japanese authorities as to the examination of public prostitutes in the open ports.   Under the direction of some English surgeons the necessary measures were put into practice, and this was one of the earliest sanitary steps taken in Japan.

Vaccina-
tion.

The next was to obtain vaccine from abroad through Dutch physicians, by which to commence vaccination. This most effective preventive against small-pox was, as everyone knows, discovered by Dr. Jenner, of England, and we ever remember his name with gratitude for his great service to mankind.

Dr.
Eldridge.

In the work of bringing Hokkaidō under cultivation we were greatly indebted to an American benefactor, for when the enterprise was about to be started, General Capron visited this country with a party, among whom was Dr. Eldridge. The latter rendered much help in developing the resources of the district, and also imparted his profound medical knowledge to many of its inhabitants.   Nor was this all, as, some years later, he took part in framing the law to prevent the importation of infectious diseases from foreign lands, and did great service in training our quarantine officers at the open ports.

Dr. Man-
ning and
Dr. Ash-
mead.

At the time of the Restoration our hospitals were exclusively confined to the use of the army, but when the ' North-Eastern Rebellion ' was suppressed, the Military Hospital in Tōkyō was turned over to the Imperial University, and later, as the Tōkyō municipality developed, a Civil Hospital was erected there, at which Dr. Manning, an English physician, and Dr. A. S. Ashmead, an American, were charged with medical duties, and delivered lectures to native physicians.

Japan at
the Inter-
national
Medical
Confer-
ence in
Philadel-
phia.

In 1876 an International Medical Conference met at the International Exposition in Philadelphia.   To this Dr. Nagayo was sent to represent Japan, and I went in attendance upon him.   This was the first time that Japan had sent a representative to a meeting of an international character, and I had the honour to be elected Vice-President of the Conference.   Since my duties were principally concerned with medical education, I took every opportunity to investigate matters bearing upon that subject.   America has always been very ready to adopt foreign improvements, and it was my opinion that Japan would do wisely to follow her in educational matters. For instance, America was then importing German medicines, and I could not but admire her eagerness to correct her own shortcomings by the example of other nations. Dr. Nagayo's chief aim being on the side of sanitary administration, he studied, among others, the following measures for preventing infectious diseases, namely, the method of taking statistics of births and deaths ; the regulations concerning water-supply and sewage ; the treatment of refuse ; industrial hygiene ; regulations concerning food and drink ; the sanitation of railway carriages, omnibuses, and other means of communication, &c. The plan of introducing Dutch sanitation had, for some reason, been postponed in Japan, and when Dr. Nagayo returned from America with the results of his investigations, the time was fully ripe for executing the new plans, for very shortly afterwards the country suffered from a severe epidemic of cholera, which proved to be an unlooked-for piece of good fortune, for it saved the inauguration of the new measures from difficulties and obstacles which might have arisen at other times. The prosperous condition of sanitation in this country at present is due mainly to the good influence of the Americans, who, in their turn, were indebted to their model, England.

Whilst to the east of us we have a highly civilized neighbour, America, beyond a narrow strip of water on the west we have China and Korea—countries where even the numbers of births and deaths are not accurately known. Hence we are liable to be attacked by pestilence at any moment, and this is a circumstance that renders our attention to public health particularly necessary. It is, therefore, a source of satisfaction that means of preventing infectious diseases are carefully taken, that sanitary rules are strictly observed, that in the principal towns water-works have been completed, and, finally, that food and drink are placed under strict supervision. Also, I may add that all sea-bathing and hot-spring resorts are submitted to proper superintendence. We have, therefore, no anxiety in these respects, and foreign tourists may now travel in this country with little inconvenience and no danger.

That we have become able to enjoy the benefits of advanced

Sanitary administration.

sanitation in so short a space of time is, we are fully aware, due to the example and guidance of our respected friends, the English and the Americans.

Let me, in conclusion, make a few short remarks upon the present state of medical progress in Japan.

Sanitary condition of the Japanese Army. In every war we have undertaken we have been accustomed to witness an enormous increase in the sick, the number often reaching hundreds of times the casualties in actual fighting. There have also been abundant instances of epidemics appearing among the troops, and spreading thence over the whole land. In the last war, contrary to this rule, our soldiers suffered little from epidemics, in spite of the trying climate and innumerable hardships they had to undergo. This goes to prove that the sheltering of the troops and the commissariat arrangements were good, that the supplies were ample, and that all sanitary rules were satisfactorily observed. Further, that our wounded recovered their fighting power in a little time may be regarded as another evidence of the above facts.

Medical administration. To attend to the sanitary condition of the empire is one of the chief duties of the Home Department. Its Sanitary Bureau superintends physicians, apothecaries, and midwives. At a recent census there were 35,160 physicians, 2898 pharmacists, 26,837 apothecaries, and 25,959 midwives.

Veterinary surgeons come under the purview of the Agricultural and Commercial Department, and numbered at the same time 4034.

Unions of medical practitioners. Most of the above practitioners are members of ' Unions,' which are under the control of the respective local governments, their objects being to protect their business rights and look after their members. Apothecaries and midwives also have something corresponding to the physician's ' Unions.'

Medical education. Physicians and apothecaries get their training in Government, public, or private schools, or under private teachers ; but some of the latter are trained in apothecaries' shops. Those who have had their training in private institutions are, in all cases, compelled to undergo a Government examination before commencing to practise. There are five medical and pharmaceutical schools established by the Government, and four public and about twelve private ones. In some of the Government and public schools special short-term courses are provided, and only licensed persons may take them up. To give an example, the Tōkyō Imperial University has a course called the State Medicine Course, and the outlines of that subject are taught in a term of three months. The schools of dentistry are mostly private, and some of them are fairly good. A graduate goes through a Government examination, and if successful is given a diploma, and is allowed to open business in much the same way as a physician.

In nearly every part of the empire one sees medical associations, and thirty-nine are in a particularly prosperous condition. They deal with nearly all branches of medicine. Subjects relating to the science of medicine, with the exception of physiology and pathology, have each a special association. The associations hold regular meetings monthly, in which the results of various investigations are reported, and general meetings are held annually or bi-annually. Sometimes a joint meeting of all associations is held. Each association publishes a journal, of which there are about seventy. Again, some have their special laboratories, and schools and hospitals, as means of new and exhaustive research. Most of their reports are in Japanese, but some—e.g. the '*Séii Kai Geppō*' ('Memoirs of the College of Medicine') — are in English, while some others—e.g. the '*Ika Daigaku Kiyō*' — are in German. *Medical associations.*

The most celebrated of the laboratories is Dr. Kitasato's Bacteriological Institute. Here licensed physicians, either Japanese or foreign, may be taught the principles of bacteriology in three months. There are, likewise, several Government and private hygiene laboratories. Their chief business is to examine, on application, foods, drinks, utensils, chemicals, and mineral waters. *Medical and hygienic laboratories.*

With the object of promoting the health of the younger generation, much importance has been attached to bodily exercises in all schools. Thus gymnastics has been placed among the compulsory subjects, and various sports have been encouraged. The schools, moreover, have school physicians, whose duties are to look after the general health and the sanitary conditions in their respective schools, and to make *Physical culture in schools.* *School physicians.*

physical examination of the pupils at fixed intervals. There were at a recent census 9664 school physicians in the country. Again, there are a number of societies and clubs **Hygienic** which aim at physical training and athletics. Hygienic **societies.** societies are almost innumerable, and of them the specially important are the Japan Hygienic Association and the Japan Women's Hygienic Association, each having several thousands of members, spread over the whole of Japan. These societies hold lecture meetings every now and then, in order to propagate hygienic knowledge.

Hospitals. The country abounds in hospitals. The most important of these number nearly a thousand. This figure includes charity hospitals, of which some are for lepers, and others for the sick children of the poor. A society for the help of lunatics has lately been organized. All these charity institutions are supported in the main by ladies of the higher classes.

XVII

THE RED CROSS IN JAPAN

Surgeon-General Baron Tadanori Ishiguro (Ret.)

Occidentals seem to hold, with a certain amount of pride, that the spirit of humanity which in these days tends to alleviate the horrors of war, is a product peculiar to their own modern civilization. But this magnanimity, which enables men to treat enemies who have lost their fighting power no longer as adversaries but as brothers, and to extend kindness and protection to those who have surrendered, has been a special characteristic of our nation from all time. It is not a mere accident that the people of Japan have of late years devoted so much attention to the development of the philanthropic work of the Red Cross Convention of Geneva; it is rather attributable to a love of mercy deeply rooted in the hearts of all true Japanese, and transmitted from their forefathers through many a generation; a spirit which has ever led them, during the twenty centuries of the existence of the Japanese Empire, to endeavour to mitigate the unavoidable miseries of war by acts of benevolence and generosity. The pages of our history abound in deeds of chivalry on the battlefield, in the form of care for a wounded enemy, or of generosity towards those who have voluntarily surrendered.

The Japanese naturally humanitarian.

It is recorded that in the expedition undertaken by the Empress Jingō against Korea, one of five famous orders issued by her was, ' Spare all who surrender, but destroy all who refuse to yield.' As this expedition took place during the third century of the Christian era, it will be seen that this humane decree preceded the introduction of Chinese civilization into Japan and also the ethical teachings of Confucius.

The Empress Jingō's attitude towards her enemies.

In the fourteenth century, when the country was distracted
by a disastrous civil war, it is recorded of the great general
Masashigé Kusunoki, that on many occasions, after treating
his captives with extreme kindness, he set them free, having
first presented each with a new suit of clothes.

Later, towards the close of the sixteenth century, when the
country was again plunged into prolonged internal dissensions
owing to the struggle for mastery among numerous clans, the
horror and bloodshed in which these struggles abounded
served to throw into strong relief many a deed disclosing the
bright and humane side of the Japanese. Two of the most
formidable rival chiefs of that time were Kenshin Uyésugi and
Shingén Takéda. The clan of Takéda occupied the inland
mountainous district of Kai and Shinano, and had to depend
for their supply of salt entirely upon the seaward provinces of
Suruga and Sagami. Imagawa, the Lord of Suruga, and Hōjō,
the Lord of Sagami, conspired to harass and injure their
powerful neighbour, Lord Takéda, by cutting off the supply,
and the whole of his two provinces of Kai and Shinano were
reduced to grave straits for lack of this necessary adjunct of
life. But when Uyésugi, Takéda's most uncompromising foe,
heard of this conspiracy, he denounced their unmanly conduct
in unmeasured terms, saying that they were no true warriors
who could be so mean and cowardly as to injure the peaceful
and helpless people of a chieftain, instead of meeting him in
fair fight and strategy, and he at once directed the merchants
of his own dominions of Échigo to supply the commodity to his
suffering enemies.

The Korean expedition of Hidéyoshi in the same century
was one long triumph, but on his return he erected a monument
to the memory of the souls of his enemies who had fallen in the
field, and the Lord Shimazu, who took a most distinguished
part in that campaign, set up a monument in his own family
cemetery on Mount Kōya, a monument still in existence,
inscribed with the words : ' In memory of Friends and Foes
who fell in the War.' A large number of Korean captives who
were brought to Japan during that campaign were also gener-
ously treated. Plots of land were bestowed upon them, and
they were assigned occupations suitable to their abilities ; the

descendants of these naturalized Korean captives are still to be found in some number in Kagoshima and elsewhere in South Japan.

These instances serve to show that in the past Japan has shared with other nations of the world the virtues of chivalry and mercy in war.

I will now proceed to give a brief review of the organization of Red Cross work in Japan.

In 1871, soon after the Restoration, the Imperial Government, in establishing a War Department for both the Army and Navy (*Hyōbushō*), included therein a medical bureau. Surgeon-General Jun Matsumoto was appointed director of the bureau, and he and Surgeon Ki Hayashi and myself were keenly interested in rumours which had reached us of an association existing among civilized countries of the West for the purpose of giving medical aid impartially to friends and foes in time of war, and whereby surgeons and nurses engaged in such work were exempted from the usual risks of war. *Japanese Government first informed of Red Cross work.*

Not possessing any definite knowledge on the subject, which we wished, if possible, to adopt, we made inquiries everywhere. Our well-meant efforts were not, however, very successful, for in those days Japan had no specialist on International Law, and we therefore lacked the means of carrying out our investigations. One thing only was clear, namely, that the sign of a Red Cross was used in Europe to distinguish a military surgeon, a field hospital, or a sick or wounded man ; also, that a person carrying this badge, or a place indicated by it, was regarded as neutral in time of war, and therefore immune from belligerent risks. Thus far we obtained information, but of the why and wherefore we were still ignorant.

At that time peace reigned in Japan, and there was apparently no possibility that it would ever again be disturbed either by civil or foreign war. General Saigō was Commander-in-Chief of the Imperial Body-Guard, and that such a distinguished soldier should instigate, as he did many years afterwards, a disastrous domestic war, was the last thing the public could have anticipated.

But most of the intelligent thinkers of those days were of the opinion that, if Japan were ever again involved in war,

First step
towards
the
adoption
of the Red
Cross
system.

it would be with a foreign country, and therefore they thought it well to adopt the sign in common use among other countries to distinguish surgeons, nurses, hospitals, and medical stores. Accordingly, the Director of the Army Medical Staff represented matters to the *Dajōkan*, or Council of State, and petitioned that the distinctive sign of the ' Red Cross ' should be adopted by our Army Medical Service. The uniform of the Army and its standard had meanwhile been determined upon, but to our deep regret the petition for the sign of the ' Red Cross ' was rejected on the ground that it was an absurd idea, worthy only of ' abject followers of Western Medicine.' In such a light was it that the Director and we, his colleagues, were regarded by a certain section in official circles at that time.

The ' abject followers of Western Medicine ' could only console themselves with the certain assurance that, sooner or later, the time would come when their supposed ' heretical ' idea would secure public support and be adopted perforce by the Service. Balked in their first attempt, the Surgeon-General and his coadjutors resorted to a further expedient: they suggested to the Council of State that a red horizontal line on a white ground should serve as the distinguishing mark of the Japanese Army Medical Service, hoping that if this were granted, they would in time be able to add a vertical line, and thus easily convert the badge into the world-worn ' Red Cross ' of their original intention. This suggested compromise obtained the approval of the august Council of State, and from 1872 was used to designate the Medical Service. It may therefore be regarded as the inauguration of the Geneva Convention in Japan.

The scheme thus promoted by a handful of army surgeons received powerful support from altogether unexpected quarters.

Ōyama
and Sano's
visit to
Europe.

Soon after the termination of the internal struggles which attended the work of the Restoration, Mr. (now Marshal Prince) Ōyama was sent to Europe to prosecute the study of modern military science, and while in France and Switzerland for that purpose he witnessed the sanguinary operations of the Franco-Prussian War. He saw young officers and soldiers alike, both French and Prussian, brought into France by trains flying the flag of the Red Cross, or cared for at field hospitals over which it was hoisted, while all those who treated or attended to the wounded bore the same badge.   Our student officer was deeply impressed by the way in which these humane deeds were carried out in the midst of so much carnage, and when he returned to Japan, he never ceased to narrate to Ministers of State and other distinguished personages, as well as to the public at large whenever opportunity offered, the experiences which had impressed him so deeply. Somewhat later, Mr. (afterwards Count) Tsunétami Sano was appointed Minister to the Japanese Legation in Vienna, and, being a scion of a medical family, was highly interested in the Red Cross exhibits which he saw at the World's Fair in Vienna in 1873.   He became still more interested in seeing the work in the field of a Red Cross Ambulance Corps upon imaginary cases during the manœuvres. The Count returned home, carrying with him a strong conviction that a Red Cross organization was a vital necessity for his country.

Pressure was thus brought to bear on the Council of State, from within by the Surgeon-General Director of the Army Medical Staff, and from without by the two influential men newly returned from Europe, Ōyama and Sano.   At last the empire's statesmen were able to understand the spirit and meaning of the ' Red Cross,' and in 1875 the proposal of Surgeon-General Matsumoto to adopt the sign for official purposes was approved by the Council. In the meanwhile, they had gradually acquired some knowledge of International Law, and had appreciated that without the consent of the nations concerned it was impossible for Japan to arbitrarily adopt the regulation badge of the Geneva Convention. Therefore, while Sano was actively promoting a scheme for establishing a Red Cross Society in Japan, the Surgeon-General and myself lost no opportunity of representing to the authorities that Japan must formally join the Convention. But meanwhile, in 1877, before either object had been accomplished, a rebellion in Kagoshima, led by General Saigō, occasioned a most sanguinary civil war. The fighting was severe and the casualties appalling, the opposing detachments sometimes losing two-thirds of their number in killed and wounded. In compliance with my earnest representations the authorities

Proposal to join the Red Cross Convention.

Military
hospital
during the
civil war.
established a temporary military hospital at Ōsaka, in which were received casualties of both sides.   Sano also was not idle, but was doing his utmost in Tōkyō to create an organization based on the lines of the Red Cross work he had witnessed in Vienna, and in Viscount Ogyū he found an enthusiastic helpmate.   The two philanthropists consulted Baron von Siebold of Austria, then resident in Tōkyō, as to the internal arrangements of European Red Cross Societies, and guided

Pre-
cursor
of the Red
Cross
Society of
Japan.
by the information thus obtained, they drew up a set of rules, collected funds from all possible quarters, and at last organized a philanthropic body, which was duly inaugurated under the title of *Hakuaisha*, or the 'Society of Universal Love,' with His late Imperial Highness Prince Komatsu as honorary president.

The newly created society hastened to obtain from the Commander-in-Chief of the Imperial Army permission to undertake the care of the wounded on both sides during the civil war then raging, subject of course to the Army Medical Department.   This sanction secured, a small medical corps, commensurate with the few thousand *yen* then at the disposal of the association, was at once dispatched to Kumamoto, the seat of war.   The Imperial troops looked somewhat askance at such an innovation as the *Hakuaisha*, but ultimately entrusted it with the care of fifteen or sixteen wounded prisoners, and these were tended at the *Hakuaisha's* temporary hospital improvised in an untenanted house leased for the purpose. Thus unpretentiously was organized the Red Cross Society of Japan, which now exercises a wide-felt influence throughout the length and breadth of the empire and is rendering valuable service to the State.

The sign adopted by this embryo Red Cross Society in 1877 was a dot placed over a horizontal red line.   Simple enough, it is nevertheless memorable in that it represented the second stage of the progress of Red Cross work in Japan.

At the termination of the civil war, the dissolution of the *Hakuaisha* was mooted, but this was strongly opposed by its president, Prince Komatsu, as well as by Count Sano and others of its founders, who not only averted this, but ultimately gained for it a position of greater stability.

In 1884 General Ōyama, Minister of War, with a staff of officers made an official tour of inspection of military affairs in Europe, and this inaugurated a new career for the *Hakuaisha*, a thorough reorganization being made in order to give it more complete efficiency.

General Ōyama's visit to Europe.

The question of how Japan could join the Geneva Convention, and how Japan's quasi-Red Cross institution, the *Hakuaisha*, could best be converted into a *bona fide* branch of the international humanitarian league having its head-quarters in Geneva, was carefully inquired into by General Ōyama and his suite, including Surgeon (now Surgeon-General) Hashimoto.

Baron von Siebold, who had returned to Austria, gave further valuable aid, and thanks to his friendly services a way was opened, and in November 1886 Japan was admitted to the Geneva Convention, and the *Hakuaisha* consequently changed its title to that of the ' Red Cross Society of Japan,' and adopted the badge of the Red Cross.   Count Sano became president of the society, and after manifold trials and difficulties it attained its present condition, which leaves little to be desired.

Japan joins the Convention.

But although Japan was thus admitted to the Geneva Convention, she was unable to enter the International Red Cross Society for lack of supporters and the necessary means, so long as the efforts of those most interested in the institution's extension were attended by the smallest results so far as the general public was concerned.   But a new plan of canvassing, giving the public something which they could see as well as hear about, brought a change for the better.   This was aided by the acquisition from the War Office, first of a plot of land and some old buildings at Iida Machi, Tōkyō, then of some adjacent land from the Imperial Household Department, and lastly of contributions, more or less compulsory, from military surgeons.

A new departure.

Upon this site was established a hospital on a small scale, to be used primarily as a training school for surgeons, and to enable female nurses to qualify for ambulance work in time of war, but also as a hospital for giving free treatment to the destitute.   Its opening was honoured by the presence of H.I.M. the Empress, and enlivened by a show of ambulance field work.

The Red Cross Hospital.

This, the first Red Cross Hospital, was subsequently rebuilt on a far larger scale at Shibuya, a suburb of Tōkyō, where a piece of ground belonging to the Imperial Court was granted to the society together with a sum of money.

The Fourth International Conference of the Red Cross Society was held at Karlsruhe, Germany, in 1887, and as this was the first function of the Red Cross Society since Japan had joined the Geneva Convention, I was commanded by the Government to represent my country at the Conference, while Viscount Noritsugu Matsudaira attended on behalf of the Red Cross Society. Accompanying me as my assistants were Dr. Taniguchi and Dr. Mori, the latter having in the late war been Chief of the Medical Staff of the Second Manchurian Army, whilst the former was Chief of the Medical Staff of the First Division.

We four Japanese were the only Asiatics among several hundred delegates representing different Occidental Powers, and in appearance and every respect we felt ourselves in strange contrast with our confrères.

The Conference lasted for seven days, during which many important questions were debated and discussed. One of these was, ' How is antiseptic surgery to be effectively performed on the battlefield ? ' I told them that among the Japanese troops, rolls of disinfected bandages were sewn inside the uniform of the soldiers, and as the latter in time of peace were regularly instructed in the methods of using these bandages, they could, whenever occasion demanded, easily bandage themselves or one another according to the location of the wounds and other special circumstances. Japanese soldiers were thus well qualified to care for their own wounds, until it was possible for them to receive regular surgical treatment. I then showed the assembly some samples of these antiseptic bandage-rolls which I had brought with me.

Now at that time the Prussian troops alone were in possession of these disinfected bandages, and my remarks were very well received by most of the delegates present, but a few commented on them in a somewhat depreciatory manner, saying that, though that method might answer in a small army, such as that of Japan must necessarily be, it was doubtful whether it could be equally practicable for European Powers possessing large armies. However, Dr. von Coler, Surgeon-General of Prussia, and Surgeon-General Sir W. Longmore of England, spoke in high terms of the antiseptic surgery of the Japanese Army, and the latter desired me to give him some bandage-rolls as specimens for future use. Another topic for discussion was, ' How can the spirit of the Geneva Convention be most effectually inculcated among the troops ? ' It was rightly anticipated that, unless the spirit of the Convention were clearly inculcated upon both the general public and the troops in time of peace, it might fail of fulfilment in time of war. The opinion of the assembled Red Cross delegates was therefore sought. I offered a reply to that question also, by stating that when, in the preceding year, Japan had joined the Geneva Convention, the Minister of War had at once caused the Compendium of the Red Cross Convention to be printed, and had caused copies to be largely distributed throughout the Imperial Army. Further, the commander of each company was directed to explain to his men the main particulars of this humanitarian scheme for the brotherhood of the world. Fortunately I had a copy of this compendium with me, which proved of much interest to the assembly. At the close of the sitting I had the honour of a summons from H.I.H. the Duchess of Baden, eldest daughter of the Emperor William I of Germany. She had been present in the strangers' gallery during the debate, and graciously said she wished to personally express her approbation of the highly conscientious way in which Japan strove to inculcate the true spirit of the mission. Her Grace also asked for a copy of the compendium I had shown during the debate, as a memento of the occasion. So far Japan had won the favourable opinion of the Conference in connection with her methods of camp surgery and for the diffusion of the sentiments of the Geneva Convention. But, on the fifth day of this international meeting, we were startled by a proposition which practically amounted to invalidating the admission of Japan into the Red Cross League. The question placed before the Conference, by the Red Cross Society of a certain Power, was, ' Whether or not the assistance and protection which the Red Cross League mutually rendered in time of war should be

A hard problem introduced to the Conference.

extended to countries outside the boundaries of Europe, even when those countries happened to be members of the League ? ' This extraordinary proposal put the delegates from Japan on their mettle, and we agreed unanimously that if such a proposition, so diametrically opposed to the spirit and principles of the Red Cross organization and betraying it into differentiating its benefits according to mere accidents of race, religion, politics, manners, customs, and geographical divisions, should be suffered to pass, we should without hesitation withdraw from the Conference as delegates, and immediately return to Japan to urge the Government to resign all connection with the Red Cross League.

It was with that uncompromising resolution that we four Asiatics attended the meeting of the following day. When all other items on the agenda for the day had been discussed and disposed of, the proposition was brought forward for discussion. I rose at once, and stated in plain terms that the delegates from Japan considered that even to entertain such a proposition was to do gross violence to the spirit of the Red Cross Convention, and that were it allowed to pass the Conference, we should have no alternative, though with much reluctance, but to withdraw from the hall. Professor Shultze of the University of Heidelberg, and M. Oom, member of the Russian Privy Council, both present as delegates, rose one after another, and fully endorsed my view. The chamber soon presented an animated scene, but eventually our contention prevailed and the motion was withdrawn. Before the close of the Conference the Red Cross Society of Japan concluded arrangements for formal connection with the head-quarters at Geneva and with its sister institutions throughout the world. The ordeal of the first Conference being over, we felt at its close that Japan had come into closer and not altogether discreditable contact with the outside world, and the outside world with us.

Extension of work.

What I saw and heard at this Conference impressed me acutely with the insignificance of the funds and scope of our Japanese institution as compared with those of the sister societies of Europe. On my return I consulted with President Sano and others upon the best means of remedying this state of things and making the institution popular with the general public. It was suggested that a special badge should be worn by the members of the Society, and with the approbation of the Government this idea was put into practice. It proved a decided success, for, in the year of the creation of the badge, the society obtained more than 10,000 new members. I next conceived the plan of undertaking lecture tours in the provinces with a magic-lantern. The slides were all specially designed to bring home to an audience the benefit of the work of the Red Cross Society, and so to appeal to their sympathy and gain their support. In these lecture tours, which were generally undertaken during the summer holidays, my wife assisted me by throwing the pictures on the sheet, while I performed the part of lecturer.

President Sano's endeavours on behalf of the Society were most noteworthy, and zealously did he identify himself with its work, especially when relations between Japan and China became strained, and there was every incentive for the President and his coadjutors to bring the Society into a state of perfect working efficiency in readiness for any emergency which might arise. Eventually the worst apprehensions were realized, and in 1894 Japan and China declared war against each other. The Red Cross Society immediately dispatched a staff of surgeons and nurses (both men and women) to whatever part of the field they were required. China-Japan War.

At that time I was in charge of Field Sanitation, and, for the first time in Japanese history, by utilizing the services of the Red Cross Medical Staff, female nurses were employed in the Reserve Hospitals, these nurses having been trained for years at the Red Cross Hospital in Tōkyō under the supervision of its chief, Dr. (now Surgeon-General Baron) Hashimoto. This employment of female nurses met with loud opposition from some quarters because of antiquated notions regarding the relative status of men and women in Japan. But I stoutly maintained my original position, and employed the Red Cross Hospital nurses in the military hospitals of Hiroshima and elsewhere. The result amply justified my course of action, for all these nurses proved an unqualified success. The medical staff dispatched by the Red Cross Society to the military hospitals established in various places numbered 1587, and besides their duty for our wounded and sick, they were also entrusted with the care of all wounded Chinese prisoners.

At the close of the war the Society was honoured by special messages of appreciation for notable services from Their Imperial Majesties, the Emperor and Empress, and decorations or presents of money were bestowed upon such members of the Society's staff as had been on active service. A number of head lady-nurses were also decorated with the Order of the Crown, which Order had been specially created some years previously to decorate women for distinguished service. This was the first occasion on which it had been granted to any save those of high rank.

The result of these services was also recognized by the public at large, and in one year the Society's roll was increased by no less than 60,000 names.

The first hospital steamers.

A valuable experience was gained by the Society during this war, namely, the absolute necessity of possessing hospital steamers for the transportation of invalids, and without loss of time the Society procured, in 1897, two good boats built for it in England, named the *Hakuai Maru* and the *Kōsai Maru*.[1] In times of peace these steamers are used by a passenger line of the *Nippon Yusén Kaisha*, but on the understanding that in case of emergency they will in seven days be fully equipped as hospital steamers.

In 1900 the Boxer trouble, which broke out in North China, put the efficiency of the two steamers to a practical test. Speedily equipped and sent to Taku with medical stores for the army corps stationed there and in the vicinity, they brought not only our own invalids, but those of France and Austria to Japan for treatment, and during the continuance of the disturbances the Red Cross Society dispatched 491 members of its staff, most of whom found a novel experience in the discharge of hospital duties on board a steamer. The French Government, deeply appreciating the services thus rendered to its wounded soldiers, presented several tokens to the Institution, also sending decorations to those who had individually cared for its men.

---

[1] *Hakuai* literally means ' universal love,' and *Kōsai*, ' general assistance.'

The work of the Society has not been strictly confined to medical service during time of war, for whenever any part of Japan has been visited by tidal waves, earthquakes, or any other disastrous calamity, the surgeons and nurses have been immediately dispatched to extend helping hands to the sufferers. Such occasions have been sadly numerous.

In looking back over the history of the Society, one cannot but be astonished at its marvellous development since its first inception.

When the *Hakuaisha*, the Society's forerunner, was founded in 1877, its members numbered only 38, and the yearly subscriptions amounted to only 150 *yen*. At the end of March 1906, when this article was compiled, the Society's statistics stood as follow : *Present status.*

Number of members	..	1,127,111
Value of property	..	9,664,835 *yen* (approximately)
Hospital steamers	..	2
Hospitals	..	4
Surgeons	..	369
Dispensers	..	171
Female nurses	..	2,874
Male nurses	..	1,544
Business officials	..	176

The Red Cross Hospital at Shibuya is the most noteworthy as to scope, internal arrangement, &c. It was built in 1891, as has been previously stated, under the patronage of the Imperial Household Department. It is provided with all the necessary means for training medical attendants, and in times of peace it is open to the public, and also receives, free of charge, destitute persons needing treatment. The Society is endeavouring to establish similar institutions in all the principal cities in addition to those already in existence. *The Tōkyō Red Cross Hospital.*

The Red Cross Society of Japan is honoured by the patronage of Their Imperial Majesties, the Emperor and Empress, and is placed under the joint control of the three Departments of the Imperial Household, War, and Navy. A Prince of the Blood is chosen as Honorary President, and, as already stated, this office was filled by H.I.H. Prince Komatsu upon the *Control and jurisdiction of the Society.*

foundation of the Society, and he continued to hold it until his death in 1903. During that long period, the Prince used his best efforts to advance the prosperity of the Society. An Executive President and a Vice-President are appointed, both of which appointments must receive the sanction of the Emperor, while a Board of Directors, consisting of thirty members, is elected by all the members of the Society by ballot. All the business of the Society, including general affairs and finance, is dealt with by this Board. Two auditors are appointed to supervise the accounts.

Count Sano may not inappropriately be called the ' Father of the Society.' With such rare constancy has he devoted himself to its affairs, that it owes more to him than to anyone else for the prosperity which it now enjoys.

The post of Honorary President is now filled by H.I.H. Prince Kan-in, and that of Executive President by Count Matsugata. The Society arranges its provincial affairs somewhat on the local administrative system, a branch office being located in each Prefecture, and an administrative chief appointed to administer the business of the branch.

Membership.

There are three kinds of membership, viz. honorary members, special members, and ordinary members, and all members are presented with a badge differing according to grade. These badges may be worn in public, just in the same way as ordinary decorations. ' Medals-of-honour ' are conferred on those who have rendered any specially meritorious service, and the fact and name of the recipient is reported to the Emperor on each occasion.

The Volunteer Lady Nurses Association.

The Volunteer Lady Nurses Association was created in 1887, and has been affiliated with the Red Cross Society. This Association is largely composed of ladies of the higher circles, including Princesses of the Blood, who, in order to qualify themselves to give practical aid in times of war, devote much of their leisure in times of peace to both the theory and practice of nursing.

During the China-Japan War these ladies personally prepared numberless antiseptic bandages and distributed them amongst both the Army and Navy, and many became nurses in the hospitals. Similar service was done by them on the occasion of the Boxer trouble, nor are they ever in the background when any extraordinary calamity lays claim to generosity and benevolence.

It is needless to add that the members of the Association zealously responded to the serious call made upon the country by the late war with Russia. The excellent example set by these high-born ladies in the work of humanity did more to elevate the profession of nursing in the eyes of the general public than anything else could have accomplished. The Association has for its President a Princess of the Blood, under whom is placed an Executive President. It possesses thirty-one branch offices, located where the Red Cross Society has its branches, and its list of members contains more than 3500 names. *During the Russo-Japanese War.*

The Russo-Japanese War supplied a unique opportunity to our Red Cross Society for carrying out on an unprecedented scale its mission of benevolence and relief. The Imperial troops actively demonstrated the spirit of the Convention towards their enemies in the field, and the soldiers of the Tsar were not slow to express their surprise and gratitude. In addition to the two hospital steamers, many relief corps were sent to the front and actively assisted the Army Medical Corps in the discharge of their heavy duties.

The war brought about among all classes of society, both at home and abroad, a wonderful manifestation of the true spirit of the Geneva Convention. Her Imperial Majesty the Empress, the August Patroness of the Society, presented our hospitals with a quantity of bandages prepared with her own hands, and she also bestowed artificial limbs or eyes, as the cases required, on the maimed among both Russians and Japanese, impartially. The sister societies of the world also offered their assistance in this special work of love, and volunteer nurses from England, America, and Germany worked side by side with our own nurses for invalid Japanese and Russians in our reserve hospitals.

The history of Japan has never been stained by deeds wilfully outraging the sentiments of humanity and moderation, and, thanks to the development of our Red Cross work, the spirit of magnanimity and benevolence inherent in the Japanese race is now acknowledged by foreign nations. *Conclusion.*

The Russo-Japanese War served to display the progress made by Japan on the stern and materialistic side of modern civilization, and the work of love and mercy carried out by our Red Cross Society established, not less emphatically, the fact that the claim of Japan to be regarded as a civilized Power rests on a sound and solid basis.

XVIII

THE FINE ARTS—PAINTING, SCULPTURE, ETC.

NAOHIKO MASAKI (FORMERLY DIRECTOR OF THE
GOVERNMENT SCHOOL OF ART)

INTRODUCTION

THE Japanese stand perhaps alone in the history of the world
as a people who, seeing what is excellent in the products of
other countries, have never hesitated to profit by them, and
by thus making good their deficiencies have striven to improve
and to advance. And so, in adopting the excellences of
foreign civilization, the Japanese have done so with a mind
well prepared to receive them, and with such a strong power
of assimilation that they have for the most part divested them
of their exotic forms and have wedded them happily to native
energy, which will involve in the future a new and yet higher
form of civilization. This is why we, living almost isolated in
a corner of a far-eastern ocean, have not lagged behind in the
world's progress. We see this fact especially exemplified in
the history of the Fine Arts in Japan. During the fifty
years since the opening of our country, while every kind of
social activity has taken after Western models, and, shaking
off its conventional crust, has striven to ameliorate and to
produce the civilization of New Japan, Art, too, has been
stimulated and subjected to change by new, alien influences.
But far from being metamorphosed into a mere plagiarism, it
has held firmly to its time-honoured traditions, and, whilst
enriching its ancient methods out of the Western store, has
done little more than freshen up old aspects and develop
what was already there. In painting alone we see that Western

Art has not merged into our own as yet on account of the wide difference both in tradition and in method, and that it exists now in our country as a flower of a totally different order, springing, as it has done, from a seed fallen on virgin soil. So our Art stands in its singular splendour, not only representing the culture of the Japanese race, but also aiding in no small degree the Fine as well as the Decorative Arts of the West to produce a simpler and chaster style.

In tracing, however, the progress of the Fine Arts in Japan since the opening of the country, some knowledge of its Art history prior to our own time is imperative, and we will therefore first of all review it briefly.

I.—The Fine Arts in Old Japan

Art in primitive Japan.

All that is known to us of the Art of primitive Japan consists mostly of articles connected with funeral rites and customs, and possessing as they do, for the most part, an anthropological interest, are to be considered only as buddings on the Art stem. The same is true with architecture and other industrial arts, but these primitive arts had some slight development in course of time, and were, indeed, the stem on which the continental art was to be grafted, and on which, through an assimilative process, the ultimate forms peculiar to the Island Empire were to blossom.

Introduction of Korean civilization.

The continental civilization of China, which came to Japan first through Korea and which influenced our country from ancient times, left its traces as early as the era of Han (206 B.C.–220 A.D.), as seen in the adoption of Chinese characters.

Chinese civilization was in quite an advanced state in the days of the introduction of Buddhism (67 A.D.) ; and as it passed on from the era of the Three Kingdoms (222–64 A.D.) to that of the Six Dynasties (265–617 A.D.), it produced famous painters and sculptors, and its occasional influx into our country may be seen in the foundation of the two houses of painting of Yamoto-Éshi and Kawachi-Éshi, by the naturalized family of a Chinese painter in the time of the Emperor Yūryaku (about 470 A.D.).

The Indian religion spread eastward, and, entering Korea (373 A.D.), made Art flourish; it ultimately came to our country in the reign of Kimméi (552 A.D.), and the islanders seeing the marvellous arts of the Continent tried to learn them, and within half a century began to produce their own Art. Japanese Art proper may therefore be said to date from that time. In the reign of the Empress Suiko (about 600 A.D.), the noted sculptor Kuratsukuri-no-Tori appeared and displayed rare talent in carving images, whilst the art of painting was much cultivated, as is seen in the pictures of the Mandara on drapery, and the paintings of Buddha, which still charm us with their lingering beauty. Architecture, too, assumed a new aspect as many Buddhist temples were built, the style of construction and the beauty of appearance being seen in the Hōryūji monastery (finished 607 A.D.), with seven edifices complete, from the Tower Gate and the main temple to the five-storied *stupa*.

When China reached the splendid era of the Tang dynasty (618–906 A.D.), Japan eagerly opened intercourse with her (630 A.D.), and the dispatch of official envoys as well as the transmission of students and priests was a frequent occurrence. Thus Chinese civilization filtered in and produced a great improvement, and the famous Reformation of the Taika period (645 A.D.) was thus effected. The civil institutions were even better systematized, whilst through the influence of Chinese learning schools were improved, and the writing of a national history was undertaken. The alien literature of the Tang school with balanced, antithetic construction was cultivated, while the national poetry flourished, and, treasured in the '*Manyōshū*' and the '*Kokinshū*' (the former with antique grace and the latter with classic stateliness), was destined to become the glory of Japanese literature. Moreover, with the introduction of the Buddhistic doctrine of Guhya-yana (805 A.D.), a new impetus was given to building temples and making images. No wonder that Art developed speedily under such favourable circumstances, sculpture and painting being cultivated on the new line of the Tang style through the influence of Buddhism, with its demand for Buddhist pictures and idols.

Introduction of Tang culture.

Sculpture.   In sculpture, in the reign of the Emperor Kōtōku (about 650 A.D.), we had some artists who raised the art to a high level of workmanship in the new style. It speedily developed through the reigns of Tenchi, Temmu, and Jitō (660–96 A.D.), and being freed at last from merely imitating the Tang style, displayed much skill in copying from the life. What artists were then capable of may be judged from the sole production of the age still remaining, namely, the famous bronze statue (53 feet in height) of the Great Buddha at the Tōdaiji, Nara, which was completed in 749 A.D. The reigns of Kōkén and Shōtoku (749–69 A.D.) saw still greater activity in the production of Buddhistic statues, and as the continental method of papier mâché was added to the already existing methods of bronze-casting, wood-carving, and clay-moulding, craftsmanship became increasingly varied. The works, being noble in treatment, stately in expression, and graceful in drapery, were rarely excelled by those of the following periods ; and although the introduction of the esoteric Shingon sect a little later gradually opened the way to the evils of conventionality, glyptic art in Japan found a wide range in expression.

Painting.   In painting we had, after the legislation of the Taihō period (702 A.D.), Court painters, who ornamented furniture for the Imperial household. Later they also undertook the painting of Buddhist figures, partly in the style of Tang. These becoming more natural, and the drawing of landscape approaching somewhat to the realistic, the artists showed their feeling in force of stroke and brush-work and their fondness for rich colouring. Many Buddhistic frescoes done by these men on the walls of the Hōryūji are still preserved. It is also recorded in old writings that at this period a great number of large pictures (more than 10 feet in length) were made. Many new pictures painted according to the doctrine of Shingon were produced by the priests Kūkai, Enchin, and others ; so we come to Kudara-no-Kawanari (782–853 A.D.), who showed marked progress in painting, and excelled not only in Buddhistic pictures, but also in those of landscapes and trees, in portraits and in historic pictures. After him we have Kosé-no-Kanaoka (in the second half of the ninth century), who, focussing in himself the skill of the generations before him, painted Buddhistic pictures in correct and minute style, and in fine, delicate colouring. He also excelled in landscape, the human figure, and horses. His pictures, like the sculptures of the era of Tempyō, were evolved out of the Tang style in tone, but surpassed it in technical grasp.

Remarkable progress was made also in architecture, notably in Buddhist temples. Elaborate frame-works, ceilings, and other constructions were perfected, and plans and forms were varied and designed more attractively. As more temples came to be built, a new style of plan rose, and as the strict symmetrical distribution of seven edifices was no longer followed, in design and workmanship they became freer and richer. For other kinds of architecture we find the Dairi, or Imperial Palace, which was erected in imitation of the Chinese method prevalent in the Tang dynasty, when Nara was made the capital in 710 A.D., with Imperial residences and official buildings beautiful with tiled roofs, plastered walls, and red pillars. As the Emperor Kwammu moved his capital to Héian (now Kyōto) in 794 A.D., the grand Dairi was made perfect at last ; especially as regards the Chōdōin, where the nation's great ceremonies were performed, comprising the Daigokudén, the Twelve Halls and the Towers of the Green Dragon and the White Tiger, in marvellously beautiful construction, each main building having red pillars and green tiles with golden grampuses on the ridge ends. *Architecture.*

Industrial arts also made progress, through contact with the products of Tang. In the beautiful collection at the Shōsōin, or Imperial Treasury at Nara, where the riches of the day were preserved, we see every kind of household article executed in all manner of styles, holding the mirror up to the life and culture of that time. Pottery, metal work, lacquer, inlaying, dyeing, weaving, and embroidery all seem to have been cultivated to a wonderful degree of perfection. In pottery, coloured glaze was used, and glass beads and enamelled backs for metal mirrors showed great skill. That displayed in metal work will be seen in such articles as copper mirrors and silver basins, and in the manner of casting and engraving *Industrial arts.*

ornaments. Lacquer, an industry peculiar to Japan, was already in a high state of development at this age, the methods of *hyōmon*, *makkinrō*, and mother-of-pearl lacquer work, then applied on scabbards, being in frequent use. Marquetries of ivory and wood found on musical instruments and *go*-boards are so excellent, both in felicity of design and in minuteness of workmanship, that the work of later ages can hardly surpass them. Such is also the case with painted decorations upon wooden articles. The art of making masks made much progress in consequence of the fashion for *gigaku* and *bugaku* (musical performances or dances). These were either carved out of wood or made of dry lac, usually with grotesque faces conceived by vigorous imagination, and they show much skill in design and workmanship. In dyeing, excellence was observable in such methods as *rō-kéchi* (laying of patterns by wax), *kō-kéchi* (dyeing in the skein), and *kyō-kéchi* (dyeing by means of open-work boards). In weaving, brocade was known, figures of birds, beasts, flowers, and leaves being woven in colours, intermingled occasionally with gold and silver thread, and not infrequently the method of *tsuzuré* (a sort of gobelin) was resorted to.

Formation of national character in Art.

While Art and Culture thus ripened under the sun of the civilization of the Tang period, China was thrown into disorder by civil wars, so that the Emperor Uda suspended sending official envoys thither (895 A.D.), and communication with the Continent was entirely discontinued. War succeeded war for fifty years, during which five dynasties rose and fell, and as there was nothing in which Japan could profit in her civilization even in the next era of the Sung dynasty (963–1279 A.D.), the intercourse was never renewed as freely as before. So during three hundred years our people built by their own initiative, on a basis of already acquired culture, and perfected a purely national character. As an instance, the Chinese style of writing, which had been much in use, was gradually discarded for one with a Japanese syllabary, which gradually developed from about 923 A.D. It reached its zenith in the reigns of Ichijō and Go-Ichijō (987–1036 A.D.), and the journals, essays, and novels of the time in this purely national style, represented by such masterpieces as the ' *Genji*

Monogatari' and the '*Makura-no-Sōshi*,' are unrivalled in grace and delicacy of feeling and of diction.

The painting developed in this period was the so-called Yamato '*Yamatoyé*,' which in the hands of such men as Kimmochi painting. (about 950 A.D.), Hirotaka (about 1000), Motomitsu (about 1090), and other artists of the old Tosa school, came to be perfected in purely national style. By this time, however, a sort of variation of this school appeared in the simple yet vigorous style of Toba-Sojō's caricatures (1053–1140), which, harmonizing well with the spirit of militarism of the next age of the Kamakura Shōguns (1185–1333), was directly opposed to that of the former. With the prevalence of a simpler and more robust form of religion, it developed into the style of the *émakimono*, which practically covered the whole painting of the time. *Émakimono* consisted of a collection of illustrations to a romance, drawn in an off-hand way and, though small in size, showing freedom and vigour in the use of the brush, and catching skilfully the general aspects of life. Those who excelled particularly in drawing the *émakimono* were Mitsunaga (1166–98), Kéion (about 1190), Takanobu (1142–1205), and Nobuzané (1177–1266), and later, Yoshimitsu, Nagataka, Nagaaki, and Koréhisa (all about 1264–1301), and Takakané (about 1308–18). Many of their works are still in existence, so the characteristics of this later national school can still be studied.

Sculpture was affected in a similar manner to painting Progress when the communication with Tang was given up : a purely of national style was formed, characterized by grace and delicacy. sculpture. In the works of Éshin (943–1018 A.D.) the national quality is especially conspicuous, and through the influence of the much-developed lacquer industry due to the luxury of the day, gold-wire damascening and gold-lac coating were made use of in colouring with much effect. Jōchō (died 1057), as a sculptor of Buddhist statues of extraordinary skill, stood second to none in his day. By him, it may be said, the general form and proportion of the parts of a statue were finally fixed. The next period of Kamakura saw such renowned artists as Unkéi (1173–1256) and his contemporaries, Tankéi, Kwaikéi, and Jōkéi, all of whom following the school of Jōchō, developed the national quality to a higher degree.

Architec-
ture
Architecture also followed the national tendency taken by painting and sculpture, and was known for elegance of form and richness of decoration. For the latter, *makiyé* and inlaying of mother-of-pearl were profusely used with brilliant effect. As to construction, in the building of *Shintō* shrines, which had hitherto preserved the primitive style, the new styles called *kasuga-zukuri* and *nagaré-zukuri* arose through an infusion of the fashion of Buddhist temples. For private houses the *shindén-zukuri* style came into vogue. The main building, which was called *shindén*, had a roof of *hinoki* bark shingles sloping in fourways, balconies, stairs, and verandahs, and was furnished with sliding doors, paper partitions, bamboo shades, screens, folding screens, *étagères* and such-like, all of which were designed for the first time in purely national style. In the Kamakura period a modified form of the *shindén* plan called the *buké-zukuri* came into fashion, being remarkable for its simplicity as opposed to the gorgeousness of the *shindén*.

Art
industries.
In Art industries the national culture left more marked impress on lacquer than on anything else. It was perhaps best suited to the luxurious taste of the time and for the use of the upper classes. So the methods of *hiramakiyé* (flat work) and *togidashi* (ground work) were started and cultivated with the use of *héijin* (flat gold dust), *ikkaké* and *kirikané* (gold or strip wire), as well as mother-of-pearl inlay, which were handled with marvellous skill. These were applied to *ashidé* (pictures interpolated with poetry), which were designed with much freedom, and in idealized pictures of flowers, birds, and landscapes. The arts of weaving and dyeing were also improved as splendour of official robes was much affected. All sorts of beautiful *nishiki* (brocade) and *aya* (silk damask) with a great variety of patterns were made, while a process of dyeing called the *ungén* (checker work of red and blue and their shades) was invented.

The
influence
of Sung-
Yuan.
In China a revival of Art and Learning took place when the wars of the Five Dynasties were brought to an end by the founder of the Sung dynasty, but since Japan had itself developed on the basis of the ripened civilization of Tang, as

shown above, no need of sending official envoys to keep up the international good feeling with China, or students to complete their studies, was felt; besides, the reopening of intercourse could not be effected quickly. In the meantime, in China the era of the Northern Sung (963–1126 A.D.) passed, and that of the Southern Sung (1127–1279) began, when, as Priest Éisai brought back with him the Rinzai sect (1192), and Priest Dōgen (1250–53) the Sōdō sect, religious intercourse became more frequent. From that time onwards many Chinese priests became naturalized in Japan, while Japanese Buddhists went over to China to study. This close contact with Sung thought brought a new influence to bear on our Art.

First as regards painting. In the school of Takuma *Religious* we have Shōga (about 1200) and Éiga (about 1310), and later *pictures.* Chōdensu (1352–1431), who, following the style of Li-Lungmin of Sung, painted images of Bodhisatvas and Arhats, producing an effect hitherto unknown under the Sung influence. Another effect of this influence was the prevalence of *bokugwa* (black-and-white sketches). This fashion was started by Chinese priests, Ning-Ishan (died 1317) and Fanshien (1292–1348), who came to Japan and painted so many *bokugwa* in the Sung style that it soon came to be the fashion among priests to study the art as an avocation. Laymen, too, began to take it up as a diversion along with the tea ceremony, and many became proficient in it. It received, however, a purely artistic treatment for the first time, and was perfected by Shūbun (about 1450) through Josétsu (about 1440). He was followed by such famous artists of this school as Sesshū (1420–1506), Sōtan *Sesshū* (contemporary with Sesshū), and Masanobu (1454–1550), *and Kanō.* all of whom flourished under the patronage of the Shōgun Yoshimasa (1449–90), which made the style at once popular, producing the so-called 'paintings of the Higashiyama era.' Sesshū ranks, indeed, at the head of our old painters of landscape, and combining in himself all the excellences of the Chinese styles of the Sung-Yuan, is known for his severe, robust style. Sōtan followed Shūbun, and, studying only the Hoang style of Sung, painted principally flowers and fruits. He stood almost by himself in the matter of peculiar charm. Masanobu was the founder of the house of Kanō. He studied

under Shūbun and Sōtan, and was skilful in painting landscapes after the Northern Sung style. Thus the flourishing Art
epoch of Higashiyama seemed as though the famous eras
of Senhoa and Shaohsing during the Sung had been revived
in Japan. But the strange thing is that, though China was
at this time in the next era of Ming (1368–1643), and
though her style of painting had changed, in our country
the Art school of the previous period was cultivated continuously, and the Southern Sung school of landscape, together
with the Hsü style of flowers and birds, both of which had been
much in vogue in China since the period of Sung-Yuan, were
not introduced at all.

Sculpture
and archi-
tecture.

In sculpture, as the building of temples of the Zen sect was
frequent, numbers of images of Arhats and statues of Zen
priests were made with much infusion of the Sung style.
Architecture also felt the influence of the Sung by the propagation of the Zen sect, and a new plan of temples was established; such new features in construction as polished ceilings
arose, *kumimono à la Chinoise* and fan-shaped rafters being
adopted. For private houses the architectural style underwent a change to that of *shoin-zukuri*. In Art industry the
potter Shunkéi, who went to the Sung at the beginning of
the Kamakura era (about 1230) and studied applied art, on his
return produced the new pottery of *ko-séto* and *ki-séto*.

Influence
of con-
tinental
Art
industry.

As the Ashikaga Shōguns had a great liking for *bibelots*,
the tea ceremony, which made use of utensils of value, came
into fashion. But since ceramic art in Japan was still undeveloped, imported articles were most highly prized, and not
only did people buy wares from China, but they induced Spanish
or Portuguese merchantmen to import similar articles from
Cochin China, Luzon, and India. These were of use in stimulating native art in pottery, which soon showed signs of development. In 1513 Shōzui went to China, and came back,
having studied the art of making under-glazed porcelain.
Later, Sōkéi, a Korean, became naturalized and opened a kiln,
and his son Chōjirō invented *rakuyaki*. Thus kilns came
to be opened in several provinces. In 1598, however, when
Hidéyoshi returned from his Korean expedition, many of his
generals brought over Korean potters, and took them to their

castles, where they opened kilns. From this time the ceramic art in Japan made speedy progress.

Besides, earthenwares, copper vessels, carved lacquer wares, and fabrics were imported from Ming, to the great benefit of our industry. Again, by European vessels such fabrics as *shuchin* (setine), *birōdo* (velluda), *santomé* (San Thomas), and *mōru* (Mogul), as well as Indian and Persian leather, were brought in and utilized.

After the Chinese influence of the Sung-Yuan had had its full effect in the era of Higashiyama, Japan was plunged in a succession of wars; but fortunately Art industry was not much affected, and when the age of restored peace under the Tokugawas after the many wars arrived, Art revived and made unprecedented strides. Hitherto it had been mostly Buddhistic, and even the *bokugwa* of the era of Higashiyama were pervaded with the religious spirit of the Zen. But from the days of the Toyotomis (1585–1602), Buddhism gradually ceased to supply moral principles, and was superseded by Confucianism. So Art broke free from its restraints and, following the natural inclination of the human mind, progressed in all directions. Again, as civilization was aristocratic in olden days and the masses had little to do with progress, Art was localized in the upper classes. But when we come to the period of the Tokugawas (1603–87), culture diffused itself gradually down to the lower classes, with the result that new schools which conformed to their taste arose in abundance, and thus introduced greater variety in Art. *Assimilation and development of Art.*

The first sign to be seen in the development and perfection of painting is the appearance of Motonobu Kanō (1476–1559) towards the end of the era of Higashiyama. This talented artist was first trained in the school of Southern Sung by his father, Masanobu, and, studying also from the Tosa school the beauty of national style, originated his own, which was hereafter to be known as the ' Kanō School.' He was skilful in everything—human figures, landscapes, birds, and flowers, and was known for the elegance and freshness of his work. His grandson, Éitoku (1543–90), appeared in the time of Toyotomi, and, embodying the *Painting.* *Kanō school.*

heroic and extravagant spirit of the day, painted profusely on the screens and golden walls of the castles built by Hidé-yoshi. His works are known for largeness of design and brilliancy of colouring, giving the painting of the so-called Momoyama period a distinctive quality of its own.

Among the more noted of Éitoku's pupils we may mention Yūshō, Sanraku, and Tōgan, all of whom varied the style somewhat. As we come to the Tokugawa period, we have Kōi (died 1636), pupil to Éitoku's son, Mitsunobu. He is known for his graceful style, which shows much of the national quality. Under him we have Tannyū (1602–74), who, studying old and new paintings of different schools, struck out in an original style, and, improving on the traditional methods of his school and infusing more of the native feeling, gave a new standard to the Kanō style. Among many of his pupils who reached distinction afterwards we may mention Naonobu (1607–50) and Yasunobu (1613–85), his younger brothers, his nephew Tsunénobu (1636–1713), and Morikagé. Their works on screens and walls retain the gaudiness of the Momoyama period, possess grace, the sign of a peaceful age, but lack the vigour and boldness of Éitoku. After these artists, as the spirit of heredity pervaded society, their descendants blindly adhered to the rules handed down to them, and committing themselves to the evils of merely copying model pictures and leading a life of ease by means of their pensions, they did not essay to rise above mediocrity.

Tosa school.

In the Tosa school there were Mitsunobu and Mitsuoki (1617–91), who made it popular for a time, but after the appearance of Jōkéi (1598–1670) and Gukéi (1631–1705) it sank to a low ebb. Moreover, with the exception of Totsugén (died 1823), Ikkéi (1795–1859), and Tamétaka (1778–1844), who revived the old Tosa style and painted the so-called *yūshoku-gwa*, the Tosa school fared no better than the Kanō school.

In the so-called Genroku period, embracing the eras of Teikyō (1684–87) and Genroku (1688–1703), culture pervaded all classes, and Art and Literature were appreciated everywhere, while, in consequence of the development of trade and industry, people grew rich and towns wore a far more flourishing aspect than heretofore. The standard of living rose, and the demand for Art became unprecedentedly great. On account of this, painting had to undergo a change to suit the time. So we have Kōrin (1665–1716), who, reflecting Kōrin the wealthiness and extravagance of the age, showed much school. of decorative beauty in his art, and Itchō (1652–1724), who, seeing that the motives of the Kanō school were fettered by the formality of the Chinese style and were deficient in life, endeavoured to paint things as he actually saw them. Moronobu also (died 1694), finding that the Tosa school took subjects mostly from medieval aristocratic life, and never touched the modern, and therefore was out of sympathy with the general mass of the people, sought motives for his pictures in the scenes and figures of every-day life, and founded the *ukiyoyé*, or school of ' *Ukiyo-* genre pictures, as well as the art of modern xylography. *yé* ' school The new artistic movement was now general, and many artists of note appeared and brought palmy days to Japanese painting. Kōrin's style, originating in Kōétsu (1552–1637), was unique in that it aimed at an imaginative, and hitherto unknown, treatment of nature, producing fresh designs and rich effects. Flowers and leaves were mostly drawn, often in ink thick with gold dust, and the result surpassed everything, even those of old Oriental production, for decorative purposes. The school of Kōrin declined somewhat after his death, but revived again with Hōitsu (1757–1828). The paintings of this school have not only been greatly utilized in dyeing and weaving in modern Japan, but they have influenced Western design more than any other. Moronobu was somewhat immature in his technique, but with his creation of a new school of *ukiyoyé*, such noted artists appeared as Chōshun and Harunobu in the early part of, and Shunshō, Kiyonaga, Sukénobu, and Masanobu in the middle of, the eighteenth century. Moreover, the arts of wood engraving and chromoxylography gradually improved, and the so-called *nishikiyé*, of women and scenes from every-day life in gay colours, was perfected at last. Later we have Eishi (about 1780), Utamaro (about 1790), and Toyokuni (early in 1800), all of whom excelled in pictures of women, and Hiroshigé (about 1830), who was skilled in topography. As we come to Hokusai

(1757–1849) we find a rare painter who, with vigorous yet facile strokes of the brush, towered above his fellow-artists, and who for his book illustrations and printed *mangwa* is now famed even across the seas.

During the eras of Hōréki and Méiwa another wave of considerable size rose in the artistic world of Kyōto on the appearance of Ōkyo (1733–95), who, by dint of remarkable originality, founded a new naturalistic school of painting. He painted landscapes, birds, and flowers so realistically that the whole world stood astonished at his skill. The progress of Japanese painting made a sudden leap with him and reached

Maru-
yama
school.
at once its apogee. The school is known as the Maruyama. Among his noted pupils were Rosétsu and Goshun. Goshun, however, started what is known as the Shijō style, which had

Shijō
school.
lightness in touch as compared with Ōkyo. His brother Kéibun and his pupil Toyohiko were distinguished followers. But the Maruyama and Shijō styles became indistinguishable in later days, and we may regard the latter only as a variation of the former. Mention should be made also of Jakuchū, Shōhaku, and Ganku, who were contemporaries of Ōkyo and who rivalled him in skill and methods.

Sculpture.
In sculpture there was no artist of fame for a long period after that of Ashikaga. The making of Buddhistic images was no longer considered in the same way as painting, and only the *Shichijō Bussho* in Kyōto could maintain its prestige, and that but feebly, until we come to the prosperous era of Genroku, when Ryūkéi appeared and exhibited his minute and graceful art. Carved ornamentation in architecture came into fashion as the *shoin-zukuri* inclined to be elegant, till it was driven to excess in the shrines at Nikkō. Mask-making had been almost abandoned, but the prevalence of the *Nō* dance in the Ashikaga period caused a revival, and in the hands of Zékan Démé (about the end of the sixteenth century) it reached such a state of perfection as has never been excelled since. *Nétsuké* carving was also cultivated for *inrō* and tobacco pouches, and came into wide use in the eras of Kambun and Émpō (1661–80), and many noted craftsmen appeared and opened the way to the ivory carving of to-day.

In the progress made in architecture through the influence Architecture. of Sung the tea-room ranks next to the Zen temples. Its plan is very small, but nothing else is comparable to it for the quiet, reserved note pervading it. Gardening was also changed to suit this cult. As Hidéyoshi Toyotomi erected many buildings owing to his love of extravagance, the *shoin-zukuri* style was greatly improved upon : the plan was made larger and more grandiose, and carvings and paintings as ornamentation on walls, screens, ceilings, and lintels were freely resorted to. At the same time, the building of castles made a new start. With stone walls, corner towers, and a watch tower called the *tenshu-kaku*, the castle became an imposing sight. As we pass on into the Tokugawa period, architecture made yet further advances in point of workmanship : the two styles of temples and shrines were blended into one, producing such new styles as the *yatsumuné-zukuri* and the *gongén-zukuri*, and reaching the height of complexity in the mausoleums at Nikkō, Shiba, and Uyéno.

In the era of Genna (1615–23) we find the potters Faience. Ninséi of Kyōto providing the use of colours and glaze, and Joén of Hizén making perfect porcelain for the first time in Japan. About the era of Shōhō (1644-48), Kakiémon of Arita invented *kinrandé*, or gold-brocade-painted porcelain. Presently kilns were opened at Awata and Kiyomizu, and fine Kyōto wares were produced at the hands of Rokubéi (about 1790), Dōhachi (about 1810), and Mokubéi (about 1820). The Kutani ware was started by Saijirō Gotō in the era of Kambun (1661–72), and the porcelain of Séto by Tamikichi Katō early in the nineteenth century.

In metal work the manufacture of armour became notable Ornamentation of sword furniture. mainly through the requirements during the warlike period of Minamoto-Taira, but as we come to the Higashiyama period its decoration made considerable progress. Of armour-smiths we have the house of Myōchin, from which in the era of Tembun (1533–54) the famous artist Nobuiyé appeared, who stands first among the noted Myōchins. At an earlier period Yūjō Gotō (1440–1512), the founder of the Gotō house, produced works of the highest quality in sword furniture, and handed on the art to his successors. The Gotōs, like the

Kanōs in painting, stood for four hundred years as representatives of the academic style in metal work in Japan. Besides the Gotōs there were the two houses of Nara and Yokoya. Of the Naras, Toshinaga (1667–1736), Jōi (died 1761), and Yasuchika (1670–1744) are noted. Of the Yokoyas, in the era of Genroku, the famous Sōmin originated a new style of designing and gave new life to metal work. He and Nagatsuné Ichinomiya (1720–86), realistic in his style, may be called the double stars in metal carving of the eighteenth century.

Lacquer.   In the lacquer industry, the method of decorating with gold made great progress in the Higashiyama period. The making of gold dust, gold sheet, and *nashiji* lac were perfected for the first time ; the art of *takamakiyé* advanced, and landscapes, trees, and rocks were introduced into the designs. The processes of making ground lacquer also were greatly improved. At this time the Kōami family in Kyōto excelled in the manipulation of gold lac. The civil wars of the late sixteenth century, however, dispersed the lacquerers of Kyōto, and brought a decline in the art for a while, but after peace was restored the industry revived, and though poor in technique, the works known by the name of *Kōdaiji-makiyé* are noted for their vigour of design. In the Tokugawa period peace and luxury induced speedy progress in the art. We have first such artists of great distinction as Kōétsu Honami, Nagashigé Kōami, and later, Chōkyū Kōami, Kōrin Ogata, Haritsu Ogawa, who developed the art of *makiyé* to perfection. But it was Kōétsu and Kōrin who applied their skill in painting to *makiyé* and produced unique decorative pictures, originating a new school of marvellous vitality. Originally *makiyé* had nothing but delicacy and prettiness, but in the works of Kōétsu and Kōrin it acquired a totally different note by the use of inlay of mother-of-pearl and pewter, overflowing with surprising vigour and marked by such freedom from conventionality as almost verged on eccentricity.

Weaving and dyeing.   Weaving, like *makiyé*, declined in the period of the civil wars, but afterwards it revived at Nishijin in Kyōto. Several kinds of brocade, as *yamato-nishiki, ito-nishiki, karaori-nishiki, kinran,* and *tsuzuré-no-nishiki,* as well as *rinzu* (satin) and *donsu* (silk damask), were produced, and from the latter *shichi-shidonsu* and *mon-jusu* were evolved with beautiful designs of great complexity.   In the era of Tenna (1681–83) figured crape and figured taffeta were invented, followed by heavy *shuchin-ori*.   Since then every kind of textile fabric has been produced.

In dyeing, in the era of Kanéi (1624–43), Yūzén started what goes by his name, with beautiful figures of birds and flowers in brilliant colours, a style which has since been much improved.

When trade at Nagasaki became, in the beginning of the Tokugawa period, a considerable factor, a Chinese priest, Ih-yen, came there (1645) with many others, escaping from the war at home, and produced paintings in the Ming-Ching style.   Shūséki (1639–1707), Jakushi, and others studied this style and opened the way to a new school.   In the era of Kyōhō (1716–35), more Chinese—Ih-Fuchiu, Shen-Nan-pin, Fei-Han-yuan, and Sung-Tsai-yen, for instance—also came to Nagasaki, and Ih-Fuchiu and Fei-Han-yuan with landscape paintings of the *bunjingwa* style, and Shen-Nan-pin and Sung-Tsai-yen with pictures of flowers and birds of improved Hsü style, introduced pictures of the early Ching.   Besides, Ming-Ching paintings in albums, scrolls, and sheets were much imported from about the era of Genroku onwards, as we know from the fact that an office of examiner of painting was established at Nagasaki.   This stimulus from outside was aided by the change taking place in the literary tendency of the time, which had its effect on Art and brought about the palmy days of the Southern Sung style which followed the eras of Hōréki and Méiwa (1751–71); for the study of Chinese was witnessing a great revival at this time, such scholars as Sorai Ogyū (died 1729) and Nankaku Hattori (died 1759) not limiting themselves only to the ethical aspect of the subject, but paying much attention to poetry and essays.   As these came to appreciate the writings of the Ming-Ching period, they prized sketches with verse-themes of the early Ching style, in which the Southern Sung elements predominated, and took delight in the literary amusement of sketching and giving themes in verse.   So, too, Nankai Gion,

Influence of Ming-Ching.

Hyakusén Sabaki, and Rikyō Yanagisawa devoted themselves to painting in the Ming-Ching style, and thus we arrive at Taiga, who was the master-artist in the *Nangwa*. Sparing of line and subdued in tone, his refined work was held in great admiration in his day. At the same time there was another artist called Buson who started a new style on the basis of the *Mingwa*, excelling that of Taiga in fineness of workmanship. After these men the school of *Nangwa* flourished, and with the rise of a number of famous artists everywhere in the first half of the nineteenth century, led by Chikudén and Kazan, it monopolized for a time the artistic field of Japan. It also exercised its influence over artists of other schools, among whom we have the famous Bunchō (1763–1840), who went so far as to make it his principle to blend the *Nangwa* and *Hokugwa* school, and by his superb skill towered over his fellows.

Ming influence upon sculpture and architecture. The influence of Ming outside of painting is seen mainly in sculpture. A Chinese sculptor, Fan-Tao-sheng, came over with his master In-yuan (Ingén) (1653), and carved the Buddhist images at the temples of the Ōbaku sect. His style, which was henceforward known as the Ōbaku, differed from that of the Tang mainly in following the natural folds of drapery. He was followed by Shōsétsu (1648–1710), and many other sculptors of Yédo. In architecture, as the Ōbaku sect was propagated, its temples were executed in the pure Ming style. In Art industry, with the prevalence of Ming-Ching music and the Chinese way of making tea, called *sen-cha*, utensils or instruments decorated in the so-called *bunjin-kazari* style came into fashion, while a wider application of the *Nangwa* may be seen in all sorts of ornamentation.

Western painting before the opening of the country. Western nations began to explore the Far East as early as the fifteenth century, but it was only in 1541 that the Portuguese came over to Japan for the first time. Spaniards followed and started trading. Missionaries accompanied them, propagating Christianity, and bringing with them Western paintings of Christ and the Virgin Mother. But consequent on the disturbance of Amakusa (1634), Christianity was put under the ban, and all such objects were destroyed. There was, however, a Christian artist

named Uémonsaku Yamada who was forgiven because of
his skill in Western painting. He was ordered by the
Tokugawa Government to paint a picture of an incendiary
being executed, which afterwards was exhibited on a
public road. Through this work of his, oil-painting may
be said to have escaped utter destruction. Dutch merchants,
however, continued to come and import many foreign works
of Art. With the study of Dutch becoming prevalent, we
find in the middle of the eighteenth century Gennai Hiraga,
who attempted Western painting. He was followed by
Kōkan Shiba, a better artist than his predecessor. Their
endeavours were, of course, crude, but there is no doubt
that they contributed something by way of preparation for
the study of Western painting after the opening up of the
country. The works of these men failed to influence the
native Art, and, although it is said that Ōkyo and Kazan
learned something from the West, their pictures show little trace
of it. The perspective pictures of Hokusai are mere imitations
made out of curiosity, and cannot be said to be the result of
assimilation or even adaptation.

II.—The Fine Arts subsequent to the Opening of the Country

We have traced thus far the history of the Fine Arts in
Japan in their main aspects before the opening of the country
to foreign intercourse, a survey which has shown us that
the Japanese again and again assimilated the arts of China
and Korea, and digesting them thoroughly, raised them to a
higher degree of perfection. We will now look at what followed
after this in the province of Art upon the inflowing of Western
civilization after the Restoration.

First as regards painting. At the outset a change was
slow in making itself felt, doubtless on account of the inertia
of the preceding period, and of the people being concerned with
things more immediate than Art. Consequently no artists
of talent appeared for some time. With the death of such
men as Bunchō and Kazan, the flourishing eras in Art passed
away, and naturally, when the Tokugawa Government fell to

pieces, when all the lords yielded up their revenues to the
Crown, and *samurai* were without the means of livelihood,
and merchants and artisans who had lost their trades abounded
everywhere, at such a time Art was bound to be entirely
neglected, and in consequence precious works of Art and
valuable paintings were prized no more than rubbish. Even
when peace and quietness ensued, the people were too occupied
with their immediate concerns and too busy adopting the
material civilization of the West, to attend to anything like
Art. Such was the condition of Japan for about twenty
years from the era of Genji (1864).

Condition
of the
hereditary
artists.
In those days hereditary artists were reduced to such
straits as defy description. The Kanō family were broken
up with the downfall of the Tokugawa Government, and their
traditional art was no longer cared for, while the official
artists of the Tosa school were relieved of their duties upon
the reformation of the Court institutions. Almost every
artist either changed his profession or barely lived on some
vulgar handicraft. A few only there were who persevered
through all these adverse circumstances, and who managed in
one way or other to keep the artistic tradition from perishing.
Such were Yōsai, Gyōsai, and Zéshin. Yōsai professed the
yūshokugwa style, which rose with the study of national
classics in the preceding period, and with his historical accuracy
of costume and skill at realism, improved historical painting.
The *yūshokugwa* of Totsugén, Ikkéi, and Tamétaka in the
previous period were no more than a mere enlargement of
the *émakimono* of the Tosa school, but Yōsai differed from
them in selection and composition, and made really original
historical pictures.

Yōsai.
His skill in naturalistic portraiture also reached a standard
that had hardly been met with in Japanese pictures of human
figures before him. He was really spurred on by the spirit
of the day which, in the Restoration, again reflected much
of the past, and he had the honour of being given the name
of ' Painter-Chronicler of Japan ' by the Emperor. Yoshi-
toshi Tsukioka studied with him and established a new style
of *ukiyoyé*, which for a while appeared in newspaper illustrations and *nishikiyé*. Its fault, however, lay in too much

confusion of lines. Gyōsai and Zeshin were of the Kanō school
and the Shijō school respectively, and each established his
own style. The former had much vigour and excelled in
caricature, while the latter was noted for humorous representation.

There was one school of painting, however, which, through *Nangwa.*
this period of artistic depression, was in popular favour, and
remained in just the same flourishing state as in the previous
period. This was the *Nangwa*. The reason for this is evident.
In the first place, what inspired the spirit of the Restoration
was rather the study of the Chinese classics than of native
literature, and in the second, the task of the Reformation
was entirely effected by men trained in Chinese ethical ideas.
So, for over ten years after the Restoration, the study of Chinese
formed the basis of culture in Japan, and its popularity was
even greater than in the preceding period. It was not strange,
then, that the school of *Nangwa*, which was first started with
the revival of Chinese study, should not only endure but
be popularized by the diffusion of that study. But when
movements culminate, degeneration sets in. The prevalence
of the *Nangwa* induced everybody who had learned Chinese
and knew something of its literature to attempt landscapes,
orchids, or bamboos, by merely smearing India paper with ink.
These men had no eyes for Art, and took crudeness for elegance
and coarseness for grandeur. Lowering the artistic taste of
the day, they made the *bunjingwa* of the time a worthless
possession. Such ignorance prevailed that almost anyone
who tried his hand at the brush was looked upon as a master-
artist. Such a condition could no longer be regarded with
any artistic seriousness. Yet we must not overlook a few
gifted painters among the crowd, who fortunately kept the
lamp of Art-truth burning. These were Sōun in landscapes,
and Yūkoku and Kwatéi in flowers and birds. Even now the
school has some influence, and, judging from the number of its
professed artists and from some of the works it has produced,
it does not rank far below the most notable of our schools.
This is due mostly to the impetus of a long period of prosperity, but partly to the nature of the style itself, which is
rich in such methods as *sensen* (washing), *ten-pō* (dotting),

and *shun-pō* (wrinkling), and is so flexible and adaptable to realistic representation as to make it but little inferior to the Maruyama style, though there is room for improvement. If the best of other native or Western schools be infused, it should not be impossible to evolve a new style out of the *Nangwa*. It should be noted that in painting flowers, trees, bamboos, and birds the method of *bokkotsu*, namely, the application of a wash and the painting of light and shade by a single stroke of the brush, is peculiar to this school: it is a device which Ōkyo seized upon, and improving it with his realistic skill, made it a special characteristic of his work.

In the school of Maruyama we had recently such artists as Kwansai, Bairéi, and Hyakunén, and have now Gyokushō and Kéinén, men of much distinction. The school has a good many followers and is in a more flourishing state at present than any other. The reason for this is obvious : the Maruyama is the most recently developed of all Japanese schools of painting, and as it was specially adapted by Ōkyo to the needs of his day, taking hints from the *bokkotsu* method of the Southern Sung school, and also from the laws of perspective in Western painting, so in our time, when scientific knowledge has been diffused and Art has come to be judged by Western canons, such a style should live. We are not surprised, then, to see that the new schools which promise great development are mostly evolved out of the Maruyama, or from a fusion of that and the Western school. The great work of Ōkyo may be said to be still a power in the present Art world of Japan. In the Kishi school we had Chikudō, who excelled much in painting from nature, but whose style was almost assimilated to that of Maruyama.

As to the Kanō family, which were once in a most flourishing state, monopolizing the patronage of the feudal government as well as of the clan lords and being their hereditary artists, they were almost ruined when their pensions ceased. Though we have had recently such a master as Shōsén out of the school, and also Hōgai and Gahō as students of Shōsén, there are hardly any followers at present, while Hōgai and Gahō are no longer orthodox Kanō, having entirely changed their styles. So the school cannot be said to survive. As

[marginal notes:]

Maruyama school of recent years.

Kanō artists.

for the Tosa school, its decadence has been still more thorough, and except for Kwangyo Morizumi, who attained to some prominence recently, it has gone totally out of fashion. This school, which first originated in depicting the ancient Court life (just as the *ukiyoyé* painters restricted their subjects to modern low life), never went outside its province, and thus it has left no more than a trace in a few modern historical paintings. As for Buddhist painting, with the decline of image worship in modern Japan, the demand and supply has inevitably decreased. The pictures and statues (required for the purpose of rituals) in Buddhism are amply provided for by copies of old works done by ordinary craftsmen; and just as is the case with Christian Art in modern Europe, they are no longer painted by artists of distinction. It is true that some artists of the idealistic school seek new subjects in the Buddhist mythology, fables, or legends, and execute them in new styles and methods, but the old tradition of Buddhist art has been totally abandoned.

Genre pictures (*ukiyoyé*) were used mainly for book illustra- tions or printed as sheet *nishikiyé* in former times, and though artists of the school sometimes produced hanging pictures, as their subjects were almost confined to actors or women of the town, the works were not used for ornamental purposes, like those of other schools, and consequently could not rank with the latter in the Art world. But with the advance in Art theories this barrier has been removed, and the school is accorded in the classification of motives equal treatment with others. At present there are quite a number of painters of this school.

Since 1882 and after the Kanō and Tosa died away, painting has been revived by the appearance of several noted artists of different schools. Formerly we had not the term *bijutsu* (beautiful or fine arts), which is in use now, painting only being thought of as a noble art. Sculpture indeed was once so considered, but this was due to its connection with Buddhism, and from our middle period it passed into an ordinary handicraft. In 1873, however, our Commissioners to the International Exhibition at Vienna came back much enlightened on matters concerning Art industries, and finding that painting

and sculpture are nobler than other arts, used for the first time
the term *bijutsu* for them in their reports. They, moreover,
saw the folly of blindly imitating foreign styles, at the expense
of national characteristics, as had been done in Art industries
to suit the foreign market ; and four years later, when the
National Industrial Exhibition was held, the Government
took means to encourage national applied arts by providing
a special department for them.   Just then, that is about 1880,
several foreign Art critics, including Fenollosa, Bigelow, Wagner,
and Chiossone, were assiduously engaged in expounding the
beauty of our native Art ; and as their views were accepted by
certain men of influence at a time when everything was under
the spell of Western influence, Art alone maintained its independence, and was encouraged to preserve and develop its national
characteristics.   In 1882 and 1884, National Art Exhibitions
were held in Tōkyō ; in 1887 the Japan Fine Art Society was
formed, which since then has held exhibitions annually.   In
1888 the Commission for investigating National Painting was
changed into the Tōkyō Art School, where national arts were
principally taught.   In Kyōto a City Art School had been
started in 1880.   Upon this the Art feeling in Japan, which
had fallen to a low ebb, suddenly revived, and with the
institution (1890) of the office of Court Artists presented a
very thriving aspect.

   In this connection we must remember the direct and
indirect efforts of such men as Professor Fenollosa, Kakuzō
Okakura, then Principal of the Tōkyō Art School, and Baron
Ryūichi Kuki, Director of the Imperial Museum.   The establishment of the Bureau of Art Treasures in the Department
of the Imperial Household, to catalogue old Art works, as
well as the creation of the office of Court Artists, were brought
about by Baron Kuki, while the Tōkyō Art School and the
Art magazine ' *Kokka* ' were started mainly through the efforts
of Professor Okakura.

   The Government Exhibition of Paintings and the Art
Exposition of the Japan Fine Art Society greatly encouraged
painters of the national schools.   Every school produced
some artists of note, and it looked as if the flourishing eras
of Bunka and Bunséi were to be installed again.   But it

was a mere temporary struggle against decline ; the new
schools of modern Japan had not appeared as yet when Hōgai
and Gahō were appointed Commissioners for investigating
National Painting. They, following the opinions of Professor
Fenollosa and others, tried to improve national painting, and
studied hard the motives to be aimed at and the decorative
effect of lines, shades, and colours. Hōgai was bent on catching
elusive ideals executed in heavy colouring, and attempted
new interpretations of abstract subjects and human feelings,
while Gahō followed the same course and, improving also the
composition of landscape painting by adapting the laws of
perspective, taught his new style at the Tōkyō Art School.
It was given the name of *Gakkō* (School) style, and was
even called by some fanatical. By this time young artists in
the Japan Art Society, who could not gain currency for their
opinions, left it and formed, on their own account, a society
called the Young Painters Association. Later young artists
from the Tōkyō Art School joined them, and naming the
new society the Japan Painting Association, they gave exhibitions of works in the modern style and competed with the
Japan Art Society. A difference of opinion rose shortly
among the faculty of the Tōkyō Art School. The progressive
party organized themselves a private school called the Japan
Art Institute (*Nippon Bijutsuin*), and, amalgamating with
the Japan Painting Association, did their best to cultivate
the new style. But their works showed over-hastiness in
embodying ideals and neglect of realism, and though some
struck a refreshing note, most of their paintings resembled
decorative pictures. Theirs was spoken of as the *Bijutsuin*
School, or the ' chaotic style,' but it was so much in fashion
at the time that almost all the painters followed it ; and though
its evils were sometimes emphasized too much, it served to
arouse the lethargy of the Japanese Art world. The movement,
be it observed, was brought about chiefly by Professor Okakura,
who was at first Principal of the Tōkyō Art School and later
directed the Japan Art Institute. Since then, with the exception of a few aged masters who have tried to wind up their
careers by large works, artists of all schools have competed
in cultivating new fields, and we see in the last few years

Present
condition
of paint-
ing in
national
schools.

a development of new styles on all sides.   The general tendency is to base them on the least conventional, and therefore the naturalistic, styles in native painting, to adapt from Western Art the law of perspective and the methods of light and shade and colour harmony, and to seek originality in subject and composition.   Artists of course differ in utilizing the best portion of Western Art in quantity as well as in quality : some introduce only the law of perspective in their landscapes, whilst others shade garments, trees, rocks, flowers, leaves, and so forth.   Their efforts are thus diversely directed, but all concur in this, that being tired of the rusty Art of the old native schools, they are aspiring to higher developments, under the stimulus and tutorship of Western painting and the pressure of modern æsthetic criticism.   So the traditions of the old schools, clearly distinguishable before, are now mixed together, and out of such chaos the new school of the era of Méiji may produce splendid results.

Western painting.   Western painting in Japan, which was first introduced through the Dutch and made only a feeble start, has developed rapidly since the opening of the country.   While the Conservatives were still harping on seclusion, foreign intercourse was resolutely started, and the men who quickly recognized the excellence of Western Art and Science induced the Tokugawa Government to found the Institute for the Investigation of Foreign Books in 1857.   Here Western painting also was taught, with Tōgai Kawakami as instructor.   He was very apt and showed much skill, but he had learned it only through Dutch books and not directly from any foreigners, and his oil paintings were no more than improvements of the style of Kōkan.   Tōgai was formerly a *Nangwa* artist, and thus his landscapes were still in that style, with infusion of the laws of perspective, and light and shade.   His pupil, Yuichi Takahashi, however, was able to study under an Englishman named Wirgman (who was thus the first foreigner to teach Western Art to the Japanese), and, going to Shanghai, prosecuted his studies further.   In 1873 Takahashi started a private Art school called the *Tenkwai-sha* and had a number of students.   His works were a step in advance of those of Tōgai and had much more of Western Art in them.   Besides Yuichi, Hōryū Goséda and Hōsui

Yamomoto, both of whom became afterwards distinguished artists, also learned under Wirgman. In 1874, Shinkurō Kunisawa, who had been to England to study painting, came back and started a school called the *Shōgidō*, where he taught many students. On his sudden death his pupil Kinkichirō Honda took his master's place. In 1876 the Imperial Engineering College (*Kōbu Daigaku*) was founded, and included an Art Department, over which the Italian artist Fontanesi was placed. He was the first instructor of Western painting who came to our country as such, and sound methods were for the first time inaugurated through his efforts. Many young men who had been in the *Tenkwaisha* and the *Shōgidō*, or followers of Tōgai, entered the new school and received instruction there. Most of the present artists of note were of the group, of whom we may mention Shōtarō Koyama, Chū Asai, and Hisashi Matsuoka, the two latter afterwards completing their studies in Europe. After Fontanesi's return home two other Italians, Ferretti and San Giovanni, followed in succession ; but, in 1883, the school was closed, causing a temporary halt in the progress of Western art in Japan. Two years before this, however, Kiyoo Kawamura, who had been for a long time in Europe and America, and some time after Naojirō Harada, who had been in Germany, came back and contributed much to the furtherance of Western Art.

One reason that led to the abolition of the Art Department in the Imperial Engineering College was the rise of the nationalistic movement in Art above mentioned, for as the real value of native Art, neglected for so long a time, came to be again recognized through the enthusiastic appreciation of foreigners, the awakening reacted on Western Art. Consequently, with this renaissance of national painting the Government of Paintings Exhibition stopped accepting Western paintings, the newly established Art School stayed its courses in Western painting, and in public schools pencil drawing, which until then had been in vogue, was replaced by brush drawing. For some years after that Western painting was at a low ebb, but its adherents still cultivated it, and training what pupils they had, bided their time. Especially those who had studied under Fontanesi ripened in their art as years went by, and, in 1888, such men

as Koyama, Matsuoka, Asai, and Kawamura rose at last in
defiance of the tendency of the time, and formed the Méiji Fine
Art Association, giving an exhibition annually, and attempting
to arouse public interest. Six years later, Kiyotéru Kuroda
and Keiichirō Kumé came back from France and introduced
a new school of painting.   Having received a thorough education in Paris *ateliers*, they moved the public to wonder by their
canvases, and they induced the Tōkyō Art School, which had
been established under the principle of preserving national
painting, to start a new course in Western painting in 1896,
and to appoint them as professors. Thereupon Western
painting, which had been moribund for a while, revived
suddenly with more vigour than ever.   Kuroda and Kumé
championed the French impressionist school, and as they
differed from the artists of the Italian school of the Méiji
Art Association, both in style and taste, they formed a new
Art association called the *Hakubakai*, giving their own exhibitions, and also opening a studio for instruction.   To the
Hakubakai students of the Tōkyō Art School belonged ;
to the Méiji Art Association, the pupils of Koyama and Asai.
The rivalry of the members of the two associations certainly
gave an impulse to the Art world.   The Meiji Art Association
was later renamed the *Taihéiyō Gwakai* (Pacific Painting
Association).   Both associations are now producing talented
artists, while the Tōkyō Art School sends out many graduates every year.   Western painting in Japan is thus on its
way to further development.

Sculpture.   In glyptic art there were, at the end of the seclusion period,
men of note such as Hōun Takahashi and Tōun Takamura,
as sculptors of Buddhist statues, reflecting the splendour of
the preceding period, as well as many skilled carvers of *nétsuké*.
But the Restoration War swept away their trade, and their
art reached the depths of decline, and nothing of note was
evolved for a considerable time, although hope of revival
soon appeared from two directions. With the increase in
foreign trade, the demand for *nétsuké* increased largely, and
this led to the revival of ivory carving. As *nétsuké* were
exported by thousands in the beginning of the Méiji era,
the works of the preceding period were soon exhausted, and

the demand had to be met by new productions. Foreigners cared most for carved ivories, so that the efforts of artists were directed mainly to that work. From *nétsuké* the demand extended to *okimono* (alcove ornaments) in ivory, and the supply could hardly keep pace with it, so much so, that every craftsman in carving who had lost his trade in the national disturbance, whether he was a mask maker, an ornament carver of shrines, or a sculptor of Buddhist statues, found employment in this new business. Small works in ivory reached the highest state of artistic excellence between 1877 and 1887, and artists of note were produced, with Gyokuzan Asahi, Kōméi Ishikawa, and Shumméi Shimamura as their leaders.

The Japan Art Society, and the Tōkyō Art School also, had departments of sculpture. The Tōkyō Sculptors Association was subsequently founded, and in these three places the national style of carving was principally cultivated; and besides ivory carving, which was brought to a high degree of perfection through the foreign demand, carving in wood was practised after the manner of ancient Buddhist artists. Among the artists of note in this line we may mention Kyūichi Takéuchi, who, studying old works at Nara, revived the Tempyō style, and Kōun Takamura, who, as the pupil of Tōun, mostly carved animals. In the Tōkyō Art School wood carving was principally taught, and as young artists flocked thither, the art was in a very flourishing state from 1887 to 1897, showing much advance in workmanship over that of the preceding period. The second favourable factor was the establishment of a course in sculpture in the Art Department of the Imperial Engineering College. This was formed purely on Western lines, and with Ragusa, an Italian, as instructor, the European art of modelling was taught there for the first time in Japan. After a while such men as Bunzō Fujita and Ujihiro Ōkuma, who finished their studies there, came out with high aims, although unfortunately these were checked in their advance by the rising spirit of nationalism. In the meantime, Shukéi Naganuma, who had been studying Western sculpture in Italy for a long time, came back ; and, though things Western were not in favour then, his works were much respected for their idealism. Soon, however,

Western sculpture.

with the growing knowledge of Western Art, dissatisfaction was aroused at the carvings of the day with their monotony of style, their lack of realism, and their old-fashioned methods. The advance of æsthetic criticism, and its severe attacks upon the sculptors, urged them to reform ; and so, in 1898, Hidéo Takaminé, Director of the Tōkyō Art School, decided to adopt Western methods in the department of sculpture, and, appointing Shukéi Naganuma and Bunzō Fujita as professors, encouraged modelling from the life in clay.   On this the young carvers of the national school did not hesitate to give up their old-fashioned methods, and, following the lead in copying from nature, attempted to improve their style. The Western art of modelling became diffused at once, and young artists formed the Carving and Modelling Association to further investigate the new methods. Statues from the life in plaster, which were rarely seen formerly, came to be exhibited more and more, as well as casts made after them. Wood carvers, too, used clay in modelling, and came to work exactly in the same manner as sculptors ; while workers in ivory, following this example, improved their art also. Compared with the products of former days, when the use of soft material for modelling was unknown, and the wood or ivory was, from the start, carved from imagination, the new productions were far more meritorious. Thus in sculpture, unlike painting, the national and the Western styles have blended completely and are on the road to speedy development. That such perfect union was possible in this field is due to the nature of glyptic art itself. In the case of painting, objects are only made to appear to stand out from the plane ; and as there is ample room for the exercise of diverse methods, leading ultimately to diversity of schools of Art, native painting, which is far removed from the Western art in the tradition and in the manner of presentation, cannot be easily blended with it. But with sculpture, which aims at the reproduction of a solid body in the solid, whatever the style may be, concave portions cannot be represented in any other way than as concave, nor convex portions except as convex. There may be a wide difference in technique between the works of native and foreign schools, but no great dissimilarity in the methods of their representation can be found. So it was not difficult from the start for our glyptic art to blend with Western.

Western architecture was introduced with the opening of the country and was first used in Government buildings, and subsequently in those for commercial firms and banks. Stone and brick houses quickly rose in great numbers, and have increased steadily until nearly all the important buildings in our great cities are now in Western style. This is, indeed, as great a change in the history of architecture in Japan as when the Tang style was introduced some twelve centuries ago. But houses in Western style are as yet mostly built for practical purposes, and real artistic architecture with rich ornamentation has still to make its appearance. It is now a fashion with the nobility and millionaires to build their residences in the Western mode, but on account of the costume they wear in domestic circles, the living rooms still continue to be in native style. With average well-to-do people houses are in Japanese style, with one or two rooms furnished in the Western way for receiving guests. The science of architecture is taught at the College of Engineering, Imperial University, and a number of trained architects in Japanese or Western style have been produced, and both in design and in execution the art is progressing steadily. The native style of residence most in vogue is a variation of what was known as the *shoin-zukuri*, while several styles of the *sukiya* are used conjointly with it. In the building of temples and shrines the old styles are still severely followed.

The Art industries of Japan also fell into a pitiable condition in the great national disturbance of the Restoration. Especially was this the case with workers in metal, who were engaged mainly in chiselling sword furniture, as the wearing of swords was prohibited; and as *inrō* and other decorative articles fell into disuse with the changed ways of living, workers in gold lac were reduced to a miserable state. But with the rise of foreign trade and with encouragement given by opening the National Industrial Exposition, these old Art industries soon revived, and presented a more flourishing aspect than before, alike in the amount of production and in workmanship. Pottery, porcelain, and weaving have been assiduously

Western architecture.

Art industries and their encouragement.

cultivated by introducing Western methods, since Japan took part in the Vienna Exposition of 1873. Besides, the demand for exportation and the policy of industrial encouragement, together with the progress in painting and sculpture, induced a marked improvement in design, whilst recent productions have come to excel any former period in point of workmanship. Two facts which contributed most to this end were, first, that Tsunétami Sano, Chief Commissioner to the Vienna Exposition, took with him artisans and made them acquainted with Western methods; and secondly, that Toshimichi Okūbo, then Minister of the Interior, established the National Industrial Exposition in 1877. The National Industrial Expositions, opened one after the other since then, have encouraged progress, while the display of our works at foreign exhibitions from time to time served to increase the export. It is owing to such causes that the present flourishing state of Art industries in Japan has been reached.

In conclusion, let me now describe the present state of each Art industry, but only briefly, so as not to intrude on the province of industries which receive separate treatment.

Ceramics. In ceramics Western methods of manufacture as well as new pigments have been utilized for improvement since the opening of the country, and with the increase of trade and the rise in Art production far finer works have been turned out. In Tōkyō we had formerly nothing but crude pottery, called Imado ware, but since 1877, when the Yédogawa Porcelain Manufacturing Plant was established, such craftsmen of note as Tomotarō Katō and Hayata Takémoto have appeared. Takémoto used plaster moulds for the first time in Japan, and is famed for his management of stoving to produce a special glaze. In Yokohama we have Kōzan Miyagawa, whose porcelain wares are said to be the finest now in Japan. Kyōto has been noted for ceramics from olden times, and the wares of Awata and Kiyomizu are abundantly produced now. Tōzan Itō and Sōbéi Kinkōzan are famed for pottery, and Yohéi Séifū, Dōhachi Takahashi, and Chikusén Miura for porcelain. Their works are celebrated for technique, showing a diversity of beautiful effects which command the highest appreciation. Séifū and Miyagawa are both artists in the Imperial service, and rank very high in their respective fields. In Arita the ware of the *Kōransha* is the best. Séto produces mostly wares for daily use, but its painted earthen tiles are without equal in Japan. Kutani makes artistic porcelains in large quantity. Satsuma pottery has made steady progress, and that of Chin at times excites our admiration for dexterity of ornamental open-work and beauty of decoration. A few years ago the Association for Ceramic Industry was formed, and, holding exhibitions, is encouraging fine workmanship.

The making of cloisonné was undertaken in earnest only recently, but its progress is indeed surprising. The art was known to the ancients, but was given up for a long time. It was revived in later days, but never reached a state of artistic excellence, and its production was very small. In the period of Méiji, however, the art has been greatly cultivated in Nagoya, Kyōto, and Tōkyō, and quickly reached its present state of development. Séishi Namikawa of Kyōto and Sōsuké Namikawa of Tōkyō, both Court artists, and Shibatarō Kawadé of Nagoya are distinguished in this branch. They all produce works of the finest technique and export abundantly. Especially Sōsuké Namikawa is noted for his invention of cloisonless enamels (*musén*), and for the lightness and delicacy of his designs. Séishi Namikawa, on the other hand, is known for the fineness of his cloisonné pictures. The town of Nagoya excels all others in the amount of its production, and it not only turns out fine works in lined or lineless cloisonné, but has invented recently such wares as *moriagé*, or cloisonné in relief, and *mutaiban*, or bodiless cloisonné.

Metal engraving has also made marked progress since the Restoration. Decorated sword furniture, which was in such a flourishing state of production in former periods, fell entirely out of demand, but other articles needing ornamentation have supplied its place. Foreign trade, as in other cases of Art industries, must be counted a great factor in contributing to revive this branch also, while the progress made in the whole province of Art brought improvement in the traditional styles of carving till they reached the present state of high excellence. Lately Natsuo Kanō attained to great celebrity

Cloisonné.

Metal work.

for his *katakiri* process in realistic painting-like style, and at present we have artists of such fame as Shōmin Unno and Katsuhiro Kagawa, who excel each in his own peculiar process. The two latter are the Court artists for metal engraving. In *repoussé* work Chōzaburō Yamada is noted : he works mainly in iron, and produces pieces showing great ease and dexterity in representing all kinds of objects ; they are, however, still on the way to further development, with a promising future. The Tōkyō Art School has departments in metal carving, casting, and hammering, and sends out many graduates yearly. As an organization of artisans, we have too the Metal Workers Association ; while the Japan Art Society and the Carving and Engraving Association have each a department of metal work and give public exhibitions of their productions.

Lacquer.   In lacquer we had, in the early part of the Méiji era, such noted artists as Zéshin Shibata and Shōmin Ogawa, who served as transmitters of the advanced Art of the former period. Zéshin, who was also an artist with the brush, invented lac drawing in colours and opened the way to polychromatic decoration in lac. Since 1887, with the thriving condition of Fine Art and Applied Art, the lacquer industry has prospered greatly, and decorations in gold lac now include pictures of different schools, and are not restricted, as in the former period, to the Tosa and the Kanō styles. There has been some improvement, but this branch of the art seems to have exhausted its resources, while polychromatic lac is still very limited in use. The wares, too, are mere reproductions of old-style boxes, cabinets and so forth, and are never articles of more modern application. A great change must be made if the art is to be further developed. The reason for this stationary attitude may, perhaps, lie in the fact that the industry has no equivalent in the West, and has therefore had no Western influence to revivify it. Lacquerers much noted for *makiyé* at present are Itchō Kawanobé and Shōsai Shirayama, both of whom are Court artists. As an organization of artisans we have the Lacquer Association, while a lacquer department is found in the Japan Art Society and the Tōkyō Art School, as well as in the Industrial Schools in the country.

What dyeing, weaving, and embroidery have gained from the West since the opening of the country consists mainly in the improvement of looms and in the importation of dye stuffs.   As for progress on their artistic side, it has been made principally on the basis of our national Art, side by side with other Art industries.   Foreign influence in this respect is only traceable in some infusion of Western designs in embroidery and fabric, and also in the adaptation of forms to new demands which have called forth new inventions.

THE FINE ARTS—MUSIC

Suyéharu Tōgi

Ancient music.

THE genesis of singing and dancing dates very far back in Japan, but traditions handed down from time immemorial suggest how they originated. According to some the prehistoric divine couple, Izanagi and Izanami, happened by chance to utter a cry of *anasniéya* (how lovable!) harmoniously in salutation to each other, and the celebrated song of *Yakumotatsu* was composed and sung somewhat later by Susanō-no-Mikoto. These may be regarded as the beginnings of the art of song, while, as to dancing, others tell us that Honosusori-no-Mikoto announced to Hikoho-hodémi-no-Mikoto his intention of becoming a professional actor, and that singing and dancing were performed by Amé-no-usumé-no-Mikoto in front of the cave in which the Sun Goddess by hiding herself had withdrawn all illumination from the world. It goes without saying that traditions such as these can throw but little light on the actual condition of music in primeval times; but it may safely be inferred from them that a taste for it existed in our country long before the dawn of history, and that this taste has done much in forming the scales of our present national music.

Martial music.

There is good reason to believe that the inhabitants of our insular empire were distinguished even in prehistoric times for their love of music, which served both to foster their brave and warlike character and to encourage its ardour. Warriors seldom went on expeditions without being accompanied by military music and a number of war-dancers. In later times when the Emperor Jimmu, founder of the empire, marched at the head of a great army to subjugate the natives of the Eastern districts, he is said to have stirred the martial spirit of his soldiers by making them sing a song he himself had composed for the occasion. This song has been handed down to the present day under the name of *kumé-uta*.

Dancing accompanied by music was one of the most important forms of worshipping the *kami*.[1] When the tenth Emperor, Sujin, removed the Imperial shrine of the Sun Goddess to the province of Yamato, he ordered a *kagura* (a dance accompanied by music and performed to entertain the *kami*) to be danced in celebration of the event. Besides the *kagura* performance, there were several kinds of song then in vogue, such as the *shinénka*, the *shihōka*, the *kusu-uta*, the *amataburi*, the *ebisuburi*, the *katashita-uta*; but, with the exception of those of the *kagura*, their airs have not been preserved. Concerning the non-religious performance of dancing, history tells us that, in the reign of Inkyō, the nineteenth Emperor, the Empress danced a dance to the sounds of the harp played by her Imperial consort, at the fête celebrated upon the completion of a new Imperial palace, and that, a little later, a dance called *tatsumai* was performed by two Imperial princes, both of whom subsequently became emperors in succession under the names of Kensō and Ninkén. Of musical instruments, only the harp and the drum are known with certainty to have been employed in these performances, but it is probable that the flute was also made use of.

Music in religious rites.

It was the practice in those days for young men and maidens to assemble together for singing and dancing, and to avail themselves of the occasion to make love to one another, and such was the case with the Emperor Kensō, who secured the affection of Kagéhimé while dancing with her. Such a mode of courtship was called by the name of *utagaki* or *kagahi*. The custom, however, disappeared upon the introduction into the empire of foreign modes of dancing and singing.

Music in love-making.

Korea, separated as it is from Japan by a very narrow channel of water, has usually been the medium through which innovations from the Continent have been introduced into this insular empire. The first mention of foreign music is

Introduction of Korean music.

---

[1] *Kami*: see Vol. I, p. 2.

at the time of the Emperor Inkyō's death, when it is recorded
that musicians to the number of eighty were offered to our
Imperial Government as tribute by the King of Shiragi (one
of the four contemporary kingdoms of ancient Korea), and it
is highly probable that similar homage may also have been
paid by two of the three other Korean kingdoms, namely,
Kudara and Koma. Further, according to the ' *Taihō-ryō* '
(code of laws established in 702 A.D.), the instruments these
foreign musicians used consisted of a wind instrument made
of short pieces of bamboo put together (*shō*), a flute (*wotēki*), a
seven-stringed instrument (*kin*), a twenty-three-stringed harp
(*kūgō* or *kudara-goto*), and a drum (*yōko*).

Indian music.

Early in the seventh century intercourse with China
first began to be cultivated, and Buddhism was introduced
into our country, and it is not altogether unreasonable to
conjecture that Indian musical instruments must have made
their way here along with the Indian religion. The famous
Imperial Prince Shōtoku, who is said to have transmitted
the art of the *shisimai* (a kind of dancing performed by a
man wearing a mask shaped in imitation of a lion's head), set
great value on the beneficial use of music, and exerted himself
to diffuse a musical taste throughout the empire. In the twentieth year of his regency (612 A.D.), a naturalized Japanese
from Korea, Mimashi by name, brought with him a method
of dancing called *kurémai*, which the Prince skilfully introduced into the Buddhist services, and which was in universal
use afterwards in conjunction with Korean music. The
kurémai was performed by men wearing masks, and accompanied by the flute and the *yōko*. In a word, the eastward
march of Buddhism and our intercourse with China each gave
an impulse to the advance of civilization, which resulted in
the development of music and dancing in our country.

Diversifi-
cation of
national
music.

Later, several kinds of song and dance came into fashion,
such as the *tamai* in the reign of the Emperor Tenchi (seventh
century) ; the *charitamai* and the *gosechimai* in that of Temmu
(seventh century), the latter of which was composed by the
Emperor himself ; the *tatefushimai* and the *tōka* in that of
Empress Jitō (end of seventh century) ; and one called the
yoshinomai, which was, it is believed, first performed by one

Abé at the festival of thanksgiving after the triumphant
return of the Empress Jingō from her Korean campaign.
All these songs and dances were of purely native growth,
but it is probable that they had become comparatively perfected by those days and were far in advance of anything
previously known.

As to the key-note or tone of music in the early days, it
is now altogether unknown. Though the Emperor Jimmu's
kumé-uta has still much that is peculiarly its own, even when
sung to the music of to-day, we can by no means affirm that
on that account the song had this characteristic from the first.
Moreover, none of the musical books or instruments of that
remote antiquity, by means of which we might have been able
to learn what the note of music then was, have been handed
down. But this much we can say with perfect safety : that
the peculiar tone of our national music has been developed
out of the mixed notes of the purely native *kagura-uta* on the
one hand, and the *kumé-uta* and the *ta-uta* (a song accompanying
the *tamai*) on the other. These were, however, so much
modified by foreign influence in the Middle Ages that all their
notes have come to agree exactly with the five principal notes
or scales of Chinese music, named, respectively, *kyū*, *shō*,
kaku, *chō*, and *u*.

In the Nara epoch (690–783 A.D.) the development of music
again progressed. Large foreign contributions and great
efforts on the part of the Government at home aided this.
Masters were officially appointed to give lessons in singing
and dancing, not only of the *yamato-uta*, the *yamatomai*, and
those above mentioned, but of the later dances and songs,
such as the *tsukushimai*, the *shokénmai*, and the *tōgokumai*.
As to the folk-songs and dances in the various provinces,
the governors were ordered to see to their being properly
taught. A performance of these was given before the Emperor
Genshō in the first year of Yōrō (777 A.D.), when he was travelling through his empire. But those practised by the *Hayato*
(the bold and daring race of men) in Satsuma and Ōsumi are
said to have originated in prehistoric times, and were taught
only by special masters belonging to the War Department.
First and most conspicuous was the women's *tōka* and the

(margin notes:) Key-note of early music.

Music during the Nara epoch.

utagaki, performed in the *Naikyōbō* (a kind of school attached
to the Imperial Palace where music and dancing were taught
to ladies), the performance of which latter appears to have
been carried to excess in the reign of the Empress Shōtoku
(the second half of the eighth century).

Bureau of
Music.   After the Reformation of the Taika era (649 A.D.), when
everything in the empire was put on a new and better footing,
musical performances also improved to a degree before unknown. The *Uta-ryō* (Bureau of Music) was established, in
accordance with the provisions of the ' *Taihō-ryō.*' A number
of instructors and performers of Japanese music, especially
of singing, dancing, and fluting, as well as of foreign music,
Chinese and Korean, and the *kurémai*, were maintained at
the expense of this bureau, that they might be ready at a
moment's notice whenever a Court festival or a Buddhist
service took place.

The
shōmyō
and the
bombai.   In the reign of the Emperor Shōmu (about 730 A.D.), the
number of musicians belonging to the *Uta-ryō* was doubled.
The *shōmyō* (a species of hymn prosody) and the *bombai*
(reciting from the Buddhist sacred books) were brought over
from China by Chinese Buddhist priests, who became naturalized in Japan about the same time. The eighth year of Tempyō
(736 A.D.) saw the introduction of two modes of dancing to
music, the *battō* and the *bosatsu*, also by Chinese priests who
came over to Japan.

Foreign
instru-
ments.   The instruments employed in these foreign musical performances, it is needless to say, differed more or less at different
times and according to the nature of the pieces to be played ;
but it is certain that, in addition to the *shō* and the *hichiriki*,
flute, (both wind instruments), they included the *wagon*,
the *koto*, and the *biwa* (stringed instruments), the *kakko*, the
taiko, and the *shōko* (the last named being made of metal),
all of which are still used by musicians, as well as the *kin*, the
kūgō, the *gogén*, the *shakuhachi*, &c., all of which were popular
in the Middle Ages, but which we do not use at present, and
of which we know only from the specimens which are kept
at the Shōsōin at Nara.

During the Héian epoch (784–1186 A.D.) musical development
in Japan may be said to have reached its highest stage, for

almost all the pieces that are now regarded as of greatest value from a musical point of view then came into existence. After the removal of the Imperial capital from Nara to Héian (Kyōto), everything remained for a time as it had been, but the two Emperors, Saga and Nimmyō, who were both addicted to and well versed in Chinese music, spent much of their time in studying the comparative value of various musical pieces: this resulted in bringing about the amalgamation of different elements of music, domestic and foreign. Imported arts and sciences now began to be digested so fully, and settlers from abroad came to be so assimilated with the natives, that foreign music could never be popular so long as its modulation remained as it was when first introduced ; something had to be done to adapt it to the altered condition of things in the empire, for the time was past when two species of music, domestic and foreign, could co-exist independently of each other. Fortunately, at this juncture, Owari-no-Hamanushi, Ōdo-no-Kiyokami, Wanibé-no-Ōtamaro, and Fujiwara-no-Sadatoshi, the greatest masters of music in ancient Japan, successively appeared, and devoted themselves to the task of altering the Chinese music and of evolving out of it a national one.

Apogee of Japanese music in the Héian epoch.

Domestic and foreign music.

In this they were aided by a celebrated Buddhist priest, Kūkai, who introduced fundamental changes in the airs of *shōmyō*, the result being one of the greatest epochs in the history of our national music. The newly arranged music came into high favour with the public, and the *Uta-ryō* became filled with musicians belonging to the new school, while purely Japanese music was entirely left to the care of the *Ōutadokoro*, another bureau of music. It may be mentioned that the time we are now speaking of was noted especially for the development of instrumental music. As to vocal music, it appeared for a season to be on the wane, and it was not until the reign of the Emperor Séiwa (in the middle of the ninth century) that it revived in the same way as instrumental music just described. Then it was that regulations concerning musical performances were enacted for the first time in the ' *Jokan-shiki* ' (a code of laws formed in 869 A.D.), and in the ' *Engi-shiki* ' (promulgated in 908 A.D.), according to which the *kagura* and the *azuma-asobi*, handed down from time immemorial, were reserved for festival days, while the *kumé-uta* and the *yamato-uta* were to be performed only on ceremonial occasions.   The musical instruments to be employed in these performances consisted of the *hichiriki*, whose tone was the most adaptable among the Chinese musical instruments, and the Japanese flute and the *wagon*, the playing of both of which had originated early in the empire.   From this it will be seen that any difference between Japanese music and Chinese had by this time disappeared, so far as modulation was concerned.

Saibara.   About this period a peculiar kind of operatic performance known by the name of *saibara*, which aimed with success at representing the condition of society and humanity in the Héian epoch, made its appearance on the scene and soon came into great favour with the public.   It had been popular in the Nara epoch, but early in the Héian, when, as mentioned above, great fundamental changes took place in the system of music in general, this *saibara* was remodelled in the manner of Chinese music and became distinguished for its sweetness and elegance : it is eloquent of the taste of the Fujiwara family, under whose auspices the transformation was effected.   A little later, in a period between the two eras of Engi and Tenryaku, when poetry and prose were much in vogue, there appeared a species of recitation called the *rōyéi*, which con-

The *rōyéi*.   sisted in the singing of verses selected from famous literary works, both Chinese and Japanese, and melodized for the purpose.   It was principally used, together with the *saibara*, at Imperial festivities.   Thus in the middle of the tenth century our national music and dancing reached their highest point of excellence.   Minamoto-no-Hakuga, one of the greatest musicians Japan ever produced, flourished in this remarkable age.

Music in the Court circles.   The period of some two centuries following the reign of the Emperor Ichijō (987–1011 A.D.) was the golden age of the arts of music and dancing.   The newly ordered scheme of Japanese music had come into prominence by this time ; and not only every person belonging to the Imperial Court was more or less skilful in performance, but not a few celebrated musicians appeared from the ranks of the aristocracy.   Of these the Emperor Horikawa stood pre-eminent, having never been surpassed even by professional musicians. At this time every branch of art and science had its own school, which was monopolized as a rule by a certain family recognized as its head. Among the noble families admitted to Imperial intimacy there were two, the Minamoto and the Fujiwara, to whom the special duty of everything connected with the *téikyoku* (a general name for all performances of vocal music) was entrusted. In these families musical accomplishments were handed down from father to son. There were also, similarly attached to the Imperial Court, certain inferior families, to each of whom the privilege was granted of exclusively performing a special branch of music. These kept their specialities strictly to themselves for so long a time that the arts finally came to be regarded as attainments beyond the reach of the people at large.

The taste of the governed is, for the most part, little else than a reflection of that of the governing. So it happened in regard to the musical taste of the age we are speaking about. There were performances of music and dancing particularly popular amongst the lower classes, as well as those enjoyed by the higher. A comic dance, the *sarugaku*, first begun by *sangaku* players—players belonging to the *Uta-ryō*—and a kind of dancing to music called the *senshū-banzai*, which was a changed form of the *tōka* (or the *mannen-araré*) and performed only at the beginning of the New Year, came into favour with the public in the reign of the Emperor Murakami (the middle of the tenth century), along with other popular amusements, such as the *kyokumai*, the *monogatari*, and the *kukutsu*. In the reign of the Emperor Toba (early in the twelfth century), two girls employed in a saloon, Shima-no-Chitosé and Waka-no-Maé by name, originated a dance to the sounds of, not any stringed instrument, but a drum, a flute, and a cymbal, and attained great popularity at the time. Thus originated the form of dancing since known by the name of *shirabyōshi*. *Popular music.*

But with the decline of the Imperial power at the end of the twelfth century, the forms of music which had flourished under its patronage disappeared like a dream. For four hundred years from that time down to the end of the Ashikaga *Transitional period.*

Shōgunate, the arts of popular music and dancing were in constant progress, whilst those of a refined nature were thrown into the background.

Origin of the *Nō* performance.

Under the Kamakura Shōgunate the *shirabyōshi* and the *dengaku* superseded the newly risen *sarugaku*, the *dengaku* especially being exceedingly popular among all classes of people, its professional players being bonzes (or *hōshi*), who vied with one another in skilfully performing their entertaining feats. In addition to their regular arts, the *dengaku-hōshi* commenced for the first time a kind of operatic performance, and gave it the name of *nōgéi*. This may be regarded as the earliest operatic performance in Japan. Not long afterwards the *nōgéi* of the *sarugaku* was introduced, in addition to the *nōgéi* of the *dengaku*. It was played at the public services held at the Kōfukuji temple, at the temples of Hiéizan, and at the Isé and Sumiyoshi shrines. Early in the era of Ōyéi (from the latter part of the fourteenth century to the beginning of the fifteenth), Matasaburō Yūki, or Kan-ami, a player of the *nōgéi*, served the Shōgun Yoshimitsu Ashikaga as page, and was treated by him with special favour. Both his son Sōzén, who became the first ancestor of the Kanzé family, and another famous performer, Komparu of Nara in the province of Yamato, composed many new pieces of the *nōgéi*, in which the drum, the *ōtsuzumi*, the *kotsuzumi* (both drums struck with the hand), and the flute were used. This was the origin of the *Nō* performance of to-day. As to the *mono-*

Origin of the *mono-gatari*.

gatari, another species of music, it originated at the time when Ikibotoké, a blind lutanist of Kyōto, first recited the *Héiké Monogatari* (family history of the Taira), accompanied with the sounds of his instrument.

A blow to the development of music.

Up to the middle of the Ashikaga Shōgunate, both the *dengaku* and the *sarugaku* had been in great vogue, but they received a crushing blow from the disturbances caused by the general war in the era of Ōnin (1467). This war not only retarded the advance in our national music, but nearly destroyed the *nōgéi*. It also dispersed the musical performers, who passed into the employ of *daimyō* of various provinces, and Kyōto, the Imperial city, was utterly denuded of those who could have fostered the art of music.

It was not until the time of Hidéyoshi Toyotomi (in the sixteenth century) that the Imperial Court was restored to its former honour, and its ceremonial forms were brought back to the condition they had been in before the long civil wars. The Emperor Ōgimachi was able, in consequence, to invite musicians from the Tennōji temple at Ōsaka to his palace, and in the era of Bunroku (1592–95) others from Nara were engaged by the Emperor Goyōzéi. In this way Court music was gradually restored to its original condition, and the scattered Kyōto musicians were once again collected and became a feature of the capital. *Restoration of classical music.*

Contemporaneously the prestige of the *Nō* performance began to revive. Hidéyoshi was so enamoured of the *Komparu* style of *Nō* dancing, that he himself performed it, his great vassals following his example. *Revival of the Nō.*

When the Tokugawa Shōgunate was established in Yédo (Tōkyō), the *Hōshō* style (introduced by the Hōshō family of the feudal clan of Odawara) became the mode there, and was followed a little later by the three styles of the *Kanzé*, the *Komparu*, and the *Kongō*. Of the four, the *Kanzé* and the *Hōshō* styles from Kyōto were called the *kamigakari*, and the other two from Nara the *shimogakari*. Thus it will be seen that the national music in the time of the Tokugawa Shōgunate consisted of three kinds, namely, the refined music prevailing at the Imperial Court, the *Nō* performance, mainly in favour with the military class, and the *sangéngaku* (vocal music accompanied by the *samisén*), which originated about this time, but was destined before long to become very popular among the lower classes. *Three main branches of national music.*

The civil and military peace which Japan enjoyed during the next two centuries and a half gave a rare opportunity to all three kinds of music to develop, and they were not slow in so doing. The *sangéngaku*, which made greater progress than the others during this period, divides itself naturally into two classes, one being the *utaimono* (a general name for songs, ballads, &c., such as the *naga-uta*, the *ha-uta*, &c.), and the other the *katarimono* (a general name for all kinds of dramatic recitation, such as the *jōruri*). The *katarimono* or the *monogatari*, originating in the recital *The sangéngaku.*

of the *Héiké Monogatari*, was at first sung by the *gozé* alone (blind women who go about seeking alms by singing songs), who used to travel through the country singing, to the accompaniment of a drum, always the same operatic song, namely, about the Soga brothers having killed their enemy in revenge.

Development of the *jōruri*.

The *jōruri*, which the *gozé* took up soon after the disturbance of the era of Ōnin, was much improved at the time of the establishment of the Tokugawa Shōgunate at Yédo, by being made to rest upon the basis of the *Héiké* style and having some important ingredients added to it from the *yōkyoku* (*Nō* singing), the *sekkyō*, the *saimon*, &c. The *sangén*, a three-stringed musical instrument, was first brought over from the Loochoo Islands and rapidly became popular, especially amongst the *kengyō* and the *kōtō* (the first and second rank in the Guild of Blind Shampooers). In the era of Kéichō (towards the end of the sixteenth century), a *kengyō*, Sawazumi by name, who was skilled in performing on this instrument, invented the art of playing it so as to harmonize with the singing of the *jōruri*, and then Chōzaburō Ménukiya, one of his pupils, applied this musical art to a puppet show. The *jōruri* was thus made to assume the character of a musical drama as it is at present. The style of singing the *jōruri* was subdivided, towards the second half of the sixteenth century, into several branches, such as the *Yédo-jōruri*, the *Satsuma*, the *Toraya*, the *Sanai*, &c. These were still further divided, during the next one hundred years, into numerous schools, of which the chief were the *Yédo-bushi*, the *Bungo-bushi*, the *Tokiwazu*, the *Fujimatsu-bushi*, the *Shōdén-bushi*, and the *Sonohachi-bushi*.

The *gidayū*.

The *gidayū-bushi*, now sung almost invariably in a puppet show and a theatre, originated in Ōsaka with a *Toraya-jōruri* performer named Harima Inouyé from Kyōto. In the era of Genroku, another performer of the same school, Chikugo Takémoto, appeared and completed the system, changing the name of *jōruri* to that of *gidayū*. The first *gidayū* songs sung in puppet shows in Ōsaka were written by Monzaémon Chikamatsu, the greatest dramatist existing at that time. As to the *kabuki* (dramatic performance), it originated in the *nénbutsu-odori* (a kind of dance), danced to the musical sounds

The *kabuki*.

of a flute and a drum, first of all by Okuni (a virgin who danced at the Izumo shrine to entertain the gods) and Sanza Nagoya (of Owari) at the beginning of the seventeenth century. There were actors and actresses attached to the *kabuki*, respectively called the *wakashū-kabuki* and the *yūjo-kabuki*. The three-stringed musical instruments came a little later to be employed in the performance, and the dances were danced in harmony with the singing of a song popular at the time, as well as of a *jōruri*. When the puppet show, accompanied by the *gidayū-bushi*, became popular in Ōsaka, its method of performance was imitated by *kabuki* players, and from the eighteenth century onwards the *kabuki* grew more and more in favour with the public, especially in the three chief cities of Tōkyō, Kyōto, and Ōsaka, till it has been made what it is. The *naga-uta*, a kind of popular song, is said to have had its origin in the playing of the *sangén* in a *kabuki* performance, got up at Yédo by a certain Kangorō Kinéya from Suruga, at the beginning of the seventeenth century.

The *ha-uta* or *ko-uta* was a general name for folk-songs popular in the Tokugawa era, just as the *fūzoku-uta* in the Nara epoch, the *imayō* in the time of the Fujiwara regency, and the *Ichirikengyō* and the *Nimonjō* in that of the Kamakura Shōgunate. In the earlier part of the time, the airs (styles of singing), each of which prevailed at a certain epoch, appear to stand in the following chronological order—the *Ryūtatsu-bushi* in the era of Bunroku (1592–95), its modified form being *Rōsai-bushi*; the *Shibagaki-bushi* in that of Méiréki (1655); the *Doté-bushi* and the *Kaga-bushi* in Kambun (1661); the *Nagé-bushi* in Teikyō (1684); and, lastly, the *Dōnen-bushi* and the *Kokon-bushi* in Genroku (1688). Later, in the era of Anséi (1854), the *Utazawa-bushi* appeared and became very popular. The *Shinnai* and the *Ōtsuyé* of to-day are nothing but transformations of this style. Of many others prevailing in various provinces, the *Kamigata-uta*, mainly in vogue in Kyōto and Ōsaka, is the most noted, and has always had something peculiar to itself.

The *ha-uta.*

The thirteen-stringed *koto* (a kind of harp) or the *tsukushi-goto* originated in the western province of Tsukushi (now Kyūshū) towards the end of the time of Ashikaga; and the

The *koto.*

songs sung to the *koto* were first composed by Yatsuhashi, a blind musician, in the latter part of the era of Kanséi (1640). The art of playing on this instrument has been much improved since then. Musical points marked in its pieces have been classified by his successors, according to the degree of their abstruseness, into four parts, respectively called the *omoté*, the *ura*, the *naka*, and the *oku*, and various new styles have emanated from it in consequence, so that it is now in general favour with the ladies of the middle and higher classes. The *Ikuta* and the *Yamada* style, however, are most popular at present, and are taught in girls' schools throughout the empire. In the present mode the *koto* is not employed by itself, but is often accompanied by the *sangén* and the *shakuhachi* or the *kokyū* (a three-stringed fiddle) played in concert, forming what is called the *sankyoku gassō* (the three musical instruments played in concert).

Introduction of Chinese music.

The introduction of Chinese music into our country appears to have taken place in the era of Bunséi (early nineteenth century). There are two particular styles of performing it, called respectively the Ōsaka and the Tōkyō. The former was propagated by one Katō-Ikkéi, and the latter was originated in Nagasaki and was brought to Yédo by Eisenren, a musician, in the era of Tempō (1830–43).

Decline of music at the Restoration.

Music, with almost everything else that was old, was practically swept away by the Restoration. It is true that musical performances practised on occasions of ancestral worship at the Imperial Court were soon restored to their former condition, and that the *Utakyoku* (Bureau of Music) was established in the *Dajōkan* (Council of State) in 1870, but it is also true that these feeble efforts were counteracted by various potent influences which stood in the way of music in the earlier part of the Méiji era. The only kind of music that might be called national was to be found at the Imperial Court, where, however, it was kept secret from the public by its special performers. The Court nobles, amongst whom it had formerly been popular, were now not only too busily engaged in other directions to take any pleasure in listening to music, but they had begun to be influenced by Western ideas and tastes, that tended to make them indifferent to such matters.

The *Nō* performance, which had been in such favour with the
military class, disappeared with the abolition of the feudal
system; and though European music was adopted in our
Army and Navy, and even began to be learned by musical
performers belonging to the *Shikiburyō* (Bureau of Rites
and Ceremonies), it could scarcely be taken into account,
being still in an embryo stage. The musical art peculiar to our
country having thus fallen into decay, and the imported art
being not yet developed sufficiently to be a substitute, it was
only natural that there should be no encouragement bestowed
on popular native music or song.

But about 1878 the musical atmosphere showed signs of
lightening, and musicians as a beginning set to work composing
pieces for the benefit of school children. Two songs, entitled
' *Kazaguruma* ' (The Windmill) and ' *Fuyu-no-madoi* ' (Sitting
at Home in a Circle in Winter), were first composed at that time
by a musician named Tōgi Suénaga at the request of the Tōkyō
Girls' Normal School. They were purely musical in composition, and were sung as a lesson in that institution. Other
pieces of a similarly instructive nature presently followed
them, each composed by distinguished musicians of the day
in a mixture of classical and popular dictions. In 1879, when
a new national anthem was to be adopted at the suggestion
of the Naval Department, the Section of Music in the Bureau
of Rites and Ceremonies was entrusted with the work of
selecting one, and acquitted itself with success, the choice
being our existing national song, ' *Kimiga-yo*,' composed
by the late Hayashi Hironori. At the same time, Tōgi Sué-
yoshi's ' *Umi-yukuba*,' a song to be sung to salute an admiral,
was selected in like manner. Strange as it may seem that
such compositions in purely Japanese music should have
made their appearance at a time when the Europeanizing
influence was at its height throughout the empire, the fact is
merely to be regarded as one of the natural results of singing
having been included in the regular courses of school study,
in imitation of the educational system of the West.

Western music, which became a fashion about this time,
was curiously enough first introduced to the public through
Christianity and military bands. The former not only

School songs.

The national anthem.

Introduction of Western music.

originated hymnal singing in church, but began early to give lessons in music on the piano and the organ in the mission schools for girls. Many an unknown musician from these seminaries came to have a home of her own, where she practised her accomplishments, and thus contributed not a little to the

Naval and military bands. development of Occidental music. The bands of our naval and military services played a scarcely less important part in the importation of foreign music in modern Japan. Something like a band existed even before the era of Méiji in the army of each feudal clan, but it could hardly be called musical, for it was merely a company of drum-beaters, trained and equipped either in Dutch, English, or French style, according to the practice of the clan it belonged to. It was in 1871 that the *Hyōbushō* (the War Department) first set on foot the organization of a central military band, having previously summoned drum-beaters from various clans for the purpose. In the same year, when the *Hyōbushō* was divided into two departments, the Navy and the Army, an Englishman named Fenton was appointed Master to direct the musical band in the former, and a Frenchman by the name of Dagron in the latter. No clear distinction, however, was yet made between a musical band and a band of trumpeters ; and it was not until 1874 that the foundation was laid of our military band. In 1882 some musicians belonging to the Military Band Bureau were sent to France to prosecute their studies.

German school of band music. Up to 1890 our military band had been trained entirely in the English and the French style. Then, however, a German element was imported, Mr. Eckert, a musician of that country, being engaged as bandmaster. The naval band, which had been organized at the outset according to the English system, had previously employed him as a teacher, and had in consequence

The first naval band. become partly Germanized. In 1883 a new band of eighteen musicians was formed for the first time and placed on board a man-of-war named the *Fusō*. In 1889 a training school for naval band musicians was formed, and Kōzō Yoshimoto, one of the students, was sent to Germany to prosecute his studies there.

That the manner of teaching both naval and military music has much improved since then was clearly shown in the recent wars with China and Russia, when the martial spirit of our fighting men was greatly stirred by means of spirited band music. Our naval and military bands now serve at once as organs of social intercourse and as a means of elevating the musical taste of the people at large, musical entertainments being given by them to the public at the music hall in Hibiya Park, Tōkyō.

Recent progress of military music.

A word must now be said concerning the order in which other kinds of foreign music were introduced into Japan. In 1876 the Music Section of the Bureau of Rites and Ceremonies engaged Fenton, who, as we have seen, was then teacher of music to the Navy, and made some native musicians learn under him the art of Western music (especially that of wind instruments), which they played on the Emperor's birthday, the 3rd of November, in the same year. This was the first time that European music had ever been performed in the Imperial Palace. Two years later, in 1878, a musical performance was given to the public at the training school of native music (attached to the Bureau of Rites and Ceremonies), and various pieces were played on instruments newly imported from the West, as well as on those of Japan : this was, perhaps, the first musical meeting or concert held in public where European music was included in the programme. When, a little later, the *Ongaku Torishirabé-jo* (Office for investigating Music) was established in the Educational Department, some of the native musicians also organized themselves into an association called the *Yōgaku Kyōkwai* (European Music Association) for the purpose of studying the orchestra of the West. Under Eckert they learned to play on stringed instruments such as the violin, the viola, the contra-basso and the violoncello. In July 1881, musicians belonging to this private association entertained those present at a banquet given by the Emperor in his palace with music performed on European instruments. The name of the association was then changed to *Ongaku Kyōkwai* (Music Association), its scope was enlarged. and in the following year a great concert was held by its members at the Hongwanji temple in Asakusa, Tōkyō. Shortly afterwards, European orchestral music was adopted by the Imperial household as a regular part of its music.

European music in the Imperial Court.

The first concert of European music.

European Music Association.

School
music.

First text-
book of
school
songs.

Develop-
ment of
school
songs.

The *Ongaku Torishirabé-gakari* (Bureau for investigating Music), forerunner of the present Tōkyō Music School,
has contributed much to the propagation of Western music,
especially in regard to its adoption as a course of study in
schools. It was established in 1879, with Shūji Izawa as its
head, and placed under the jurisdiction of the Educational
Department. To make the imported music more popular
amongst all classes of society, and to investigate at the same
time the condition of our musical art, the Bureau engaged an
American named Whitting Mason as a teacher, whilst it
entrusted the work of investigating the national songs to two
native musicians, Kacchin Shiba and Shōin Yamasé. The
task of compiling songs for school children, which had been
commenced some years previously by the Bureau, was completed in 1882, and the collection was at once adopted as
a text-book in primary schools. It should be observed, to
the credit of those belonging to the *Ongaku Torishirabé-
gakari*, that they not only acquitted themselves with success
in their duty of promoting the progress of European music,
but also contributed not a little to the improvement of
music in general, especially of the art of performing on the
koto ; still more do they deserve our commendation for having
completed a collection of school songs in the short space
of a few years, and thus added singing in European style to
the regular courses of study in the primary schools throughout the empire. Foremost amongst these teachers stood
Mason with his great services ; and next to him came his first
pupils, Uyé, Oku, and Tsuji, who assisted him in his task.
There is still another successful assistant in the work whom
we must not overlook : namely, Miss Shigéko Nagai (now
Baroness Uryū, wife of Vice-Admiral Baron Uryū), the
first female student sent by our Government to study music
abroad. During 1883 those who had studied the new songs
in the *Ongaku Torishirabé-gakari* amounted to 1158, not
a few students of the Men's and Women's Normal Schools
and the *Gakushūin* (now the Peers' School) being included
in the number. In 1885 a society was set up by some professors and students of the Tōkyō Imperial University for
studying singing and music ; and about the same time a

similar association was formed for the benefit of the teachers of the primary schools of the Tōkyō prefecture. These are to be regarded as the first associations in our country for studying singing in a systematic manner. In less than twenty years from the outset, every school in the empire, both elementary and secondary, came to have singing lessons given to the pupils as a regular course of study. What is particularly worthy of note in this connection is that the new improved school songs almost entirely superseded the vulgar and often indecent nursery songs formerly in vogue among the lower classes. This is only one instance of many beneficial effects, but it sufficiently proves that the amelioration of popular manners depends largely on the nature of the songs sung by the people.

In the period between 1882 and 1891, during which our national music made the greatest progress, many important events took place in the musical world. For instance, the Court musicians belonging to the Bureau of Music in the Imperial Household Department exerted themselves to preserve our ancient music, compose new pieces, and study the art of playing on Western stringed and wind instruments. The *Ongaku Torishirabé-dokoro*, which changed its name to the Tōkyō Music School, greatly enlarged its sphere, sending a number of students abroad for the prosecution of their musical studies. In 1890 the composition of songs to be sung on national holidays was effected after a year's labour. Many societies came into existence and vied with one another in entertaining the public with their concerts, whilst temporary associations which had arisen in various places for studying singing were countless; private bands were also formed in numbers to meet the popular demand. *New epoch for music. Tōkyō Music School. Musical organizations.*

The *Nō* performance, which had fallen into decay since the time of the Restoration and apparently lost all its former popularity, began to revive in 1881, and had its dancing hall rebuilt in Shiba Park. From that time onwards it has been in favour with people of rank and wealth, all its different styles of performing being equally in vogue. *Revival of the Nō.*

Popular songs played on the three-stringed instrument began again about the same time to attract the attention of the

Sangén-gaku or popular music.

public, and they have now reached a height of popularity never attained either by classical music or by the *Nō* dance. The *gidayū-bushi*, which had originated in the city of Ōsaka, is most in favour with the public. The *naga-uta*, being the most refined of all common songs, appears most frequently in the programme of a concert, and is always welcomed by the audience in preference to the *tokiwazu* and the *kiyomoto*, two other very popular airs on the same instrument.

The war between Japan and China in 1894–95 naturally called a halt in all the fine arts, especially music, but, notwithstanding, martial airs naturally prospered, because of the readiness with which people accepted anything calculated to excite their patriotic feelings. Not in the capital alone, but in every rural district where any number of troops were stationed, there was always some kind of privately organized band playing spirited war songs, and officers and men returning from the war were welcomed home by the grateful nation with songs of victory. Under these circumstances, it is but natural that collections of war songs should have been published in great numbers.

Méiji Music Association.

In 1898 a musical society, called the *Méiji Ongaku Kwai*, was established conjointly by some of the graduates of the Tōkyō Music School and by young musicians who had studied their art at the Section of Music belonging to the Bureau of Rites and Ceremonies. This society, in which the two different exponents of the foreign music then prevailing in our country agreed to go hand in hand, has devoted itself to the work of introducing the European orchestra to the public. Under the guidance first of House, an American, and later of Dubravitch, an Austrian (employed as a teacher in the Imperial household), its members not only have held many concerts in the capital, but also have toured the different provinces with a view to improving the musical taste of the people. The Music School has also added a European orchestra to its curriculum. In 1903 Gluck's opera, ' Orpheus,' was presented in public by some of the students, the first of the kind ever performed by our countrymen.

Restoration of all sorts of music.

Operatic performances.

The effect of the war with Russia upon the musical world was not so harmful as was that of the China-Japan War. This may be partly accounted for by the fact that the musical performances, native and imported, had by this time made considerable progress, and public taste had also improved. Besides, the number of private music schools is continually increasing as the art of playing on Western instruments is becoming more and more in favour with male and female students. This has called for the manufacture of musical instruments, which are now being made on such a large scale that enough are produced not only to supply the domestic demand, but also to allow of export to the various countries in the East.

Effect of the Russian War on music.

Manufacture of musical instruments.

In conclusion, it may be briefly stated that the musical performances peculiar to the insular Empire of Japan are wholly indigenous, having originated far back in the primitive ages, but they have reached their present flourishing condition after assimilating various elements imported at different times from China, Korea, and other countries, and after passing through many a stage of development of their own. The imported arts of playing on the flute and the harp, for instance, have been preserved in our country for more than a thousand years, long after they became extinct in their mother countries, China and Korea. More lately, when the three-stringed instrument was brought over to our country, it was soon made use of by the people in their various singing performances, and thus it contributed not a little to the development of vocal music in Japan. The recent introduction of European music has wonderfully influenced our musical profession, whose scientific investigation into the imported art has been most thorough. We cannot, of course, tell in what direction, or to what extent, our music may be developed in future through the influence of this new and important element, but we have sufficient faith in ourselves to affirm that Japanese musicians will surely adapt and assimilate in the future, as they have done in the past, only the choicest parts, and thus enrich our national music, with all its distinctive characteristics preserved, but perfected.

Conclusion.

XX

THE FINE ARTS—THE DRAMA

Professor Yūzō Tsubouchi, D.Litt. (Japan) (Professor of Waséda University)

I.—The pre-Restoration Period

Those who have studied the various phases of our history as set out in the pages that have preceded this, will be prepared to find that the strict demarcation of the classes and the masses which placed an impassable gulf between peer and peasant, nobleman and commoner in olden days extended even to the performances of our pastimes and amusements—in which, indeed, the separation was even, if possible, wider. The Imperial household, for instance, had a form of music, known as *Gagaku*, which was introduced into the country from China and Korea and was brought to perfection a thousand years ago. It consisted of instrumental and vocal music and dancing, and became a ceremonial only indulged in by the Court, so much so that the Shōgun even, notwithstanding his great power and authority, was debarred from its use in his private palace. It is not surprising that under such circumstances there arose, towards the close of the Hōjō Regency (i.e. early in the fourteenth century), a new form of music for the Shōgun and his followers, and this was subsequently known as *Nō*. But again, this *Nō* was enjoyed exclusively by the military class, the common people being unable to participate in it, and as from the Genna era (early in the seventeenth century) these latter began to acquire affluence, there arose in response to the demand and taste of the middle and lower classes of society, that is, of the mercantile, industrial, and agricultural classes,

378

other forms of entertainment—namely, a kind of musical drama, called *Ayatsuri-shibai*, in which puppets were skilfully manipulated to the accompaniment of a complicated melange of dialogue and song known as *Jōruri*, and a kind of melodrama called *Kabuki* or *Kyōgen*, subsequently known as *Shibai*. Not only the Court nobles of Kyōto, but also the military families in Yédo and the provinces, considered it undignified to witness these performances. The characteristics of these forms of entertainment may be summed up by saying that, while the *Nō* is refined, but monotonous and unexciting, the *Jōruri* and *Kabuki* are coarse and vulgar, but rich in incident and passion. In short, in their strong and weak points alike, the former resembled the classical, and the latter the romantic, dramas of Europe.

The *Shibai* or popular drama.

Of the four forms mentioned in the preceding paragraph the *Gagaku* is not drama, and as its influence has been very slight, even on the *Nō*, we may leave it out of consideration, and proceed at once to touch upon the origin and evolution of the *Nō*, or aristocratic drama.

Nō, or Aristocratic Drama

The *Nō* was at first only performed by *Shintō* priests in shrines to propitiate the gods, and was probably similar to the shrine music now played in country places under the name of *Nijūgoza*. Coming into vogue, as before mentioned, in the fourteenth century, it became the ceremonial music of the military class, and was performed during the offering of prayers for fortune in war or congratulations on military exploits ; it was at the same time the principal form of entertainment among the *samurai*.

Origin of the *Nō*.

But as the period in question constituted our Dark Ages and all literature was in the hands of Buddhist priests, the texts of the *Nō* also emanated from the same source, and even the language of the congratulatory *Nō* was not free from Buddhist influences. And as the *Nō* so far developed as to take a form similar to that of the Chinese or Greek drama, the motive, irrespective of the subject, was commonly Buddhist. It dwelt more or less clearly on the inevitableness of retribution,

Buddhism and the *Nō*.

insisted upon the transitoriness of life, and urged the abandonment of this world. It is owing to this peculiarity that there are so many *Nō* which have for their principal characters ghosts, apparitions, and other forms from the spiritual world, and the object that of deliverance from the spells they are under. It is true there are other *Nō* resembling ordinary plays in their attempt to picture the working of human passions, but their number is extremely small, and even in their case the language, idea, or music, usually has in some degree a Buddhist note.

Development of the *Nō*. Passing through Hidéyoshi's time down to the nineteenth century and the close of the Tokugawa *régime*, the *Nō* was brought to such a degree of perfection that it hardly admitted of further development, so when the ' black ships ' from America appeared off Shimoda, and the country went through the throes of dissolution, the occupations which engaged the leisure hours of the upper and middle classes were **Decline of the *Nō*.** abandoned, and the *Nō*, which occupied the foremost position among accomplishments, fell into such disfavour that at one **Revival of the *Nō*.** time it seemed likely to be entirely forgotten. But, happily, the fashion turned later on, and within the last twenty years it has recovered a great part of its former vogue. This rehabilitation, although in a large measure due to its own merits, is in no little degree owing to the protection and encouragement extended to it by the late Prince Iwakura, and to the labours and perseverance through adverse years of great artists like Kurō Hōshō and Minoru Uméwaka.

Characteristics of the *Nō*. There are at present several hundred *Nō* plays which are commonly acted. The principal characters in them are usually one or two, and the scenes are two. Unity of action and place is strictly observed, while the plots and the language are stereotyped. The *Nō* is always melodramatic, solemn, and imposing, being mostly tragic ; and, by way of relief, a simple **The *Kyōgen*, or farce.** one-act farce called *Kyōgen* (not to be confounded with the same word used as another name for *Kabuki*) is played between *Nō* plays. It belongs to the same family as the interlude of medieval Europe, or the farce, and the Greek comedy, but it is less complex and is always written in prose. Several hundred *Kyōgen* are played at the present time.

The *Nō* acting was from the earliest times divided into many
schools, and even in our day there are still five different
schools, namely, *Komparu*, *Kanzé*, *Hōshō*, *Kongō*, and *Kita*.
Although to the uninitiated little difference is observable
among them, as a matter of fact there are few things in which
family tradition, usages, professional secrets, and musical forms
are more jealously guarded.   Hence each school is differentiated
from the rest by various minutiae of the art ; each strictly
observes its own usages and takes care that not a single note
shall leave the accustomed groove.   Conservatism, in truth, is
the life of the *Nō*.   During more than four centuries that have
passed since the Ashikaga period, its main characteristics
have remained unchanged.   It is, in short, a crystallized art,
and is a worthy memorial of military Japan. *The five schools of the Nō.*

Of recent years many foreigners who are interested in Japan,
or are of a musical turn of mind, have begun to appreciate
the *Nō*.   There are also not a few Japanese who are concerned
about the future of the *Nō* and are anxious as to its preservation,
for the tendencies of the new era do not appear to them to
be favourable to the art.   If these foreigners and Japanese
could be brought together so as to co-operate, it is quite possible
that some change might be effected in the *Nō*.   But there
are others, again, who insist that to reform the *Nō* would be
practically to destroy it.   At any rate, since the *Nō* came
into existence in response to the requirements of the higher
military class, in the same way as the *Gagaku* owed its origin
to the taste of the Imperial Court, one is, like the other, too
refined, solemn, graceful, and antique to suit the tastes of
the middle and lower classes.   If we compare the *Gagaku* to
the ancient school of pictorial art in the time of Kawanari and
Kanaoka, we may fitly liken the *Nō* to the Tosa and Kanō
schools, which appeal chiefly to the upper and middle classes.
Hence, whatever the future may have in store, the sudden
rise of the puppet play known as *Jōruri*, and the popular play
known as *Kabuki*, in the latter half of the seventeenth century,
to meet the requirements of the commercial and industrial
classes, must be admitted to have been unavoidable.   They
may be fitly compared to the *Ukioyé* or Genre school in
the domain of pictorial art. *Future prospects of the Nō.*

Jōruri, or Puppet Drama

The Jōruri and the Kabuki.

The *Jōruri* and the *Kabuki* arose almost simultaneously, and reached maturity at the same time.　They began gradually to develop at the close of the Ashikaga Shōgunate in the latter half of the sixteenth century, reached maturity at the most prosperous period of the Tokugawa *régime*, namely the close of the seventeenth and the beginning of the eighteenth century, and are still in great vogue at the present day.　Though these dramas subsequently presented new forms, they were evidently modelled on the aristocratic prototype already described.　The *Jōruri* is indebted to the *Nō* music for its ideas and intonation, while the *Kabuki* owes even more for its delivery and action to the *Kyōgen*, for which reason it is also known as *Kyōgen*.

Nature of the Jōruri.

The *Jōruri* is a species of dramatic ballad written to be sung or recited to the accompaniment of the *samisén* and in unison with the movements of puppets.　It is a romance composed in such untrammelled verse as to be almost mistaken for prose : a ballad, in short, of the most complicated structure. Formed in part of narrative and description, it nevertheless consists mostly of plain dialogue, and, in parts where intense passion is depicted, it contains lyrical passages of great beauty to accompany the so-called posture-dance.　Taken as a whole, it is too complicated, diffuse, and full of episodes and characters, and too absolutely wanting in unity ; but if the individual acts are considered by themselves, they are often found to be fine dramatic poems, which remind us at times of the products of the brilliant group of Elizabethan dramatists.

Origin of the Jōruri.

The *Jōruri* is, furthermore, a generic name like the ‘ romance.’　Tradition traces its origin to the composition of the ‘ *Jōruri Jūnidan Sōshi* ’ (the ‘ Story of Lady Jōruri,’ in twelve acts), by O-Tsū Ono, a waiting-woman of Lord Nobunaga Oda, master of the great Hidéyoshi.　But what truth there may be in this it is impossible to say.　There have been various forms of *Jōruri*, namely *Itchū*, *Tokiwazu*, *Tomimoto*, *Kiyomoto*, and *Shinnai*.

Birth-place of the Jōruri.

The *Jōruri* first came into existence in Kyōto, whence it was transferred to Yédo, and later to Ōsaka, where, under the dramatist Monzaémon Chikamatsu (1653–1724), to whom has been given the title of the Japanese Shakespeare, and the musician Gidayū Takémoto, a man of extraordinary genius, this art of musical recitation made such wonderful progress that the term *Jōruri* came to be regarded as synonymous with the great singer's name, Takémoto or Gidayū. As this puppet drama prospered for more than two hundred years under the Tokugawa Government, it gave employment to an enormous number of dramatists, musicians, and singers ; and during the golden age of that *régime* hundreds of *Jōruri* were produced—Chikamatsu himself being responsible for over a hundred. There still stands in Ōsaka a theatre, called the Bunrakuza, where the puppet drama is played in the old style by singers and musicians of the first rank.

Kabuki, or Plebeian Drama

The word *kabuki* appears to be derived from the verb *kabuku*, which means to dally or jest. Hence *kabuki* signifies buffoonery. The first *Kabuki* player was a woman named O-Kuni, a dancer in the Izumo shrine. When she played, however, with her husband, before Nobunaga, Hidéyoshi, or Hidéyasu, the son of Iyéyasu, it was nothing more than the singing and dancing together of a few men and women, to the accompaniment of simple musical instruments. It was more properly called a dance than a play. *The word kabuki.*

O-Kuni, the first Kabuki player.

Presently companies of young actresses, known as *Onna Kabuki* (female players), appeared in various places and were at one time in great vogue, but, on account of their evil influence upon public morals, they were stopped, and thus arose the prohibition against actresses, long enforced in Japan. But shortly afterwards companies of good-looking youths, known as *Wakashu Kabuki* (youthful players), made their appearance. The *Wakashu* were handsome boys who made up their lovelocks over the forehead like girls, and tied them into pretty knots. Although their art was at first, like that of the female *Kabuki*, no more than a kind of dance, it began, upon the adoption of the *samisén* (about 1633), to assume a dramatic form. The star of a company at this period was always the best-looking youth of the troupe, and was called the *Tayū*, his duty being to sing and dance in woman's guise. *Female players of the Kabuki.*

Youthful players.

An older person acted as the *Tayū's* leading man, so to speak, and amused the audience with mimicry and comic speeches. But the *Wakashu Kabuki* was in course of time found to be as injurious to public morals as the female *Kabuki*.   It, too, was prohibited by the Government, which at the same time forbade the wearing of lovelocks.   Thereupon the *Wakashu Kabuki* became the *Yarō Kabuki* (players without lovelocks).

The *Yarō Kabuki*.

From this time great improvements began in the composition of plays, in the art of acting, in the construction of theatres, in the get-up of the stage, and in the costumes and general stage properties, until, after many evolutions, they came to be what they are at the present day.

Play-wrights and actors.

At first there was no definite distinction between the play-wright and the actor : in fact, the actor was usually his own playwright.   But in time the two professions became separate and distinct.   The earliest actor of note was Tōjūrō Sakata (1645–1700) in Kyōto, and Danjūrō Ichikawa the first (1660–1704) in Yédo.   The former excelled in domestic drama, called the *Wagoto* or *Séwamono*, and was realistic and graceful in his acting ; but the latter was strongest in historical drama, or the *Aragoto* or *Jidaimono*, and was fierce and rough.   Monzaémon Chikamatsu, who, as already stated (p. 382), usually wrote for the puppet shows, produced plays also for Tōjūrō.   From his time the puppet shows and the stage worked on common plots and materials, and strongly influenced each other in their manner of acting.   From the beginning of the eighteenth century it became the fashion to put the *Jōruri* on the stage, so that before long the only differ-ence between the theatre and the puppet show appeared to the casual observer to lie in the fact that, in the former, men acted instead of puppets, while in the latter music pre-dominated.   The most noted playwrights were Gohéi Namiki in Ōsaka, and, in Yédo, Jisuké Sakurada, Namboku Tsuruya, and Mokuami Furukawa, the last of whom died in 1893.

The theatrical perfor-mances and the puppet show.

Some famous play-wrights.

Character-istics of the *Kabuki*.

The characteristics of the *Kabuki* plays may be summed up as follows :

1. They invariably included one or more mimetic posture-dances, called *Shosagoto*, which developed from a mere medley of dance and mimicry into independent intermezzi.

2. Taking variety and claptrap as their principal object, they were full of inconsistencies in their plots and absurdities in their climaxes ; they made a reckless jumble of past and present, truth and falsehood, and they utilized every occasion to display wit and fancy, with the result that the whole fabric appeared like a mosaic, a maze, or a phantasmagoria. The spectators were therefore bewildered by the interminable entrances and exits of the characters and frequent changes of scene. I once gave it the name of *Mugen-géki*, or 'phantasmal drama,' as it resembles such visions as we see in dreams.

3. As actors were more powerful than playwrights, the latter, completely at the former's mercy, made it their principal aim to write plays to suit the personal peculiarities of the actors for whom they were working, rather than to develop independent plots or depict character.

4. The object of the *Kabuki* being to give pleasure for the moment, wonderful progress was effected in such mechanical contrivances as the get-up of the stage, scene-painting, costume, toilets, and wig-making. Consequently the playwright, relying upon these improvements to entertain the public, did not take much pains to give a literary quality to his productions.

5. When, later on, realistic social dramas began to be produced, the majority were sensational, making prostitutes and robbers their heroines and heroes. Their motives were the evil influences of the spirits of the dead, tricks of villains, or illicit love, and they abounded with coarse, obscene, or barbarous scenes and speeches.

6. Though actors were admitted and patronized by the middle and lower classes, many persons despised them and still harboured against them the prejudices of the tradition that they were put under the control of the *éta* (pariahs) during the Kamakura Shōgunate. Even at the close of the Tokugawa rule they were not looked upon as respectable citizens, and consequently the military class studiously shunned intercourse with them and refrained from visiting theatres.

II.—THE POST-RESTORATION PERIOD

With the great political and social changes brought about by the Restoration, the power of the Shōgun, chief patron of the

Nō, crumbled into dust, the political and social class distinctions disappeared, and the era of free competition was opened.

The *Kabuki* gaining ground.

The effect of all this was felt in the theatrical world also, for simultaneously with the decline and decay of the aristocratic *Nō*, the plebeian *Kabuki* began to flourish under the patronage of the upper and middle classes. There was a steady increase of playgoers among the nobles, high officials, men of wealth, and scholars. These new patrons of the stage, men of great social influence at the time, of comparatively high intellectuality and of advanced ideas, had been all brought up in the atmosphere of political reform, and had been gainers by its success. They were in their views worldly and utilitarian, preferring actualities to phantasms. In their manner of life, their ideals, and their tastes they differed in a great measure from both the upper, the middle, and lower classes of the pre-Restoration days. When they first visited the theatre they felt as if they were in dreamland, and looked upon playgoing simply as a means of beguiling time ; but when they came by and by to appreciate the plays they witnessed, there arose a collision between the old

New taste for the stage.

and new taste for the stage. The new school began to condemn the character of the acting which had developed under the old school, and every effort had to be made by managers, actors, and playwrights to retain the patronage of their audience of the new era. Hereupon the progress of the stage and that of society acted and reacted upon each other, and the foundation was laid for great changes in the character of plays and the art of acting. Becoming convinced of the inferiority of the old plays, the new critics, at first by speeches and later in newspapers, condemned the want of uniformity and consistency in plots, and attacked the vulgarity and absurdity of their development. Thus commenced a great movement for theatrical reform.

Jidaimono, or Historical Drama

Reform of the historical drama.

The first step in the reform movement was a cry for the improvement of the *Jidaimono*, or historical drama. This was probably a reaction against the prohibition which had been enforced for political reasons under the Tokugawa Government against the production on the stage of recent or contemporary events. It may also be attributed in part to the facts that the stirring incidents of the Restoration period had increased the historical knowledge of the people and made them take interest in historical drama ; that the theatrical reformers mostly took loyalty and patriotism as their ideals ; that the nobles, high officials, and men of wealth who were the new patrons of the theatre, being mostly provincials, neither understood nor cared for the domestic drama which dealt with the bourgeois life of Yédo ; and finally, that Danjūrō Ichikawa, the ninth of that name, who came to the fore during the new era, shone especially in the presentation of historical plays.

The persons who wielded most influence in the new movement were, among the officials, Michiyuki Matsuda, Governor of Tōkyō at the time, and in the theatrical world, Kanya Morita, a manager, Danjūrō Ichikawa, Kikugorō Onoyé, and Sadanji Ichikawa, actors, and Mokuami Furukawa, a playwright. *Some prominent stage reformers.*

The presence of the ex-President General Grant at a performance in the Shintomiza Theatre (1879), and the playing of Danjūrō and Kikugorō before the Emperor when His Majesty visited Marquis Inouyé (1887), were events unprecedented in the history of the Japanese stage.

The Dramatic Reform Association, which was organized at the instance of Viscount Suyématsu, was a body representative of the playgoers of the upper class. Among its promoters were Marquis Inouyé, Professors Nobushigé Hozumi and Kenzō Wadagaki, Baron Kikuchi, Baron Éiichi Shibusawa, and the late Génichirō Fukuchi, and among its supporters were many noblemen and high officials. *The Dramatic Reform Association.*

Almost simultaneously with the formation of this Association views respecting the reform were put forth by well-known scholars in official circles, especially by those of the new school lately returned from abroad. Among those who thus gave expression to their views by speeches or by publications were Viscount Suyématsu, Mokichi Fujita, and Dr. Masakazu Toyama, while new plays were written by a Confucian scholar, Hyakusén Yoda. The views of these scholars were, roughly speaking, formed from different standpoints. Some condemned the low moral tone of the old drama, and proposed *Views for stage reform.*

to replace its obscenity, barbarity, vulgarity, and frivolity with loyalty, filial piety, fidelity, elegance, and refinement ; while others objected to the absurdity and wildness of the plays hitherto on the stage, the unnaturalness of the make-up and dialogues, and the untruthfulness to nature of the singing, dancing, and music, and wished them to be, if possible, absolutely realistic, or at least to resemble the Western drama. In the representation of historical plays, therefore, the ideal became to present scenes from ancient history and biography ; to make, as it were, the figures on ancient picture-scrolls leap out upon the stage. From this arose the name and histrionic style of *Katsuréki*, or ' living history.'

Weakness of reform leaders.

The weakness of the latter ideal lay in its confusion of the good and the beautiful, its lack of poetic taste, and desire for superficial realism. It failed to note that the national drama was essentially musical. When, later on, the preservation of national excellences was loudly advocated by reactionaries against the excessive craze which had come to prevail for every-thing European in political and social matters, a similar reaction took place also in the theatrical world and checked its progres-sive spirit, which at one time produced domestic drama with characters dressed in European clothes, or made up as Euro-peans, or proposed to engage artists from the West. The Reform Association, resuscitated under various designations, died after each rebirth, and the old-style drama seemed likely to be revived. Fortunately, just at this time, the late Génichirō Fukuchi (whose pen-name was Ōchi), well known both as a political writer and as a *littérateur*, entered the theatrical world as a playwright, and, in conjunction with Danjūrō, wrote or revised historical plays with the special object of bringing out the great histrionic talents of that celebrated actor, and at the same time revived thereby the dramas of ' living history ' which were at one time threatened with extinction. Though unqualified praise cannot be given to Fukuchi's plays as literary productions, still credit must be accorded to him for forwarding the cause of historical drama by depriving it of its excessive unnaturalness and commonplaceness. Fukuchi's plays, however, numerous as they were, did not, with the exception of two or three, meet with a warm reception from

Génichirō Fukuchi.

the public. Hence, from 1895 onward, not only the 'living history' dramas, but new plays of every kind, became rare. Even Danjūrō Ichikawa, the principal advocate of 'living history' drama, came to produce the old phantasmal plays in rapid succession, under the pretext that they were to be his farewell performances of those old-fashioned plays. Thus the old drama appeared to have recovered its former prosperity. There were also several direct causes for this reversion to the old style, two conspicuous ones being : first, the success in the old style of Kikugorō Onoyé, who differed from Danjūrō in temperament and histrionic style, which aroused a spirit of rivalry in the latter ; and, secondly, the desire to put down the Sōshi acting which had arisen, by developing to the utmost the special characteristics of the actors of the old school.

Decline of the 'living history.'

Séwamono, or Social Drama

Before touching upon the rise of the Sōshi drama, it will be advisable to say a few words on the state of the Séwamono, or social drama. The Kabuki play is always a medley of comedy and tragedy ; there is an equal proportion of serious and comic elements in it. In this respect there is little to choose between historical and social plays, and considerable ambiguity attaches to the meaning of the word séwamono as it is understood to-day. The term was applied generally, it would seem, to the more or less realistic presentation of the life of the lower classes in the Tokugawa period, in contradistinction to which the picture of Méiji society has been called Zampatsumono, or 'cropped-hair' drama. At any rate, upon the coming into vogue of the 'living history' drama and upon the death of Mokuami Furukawa, the last of the old-style dramatists, the Séwamono declined, and there has not since been a single Séwamono dealing with the Méiji era worth speaking of, nor have there indeed been any actors willing to figure in a new play of the kind. Probably their old-style education and lack of the new knowledge disqualified them from portraying the social phases of the Méiji era. At this juncture arose a body of new actors whose object was to make good this deficiency in the old actors and meet the demands and tastes of the new generation. They are called Sōshi actors.

Nature of the Séwamono.

Decline of the Séwamono.

Sōshi Drama

Circum-
stances
giving rise
to the
Sōshi
drama.

The primary cause of the rise of the *Sōshi* drama is to be sought in Government decrees, issued when the agitation for the rights of the people first broke out. When the younger members of such political associations as the *Jiyūtō* (Liberal party) indulged in the expression of extreme political views, strict laws were promulgated for restraining the freedom of speech, and, to evade these restrictions, many young politicians became public story-tellers with the object of making indirect attacks upon the Government in the story-tellers' halls. The pioneers of the *Sōshi* drama, as Sutō and Kawakami (Otojirō), were at first nothing more or less than impetuous students.

Birth-
place of
the *Sōshi*
drama.

The *Sōshi* dramatic companies were subsequently reinforced by a new element : that is, by men who had drifted from student life. Thus companies were formed in various localities. The oldest of them came into being in Ōsaka, probably for the reason that there were in that city no great and influential actors like Danjūrō and Kikugorō in Tōkyō, and that, being a purely commercial city, its inhabitants are poor judges of the dramatic art and ready to welcome any novelty. However that may be, new *Sōshi* companies, like those of Sutō and Kawakami, appeared on the stage, making specialities of

Nature of
the *Sōshi*
drama.

political allusions to current events and a rough and shallow delineation of the society of the Méiji era. Their idea of the histrionic art was to make speeches in a style peculiar to themselves, to put in practice the forms of the *jūjutsu*, and to imitate a vulgar kind of farce known as *Ōsaka niwaka*. The subjects they took were political incidents, detective cases, actual judicial trials, and others relating to contemporary events ; the plays lacked order and coherence, and were utterly valueless as literature ; their language and action were rude and unseasoned, and worthless from an artistic point of view ; and yet, as they enjoyed the patronage of the common people, who had been long waiting for the appearance of the Méiji social drama, and as they improved with time, these *Sōshi* players were favourably received everywhere as exponents of a new school.

The war with China in 1894–95 gave them a subject well suited to their ability, and afforded them an opportunity of raising themselves to the same rank in popular estimation as the actors of the old school, for their war plays were well received wherever performed. This triumph, however, was but temporary. The new *Sōshi* school, whose experience of the stage is still of short duration, must be considered to be yet struggling for existence. If, however, a great dramatist should appear and produce a fine social drama of the Méiji era, and then get the ablest among these *Sōshi* actors to play it, there can be no doubt that such drama would become indisputably a speciality. There are among the *Sōshi* not a few of more or less promise, and of these the principal are Takata, Kawakami, Ii, and Kawai.

Popularity of the Sōshi drama.

The Playwright, Critic, and Actor

Mr. Fukuchi (who died only a few years ago), of the Kabukiza Theatre, was not the only dramatist attached to a theatre, for every theatre has its own playwrights. But very rarely now are original plays produced. Usually serial stories from newspapers or new novels are made into plays, or European novels and plays are adapted. Two or three of Shakespeare's plays have been transformed into Méiji social plays and put on the stage, but they were none of them worth a visit.

New dramatic productions.

Dramatic criticism has been active since the beginning of the eighteenth century, but the best-known critics at the present time are Aéba ('Kōson'), on the staff of the *Asahi Shimbun*; and Ibara ('Séiséiyen'), author of the 'History of the Japanese Stage.' Mori ('Takéji Miki') was a famous critic as editor of the *Theatrical Magazine*.

Dramatic critics.

Among the actors, the three most experienced—Danjūrō, Kikugorō, and Sadanji—have died one after another within a decade, and there is now no one who stands head and shoulders above his fellows. Danjūrō's traditions are being followed by Yaozō, Shikan, Komazō, and Ennosuké; while to Kikugorō's art have succeeded Uzaémon and Baikō. Noted among the older actors are Danzō and Matsusuké. The foremost actors in Ōsaka are Gatō, Ganjirō, and Fukusuké. There are now several companies formed exclusively of actresses, and a few occasionally join *Sōshi* companies,

Contemporary actors.

but in the principal theatres actresses are not yet engaged, female parts being played by actors known as *Onnagata* (female-character players).

There are some parts of the theatrical organization which cannot, for various reasons, submit to reform. In short, so long as appropriate new plays are lacking, the future of the actors of the old school is gloomy indeed.

Shosagoto, or Dramatic Posture-dance

Nature of the *Shosa-goto*.

It has already been stated that the *Kabuki* owes its origin to a certain kind of dance, and that, even after its full maturity, it always retained to some extent its original terpsichorean characteristic. This element eventually developed into an independent dance under the title of *Shosagoto* or *Kéigoto* ; or, to speak more correctly, into a kind of operatic inter-mezzo, with *Furigoto* (or mimetic posture-dance) as its principal feature. The shortest of these consists of one act of one scene, while the longest may be an act of several scenes. Some have rude, disconnected plots, while others have pretty music and dancing, as if their sole object were to delight eye and ear. Most of them have love for their motive. The actors themselves make the dancing their principal duty and do not sing, nor do they, in many cases, even utter the speeches themselves, in all which respects they differ radically from the *Nō* performer. The feeling and passions of the characters are depicted by a singer to the accompaniment of the *samisén* or other musical instruments, and the actor dances in tune with the singer. The dances exhibited by *Géisha* girls before their guests are often no more than portions of these dances of the stage, or else closely related to them.

The most popular of these posture-dances are those per-formed to the accompaniment of the *Naga-uta* or *Tokiwazu* music. These must be subjected to drastic reform if they would retain popularity, for they do not, in either their design or their tunes, meet the requirements of the changed taste of the new era.

JAPANESE JOURNALISM AND LITERATURE

THE LATE SENTARŌ TOYABÉ, EDITOR OF THE 'SUN'

THE EARLIEST NEWSPAPERS

THE development of the Press is one of the most important *The* phenomena in the civilization of New Japan, for, while there *germs of Japan's* were what may be recognized as the germs of news-sheets in *news-* Old Japan, newspapers in the strict sense of the term were *papers.* only introduced from Europe after the opening of the country. The earliest known of these germs will be found in 1702, when the Forty-Seven Akō Rōnins' vendetta took place, tile prints (something like papyrographs), containing a full account of that event, being read aloud and sold through the streets of Yédo. About that time printed matters thus hawked about were quite common, the ' *Shimpan Uta-Saimon,*' the ' *Imosé - no - Kadomatsu,*' and the ' *Yomiuri Mitsu - tomoyé* ' being among the most conspicuous, and each reporting incidents which had occurred in the city. But these publications, though they partook of the nature of newspapers, were rather a kind of pamphlet, and could not be properly regarded as journals.

The first newspaper that appeared in Japan was probably *Japan's* the ' *Batavia Shimbun,*' published in October 1861. Prior *first news- paper.* to this, the Dutch merchants resident at Nagasaki selected important items from newspapers brought by Dutch merchantmen once a year, and submitted them to the Nagasaki magistrates, who had them translated into Japanese and sent them, together with the originals, to the Tokugawa Shōgunate. This is what was called the *Dutch News* (' *Oranda Fūsetsusho* ').

Subsequently to the conclusion of the Anséi Treaty, the
Shōgunate, feeling the necessity of acquiring an accurate
knowledge of the state of foreign countries, ordered the *Bansho
Torishirabé-dokoro* (Foreign Books Investigation Office) to
translate several European and American papers, but those
who read the translations were confined to officials of the
Shōgun's Government and a few men in higher circles.   It is
true that at times these translations were copied and circulated
among the people, but the reading public was limited, the
documents not being sufficient to satisfy any general demand.
Lord Oguri (Kōzuké-no-suké), who was sent to America
as an envoy of the Shōgunate and learned the influence of
newspapers there, attempted, after his return home, to
publish a journal as an organ of the Government, but his
proposals were not put into practice.   But so soon as the
light of European civilization dawned in the East, the usefulness of newspapers was quickly recognized by the people,
and it was but a short while before the above-mentioned
'*Batavia Shimbun*' appeared.   The publisher was Yorodzuya
Shirō, a bookseller, and the paper took its name from Batavia
in Java, whence a certain Dutchman brought some foreign
journals, translations of which were printed on ordinary
Japanese tissue-paper, printing blocks, and not movable types,
being used for the purpose.   Unhappily, the editor was not
the right man for the enterprise, so it fell through after the
publication of the first number.

The
second
news-
paper.

On March 1, 1864, a paper, entitled the '*Shimbunshi*,'
was published in Yokohama.   Ginkō Kishida was its editor,
and Senzo Homma and a Japanese who had wandered to
America and been naturalized there, John Hikozō by name,
were the assistant-editors.   Hikozō orally translated foreign
news from American papers, and Kishida rendered it into
Japanese.   As for domestic news, Kishida himself collected
any novel or interesting items and inserted them.   The
comparative freshness of this journal's descriptions and its
endeavour to report domestic news, not limiting itself to
foreign affairs, showed a step of advance compared with the
'*Batavia Shimbun*.'   It was published twice a month and lived
till September of the same year, when Kishida went to China,

and Hikozō went back to America, having published ten
numbers. Upon Kishida's return the insurrection had broken
out in the north-east, and, although the whole empire was consequently thrown into confusion, he again published a paper
called the ' *Moshiogusa*,' whose chief contents were war corre- The third
spondence, mixed with domestic and foreign news. At first it news-
appeared twice a month, but before long it became a weekly, paper.
and the contents as well as the get-up being satisfactory,
it gradually attracted a considerable circle of readers. But,
unfortunately, it was soon discontinued, owing to Kishida's
having turned his attention to the more profitable business
of shipping and transportation business between Tōkyō and
Yokohama.

Before and after the publication of the ' *Moshiogusa* ' there Papers
appeared several papers, of which the most important were before the
the ' *Chūgai Shimbun*,' edited by Shunzō Yanagawa ; the tion.
' *Bankoku*,' by Bailey, a missionary ; the ' *Kōko Shimbun*,' published by the co-operation of Génichirō Fukuchi and Dempéi
Jōno ; and the ' *Enkin Shimbun*,' promoted and planned by
Shinji Tsuji and Tadaichi Suzuki. There also followed several
other journals, such as the ' *Rikugō Shimbun*,' the ' *Naigwai
Shimbun*,' the ' *Shimbun Jiryaku*,' the ' *Kōjō Nisshi*,' and the
' *Zuiji Shinshi*.' But these were almost all weekly or monthly
papers, printed by means of printing blocks, the compilation
being very crude and imperfect, without any systematic
method ; they were but a rude form of magazine as viewed
by present standards. As yet no foreign printing machinery
had been introduced into Japan, so there could be no newspaper
published on a large scale ; besides, as anyone who wished
to retain his place in society could not do so were he an editor
by vocation, those so employed regarded their work as a mere
diversion, and thus the influence of journals upon the nation
was insignificant. This was the state of journalism in Japan
until the beginning of the Méiji era.

But at this time there was one paper distinguished from Attack on
others by having a peculiar political colour, namely the ' *Kōko* the new
Shimbun,' which in every issue filled its columns with articles ment.
or notes severely attacking the Satsuma and Chōshū clans. In
consequence, it not only came under the ban of the censors,

but Fukuchi, the editor, was tried and condemned to imprisonment. Hitherto the Government had not exercised any supervision over newspapers, but it now felt the necessity, and
prohibited the publication of all journals issued without official
permission ; in consequence, the ' Kōko Shimbun ' and several
other papers were annihilated by the first blow of the Press law.
In fact the ' Dajōkan Nisshi,' first published in 1868, the
forerunner of the Official Gazette, and the ' Chinshōfu Nisshi '
alone survived the prohibition, because they were both official
organs.

The Rise of Daily Papers

But whilst almost every paper was banned, there were
not wanting officials of progressive views who recognized
that it was to the interest of the country to encourage
the publication of papers under proper supervision. So in
1871 Sanshū Chō and Tokusuké Séki started a journal
entitled the ' Shimbun Zasshi,' under the patronage of
Councillor Kido ; it was a periodical appearing six times
a month, and was discontinued without ever becoming a
daily paper. Later on, subsequently to the publication of the
' Yokohama Mainichi Shimbun,' for which a foreign press was
first used, a new era of daily journals began, and every department of editorship, printing, &c., was arranged in some order :
the ' Mainichi ' was not only the father of daily papers in Japan,
but it had the honour of being a model journal. Afterwards
it removed its office from Yokohama to Tōkyō, changing its
title to the ' Tōkyō Yokohama Mainichi Shimbun.' Morikazu
Numa, Saburō Shimada, and Ryū Koyezuka undertook its
management, and it assumed the position of the North Star
on the literary horizon.

The pioneer of daily papers.

On or about the time that the ' Yokohama Mainichi
Shimbun ' first saw the light, daily papers, such as the ' Tōkyō
Nichinichi,' the ' Yūbin Hōchi,' the ' Chōya Shimbun,' the
' Akébono,' the ' Yomiuri,' and the ' Tōkyō Eiri,' were estab-
lished, and in 1875 the newspapers in the empire, daily as well
as periodical, amounted to more than one hundred in number.
The ' Tōkyō Nichinichi ' was a resuscitated ' Kōko Shimbun,'
and having become a daily paper, its first number was published

in 1872. At first Ginkō Kishida was editor, but afterwards Génichirō Fukuchi became editor and proprietor, and his lucid and vigorous style greatly assisted the paper; he invented many new plans and novel methods in the art of compilation—as, for instance, utilizing the margin of the paper for printing advertisements and price lists, issuing extras from time to time, getting ahead of others in engaging reporters, and so forth. The ' Tōkyō Nichinichi' was followed by the ' Yūbin Hōchi' in the same year. This was started by Hisoka Mayéjima, the then Postmaster-General, and was managed by a subordinate official, Konishi. It seems that Mayéjima's opinion was that the development of communications depended largely upon newspapers. At first the ' Yūbin Hōchi' was a periodical, published five times a month, but in 1873 it became a daily paper, and enlarging the size of its sheet, it became a rival of the ' Tōkyō Nichinichi.' Joun Kurimoto was its editor, but the duty of writing editorials devolved mainly upon Shigéru Furusawa. While the ' Tōkyō Nichinichi,' representing the party of Councillor Kido, set forth progressive views, the ' Hōchi' advocated the principle of radicalism, so that disputes between these two papers constituted for a time a prominent feature of our literary circle. Subsequently, when Fumio Yano, Mokichi Fujita, Kowashi Inukai, and Katsundo Minoura came to take up their pens for the paper, it shone with great brilliancy. To these ventures succeeded the ' Chōya Shimbun,' with Ryūhoku Narushima as editor and proprietor, and in 1875 the ' Akebono Shimbun,' with Shu Aoyé as proprietor and Shigéyasu Suyéhiro as editor. These two papers, together with the ' Yokohama Mainichi,' the ' Tōkyō Nichinichi,' and the ' Yūbin Hōchi,' were called the five great journals of Japan.

The five great newspapers.

About this time the Government became sensible of the no small influence of newspapers, and eventually even became afraid of them. Before this recognition came about the ' Nisshin Shinjishi,' which appeared a little later than the ' Yokohama Mainichi,' had devoted a separate column to editorials, and attracted the attention of the public by inserting political essays written by Kentarō Ōi, Shigéru Furusawa (afterwards editor of the ' Yūbin Hōchi'), and others. So too, in 1873, it created

a sensation throughout the empire by a ' Memoir on Finance,'
conjointly signed by Kaoru Inouyé, the then Vice-Minister of
Finance, and Éiichi Shibusawa. This was directed at the
Government, and exposed the real nature of the divisions in
the Cabinet. After this, the influence of journalism suddenly
became recognized in Government circles, as well as by the
people at large. Again, in the next year, when there were
renewed ruptures in the Cabinet concerning the Korean
Question, and petitions were sent to the Government asking
to have a popular assembly summoned, several newspapers
discussed and criticized severely these current topics. Among
the rest, such journals as the ' *Tōkyō Nichinichi*,' the ' *Yokohama
Mainichi*,' the ' *Yūbin Hōchi*,' the ' *Chōya*,' and the ' *Akébono* '
daily inserted editorials upon political questions, pointing out
maladministration on the part of the authorities. Their arguments, however, sometimes went too far, and the Government
took the course of enacting a law of libel in 1875, which provided
for the fining and penalizing of journalists, as well as putting
all the news-sheets under a censorship. The first to feel this
law was Shigéyasu Suyéhiro, of the ' *Akébono*,' who was
sentenced to a fine of twenty *yen* and imprisonment for three
months. The next victims were Kageo Hokiyama of the
' *Tōkyō Nichinichi*,' Ryūhoku Narushima of the ' *Chōya*,' and
Kéikō Oka of the ' *Yūbin Hōchi*,' who were also sentenced to
fine and imprisonment ; in fact, the men who at this time
suffered the ' penalty of the pen ' amounted to as many as a
score, some of them being condemned more than once. But
the effect of this restraint put upon the freedom of the Press
only increased its readers and developed its influence.

    In the early 'seventies the five great papers all laid stress
upon editorial articles, even miscellaneous reports being
written in essay style. Thus, the standard of journalism
being generally above the comprehension of the masses,
subscribers were confined almost entirely to the cultivated
classes. There was, however, one Masao Suzukida who, in
1874, in co-operation with Shun Koyasu, Seikō Motono and
others, established a paper called the ' *Yomiuri Shimbun*.'
Its miscellaneous reports dealt with things domestic, and
the whole paper was written in familiar style with *furi-kana*,

so that it was welcomed by the middle and lower classes. In the following year the ' *Tōkyō Éiri Shimbun* ' opened a new chapter in Japanese journalism, being the first illustrated paper, as well as the first to insert novels. These two papers were noted for the space given to social matters, in contrast with the five large papers which were mainly occupied with political topics, and thus they too gave a fresh colour and hue to Japanese journalism. The editors of these papers, however, were mostly comic writers, or at least belonged to that class, and, as they lacked erudition and culture, they were looked down upon by the general public. On the other hand, the editorial staff of the five great papers consisted of men of good station, of high character, and profound learning, so that, in spite of their imperfections, their arguments were cogent enough to represent, as well as to lead, the spirit of the age.

The Political Press

In April 1875 the Imperial edict, to establish in due course constitutional government, was proclaimed, and several years afterwards, that is in 1879, the prefectural assemblies were first summoned. Thereafter Japan entered upon an era of political discussion and contention. Petitions for the convening of a Diet began to be sent to the Government, and the organization of political parties commenced. But it was not until 1882 that the Imperial edict for the summoning of a Diet was issued. Thereupon the number of papers greatly increased, most of them being organs of political parties, as few journalists were non-politicians. Some of these papers had the names of political parties prefixed to their titles: for instance, when the constitutional party was organized in Ōsaka, the ' *Ōsaka Nippō*,' which had been established in 1876, called itself the ' *Rikkén Séitō Shimbun* ' (the *Constitutional Party Paper*). Thereafter even papers hitherto classed as minor journals, which had made miscellaneous reports their chief feature, began to discuss politics and assumed some features of political journalism. About this time a paper called the ' *Ukiyo Shimbun*,' published by Itsuga Jikémura,

Political papers.

which had originally existed by reporting incidents by the wayside, or events happening at the houses of ill-fame, changed its tone and, under a new title of ' Kaishin Shimbun' (the Progressist Paper), professed itself an organ of the Progressist party, while the ' Tōkyō Éiri Shimbun' also changed its name to the ' Yeiri Jiyū Shimbun' (Illustrated Liberal Newspaper), and professed itself an organ of the Liberal party. Hitherto novels composed by comic writers had not infrequently been inserted in papers, but now those interwoven with politics superseded them. There were also journalists who, whilst at home in politics, expressed their ideas and sentiments with the pen of novelists, so that newspapers of all forms and shapes inclined towards politics, and the journalistic currents one and all flowed into a whirlpool of political discussion. The influence of the Press in the political world thus developed to a wonderful degree.

But, as almost all the papers throughout the empire stood in opposition to the Government, its officials felt it advisable to establish organs of their own, for the defence of their policy. Consequently, besides the ' Tōkyō Nichinichi Shimbun,' which was called the 'Semi-official Gazette,' the Government employed Sakura Maruyama to publish the ' Méiji Nippō,' and Torajirō Mizuno to issue the ' Tōyō Shimpō,' and these, engaging university students as their assistants, preached the German doctrine of State autocracy, thus combating the principle of popular rights and freedom. These papers were commonly called ' Government papers,' an appellation which originated in the columns of the 'Tōkyō Nichinichi Shimbun,' which in 1875 declared itself to be ' under the special patronage of the Council of State.'

Semi-official gazettes.

But their influence was not at all equal to that of the opposition journals, especially as the Government very soon adopted the ' policy' of over-riding all political parties, and consequently its relations with its organs quickly cooled off. The ' Méiji Nippō' and the ' Tōyō Shimpō' were discontinued within a few years, and Génichirō Fukuchi also withdrew from the ' Tōkyō Nichinichi,' leaving the stage of the literary world to the sole use of the opposition papers.

As a natural consequence of the political debates and

discussions in vogue at that time, newspapers were narrow and limited in their character. In other words, political discussion being their sole aim, their contents became monotonous, with a tendency to neglect matters relating to vital questions which concerned those outside political circles. What was worse, from the time that newspapers were established as organs of political parties, it became absolutely impossible to find independent opinions or unbiased news in them. For these reasons the reading public was naturally limited, and the newspapers, unable to make both ends meet, were one by one discontinued. It is quite certain, that whilst political parties' sponsorship on the one hand greatly helped the rise of newspapers, it is also unquestionable that it hindered their healthy development and progress.

Monotony of political papers.

THE TRANSITION PERIOD OF NEWSPAPERS

About this time a powerful newspaper, professing itself to be impartial and independent, and standing on the basis of self-esteem, appeared on the stage. This was the ' *Jiji Shimpō* ' of Tōkyō, first published in 1882. The real director of the paper was Yukichi Fukuzawa, founder of the Mita school of learning. According to its prospectus, it was called the ' *Jiji Shimpō* ' (*Times*) because its chief object was to describe modern civilization, to discuss the ways and methods of attaining this civilization, and to furnish such information to the public that it might not fall behind in an age of continuous progress. But the principles that the paper really espoused were the independence of individuals, of families, and of the nation itself. Politics were not within its field of activity, but it described itself as a paper of wide liberal principles, which took upon itself the responsibility of being the leader of civilization and enlightenment. It endeavoured to avoid monotony, and its press reports were rich in material and various in kind. Above all, it abounded in economic and social matters, while its style was simple and familiar after that of the Mita school, so that within a year it attracted many readers, and sowed in the Japanese journalistic circle germs of a salutary reform.

Tendency to a change of tone and contents.

Next to the 'Jiji,' a newspaper which remodelled its form and contents was the 'Yūbin Hōchi Shimbun.' From 1882 the proprietor of the 'Hōchi' was Fumio Yano, and the editorial staff consisted of such young and active politicians as Mokichi Fujita, Kowashi Inukai, Katsundo Minoura, and Yukio Ozaki. It was an organ for setting forth political principles, and as it had no venal objects in view, it endeavoured to maintain to the utmost the dignity of a great journal. The proprietors increased the size of the paper and raised its price, regardless of the extent of its circulation. When Fumio Yano, after visiting Europe, returned home in 1885, he immediately put his hand to a further remodelling of the 'Hōchi.' The pages were reduced in size, the journalistic matter had furi-kana as an aid to the interpretation of the square characters, novels were inserted, and the price of the paper was at the same time lowered. Thus it became accessible to people below the middle class, and consequently the circle of its readers was widely extended. Soon afterwards, the 'Hōchi' published an evening sheet, but this new venture failed after a time, owing to imperfections of the press and the deficiency of means of communication. The fact that the 'Hōchi,' hitherto regarded as the great leader of newspaper progress, had to change its form and get-up and transform itself into a popular news-sheet, proved how difficult it was in those days to carry on the so-called 'great papers,' or purely political organs. Several journals, which appeared about this time, were published chiefly with the object of gaining as many readers as possible. The 'Tōkyō Chū Shimbun,' the 'Miyako Shimbun' (forerunner of the 'Chūō Shimbun'), the 'Yamato Shimbun,' and others were all born during this transition period.

The 'Kokumin Shimbun,' first published in January 1890, exactly fitted the needs of the time and was the best model paper of the day, and its contents demonstrated that Iichirō Tokutomi, its editor, was not only an acute and original critic of the times, but also that he had extraordinary talent in the editorial art. Whilst it was characteristic of this paper that its press accounts were full of variety and that it catered for various tastes, so as to obtain popularity with every class of readers, it also took pains to write in a familiar and easy style, and endeavoured to avoid falling into vulgarity and to infuse a fresh and pure spirit into its columns. It set up an illustrated department and produced pictorial designs, by which it strengthened its hold on its readers.

But the newspapers of those days, including even the '*Jiji*,' the '*Yūbin Hōchi*,' and the '*Kokumin*,' had not as yet the character of business undertakings, for their managers, having been originally journalists, did not possess financial training. However, when the '*Ōsaka Asahi Shimbun*,' started in 1879, came into the possession of Ryūhéi Murayama, it gradually assumed that character, showing that the development of newspapers, as in other businesses, depended largely upon the force of capital. Though Murayama had neither ability nor the qualifications of a journalist, he clearly understood the special requirements of a newspaper proprietor, and he devoted his attention to producing a journal such as should attract the greatest number of readers. In the first place, determined to grasp the sceptre of sovereignty in journalistic circles by giving the freshest news on every topic, he concentrated his energy on making the best use of organs of communication. The result appeared in the form of home and foreign telegrams and the establishment of special correspondents, upon which he stinted no outlay. Thus competition between capitalists in newspaper enterprise began for the first time. In 1883 the '*Ōsaka Rikkén Séitō Shimbun*' had changed its name and appeared as the '*Ōsaka Mainichi Shimbun*,' Shirō Shiba and Séishi Takénouchi being its editors, to be followed by Osamu Watanabé, who greatly improved its form and contents. When the '*Ōsaka Asahi*' suddenly rose to distinction by means of telegrams and correspondence, the '*Ōsaka Mainichi*' also greatly improved its organs of communication, and the two competed in the quantity and variety of telegraphic intelligence. Already, in Ōsaka, there were the '*Ōsaka Shimpō*' with Téi Tsuda as editor-in-chief, the '*Daitō Nippō*' with Kéi Hara as editor, and the '*Shinonomé Shimbun*' with Tokusuké Nakaé. But all these papers, unable to stand the competition of capital, gave in one by one, and, at length, the palm of the Ōsaka literary world was divided between the '*Ōsaka Mainichi*' and the '*Ōsaka Asahi*.'

In 1888 Ryūhéi Murayama, the capitalist giant of news-

The competition of capital.

paper ventures, issued the ' *Tōkyō Asahi Shimbun* ' in Tōkyō, independently of the ' *Asahi* ' of Ōsaka. In co-operation with the ' *Ōsaka Asahi*,' he spent large sums on correspondence and undertook to secure greater rapidity of reports than ever, so that his journal threatened to extinguish every other newspaper of the day. For instance, in 1889, when the Constitution was first promulgated in Japan, the ' *Ōsaka Asahi's* ' correspondent telegraphed the Constitution at full length, and an extra was immediately issued and distributed among its subscribers. Again, in 1890, when the Imperial Diet first met, the ' *Ōsaka Asahi*,' receiving full records of the debates by wire, issued an extra sheet for the special news. This was something that other papers could not imitate, and at last newspaper publishers came to perceive that the great papers hitherto compiled chiefly for discussing politics did not satisfy the need of readers at large, and that newspapers must be topical in their nature and also organized as money-earners.

Among the journals of that time there was one which had a peculiar colour, namely, the ' *Nippon*,' established in 1889. Representing the Conservative principle entertained by Viscounts Kanjō Tani and Gorō Miura and others, and opposing the ' Policy of Westernization,' it preached thrift and industry, and encouraged the spirit of chivalry. Though its arguments were at times greatly biased, its style, as well as the personal character of Minoru Kuga, the then editor and proprietor, made the ' *Nippon* ' a lighthouse in the sea of journalism. It was a paper essentially of editorials and articles, and even its press accounts were tinged by this style, but it claimed to be a great paper, standing far above the common herd of journals, and to discharge its mission of high and noble criticism amid the struggles for popularity of its *confrères*.

THE DEVELOPMENT OF NEWSPAPERS

The
House of
Represen-
tatives
and news-
papers.   In 1890, when the Imperial Diet was summoned, every newspaper throughout the country, whether an organ of a political party or not, returned to politics. Many journalists were elected to the House of Representatives, and many leading

members of the Diet had connection, direct or indirect, with one paper or another. Thus the Diet and the Press, co-operating with and aiding each other, produced the so-called ' public opinion,' and from the first session onwards there was not a subject of any importance that was not discussed in the Press. The questions which led to the dissolution of the first Diet were all journalistically treated, and no formal public opinion could exist that was not endorsed by the Press. For example, if the question of curtailing expenditure or cultivating national strength was raised in the Diet, behind the curtain there were always some newspapers which, having approved the motion, would pose as leaders of public opinion. If an address to be submitted to the Throne suggesting a stalwart foreign policy was proposed in the Diet, newspapers were always to be found advocating it. Again, if in the Diet members contended for administrative or financial reform, some newspapers always backed them, and eventually the topic became a burning question of the day. Therefore, if the Government occupied the first grade of political power, and the Diet the second grade, newspapers certainly were a good third. Sometimes the Government appeared to fear the news-sheets more than it feared the Diet itself, so that their suspension became more and more frequent as time went on.

While newspapers, on the one hand, still felt a difficulty in maintaining themselves on account of frequent suspension, on the other they had already entered the era of self-support and competitive life, so that the editorial art was greatly improved, and they became at once more businesslike, technical, and venal. As a result, in the first place, all the chief newspapers secured permanent correspondents in the most important places at home or abroad, and when any great event occurred they competed in dispatching special correspondents to the place. Secondly, recognizing the value of foreign telegrams, they obtained a supply from Reuter, some of them publishing cablegrams by special contract. Thirdly, several kinds of correspondence companies were established, and these became in turn organs for supplying news materials which were again refined or sifted by newspapers, so that journalists became skilled in the art of selection, and

Great improvements in the editorial art.

the contents of newspapers were gradually improved. Fourthly, many newspapers laid stress upon police accounts as 'third-page items,' and these attracted great interest. By thus describing the dark side of society, they sought to appeal to the sensuousness of readers. The representatives of this tendency were the '*Yorozu Chōhō*,' established in 1892, and the '*Niroku Shimpō*,' which saw the light in 1893. The '*Yorozu Chōhō*' had for a time the reputation of being the worst of the yellow journals. Shūroku Kuroiwa, its proprietor, generally recognized as a perfect type of a backstairs editor, greatly pushed its circulation. Fifthly, novels inserted in papers ceased to be political, and party and clique were replaced by realistic *affaires-du-cœur* romances and detective stories, which came into fashion at that time. The original works of Professor Tsubouchi, Kōyō Ozaki, Rohan Kōda, Ōgai Mori, and Bimyōsai Yamada, and the translated novels of Shikén Morita, were most welcomed. Sixthly, editors of the political type gradually lost their influence, and genuine journalists came to occupy the leading positions in the kingdom of the Press. Such journalists as Chisén Asahina, Iichirō Tokutomi, Minoru Kuga, Yūjirō Miyaké, Kamméi Ishikawa, and Yosaburō Takégoshi stood prominent on the stage of literature in Japan, each with his own original style and argument. Seventhly, most of the articles and editorials published prior to the creation of the Diet were inclined to be of an abstract and theoretical character, but now they dealt with practical questions. Eighthly, in 1890, when the Government bought a revolving cylinder press from France and used it in printing the Official Gazette, the '*Tōkyō Asahi*' and the '*Ōsaka Asahi*' adopted similar plant, and the '*Jiji*' followed their example. Thus newspapers which still employed the old hand press could not possibly live with journals printed with the newest machinery, and consequently they became all the more conscious of the power of capital.

In 1894 and 1895, that is when the China-Japan War broke out, the lower classes, who had hitherto never opened a paper, began to find enjoyment in reading journals, so that, on the one hand, the circulation of papers made sudden and wonderful leaps, and, on the other hand, as each journal

strove to attract as many readers as possible, it need hardly be The effect of the China-Japan War.
said that editorial art made great progress. If we enumerate
the things which derived great advantage from the war, we
must count journalism among the number.

RECENT NEWSPAPERS

Newspapers after the China-Japan War inclined, for the
most part, towards venal motives. Competition was fierce in
every direction, extras and supplements were given, advertisement rates were cut, prices were reduced, and some journals
were, naturally, ruined in the struggle, although others came
out victorious and attained wonderful expansion. At this
time the ' *Yūbin Hōchi Shimbun*,' after many vicissitudes of
fortune, finally passed into the hands of Zempachi Miki
and Gensai Murai, cast off its first appellation ' *Yūbin*,' and
renamed itself simply ' *Hōchi*.' It professed to have no longer
any relation with political parties, and thus, having made clear
its nature and attitude, simplified its language and laid stress
upon news items, especially the contents of the third page,
converting itself into a ' high-class miscellaneous reports
paper,' chiefly for family reading. It also published ' *Hino-
déshima*,' a novel by Gensai, which might be called a by-product
of the war literature. This policy being well suited to the
taste of readers who had been led to read newspapers through
the influence of the war, the number of copies sold mounted
up day by day, and from having had only five or six thousand
readers before the war, within a few years they increased
tenfold. This success was due to the new managers foreseeing that readers after the war would be mostly below
the middle class, and thus cleverly anticipating their tastes.
Further, they took the lead in devising plans which brought
the paper and its readers into closer connection, as, for instance,
by assigning a column to a ' business guide,' a ' sanitary
guide,' a ' legal adviser,' and so forth—an innovation which
many other papers afterwards imitated.

What contributed, in the next place, to accelerate the
development of newspapers was the business boom that
followed the war. The effect of this was that things economic

Influence
of the
*post-
bellum*
business
boom.

came to occupy the most important position in newspaper columns, men of commerce being thus brought into close contact with newspapers. As a result, the number of journals circulating among business men greatly increased, while the rapid growth of new tradal undertakings expanded the wealth of the nation and increased the people's power of purchasing newspapers. Again, information about economic events demanded the greatest accuracy and promptitude, so that the reporting organs of every newspaper were compelled to great activity, and the use of telephones and telegraphs came into vogue—some of the most influential papers possessing long-distance telephones for their exclusive use. Further, the use of the revolving cylinder press increased by degrees, and not a few newspaper offices now used two or three of these machines.

The
policy of
getting
the
greatest
number of
readers.

Although Japanese newspapers made rapid progress after the China-Japan War, yet it seems that the journals which most largely increased the extent of their circulation were those which put into practice the policy of catering for the people below the middle class : that is to say, made their language easy and familiar ; inserted as many pictures as possible, so as to attract the readers' notice ; devoted a larger space to sensational items rather than to philosophical matters ; endeavoured to report, with exaggeration, incidents calculated to excite the curiosity of readers ; supplied for family consumption accounts of family amusements ; reported quickly such economic matters as had immediate relation to the living questions of the nation—and thus supplied the whole of what is called ' editorial art.' This was one natural result of the fact that all the newspapers came in time under the ban of a venal policy. Looked at from the point of gain, a newspaper became a product having little to distinguish it from other kinds of merchandise. Hence the ideals of high-class journalists had often to be subservient to the will of capitalists, and even the ' *Nippon*,' which had never compromised its dignity, but always maintained its ground far above its *confrères*, changed its tone at last with a change of proprietor, its contents thereafter becoming entirely prostituted to business principles. If such were the case with the ' *Nippon*,' not much need be said about other newspapers.   Nowadays the cost of printing and other expenses have increased so much with the development of the journalistic sphere, and, at the same time, competition among papers is so great, that a reduction of price, followed very often by distribution of copies gratis, is nothing extraordinary.   Consequently, even the journals of widest circulation have found that they cannot support themselves solely by the sale of copies, and they are obliged to rely largely on advertisements.   Naturally, therefore, they spare no pains to become suitable organs for advertisements of every kind, the credit of a newspaper being mostly measured by the number of advertisements it publishes. The age in which the editorial bureau controlled the management of a journal has gone, and the power of guiding its policy, it may be justly said, has been transferred to the manager of the advertisement department.   The ' Ōsaka Asahi' and the ' Ōsaka Mainichi' are the most evident instances of a tendency that became more marked after the Russo-Japan War. *The policy of advertisement.*

But notwithstanding this, there are journals whose proprietors entertain right ideas about the mission of their craft and the august position of their profession, and who pay constant attention to journalistic credit, and do not make pecuniary gain their chief end.   These papers not only carefully select their materials, but also attach much importance to editorials.   Even the journals with mercenary aims, when their circulation has attained fair proportions, become conscious of the greatness of their influence upon readers, and there is no doubt that they too gradually come to feel self-respect and self-esteem.   Among present-day newspapers there is none, even of the lower class, that does not insert at least a short editorial in every issue.   But the editorials of to-day, when compared with those of former times, contain very little of the editor's own personal sentiments or of what may be called pleadings for political parties.   They serve rather to describe and elucidate topics of immediate interest.   Some of them doubtless aim at exciting their readers by the use of impulsive and dangerous language, but, on the whole, it is patent that the tone of editorials of present-day newspapers is by degrees *The self-respect of journalists.*

aiming at a standard proportionate to the progress of the
nation.

Number of newspapers. In 1877 the newspapers throughout the empire were not
more than 100 in number, but according to recent records the
number of such publications in Japan has reached 375, of which
54 are published in Tōkyō.

Principal vernacular papers. The principal newspapers now published in Tōkyō are the
'*Tōkyō Nichinichi Shimbun*' (Séiichi Honda, proprietor), the
'*Jiji Shimpō*' (Ichitarō Fukuzawa, proprietor), the '*Hōchi Shimbun*' (Katsundo Minoura, proprietor), the '*Kokumin Shimbun*'
(Iichirō Tokutomi, proprietor and editor), the '*Chūō Shimbun*' (Ikuzō Ōoka, proprietor), the '*Tōkyō Asahi Shimbun*'
(Kichitarō Ikébé, editor), the '*Yoruzu Chōhō*' (Shūroku Kuroiwa,
proprietor and editor), the '*Tōkyō Niroku Shimbun*' (Teisuké
Akiyama, proprietor), the '*Yomiuri Shimbun*' (Séikō Motono,
proprietor), and the '*Nippon*' (Kinryō Itō, proprietor). The
'*Ōsaka Asahi*' and the '*Ōsaka Mainichi*' are said to surpass all
other Tōkyō newspapers in influence.

English newspapers. Besides the above, English newspapers published by Englishmen or Americans number five in Yokohama and two in Kōbé;
of these the *Japan Daily Mail*, issued by Captain F. Brinkley,
an Englishman, is the most notable. There is one newspaper
published by Japanese in English, namely, the *Japan Times*.

Number of copies sold. As regards the circulation of papers, in 1877 there was only
one journal which issued daily over 10,000 copies, but now there
are local papers whose daily number reaches 30,000. Of the
most influential newspapers, there are not a few that issue
between 100,000 and 200,000 copies daily. It is quite probable
that before long some will attain to over 500,000 copies a
day, a result due to the propagation of national education
among the people at large.

The Development of Magazines

The publications which originally appeared in Japan under
the name of newspapers were mostly periodical pamphlets,
not distinguishable from ordinary magazines in form. But
afterwards, when daily news-sheets came to be issued, journals
and magazines came gradually to be distinguished in form as

well as in contents. In 1873, Arinori Mori, on his return A
home from America, saw the necessity of forming an magazine
association of literates, and he, together with Shigeki literates.
Nishimura, Shindō Tsuda, Masanao Nakamura, Shū Nishi,
Hiroyuki Katō, Yukichi Fukuzawa, Shūhéi Mitsukuri, Kōji
Sugi, and Rinshō Mitsukuri, organized a literary society
called the *Méirokusha* (Society of the Sixth Year of Méiji),
which derived its name from the sixth year of Méiji (1873),
when it was first founded. Shortly afterwards they published
a magazine called the '*Méiroku Zasshi*' as an organ for
expressing their sentiments, and in its pages they earnestly
advocated Western ideas.

Following the '*Méiroku Zasshi*' there appeared the '*Katéi
Sodan*,' which was edited by Yukichi Fukuzawa himself; but it
soon gave place to the '*Minkan Zasshi*,' edited by Masanosuké
Katō, which became the organ for expressing the ideas of the
Mita school of learning. The '*Tōkyō Kéizai Zasshi*,' established
by Ukichi Taguchi in 1879, at once took firm root among the
reading public, and has continued to do so ever since. Its A free
success was due to its constant advocacy of free trade, thus trade
greatly influencing a section of the people, and also to its magazine.
excellent management. A little later appeared the '*Tōkai
Kéizai Shimpō*,' superintended by Kowashi Inukai, which advocated a protective trade policy, representing the Listian school
of Germany ; it stood in opposition to the '*Kéizai Zasshi*,' but
soon collapsed.

In 1875 Sen Tsuda, founder of the Gakunōsha School, the
first agricultural school, began to publish the *Agricultural
Magazine* ('*Nōgyō Zasshi*'), the pioneer of its kind, and still
existent. The '*Jogaku Zasshi*' (the *Woman's Magazine*), which
was established by Zenji Iwamoto in 1885, was the first magazine
for the other sex in Japan, and it had a great influence among
progressive young women for many years.

The two periodicals that did most honour to the magazine
world of Japan were probably the '*Kokumin-no-Tomo*' and the
'*Nipponjin*.' The former, established by Iichirō Tokutomi in
1887, exercised great influence in the department of literature
by using a new style, happily harmonizing the three different
dictions and phraseologies of Japanese, Chinese, and English.

Its arguments, thoroughly popular in principle, were in harmony with the spirit of the age, and were thus welcomed by the youth of the country. The latter, published in the following year, was mostly written by Yūjirō Miyaké and Shigétaka Shiga. It opposed Western ideas, advocated Conservative principles, and breathed Oriental rather than Occidental thought.

The Haku-bunkan. The '*Nippon Taika Ronshū*,' which appeared in the same year as the '*Kokumin-no-Tomo*' was born, attracted many readers, its first issue especially being so popular that it ran through many editions. This magazine was a monthly, published by the Hakubunkan, an institution founded by Sahéi Ōhashi. In succession to this, the '*Nippon-no-Jogaku*,' the '*Nippon-no-Kyōgaku*,' the '*Nippon-no-Shōnen*,' the '*Nippon-no-Hōritsu*,' and others, were issued by the same publisher; and the name Hakubunkan gradually came to be respected as that of a great publishing firm, especially of magazines. The Hakubunkan of the present day publishes also the '*Taiyo*'—a monthly, which is really the '*Nippon Taika Ronshū*' in another form—the '*Taihéiyō*,' the '*Shōnén Sékai*,' the '*Bungéi Kurabu*,' the '*Shashin Gahō*,' the '*Yōnén Gahō*,' the '*Bunshō Sékai*,' the '*Chūgaku Sékai*,' the '*Jogaku Sékai*,' the '*Shōjo Sékai*,' the '*Gogaku Sékai*,' the '*Shōgyō Sékai*,' the '*Eigo Sékai*,' and the '*Nōgyō Sékai*'—fourteen magazines in all. Among new designs and plans for the illustration of magazines there is scarcely one that does not emanate from the Hakubunkan. The most remarkable are the photolithographs, collotypes, coloured wood-cuts, and three-colour engravings for frontispieces.

Literary magazines. One of the earliest pure literature magazines was perhaps the '*Garakuta Bunko*,' published by the *Kényūsha* in 1888. What was called the *Kényūsha* was an association of young novelists, with Kōyō Ozaki as its centre. Succeeding this, the '*Waséda Bungaku*' appeared in 1891, under the superintendence of Yūzō Tsubouchi ; it was compiled by men in connection with the Department of Literature in the Waséda University. About this time also the '*Shigarami Zōshi*' appeared, edited by Ōgai Mori. Whilst the '*Waséda Bungaku*' represented the ideas of the English school, the '*Shigarami Zōshi*' advocated those of the German school, and both were for a time landmarks in the literary world of Japan. In 1895, when the '*Téikoku Bungaku*,' a monthly magazine compiled by graduates of the College of Literature in the Imperial University, appeared, the '*Waséda Bungaku*,' the '*Shigarami Zōshi*,' and the '*Téikoku Bungaku*' formed, as it were, a triumvirate. But the life of the two first named was short, although in 1906 the '*Waséda Bungaku*' came to life again. With the progress of modern literature and art, many poets, original writers, and critics arose, the consequence being that works dealing with literature and art increased year by year. They are now so numerous that we cannot speak of them in detail.

Besides those mentioned above, magazines and periodicals published by associations, and magazines of science, education, religion, philosophy, arts, and industry, now reach over one thousand in number. According to the latest statistics, the magazines issued in Tōkyō alone number 380. Among them, those which have business people and the fair sex for subscribers are the most numerous.

PRINTING AND BOOK PUBLISHING

Printing in Japan had already made marked progress in the Tokugawa period, a fact of which we may speak with some pride. This was due chiefly to the encouragement given to publications by the Shōgunate as well as by feudal chiefs. Above all, the Chinese classics and histories reprinted at the Séidō (the university) by order of the Shōgunate, were far superior to their originals as regards binding, printing, and paper, so that they were greatly appreciated by the reading public. This is what was called the 'Government Press.' Outside this press, the best known were the so-called clan presses of Mito, Kanazawa, Tokushima, and Tsu, of which the Mito stood at the head. Mitsukuni Tokugawa, the second lord of the Mito clan, having paid great attention to the cultivation of literature, and himself superintending many Confucian scholars, compiled and published the '*Dai Nihonshi*,' consisting of 243 volumes. In addition to this, he published several Japanese and Chinese works, conferring considerable benefit on

Publishing in the Tokugawa age.

scholars. Other clans in imitation produced bulky volumes and gave patronage to book publication. Following them came the Buddhists in Kyōto. Books from the Wōbaku Press or the Éizan Press were all published at Buddhist temples. The famous 'Issaikyō,' one of the productions of the Wōbaku Press, which consists of 6930 books and 2094 volumes, is perhaps one of the most voluminous works in the world. Illustrated novels, all of them written with the *hira-kana* syllabary, and printed in small characters with minute pictures inserted, were much in vogue, many remarkable and admirable specimens of art appearing in their pages. Wooden types, called *Shokujihan* or *Ichijihan*, have been in use in Japan for over four hundred years. Iyéyasu, after the campaign of Sékiganara, gave 300,000 wooden types to the Ashikaga school, and caused it to reprint many old books. Afterwards, in 1614, 200,000 copper types were cast which were given to the Konjiin, a temple in Kyōto, for the purpose of printing the '*Daizō Ichiran.*' The '*Gunsho Chiyō,*' printed in the earlier part, and the '*Shisho Shūchū*' and '*Shūéki Hongi,*' printed in the latter part of the seventeenth century, and the '*Rikuyu Éngi,*' the '*Tōi Hōkan,*' and the '*Zōkō Taihéi Wazai Kyokuhō,*' printed in the earlier part of the eighteenth century, were all produced by means of wooden or copper type. The most bulky book printed with such type was the '*Daihannyakyō,*' published by the Denzūin temple in the Bunkyū period (about 1862). This work consists of three hundred volumes, and they were all printed by means of wooden types.

In the latter days of the Tokugawa Government, one Shōzō Motoki of Nagasaki first studied the art of European printing under a Dutchman, and in 1869 he established a school to teach printing, himself casting leaden type which he supplied to publishers. The use and advantage of this new type attracted the attention of the community by degrees, and finally led to the establishment of the Government Printing Bureau and the Tsukiji Type Foundry in Tōkyō. Thereafter, when such printers as the Kokubunsha, the Shuyéisha, and the Kurata Printing Office set up printing establishments one after the other, the publishers of Japan came to use leaden types. So, too, in printing machinery, the hand was changed for the cylinder

Movable types of the time of Iyéyasu.

European printing.

press, thus keeping pace with the increase of new publications, which were then in great demand. Owing to the call for translations of foreign literature, printing businesses made rapid and great strides.

The following comparative table of publications may be of interest : Table of publica-tions.

Years.	Original works. Vols.	Translations. Vols.	Reprints. Vols.	Total. Vols.
1877	4,745	232	464	5,441
1882	8,751	281	616	9,648
1887	8,885	692	875	10,452
1892	21,409	173	262	21,844
1897	25,381	141	—	25,522
1900	18,505	111	—	18,616
1903	24,738	17	—	24,755
1904	26,582	28	—	26,610
1905	27,078	17	—	27,095

It will be seen from the above that, whilst the total number of publications in 1877 was 5,441 volumes, of which translations were 232 and reprints were 464, in 1905 the publications had increased to 27,095 volumes, but translations were only 17 volumes, and there were no reprinted works. This was due to Japan having joined the International Copyright Protection League, which made it difficult to translate or reprint any foreign books, but it was also a result of the fact that Japan now contains a large number of persons who are able to read foreign works in their original form without resorting to translations. Increase of original works.

But when we compare the publishing records of Japan with those of Europe, it must be admitted that the former are far inferior to the latter; for though in Japan the number of new publications is increasing day by day, really good works are very few, and Japan is still the Grub Street of the East. Subjoined is a list showing the average fixed prices per copy of several publications put upon the market by the Tōkyō Book-publishers' Guild in the years 1904-06 : Average prices of books.

Table showing the Average Fixed Prices per copy of various publications, given in decimals of the yen, which may be taken at 2s.

	Theology and Religion.	Philosophy.	Education.	Elementary School Text-books.	Books for Young Folks.
	Yen.	*Yen.*	*Yen.*	*Yen.*	*Yen.*
1904	·323	·542	·510	·400	·106
1905	·632	·528	·688	·210	·128
1906	·574	·424	1·090	·234	·202

	Literature.	Novels.	Japanese Literature and Language.	Foreign Literature and Language.	History and Bio-graphy.
	Yen.	*Yen.*	*Yen.*	*Yen.*	*Yen.*
1904	·444	·574	·398	·414	·815
1905	·390	·362	·425	·512	·505
1906	·389	·351	·430	·530	·632

	Geography, Travels, and Maps.	Law and Ordinance.	Politics, Political Economy, Sociology, and Statistics.	Physics, Chemistry, and Natural History.	Mathe-matics.
	Yen.	*Yen.*	*Yen.*	*Yen.*	*Yen.*
1904	·727	·976	·433	·962	·498
1905	·791	·763	·760	1·016	·423
1906	·391	·770	·500	·686	·540

	Medicine.	Engineering and Technology.	Commerce.	Agriculture.	Military Subjects.
	Yen.	*Yen.*	*Yen.*	*Yen.*	*Yen.*
1904	·992	·743	·505	·577	·276
1905	·847	·974	1·169	·760	·394
1906	1·167	·505	·880	·762	·497

	Fine Arts.	Music and Dancing.
	Yen.	*Yen.*
1904	·215	·118
1905	·277	·219
1906	·326	·290

	Games.	Household Management.	Yearly average price.
	Yen.	Yen.	Yen.
1904	·306	·414	·533
1905	·311	·382	·514
1906	·297	·464	·518

It will be seen from this that the average price of publications is from 10*d.* to 1*s.* per copy, and the number forming an edition of each of these publications would be generally between 1000 and 2000 copies. From this it will be seen that the reading taste of the Japanese in general is still undeveloped.

Although there were many distinguished publishers after the Restoration, the majority gained but temporary success, and many failed. The Hōbunkan, once leader of the publishing circle, reprinting mainly Chinese classics by means of copper plates and printing blocks ; the Hakubundō, famous for publishing works on politics, economy, and literature ; the Hakubunsha and Yao, both of which stood prominently in the publishing circle as law-book publishers ; the Usagiya, renowned for publications adapted to the season ; the Kingyoku, famous for reprints of fictions and novels of the Tokugawa period—all these no longer exist. Even such old and noted publishers as Suwaraya and Yamanaka were doomed to pass out of existence. Although failure in many instances was mainly due to bad business management, yet it also proved the difficulty of achieving success in the publishing trade. Those publishers who were engaged chiefly in bringing out elementary school text-books, the demand for which is generally believed to be great, were more fortunate, and among them the Kinkōdō was most prominent. They were generally called ' the text-book publishers.' But, when elementary school text-books came under Government management, even these lost the principal part of their business and could no longer maintain their position in the publishing world. It is no wonder that in such circumstances no great publishers exist.

The rise and fall of publishers.

Many books, the majority in fact of those that are reprints, have been published by subscription. For example, the '*Shiséki Shūran*' (of 533 volumes), the '*Gunsho Ruijū*' (26 volumes),

Publications by subscription.

the '*Kokushi Taikei*' (29 volumes), the '*Tokugawa Jikki*' (7 volumes), the '*Gagen Shūran*' (57 volumes), the '*Kojitsu Sōsho*' (131 volumes), and the '*Manyōshū Kogi*' were all brought out in this way. As for more bulky publications, we may instance the '*Dai-Nippon Shiryō*,' issued at indefinite intervals, two or three volumes per year, and spread over several decades, although brought out by the Tōkyō Imperial University; the '*Koji Ruiyen*' (divided into thirty-six departments, each consisting of from three to thirty volumes and published in sections), brought out by the Jingūshichō; and the '*Issai Zōkyō*' (which comprise all Chinese and Japanese writings, essays or posthumous works on Buddhism), brought out by the Kyōto Zōkyō Shoin. But these three great works are publications which have a special character, and are not produced for pecuniary ends, so that ordinary book publishers could not undertake them. The usual number of subscribers for publications by means of a previous contract is generally from 1000 to 2000, and even the most popular publications welcomed by the reading public seldom find 5000 subscribers.

The prince of the publishing circle.

There is, however, one book-publishing firm that has attained great success without either printing text-books or issuing books by subscription, and that is the Hakubunkan. From 1888 to 1897 they published over 3380 volumes, of which the most important was the 'Series.' The chief books in this 'Series' were the '*Teikoku Bunko*' (100 volumes), the '*Nippon Bungaku Zénsho*' (20 volumes), the '*Shina Bungaku Zénsho*' (24 volumes), the '*Teikoku Hyakka Zénsho*' (200 volumes), the '*Nichiyō Hyakka Zénsho*' (50 volumes), the '*Kōgei Sōsho*' (50 volumes), the '*Tsūzoku Kyōiku Zénsho*' (100 volumes), the '*Shōnen Bungaku*' (32 volumes), and the '*Nippon Otogibanashi*' (24 volumes). The publications of the Hakubunkan have during the last ten years increased more than three hundred per cent. compared with those of twenty years ago, and they have taken steps to propagate the largest amount of knowledge by supplying the public with the cheapest books of a scientific, literary, educational, and social nature. Again, they have devoted one-half of their business to the publication of magazines, and during the past nineteen years have brought out some forty magazines, those now published being fourteen. Lately the Hakubun-kan started printing works, and besides the publication of their own books, they carry on a printing business. They have a revolving cylinder press and more than thirty other machines. They have also a department of engraving, and are successfully manufacturing many kinds of engraved blocks and plates. They may well be called the Prince of Japanese publishers.

At present the number of members of the Tōkyō Book-publishers' Guild is about four hundred, among whom the most distinguished, besides the Hakubunkan, are the Tōyōdō, which mainly publishes pictorial pamphlets and picture books ; the Shunyōdō, which publishes new novels; the Sanséidō, which publishes works on politics and law, and also all sorts of dictionaries ; and the Fusanbō, which publishes text-books for secondary education—all these are firms started during the Méiji period. *A Book-sellers' Guild.*

Coloured wood-cuts may well be called the pride of Japanese publications. The art of wood-cutting had already made high progress in the time of the Tokugawa Government, and the Azuma chromoxylograph, commonly known in the West as a ' Japanese colour print,' which was first produced at that time, is one of the Japanese fine arts, much admired and esteemed nowadays all over the world. After the Restoration, simultaneously with the introduction of foreign engraving, the art of wood-cutting indigenous to Japan gradually began to decline, but in 1889 Kenzō Takahashi and Kakuzō Okakura published the ' *Kokka*,' a monthly magazine of fine arts, with the intention of promoting the beautiful art of Japanese chromoxylography. They reprinted famous old Japanese pictures by means of wood-cuts and published them in the magazine, which gained much esteem at home and abroad. Afterwards Naohiko Masaki promoted and established the ' *Shimbi Shoin*,' and published the ' *Shimbi Taikan*,' which was the same sort of magazine as the ' *Kokka*,' but on a larger scale, By these means the arts of Japanese engraving and coloured wood-cuts were greatly improved, and a new era was opened for them. But some of the more minute and subtile kinds of chromoxylographs require from thirty to one hundred printings, *Coloured wood-cuts.*

and the result is a high price which naturally decreases the demand. There is now a tendency to reduce the number of Azuma chromoxylographs, which have been considered a special art in the Japanese publishing world, while, on the other hand, the art of foreign engraving has gradually come to be welcomed, and every sort of engraving—in addition to wood-cuts and lithographs, such as photogravure, electric copper-plate, photo-lithography, common copper-plate, aluminium-plate, concave and convex plates, collotype and three-coloured engraving—has passed into active use, and the art itself has greatly improved.

The future of publishing.
Nevertheless, upon the whole, the publishing world of Japan is still young compared with that of Europe and America. Although this is largely due to the fact that the taste of the reading public in Japan has not yet fully developed, still the main cause is doubtless due to the narrow sphere of the use of the Japanese language. Of late, as the influence of Japan spreads over China and Korea, it would seem as though the publishing business of this country were destined to turn in those directions for its future development—a matter for hearty congratulation.

XXII

THE LITERATURE OF THE MÉIJI ERA

Professor Yaichi Haga, D.Litt. (Japan)

The following sketch has been prepared, in compliance with a request of Count Ōkuma, with a view to its taking a place in his monumental work. It claims to little more than a brief notice of some traces left by alien influences, by translations and by current Occidental literature, on our literature.

It is nearly three centuries since the light of Occidental civilization first dawned on Japan and a European, Kaempfer, first wrote upon it. The Island Empire has been a world's wonder ever since, and if all the works catalogued in Wenckstern's Bibliography could be brought together, an extensive library, composed entirely of books on Japan, could be formed. There is hardly a branch of our literature that has not been translated, at least in the form of fragmentary specimens, into some European language. The oldest chronicles, from the ' *Kojiki* ' and the ' *Nihongi* ' down to the ' Tales of the Middle Age ' ; chronicles of warlike days ; the *Nō* and the *Kyōgén* literature of the military epoch ; various novels ; and the *Hokku* of the Yédo period, have been so rendered. It is, however, only comparatively recently that foreigners have begun to view our literary activity from an historical standpoint, the translations of the above-mentioned works having been known only to the rather narrow circle of specialists. In the so-called history of universal literature, by Hart, Kerpeles, or Scherr, we find only two or three pages set apart for our country's literature, the co-existent syllabaries (*kata-kana* and *hira-kana*), and the two names, ' *Genji Monogatari* ' and ' *Gempéi Séisuiki*,' being considered by those historians as the only things worth mentioning out of an extensive range of facts. Mr. Aston was

Japan in Occidental literature.

the first to write our literary history, and his work, ' History of Japanese Literature,' exists also in a French version. Professor Florenz, of the Tōkyō Imperial University, also is busy at his ' Geschichte der Japanischen Litteratur,' several parts of which have already been published. Besides these there are two or three similar publications in European languages. Though not separately published, the fairly comprehensive article on our literature contained in Meyer's ' Conversation Lexicon ' should be recommended as a praiseworthy attempt at a fuller analysis of Japanese literature. This being so, we may be permitted to leave untouched many things already treated of in ordinary manuals, and confine ourselves to those of more recent date.

Chinese literature as our semi-national literature.

The national literature of a people should be always in their mother tongue. Hence all literary historians, native and foreign, naturally declined to assign any position to works written in a foreign language. Thus the translations, as gems of Japanese literature, by Chamberlain, Satow, Aston, Meyer, and others, were always selected from compilations in the purely native tongue. This, however, requires some modification in the case of Japanese literature, for throughout its long centuries of evolution it has never ceased to find an important complement in Chinese literature, and most of our philosophical, biographical, historical, and geographical works, nay, even our lyrics, were written in Chinese. This custom, which obtained even down to quite recent years and is still far from being abandoned, should not be confounded with the apparently cognate phenomenon in Europe, where Latin and Greek once held a classic prestige.

When Chinese classics in ideographic monosyllables were in use, our ancestors, unwilling to abandon their own original pronunciation, invented a convenient method of reading Chinese characters by rendering them into Japanese, by which means any Chinese literature in Chinese became as readily appreciable as that in the mother tongue. This was achieved by a simple system of suffixes and by the employment of the auxiliary verb and the *téniha* particles. Such a method of rendering may surely be disassociated from translation in the ordinary sense of the term.

In our early days Chinese classics were practically turned into Japanese by attaching dots at the four corners of each of the ideographs, which plan was subsequently replaced by writing Japanese *kana* beside the ideographs. Thus, even in the nineteenth century as in the fifth or sixth, we uniformly treated our neighbours' literature as if it were our own.

Chinese literature as Japanese classics.

The natural result of such a method was the appearance of a peculiar vernacular Chinese mingled with various Japanese idioms—a vernacular so changed from its original that it finally ceased to be intelligible to the Chinese, even when written in the Chinese way without any *kana*, for the grammar regulating it was entirely home-bred and words were used in their Japanese sense. It was, in fact, nothing more than Japanese written without the *kana*. It is not, therefore, too much to say that our modern Japanese may be considered a corruption, or rather a modification, of Chinese, *kana* replacing particles used, when the method of syllabic rendering of Chinese was first invented. The time-honoured prestige tenaciously held by Chinese ideographs, even in our progressive age, may be ascribed mainly to this singular relationship, and were books written in Chinese to be excluded from our literature, the loss would be almost incalculable.

Chinese of the Japanese.

During my sojourn in Berlin I was surprised to find that the ' Nihon Gaishi,' one of our most famous war chronicles, written by the celebrated Sanyō Rai, was registered in the department of Chinese Literature in the Catalogue of Oriental Books, and I remember a conversation between a literary attendant and myself, in which I tried to make him aware of this gross mistake, by explaining that this very work enjoys a wide circulation as a purely native classic, although apparently written in Chinese characters. My representations produced no effect. I may mention that Sanyō Rai is also known as the author of the ' Nihon Séiki ' and the ' Tsūgi,' and his poems are still favourites with students, who sing them to certain music while they dance with a sword. Indeed, his writings have done much to inspire later generations with the patriotism which directly contributed to the restoration of the Imperial authority, and indirectly to the repeal of the exclusion policy. Similarly, many other important literary productions which

The ' Nihon Gaishi ' in the Royal Library of Berlin.

gave a powerful impulse to national activity and evolution were, strange to say, written in Chinese.

Greater part of Japanese literature written in Chinese.

Thus Chinese was considered for many a century as the sole medium in which a cultivated person could convey his thoughts, and novels and dramas written in the Japanese vernacular were looked down on as unworthy of serious attention. Therefore, one who has a mind to form any adequate estimate of our national life and sentiments cannot possibly neglect the careful investigation of books in Chinese, independently of the rich productions in pure Japanese which were produced under cruel depreciation. By neglecting so to do he would miss the greater and perhaps the better half of his pursuit, since so far as quantity is concerned the former are twice as numerous as the latter.

Decay of Chinese studies.

With the advent of the new era, which brought the worship of Occidentalism in its train, Chinese studies all but disappeared. The nine classics, in which the youth of former generations had been educated, gradually gave way to text-books specially prepared for primary schools under the new *régime*, and thus the very source of the nation's moral education for nearly ten centuries was allowed to dry up, as it were, and its place was taken by readers based on Wilson's and by grammars modelled on Pineo's or Quackenbos's. Those who had prepared the way for the glorious Restoration by an elevation of the moral ideal and by stirring up patriotism—that is, the Chinese scholars and the admirers of our old national literature—were contemptuously thrust aside in the rush for Occidental civilization.

Assimilation of Occidental civilization.

The Restoration brought about as its immediate consequence the rapid assimilation of Occidentalism, which with marvellous success was grafted on to our prescriptive politics, economics, tactics, education, and so forth. The people, trained for nearly ten centuries in Buddhist and Chinese philosophy, were on that account fully competent to digest the most profound doctrines of Occidental philosophers. Nor was the change from the feudal age to the nineteenth century so abrupt as it seemed, for it must not be forgotten that science, biology, and medicine of a kind had been introduced from Holland during the long peace of nearly three centuries, as had astronomy and mathematics from China.

Dutch was the first European tongue to be learned by the The first European language in Japan. Japanese, and about two centuries ago there were already a number of scholars well versed in that language. Many students of science, geography, and especially medicine, devoted themselves to acquiring this language at the risk of incurring heavy penalties. In the wake of Dutch other languages came to be introduced, their order being English, French, and German, the main traces of which languages in our literature are briefly discussed in the following pages.

Amongst the various branches of learning introduced since Influences of the English language. the Restoration, the study of English is perhaps that to which we have paid and are paying the greatest attention. It has always been through books in that language that we have formed our conceptions of things European and obtained glimpses of the general features of the outside world. Even when the *Bansho Torishirabé-béjo* (Institute for Investigating Foreign Books), established during the Yédo epoch, and afterwards called the *Yōsho Torishirabé-béjo* (Institute for Investigating European Books), was turned into the *Kaiséi Gakkō* and then into the Tōkyō University with its several Tōkyō University. departments, the sole vehicle for conveying the new learning was the English language.

The University at its inception consisted of the three colleges of law, science, and literature. Professor Toyama, dean of one of these colleges, was a graduate of Michigan University, Professor Hozumi was an English barrister, and Professor Kikuchi a graduate of Cambridge University. In private establishments of a similar nature the late Yukichi Fukuzawa of the *Kéiō Gijuku* and the late Kéiu Nakamura of the *Dōninsha*, the most distinguished exponents of the new learning, used English as the medium in which to convey their ideas. The Anglo-Saxon practical tendencies, in fact, harmonized entirely with ours, and the American progressive spirit in matters of material civilization served us as a guide on our career of progress.

The late Mr. Yukichi Fukuzawa, not only as an eminent Yukichi Fukuzawa. educationalist but also as a writer, did a great deal towards the popularization of European knowledge by writing a number of books in the plainest style—among others, popular lectures on geography, history, natural history, and physiology, as their titles show : ' The Nations of the World,' ' Things European,' ' True Analysis of the Human Body,' ' Wonders of Nature,' &c.   He left also two works on ethics, ' *Kanzen Kummō* ' and ' *Dōmō Oshiégusa*,' the original of the latter being ' Chambers's Moral Class-book.'

Kéiu Nakamura and his translation of ' Self-Help.'
European civilization found another able spokesman in the late Dr. Masanao (Kéiu) Nakamura, a scholar well versed in Chinese classics, who translated Smiles's ' Self-Help ' and Mill's ' Representative Government.'

In this way every effort was made to familiarize the nation not only with foreign manners, customs, and etiquette, but also with religion and administration, and all our pioneers in European languages did their best in this direction.   Masao Uchida's ' *Yochishiryaku* ' (' Universal Geography ') and Rinshō Mitsukuri's ' *Bankoku Shinshi* ' (' Universal History ') deserve passing notice here as the more remarkable among such publications.   Contemporary with these, the Department of Education undertook the translation of ' Chambers's Encyclopædia,' and in 1875 the late Jō Niishima established the *Dōshisha* (see ii. 90), with the aim of introducing Occidental civilization and seasoning it with the fundamental principles of Christianity.

French scholars.
The nation, having thus become partially acquainted with the outside world in its past and present, including its various forms of State, a demand for liberty and equality naturally arose, and people turned to the great thinkers in that special line, such as Rousseau, Voltaire, or Montesquieu.   Tokusuké Nakaé, who had been in France, translated Rousseau's ' Contrat Social ' under the title of ' *Minyaku-Ron*,' and its reception was so great that the Imperial rescript issued in 1881 promising the inauguration of constitutional administration within ten years was said to be due to the idea of popular rights widely diffused through that book.   By that time people were already able to appreciate Spencer's ' Evolution,' as well as histories of civilization by Guizot and Buckle, and these were steadily preparing the way for the coming revolution of thought.   Such was the spiritual transformation that young Japan had been undergoing down to about 1882, although there was as yet little to be said with regard to literature

properly so called. The nation was still too busily occupied
with the introduction of such knowledge as had direct bearing
on statecraft and useful sciences to trouble itself in any way
with *belles lettres,* and probably people had not yet been
sufficiently versed in European tongues to enjoy a high
standard of literary production.[1]

The old literary men who survived the Restoration were
altogether incapable of satisfying the new public, and as
indicating foreign influence in some degree, we may recall
Robun Kanagaki, a follower of Ikku and Samba, who wrote
' A Humorous Trip on Foot in the West,' imitating that laugh-
able tourist literature so popular in the Yédo age, and ' An
Analysis of a Cucumber,' a parody of ' *Kyūri Zukai*,' or ' Pictorial
Analysis of Truth.' Super-
annuated
men of
letters.

' Poems in a New Style,' published by three professors, Toyama, Yatabé, and Inouyé, in 1882, claims serious consideration
as the first-fruits of studies in Occidental literatures. The
most glaring departure made by these learned men from
the conventional short poem, which constituted the literary
classic of the Middle Ages, was the adaptation of the European
stanza and the free treatment of various subjects of wide scope,
in popular and flexible language. The same book contained
a number of renderings in verse from Bloomfield, Campbell,
Gray, Longfellow, Tennyson, and others—perhaps the first
attempt at translating Western poetry into Japanese. Too
great literary value must not be attached to the work of these
three, for no one of them was either a man of letters or a poet
in the strict sense of the term. Still, 1882 must be taken as
a memorable date in the history of new literature in Japan. The first-
fruits of
European
literature.

It was then also that the romantic literature sought out
a new channel. The names remembered in connection with
that interesting tendency are not, however, those of professional men of letters, for the novel then in vogue was political,
imbued with the fervent liberalism inevitable on the eve of a
constitutional movement.

In 1883 Lytton's ' Ernest Maltravers ' was translated under

---

[1] I leave out of this paper any mention of the side of literature which finds
expression in newspapers or magazines, as these have been dealt with at length
elsewhere (ii. 410).

Novel
transla-
tion.

the title of ' *Karyū Shunwa*,' and soon after were published Méikaku Fujita's ' *Kéishidan* ' and Naohiko Séki's ' *Shunōtén*,' the former being from Lytton and the latter from Disraeli.

Besides these books of alien origin, there were also several original works well representing the above-mentioned tendency. Mr. Fumio Yano's ' *Kéikoku Bidan* ' (' A Model for Statesmen ') was a Greek story with Epaminondas as its hero ; Mr. Suyé-hiro's ' *Setchūbai* ' (' Plum-tree amid Snow ') and his ' *Kakanō* ' (' A Warbler among Flowers ') were political novels anticipating constitutional Japan.   Thus novelists were almost exclusively politicians and their works political.   These, therefore, had very little merit from the modern literary point of view, for all they aimed at was to ventilate the author's own political ideas rather than to depict social life and psychology.   Similarly, certain scientific novels—Jules Verne's ' A Trip to the Moon,' ' One Thousand Leagues under the Sea,' ' A Trip through the Air,' &c.—won popularity because of their novel information, just as political novels were welcome because they had much to do with the absorbing topic engrossing popular attention at that time.   A glance, however, at the political literature prior to 1882 will convince us of the marked rise of literary taste in the popular estimation.   It was then that Dr. Tsubouchi gave a new adaptation of Shakespeare's ' Julius Cæsar ' under the title ' The Last Blow of the Sword of Freedom.'

Shōyō
Tsu-
bouchi.

Professor Tsubouchi, though a graduate of the Department of Politics in the Tōkyō Imperial University, seems to have been endowed with exceptional literary genius.   In his well-known ' Essentials of the Novel ' he expounded the virtues of roman-ticist literature, denounced the school established by Bakin, whose characters he condemned as inconsistent and artificial, set up realism against moralism, and recommended such realistic writers as Samba and Shunsui, at that time nearly forgotten.   These doctrines being supported by his own works, ' The Humour of Students ' and ' Man and Woman,' which embodied his professed principles, his influence over our novel-writing was great.   With his predecessors, who wrote political stories, literature was not a profession, but he was entirely a man of letters, and his productions had real literary merit. Moreover, being a refined gentleman with a complete familiarity

with the literature of both hemispheres, he was justly entitled
to be called the originator of the new literature of Japan.   It
is not surprising that he found no small number of followers.
In addition to being an author, he is a professor in the Literature Department at the Waséda University, and an assiduous
advocate of English literature in the ' Waséda Bungaku,' a
literary review started by him.   His ' History of English Literature ' is by far the most voluminous work on foreign literary
history written in Japanese.   Among followers inspired by his
university lectures, Hōgétsu Shimamura, Chūgai Gotō, and Futō
Mizutani are well known either as critics or original writers.

The spread of the English language and literature during **Expan-**
the last two decades has been in a geometrical progression, so **sion of literary**
much so that Macaulay's ' Clive ' and ' Hastings,' which were **taste.**
in the curriculum of the University in 1881, are now superseded in secondary schools by Goldsmith, Irving, Tennyson,
and Thackeray.   Such a rapid spread of Western literature
naturally inspired many of the younger generation, and a
literary coterie, called the *Kényūsha*, was formed by young **Kényū-**
students headed by Kōyō Ozaki, Sazanami Iwaya, Shian **sha.**
Ishibashi, and Bimyōsai Yamada.   They were all fervent
devotees of literary pursuits, and after several years most of
them left their academical life and became professional literary
men.   The late Kōyō Ozaki was by far the greatest of this
race of new *literati*, who each in his turn aided the progress of
the Méiji literature by their culture in modern as well as old
book lore.   Kōyō died an untimely death in his thirty-eighth
year, leaving as his disciple successors Kyōka, Fūyō, Shūséi,
Shunyō, &c., who, ably representing the *Kényūsha* school,
stand as rivals of the literary men of the Waséda.

The '*Kokumin-no-Tomo*' (*Friend of the People*), a magazine **Kokumin-**
devoted to literature, religion, and society, started by Sohō **no-Tomo.**
Tokutomi in 1887, occupies the first place in our memory
whenever the interpretation of European literature is spoken
of.   It well deserved its title, for discussions therein of acute
and novel interest, of European literature, and the development
of the new literature, found in its pages an able mouthpiece.
Translations, original works, and literary controversies also
secured a place in the periodical, and the late Shikén Morita

brought to it his translations of Hugo's works from their English forms—among others, ' The Blind Messenger ' (1888), ' Jubel, the Detective ' (1889), ' Les Misérables,' &c., while shorter compositions of various authors, as Calderon, Turgenief, Byron, Daudet, and Shakespeare, were rendered into the vernacular by other persons.

Ōgai Mori.

The activity of Ōgai Mori as an interpreter of German literature dates from 1889. A range of German poets comprising Scheffel, Heine, Körner, Lanau, Goethe, Kleist, Stellen, and others was introduced by him to our public, and his literary criticisms upon them had much weight with his contemporaries.

Literary magazines.

By this time a number of literary magazines had come into existence, the ' Miyako-no-Hana,' the ' Garakuta Bunko,' the ' Shōsétsu Hyakkasén,' and the ' Shincho Hyakushu ' being the more important. To these must be added the ' Kokumin-no-Tomo,' which was by far the most influential, owing to its original as well as critical productions in the domain of literature.

The ' Nihon Jin.'

In contrast with the ' Kokumin-no-Tomo,' represented by Mr. Tokutomi, a Christian and earnest advocate of Occidentalism in matters religious, political, and social, the conservative ' Nihon Jin ' appeared in 1888, its immediate purpose being to restrain the nation from overlooking the beauties of things Japanese in a blind worship of Occidentalism. These two magazines well illustrate the two main streams of national thought early in the third decade of Méiji, one a fervent supporter of Occidentalism, the other of conservative nationalism, the harmonizing of which two systems led Japan to her present prosperity and to the national adolescence upon which she is now entering.

Effect of Occidentalism on art.

As long as we were fettered by philo-Occidentalism the national arts were wholly neglected, and precious specimens of ancient art were exported without the least regret. It was then that temples and shrines, witnesses of former greatness, fell into semi-ruin, and Gahō Hashimoto, a master-painter of the Kanō school, was forced to earn his livelihood as a draughtsman in the Navy Department. Reaction, however, was not far distant, for in 1881 an American, Fenollosa, taught us how to admire the unique beauty of our art, and in consequence the next year saw at Uyeno an exhibition of pictures organized to encourage Japanese painting.   In 1893 the Committee for Investigating National Relics was organized, and specialist commissioners took measures for the conservation of the relics of antique art scattered throughout the empire.   Subsequently a society was formed with the object of preserving ancient temples and shrines, and now a certain sum of money is voted annually for preserving the remains of ancient architecture.

The above tendency, though partly due to ultra-nationalism seeking a wider outlook, must be ascribed mainly to the growth of national self-consciousness.   Encouraged by this reactionary movement, purely native arts, as the tea ceremony, floral arrangement, *Nō* performances, *jūjutsu*, and fencing, underwent more or less of a revival.

Nor must we ignore the important though indirect part played at this time by the revision of the foreign treaties. The codification of national laws, a collateral incident of this revision, necessitated a survey of ancient laws, customs, manners, and history, a matter of imminent urgency, and this in its turn led to the revival of national learning, which had been entirely neglected since the Restoration.   Difficulties met with in the course of revision taught us our own importance, and the establishment of a Constitution begot a due conception of the State as well as a consciousness of national duties.   In such circumstances studies in classics and history made unprecedented advances, and reprints of old books were received with increased encouragement.   In 1889, the year which saw the promulgation of the Constitution, the College of National Learning (*Kokugakuin*) was inaugurated by Count Akiyoshi Yamada, then Minister of Justice. *Revision of foreign treaties and revival of ancient classics.*

While the Constitution was being drawn up various institutions of European origin were studied, and the opinions of experts were asked for.   Among those to whom we largely owe the adjustment of State affairs was Dr. Stein of Austria, who taught our senior statesmen the idea of a State and how to manage it.   Politics were naturally formed on the same model as the institution which had been copied, and so, although the majority of those charged with the compilation of our laws *German influence.*

were not, strictly speaking, of the German school—Professor Hozumi being a representative of English, and Professor Tomii and Umé of French law—still German law, being ably represented by Professors Niho and Niida, two assistant - commissioners of the Compilation Committee, and by a number of barristers outside the Government, came to be adopted, as did autonomic local administration on the German model. Moreover, from the middle of the second Méiji decade, Government students sent abroad prosecuted their studies mostly in Germany, and on their return were looked upon as leaders of contemporary Japan. No wonder, then, that an atmosphere of philo-Germanism permeated the upper stratum of modern Japan; but although in the region of politics, education, law, music, and various sciences it was unmistakable, on the other hand this borrowing from foreign sources proceeded side by side with the renaissance of national classics.

The study of ancient literature and history. Literary activity was the principal agent in which this renaissance of old literature and history showed itself. Just as a reaction to the spoken-language style found an apostle in Bimyōsai Yamada, so the novelist Kōyō, Rohan, and other romanticists sought literary models in the writers of the Genroku age—the age when the Tokugawa literature reached its zenith and such geniuses as Monzaémon Chikamatsu and Saikaku Ihara produced their best works. This throwing off of the servile worship of Occidental literature led the masses to expect a new literature in which the old national classics would be allied with the healthy features of Western writing. This was met by the composition of historical romances, and the conspicuous progress made in epic and lyric literature in the matter of diction must be ascribed to appreciative studies of the old classics.

German literature. German literature found a never-wearying advocate in Dr. Ōgai Mori, Surgeon-General of the Army, just as English literature did in Professor Tsubouchi. There is nothing strange in the fact that German literature was introduced by a man of medicine, if we remember that the Imperial University at that time made the study of the German language an essential for students of the Medical College, while English was the principal language in the Colleges of Law, Science, and Literature.

In 1888 a special course of German literature was inaugurated in the Tōkyō Imperial University, and this in time achieved such development that in 1905 the graduates and under-graduates of the University celebrated Schiller's centennial anniversary by publishing a Schiller number of the '*Téikoku Bungaku*' (*Imperial Literature*), of which students of the College of Literature were the writers.

Dr. Ōgai Mori began his literary activity with translations of German poetry and criticisms of general literature.   These appeared in the '*Kokumin-no-Tomo*,' but subsequently he started a literary periodical called the '*Shigarami Zōshi*' in collaboration with the late Naobumi Ochiai, a scholar of old literature, and Sanjirō Ichimura, a scholar of Chinese literature.   Dr. Mori also produced many renderings of literature other than German, using German versions.   His '*Minawashū*' (1892) contains several dozen translations of epics and lyrics by Daudet, Kleist, Stern, Tolstoi, Turgenief, Irving, Bret Harte, Hoffmann, Lermontoff, and others.   His Japanese translation of Ander-sen's 'Improvisator' is also well known for its faithfulness. Even his original works, as '*Maihimé*' ('Dancer') and '*Utakata-no-Ki*' ('Dream'), are purely German in their spirit, as, for example, a love story of a Japanese student resident in Ger-many and a German girl devoted to art.   He is also deserving of praise for having taught our public how to criticize literary productions by means of Hartmann's æsthetics.   Mrs. Kimi Koganéi, his sister, is well known as the authoress of many excellent translations from German literature. *Ōgai Mori.*

Contemporary with Dr. Mori were many others who con-tributed towards introducing European literature into Japan. In 1888 and 1889, just before the first opening of the Diet, a number of literary periodicals came into existence, such as the '*Miyako-no-Hana*' (Urban Flowers), the '*Garakuta Bunko*,' and the '*Shincho Hyakushu*,' showing that the general and artistic appreciative faculty of the public had made a wonderful advance.   By that time men who had been abroad, and books published in the West, ceased to be deemed rarities, and the world's literature, no longer confined to English and German, began to be rendered into Japanese by men of various minds. During one decade, from 1887 to the time of the China-Japan *Literature after 1888.*

War, Hugo was translated by Shikén, Lessing and Calderon by Mori, Turgenief by Futabatéi Haségawa, and Dostoewski by Roan Uchida. In addition to these comparatively massive attempts a number of minor writings were rendered into Japanese, such as Burnett's 'Little Lord Fauntleroy' (by Mrs. Iwamoto), and shorter pieces from Addison, Hawthorne, Dickens, Irving, Wordsworth, Edgeworth, Tolstoi, Eichendorf, Daudet, Pierre Loti, Stevenson, Dumas, Conway, Goldsmith, &c. In a student's Manual of English Literature prepared at this time we find Goldsmith's 'Deserted Village,' Tennyson's 'Enoch Arden,' Milton's 'Paradise Lost,' Carlyle's 'French Revolution,' Emerson's 'Compensation,' and De Quincey's 'The Confession,' fully annotated.

Literature subsequent to 1892. While admitting that these attempts were sometimes unsatisfactory and the originals were rather badly mangled, the wideness of the field from which they were taken certainly deserves notice. In 1892 the '*Kokumin-no-Tomo's*' publishing office undertook to bring out a series [1] of biographical sketches of eminent Western literary men, in imitation of the 'English Men of Letters' series. Reprints and publications of old classics, national or Chinese, were also much encouraged—in short, everything was done to promote the renaissance of the old-time epic and short poems by embodying new thoughts in old-time diction, thus imparting to them a new flavour. In the realm of romance also, about this time, Kōyō and Rohan, twin magnates in their special fields, were in full production. The *hokku* and cognate brief poems were, however, not overlooked in this absorbing tendency to innovation. Much was due to Viscount Ki Inouyé, Minister of Education (1892–94), who was indefatigable in his patronage of education in the national language.

Post-bellum literature. The war with China in 1894 showed Japan in a new light to the world's eyes. During its continuance the '*Téikoku Bungaku*' was started with much ceremony by undergraduates of the College of Literature in Tōkyō University, the '*Shigarami Zōshi*' and the '*Waséda Bungaku*' having been discontinued. This magazine never tired of offering excellent criticism and renderings of Western literature, a special section being reserved for current Occidental literary news.

---

[1] 'Twelve Great Writers.'

The College, teaching as it does literature in all its various branches, such as Japanese, Chinese, English, German, French, &c., has naturally been looked up to as a cradle of learning. Among notable men of this University, the late Chogyū Takayama enjoyed a high reputation as a literary critic, contributing various articles to the '*Téikoku Bungaku*' in his earlier days, and later to the *Sun*, an important though not purely literary magazine, published by the Hakubunkan. Contemporary with him were Bin Uéda and Chikufū Tobari, able advocates of English and German literature respectively. From small beginnings, the literature course of the College, which had no more than a little over a dozen students in 1887, reckoned after ten years over three hundred names in its list of graduates and undergraduates, and the same could be said with certain slight modifications of various private colleges and universities.

The College of Literature, Tōkyō Imperial University.

Nothing is more natural than that the art of translation should be favourably influenced by the ever-widening and deepening appreciation of Western literature. Satisfied at first with a mere transcript of plots and general outlines of works, translators came gradually to strive after the exact conveyance of diction, and, from being confined to short pieces, to follow more ambitious lines. In 1904 a version of Goethe's ' Faust ' was made by Gorō Takahashi. Wasaburō Asano, a University man, well known as the translator of Irving's ' Sketch Book,' is now busily engaged in collaboration with Hakoya Tozawa, another University scholar, on a translation of Shakespeare's complete works, parts of which—' The Merchant of Venice,' ' Romeo and Juliet,' ' Hamlet,' ' Macbeth,' and others —have already been published. Kosétsu Fujisawa, a University man, translated Schiller's ' Jungfrau von Orleans,' and is about to do the same with Schiller's complete works. Ruikō Kuroiwa translated Hugo's ' Les Misérables '; Shūtō Osada, ' La Dame aux Camelias ' of Alexandre Dumas ; and the late Kōyō, even on his death-bed, ' Notre Dame.' Yōtarō Kimura's complete works of Plato has been published. Over and above these classics of established reputation, the public has become so greedy of information about current events that every leading daily in Tōkyō and Ōsaka contains in its columns Reuter's telegrams concerning the literary world.

Translation of literature.

If we enumerate the names of literary masters, who have in turn exercised an absorbing influence upon our mental life, we find, in 1894, Tolstoi and Ibsen ; in 1896, Sudermann, Hauptmann, and Björnson ; in 1897, Maupassant ; in 1898, Turgenief ; in 1901, Nietzsche ; in 1902, Gorky, Maeterlinck, Ibsen, Tolstoi, Sienkiewicz, Jokai, Merejkowski ; in 1903, Chekoff and Wagner. In this way hardly a week has passed without some fresh interpretation of Western literature. We have noted Schiller's centenary celebrated by scholars of German literature ; and an Ibsen number was published on that great dramatist's death. Such periodicals as the ' *Téikoku Bungaku* ' and the ' *Waséda Bungaku* ' (a revived form of that previously mentioned) now present us with information relating to Western literature practically up to date—that is to say, with a delay of a month only.

Continental literature as a fashion. It may be mentioned, in passing, that our reading public at the moment seems largely inclined towards Continental rather than English literature. Doubtless Russians were unaware of our familiarity with their Tolstoi, Gorky, and Sienkiewicz, even prior to the outbreak of the late war.

The amount of Western literature rendered into our language or discussed by our critics, though we may assume that it aggregates ten times that done by foreigners in the matter of our own literature, is barely more than a fraction of the whole, and if we are to have anything comparable to that valuable treasury, the ' Reclam ' series, we must look to the coming generation.

We may here interpose a remark as to the attitude assumed by our translators and readers towards translation. When the former translate, it is rather as transcribers than as interpreters, and when the latter read a translation, their first idea is to estimate how far the attempt has been successful rather than to obtain from it a clear conception of the original. It is therefore erroneous to infer Japanese familiarity with the range of European literature merely from the number of translated works, for our educated classes are qualified to appreciate the untranslated literatures of Western nationalities, just as any people of Europe bring their own linguistic acquirements to the study of a neighbour's literature. An exact precedent for this state of affairs may be found in the ancient days when the Chinese classics were greedily devoured by our nation.

Even in the realm of the drama, which I have intentionally Drama. left thus far untouched, the same may be observed in rather a marked way, though in the matter of progress this branch of literature is somewhat belated. Men's minds are at present in doubt between the traditional and the new school, although a call for some improvement of the national drama was heard as far back as twenty years ago, when men who had been abroad—Kenchō Suyématsu and Génichiró Fukuchi being the more distinguished leaders of the movement—organized a club under the name of the Association for Improvement of the Drama, seconded by a body of scholars, men of letters, and wealthy merchants.

Our national drama, originally a humble adaptation of the *Nō* literature, passed through various stages of elaboration during the Tokugawa epoch, and was finally enriched by many an excellent play, which even Aston apparently found in excess of his expectations. Still it remained little more than a mere pastime of the middle and lower classes of the population, and was far from being an object of general interest, dealing as it did too often with obscene and sanguinary subjects. Much commendation was therefore due to the Association's efforts in the cause of progress, which did much towards the removal of these defects, as well as the improvement of theatrical architecture, accommodation, and the elevation of the actors' social position, which had, until then, been little above that of beggars. So far was this last change carried that the Emperor honoured a theatrical performance with his presence in 1887, and the drama was at once raised to an eminence almost equal to that of its sister arts. Moreover, the student class, whose visits to a theatre would have been absolutely inconceivable in former days, came to assume an important *rôle* as dramatic critics, and in 1893 a playgoers' club, called the *Aoba Kai*, was formed by students of the Tōkyō and Waséda Universities.

The late Danjūrō Ichikawa, generally admitted to have Danjūrō been the greatest of modern actors, and placed by some even Ichikawa. above the English Irving, acquired such a high reputation by his repeated successes in an age specially propitious to the drama, that, in his later years, it is said, he lived in a kingly manner. As has been the case at all times, however, the fundamental reform of the drama had to commence with that of the plays.

Innovation of drama. Until now it had found its patrons solely among the elders, men of comparatively conservative taste, and this at once prevented the introduction of daring innovation, a new play being liable to evoke condemnation at the hands of devotees of the old *régime* without obtaining the appreciation of those of the young generation. Tsubouchi's adaptation of 'Julius Cæsar' (1883) and Mori's of one of Calderon's works and Lessing's 'Emilia Galotti' (1899) were valuable only as illustrations of the new ideal, not as popular plays. The gradual passing away of this older generation, and the advent of men who have received a more advanced education, raise one's hope for the advent of a national drama—a hope already partially realized.

Dr. Tsubouchi on the drama. Dr. Tsubouchi, who played the part of pioneer in romance literature, has done the same for the stage. His article 'On Historical Plays,' contributed to the '*Waséda Bungaku*' in 1893, was mainly directed towards giving a genuine conception of the drama of former days, showing that phantasmagoria were the fundamental features of the *Kabuki* drama, and inculcating the importance of personification in a play, and protesting against the superficial innovations which had been limited to the form of the drama. In truth, so occidentalized were his views, that his essay on historical plays provoked a controversy and cleared the way for a general renovation.

Tsubouchi's plays. It seems to have been Tsubouchi's cherished ambition to shine in dramatic literature. As for his novel writing, we have nothing new since his '*Imo-to-Sé Kagami*' ('A Mirror of Husband and Wife') and '*Saikun*' ('Wife'). To illustrate his dramatic principles he wrote two plays, '*Kiri Hitoha*' ('The Last Leaf of the *Kiri*-tree') (1895), and '*Maki-no-Kata*' ('The Lady Maki') (1896), the former of which deals with the tragic loyalty of Katsumoto Katagiri in the last campaign of the Toyotomi family, and the latter has the Lady Maki, Tokimasa's widow, as its heroine. In 1897 he wrote another play, '*Hototogisu Kojō no Rakugétsu*,' a sequel to the '*Kiri Hitoha*.'

His most striking innovation was the embodiment of a Shakespearean spirit in traditional forms. Though his plays could not be called popular for acting purposes, they served to stimulate young playwrights essaying the composition of historical plays.

And now as to our actors. Otojirō Kawakami (see ii. 390) deserves special notice as the founder of a new school of drama, commonly called the student or *Sōshi* drama, which was started as early as 1892. Actors of this school sought by means of vivid lifelike realism to atone for deficiencies in the consummate training in theatrical dancing and gestures possessed by actors of the old style. They chose pieces well suited to the public taste, especially depicting the hurly-burly of battle scenes, for public attention was then concentrated on the China-Japan War. Thus they won much more popularity than they deserved, being finally welcomed at the best theatres in Tōkyō and Ōsaka. Their number increased so much that, grouped under the name of ' New Players,' they were able to compete even with the old school. *Sōshi drama.*

In 1900 Kawakami, with his actress-wife, Sadayakko, visited Paris at the time of the Exhibition, and the next year they with their troupe repaired again to Europe, where, offering more or less imperfect representations of their country's drama, they won an unexpected fame. In these repeated trips to Europe and America the Kawakamis and their troupe became acquainted not only with the stage construction and machinery of Europe and America, but also with methods and impersonations of first-class actors and actresses, which lessons they could not have learned otherwise. *Kawakami.*

On their return, Kawakami, on the strength of his European and American trips, put upon the stage adaptations of ' Othello ' and ' Hamlet,' under the elevated title of the ' Classic Drama,' thus taking advantage of the fact that Japanese playgoers had tired of the traditional drama. His innovations were not confined to the choice of plays : it extended even to matters of subordinate importance in theatrical management, e.g. shortening the intervals between the acts, reforms in the ticket system, &c. *Kawakami's so-called ' Classic Drama.'*

In 1902–3 the three stars of the older school—Danjūrō,

Kikugorō, and Sadanji—successively passed away, and a sudden blight fell upon it. This was naturally all in favour of the new school, which has since grown in importance, its ascendancy being materially assisted by support from the younger generation. Translations of ' Othello ' or ' Hamlet ' could only be appreciated by men educated under the new *régime*, who are pleasantly reminded of their experiences as students in the class-room when they see a Shakespearean adaptation at the Hongō Theatre.

Transla-tions of plays.

This being so, it was of primary importance to act some-thing new to the new race of playgoers. One of the various expedients to satisfy this was the dramatization of novels by contemporary authors. In this even the older school frequently vied with new players. Besides, popular Western plays were acted in Japanese, so that nowadays ' King Lear,' ' Othello,' and ' The Merchant of Venice,' Schiller's ' Wilhelm Tell,' Hugo's ' Hernani,' Pellico's ' Francesca,' Daudet's ' Sappho,' and one of Kleist's dramas are frequently put on both town and country stages. Though far from being exact or perfect from a literary point of view, these representations are character-istic of our most recent tendency, which, every day growing more weary of the traditional stage, yearns for a more liberal cosmopolitanism. In this way much that is necessarily crude and unnatural, not to say wholly unintelligible, in these render-ings is unchallenged, simply because it comes from a foreign source, just as men had heartily enjoyed the novels of Lytton and Disraeli two decades previously without any insight into their political import. In short, Shakespeare, though in his barest outlines, and even the phantoms of the European drama, are preferred to the more substantial and original works of Tsubouchi and Mori, though the former's ' *Maki-no-Kata* ' and ' *Kiri Hitoha* ' and the latter's ' *Urashima* ' and ' *Tsuji Seppō* ' (' Wayside Preaching ') were mounted on the stage with much brilliancy.

Dramatic chaos.

Chaos is thus the term most applicable to the present state of our dramatic literature. As for the pleasure of offering something like national drama for the criticism of foreign visitors, we must look to the future, say some fifteen years hence, during which interval the new tendencies not yet fully developed will have joined hands with tradition, and plays of high literary value will be performed by actors in full sympathy with their parts.

With the revival of the Nō literature, the increasing Opera. popularity of Western music, and various essays on Wagner, people gradually began to speak of the opera. Dr. Tsubouchi was also one of the leaders here. He published an essay on the opera ('New Studies in the Opera'), 1905, in the midst of the Russo-Japanese War, together with two original opera-like pieces, 'Shinkyoku Urashima' ('A New Play of Urashima') and 'Kaguya Himé' ('Lady Kaguya'), both founded on ancient Japanese semi-mythological traditions. But however far theories may be advanced, the opera problem will remain unsolved in Japan until a musical genius arises.

A scheme is now in progress among some of the Tōkyō upper classes for the establishment of a model theatre—a welcome project, even though, as some maintain, it suggests little serious purpose for the furtherance of the actor's art.

Thus far I have tried, though cursorily, to show how eagerly, since the long-cherished policy of seclusion was abandoned, Occidental literature has been introduced and how sympathetic-ally it has been appreciated here in Japan.

The old educational institutions attached to the fiefs of New feudal days, though they ceased to have any material existence literature. after the Restoration, are now regaining something of the spirit in which they nourished and reinspired our healthy nationalism immediately blind pluto-Occidentalism gave way to a more prudent eclecticism, and the ethical system, on which our school education is built, came to be amalgamated with the moral principles believed in by our ancestors. Just the same may be said with regard to the present literary tendency. Old Japanese classics, thrown aside as worthless in the earlier years of the present era, gradually recovered their prestige towards the middle period under review, and every thinking man now looks for the renovation of our literature in a felicitous confluence of Occidental and Oriental thought. As in science, education, and military arts, so in literature we are aware of our debt to the nations of the West. The consciousness of the deep significance of literature in life, the elevation of the social position held by men of letters, the embodiments of the national spirit that we possess in a new form of poetry in our mother tongue—while, heretofore, our versification was almost entirely confined to comparatively fragmentary *hokku*, sonnet-like, epigrammatic stanza-poems, or short couplets in classic Chinese,—all these we owe to the increasing prevalence of studies in Western literature.

A knowledge of æsthetics and of the art of modern literary criticism paved the way to the comparative study of Occidental and Oriental productions, which again appreciably contributed to the evolution of the novel and the drama ; for in the novel our people, no longer satisfied with descriptions of mere facts incidental to political plots, have come to look for distinct character delineation and subtle description of minute details ; while in the drama, conventional intrigues, based solely on the transient effects of right and wrong, are replaced by the far loftier character play ; and even in music repeated attempts have been made to bring forth something like opera by mastering and utilizing Western musical principles, and excellent lyrics are now being abundantly produced.

I must end this chapter without further comment on recent interesting developments and phases in our novels, poetry, and drama, except to say that the Western influence is equally unmistakable in one and all of them. Tsubouchi, Mori, and Natsumé are well known as profound scholars of Western literature. The hero of the ' *Konjiki Yasha*,' the greatest masterpiece of Kōyō, the novelist, is such a person as would have been inconceivable in pre-Restoration times. The ideas set forth by Rohan, the novelist and poet, in his epic, ' *Shutsuro*,' would be almost entirely unintelligible to those ignorant of Western poetry.

Fortunately for us, we are now honestly assimilating the beauties and excellences peculiar to Western literature without thereby injuring in the least our own individual characteristics and personalities.

XXIII

SOCIAL CHANGES IN NEW JAPAN

Professor Sakutarō Fujioka, D.Litt. (Japan)

Supposing that a man born fifty years ago returned to Japan Japan fifty years ago. after a wandering life in a foreign country without any news from his fatherland, how many of the scenes before him would resemble those of his childhood ? Very few indeed. To commence with : he would find no trace of the Shōgun, the real ruler of his childhood, and no *daimyō*, except as peers, and these of little higher standing than the commoners, except in name. The castles of the *daimyō*, once so magnificent, would now show themselves to him as a mass of crumbling ruins ; the spears, swords, and other implements of warfare, which he regarded with awe as a child, he would only find preserved by amateurs as objects of historic interest. What were then poor sea-shore hamlets, with only a few fishermen's cottages lying scattered about, would now be transformed into great naval ports or prosperous towns, such as Yokosuka, Sasébo, and the like. Would he be able to believe that this is the selfsame country wherein he was born and spent his young days ? The bewilderment of Urashima-Tarō (the Rip Van Winkle of Japan), who found, on his return from the Dragon's Palace, that both his family and house were gone, and that the tall trees in his garden were offsprings of the tiny plants he had known, would be identical with those of our supposed *revenant*. The scientific progress of the nineteenth century has brought about general improvement, and produced a great metamorphosis in all European countries, but this metamorphosis, remarkable as it is, is as nothing when compared with that which Japan has undergone in the past fifty years.

Changes and their cause.

What is the cause of this miraculous change ? Putting aside, for the moment, the various political factors which accelerated it, we must look for an explanation in social causes. It was simply a result of the people's determination to throw off the yoke under which they had struggled during a feudal *régime* seven hundred years. The two chief reforming powers, among many minor ones, of modern Japan have been Nationalism and Occidentalism. To the casual observer it would seem that Nationalism, which insists on the rejection of foreign civilization and on the retention of national features, and Occidentalism, which admires all things Western and advocates the adoption and imitation of Western enlightenment, are from their very nature incompatible. Yet, strange as it may sound, these two apparently conflicting principles acted hand in hand in fighting the old system and old usages in Japan, and finally succeeded in completely overthrowing the influences which had so long controlled the mind of the nation.

Return to ancient times.'

The Nationalism of those days was indeed nothing but Restoration. Its adherents believed that the political, social, and other numerous evils, which had arisen since the Middle Ages, were the result of partaking of foreign civilization to excess. They argued that Confucianism, which had come from China, had given them delicate rules of ethics, but at the same time had left many evil influences, and that Buddhism, likewise, imported from the same land, had had the effect of leading the people into negativism, pessimism, and morbid sentimentalism. Owing to these two teachings, men's actions had become artificial and hypocritical. To wipe out these evils of alien civilization, people must return to their old ways —return to nature, as it were, when they were free from all foreign influences. They must retrace their steps to those of their ancestors. So they began to study ancient history and ancient literature, and some of the results soon became clearly visible.

Renaissance of ancient customs.

Funerals, for instance, which had long been conducted according to the Buddhist ceremony, are now performed to a great extent according to *Shintō* rites. Formerly *Shintō* shrines used to resemble Buddhist temples in structure, but now they follow the simple type of ancient buildings. In the present uniforms worn by legal officials, lawyers, and artists, one can clearly recognize the renaissance of the old court robes. These are some of the examples illustrating the retrograde movement caused by the cry ' Return to the old times ! '

That Occidentalism was the main cause of the recent changes we need hardly say. Up to half a century ago, the nation, avoiding all intercourse with foreigners, indulged in the happy dream that the Japanese were the mightiest nation under the sun. What was their surprise, then, when they were brought face to face with the civilization of the West ? An ignorant man, born in a mountain village and suddenly taken to the seashore and shown the boundless expanse of water and the rolling of gigantic waves, could not be more astounded than they were. Western civilization, which was the fruit of Christianity and of the scientific progress of the nineteenth century, seemed a marvel of marvels to them. But soon wonder gave place to admiration, which, in its turn, became a desire to import this civilization into their own country. As a reaction from their former pride, they now passed to the other extreme, namely, a sense of humiliation, and they became keenly anxious to take in everything Western. Thus politics, economics, natural science, and art—everything was taken from the West with insatiable avidity, and the customs and usages of the people underwent a complete change, so complete that those alone who witnessed it can believe it.

Admiration for Western civilization.

Naturally most of these changes originated in Government offices, companies, and other public concerns, and then gradually found their way to the people at large. To cite some instances of the change : European clothes were at first used by officials as ceremonial costumes ; then they were found very convenient to work in, and consequently came into popular use. Formerly holidays were limited to the five *sékku* festivals and a few other occasions, but now Sunday has been made a day of universal rest. To-day even private people, who can afford it, live in large European houses, and many in the middle class furnish one or more rooms of their Japanese houses in European style and use them as studies or drawing-rooms. Foreign restaurants are met with almost everywhere, and often the tourist finds European dishes served in a Japanese hotel.

Instances of European influence.

Indeed, there is no Japanese homestead wherein one does not find some marks of Western influence.

Women's dress. What determines the mode of women's dress is, in all countries, beauty of appearance rather than practical convenience ; and since each nation has its own fancy, any change in female costume is naturally not so rapid as in that of men's. Nevertheless, the now popular use of the European style of hairdressing cannot fail to strike any observer, as also the prevalence of the *hakama* or skirts among the school-girls, though doubtless this is an imitation of the man's skirt, and supported by ancient usage, but it must have been encouraged by the dress worn by the fair sex of the West.

More instances. Until fifty years ago people did not know that the flesh of pigs and cows was eatable, or that coal was combustible ; they had no petroleum lamps and no waggons drawn by horses. They had only black-and-white drawings and paintings in light colours, and they pleased their ears with the *koto* (harp) and *samisén* (three-stringed guitar). But to-day foreign oil paintings and water colours have many admirers, and the piano and the violin are more fashionable than the native instruments. Formerly novelists and dramatists received no honour, while actors were despised as an inferior class of men, but now the drama is recognized as the highest form of art.

Change and the national spirit. To go into further examples would be only tedious and unduly swell the present article ; so I shall confine myself to a general statement, and will proceed to consider the spirit which has governed and directed all these changes. It should be clearly understood that, wonderful and complete as the outward transformation has been, not one jot or one tittle of the nation's innate character has been allowed to change. Consequently we rest perfectly content with our altered aspect, and even pride ourselves on the successful introduction of a new civilization. True, there are some aged people who lament the good old days and old customs, and we too are aware that in some instances the change has been too uncontrolled and that some old customs might have been preserved. Still, we regard our new garb as an improvement, on the whole, and when we speak of the social change, we naturally dwell more upon the evils that have been done away with than on the good features that have been unfortunately lost.

The first of the series of social changes in modern Japan was the destruction of social rank.   Before the Restoration it was necessary, for the maintenance of peace and order, to attach great importance to classes and ranks.   Roughly speaking, people were graded into four classes : *samurai*, farmers, artisans, and merchants, or more roughly into the two main classes of aristocrats (*shibun*) and commoners (*héimin*).   These ranks were strictly defined, and every individual had to rest contentedly in his own sphere.   The *daimyō* were placed at the head of the aristocrats, and such was their authority that, if a merchant or a farmer met a *daimyō's* procession, he was bound to take off his shoes and prostrate himself on the road.   Should a commoner offend a *samurai*, the latter was at liberty to slay him with his sword.   It was regarded as a special honour for a commoner to be permitted to assume a family name or to wear a sword.   A commoner, however wealthy, was not allowed to wear clothes made of *rinzu* (figured satin) or to ride in a palanquin.   There were many varieties in the use of honorific terms according to rank, and complicated rules had to be observed in writing to and in addressing a superior.

Destruction of social rank.

This gulf between the two classes finally brought on a difference between them in literary and other tastes.   Thus the *samurai* composed Chinese and Japanese poems, while commoners expressed their sentiment in less dignified forms of poetry, *kyōka* and *haikai*.   The former class took delight in the paintings of the Tosa and Kanō schools, but the latter's favourites were the *Ukioyé*, which were more gorgeously coloured, and appealed to the popular taste.   The *Nō* (opera) and the *koto* belonged to the former ; the theatre, the *jōruri* (drama-songs), and the *samisén* to the latter.   The former played *go* (checkers), but the latter diverted themselves with *shōgi* (chess).

Difference of tastes between the two classes.

The upper class was conservative, and adhered to old traditions with fidelity ; the lower class was progressive and inclined to novelties, though their tastes were vulgar and their manners unrefined.   Yet this system of classes, strict as it was, was shattered by the reformation as completely as if it had

Growth of equality.

been a piece of glass struck by an iron hammer. There exists, it is true, a distinction between the *samurai* class (*shizoku*) and commoners (*héimin*), but the distinction is entirely nominal. Now every one is perfectly free to use any style of dress that pleases his fancy, except at court or on ceremonial occasions. Now in addressing another, *anata* (you) is polite enough for most people, and *watakushi* (I) humble enough. The sharp difference in tastes between the two classes has been toned down to a considerable extent, and equality is gaining ground day by day.

Impor-
tance of
genealogy
in feudal
ages.

The strict class system of former days was necessarily attended by the attachment of great importance to genealogy. From time immemorial people took fond delight in inquiring into the genealogy of one another, and the class system itself was to a great extent encouraged by this fancy. The mighty Hidéyoshi, having no ancestors to be proud of, found it necessary to conceal his humble origin by assuming the family name of Toyotomi. Iyéyasu, too, thought it wiser to use his forefather's dignified title, *Junna-Sōgaku-Ryōin-no-Bettō*, and thereby invest himself with greater authority. Even the mightiest general dared not endorse openly the well-known Chinese saying :

Is there a seed decreed to grow
A king, a general, a chancellor ?

Since genealogy was so important, people were in mortal fear lest their houses should come to an end, and thought themselves bound by duty to see that such a disaster did not happen in their generation. In their eyes the family was everything, and the individual nothing. A man was worth regarding only in the capacity of a member of a family. He worshipped the guardian gods of his house, but none of his

Develop-
ment of
indivi-
dualism.

own. His retainers, for the most part, were not hired servants, but constituted a sort of real estate which might be bequeathed to later generations. The house, with its entire property, was practically entailed upon eldest son and eldest grandson, this custom being an outcome of the high estimation in which the ancestral line was held, and of the desire to keep the property of the house undivided. Should a man have no male issue, he adopted some one to continue the house ; and should his son—even a real son—prove unworthy of maintaining the family honour, he was liable to be disowned and expelled. This family system, so strict and so important, began to die away with the collapse of the social classes, and now few would listen with reverence to any boast of heraldry or of the exalted names of ancestors. People have been converted to the new notion that man should create his status by his own capacity, and that self-made dignity alone adorns him.

When the class system was preserved with so much strictness, people naturally pursued the avocations of the house rather than their own choice. For instance, the carpenter's son became himself a carpenter, and a farmer's children were all brought up to follow the plough. A son who departed from his father's business was despised, and it was taken for granted that he would fail. Consequently, each man had a peculiar appearance which his respective family occupation conferred on him, so that on sight of him even a stranger could tell whether he was an artist, carpenter, or mason. Disappearance of family occupations.

Another institution which grew up side by side with this hereditary succession of occupations was the strict custom of revering and following one's teacher. A pupil was taught to walk ' seven feet in the rear of his instructor, lest he should tread on the latter's shadow.' The teacher showed the way and the pupil had only to follow it. Hence the pupil was not allowed to depart a step from the teacher's instructions : he was permitted to reproduce but forbidden to improve. It is not surprising, therefore, that the teacher should have become more sparing of his teaching as the pupil advanced, or that he should have tried to sanctify his art by surrounding it with all manner of mythical traditions. If the pupil happened to be of a free and ungovernable turn of mind, and attempted to add his own devices to what was imparted to him, he was certain to provoke his instructor's wrath, and even became liable to be ' excommunicated.' With the advent of the Méiji era, however, everything became free, and every individual was set at liberty to do anything or follow any course. In the choice of occupations, there is no longer now any restriction to fetter the ambition of young people, and the son of a statesman may become an engineer, and a farmer's boy Decline of respect for teachers.

may join the army. At the same time, the teacher's word
has ceased to be immutable law, and a school-boy regards
his master as nothing more than a temporary guide along the
pathway of practical business life. This new tendency has
been pushed to such an extreme that 'strikes' amongst students
are not unseldom, as though they were labourers. With
such freedom in the choice of business, the typical appearances
which formerly marked the different classes of people have
disappeared, and by a mere glance at a man in his *haori* and
hakama, it is hard to tell whether he is an official or a merchant.

Results of the negative policy.
    In the days when avocations were handed down from father
to son and when social ranks were observed strictly, things
were bound to be in the negative, and consequently men
had to live in contentment and frugality. In such a time
a trader, however clever and able, stood no chance of ever
becoming a *daimyō*, and if a son should lose his family's
property by reason of inordinate ambition, he would be called
an unnatural son and be despised by all men. Every man
naturally chose to live, under these circumstances, in his
ancestral homestead, to engage in his hereditary occupation,
and to lead a peaceful life, rather than to run so much risk.

    Such was, doubtless, the result of the policy followed by
the Shōgun's Government, which tried to maintain the order
of society by diminishing as far as possible the difference in
the wealth of the people and removing the cause of their
complaints. Nevertheless, we cannot deny that it went far
to check progress and fossilize the nation. The policy of
seclusion and the prohibition against new theories and inventions were alike the outcome of this principle. A season was
prescribed by law for each kind of land produce, and green-
grocers were warned, on pain of punishment, against introducing to market vegetables and fruits previous to these seasons.
Clothes, too, were placed under restrictions, and each man
was allowed to use materials only worth so much, according to
his status. At one time the use of lacquered *géta* (clogs) and
hairdressing by professional coiffeurs were deemed extravagant,
and prohibited. People were not permitted to use the crest of
the hollyhock leaf, since it was the arms of the Shōgun's family.
The flesh of storks was served only at the Shōgun's table,

so they might not be caught. Silver was the costliest material of which hair ornaments for commoners' wives might be made. They used silk as the lining only of their dresses, and hawk's-bill turtle-shell was employed under the name of tortoise-shell, so as to avoid the charge of luxury. A traveller in the interior even now finds papers bearing two Chinese characters signifying ' frugality ' stuck up on the posts of houses side by side with periapts, and is strongly reminded of the negative policy that was encouraged and followed up to our father's days.

This hermit people, which led such a peaceful and simple life, were happy and contented in spite of the low grade of their material progress, yet the mighty whirlwind of the Restoration, which shook the community to its very foundation, could not but crush this policy also. Thus, when old bigoted restrictions were removed and a new world dawned on the principle that where there is genius, there also are position and wealth, how could young people, full of energy and ambition, remain contented in the old homes of their fathers ? Everyone, therefore, formed new schemes and attempted new enterprises, and out of the struggle poor people came out millionaires, while many a *samurai* of noble family sank to the rank of a beggar. Peer or commoner, one is now free to do anything and to indulge in any luxury. If one is rich enough, nothing prevents one from living like a king. In a word, the extremely negative age has given place to an extremely positive age.

It need hardly be mentioned that, with the loss of ranks and classes, the gulf between the city and the country has also been filled up. In the feudal age, when the *daimyō* ruled their respective dominions and governed their people according to their liking, the inhabitants of some districts lived in comparative ease and happiness, while the people of other districts were grievously oppressed. And it was by no means uncommon for people in adjoining fiefs to be on bad terms and even to fight with each other. The Shōgun's Government had made it a point of their policy to take advantage of this, and had placed the *daimyō* in such positions as to restrain one another, thus rendering impossible the concentration of united power against the Shōgun. To that end the empire was parcelled out into different sections, and no attempt was made to facilitate

Gradual disappearance of local differences.

traffic in the country. Even the busiest route, that of the
Tōkaidō, was blocked at the two *sékisho* (guard stations)
Hakoné and Arai, where all travellers were subjected to exami-
nation, and no bridges were allowed to be built over the
Fujikawa, Ōigawa, and Tenryūgawa. The result was that
Kyōto and Ōsaka, only twenty odd miles apart, had each its
peculiar customs, not to speak of the two capitals Kyōto and
Yédo (Tōkyō).

Formerly, by glancing at the accoutrements of a procession,
one could tell what *daimyō's* it was, and likewise the *samurai*
belonging to each *daimyō* had their own peculiar language and
manners. But the introduction of the telegraph and telephone,
the steamer and the railway has contracted ten thousand
miles to ten steps, and these facilities, assisted by the general
diffusion of knowledge among the people, are yearly lessening
the distance between districts, and bridging the gulf between
city and country. Every new fashion in the capital finds its
way to all parts of the land in a short time ; the different
manners and customs in the land have become fairly uniform,
and the variety of dialects, one of which used often to be
entirely unintelligible to the speakers of another, are now
gradually settling into a common form.

Criticism that Japan is now essentially the same as before the Restoration.

To sum up, until the Restoration a family formed the
unit of the community, whereas an individual is the unit
now. Formerly, with the view of maintaining order, social
ranks were emphasized ; now equality is the ruling principle.
Formerly obedience was exacted ; now freedom is granted.
Naturally these changes in principle and policy could not fail to
affect every phase of life, and the consequent transformation
was quite unprecedented in the annals of this country, and
probably in those of other countries also. This is, as I have
said, the result of Nationalism and Occidentalism—especially
the latter. Some argue that all these changes in modern
Japan consist in imitation of foreign civilization, that her
progress is only outward and superficial, and that she remains
essentially the same as before. ' Whereas,' say they, ' there
is so much talk about philanthropy, liberty, and the like in
Japan, how much are the individual's rights regarded ? People
use machines cleverly, but have any Japanese tackled the

heights of science and attempted original inventions ? Many discuss Shakespeare and Goethe and criticize Michael Angelo and Raphael, but in what chaos are their own literature and art ! Rome was not made in a day. Clever as the Japanese may be, it is not possible for Japan to equal Europe and America all of a sudden. What they have done is artful disguise and nothing more.'

This argument has a semblance of reason, but in reality it is a superficial view. Japan never could jump to the top of a tower without climbing the stairs step by step. Her civilization is a bridge built on sound abutments, and challenges any flood. She has a history of twenty-five centuries, and this history is the basis of all her present progress. Western enlightenment has acted as her guide, but she has had the power of discriminating and weighing every part of it. The West gave stimulus and Japan advanced ; that has been the true nature of her development.

Some foreign critics have said : ' The Japanese people are incapable of appreciating colours. Their paintings chiefly consist of lineal strokes, and though occasionally thin colouring is used, the results fall far short of accurately depicting objects. Their garments are mostly dark-striped and they dwell in poor buildings with little decoration. Their taste has no place for brilliancy or grandeur, and they do not understand harmony of colours. Their conversation is marked by monotony of tone and meagreness of gesture ; it is all level-toned and gloomy. Their countenances seldom express emotion. In a word, the Japanese are an extremely uninteresting and prosaic nation.' *Criticism of Japanese character.*

This criticism by no means does justice to the true nature of the Japanese people. Among the traits of the Japanese mind and character there are some which have persisted since the Middle Ages, while others are deformation and distortion of ancient characteristics. And though we are indebted to Western influences for much of our recent change, yet we may also say we have returned in many respects to pre-medieval ages. The scholar of Japan and the Japanese of modern times should not study only her feudal age, but should also take into consideration the fact that the people are the descendants of the refined men and women of the old Imperial ages.

*Bushidō
and its
effects.* It is universally thought that the term *Bushidō* is one that best expresses the Japanese characteristics, but it should be remembered that its signification has not been the same through all ages. Of course such virtues as loyalty, patriotism, and bravery have always constituted essential elements of the Japanese spirit, but other elements were gradually imported into it during feudal ages. *Bushidō* was influenced and modified by a long succession of terrible wars, by the teaching of Confucius, who encouraged practice and disdained theory, and, lastly, by the doctrine of the Zen sect of Buddhism, which teaches that ' the Three Worlds exist only in the mind,' and that 'life and death are but one and the same thing.' To this were added many more qualities, such as self-control, self-renunciation, and contentment with a simple life. Hence it was the duty of a *samurai* to equip himself with all chivalrous accomplishments and to study the art of governing a country and a house, and it was considered unbecoming for him to indulge in the drama, fiction, or singing. He also thought it beneath his dignity to weep or laugh, and he tried to prevent his sorrow or joy from showing in his face. Nay more, he must not grieve or rejoice. Life is like a die ; which side turns up one knows not. If one attains to wisdom one may live in tranquillity, leaving all the rest to destiny. But he must guard against extravagance, as it is the source of all evils. Since much treasure is the cause of much anxiety, the best way to live is to put up with want and restrain one's desires.

That is the gist of the doctrine of modern *Bushidō*. But, as may easily be seen, it was fatal to the flowery life of the Nara age, whose traces were completely wiped out in time. Thus the making of butter was given up ; the spoon was supplanted by a pair of chop-sticks ; hats and shoes were put out of use ; the long pendant sleeves of the *hitataré* (robe) were cut down; and the women's rich long hair was tied up to facilitate work. Furthermore, women's *hakama* (skirt) was abolished, all gorgeous colours were despised, and clothing, furniture, and house decoration assumed the dark rusty tints we now see in them to-day.

But it would be a mistake to think that the Japanese were like this in all times. Every tourist is acquainted with Nara—that beautiful spot where so many spend a pleasant half-day playing with the tame deer in the woods of the Kasuga shrine—this Nara had its flourishing era many ages ago. It was the ancient capital of Japan. It was, like Italy in Europe, a centre of art and literature, and to-day it is the resort of antiquaries who go about in quest of relics. The age of Nara was an age of beauty and pleasure; its people led, as it were, a life of eternal spring. Just as the medieval Japanese were a nation of will, so the ancient Japanese were a nation of sentiment. They read much poetry and other literary works, but little of ethics and tactics; they were not people of the sword, but people of the pen and the lyre. The Héian shrine, recently built in Kyōto, represents the main edifice of the Imperial Court of that time. How dazzlingly bright are the golden pheasants, the emerald-coloured tiles, and the vermilion pillars. The Court robes, too, were richly and attractively decorated with patterns of flowers, while the houses were no less picturesque. All these were the reflection of the people's extravagant fancy and warm emotion, for self-denial and frugality were not virtues required in those days. Singing Narihira's madrigals in the 'Isé Monogatari' and shedding tears over the characters drawn by the authoress of the 'Genji Monogatari,' the people of the period affected lovers and dilettanti without any thought of effeminacy. Thus the rich tastes and the fiery passions of those ancient people were in strange contrast with the characters of the subsequent feudal ages. The present generation, though in the main they have succeeded to the character and usage of the post-medieval people, have been compelled by the influence of the time to depart in some respects from the Tokugawa period and return to the ancient time. The marvellous change of modern Japan is not the result of copying the West alone, it is also a renaissance of her own ancient civilization.

Flowery days of ancient Japan.

Some people may traverse my argument and say that it is a wrong view of things, and that I have intentionally distorted the picture, so as to minimize the influence of foreign civilization. That is by no means the case. I hold that no nation could have achieved the great development that the Japanese have, without some element of its own to help it, however strong the external influence. My argument is intended for those who insist, through ignorance of historical evidence, that the Japanese characteristics are wholly manifested in *Bushidō*, and therefore the Japanese are deficient in appreciation of literary art. On the other hand, I thoroughly acknowledge the great obligation Japan owes to Europe and America.

Foreign
critics and
Japanese
conserva-
tives.
However, some of our conservative scholars, who take it to heart that the customs and things of Old Japan are daily giving place to Western innovations, cry out that our ancient form must be preserved. Some foreign critics have even been known to say that Japan is losing her peculiar charm year by year, and that the beautiful Eastern paradise is transforming itself into a comical admixture of East and West. Japanese conservatives, pleased to find foreign criticisms chime in with their own argument, warn their countrymen with increased vehemence against foolish imitation of the West. My answer to them is this. We do not doubt the foreign critics' intention to be just, yet most of them look on us with an eye of curiosity. They visit Japan in the hope of seeing something new and strange, and though they have heard of Japan's recent transformation, yet the impression they formerly got from writings such as those of Kaempfer and Siebold led them to expect many traces of Old Japan. They are disappointed to find, on coming over, that Japan is becoming more and more like their own countries—what they wished to see they cannot see. So they rebuke the Japanese, saying: ' Japan has degenerated ! Why does she abandon her own charming disposition for a weird hybrid of native and foreign civilizations ? ' It is for the same reason that foreigners like Kyōto more than Tōkyō. Not only foreigners, but we too regret to return from our visits to Nara or Nikkō. It is not because these places represent Japan of the present day, but because they are full of relics and tell old stories. Likewise, foreigners love paintings by the old masters of the Tosa, Kanō, and Maruyama schools rather than those of

the Méiji era. We also are grateful to these old masters for bequeathing to us beautiful works of art, nevertheless we know that Japanese art cannot remain within its old boundaries, nor must we admit the opinion of conservatives who flatter themselves that their views are endorsed by foreigners, when the latter are really criticizing our things as though they were criticizing curios. For Japan, this is the day of reformation ; the time of conservation has already passed.

That Japan is in a chaotic stage, no one can deny. Nationalism and Occidentalism have, as we have seen, united their powers to grapple with the evils which infested the country before the Méiji era, but now, their common enemy having fallen, they are at variance with each other, sometimes the one getting the upper hand and sometimes the other.

Present chaotic state and future of Japan.

The Japan of the present day gives one the impression that time and space are mixed up in this country, for we see in it a revival of ancient customs and at the same time Western civilization rapidly flowing over the land—in fact, the progress of many centuries and many countries seems to be crammed into one period and one place. Yes, Japan is in a chaotic stage ; yet did not the Russo-Japanese War prove that her old *Bushidō* has harmoniously blended with the latest science and brought about her victories ? Chaos is the avenue to assimilation ; unity must needs be preceded by temporary confusion. What Japan has to do is to hammer and weld the civilizations of the two hemispheres and shape them into one harmonious whole. Things may be in disorder for a time, but this cannot be avoided, and after a while magnificent results will be reaped. In early ages Japan looked to China and Korea for enlightenment, but she has not only surpassed them, but also gained undisputed supremacy in the East. The past is a sure guarantee for the future. In Japan social change is still going on, and while we must acknowledge that things are confused and more or less out of harmony, the fact remains that the change, confusion, and the discord itself are in reality the strongest evidence of the rapid progress of the Japanese nation.

XXIV

THE INFLUENCE OF THE WEST UPON JAPAN

PROFESSOR INAZŌ NITOBÉ, D.AGR., D.C.L. (JAPAN), D.PH.

General
tendency
of the
world.
As microscopy and cytology have discovered organic units in cells, so steam and commerce have reduced sovereign nations into mere units of a larger cosmopolitan form of life. Men, no more bound in spirit to their narrow immediate surroundings, are expanding to be citizens of the world. Aristotle's definition of man as *zōon politicon* applies nowadays to a larger organism than an individual. National isolation is no longer tenable, exclusion is for ever excluded from international politics. The Great Wall of China affords a barrier neither to the aggression of any foreign power nor to the greed of European capital seeking investment within it. The utmost one people can do to exclude another is to erect a high defence of prohibitive tariff and of immigration restrictions—neither of which is strong enough permanently to resist attacks from without or assaults from within. Wonderfully indeed has mankind grown in political instincts, from being a member of a village community to becoming a voice in the federation of the world. This is the undisputed tendency of the modern age— that nations are coming closer and closer in touch one with another, and whoever refuses to join in the union is doomed not only to decay but to destruction.

Neither in Plato's ' Republic ' nor in More's ' Utopia ' is foreign trade highly prized or courted. Bacon advocated exclusion for his ' New Atlantis,' because he ' doubted novelties and commixture of manners.' Campanella, too, did not allow commerce to be carried on within the walls of his ' Civitas Solis.' Fichte in his ' Geschlossene Handels-staat ' is far

458'

from favouring foreign intercourse, upon which he looks as a necessary evil.   Only the latest ideal state, such as Wells or Ellis describes, is co-extensive with or more extensive than the planet.

Japan has learned late, but fortunately not too late in her history, that it is hard to keep aloof from this universal trend of cosmopolitan comity.   Many a psychological explanation is attempted of the sudden emergence of the country into the brotherhood of nations.   Perhaps her rise was no more sudden than that of the sun—slowly and steadily below the horizon it has been rising, rising ; but until its disc appeared above it, few cared to notice what it was doing in the obscurity of the night. *Japan's open door.*

How we have come to abandon the time-honoured policy of exclusivism is now a well-known page in the general history of culture.   The causes which led Japan to take this step belong to what I may term her medieval history, and the chapter of her modern history dates from the influence of the West upon her, as her recent history began with the end of the war with Russia.

What I have now to do is to review the influence of the West—the Europeanization of Japan, or, as it may perhaps be more fitly termed, the Japanization of European influences. I have to depict the approachment—at first shy and suspicious, then more confiding, later blindly bold, and lastly, discriminating and rational—of the West and the East.   This means a study of the blending of two culture grades or the welding of two different types of civilization. *Europeanization of Japan.*

I have said above that I shall treat of the influence of the West upon the East.   I should perhaps be more explicit concerning these terms.   I do not mean by influence, as is often the case, any Western domination, by means of power, money, or intellect.   I use the word in the literal sense of an inflowing of ideas and methods of the Occident into our intellectual, social, and political fabric.   The word ' Occident,' also, is too broad.   Its general use amongst us takes for granted the solidarity of Europe and America, at least as far as culture is concerned, but it is a convenient working term, more comprehensive than a ' state,' which is necessarily selfishly *Influence of the West.*

disposed, and less comprehensive than ' Christendom,' which is too ideal and vague. The Japanese do not always distinguish between different nationalities of the West, for they are content with the larger features of Western civilization, disregarding national idiosyncrasies and details. To them Christianity is a Western religion, and the differences between Protestantism and Catholicism do not trouble them. Demo-cracy is Western, notwithstanding German absolutism or Russian autocracy. Progress is identified in our mind with the West, though geographically Spain and Turkey lie in Europe. Just as, upon first contact, all Japanese look alike to a European, and *vice versâ*, simply because racial character-istics strike us first and individual peculiarities only grow clearer after close acquaintance, so was Aryan culture undivided in Japanese eyes and the whole white race was one. We have but lately come to know the differences between different ethnic groups. Every Japanese knows, and does not forget—nor will Heaven forgive—that it was Russia, Germany, and France that snatched from her the prize of her war with China. The very peasants are aware that England is our ally and America our friend. Friend or foe, we owe much of what we are to the West, and it is this indebtedness which is our present theme.

Things Eastern and things Western.

Very often it is difficult to distinguish the national origin of what we have received. Equally difficult is it to tell what is Eastern and what is Western in the thoughts which guide us. In the spaceless sphere of ideas there exists neither a scientific nor an arbitrary longitude to divide us into East and West. The points of the compass show only directions and not boundaries, much less ideas. To Europe, the East stretches from the Balkans across Syria, Persia, and India to China and Japan, and yet ethnologically and historically what a far cry it is between Syria and India and Persia and Japan ! Is loving one's enemy an Eastern or a Western virtue ? Was it taught by Christianity or some Asiatic religion ? Of course we can put back the inquiry : Is Christianity itself to be called an Eastern or a Western religion ? So again, is local self-government of Eastern or Western origin ? Are trousers a European invention or an Asiatic ? Was it a yellow wife or

a white that made the first dumpling ?   Questions as numerous
as there are objects and subjects might be put.   The constant
exchange of ideas, the action and reaction and counteraction
going on for generations and for centuries, among tribes and
nations, have obliterated many original marks of nationality,
and in some cases even of racial distinctions, so that only by
exaggerating a comparatively few points of difference can one
endorse the language of the poet that

East is East and West is West.·

Differences—the quainter the better—are noticed and stretched
beyond their logical deserts.   Differences there must be
between races and peoples, as there are between tribes and
families—indeed, as there are between brothers and sisters.
But besides differences that run parallel—that will never meet
—are there not many that tend to grow less and less, finally,
perhaps, to merge into unity, and such as are causes of further
differentiation ?   In other words, are not differences either
convergent or divergent ?   The terms East and West, showing
opposite directions, convey on the surface divergent differences,
but we forget that the earth is round, and the so-called farthest
East touches the farthest West.   The East and the West, then,
are also terms denoting convergent and converging differences
on a globe.

The matters in which Japan differs from the Occident are ‘ Topsy-
not always of a divergent kind.   He whose sight is blurred by turvy-
the manifold details of every-day life, customs, and manners, dom.’
might think that Japan is a land of topsy-turvyness, as a good
lady missionary once remarked to an American friend of mine.
‘ Everything is different in Japan,’ she said—‘ cats have no tails,
dandelions are cream-coloured, and chickens’ feathers grow
the wrong way.’   Her interest in heaven had evidently made
her oblivious of a few earthly facts—that in her own country
horses are ‘ bobbed ’; that, while the rarer cream-coloured variety
is peculiar to Japan, she shares with the West the golden
abundance of the orthodox dandelion; that the heterodox breed
of fowl which perturbed her faith in the unity of the human
race is an importation into this country, perhaps from her own.
These things are trivial, but they are symbolic of an attitude

of mind more serious where graver matters are concerned. Beneath all the quaintest and queerest excrescences of social life man remains man—white or black, yellow or brown. In the noble words of Lowell—

> For mankind are one in spirit, and an instinct bears along,
> Round the earth's electric circle, the quick flash of right or wrong.

Moral notions of all races.

Time and place may impose deviations in outward things. They may favour this race with more of this and provide that race with more of that ; but all races can be reduced to a common denominator—which may be broadly called their moral notions. Take any anthropological or ethnological standard, and one easily finds that the variations in our species are more quantitative than qualitative, and especially is this true of an ethical standard, or what the poet called ' the flash of right and wrong.' We are told that a cannibal tribe feels no compunction about homicide. We are told that a certain people deem it an honour to lie, and we are invariably informed in such cases that white men have very soon brought about changes in their notions. The very fact that such changes can be so easily wrought is a sure evidence that the crudest of races can respond to advanced moral ideas. That is to say, that they have something within themselves which can apprehend what is good. George Fox very fitly calls this inborn power ' the Seed.' Do not be surprised, therefore, that cannibals can be made to grasp, without cogitation, principles of European ethics, feel the Hegelian difference between *Moralität* and *Sittlichkeit*, and even comprehend in a good measure the Categorical Imperative of Kant. For my part the surprising thing is that European ethics can be so atavistic as to stoop to a sort of cannibalism ! The most primitive mind can respond to noblest sentiments. Response means affinity and excludes divergence.

Imitation.

It is still a custom among ethnologists, especially of that exceedingly shallow school of Le Bon (if, indeed, a shallowness like his can breed any followers), to neglect this mental affinity and moral sympathy, to accept without due proof that racial differences are irreconcilably distinct, and to infer from this premise that all the changes in Japan during the last five decades are due to mere childish imitation. They little remember that imitation itself—to be good, as ours is said to be —is not possible beyond a certain range unless there is faculty to imitate, nay, intelligence enough to perceive how, why, and what to imitate. Imitation—including adaptability and receptiveness—is a biological and ethical process of the highest importance. As among animals mimicry is a principle of self-preservation, so among individuals it has been a large part of education, and, practised among nations, it has preserved and educated them.

Learn of Emerson, who taught us : ' Great genial power, one would almost say, consists in not being original at all, in being altogether receptive, in letting the world do all, and suffering the spirit of the hour to pass unobstructed through the mind.' If this is true of 'great genial power,' how much more is it so of a large agglomeration of mediocrities, which we call a people. The cultural history of mankind is largely the history of imitation. As Giddings says : ' Modern civilization is the continuing imitation of Greece and Rome.' Only recently, Professor Woodberry, in treating of the ' Race Power in Literature,' has emphasized the fact that always some great culture is dying to enrich the soil for new harvests, some civilization is crumbling to rubbish to be the hill of a more beautiful city, and some race is spending itself that a lower and more barbarous may inherit the stored treasure-house. But how ? Mainly by the lower, or rather a newer and younger race studying, admiring, and imitating its predecessor. 'Follow Me ! ' says the Master, and like sheep on the green meadows, by the still waters, or even to the shambles and sacrificial altars, they follow. The highest that mortals have attained has consisted, like Thomas à Kempis, in imitating Christ. *Civiliza-tion and imitation.*

This is all very well, you say, provided there is a perfect political or social model to follow. But is there such a model ? I contend that the model need not be perfect, if it is only higher than one's own level. ' Find what is superior in your neigh-bours, practise it yourself until you have attained unto it,' has been our teaching. One of the five articles of the Rescripts,[1] with which the present Emperor began his reign, clearly declared this as a guiding principle of his government. We

[1] See Vol. I, p. 141.

have faithfully lived up to it, not without some hope of surpassing our models in a few points.

Japanese
eclecti-
cism.
Japanese eclecticism is a concrete method, whereby Western ideas were adopted and consciously and voluntarily adapted to our own ends. I employ intentionally the word ' ideas,' in order to avert the conception not at all uncommon among misinformed people, that our adoption of Occidentalism—whatever that ' ism ' may imply—is only material and materialistic—that it is only in forms, formalities, and formulae, and therefore merely a superficial veneer. Sure enough, Tōkyō and other large cities are full of trousers covering bow legs, and high collars encircling drooping necks, of silk hats resting on straight black locks. Tourists' eyes are amused at the sight, but this sight, indicative as it is of foreign influence (for clothes are, indeed, the first indication of a psychological change, as they were the first invention after the Fall), is far from being its most serious side. Samples of Western architecture dot many a street in many a town, and they are increasing. They, too, indicate much, but not all. Superficial observers take these as indices of foreign influence, and judge therefrom how far short of the mark we still are. The less superficial study our laws, our courts of justice, our schools, our military system and our navy, and find in varying degrees their efficiency, and conclude therefrom how near the model we have come. What we have accomplished is, as Adelaide Procter beautifully puts it, only ' things of Time,' that ' have voices, speak, and finish,' whereas within our race-capacity lie still, unexplored and unexpressed, illimitable forests and unfathomed seas, whose existence is only surmised by their waves and sighings.

New
Japan.
He alone knows us who can penetrate through the outward covering, the social wraps, the parliamentary garb, the military uniform, and can see the underlying motive by which all these changes were adopted and adapted, and such an one will confess that fifty years of New Japan are no buffoonery. New Japan is, indeed, not an accretion from without of foreign culture. It is the application of innate race-energy to new circumstances, the self-realization of our own strength, the conscious and purposive utilization of world forces.

At the cost of modesty, I may say that there were powers latent, energies dormant within us, or what Aristotle calls *dunamis* (potentiality). To follow the Stagirites a little further, no actuality is possible without potentiality, although, as a matter of fact, the former always precedes the latter. Japan's adoption of Western ideas proves her own *dunamis*, and her adaptation to them is the *entelecheia* so closely related with her energy.

We have had ample experience in assimilating alien thoughts and alien institutions—or, what amounts to the same thing, in adapting ourselves to them. We may say that we have been in the habit of skimming the cream from the milk, irrespective of the breed to which the cow belonged. For centuries previous to the opening of the country, we had been accustomed to view ' the infinitude of social customs and political institutions and vast congeries of philosophical opinions and religious beliefs existent on the Asiatic continent ' as a convenient storehouse from which we could exploit what we best liked for our own peculiar needs. It is but little known, outside of a scientific circle, what a vital place is filled in the evolution of a race by adaptability and receptiveness, two of the primary factors of progressive variation in ethnic psychology. Professor Vierkandt maintains that the real source and centre of all differences between the culture grades of human groups is the one difference between their voluntary and involuntary activities. Brinton, elaborating upon this remark of Vierkandt, adds that ' the latter are instinctive, the former reflective ; the latter are mechanical, the former rational ; the latter are of bondage, the former of freedom.' [1] To any student of the modern history of Japan, it must be obvious to which category the activity of our nation belongs. It is far from me to assert our eclecticism to be a facile and comfortable process of growth like the play of a thriving child. On the contrary, it is accompanied with pains and sorrows of sacrifice—sacrifice which Lord Morley recently and truly calls the law of society and progress. Says he : ' Selfishness and interested individualism have been truly called non-historic. Sacrifice has been the law—sacrifice

Assimilating power of the Japanese.

[1] See Brinton, *The Basis of Social Relations*, pp. 52–61.

for creeds, for churches, for dynasties, for kings, for adored teachers, for native land.' [1]

Difficulties of Europeanization. The history of what I have above called medieval Japan terminated with the opening of its long-closed doors. This act was largely one of non-resistance, or, at least, of passivity. It meant the sacrifice of a national tradition of long duration —the sacrifice of national pride. The conscious and active Europeanization of modern Japan means the sacrifice of the Chinese models of administration and morals. Mr. Boxall, in his ' Anglo-Saxon,' reiterates over and over again the necessity of doing away with the Latin elements in the culture of that race, should it develop to its fulness the measure of stature allotted to it. May we not say that Japan can really and truly be Japanese only by sacrificing Chinese idolism, by a brave iconoclasm that will shatter the joss-houses of the sons of Sinim—that is, by tearing down the Celestial scaffolding whereby we had largely built our edifices ?

To wrest Chinese culture from us will not bleed us to death. It will be like amputating a limb, but never like tearing out a heart ; for in temperament the two peoples are very different. The greatest radical difference, which the most casual observer must notice, between the constitution of Chinese and Japanese society and principles of ethics is the highly developed economic individualism of the Celestials and the equally developed moral individualism of our people. China is a country of shopkeepers, Japan of *samurai*. Whether China is an economic entity or not, it certainly is not a political, whereas Japan is a compact political and moral entity. Foreign influence in China must enter through the warehouses of Shanghai and the workshops of Hangchow. In Japan it works best through the organs of the state and education.

The Occidentalization of Japan is not a natural process in the sense that it takes place under the *régime* of *laissez faire*, being decidedly unnatural in the sense that it is directed by the fostering care of a paternal government. If the breakdown of the system of exclusivism was a passive work, the systematic Occidentalization which followed, and which marks the new era, has been an active and even an aggressive labour of the State.

The Occidentalization of Japan a natural process.

[1] *The Nineteenth Century and After,* April 1905.

A summary glance at the last fifty years of Japan's progress will show that Occidentalization has been a systematically planned work, and that it has gone in an order surprisingly wise and fortunate, and, I might state, truly natural, if not naturalistic. The rapidity with which this process has taken place is the best proof that it has progressed in natural channels. At least, conforming to Tarde's first law, imitation has spread among us in a geometrical progression. I had said its velocity has been in a saltatory ratio. Again, true to his second law, our imitations have been strongly refracted by their media, i.e. by our own national character. Just compare the experiences of the similar process in the Muscovite Empire, as described by Bruckner,[1] and let his readers judge which race understands the West better, Slav or Japanese. Let them compare the wisdom and order by which the work progressed under Peter the Great and Mutsuhito the Enlightened.

It is usual for political philosophers to treat the objects of the State as threefold—might being its primary object, to be followed by the legal safety of its subjects and the cultural care of its citizens.

The oft-repeated tale of the study of Dutch medicine in the latter days of exclusivism belongs, as I have said before, to our medieval history. The new era opened with the application of Dutch knowledge to military research. In fact, prior to the advent of Holland on our shores, simultaneously with the first appearance of Europe in the persons of Portuguese merchants in the sixteenth century, we began foreign trade with the importation of musketry and the knowledge of its manufacture, and even the embassies sent by several *daimyō* to the Papal Court, in the same century, made constant and diligent inquiries. How do Europeans fight? With what engines of war? How are armies formed? How are they fed and clothed? How are they mustered and drilled? In what ways are frontiers guarded? How are forts and fortresses built? Questions like these most naturally exercised the mind of the *samurai* class. Even those who began the study of the Dutch language—yes, the very ones quite advanced in anatomy and *materia medica*—gave up the

---

[1] *Europäisierung Russlands.*

examination of bones and herbs in order to devote themselves
to the more alluring and ambitious task of national defence.
From the study of the body natural to that of the body politic,
there was no impassable barrier.   The study of fortifications,
of naval architecture, of military tactics, of gunnery, were
soon clandestinely carried on.   We had men enough to stand
behind the guns and on the conning towers, but the trouble
was that there was neither a good gun nor a conning tower.
The technical knowledge of war and of coast defence was
the thing most needed and first attended to.   Personified
in Shōzan Sakuma, the introduction of military knowledge

The
Army

was the first effect of foreign intercourse.   Gunnery was
represented by Égawa and military organization by Ōmura.
The military profession, hitherto confined to the *samurai*, was
made general by the law of conscription in 1870, and this,
instead of degrading the two-sworded order to mere boors
in uniform, raised the whole nation, inclusive of the *éta* (pariah),
to the level of defenders of the land.   Great fears were at
first entertained lest such a summary elevation of peasants to
the rank of warriors might weaken the fighting force of the
empire, but there was not lacking an occasion for proving
the calibre of the newly organized army.   The Saigō trouble
in 1877 was an experimental contest between two armies—
one consisting of the pick of the Satsuma *samurai* and the
other of a mixture of all classes.   That war was decided in favour
of our army by conscription, and Japan continued her military
reforms along the lines in which she had already started, first
looking mainly to France for her model, and later to Germany.
The efficiency of the people at large as a fighting force being
now demonstrated, the rest was but a bolder adoption of
foreign means and materials of warfare.

The
Navy.

So with the Navy—the country abounds in sailors and
fishermen, enamoured of the winds and waves, accustomed
to their dangers, and familiar with the crude contrivances of
junk-building and navigation.   Give them a few months'
training in a battleship, cruiser, or torpedo-boat, and let them
don a cap and a blouse, and you may have any number of
blue-jackets—small in stature, no doubt, compared with their
British brethren, but perhaps not less efficient.   Our instructor

in naval affairs was Great Britain, though as early as the middle of the last century the Dutch Government did us great service by demonstrating the importance of a strong navy, furnishing us with the first warship, the *Kankō Maru*, and a staff of officers to teach in the naval academy which she prevailed upon us to establish in Nagasaki.

Into no branch of State activity did foreign influence more quickly, more completely, or more effectively enter than into the art of war. The adoption by us of a Western military system and of military engineering was, in fact, a most fertile marriage of the newest invention in technology with the martial spirit of long training. The fruit of this union was exhibited in the late war, and needs no further comment here.

When the national defences of the country were set fairly agoing, the next requisite of a well-ordered State was brought under examination and found greatly wanting. Laws were discovered to be sadly defective in principles of justice—the rights of men and of citizens were not clearly defined. We may pause here for a while to consider what new principles in law and politics were introduced into modern Japan, or, in other words, how Japan advanced to a jurisdictive State.

Foremost among the ideas borrowed from the West must be enumerated civil liberty and its concomitant—popular representation. Scholars can find traces of these ideas in the early records of the nation. Ultra-patriots may go so far as to detect evidences of popular representation in the earliest dawn of our history. Such a claim may be justified in so far as any institution can be traced back to a primitive conception, there being nothing new under the sun. The Parisian dandy's cane can trace its inception back to the stick with which Adam drove his animals, or to a newer form of the club with which Cain cudgelled his brother. Comparative sociologists and jurists have done much the same thing with political institutions. If the idea of civil liberty was not new to Japan, the Anglo-Saxon interpretation of it was at least novel, convincing, and impressive. It was not surprising that Professor Kéiu Nakamura experienced great difficulty in translating Mill's essay ' On Liberty ' early in the 'seventies, because of lack of proper words in the Japanese vocabulary. Still, common sense guided

Popular representation.

scholars in comprehending what Hallam, Austin, Blackstone, Holland, and Stubbs meant by civil liberty, by political institutions, by representative government.

Liberty.   Strange to say, no one idea finds fuller response on the part of the Japanese than liberty. It is no dogma swallowed whole without due mastication. It is no doctrinaire assertion that is only repeated by rote. Not only have we put it into practice in our political life, but we stand alone for it on Asiatic soil. John Stuart Mill teaches us that civil liberty meant originally, and even now means mainly, protection against the tyranny of political rulers. Japanese history has not been free from tyrants any more than French or Spanish ; but the inborn good taste of the race, if I may say so, its natural sense of moderation and of right proportion, kept the rulers from indulging in excessive despotism. If sometimes the passion of a prince was unrestrained, it was tempered by the teaching that the sovereign is father of the people. The nation was a united family on a large scale, and if patriarchism is not consistent with liberty—they being, indeed, opposed each to the other, beyond a certain limit—the former gave no occasion to cry for the latter, since, as long as *patria potestas* was not oppressive, no need was felt for protection against it. Ignorant of its philosophy, the people had for generations a comparatively free government. It is customary to speak of Patriarchism and Feudalism as terms opposed to Democracy and Freedom, and a patriarchal feudal state is looked upon as an embodiment of all that makes for a bad government. But, strange to say, in the isolated feudal state, and in graded feudal society, there was no small amount of liberty. Certainly Capefigue uttered more than half truth when he wrote : ' La liberté réele n'est que dans l'esprit local et provincial, dans l'inégalité des classes, des contrôles, et des pouvoirs eux-mêmes. L'unité, c'est le despotisme plus ou moins brillamment habillé.' What, then, did the introduction of the Anglo-Saxon idea of liberty accomplish ? It rendered articulate this hitherto unvoiced enjoyment of privileges on the part of the people. It formulated their own sense of right, which had been theirs for generations. And as its character was analysed, its history recounted, and its limits defined, they found that there are wide fields for personal freedom whose stretches they had hitherto but dimly discerned. Thus did the English idea of liberty find easy entrance among us. Not only was it assured among our own selves, but we became its torch-bearers on the Asiatic continent. It was to rescue Korea from the successive tyranny of two despotic powers that our two recent wars were fought. Woe to us if the banner unfurled in Freedom's cause should be stained with the blood of the people over and for whom it was raised !

Closely related to the subject of liberty is that of Constitution. The annals of our history are not entirely lacking in instances of well-meaning rulers who made some attempts at enunciating the guiding principles of their polity. That a government is primarily *for* the people was an oft-repeated statement ; and from this the inference that it is to be *by* the people, though startlingly novel, did not seem unreasonable. If a constitutional government is reasonable, is it good ? If it is good, why not adopt it ? We studied the experiences of other nations, and finding the German constitution as securing best advantages for the Court and Country, we framed ours after its model. Those who clamoured for a parliament as a panacea for all the ills of the body politic are largely disappointed, but I am far from acceding to the views expressed by men so widely apart in sympathy as Pobyedonostseff and Kipling that a representative government is and will be a strictly Anglo-Saxon institution. It is, however, undeniable that a constitutional government is still in its infancy with us, and as to a party government, it is hardly yet born. Improvement on these lines can surely be made by reforms in election law and the like after the pattern of the West ; but nothing permanent can be expected until after the general spread of political education among the people.

Constitutional government.

Regarding other laws, public and private, the influence of Europe is so obvious that it scarcely requires anything more than mention. Different codes have been promulgated one after another in the last forty years. As far back as 1869 the Government began to frame a Civil Code ; but, though the Code Napoléon was taken as a model, the delicate task of adapting it to the customs and sentiments of the country

Laws.

did not advance with rapidity. In the meantime a rough sketch of a Criminal Code was drawn up and promulgated in 1870, only to be largely modified after two years, and again a year later, by additions which for the first time showed evident marks of foreign influence. In this code, which has assumed its present form since 1888, one notices that French ideas form a prominent part. The Civil Code would have been largely French, had it not been for a sudden admiration in the later 'eighties for a newly issued *Motiven* and *Protocol* of the German *Bürgerliches Gesetz*, and hence a large part of our *Mimpō* (Civil Code) as well as our *Shōhō* (Commercial Code) show German influence.

Two great factors of Occidentalization. It may be remarked *en passant* that a curious anomaly is observable between legal and economic commerce, so to speak, or commerce in law and that in trade ; for, while our legal ideas are German, in actual commercial undertakings English practice is the rule. In exchange, in insurance, and especially in shipping, the terms in vogue at the counter are English and they sometimes have no exact equivalent in German or Japanese law books ! A similar discrepancy exists in other departments of our social life. We can broadly state that while the Government and the State are largely under German influence, the people and society work under an English and American *régime*. The same is true in education. The Imperial universities and colleges are German in spirit and method ; the private institutions of high standing are repositories of English thought.

And here we may affirm without hesitation that the Occidentalization of Japan is guided by two powerful agencies, German and English. Have we selected bad models ? Are we unwise in our selection of patterns to work by ? In other words, is there a country better administered and more healthfully growing than Germany ? Is there a nation with nobler thought and higher prestige than the English ? Is there a people more energetic and more hopeful than the American ?

Gentleman and *samurai*. Thus has Japan selected the best that the West can give, while retaining what the East can least afford to spare. If there is any doubt as to the wisdom of the choice, it will concern the attitude we assume towards the moral sentiments of Europe and particularly towards Christianity. I have already said that moral sentiments are the common meeting ground of all the branches of the human family. There is brotherhood between an English gentleman and a Japanese *samurai*—a spiritual bond between them. The gentleman is a more modern type than the *samurai*, and hence he can adjust himself more readily to the new era. The latter has yet much to learn of the former in order to make his *début* into the society of the twentieth century. But this is exactly the point most neglected by our savants and statesmen. There lingers still in their minds the thought which Kamon Ii expressed in a couplet on the occasion of the inauguration of a military hall in Yédo (Tōkyō), which roughly rendered runs :

> Wherefore follow alien ways and alien thought
> When here the *samurai's* noblest virtues can be taught ?

Is it true that we have nothing to learn of the West in morals and morality ? Do we exploit the best in Europe when we borrow its systems of law, of education, and of industry ?

The greatest influence of the West is, after all, the spiritual, by which I do not mean only the religious. Christianity has influenced the thought and lives of many individuals in Japan, and will influence many more—eventually affecting the nation through the altered viewpoint and *personnel* of the citizen and the administrator. This character-changing power of the religion of Jesus, I believe to be only just now making itself appreciably evident in our midst. Christianity has not worked such obvious influence upon the social life of our people as Mr. Dennis and other zealous advocates of missions are inclined to think. When a man such as he—considered to be an authority on things evangelical—tries to demonstrate the effect of missionary enterprises on our national sanitation by affirming that the Japanese people are in the main cleanly in their habits, but that there are Ainus in the country who are very dirty, his good efforts lose much of their value and validity. His argument sounds as absurd as though one were to say that the Americans generally are well dressed, but that there are

The greatest influence of the West.

Indians among them who are nearly naked. Exaggerated statements such as the above are too frequent to mention.

What, then, do I mean by the spiritual influence of the West? I mean particularly two phases of it. To the first and more important—Christianity—I have frequently made allusion, and I hope my hearers are aware that I deem it of the utmost consequence as a transforming agency. Without further elaboration here as to its significance, I will speak of the second source of spiritual influence from the West, the vast spread of the reading knowledge of European, and, most undoubtedly, of the noble English tongue. Indeed, it is no hyperbole to say that if Rome thrice governed the world—once by its laws, then by its language, and thirdly by its religion (Catholicism)—England dominates the Far East, first by its commerce, secondly by its navy, and thirdly by its literature. The eloquent tribute of Lord Curzon to the language of his people is no mere bombast : ' Its sound will go out into all lands and its words unto the ends of the world. That this splendid future is no mere dream of fancy, but is capable of realization at no indefinite period, none who have travelled widely in Eastern Asia will doubt.' [1]

The effect of the acquisition of the English tongue on the mental habits—I had almost said on the unconscious cerebration of our people—is incalculable. Its depth depends of course upon individual minds, but its breadth covers millions

of the mediocre. The moral influence of some of the simple text-books used in our schools cannot be over-rated. The Readers of different grades, selections from English literature, Benjamin Franklin's ' Autobiography,' Washington Irving's ' Sketch-Book,' Smiles's ' Self-Help,' and other books of wholesome and edifying character have been instrumental in opening new vistas of thought and vast domains of enterprise and interest to young minds. How many Japanese minds have come under the spell of men like Kant and Hegel, Spencer and Mill, Tyndall and Huxley, Scott and Wordsworth, Gibbon and Macaulay, Shakespeare and Bacon, Carlyle and Ruskin, Longfellow and Emerson.

Intellectual and moral upheavals on a large scale were

---

[1] *Problems of the Far East*, revised edition, p. 428.

accomplished in silent ways by these men ; but, here again, foreign influence must not be exaggerated beyond its desert. People who think that modern Japan simply absorbed foreign ideas much as a sponge sucks up water, forget a psychological law well expressed by Dr. Edwin Hatch : [1] ' The truth which Aristotle enunciated,' he says, ' that all intellectual teaching is based on what is previously known to the person taught, is applicable to a race as well as an individual, and to beliefs even more than to knowledge.' Affinity is essential to a mutual understanding. There must be alliedness before there can be alliance. A scion and a stock must belong to allied genuses.

In the receptive faculty of the Japanese race there must be something which makes it near akin to the races of Europe. Is it due to the Aryan blood which may have come to us through the Hindoos, as Professor Hamy once told me he felt he had proved by craniological evidence ? Whatever the explanation, the unquestionable fact remains, that the intellectual influence which one race can exert upon another ' is relative of the latter.' During the late war Russian writers and their friends throughout Europe did their best to prove the racial affinity, if not the identity, between the Slav and other European nationalities, as though blood were the only strong bond of union. A wise man said long ago that ' there is a friend that sticketh closer than a brother,' implying that there are ties which bring strangers closer than brothers. Baron von Bruggen, in his study of Russian history, discovered that two hundred years of ceaseless effort on the part of the Czars and their servants to occidentalize their people are just beginning to tell. This argues comparatively little mental affinity, a lack of response, the unpreparedness of the Russian intellectual soil for the reception of West European seed.

The true phase of Occidentalization.

Without meaning in the least to detract from the magnitude of foreign influence upon us, we have self-respect enough to believe that the intellectual capital we borrowed from the West was largely invested in opening our own existent resources. ' The inventor only knows what to borrow,' says Emerson.

---

[1] Introduction to the Hibbert Lectures of 1888.

It may be that we shall return the sum of our indebtedness with compound interest. Our study and ' imitation ' of Europe have been what Socrates used to call the maieutic method, by which our own minds have been helped to deliver their contents, to give birth to their own fruits.

XXV

SOCIAL INTERCOURSE BETWEEN JAPANESE AND OCCIDENTALS

BARON KÉIROKU TSUZUKI

NOTHING but Count Ōkuma's urgent desire has overcome my extreme reluctance to expose myself to literary publicity, especially as the above is a subject which does not fall within the sphere of my usual studies. All, therefore, that I can do is to refute some of the most common fallacies, often purposely reiterated, in regard to the difficulties which are supposed to confront the much-desired development of social intercourse between Westerners and ourselves.

Small in stature and different in physique from Westerners,[1] having been long secluded from the rest of the world, and, in consequence, our language, customs, and entire culture being an almost unknown quantity to Westerners of fifty years ago, they had naturally been misled to consider us as a set of human beings of quite a different stuff from themselves. In my opinion, it is only the inertia of this once acquired habit of thinking that prevents the Western mind even now entirely escaping from the error of laying undue stress on this so-called difference of races. Especially in the panic-stricken imagination of 'Yellow Peril Phantoms' do I often see arguments inclining towards the belief that a skin-deep difference of colours makes friendship and intimacy between the two races a matter of sheer impossibility. No grosser mistake!

So-called difference of races.

Love and friendship are not matters of colour or form, but of heart and brain. 'One touch of nature makes the whole

[1] By the terms 'West' and 'Westerners' I include for brevity's sake America and Americans respectively.

477

world kin '—therefore let me try to prove that we have the same mental and moral ' touch ' as Westerners.   There is no greater mistake than to assume that we are only veneered by a half-century-old imitation of Western civilization, and that, denuded of our Western costumes, laced boots and silk hats, you will find something much worse than a Tartar.   It is forgotten, or not known, that we had a very highly developed moral and mental culture before we came in contact with Westerners.   Twelve centuries ago we had the civilization of Nara—still a wonder to travellers as well as to ourselves. With outward civilization came also the moral tenets of the best eras of China and India.   Then followed the civilization of Kyōto, with a marked tendency to further Japanization and idealization of the civilization borrowed at first from the Asiatic continent.   After Kyōto came feudalism, which lasted eight centuries, and which led to the unparalleled development of the code of honour, of chivalry, of fraternal love, of humanity —all under the name of *Bushidō*, that is, ' The ways which a *samurai* ought to tread.'   Thus it is our own past history which has given the impetus to each rising generation of pre-cosmopolitan Japan to endeavour to educate and develop itself in such a way as to come nearest the ideals offered by philosophy and by historical examples of the golden ages of China and of India and of each preceding generation of our own country, the practical result of the process being that an ideal gentleman has to combine in himself moral virtues, martial capabilities, and literary and æsthetic accomplishments.[1]   In short, I claim that, contrary to opinions generally prevalent in the West, we were already a cultured people before we came into contact with Westerners.   Mr. J. G. D. Campbell, in a work entitled ' Siam in the Twentieth Century,' published in London in 1904, says : ' Japan has now taken her place among the great powers of the world, and, *it may perhaps be admitted, in the fraternity of civilized nations.   Japan fifty years ago was as barbarous as Siam now is or even was twenty years ago.'* (Italics are mine.)   I wonder whether the author troubled to dip into our literature before he pronounced such hasty

Japan's civiliza-tion.

---

[1] Martial accomplishments were, of course, not expected of other than *samurai* castes.

judgments. What lofty sentiments are treasured in the inexhaus- Poetry
and arts. tible fountains of Japanese poetry! Patriotism, loyalty, filial piety, sexual love, matrimonial fidelity, maternal love, fraternal self-sacrifice, bravery, honour : all these passions and emotions have been depicted in the strongest of words and in the noblest forms of lofty idealisms. Then the peculiarly national tender-ness for anything that is beautiful and delicate in nature—the never-ending homage to, and the almost idolatrous love of, the white purity of snow, of the Nirvana-like serenity of moonlight, of the tender delicacies of flowers, and of the voluptuousness of nightingales' songs ! The Westerner's love of plums and cherries for the sake of their fruit is, to be sure, more practical, but forgive me if I say that it sometimes jars upon our feelings as prosaic, and even smacking a little of vandalism against the æsthetic. Then our paintings and sculptures ! Our sculp-tures, those who have seen the finest specimens of Nara can assure you, will stand unflinching comparison with the works of great artists of Greece. Of course we had no marble, but that does not affect the æsthetic. Then, again, the marvellous realism of religious paintings on one hand, and the highly idealistic suggestiveness of laic art on the other. Concerning the latter, let me ask which other nation has arrived at the height of aiming by its art rather at the kindling of vivid subjective imagination than at the objective impression the painting in itself shall produce ? A Western traveller who has seen landscape gardening in Japan would have observed that very often the scenery is so arranged that we hear the rippling of artificial running water without seeing its course—simply because this arrangement is more apt to produce the sense of serene repose, and serves as the fruitful source of more ideas and imagination than seeing the reality of the thing itself, which latter is liable to fatigue the mind by its unchanging sameness. This is the key-note of that branch of Japanese art which tried to appeal, not to the masses, as in the case of religious paintings, but to the educated aristocracy. What lofty idealism in all this ! Therefore let me ask, can an uncul-tured nation ever arrive at this height ? Then, in applied fine arts, dyeing, weaving, embroidery, colour prints, porcelain, and in the production of a thousand *bibelots* and articles of household usage, what nation has manifested so much skill and artistic taste as Japan fifty years ago, that is, before contact with Western civilization?

This social atmosphere of high moral culture and æsthetic development, themselves the product of society, could not fail, in their turn, to react on that very society, with the result that almost every educated Japanese, and especially women, could, when occasion required, break out into verse; while the enormous number of paintings and other works of art, including often even sculptures, left behind by celebrated warriors, states-men, philosophers, and *literati*, attest to the many-sidedness of their accomplishments and to the aspiration of our fore-fathers to develop their inner beings to as near perfection as possible in the harmonious combination of the then known accomplishments—in other words, ' to become a developed human being.' Of course, the materialistic side of modern civilization, technical and mechanical sciences, and material appliances of these sciences failed us entirely. This side of modern civilization was almost an entire blank for us fifty years ago. All that I endeavour to prove is that we had then the moral and mental fibre sensitive and strong enough to discover quickly and almost instinctively what was failing in us, and to persevere deliberately in the mental drudgery necessary to fill the gap. And, indeed, in the first impulse of a strong feeling, we went rather too far in the search after specialized technical knowledge, so much so that, of all Japanese, modern ones—I mean those born and bred in the transi-tion period, like ourselves—are the most prosaic, or at least most devoid of accomplishments other than our respective specialities.

Code of honour.

Of course, fifty years ago there were many eccentricities unavoidable in any highly developed code of honour. They were nothing but the eccentricities of over-sharp angles and apexes of crystallized and superannuated social customs and usages. For example, the idea of self-immolation, especially in the form of the now celebrated *hara-kiri*, may have been carried too far, and has often been stigmatized as barbarous. But the idea of preferring death to dishonour, besides being common to all nations, from Lucretia to the debt-burdened officers of the Prussian Army, is no more the real symptom of social conditions as a whole than the 'Lebensgefährliche' duels to which Western usages cling with a pertinacity incomprehensible to us—not to mention 'lynchings,' resorted to by one of the most civilized people of the world.   To take another example : In my opinion the literature of modern Europe lays too much stress on sexual love as the motive power of human actions.   Almost in every modern fiction sexual love, whether in its so-called pure, platonic, and sentimental forms, as in Germany, or in its more sensual forms, as in the *fin-de-siècle* literature of Paris, is represented as the fountain-head of all the noble and ignoble aspirations of human nature.   But it is evident that this late Western social exhalation does not make up the essence of its civilization.   The modern French fiction, which either shocks the reader or else leaves him more sensual after perusal, does not make the French civilization an immoral one.   Just so in our case : our eccentricities, although better known to the outside world, could not weigh against the essence of our 'fifty years ago.'   We were in some respects even more cultured then than now, so that I can conscientiously assure you that our present culture is not a veneered one, as seems to be usually believed by Western observers.   You may be surprised to hear that we, as young boys, found Plutarch's 'Lives' extremely interesting reading.   Shakespeare's 'Julius Cæsar' made our hearts throb with sympathy.   And what difference is there between Brutus's Portia and the heroines of our popular literature, except perhaps that Portia describes her feelings rather effusively in the first person, while for our heroines her feelings, though exactly the same, would be described for her in the third person by the author ?   I remember that the now so celebrated Dr. Tétsujirō Inouyé, as a boy, made a marginal note to his text-book of 'King Lear,' at the place where the Earl of Kent reads a letter by moonlight, to the following effect : 'Those who can read these pathetic lines without shedding a tear of sympathy are simply human brutes.'   Don't think we as boys were much attracted by the beauty of the English language as displayed by Shakespeare.   The study of appended glossaries was, at the best, nothing but a pleasure of the sort of driving on a

Love and sympathy.

much-broken road, if pleasure it can be called at all. No, it is the sentiments expressed therein which appealed so strongly to our youthful minds. We studied the English language simply in order to be able to cherish these sentiments so much the more. Well, you will easily admit that there must have been a remarkable similarity, or at least a strong resemblance, in the receptive sensibilities of our youthful emotions and those of our Western juvenile contemporaries. In other words, no one can deny we were as ready for and as receptive to the so-called classical education—i.e., as the Germans understand it, the education of the character of a man as he ought to be—as our Western brothers. This receptibility, I claim, is a heritage of many generations of the highest moral culture. And that heritage was existent before we came into contact with Western civilization. I lay much stress on this point, because I am really convinced that high culture on both sides is one of the foremost requisites of close intimacy and lasting friendship between different countries. The simple partnership of material interests never makes lasting friends.

Religious sentiments.   Again, difference of religion has been pointed out as one of the hindrances to our intimate intercourse with Westerners. A very superficial idea, this ! The religions which we possess are by their very nature extremely tolerant to the divinities of other religions. Moreover, Buddhism, the religion of by far the greater majority of our countrymen, is more of a philosophy than a religion properly so called. That Confucianism is nothing more than a mass of moral axioms and philosophical tenets, and that the Confucius Heaven or the supernatural is easily disposed of as unknowable, is known to everybody, and requires no reiteration here. Buddhism in its purest form—i.e., in the form ordinarily accepted by the initiated—is a system of philosophy which recognizes nothing superhuman, or, at least, nothing supernatural. Humanity can develop itself by evolution to perfection, to Nirvana, to Buddhahood. Here, again, there is no necessity of making a jump over the immensurable abyss that extends from the last footstep of human reason to the first landing-stone of divine or blind faith. It is this feature of Buddhism which makes it remarkably resemblant to the philosophical doctrines expounded by Kant, Hegel,

Schopenhauer, and other German philosophers. Change the words ' Logos,' ' Absolute,' &c., to ' Nirvana,' ' Neant,' &c., and you will be convinced of the resemblance yourself. Of course, superstition has woven quite a system of religious super- naturals around this primitive simplicity of inexpressible grandeur, just as people have dimmed the halo of the simple teachings of Christ by a complicated system of superstition and doctrines. But you can easily understand that the belief in its purest form—that is, in the form entertained by the higher and educated classes—always exercises an enormous influence on the inclinations and tendencies of the mass, and serves to restrain their idiosyncrasies, eccentricities, and fanaticism. Western correspondents at the front in the late war with Russia must have observed that our common soldiers, recruited as they were from the masses, are not so superstitious by far as the Christian soldiers of Russia. Indeed, the faith in the icons, and in the protective influences of the saints, as well as the part played by crosses and their bearers in that conflict, reminded us forcibly of the Golden Calf of the Israelites, as well as of the ideas of invulnerability entertained by the Boxers. Even in the form accepted by the mass of the people, Buddhism is usually a polytheistic, and at the best a pan- theistic, religion, which naturally and easily acquiesces in the idea that there may be other gods equally divine as those one had hitherto known. This is the only explanation which I can give for the easy fusion of *Shintō* divinities with Buddhistic ideals at the beginning of the Buddhistic propaganda, in the ancient history of our country. But *Shintō*, you say, is a fanatical religion. That is another mistake. My Western reader, suppose you stand before the tomb of your teacher or mother. I believe you naturally take off your hat, just as Frenchmen and some Englishmen do when they meet funerals in the street. *Shintō* is a crystallized system of rites for the veneration of the personalities closely connected with our existence and our national history—in other words, a system- atized and complicated form of taking off our hats before the emblems of our ancestors and national heroes. A *Shintō* temple is a monument of veneration. The servants of the principal *Shintō* temples are semi-public functionaries. They

Buddhism and Shintō.

2 I 2

do not preach, they make no religious propaganda, and they are forbidden to officiate in funeral services, the servants of less important temples being only temporarily excepted from this prohibition on account of pecuniary considerations. They have no religious dogmas, no complicated doctrines of future life and of supernatural interference in human affairs. In the first revulsion of feeling against everything foreign or imported which characterized the Restoration of 1868, they tried to weave out a religious system from original *Shintō* pure and simple. The religious associations calling themselves Shintō-istic sects are essentially post-Restoration institutions ; they have no direct relation with *Shintō* temples—the real objects of popular veneration—and can at the best be called only a partial success as yet. The Department of the Interior has a ' Section of Religion,' but *Shintō* temples do not fall under its jurisdiction. Well, reader, you will see that *Shintō* is an institution *sui generis* more closely connected with Imperial tombs and mausoleums than with religious doctrines and moral tenets. Of course, the remark concerning the corrupted superstition of the masses and the mitigating and restraining influences of educated classes applies to *Shintō* to as equal a degree as it does to Buddhism. With this exception of superstitious corruptions, neither Buddhism nor *Shintō* offers the slightest resistance to the monotheistic exclusiveness of Christianity. It is true that, in the history of our past, we have persecuted Christians, but that was entirely due to the endeavour of the Jesuits to usurp political power and influence in our country, and to their foolish trials to experiment ' empirical miracles ' before the ignorant crowd, who naturally mixed them up with the ideas of witchcraft. Monotheism is an essentially exclusive religion. Oneness is an idea that excludes moreness. Christianity, just as Mohammedanism, recognizes its God as the only true supernatural being—to the exclusion of every other belief in the supernatural. History shows us that the contact of one form of monotheism with another is followed by terrible conflict, and very often by bloodshed. Not only is Christianity more exclusive and narrow-minded towards other religious beliefs, but even one sect of Christians is much more antagonistic to and exclusive of other sects of the same religion than

Buddhism is of Christianity.   For example, a Russian Orthodox
Church will, I am afraid, consider Roman Catholics, and much
more Protestants, as more incorrigible proselytes, or even as
greater heretics, than ever Buddhists have dreamed of Christians.   I have studied Christianity deeply enough to appreciate
and respect its doctrines; but, stripped of its miraculous and
supernatural portions, I do not see any material difference
between the injunctions of the Ten Commandments and the
moral tenets preached by Buddha and other Asiatic centres of
light and learning.   I am sorry to expose in this way what you
Westerners are accustomed to cherish as your dearest sanctity
to unscrupulous vivisection by the trenchant—though occasionally erring—knife of human reason.   But that is what I
believe—and tolerance for everyone's belief is one of the
fundamental principles inculcated by Christ Himself, and
therefore I can only hope that you will read these lines with
Christian impartiality.   A German friend of mine once wrote
in my autograph album :

> Ob von Buddha oder Christ
> Nur das Licht verkundet ist
> Es versteh'n sich allerwärts
> Freier Geist und offenes Herz!

That is my opinion also.   Superficial observers have said that
Christianity teaches monogamy, while Buddhism does not.   I
do not think so.   The forms of matrimonial ties, monogamy,
concubinage, polygamy proper, and polyandry, are nothing but
historical products necessitated and justified by the successive
conditions of social existence—at least, that is the teaching of
your philosophers of the historical school.   Be it remarked,
besides, that we never had polygamy proper, but that feudalism,
with its undue consideration of real and fictitious family ties,
simply necessitated us to look with greater indulgence on the
institution of concubinage, and that with the abolition of
feudalism our society has returned to monogamy pure and
simple, without any reference to Christianity whatsoever ; and
also, that the present standard of sexual morality of our
countrymen, of the highest and lowest classes, especially of
women, stands a very favourable comparison with the scandal-
creating highest classes, or degenerate lowest scums, of the

largest cities of the West, in some of which it is really high time for ' the Writing on the Wall.'

That, in spite of the best efforts of missionaries, Christianity does not make a marked progress here is simply due to the fact that the higher and educated classes are not so prone and receptive to the miraculous and the supernatural. How can it be otherwise when Western missionaries preach us blind faith in the sanctity of the Bible, and the consequent acceptance of all the miracles contained therein, while Western teachers and professors preach us the supremacy of reason, the necessity of scrutiny, and the disbelief of anything supernatural. Indeed, it is the Westerners who teach us that the history of modern philosophy begins with the ' universal doubt ' of Descartes. And, after all, do not you confess to yourself that in the West, also, the enormous development of material sciences during the latter half of the nineteenth century has contributed to shake immensely the simple faith in the Bible ?

Then, again, we are sometimes accused of hating foreigners. Why should we ? It is true once upon a time we hated them. There was a period when we considered their compulsory advent and forcible sojourn in our country, their reckless disregard and sometimes even wilful violation of the time-honoured etiquette of our country; as something like a vandalistic raid of Mongol races upon our islands. That we were compelled, by superior force, to accept their uninvited presence upon what we had been accustomed to consider our sacred soil added only to the bitterness of the indignity we had to feel. Every foreigner present reminded us of his superiority over us. Moreover, these foreigners were only too prone to make their superiority felt at each and every step, and in their ignorance of things Oriental did not conceal their contempt and derision of institutions, usages, and ideals which we—often justifiably, but more often in the self-contented and self-conceited ignorance of the seclusion of centuries—had falsely considered as sanctified by ages of long-continued existence, and, in consequence, beyond the pale of human scrutiny. Concussion and friction were unavoidable under these circumstances. But that was long ago, before even the present writer was born; before Prince Itō and Marquis Inouyé had even had opportunities of being surprised at seeing,

No anti-foreign spirit.

for the first time in their lives, the flying cars vomiting smoke and fire ; long before our fathers made us suspicious of their soberness by the story of having travelled on a flying car swifter than kites and crows in heaven—nay, even swifter than arrows ! *Tempi passati !* Once convinced of the superiority of Westerners to us in many respects—especially in regard to technical sciences and mechanical appliances of modern age—and their consequent superiority in the struggle for existence, we were not slow in acknowledging our error. We soon learned to respect them as precursors in modern civilization, and as our teachers ; and here in the Orient you know the respect shown to a teacher is only next to that which we show to our parents. Westerners brought us sciences, learning, commerce, and material wealth, new ranges of vision concerning art, taste, and literature. What on earth, then, was there to make us hate them ? On the contrary, we were inclined to be somewhat extreme in our admiration of Western ideas and institutions, of its usages and customs, and of its habits—even to the extent of sometimes adopting corsets, high collars, and narrow and high-heeled boots. True, there were frequent recurrences of galling sensations caused by the Westerner's occasional recklessness in advertising his conviction of innate superiority, culminating in such examples as quoted below. One Mr. Lenaide A. Ragonin, in his work entitled ' Chaldea from the Earliest Times to the Rise of Assyria,' published as late as the year 1900 in London, has, in this very scientific, and therefore, I believe, cool-headed work, such words as the following in reference to yellow races: ' All the different members of this great family (Turanian or yellow race) have had very striking features in common, the most extraordinary being an incapability of reaching the highest culture, of progressing indefinitely, improving continually.' Then again : ' There are now a great number of Turanian tribes more or less numerous . . . whose day is done, which has long ceased to improve,' &c., &c. Again : ' Only there is that strange limitation to their power (i.e. of yellow races), and that want of natural refinement which are as a wall that encloses them all around.' Then the author asks : ' What is this great race which we find everywhere at the very roots of history ? ' And he hazards the hypothesis that they may be

descendants of Cain, the cursed of God, that being the reason
why the Bible does not mention them, and also why they are
by nature excluded from the boon of perpetual progress. This
author must be a learned man, as he has written much on such
profound subjects as Chaldea, Medea, Assyria, &c.   I can only
say, ' *Voilà* the prejudice of ignorance self-contented in the
idolatrous reverence of the Bible ! '   As if the differences of
forms of noses and eyes, and the differences of colours of hair
and of skins necessarily led to differences of fundamental ideas
on humanity ! As if Hungarians could not reach the same
height of civilization as Poles, Russians, and Bohemians ! As
for the descent from Cain, I can only say, ' Danke schön
für die Ehre.'   The example just quoted will show into what
errors of judgment even learned men can fall, and will also
illustrate the fact that there is very often a tendency in a
Westerner, especially when he is in the Orient, to consider
himself so transcendentally superior to people he meets with
that he considers the social intercourse with the latter not worth
the trouble.   And moreover, such a Westerner has ordinarily
the additional short-coming of desiring to advertise his assumed
superiority.   Galling as such experiences must have been, we
were nevertheless satisfied to take them, too, into the bargain,
because we knew it was our place to respect them for what
they could teach us, and thereby enable us to supplement our
shortcomings ; so that, upon the whole, we were always glad to
have Westerners as our friends.   There was another feature,
however, of their intercourse with Japan and Japanese, to
which we could not reconcile ourselves so easily.   That was in
the attitude of Western Powers towards our country in our
international intercourse.   The subject is rather outside of the
limits of the present essay ; but as the political intercourse
made at the time deep, and often very painful, impressions upon
the country as a whole, I may make a few passing remarks on
the influence which it has had indirectly on the social intercourse—our present theme.   The concert of diplomatic corps
would have reduced us to another Egypt or China if they only
could.   We had to resist obstinately, and step by step, the
attempted encroachments on the rights of a fully sovereign
State, until the Western Powers came to be convinced of the

fact that ours was also a strong Power. As the Western Powers always danced in concert to the tune of some two or three strong Powers we had to oppose our arguments against the concert itself, which fact may have often misled superficial observers to the conclusion that we were opposed to the foreigners as such. In connection with the Boxer commotion, we heard much of Chinese hatred of foreigners, and of prejudices of race and religion, &c. These accusations are certainly based on facts to some extent. We must, however, also take into consideration the fact that we of the same race and of nearly the same faith as Chinese had been included among the attacked, so that the movement must have been, to a certain extent at least, a revulsion of feeling against the concerted oppression of a weaker nation by stronger ones. Howsoever this may be, now that the stronger Powers have finally learned to acknowledge us as their equals, I hope and sincerely believe that they shall have no more occasion to see themselves under the necessity of raising the false alarm cry of Japanese hatred of foreigners in general.

Recapitulating the facts enumerated thus far, I repeat that neither differences of race, religion or culture, constitute any real obstacle to the further development of intimacy between ourselves and Westerners.

Now let me enumerate some of the real hindrances, to remove which we must endeavour to the best of our abilities.

First comes the great physical distance between us and the West. When you have to wait several weeks for an answer to your letter you naturally lose interest in writing letters at all, for the reply probably comes at a moment when you have almost forgotten the contents of your own letter. Then comes the difference of languages. This is a great difficulty. It is very difficult to write and speak in languages one is not born to, and when there is even the slightest obstacle to be overcome it is but human nature to incline towards the direction of least resistance. You must have remarked a certain amount of shyness, and even of stiffness, on the part of our countrymen who cannot speak foreign languages in their intercourse with Westerners; perhaps also the apparent desire to escape as soon as possible from the company of foreigners. Do

Real hindrances.

Difference of languages.

not misinterpret these symptoms as those of dislike of foreigners. It is more due to a fear of offending by some unconscious breach of etiquette, or of making oneself ridiculous, or, at the most, to the only too natural desire to escape from a society in which he feels himself, as Germans say, ' *unsicher.*' Westerners themselves are also to be blamed to a certain extent. It is impossible to understand a people thoroughly without mastering its language, without having made a study of its literature— the mirror of national emotions and imaginations. How many Westerners residing here—and that, too, for very long periods of time—have taken the trouble to study our written language ? When we go abroad we study the language of the country, and try to squeeze ourselves into the higher circles of its society; in short, we try to feel and think with the people of the country. However wide-awake one's eyes may be, one does not get beyond seeing the outside of a social building unless ears and tongues are exercised at the same time. ' Argus ' alone does not suffice ! Of course, we on our side must remember that we are only fifty millions of human souls, while those who make up Western civilization are more than 400 millions in number, and that the minority has always to suffer a certain amount of inconveniences for the sake of the majority, especially if that majority is our precursor and teacher. ' When you are amongst the wolves you must howl with them, and in their language,' says our proverb. But I hope sincerely that the Westerners will try to assist us in overcoming these inconveniences, and that at least those who are staying, or intend to stay, here for long will come one-third, or at least one-fourth, of the way to meet us. In that case they will surely find a much more warm-hearted people than they might otherwise have expected. On the other hand, I should like to impress upon the educators of the rising generation of our country the daily increasing importance of the study of Western languages. It is with sincere regret that I hear of late some complaints about the tendency just now to wane in this particular branch of youthful studies. This may be due chiefly to the overburdening of young brains with other and more materialistic, or rather technical, studies, but it may be due, to some extent at least, to the influence of the nationalistic tendencies of European thought in the last decade or two.

Whatever its causes may be, the effects cannot but be prejudicial to the interests of our country. For evidently, if we wish to stand up as one of the strongest nations of the world, we must try to make the outside world understand and sympathize with our national aims and missions, and if we cannot persuade 400 millions to understand us in our own language we must try to speak in theirs. I cannot but admire the present German education, which lays so much stress on the study of contemporary foreign languages, in spite of the decidedly nationalistic and imperialistic tendencies of its national politics.

Then there is another feature of our social life which may have sometimes had the influence of hindering warm social intercourse. Having been brought up in ideals like those of Sparta—rustic simplicity, robust mind and body, strong moral character, fraternal love of neighbours, loyalty to the lord, and patriotism to the State—we, at least those who were born and brought up in the transition period, were rigorously warned against effeminacy, wealth, and luxury, the result being that the present middle class of intellect and character does not exactly coincide with the middle class of wealth. Maybe it is cause for congratulation that with us intellect and character hold greater sway over the masses than wealth. Anyhow, the fact remains that exactly the middle class, in which foreigners must seek for the strength and essence of our national characteristics, is that in which the means of offering social lubricators in the form of soirées, dinners, reunions, &c., often fails, and makes it appear colder and less hospitable than it really is. *Spartan ideals of the Japanese.*

Then, again, mutual ignorance of habits and customs leads very often to embarrassing and sometimes serio-comical situations. A young man of the highest nobility here called on a Western journalist at his hotel about eight o'clock in the morning, the usual hour when the members of bureaucracy try to find each other at home on unofficial business, as they otherwise have each and all of them to be at their respective offices. But the poor journalist had to be aroused from his bed, to dress himself hastily, and speed downstairs to receive his guest unwashed! Our customs, however, are changing, and I believe the future will bring them into greater harmony with those prevailing in the majority of civilized countries. *Mutual ignorance of habits and customs.*

Our
educa-
tion.

Then, again, the education we have received, which taught us to suppress, as much as possible, the baneful influences which outbursts of passion and feeling, and all sudden impulses, are sure to exercise on the *nüchternheit* of our reasoning power, and the consequent habit of trying to suppress, as much as possible, the outward manifestations of these inner emotional waves, must often make us seem cold, and even callous, to Westerners, who are accustomed to more effusiveness. Break the ice through, you Westerners, and try to force yourselves into our society, and you will find that ' tranquil waters are so much the deeper.'

I have enumerated some of the difficulties of social intercourse with Westerners. I shall have attained my object if I have in any way contributed to the conviction that the causes which are ordinarily considered, or rather misinterpreted, as offering insuperable obstacles—such as differences of race, of religion, culture, &c.—are not at all obstacles in reality ; that they, by their very differentiation, rather serve to give more piquancy and stimulation to the social intercourse. In other words, fundamental ideas concerning the duties of humanity being the same, the apparent and superficial differences serve only to make interchange of these very differences so much the

The im-
possibility
for us of
' splendid
social
isolation.'

less monotonous. On the other hand, the real difficulties which lie in the way of further development of social intimacy are those which, by a certain amount of goodwill on both sides, can be easily overcome. And overcome them we must, at all cost. For us a ' splendid social isolation ' is an impossibility if we intend to play a part in the future development of the world's history. Ever since we came in contact with Western civilization, it has been our country's unswerving aim to be a world Power, to enter into the family of the most civilized and most powerful nations. In order to attain this object we must always remember that it does not suffice to have a strong army and navy, to stand on the footing of disconnected military equality with the most powerful, but that we must be able to act and react in unison and consonance with other nations for the further development of civilization, and for the higher common ideals of humanity. In order to act in union with others, our national aims and characteristics have to be understood by them to at least the same degree as we understand theirs. And nothing furthers this mutual understanding so much as social and friendly intercourse. It is this mutual understanding and sympathy which serves as the permeating essence to the action and reaction of international political factors.

Hence, not only is it important for us to make ourselves understood by Westerners, but it is equally so for the Westerners to understand us. Western civilization is just at this moment confronted by the difficult problem of what to do with millions and millions of swarming Asiatic populations, older in history and civilization than they, never exterminated by contact with them, and with a surprising fecundity. Speak of ' yellow peril,' if you like ; but you cannot make a *tabula rasa* of the Asiatic Continent by exterminating 400 to 500 millions of human souls ! If the Westerners do not wish to be contaminated by contact with these millions there remains no other alternative but to try to raise them as much as possible in the scale of modern civilization. How can you do this without understanding their wants and inclinations, their weaknesses and their potential capabilities ? And the easiest way to understand them is to commence by understanding us—the Occidentals of the East. Besides we can, and do, wish to play an active part in helping the Westerners in this their noble civilizing work. Indeed, we have no less authority than that of Prince Itō when we say that it is a part of our national mission to play the *rôle* of honest broker in this inevitable contact of the two widely different cultures. Besides let me point out one other point. The Macedonians who came in contact with the Persians surely gained very much by contact with the civilization and culture of the latter. But who can gainsay that Asia. then more civilized than Greece also benefited by the rustic simplicity and robust vigour of a young nation with whom it came in contact ?

Conclusion.

XXVI

SOCIALISM IN JAPAN

PROFESSOR ISOH ABÉ (WASÉDA UNIVERSITY)

To give an accurate account of the development of Socialism in Japan entails going back to the early days of our history and examining the principles which influenced our sovereigns in governing their people in those far-off times. For just as we are justified in expecting a good harvest when we sow in a well-tilled field, so we may be assured of a hopeful future for Socialism in Japan if we find that the condition of affairs there is naturally favourable to its growth. Such being the case, we will first investigate the social system of our country prior to her coming into contact with the philosophic ideas of China.

Social system of Old Japan. In ancient times we find a class of people called *tomobé*, who ranked next below the nobles in the social scale, and who were distributed throughout the country to control the common labourers. The nobles in those days were called *kami* and were divided into two branches : one including those who governed the *tomobé* and were therefore called *tomotsuko* (lords of the *tomobé*), and the other those who took charge of the management of the forests and fields in the provinces, and were accordingly designated *kunitsuko* or *agatanushi* (governors of provinces). Both were responsible for all matters pertaining to religious worship. The chief of the nobles exercised sovereignty over the people and administered worship in the central sanctuary. Such is the genesis of the Imperial Household and Peerage.

The *tomobé* were freemen, their offices were hereditary, and they formed themselves into tribes. They engaged in industry and agriculture, and paid tribute of their products to the

494

central government, supplying it also with the necessary materials for the performance of religious rites. The *samurai* of later periods originated in this class. Labourers were subordinated to the *tomobé* and were called *nuhi* (the lowest labouring class). The governors of provinces had no *tomobé* under them, but only labourers. Labourers were divided into two sections, *kénin* (retainers), who were on the same level as the *tomobé* in the social scale ; and the *nuhi*, who were mere commoners.

The above is a rough sketch of the social organization of Japan, on which were grounded the military, agricultural, administrative and social institutions of those days. Situated in the middle of the social scale, the *tomobé* class prompted industrial development, and consequently the central government held them in special esteem and called them *ōmita-kara* (great treasures), and also *tami* (citizens). This was also the case with the retainers of the governors of provinces. Commoners could be admitted into the *tomobé* class by merit, and later on, when the cultivation of land came to be more extensively carried on, princes and princesses of the blood invited the *tomobé* to their estates, giving them the names of *koshirobé* and *nashirobé*. As time went on, the numbers of the *tomobé* increased, and the tribute paid by them aided much the central government, and the armies organized and drilled by them subjugated the brigands everywhere, and maintained public order and peace. The Emperor Nintoku's (313–399 A.D.) famous utterance, ' The people's wealth is my wealth,' testifies to the aim of the Government being to promote the well-being of the people at large.

The increase in the class distinction between rich and poor was in the main due to the absorption of land by great proprietors. It is a dictum of socialism that to promote popular welfare the nationalization of land is inevitable. That system was early developed in Japan, for parcels of the public land were allotted to the people for cultivation, each household receiving its share in proportion to the number of its members and these shares undergoing revision at stated intervals. The system resembled very much that of the parcelling out of land among the Hebrews. But notwithstanding these distributions

The rich and the poor.

there were vast areas of uncultivated land and trackless forests, and these the nobles seized and rented out, realizing large profits thereby.   To stay this, landlordism was prohibited in the political reforms undertaken by the Emperor Kōtoku, and provincial governors were also inhibited against monopolizing the benefits of means of irrigation and communications, but were to share them with the people placed under their jurisdiction.

In a later decree of the Emperor Mommu, in 706 A.D., we read :

' Recently many princes and high officials of State occupy at will forests and fields and leave them uncared for ; and when people go there and gather faggots or hay, their tools and implements are confiscated.   Moreover, when these princes and high officials have some lands conferred upon them by the government, they soon make every effort to extend them in all directions under various pretexts.   Such acts are henceforth strictly prohibited.'

Again, in a decree of the Empress Gwammyō, in 711 A.D., we find the following passage :

' Lately princes, nobles, and great proprietors occupy at will forests and fields and disturb the work of farmers.   Such an illegal act is henceforth strictly prohibited.   Those who desire to cultivate free land shall apply to the " *Dajōkan* " (Ministry) through provincial governors and carry on their work in obedience to their directions.'

These Imperial decrees clearly indicate that absorption of land by great proprietors was still extensively carried on, and even these decrees had little effect in staying the determination of landlords to enlarge their estates.   Another factor, too, was that land was donated to the Buddhist temples that were being built all over the country, and consequently the religious houses also became great proprietors.   Thus the system of land nationalization was gradually undermined.   In the year 743 A.D. the Emperor Shōmu issued a decree, by virtue of which each of the princes of the blood, nobles, and provincial governors was allowed to own a certain area of arable land as his hereditary property.   Later, in the year

765 A.D., when Fujiwara-no-Nagaté was in office as Prime Minister under the Empress Shōtoku, he abolished the system of private property in land. The Emperors Kōnin and Kwammu also issued decrees to the same effect. But, in spite of all this absorption of land by nobles, shrines and temples increased with great rapidity, and as the power of landowners grew, the farmers became impoverished. Proprietors of provinces combined with nobles and priests and shared with them the profits accruing from landed property. Gradually the distinction of *daimyō* and retainers was made, and this inaugurated the feudal system which began with the Kamakura *régime* (twelfth and thirteenth centuries), and, passing through the Ashikaga period (fourteenth and fifteenth centuries), reached its height in the Tokugawa age. In short, our feudal system owed its origin to the fact that, as the number of nobles increased and their *per-capita* property was thereby diminished, their influence gradually declined until at last the military class superseded them as landowners. It was an inevitable tendency of things, viewed from the standpoint of social evolution. Be it noted, however, that in our feudal system the local lords were in perfect harmony with the soldiers and farmers on their estates, called them their followers, and united with them in defending their estates against invasion and pillage and in protecting the industry of the common people.

If we contrast the feudal system of Japan with that of Europe in the Middle Ages, we can easily trace points of difference in each. In the European system the feudal lord not only occupied the land, but also possessed the serfs attached to it, and he could grant to others, if he pleased, any portions of his land as well as any number of his serfs. In Japan the system of land nationalization and prohibition of private ownership of land, enacted by the Emperor Kōtoku, persisted continuously, though at times in name only ; and while the feudal lords monopolized the profits accruing from their estates, they were not allowed to dispose of them at will. Even when feudalism was perfected under the Tokugawa Shōgunate, the offices of the feudal lords were not hereditary, and all they had was the right to rule for life. Such being the

Characteristics of Japanese feudalism.

case, neither Shōgun nor *daimyō* had anything more than an administrative power temporarily entrusted to them by the Emperor ; and down to the time of the third Shōgun, Iyémitsu, it was the rule that when a feudal lord died with no son and heir, his family name was discontinued. Later a law was enacted permitting a feudal lord having no son and heir to carry on his family name by adoption ; but even in this case, when a *daimyō* died without appointing an heir, his death was not announced, but kept secret until the appointment of the heir had been made and the approval of the Shōgunate obtained. For the inheritance of rank, Imperial sanction was needed. In the case of succession to office of the Shōgun also, application had to be made to the Emperor for approval. Hence we may properly say that the offices of the Shōgun and the *daimyō* were not hereditary.

Govern-
ment's
policy to
protect
the weak

Before the time of the Tokugawa *régime*, a benevolent policy (*tokuséi*), had long prevailed in the interests of the poor classes, and by a proclamation of the *tokuséi* all creditors were compelled to cancel debts of long standing. Disorders often arose out of this policy, but gradually the idea prevailed among high and low that to demand of a poor debtor the fulfilment of an impossible obligation was a shameful act. Hidéyoshi Toyotomi regarded usurers as defrauders, and at times inflicted penalties upon them. It is noticeable that in those days debtors often made a statement by bond to the effect that, in case they failed to repay the amount borrowed, they would not protest against being charged with default in the presence of the people. At the beginning of the Tokugawa age it was generally considered that a settlement of money matters by reconciliation or mutual concession was better than by recourse to a lawsuit.

In the year 1790, when Lord Sadanobu Matsudaira served the Shōgunate as adviser to the then Shōgun Iyénari, and had to readjust the public finances, which were then in a miserable condition after a disastrous famine, he, at the outset of his administration, commanded all creditors to give up any debts of more than five years' standing ; but for debts of less than five years' standing, he accommodated all debtors out of the public treasury with such sums of money as were deemed necessary to repay their debts. This example was followed by many *daimyō*.

This Shōgun's extravagant living almost ruined the Tokugawa Government financially, so that when his successor, Iyéyoshi, came into office he had to carry out fiscal reforms. Amongst these was one that the courts were not to deal with any case concerning pecuniary matters, in order to put a restraint on the avarice of money-lenders. In Europe the question how to control usurers has long been discussed, but no feasible solution has yet been found. In Japan, however, the Government, ever since the eighth century, has taken the lead in solving this question, and in protecting the poor and weak, often at the cost of the rich and strong.

Following the example set by the Tokugawa Shōgunate, the *daimyō* vied with each other to prohibit luxurious living and to devise means of protecting the poor and weak. In the year 1838 the *daimyō* of a certain clan ordered all the landowners in his fief not to demand the rents due to them by the tenants for ten years, and when the term had expired he renewed the order, and even on the maturing of the second term he again carried on the same crusade against landowners. This policy served to deprive many large proprietors of their estates, and enabled tenants to appropriate their leaseholds to themselves. Nor was this all, for he enacted a law limiting to five *chō* (one and a half acres) the area of land that could be owned by one person. Thus we see that land nationalization was approved by the Japanese even at that time.

The political reforms at the beginning of the reign of the present Emperor put a check to the progress of land nationalization. The system of private ownership in land was then re-established and consequently great landlords again made their appearance everywhere. At the time of the political reform, the nation's attention was directed to politics solely ; social problems, as we interpret the term to-day, had not yet arisen. But since Count Itagaki and his associates started their political movement based upon freedom, the sense of human rights has gradually become diffused throughout the land. Labour problems were not long in coming to the front as the first of many other social problems that were to follow.

Effect of the Méiji Restoration upon nationalization.

2 K 2

Rise of
labour
problems.

In October 1880, Count Itagaki organized a political party known as the *Jiyūtō* (Liberal Party). The presence of the expression ' social reform ' in the declaration of this new party indicates the fact that the nation had begun to be interested in social problems. Kentarō Ōi, one of the leaders of the Liberal Party, started a newspaper entitled the ' *Azuma Shimbun* ' (about 1885), and pleaded for the labouring classes. In 1888 a disturbance took place in the Takashima Colliery, the result of ill-treatment of the miners employed there. In the following year a tea manufactory, run by a foreign resident at Yokohama, was involved in trouble. These caused the nation to consider labour problems seriously. In 1892, discontented with the deplorable condition of the Liberal Party, Ōi and others organized the *Tōyō Jiyūtō* (Oriental Liberal Party), declaring, among other things, their aim ' to effect a financial reform and to promote popular welfare (especially to protect the poor labouring classes within the limit of the national finances).' Prior to this time, Ōi had published a weekly magazine entitled the ' *Shin Tōyō* ' (*New Orient*), and had discussed therein a policy for protecting poor labourers. He had also published in that paper a translation of Bellamy's socialistic novel, ' Looking Backward.' Side by side with the organization of the Oriental Liberal Party, he formed the Labourers' Union and the Popular Suffrage Advocating League to undertake a labour movement. At the same time, he made an investigation of the Tenants Act question.

Capital-
ists taking
an interest
in labour
problems.

While politicians were busy about labour problems, there were some capitalists who showed great sympathy towards the working classes. The late Téiichi Sakuma, proprietor of the Shūyéisha Printing House, was amongst the first ; and in the year 1884, when the Printers' Union was formed, he offered it help in many ways. The union ended in failure, so he directed his helping hand to the formation of the Labourers' Union. His indefatigable efforts in the interests of the last-named union will never be forgotten. He was indeed, as some one suggested, the Robert Owen of Japan.

Iron-
workers'
league.

In the year 1889, under the promotion of Benzō Ozawa and others, a league of ironworkers, styled the *Dōméi-Shinkō-Gumi*, was organized. The aim of the league was to raise a fund

by means of subscriptions from among its members to construct
an iron-factory for the members themselves ; it only lasted a
few years.

The appearance of the *Rōdō Kumiai Kiséikai* (Labour
Union Perfecting Association) was an epoch-making event
in the annals of the labour movement in Japan. The origin
of this association dates back to 1890. In the summer of that
year, Tsunétarō Jō, Fusatarō Takano, Hannosuké Sawada, and
seven or eight other persons, who were then in San Francisco,
organized a body with a view to studying the conditions
of labour problems in Europe and America as a preliminary
step to their anticipated activities in Japan. Seven years
later most of them came home, and in 1897 Sawada and
Jō formed the *Shokkō Giyūkai* (Workmen's Society)
in Tōkyō. Takano, who was then on the staff of an
English paper in Yokohama, and Sen Katayama, who was
propagating Socialistic doctrines, joined it and took part in its
movement ; and backed by Téiichi Sakuma, Saburō Shimada.
and Kaiséki Matsumura, Takano held a meeting in June in
Tōkyō, which was attended by no less than 1200 persons, of
whom forty-seven pledged themselves to the society on the spot.
This number soon increased to seventy-one, and in July
the inauguration of the society was celebrated. From that
time on the members of the society increased with wonderful
rapidity. But in December of the same year, of the members
of the society the ironworkers, 1804 in all, separated themselves from the society and formed the *Tekkō Kumiai*
(Ironworkers' Union). At the same time, the ' *Rōdō Sékai* '
(*Labourers' World*), a monthly magazine edited by Sen Katayama, issued its opening number. From that time on, the
Ironworkers' Union made rapid growth, and in 1900 the
members numbered over 5400.

The Labour Union Perfecting Association arranged field-day
exercises for labourers to be given at Uyéno Park on the 3rd
of April, 1898 ; but two days previously, the police authorities
summoned the managers of the Association and commanded
them to give up the plan. This rather oppressive step on the
part of the authorities doubtless arose from fear that if
multitudes of labourers went by way of demonstration, it might

Marginal notes:

The Labour Union Perfecting Association.

Prohibition of labourers' meetings.

seriously affect public order. In 1901, at the proposal of the
'*Niroku Shimpō*' (a daily newspaper), it was decided that a social
meeting of labourers should be held on the 3rd of April in a
spacious ground in front of the Shirahigé Shrine at Mukōjima.
Admission tickets for the meeting were sold in great numbers,
which the '*Niroku Shimpō*' declared amounted to 120,000; and it
is probable that at least half that number would have attended.
Alarmed at the dimensions, the police authorities ordered the
'*Niroku Shimpō*' to give up the meeting, and upon its declining
to comply they required the journal to limit the number to 5000,
not to provide any intoxicating liquors on the occasion, not
to allow any disorder, or any persons attending to bring
weapons or sticks. Although, besides the authorities, the
employers of all factories tried to prevent labourers from attending the meeting, by seven o'clock on the morning of the
day, over 5000 people filled the appointed place and as soon
as the meeting was declared open, a great commotion arose
and all the buildings on the ground were pulled down and
smashed to pieces. This was a very unfortunate event for the
labourers themselves, since it gave the authorities a pretext the
year following, when they prohibited the holding of another social
gathering of labourers again proposed by the '*Niroku Shimpō*.'

Strike by
the
engineers
of the
Nippon
Railway
Company.

Side by side with the Ironworkers' Union already referred
to, the *Kyōséikai* a league of engineers in the service of the
Nippon Railway Company, did a great work. At the beginning
of 1898 a set of circulars were distributed amongst the engineers
of that railway company, referring to the unreasonably low
rate of their wages and urging all to unite in demanding higher
pay from the company. The step recommended by the
circulars for securing this end was that, instead of openly
organizing themselves, they should each send anonymous
letters of complaint to the directors of the company. That
was doubtless the safest step at that time, for if they had
openly demanded higher pay, they might have incurred the
danger of dismissal. The advice was promptly followed,
whereupon the company immediately dispatched one Matsumoto, a chief officer, to the north-eastern district, the scene
of the disturbance. On his arrival there, he picked out ten
who were suspected to be the ringleaders and discharged them,

believing that the cause of the trouble would thus be entirely
removed. But on the contrary over 400 engineers at several
places, with Fukushima as centre, threatened to go on strike
simultaneously. Alarmed at the prospect, the company
dispatched one Adachi to the north-eastern district, but he
barely succeeded in appeasing the discontented engineers by
yielding to their demands. The *Kyōséikai* was then
organized by them for the purpose of defence against the
oppression of their employers, and in deference to their demand
those who had been discharged under suspicion of being ringleaders were restored to their former posts. At the beginning
of 1899, the *Kyōséikai* had members to the number of 1000
and a fund of 10,000 *yen*, and by the end of the same year the
latter had increased to a total of 20,000 *yen*. According to the
regulations of the *Kyōséikai*, each member was required
to pay a day's wage every month as his subscription towards
the funds of the society, and when a member fell ill or died,
a reasonable allowance was to be made to him or his family
from this fund. It is a notable fact that there was a considera-
able number of teetotallers among the members; and as of the
ten, who had been suspected of being ringleaders, five were
professed Christians, these five started a Temperance Society
among the members of the *Kyōséikai*, of whom 200 soon
became regular teetotallers. The formation of such a systematic organization as the *Kyōséikai* is always desirable for
society in general and labourers in particular, but it is very
natural that capitalists should look upon it with fear and
aversion. The Nippon Railway Company was no exception
to this rule; for it soon opened an assault upon the *Kyōséikai*, and at last dissolved it with the help of the police
authorities. This fact deserves special mention in the history
of Socialism in Japan, insomuch as it was one of the greatest
blows delivered to the labour movement.

*Forma-
tion of the
Kyōséikai.*

All workmen were now awakened to their position in society,
and the Government could no longer remain indifferent to
labour problems. So when the High Agricultural, Commercial,
and Industrial Conference sat toward the close of 1896, the
following passage was found in a message of the Government
to it:

*The
Factory
Law Bill.*

'With the recent industrial development in our country, the old-fashioned domestic industry has gradually given way to the newly introduced factory industry. It is therefore of urgent necessity for the furtherance of the progress of our industries to enact a law with a view to bringing into harmony the relations between capitalists and labourers, preserving the balance between capital and labour, and eradicating every cause of conflict between these two factors of industry, thus safeguarding the interests of both sides. But it is a question in what way, in what fields, and to what extent the interference of the Government can be best made ?   We ask for the resolutions of the Conference in respect to these problems.'

Some members of the Government Committee were specially desirous of making a Factory Law, but for various reasons the Conference relegated the consideration of that subject to a committee appointed for the purpose. In the summer of 1898, the Government drafted a Factory Law Bill to be submitted to the forthcoming session of the Imperial Diet, and sent copies of it to the Chambers of Commerce throughout the country to ask their opinions. Most of the capitalists were opposed to it ; but, contrary to the expectation of the public, the High Agricultural, Commercial, and Industrial Conference approved of it, with some slight amendments. The Government, however, strange to say, has never submitted the Bill to the Diet.

Scientific study of social problems.

It is in the natural order of things that the systematic study of social problems should immediately follow the rise of the labour movement. Thus in response to the demands of the time, the Social Problem Study Association was organized, in 1890, by Dr. Yūjirō Miyaké, Sen Katayama, Téiichi Sakuma, Tōkichi Tarui, and the Rev. — Garst (an enthusiastic advocate of the Single Tax), with the object of studying social problems theoretically and practically. It was followed by the Social Policy Study Association, the members of which comprised many graduates of the Imperial University, having as their leaders Professors Noburo Kanai and Kumazō Kuwada. The aim of the association was declared to be ' to study how to put a stop to the class conflict of society by the concerted

actions of individuals and the State, in so far as it does not
disturb the present system of private property.'

Those who are interested in the study of labour problems
and social topics are naturally led to Socialism sooner or later. The first
The first Socialistic movement in this country was started by   Socialistic
Tōkichi Tarui. At the outset he intended to organize a social-   move-
istic body at Nagasaki in 1882, but in this attempt he utterly   ment.
failed.   Later, he again tried to unite Socialists in a league
with the assistance of Shimésu Inagaki, but again he failed.
Such being the case, we may safely say that the Socialistic
movement in our country is of comparatively recent origin.

The first association formed with the express purpose   Socialists'
of studying Socialism was the *Shakai-shugi Kenkyūkai*   associa-
(Socialism Study Association), established in the autumn of   tions.
1889.   The members occasionally met in the Hall of the
Unitarian Association at Shiba in Tōkyō and studied Socialism
theoretically and practically.   At their regular meetings they
gave, in turn, lectures on such eminent Socialists as St. Simon,
Fourier, Proudhon, Marx, &c. and on the principles laid down
by them.   This association lasted for two years, and during
that time some of the members advocated Socialism, while
others were opposed to it.   But at the end of 1900 the association decided to take up active work, and consequently it was
deemed essential that it should consist of Socialist members
only : the non-Socialist members thereupon withdrew, and at
the same time its title was changed to the *Shakai-shugi
Kyōkai* (Socialists' Association).   By this reform, however, the
members were reduced to only thirty or forty—far too small
a number to start any political movement.

In the spring of 1901 a memorable event in the history of   The
Japanese Socialism took place.   It was the formation of the   Social
Social Democrats' Party and its immediate dissolution by   Democrats'
Government interference.   What were the circumstances which   Party.
prompted the sudden appearance of such a party ?   We have
stated elsewhere how rapidly the *Kyōséikai*, the league of
engineers in the service of the Nippon Railway Company, grew
to be a powerful union.   Indeed, it then seemed as though all
the members of the league would readily join any political
party, if it only professed to stand by the labouring classes.

Encouraged by this prospect, on a certain day in April 1901, Sen Katayama, Denjirō Kōtoku, Naoyé Kinoshita, Kiyoshi Kawakami, Kojirō Nishikawa, and Isoh Abé met in the office of the Labour Union Perfecting Association, and decided to organize the Social Democrats' Party. A declaration was published on the 20th of May, according to which the object of the party was (1) to extend the application of the principle of Universal Brotherhood, (2) to enforce disarmament for the sake of Universal Peace, (3) to abolish the existing system of class-distinctions, (4) to establish public ownership in land and capital, (5) to establish public ownership in means of communications, such as railways and ships, (6) to equalize the distribution of wealth, (7) to equalize the distribution of political rights, and (8) to make the State bear the expense of free education for the people. But as these items were believed to be impossible of speedy realization, twenty-eight others were added to be carried out immediately. At this time the Itō Ministry was in power, and Baron (now Viscount) Suyématsu held the portfolio of Home Minister. By his order, Katayama and Kinoshita were summoned to the Central Police Office on the very day when the declaration was published, and were commanded to dissolve the party. Further, the authorities confiscated the printed copies of the party's declaration and prohibited the circulation of the newspapers, the ' Yorozu,' the ' Mainichi,' and two others, which had published the declaration, imposing a fine of twenty *yen* on each of them. Later, when the Katsura Cabinet superseded the Itō Ministry, the Socialists planned to revive the party under the title of the Japanese Commoners' Party, and applied to the authorities for approval, but the then Home Minister, Baron Utsumi, bluntly rejected the application.

Anti-war movement.

The year 1902 went by without any memorable event, for the Socialists, despairing of success in any political movement after the failure of the Social Democrats' Party, had returned to their educational work. In the following year, when the diplomatic relations of Russia and Japan became more and more strained, Kōtoku and Sakai, who had been preaching the Socialistic doctrine in the daily newspaper ' Yorozu,' and Mr. Kanzō Uchimura, who had been preaching Christianity in the same paper, united to protest against war, and on this account they all severed their connection with the journal. Kōtoku and Sakai planned a weekly paper of their own, with the assistance of Kōjirō Nishikawa and Sanshirō Ishikawa and the publication of the '*Héimin Shimbun*' was the result. From the very beginning the paper published anti-war articles, and after the sea-fight off Port Arthur on the 10th of February, 1904, the editors grew more vehement in expressing their opinions in the paper, and moreover, at times, held anti-war lecture meetings publicly. There may have been many reasons for the Socialists' protest against the war, but the most essential one was that the war would infinitely increase the suffering of the poor labouring classes no matter which side might win. When the war at last broke out, in spite of their desperate effort to check it, they decided to make an appeal to the International Congress of Socialists which was to meet at Amsterdam in August of the same year, sending a resolution which said : ' The Russo-Japanese War is nothing but a conflict between two capitalistic Governments, inflicting great loss upon the labourers in both countries. We, Japanese Socialists, therefore beseech each of the members of the International Congress of Socialists, to be held in August at Amsterdam, to urge the Government of his country to take steps to bring the War to an end speedily.' The Socialists not only sent this resolution to the Congress, but also appointed Sen Katayama, who was then on a tour in Europe and America, to represent them at it. The Congress met from the 14th to the 20th of August, with Mr. H. Van Kol of Holland as President, and Mr. G. Plekhanoff of Russia and Mr. Katayama of Japan as Vice-Presidents, and after its opening by the President, the two Vice-Presidents appeared at the rostrum, representing the Socialists of their respective countries, greeted each other by a warm handshake and addressed the audience. While the Congress was in session, the following resolution was passed unanimously, perhaps in response to the appeal made by the Japanese Socialists :

' Now that Russian despotism has received a heavy blow in consequence of the War, we express our deep sense of respect

The
' *Héimin Shimbun.*'

The International Congress of Socialists at Amsterdam.

for the commoners of the two belligerent countries who have been slain as victims of the present capitalistic system and governmental policies, and we declare that we will take measures to check the spread and progress of the War by the concerted action of all the Socialists in the world.'

Oppression of Socialists by the Government.

The Japanese Government might have shown more generosity to Socialists had it not been for the latter's strong opposition to the War. But as their anti-war enthusiasm knew no bounds, the Government could no longer wink at their activities, and when the ' Héimin Shimbun ' published an article against increased taxation, Sakai, the editor and publisher of the paper, was prosecuted. The persecution of the Socialists by the Government commenced with this case, and it became more and more vigorous until it culminated in the prohibition of the circulation of the ' Héimin Shimbun ' which contained the articles ' A Word to the Teachers of the Primary Schools,' ' The Confusion of the So-called Patriots,' ' The Attitude of the Educationist in Time of War,' &c., which were judged by the authorities to be injurious to public order, and the editor and the publisher were prosecuted in the Tōkyō Local Court.

Socialists' garden-party prohibited.

In commemoration of the first anniversary of the publication of the ' Héimin Shimbun,' on the 13th of November, 1904, the editors published, in the issue of the day, ' The Declaration of the Communists' Party,' drawn up by Marx and Engels. They also arranged a garden-party at Takinogawa to be given on the same day for the Socialists and their families. But on the previous evening, the Government vetoed the plan, and prohibited the circulation of the ' Héimin Shimbun,' in which ' The Declaration of the Communists' Party ' was published. Though the Government did not make known to the public its chief motive for prohibiting the garden-party arranged for harmless men and women, young and old, we have good reason to believe that it regarded the party as a step preliminary to the establishment of a secret society. Not only the Socialists residing in Tōkyō, but also those in the localities had been invited to the party, so the attendance might have numbered 500 or 600. The publication of ' The Declaration of the Communists' Party ' in the '*Héimin Shimbun*' had caused great anxiety to the Government, who considered it a substitute for a manifesto of a projected secret society. All these forms of oppression on the part of the Government only served as incentives to the activities of the discontented Socialists.

Nothing was now left undone to spread Socialism in this country, and not the least effort was the organization of an expedition to carry pamphlets in wagons for sale in the vicinity of Tōkyō or in the north-eastern district. Some of these even made their way as far west as Kyūshū, passing through the Main Island. Students also went on the same errand during their summer and winter vacations. In Tōkyō, the Socialists endeavoured to propagate Socialism by distributing printed matter and holding lecture meetings. The latter were at that time much in vogue, but it was those given by Socialists that attracted the greatest number of hearers. Seeing this state of things, the Government, not satisfied with oppressing the '*Héimin Shimbun*,' began to extend its persecuting hand mercilessly to such meetings, and on the 16th of November, 1905, commanded the Socialists' Association to be dissolved. This association, which had been working strenuously for the cause of Socialism ever since 1897, thus came to a tragic end. On the 19th of the same month, Messrs. Nishikawa and Kōtoku were punished for articles published in the '*Héimin Shimbun*,' and at the same time, the publication of the journal was prohibited, the printing-press was confiscated, and the issue of the 29th of November became the last. Prior to this, some Socialists had planned to publish a weekly journal and had applied to the authorities for permission, but the Central Police Office under various pretexts refused to grant it. An application to the Home Office met with a similar refusal. At their wits' end, they decided to turn their monthly magazine '*Chokugén*' (*Candid Opinion*) into a weekly one, publishing it as successor of the '*Héimin Shimbun*,' by the hands of the *Héiminsha*—a league of Socialists connected with the condemned paper.

On the 28th of February, 1905, Nishikawa and Kōtoku were sent to gaol. When they were released, after several months imprisonment, it was just after the Russian War had come to an end, and Japan was rejoicing over restored peace. They

Spread of Socialism.

Government oppression.

Activities of Socialists.

found to their great disappointment that the *Héiminsha* was fast declining in influence: in fact in October 1905, after a brave fight lasting over two years under the anti-war flag, it dissolved. Since then the activities of our Socialists have not been brilliant, although they have not ceased their efforts.   Those Socialists

Christian Socialists.

who are Christians have organized themselves into a body, and, with a view to diffusing Socialistic ideas among Japanese Christians, have published a magazine '*Shin Kigén*' (*New Era*), the first number of which appeared in November 1905.   San-shirō Ishikawa edited it with the assistance of Naoyé Kinoshita and Isoh Abé.   Nishikawa has also published another magazine entitled the '*Hikari*' (*Light*), intended to be the successor of the '*Chokugén*'; and Sakai has published still another periodical entitled the '*Shakaishugi Kenkyū*' (*Studies in Socialism*). Thus the activities of the Socialists have again become educational, aiming at obtaining more converts, and diligently seeking for an opportunity to resume their political movement.

As soon as they observed the generous attitude of the Saionji Ministry, they formed two Socialistic Parties—one

The State-Socialists' Party.

of which, the State-Socialists' Party, was organized in 1905, under the promotion of Yakichi Yamaji, Téikichi Shiba, Goichi Yamané, and Tahachirō Nakamura.   In a declaration they argue that in ancient times our Imperial ancestors practised Socialism in a sense, and that our people should resist the oppression of the rich in co-operation with the Imperial household.

The Japanese Socialists' Party.

The other is the Japanese Socialists' Party, organized in February 1906, by the Socialists who had formerly composed the *Héiminsha*.   Such names as Sen Katayama, Toshihiko Sakai, and Kōjirō Nishikawa are to be found among its advisers. This party did not publish any special declaration, but the first article of its regulations says that the party advocates Socialism within the limit of the laws of the State.   Neither the State-Socialists' Party nor the Japanese Socialists' Party has obtained a sufficient number of members to achieve anything great as yet, but they have never hesitated to express their opinions whenever a social problem of importance has occurred, and very often even to start a movement to solve it.   Especially noteworthy were their activities at a time when the proposal by the Electric Tramway Companies in Tōkyō to raise the fares was under consideration in the spring of 1906. Owing to the agitation caused by them, the proposal was withdrawn for a time, but in the summer of the same year the Electric Tramway Companies decided to put the proposal into practice by permission of the Home Office. The citizens of Tōkyō, angered at this, protested, and the Japanese Socialists' Party distributed circulars proposing to Boycott the companies by an undertaking not to take cars for three days running. The opposition of the citizens was so great that the companies could not run their cars at night for some time for fear of having them attacked by the mob; but as ill luck would have it, at that moment a heavy rainfall set in and continued for many days, so the citizens' resistance as well as the efforts of the Socialists were frustrated and ended in failure.

In conclusion mention may be made of some of the more important books on Socialism published in this country. Of those published before 1901, the chief were ' The Present Status of Socialism,' by the Minyūsha Publishing Co., 1893; ' Current Social Problems of Japan,' by Kinji Tajima, 1897; ' Protection of Labour,' by Kiyoshi Kawakami; ' What Labourers ought to Know,' by Junichirō Suzuki, 1897; 'Socialism,' by Tomyoshi Murai, 1899; ' Modern Socialism,' by Junzō Fukui, 1899; ' How to Harmonize Capital and Labour,' by Matao Toyohara, 1899; ' Economics of the Single Tax,' the posthumous publication of the Rev. — Garst's work, 1900; ' Comments on Modern Socialism,' by Yoshinori Hisamatsu, 1900; ' Guide to the Solution of Social Problems,' by Isoh Abé, 1901. Of later publications we may mention ' New Society,' by the Hon. Fumio Yano, ' The Essence of Socialism,' by Denjiro Kōtoku, and the two Socialistic novels by Naoyé Kinoshita, ' The Pillar of Fire ' and ' The Confessions of a Husband.' Besides the above books, the Héimin Sha published numerous pamphlets on Socialism from time to time. It is needless to say that all these books have greatly contributed to the spread of Socialism in this country.

Works on Socialism.

Socialistic ideas have been widely diffused throughout the empire in the past few years, and an increasing number of scholars and statesmen now devote themselves to its study, while a great

Conclusion.

many students take an interest in the subject. It would be a great mistake to judge of the influence of Socialism from the as yet small number of professed Socialists. The Socialistic spirit is afloat everywhere. To what, then, is attributable the fact that the political movement of Socialists is as yet very insignificant in influence? Certainly to the narrow limitation of the suffrage, by virtue of which the large number of Socialists have no qualification to participate in the Parliamentary elections. But some day, when the limits of the suffrage are enlarged, their activities will be great. It is for this reason that Socialists are crying out for the adoption of the popular suffrage system. How Socialism will develop in this country in the future is still problematical, but we cannot doubt that it will become a very powerful factor in politics when such extension takes place.

Postscript.—The author acknowledges his indebtedness to ' A Survey of Socialism,' by Mr. Yakichi Yamaji, for the account of the Nara and Héian Ages, and to ' The Labour Movement in Japan,' by Sen Katayama and Kōjirō Nishikawa, for information on the subject generally.

XXVII

HOKKAIDŌ AND ITS PROGRESS IN FIFTY YEARS

PROFESSOR SHŌSUKÉ SATŌ, D.PH., D.AGR. (JAPAN)

HOKKAIDŌ, called in ancient times ' Yézo-ga-Shima,' and some time later ' Oshima,' lies between 41° 21′ and 50° 57′ north latitude, and covers an area of 62,733 square miles. It is separated from Japan proper by the Strait of Tsugaru on the south, and from our new possession of Saghalien by that of Sōya on the north. Until nearly the time of the Restoration the island was owned by the lord of Matsumayé, though diplomatic troubles sometimes caused it to be placed under the direct control of the Shōgunate Government. The policy of the lords was to permit neither crop-farming nor stock-raising, and this was very hard on the inhabitants who had to depend wholly on marine products. Few immigrants were allowed to come to the island, the result being that the population gradually decreased, and the natural resources, of which it has many, were left undeveloped up to the time that the island passed to the Crown at the Restoration, when it was renamed ' Hokkaidō ' and a Colonial Department was established to look after its reclamation and other enterprises.

Geographical situation.

Rulers of Hokkaidō.

In ancient times, when the influence and power of the Imperial Ruler hardly extended to the northern province, constant conflicts raged between the Yamato and the Yézo races, the latter often invading the territories of the former, though the struggle always ended in their defeat ; in fact, history tells us of expeditions in almost every reign from the first century onwards.

Hokkaidō before the Restoration.

The earliest emigrants of the Yamato race that crossed over to the island, so far as history can trace them, were refugees who fled to that island when Yoritomo, the first Shōgun, destroyed the house of Fujiwara-no-Yasuhira in 1189. These soon began to form a feudal system of their own in the new colony, in imitation of that which they had left behind, shutting themselves up in natural fortresses as independent lords. They, however, were in time lorded over by a newcomer named Nobuhiro Takéda from the Province of Wakasa, who, having distinguished himself in battles under Kakizaki, one of the most powerful lords, at last succeeded, in 1454, in subduing the island which he subsequently ruled over. It was he who founded the

House of Matsumayé, which stretched a ruling hand over Yézo for so long a time. But neither influence nor popularity is to be gained in a hurry. Takéda had to make fortresses and station garrisons before he could do anything in the way of keeping down the mutinous people of Yézo, not to speak of Saghalien or the Kurile Islands, whose inhabitants always set at naught the authority of the new dominant clan. Nor does force bring popularity. Besides, the clan of Matsumayé, holding the southern part of the island, was too far off to be obeyed by the whole island of Yézo, and the lord himself was too selfish and tyrannizing towards his subjects. Neither did the clan attempt to lead the natives towards civilisation, but, on the contrary, stood in the way of progress. Almost wholly discarding agriculture, it looked for its taxes to those on marine products, and instead of giving its subjects farms or

lands, as other feudal chiefs did, the Matsumayé clan only conferred fishing-grounds on them, laying, at the same time, heavy taxes upon fishing and fishermen, and upon ships coming into the island harbours. Nor was anything done to open up any system of communications—such as roads to the interior. The central Tokugawa Government, by its closed-door policy against foreigners, which the clan of Matsumayé had to follow, increased the difficulties under which Yézo proper, to say nothing of Saghalien or other minor islands, suffered.

Russians had meanwhile appeared in the Kurile Islands so far back as 1711–35, and they came again in 1772–92 to Akkéshi and Némnro. All through the middle and latter end of the eighteenth century, their country was seeking for an opportunity to lay hold of the island of Hokkaidō. It was indeed no time for inaction, and this the clan of Matsumayé knew, as well as the Shōgunate.

Though the diplomacy of the Shōgunate in its last years was unquestionably a thorough failure, it deserves approval for its endeavour to fortify and protect the island of Yézo. In the eighteenth and nineteenth centuries, when the clan of Matsumayé was found to be too powerless to protect the island, the Shōgunate perforce gave up the closed-door principle which it had long held, so far as this island was concerned, and not only abolished the restriction on immigrants, but even encouraged immigration. Oppression was thus replaced by kindness and benevolence towards the people. Expeditions and explorations were made into unknown parts of Yézo, Saghalien, and the Kurile Islands, for long previously the Tokugawa Government had seen the necessity of exploring and reclaiming these islands. Mitsukuni Tokugawa had, at the end of the seventeenth century, sent ships to the mouth of the Ishikan River to explore the islands of Yézo, and his example was followed by many explorers and adventurers during the hundred and fifty years prior to the Restoration. Among the best known of these were Tsunénori Mogami in Saghalien and the Kuriles; Jūzō Kondō in the Kuriles; Tadataka Inō, who was the first to draw a map of Japan Proper and these islands; Rinzō Mamiya in Saghalien and Manchuria, and more recently Takéshirō Matsuura and Bumpéi Okamoto in Yézo and Saghalien. The Tokugawa Government certainly did signal diplomatic work in its last years, concerning the northern islands, and Masayasu Habuto, Yasutomo Togawa, Hiroshi Horikawa, and Norimasa Muragaki must unquestionably be ranked among politicians produced by the Shōgunate *régime*. Russia, by this time, had absorbed Kamchatka and Alaska, and having practically laid her aggressive hands on the island of Etorofu also, she was now pushing her way to Némuro in Yézo. Our officials found this out, but they deemed themselves so far beyond the reach of aggression that some of the retainers of Habuto marked 'Japan's possession as long as the heavens and the earth last' on notices posted on the island of Etorofu in 1801.

The Shōgunate's defence of Yézo.

Saghalien
question.

This appeared to check the Russians there, but in Saghalien they grew more and more overbearing towards the Japanese. The latter proposed to make the fiftieth degree the boundary line between Japan and Russia, but the former kept on pressing downwards in the island. Things went on in this way, till Perry made his unexpected appearance in the Japanese seas. This naturally prevented the Shōgunate Government from assisting Yézo, all it could do being to appoint a new governor of Hakodaté (in addition to the lord of Matsumayé), to negotiate with foreign countries, particularly with Russia, as to our northern islands. But this was altogether ineffectual, for the clan of Matsumayé proved too feeble either to open up or reclaim the islands, and Yézo had to wait for a new epoch to lead it to civilization.

Hokkaidō
under the
Colonial
Govern-
ment.

The Government was restored to the Imperial House in 1867, and Yézo thereupon became a part of the realm under direct Imperial rule. In accordance with the policy, laid down centuries before by the Emperor Jimmu, of extending the Imperial influence and dominions north-ward, a meeting was called in March 1868, to discuss, in the Imperial presence, how to reclaim the island, with the result that soon afterwards a Colonial Government was estab-lished at Hakodaté with many good and true men of the

Fugitives
of the
Shōgunate
in Hok-
kaidō.

Restoration as its officials. But meanwhile, a part of the discontented troops of the Shōgunate, under the command of Énomoto (the late Viscount), having been defeated by the Imperial armies, took refuge at Hakodaté, and lodged a petition that they might be allowed to start a Tokugawa clan there. It was of course impossible that the Imperial Court could permit such an illegal act of possession by the refugees, and consequently it at once sent out an army in May, 1869, to put down the rebels, issuing at the same time an Imperial order, in which we find the following :

Imperial
rescript.

' Yézo is the northern gate of the Empire, beyond which lie Santan and Manchuria over the sea. True, there is a boundary between this country and the others, but towards the north it is so vague that foreigners dwell mixed with the natives. After Hakodaté is quieted, We intend to take steps to reclaim and people the island. Every suggestion to that effect is welcome.'

It was the general policy of the Government to fortify the northern frontiers, on the one hand, and, on the other, to win the goodwill of the natives and the reclamation of the land. With this in view, the Colonial Government was now organized, and in July 1869, the island was renamed 'Hokkaidō,' and divided into eleven provinces with eighty-six districts. Lands were freely given to those who would devote themselves to agriculture, and the fundamental principle of reclamation was thus laid. Naomasa Nabéshima was the first chief magistrate of the new Government (soon succeeded by Mr., now Count, Higashikuzé), and the first staff officers were Yoshio Shima, Michitoshi Iwamura, Takéshirō Matsuura, &c. When these officials arrived at their posts, they at once selected Sapporo as the site of the island's government. In September 1870, a Saghalien Colonial Government was organized independently of the island government of Hokkaidō. In 1871 when Kiyotaka Kuroda (afterwards Count) was appointed Vice-Governor of Hokkaidō, he was commissioned to take charge of the affairs of Saghalien also, and he went thither to inspect the real conditions of that island. On his return he made a report in which we find the following :

Colonial Government of Hokkaidō.

Kuroda's memorial.

'. . . That a Government should be established in the Province of Ishikari to rule, under the presidency of one from the Ministry, the eleven prefectures of Hokkaidō and Saghalien ; that unworthy officials should be dismissed in order to correct tardiness in the discharge of official business ; that the Government should be benevolent towards its subjects, and that all taxes and duties should be made light ; that all the possessions of the different clans should be restored to the Imperial Government ; that the natives should be treated with affection, protected, and educated ; that fishing and other industries should be carried on as in former days ; that the yearly expenditure should be raised to 1,500,000 *yen* ; that a Minister or an Adviser of State should be sent to observe the conditions, in order that permanent laws may be enacted ; that advisers well versed in the work of reclamation should be

employed, and that some experts in mineralogy should be
engaged to inspect minerals, &c.'

These suggestions were adopted, and Kuroda was at once
sent to America to make necessary investigations as to what
measures should be taken in order to improve Hokkaidō, while
Count Tanéomi Soyéshima, Councillor of State, was sent to
Hokkaidō on an official tour.   In the meantime, Sadaaki
Nishimura received orders to make arrangements for the
removal of the Colonial Government to Sapporo, which was
effected in June 1871, with newly established branch offices
at Hakodaté and Némuro, and official stations in every
district.   Kuroda returned in the same month, bringing with
him General Capron, Chief of the Agricultural Bureau of the
United States, to be employed as Adviser in Hokkaidō.   It is
to Kuroda and this American adviser that we owe much of the
improvement of Hokkaidō, for the undertakings that were
carried out for the betterment of the island during the ten
subsequent years were planned under their supervision.   The
foundation of the administration being thus laid, Kuroda next
endeavoured to bring all the islands of Hokkaidō under the
direct control of the Colonial Government.   He caused all the
possessions and estates of different clans, lords, temples, and
individuals to be placed directly under the new Government,
and he even went so far as to abolish the Saghalien Colonial
Government with the same object.   He then asked the Central
Government for an appropriation of 10,000,000 *yen* spread
over ten years from 1872.   It was, however, a considerable
matter for the Government to grant such a large sum
as 1,000,000 *yen* a year, over and above the revenues of the
island, when the Treasury was quite empty ; but it was done,
and on a suggestion from Kuroda, a loan of 2,500,000
yen was floated to enable the administration to be
properly started.   In 1872 the official organization of the
Colony was revised, and branch-offices were established in
Hakodaté, Némuro, Saghalien, Urakawa, and Sōya ; the four
districts of Fukushima, Tsugaru, Jishi, and Hiyama, of Oshima
Province, which had hitherto been under the prefectural government of Aomori, were also brought under the same Government

at Sapporo. Thus, for the first time, all the islands of Hokkaidō and Saghalien were under the direct control of the Colonial Government.

The financial foundation of the Hokkaidō Government was laid when the Central Government granted the Colony the 10,000,000 *yen* during ten years, in addition to its own revenues. It was a wise action, for the reclamation of lands requires a greater amount of expense than any other enterprise, and it testified to the great confidence reposed in the chief official, and also the faith that the official had in his own ability as well as in that of his American adviser. For it must be remembered that colonization was something quite new to the Government, and the authorities consequently required the governor to be entirely responsible for his administration. The Emperor himself went out of his way to lay great responsibility on him, as we find in an Imperial edict of July 1871, which ran as follows : *Financial founda- tion of the Hokkaidō Govern- ment.*

' As the Governor is the chief magistrate, who is to take part in political affairs with the Emperor, and to superintend the officials in their work, he should hold himself responsible for every sign of misgovernment that may happen in the adminis- tration, and should never involve the Sovereign in trouble on this account.'

With his duty thus defined, Kuroda devoted himself soul and body to the work assigned him, and Hokkaidō now saw a new epoch in the history of its affairs. Cultivation and immigration are the two essentials in the reclamation of new lands, and this the Colonial Government did not fail to perceive, for, when both Hokkaidō and Saghalien were brought under its direct control, the very first work it did was to revise the laws of cultivation and immigration, and by an agrarian law set bounds to the extent of land that could be sold or purchased, made the standard of land value very low, and exempted land from all taxes and duties for ten years. Encouragement and protection were also given to immigration (particularly to immigrants who came in a body to such places as Yūshu, Tōbétsu, and Shizunai), and to fishery also, which had been the only financial resource of the clan of Matsumayé, although *Agrarian law.*

Encouragement and protection of immigrants.

the Colonial officials were wise enough to attach the greater importance to farming. For the assistance of the latter, seeds and agricultural implements were ordered from America through the American adviser,[1] and persons to be instructed in the employment of these implements were called for.

Education.

Again, the work required a wide application of science and art, for lands had to be surveyed and mineral veins searched for throughout the islands. Thus the Colonial Government was obliged to employ many scientists, as well as experts, and to establish schools of agriculture, both of primary and higher education. To this end, in 1871–72, many young men and women of promise were sent to study abroad at official expense.

Communication facilitated.

Like the Tokugawa Government, which, having long previously felt the necessity of opening communications with the Yézo islands, had constructed roads over the mountain passes of Sarudomé and commenced the coasting trade, so Kuroda saw that it was quite indispensable for his administration to have perfect means of communication. The first road that he constructed was that between Sapporo and Hakodaté, about a hundred miles long, at the cost of 1,000,000 *yen*. To us to-day this does not seem a great enterprise, but thirty years ago, and especially at the outset of the Colonial administration, such a work must have been regarded as something extraordinary. For the coasting trade, the Government provided ships and boats to ply not only along the coast of the island, but also to the Kuriles, to Saghalien, and as far as Vladivostock.

Industries encouraged.

Every branch of agriculture, industry, and commerce was introduced into Hokkaidō. Industries which were quite new to Hokkaidō were particularly encouraged with a view to enhancing the utility of the agricultural products. But, unfortunately, the people not being accustomed to business, their undertakings made little headway, and hence the Colonial Government had to take the lead, and flour mills, beet-sugar factories, breweries of wine and beer, manufactories for tinning salmon, trout, and venison were some of their most important undertakings. Besides, sericulture was encouraged by building

[1] These American seeds, grain, and fruit were first planted in experimental fields at Aoyama, Tōkyō, till they became accustomed to the soil and climate of Japan, when they were removed to the different experimental fields in Hokkaidō.

filatures, coal-shafts were sunk at Horonai, and a railway was constructed between Horonai and Otaru, chiefly for the exportation of coal.

Fortunately the marine products increased year by year, until a market for them extended over sea to China; and while, on the one hand, the Government encouraged fishermen by grants, and made scientific researches and investigations into the fisheries, on the other, many officials were sent as far as Vladivostock to ascertain what Japanese articles were in demand there.

The Colonial Government had to attend not only to the financial affairs, but to the defence, jurisdiction, and diplomacy of the island. In 1873 Kuroda sent in a petition concerning the organization of a Colonial Militia : *Militia.*

' The work of reclamation has just been initiated, and the number of immigrants is ever on the increase. It is now of urgent necessity, therefore, to provide some means of defence and protection, especially since the island of Saghalien has been a constant source of trouble to the Empire. It is very desirable to have a standing army, besides some men-of-war, to protect the coasts, but this would cost too much money. My plan, therefore, is to organize a Colonial Militia, which could serve the country alike in time of war and peace.'

The Colonial Government had also its own judges. Whilst as to diplomacy, Hokkaidō was not by any means free from serious questions, for the Colonial Government was called on to deal with such an extraordinary diplomatic question as the exchange of the Kurile Islands for Saghalien. This had been one of the most perplexing problems demanding solution by the Shōgun's officials, of whom Hori, Muragaki, and their colleagues (who were afraid of coming into collision with Russia), insisted upon giving up Saghalien altogether, while his opponents, headed by the lord of Mito, advocated that Japan should never abandon her grip on all the islands of Yézo, inclusive, of course, of Saghalien and the Kuriles. No satisfactory solution had been found when Kuroda was appointed. He saw that it would be on the whole far wiser to effect the exchange of Saghalien and the Kurile Islands, and, by thus at once ending *Justice and diplomacy.*

further trouble with Russia, to devote the whole energy of the
Colonial Government to the administration of Hokkaidō only,
and he gained his point in spite of great opposition. The system
of civil administration that the Colonial Government adopted
was that of representation of towns and villages, and it
included the creation of lines of communication both postal
and telegraphic, the establishment of light-houses, the buoying
of channels, and the building of penitentiaries.

Civil administration.

Unfortunately blunders on the part of certain officials in
selling official properties caused great public discontent, which
led the Central Government to abolish the Colonial Government,
and its work was thus arrested in 1882, at the moment of bearing
fruit, and when many further improvements were imminent.

Colonization work arrested.

The Colonial Government passed away in 1882, and the
administrative authority was divided among the new Prefectural
Governments of Hakodaté, Sapporo, and Némuro. All other
branches of administration were transferred to different departments—viz., jurisdiction to the Department of Justice ; the
Colonial Militia to that of the Army ; railways, shipping, and
other means of transportation to that of Industries ; taxes,
taxation, and matters, which pertained to subsidies for fishermen, to that of Finance ; and agriculture, cattle-breeding, and
farming education to that of Agriculture and Commerce. Instead of one government, Hokkaidō was now under the charge
of three governments and different Departments of State.
During the ten years of its existence, since 1872, the Colonial
Government did all that it could for the management and
improvement of the northernmost islands. It laid the foundation of government, and was just beginning to lead the islands
into the fair road to civilization, when it was thus suddenly swept
away ; had it not been abolished so soon, Hokkaidō would
no doubt have achieved far more progress than it has since
made. The new governments of the three prefectures followed,
as much as they possibly could, the policy adopted by the
Colonial Government, but the population was yet too small, lands
were too little reclaimed, and industries were in too imperfect
a state of progress, so that, earnest as the three governments
were, they could not make their administration successful in
proportion to its cost. They left the institutions established by

New Prefectural Governments.

the former government *in statu quo,* nor did they make many changes in the law. Nevertheless no great progress in administration seemed to be within their reach, and undoubtedly the Central Government blundered in this at least, that instead of considering Hokkaidō low and uncivilized, as it really was, and treating it as such, they tried to put it into the same administrative mould with the prefectures in Japan proper. Naturally, no sooner had the new governments begun their administration than they found themselves surrounded by every sort of opposition and obstruction, and Hokkaidō stumbled on the very road towards a progress which would have been good, had the island remained under the sway of the Colonial Government. At last, therefore, the Central Government established a Hokkaidō Works Inspection Bureau in the Department of Agriculture and Commerce, in order to look after the enterprises, industrial as well as agricultural, that the Colonial Government had started, and also to supervise the railways in charge of the Industrial Department. The new Bureau was to take charge of the government works which the Colonial Government had begun. But these required to be constantly improved in unison with the changes of the times. What, then, could the new Bureau accomplish, when it merely copied and followed the principles laid down by the abolished Colonial Government ? Besides, these official works were, at the start, never meant to be financial resources of the island government, but only to serve as examples to give encouragement to the people, and to lead them into the path of industrial development. Whilst therefore it was wise and far-seeing on the part of the Colonial officials to have introduced, years previously, every branch of science and learning to be applied to the works on the island, such works and enterprises had to be constantly improved, as time advanced. But unfortunately the Inspection Bureau was incompetent for the task, was quite impotent to direct the works, and could only keep them going, so Hokkaidō, promising and improving though it had been, naturally failed to continue its progressive course.

But whilst the Central Government followed a negative policy with regard to the ordinary administration, it was very active in doing all that it could to augment the Colonial Militia.

Aristocratic immigrants.

which served at once to fortify and reclaim the island, and when, in default of encouragement and protection, settlers on the island did not show such an increase as was desired, the Government issued an ordinance to the effect that every prefecture should send yearly to Hokkaidō 350 families of its *samurai* class. These were probably the only two meritorious acts that were

Incompetency of the new administration. done under the three governments plan, which otherwise, during their four years existence from 1882 to 1886, did nothing except to keep the institutions and establishments in the same state and condition that they had been under the Colonial Government. In this they blundered and were short-sighted. Especially was this the case, when one bears in mind that New Japan was in great need of financial resources which Hokkaidɔ alone could furnish, and therefore it was of urgent importance both for Hokkaidō and for the Empire at large to open and reclaim the islands as soon and as much as possible, and thus to carry out the Imperial behest with regard to their reclamation. But these incompetent and negative-principled governments proved themselves unworthy of undertaking any such responsibility, and failing to do so they found themselves confronted by opposition and difficulty on every side. At last, therefore, in January 1886, the Central Government resolved to abolish the three prefectural governments system as well as the Hokkaidō Works Inspection Bureau, and to transfer the administration as well as the reclamation of the island to a newly established Government of Hokkaidō.

Third Hokkaidō Government. The new Hokkaidō Government, established in 1886, was, so to speak, a second Colonial Government, but in its policy of administration it was one of quite a different nature. Although what was required in Hokkaidō remained the same as had been defined in the Imperial words spoken at the time of the Restoration, the administrative government of the island changed with the changes of the times, of its officials, and of public opinion. In the last years of the administration of the three prefectural governments, the Central Government sent various officials to the island to inspect the real conditions. It was then found, much to Tōkyō's surprise, that the Colonial officials were unworthy of their trust and that their government was an entire failure, for they, being quite ignorant of the principles of reclamation had abused the privileges and protection of which the Colony was in receipt. These Colonial officials had, as a fact, encouraged many official enterprises, while keeping down private ones, and, so far from leading the island to civilization, had stood in the way of its progress. These unexpected discoveries led the Government to a sudden abolition of the three governments. It was indeed a timely step.

Michitoshi Iwamura was appointed chief of the new Hokkaidō Administration. He had been in the Colonial Government before, and once again he applied his whole energy to the administration of the Colony. But the real conditions of the island were at this time quite different from those at the time of the Restoration. Japan, to begin with, was no longer weak and powerless. The political agitation, which followed the Satsuma rebellion, had been allayed by the Imperial promise to establish a constitutional monarchy. The whole country was now turning to peaceful work. Every branch of science, making great advances, found a wide field of application not only in politics and legislature, but in colonization and reclamation, and new works in agriculture and industry were constantly springing up. Hokkaidō was now a place of attraction, for it offered hopeful prospects for enterprises. Such of the official works as had been successful were transferred to the hands of private persons, and special protection was given to many new works of agricultural industry, such as the manufactures of sugar and hemp. The new Government made special investigations into the economics of farming, which had been an object of attention since the establishment of the Colonial Government. Steps were taken at the same time to introduce new methods of farming by replacing the hand-plough by the horse and ox. In order to afford every possible inducement to the method of large farming, the land regulations were revised, and surveys were made to ascertain how much of the land was reclaimable for arable. Taxes and duties, which had formerly been paid in kind, were henceforth to be paid in money at greatly reduced rates, and land was exempted from all imposts for twenty years after reclamation. The Colonial troops were distributed among unreclaimed parts of the island, and their efforts at industry were specially encouraged. Ports and

Governor Iwamura.

New works in agriculture and industry encouraged.

harbours were constructed on the coasts for purposes of communication and commerce, and prisoners of the Peniten-

Organiza-
tion of
communi-
cation
left un-
touched.
tiary were employed in opening and constructing roads. It is greatly to be regretted that, in spite of all that the different governments of Hokkaidō did in regard to administration, the organization of communications and especially of internal intercourse was left almost untouched. The Colonial officials failed to see what rapid progress the island would make within a few years, and deterred by the financial situation, they left the traffic management on the official railways, for instance, in the hands of private promoters. Nor did they attempt to extend the lines. In fact, the new Hokkaidō Government resembled the Colonial Government in its activities ; like the latter, which engaged many foreign advisers and engineers, the former also employed several foreigners for the construction of harbours as well as for the manufactures of sugar and flax. Numerous scholars of promise were sent out to study and investigate abroad. The Sapporo Agricultural College, the only organ of high education in the island, was much expanded and extended both to give new learning and to set an example in agriculture, and so, for a couple of years, the new Government showed much activity in the organization of the administration and in reclamation.

Hokkaidō
under
Governor
Naga-
yama.
In 1888 Takéshiro Nagayama, Commander of the Colonial Militia, was ordained to be chief of the Hokkaidō Government in succession to Iwamura. Being a soldier he combined the civil and military administrations in one. With the knowledge acquired during a sojourn abroad and the support given by the Kuroda Cabinet, Nagayama put forth his whole strength for the opening up of Hokkaidō. He naturally attached great importance to the organization of the Colonial troops, and it was about this time that the two successful military villages of Uryū and Asahigawa were founded. Nor did the pervading spirit of enterprise allow the productive Province of Ishikari to remain uncultivated, as by this time immigrants had flowed

Increase
of the
popula-
tion.
into its northern parts, and they added to the population of Hokkaidō some 40,000 persons a year. Japan had now made leaps in civilization, her financial conditions had improved, and both commerce and industry showed a very favourable outlook.

Thus the whole country being completely pervaded by the spirit of enterprise, Hokkaidō could not escape from becoming involved in the movement. Consequently, we see about this time the Muroran line of railway being constructed and the Hokkaidō Coal-Mine Railway Company organized to prolong the railways and to extend the mines, and everything in the Hokkaidō business world becoming very active and promising. But in 1890, just before the Imperial Diet was opened, the Kuroda Cabinet gave way to the Yamagata Cabinet, and this change removed Nagayama from the post of chief and put Chiaki Watanabé in his place in June 1891. Watanabé did not remain in Hokkaidō longer than a year, and during that short time the Central Government was too much taken up with Parliamentary troubles to turn its attention to its affairs. He began no new works during the year of his administration, nor indeed did anything, except perhaps that, by resuming the old negative principle, he consolidated the works started by former governments. It was also in the course of Watanabé's administration that Hokkaidō, which had hitherto been under the direct control of the Cabinet, was brought gradually into connection with the Home Department.

Hokkaidō Coal-Mine Railway Co.

Governor Watanabé.

Watanabé was succeeded by Kunimichi Kitagaki, in July 1892. He found that Hokkaidō was progressing, and that new industrial works were springing up everywhere—for the prosperous condition of the business world in Japan Proper in 1889–90 had sent hundreds of thousands of immigrants to Hokkaidō, besides many large capitalists—and so in spite of the negative principles of Governor Watanabé, Hokkaidō presented a very hopeful prospect in industries and agriculture. What attracted Kitagaki's attention most was the completion of the *post-bellum* undertakings after the China-Japan War, and projects of harbour and railway constructions which were being gradually carried into effect. The first harbours constructed were at Hakodaté and Otaru, and the first new railway built was the Kamikawa line. Canals and drainage were also carefully attended to. But the close of the China-Japan War, which caused the Department of Colonization to be established in the Central Government on account of the annexation of

Governor Kitagaki.

Post-bellum undertakings after the China-Japan War.

Formosa by Japan, removed Kitagaki from Hokkaidō to the
ministerial chair of the new Department, and Yasutarō Hara
took the whole responsibility of governing the northern islands
in the place of Kitagaki. Like Nagayama, who, as successor
of Iwamura, copied the policy of the latter, the new governor
of Hokkaidō adopted the same principles and policy that his
predecessor had followed. He merely carried out the schemes
and undertakings of Kitagaki. Besides, Kitagaki, though
removed from Hokkaidō, was still in the Colonial Department,
which practically ruled over Hokkaidō and the other colonies,
and consequently the policy of administration with regard to
Hokkaidō suffered no change, and Hokkaidō affairs seemed very
hopeful in every respect. In the meantime, the Ministry
underwent frequent changes after the close of the China-
Japan War, the administration being given over sometimes to
militarism and sometimes to political parties, and every new
Cabinet renewed the Governor of Hokkaidō. Still, the enter-
prising spirit of the Empire continued, so that while the
general tendency was to make national expansions abroad,
the prospective condition of Hokkaidō attracted the attention of men of enterprise who went over to the island and
started new works, which gradually became so numerous that
no alterations in administrative policy on the part of the
ruling classes have been able to affect them.

When Yasukata Sonoda was appointed the Governor in
1898, the Colonial Government made a step further by giving
increased importance to local self-government. Hitherto
Hokkaidō had known nothing in the way of self-government ;
it was, as it were, a pure colony, and no distinction was made
between State and local finance. By this time, agriculture
and industry had made leaps and bounds, the population of
the island had increased several fold, and the financial conditions had very much improved. Why should the people not
have their own self-governments ? Hakodaté, Otaru, and
Sapporo in particular, were as well qualified for self-government
as any prefecture in Japan Proper. Nor was the interior behind
in civilization, for the construction of railways had placed the
newly opened towns and villages on the same level with every
other part of Japan.

Governor Hara.

Recent progress.

Governor Sonoda, therefore, made great efforts to have Self-government. a completely organized self-government in Hokkaidō. He opened the Hokkaidō Assembly to discuss the local finances of the islands, and thus, for the first time, the local treasury was made independent of the National Treasury. At the same time, Sonoda proclaimed the ward system and the town and village regulations—certainly one of the greatest advances that Hokkaidō has made in administration. He also carried into effect so much of the ten years' project of railway construc- Railway. tion, which Kitagaki had planned, that the connections of Ishikari, Tokachi, and Kushiro were nearly completed, though the Russo-Japanese War suspended all these works for the time being. Another important matter that Sonoda carried out was a ten years' project for extending common roads into the interior. It was beyond doubt very far-seeing of him to detect how important and necessary it was for purposes of reclamation and administration to make the common roads keep pace with Roads. the railways. Hokkaidō has now Mr. Kawashima as Governor. Agriculture has showed a wonderful progress of late, and its products are now widely exported to foreign markets ; other enterprises—such as fisheries, manufactures, forestry, and what not—have increased in equal proportions, and the natural Agriculture, &c. resources of Hokkaidō, which had lain undiscovered for centuries, are now being vigorously developed, to the great increase of Japan's wealth and practical strength. We have, therefore, little doubt that Hokkaidō will soon prove itself quite worthy to be called, as it has been sometimes, a storehouse of natural treasures.

XXVIII

THE ADMINISTRATION OF FORMOSA (TAIWAN)

Baron Shimpéi Gotō

Acquisi-
tion of
Formosa.

The island of Taiwan, or Formosa, was ceded to Japan in 1895 by a treaty concluded at the end of the war with China. While negotiations for peace were being conducted at Shimonoséki between Marquis (the late Prince) Itō and Li-Hung-chang, the latter remarked : 'Formosa will, I think, present immense difficulties in the matter of administration, inasmuch as the people there are deeply addicted to the vicious habit of opium-smoking ; and should the island come under Japan's rule, it will cause no small trouble to her.'

Lack of
prepara-
tion for its
adminis-
tration.

With regard to the transfer of Formosa, it may be noted that Japan had made no preparations whatever for the administration of the island at the time of its acquisition, notwithstanding the fact that, in the case of other nations confronted by a similar occasion, elaborate schemes are generally formulated to meet contingencies connected with the occupation of a new territory. Under these circumstances there was every reason to doubt whether Japan could ever succeed as ruler of the island. Experienced men of other countries, who had practical experience of the difficulties in governing a new territory, were inclined to predict that Japan would, like Sparta of old, certainly fail as a ruler in peace, though she might succeed in war. This was not a mere conjecture based on Viceroy Li's remarks ; it was the outcome of doubts entertained by eminent men in great colonizing countries, who had had ample experience in forming designs for the administration of new territories. Japan was regarded as lacking the requisite genius in territorial enterprises, and was known to have many

Predic-
tions by
foreign
observers.

manifestly weak points. The most conspicuous of these latter
was a defect in her religion. How far religion affects colonization it is needless to conjecture here, but it may be confidently
asserted that all colonies, prior to the development of modern
Imperialism, owed their prosperity to the influence of religion,
and that has been proved to be the case even at the present
day. The question therefore arises whether Japan had any
such religion to rely upon. To this the answer, I am sorry to
say, must be in the negative.

It must be admitted, too, that instances can hardly be found
in the history of modern times where an Asiatic people has ever
governed its dependencies with any degree of success. There
was, therefore, every reason to doubt Japan's efficiency to
administer her new territory.

The first Governor-General of Formosa was Admiral Count
Kabayama (appointed May 1895), who was succeeded by
General Count Katsura, who in turn gave place to General
Baron Nogi, the chair of the Governor-General often changing
its occupant and none remaining there long.

I was appointed to the post as Chief of the Bureau of Civil
Government under the fourth Governor-General, the late
General Kodama, at the beginning of 1898. It would seem but
proper for me to state here the condition of affairs prior to my
appointment, so as to give materials for comparison with those
which followed, but I am unwilling to do so for various
reasons, for undoubtedly blunders had occurred in the first
three years, for which the authorities must be held responsible.
When General Kodama, the fourth Governor-General, assumed
the direction of affairs, he made no declaration whatever as to
the course he intended to pursue, his policy being ' deeds   Policy of
rather than words '—execution rather than exposition. It   Governor-
                                                              General
would have been easy to outline a policy, either written or   Kodama.
oral, in flowery diction, but practical, executive administration
is not a matter for poetical outbursts. Governor-General
Kodama was better informed than other government officials
in the Empire with regard to the affairs of Formosa, for he had
sat in council as Vice-Minister of War, and also as a member of
the General Staff at the time of the war between Japan and
China, and when Formosa was placed under military control,

immediately after its cession to Japan, he himself was deputed
to overlook the matter at home, and again when a Bureau of
Formosan affairs was established in the Central Government,
he undertook the management of its business as one of the
committee. Yet, in spite of his great knowledge concerning the
island, he remained silent as to the policy he would adopt, and
this singular attitude on his part must have arisen from the
firm convictions he entertained in view of the situation.
So, at least, I believed at the time, and I am now in a
position to verify my opinion by reference to the results
he actually achieved through an administration in which I
also participated.

Distur-
bances
caused by
insur-
gents.
At the time of my initiation into office the affairs of the
island were said to be getting into order, but such was far
from being the case. On the contrary, disturbances caused
by native insurgents were everywhere prevalent, even in
the vicinity of Taihoku, where one occurred not many
months after Governor-General Kodama's arrival—the wife of
a government official being killed in broad daylight by the
insurgents at a place very near the city. From this it was
clearly seen that the native insurgents were yet far from
being pacified.

Want of
official
order and
discipline.
If disorder was rife amongst the natives, order was hardly
better maintained among the functionaries of the Government.
Abuses were rank (the consequence of a military government),
and discipline was almost unknown. This too was the time
when the famous judicial question, burning fiercely both at
home and abroad, tended to augment the difficulty of enforcing
obedience and discipline in the ranks of officialdom.

Reduction
of
subsidy.
Another and far greater difficulty felt at this time was
the reduction—an immense reduction—in the subsidy from
the National Treasury. The sum of 6,000,000 *yen* hitherto
allowed yearly was suddenly reduced to 3,900,000 *yen*. Could
anything cause greater consternation to the executive body
than such a sudden change in its finances—especially at
a time when administrative reforms had to be carried out ?
Under such overwhelming difficulties we struggled for the best.
The most reliable source from which to derive valuable help
would have been religion, by means of which we might have

won the hearts of the people, as in the case of other countries. But religion, as I said before, was entirely wanting in our case. So the embarrassments under which we laboured may easily be imagined.

The question of foreign residence had a tendency to foster troubles in connection with many alterations brought about at the time of the transfer of the territory. Hence the territorial administration at this stage furnished to domestic and foreign journals many a chance of attacking it. Besides all this, we were not cognizant of the real state of popular feeling. Little was known about the savages living in the islands, and there were few officials, professional interpreters excepted, who understood the vernacular tongue. The language is Chinese, it is true ; but there are at least three distinct languages among the Chinese inhabitants, while twenty different tongues are spoken by the savages. The settlers speak various languages, having lived under many different rulers ; for the island has in turn belonged to Holland, Spain, China, and Japan. The greater part of the inhabitants are Chinese ; but most of these being, so to speak, descendants of rebels and insurgents, they lack the character of a people who have lived an orderly life under an hereditary government.

Question of foreign residence.

Language difficulty.

The native religion shows many different forms ; but, speaking broadly, the principal creeds are two—Christianity and Taoism. Religious belief is of the lowest kind—a mere superstition rather than a creed based on conviction. As to Christian believers, there are very few.

Religion.

Thus the want of mutual understanding owing to different languages, the conflict of habits and feelings, and the existence of distinct classes of society—all these things contributed to furnish trouble for the administration. Such was the state of affairs in the third year after the annexation of the island to Japan, and when the seven years' administration by Governor-General Kodama began.

The first thing the Governor-General did on his appointment to his new post was to suppress the broils then existing among the officials, and to clear the way for exercising full control over them, and to this end he dismissed no less than one thousand of all ranks.

Selection of officers.

Revision
of political
districts.

The political districts, which formerly were six *ken* [1] and three *chō*,[1] were reduced to three *ken* and three *chō*. Schools were established for the education of those officials who had direct dealings with the people—such as the police officials—and there they were taught the vernacular tongue along with other studies.

Diffusion
of medical
know-
ledge.

Medical schools were also opened for native students of medicine, in addition to an institution already provided for public physicians.

Develop-
ment of
education.

National language schools were also established whose object was to instruct the native population concerning Japan.

With a view to tabulate the lands belonging to the Government and those belonging to individuals, and to settle the claims of land-owners—concerning which complications had existed since the close of the War—a Land Investigation Bureau was provisionally organized.

The
insur-
gents.

One matter, however, demanded more than anything else the urgent attention of the authorities—namely, the suppression of the native insurgents (*dohi*). Most people considered that, until their rebellious attitude had been completely broken, no new undertaking could be safely started, but the Governor-General thought otherwise. He knew of course that their suppression was necessary, but he did not consider that the transaction of all other business need be postponed until after that had been effected. So while suppression was never disregarded, care was taken that innumerable other affairs should be transacted in the meanwhile.

Pro-
ductive
resources.

The great productive resource of the island is agriculture, and its principal exports are tea, camphor, rice, and sugar. The industrial arts are yet in a primitive stage, and present no prospect of great development in the near future. As for mining industries, there are many collieries, gold-mines, and alluvial deposits, as well as petroleum oil-wells. These, however, are for the most part in a wretched state, and are not in

Revenue.

a condition favourable to rapid growth. The revenues of the State for the first year after the transfer amounted to about 2,000,000 *yen*, while in the second year they were 5,000,000. Such an income was altogether insufficient to cover the expendi-

---

[1] *Ken* means literally prefecture, and *chō* office.

ture of the Government. To supply the deficiency, therefore, a subsidy, amounting to 6,000,000 or 7,000,000 *yen*, had to be obtained from the Home Government, as already stated. But after investigation into the financial resources of the island, monopolies of the three products—camphor, opium, and salt —were organized, and in consequence the revenue for 1904 reached the amount of over 17,000,000 *yen*, thus increasing threefold in seven years. *Mono-polies.*

Position of the Island in Relation to the Fatherland

The island of Formosa was placed under military government for a while after its cession to Japan; and when it was handed over to civil government, a part—and later almost the whole—of the constitution of Japan was put into force, and has since become law. Though there have been some disputes about constitutional rights, yet—at least in form— constitutional procedure is as follows : The Governor-General has a right to issue orders equal in effect to laws, by the power given him by an act of the Imperial Diet, and so bears the responsibility of governing the whole island, as there is no legislative body, but only a council under him. The Budget is presented for discussion to the Imperial Diet. Courts of justice were of three grades at first, but have been reduced to two, the appointment of judges being regulated in the same manner as in Japan; proper licences are given to lawyers, there being two classes, one class having the same qualifications as those required in Japan, and the other being of limited capacity, the validity of their licences being confined to the island.

The Constitution of the Government

The division of the Island for administrative purposes, after many changes, is now as follows : There are under the jurisdiction of the Taiwan Government, twenty districts, which are subdivided into smaller sections called *gai, shō,* and *sha*— corporate bodies of the lowest grade. There is also an institution peculiar to Formosa, called the *Hokō* system which had its origin in China. *Ho* means a hundred, and *kō* ten houses. Under this system, the smaller corporation consisting of ten houses, and the larger one of a hundred houses, has each *Executive districts.*

Hokō system.

a chief of its own, and being a self-governing body, its members are bound to help one another in time of need.   This institution has been powerful enough to keep the native insurgents in check and preserve the peace of the community.   It is said to be the remnant of the institution which existed under the Chu dynasty of China, and with some modifications has been adopted by the present Government.

THE POLICE

In Formosa the police system as first introduced was the same as that in Japan proper.   But in 1900 a reform was effected, by which a police-inspector-general was created for the inspection of the police of the whole island, so that all the business connected with them might be brought under the management of one head.   This arrangement was found to be necessary for enforcing discipline in Formosa, whilst native insurgents were everywhere doing mischief, and the movements of police officers were incessant.   The Governor-General paid particular attention to the education of police-constables as well as to that of police-officers, and encouraged them to study the vernacular tongue ; he even employed natives as police-assistants—an act which, although it provoked some criticism at first, is now considered a matter of necessity for administrative purposes.   Their usefulness is now apparent to everyone.

Aiyū *police.*   There is yet another feature peculiar to the Taiwan police-system.   A branch of the police called *Aiyū* are employed to defend the frontiers of their districts against the savages, being armed with rifles for that purpose.   The line of defence which they have to protect, is the boundary strip lying between the region where the ordinary native inhabitants are settled and the forests inhabited by the savages, and it is the business of the *Aiyū* not to allow any savage to cross that line.   This line is being constantly advanced.   In 1901 it extended to a distance of 71 *ri*, in 1902 to 129, and in 1903 220 *ri* [1] into the aborigines' land.   It is only by means of this system of defence that the camphor industry and agricultural pursuits within the boundaries of the aborigines, can be carried on with safety.   Nevertheless, it still sometimes happens that labourers

---

[1] 1 *ri* = about 2½ miles.

are attacked by the Malay savages, who cut off the workmen's
heads and carry them as trophies to their tribes.   Such occurrences are, however, growing fewer with the development
of the defence system.   The *Aiyū's* duties are quite different
from those of ordinary policemen, the men being all native
Chinese under the direction of Japanese police officers : their
number at present is over 2900.

The regular police number 3240, and the assistant police
1610.   There are also town or village police who may be
termed self-governing ; they give military aid to the regular
police forces and serve as a subordinate body for all kinds of
police business.   They are called *Sōtéidan* (young men's
corporations) and belong to the *Hokō* system above referred
to.   Each *ho* and *kō* has a certain number of young men called
sōtéi who are ready to assist in time of danger—especially
against native raiders.   This institution, left by the former
Government, though not effectively organized while it was in
power, has been brought to perfection by the present administration.   The number of *sōtéi*, or young men, belonging
to the *Sōtéidan* is 124,612, and the number of officers—such
as chief-officers, sub-officers, &c.—is 4410.   When this system
comes into full operation it will be more than enough to suppress any disturbance caused by the natives, and in assisting
the *Aiyū* in defending their line in time of emergency.

*Sōtéi-
dan
police.*

There is a keen rivalry between the different districts as
to which can show the best organization.   Indeed, it is largely
owing to this institution of *Sōtéidan* and the co-operation of
the native Chinese inhabitants with the *sōtéi* that the restoration of order and the success of the present administration are
due.   It can readily be perceived by those versed in history
that the requirements of the island cannot be satisfied by
police-regulations such as would answer for a civilized native
population.   Possibly, in time to come, military operations on
the part of police will be found unnecessary except against
an attack from the savages; but such operations formed
one of the ordinary functions of the police in Taiwan until
very recently, and consequently in the police schools, the use
of arms and military drill have formed and still form a regular
part of the teachings.

BRIGANDAGE

Nature of aboriginal rebel tribes.

The aboriginal rebel tribes of Taiwan, or *dohi*, have been much in evidence since the island came into the possession of Japan. These banditti existed long prior to our occupation. One or other of the tribes rose from time to time against the Government, but as a rule their doings bore no political character.

At the time when we first occupied the island, so little was known about these brigands and their history that we greatly misunderstood them, partly through misrepresentations on the part of our hired interpreters, and partly owing to tricks played by the detectives we employed. Judging from reports addressed to the Governor-General, or to the Head of the Civil Administrative Bureau, or to other officials of the Government charged with the doings of the *dohi*, our troops, gendarmes, and police-officers should have been well-informed about the action and movement of the bands. But they were not, and consequently were often taken by surprise. The report and the actual occurrence did not at all tally, and this at last made us suspect that something was wrong, and that the existing arrangement must be reformed. Hence it was that I began to pay close attention to the facts, and that the Governor-General determined to have recourse to a new system entirely different from that hitherto pursued.

The lowest class of interpreters—Japanese interpreters of course excepted—were in fact in collusion with the rebels whilst professing to act with the gendarmes and policemen, and were drawing money from both sides, and the same was the case with the detectives, as was afterwards ascertained when the outlaws came to surrender. Further there was a tendency among the people in general to conceal the movements of the brigands or the injury done by them, even when the people themselves were the sufferers, owing to apprehension of being victims of subsequent revenge. Thus when questioned by the authorities about the incidents of an affair, they used to deny the fact or defer any report until after the occurrence, when the arrest of the outlaws had become impossible.

Moreover, it often happened that the gendarmes and police-

officers did not agree in dealing with outlaws, and the result
was occasionally that *dohi* who had made acts of submission to
the gendarmes were arrested by the police, while those who had
surrendered to the police were seized by the gendarmes. It
also happened that innocent people were sometimes punished
as *dohi*, through the misrepresentations of interpreters and
detectives. Consequently, I devised various ways of ascertaining the actual circumstances connected with the brigandage,
and adopted a plan in spite of all antagonistic opinions, of
bringing the *dohi* into subjection. I was fortunate in inducing
Lin-Hoawang, a notorious chief among them, to take formal
oath of allegiance, and subsequently, Chên-Chükü and Han-
Taishi, captains of the banditti in the North, also submitted.
The *dohi* who thus gave in to the Government were then
employed, some in repairing roads and others in the camphor
factory. Some of them reformed, but others, having again
revolted, were put to death. Chên-Chükü succeeded so well
in the camphor business that he made a fortune, and is now
worth many tens of thousands of *yen*. Han-Taishi revolted
again more than once, and was at last executed.

So much for the *dohi* in the North, where suppression has
been complete, and where, at the end of the year 1899, the
whole region presented an aspect of peace never dreamt of
under the former Government.

The Middle and Southern parts took longer to pacify,
although gradually the above means were put into execution;
so that whereas in 1902 4043 of the banditti were executed,
in 1903 only eighteen executions took place.

The most powerful chief in the South was Lin-Shaomiao,
who lived like a prince, inhabiting a fortress and having four
or five hundred followers, and under his sway a town filled with
gambling-dens, houses of ill fame, &c. He levied taxes from
the neighbouring villages for miles around, and even after
submission continued to gather them, though pretending that
he did not. His people, although robbed of their money, did
not venture to tell the truth for fear of revenge; and the
same happened to merchants that passed through his borders,
he inflicting injury on all who refused to satisfy his demands.
His so-called tax had to be paid yearly in money or kind by the

large farmers and merchants for protection against the injuries
which might otherwise be inflicted by his gangs of outlaws, the
fact being that these brigand chiefs had so much power and
influence over the people in general that the latter were glad
to purchase immunity, and the custom was prevalent all over
the island.

Lin-Shaomiao alone, however, dared to continue the exaction
secretly of this impost up to the very time of his execution.   But
in the year 1902, this objectionable practice was completely
put an end to, and ever since 'Peace has set in to reign supreme';
so that a child may now walk alone and unmolested about the
streets at night, to the profound astonishment of the native
population whose impression from infancy had been that their
island could never be freed from the troubesome *dohi*.   Nearly
the whole island being now pacified, the progress in the cultivation of land is astonishing.

Encouragement of Industries

With a view to the encouragement of industries the Governor-
General specially convened, in 1901, a meeting of the leading
landowners and merchants of the island, and explained to
them the official views, and these were translated into the
vernacular and distributed.   The document ran as follows:
' In considering the encouragement of agriculture, we must not
lay too much stress on the labour of the people alone, for the
Government also must discharge its proper functions, without
which full development will be hopeless.   Agriculture, unless it
is conducted on lines parallel with the world's progress, will
not enable the people to reap abundant fruit in return for the
labour expended.   The Government will therefore appoint men
specially qualified to instruct and direct the people, who in
turn must strive for the best under such guidance.'   Tables
showing the results of analyses of tea, sugar, rice, and camphor
were also submitted for inspection, in order to demonstrate the
necessity of reforming the old system, and to show the merits
of modern science.   Thus the people for the first time conceived
the idea that the agriculture of to-day must be consonant
with the world's progress. Soon afterwards, Dr. Nitobé **was**

appointed head of the Industrial Bureau. He explained to all the people that development of agriculture could not be expected unless it aimed at reaching the world's highest standard.

On the part of the Government, investigations were conducted as to the comparative merits of the proposed improvements in the production of rice, tea, and sugar, and in the sequel sugar was first taken in hand, and it is now calculated that the production of sugar in Taiwan, when it attains its full development, will reach an amount worth about 30,000,000 *yen* per annum, enough to fully supply the needs of all Japan. For the purpose of encouraging its culture, the best sugarcanes were introduced in 1901, and a company was formed with a capital of over 1,000,000 *yen*, under the protection of the Government, and a new factory was built in the most improved style. As historic mementoes of the condition of the country only a few years ago, port-holes for guns here and there are to be seen in its walls. The outset of the company was not propitious, for when it attempted to buy sugar-cane and land for its cultivation from the native farmers, so many objections were raised by the peasants generally, that it seemed at one time as though an understanding was impossible, and the future of the company looked precarious. But now the motives of the Government as well as of the company having come to be appreciated, the sentiment of the people has undergone a complete revolution. *Sugar.*

The same was the case with the introduction of new and improved sugar-canes. All attempts to recommend the canes elicited only unfavourable replies from the leading farmers, who insisted that Taiwan had good enough canes of its own. When, however, I showed them the actual results of the experimental farm, they were so thoroughly convinced that the cultivation of the new canes not only became general but the insufficiency of the supply was keenly felt. *Sugar-cane.*

In my last official tour through the South I was extremely surprised to note the change wrought in the popular mind. The people now make applications in the interests of industrial concerns, instead of complaining about the *dohi* as they did some years ago.

Rice.

So too with regard to the production of rice; when a Competitive Exhibition was opened for agricultural products, the eagerness of the people for improvement was manifest on every side.

Tea.

Considerable progress has also been made in tea production. The Taiwan tea is the well-known Oolong of commerce, which was extensively exported to America and sold at high rates. But its leaves were formerly treated by being trampled on by human feet, and this crude method of manufacture was taken advantage of by the Ceylon merchants when competing for the American market. They distributed circulars with illustrations showing this repellent manner of manufacture, and did it so satisfactorily that Ceylon tea greatly extended its sale. Oolong tea, however, could not be driven out permanently, owing to its specially excellent flavour and wholesome quality, and after a while it recovered the position it had originally occupied in the American trade—when it could be shown that it was no longer manufactured by the trampling process but by a machine, lately invented, which did not impair its flavour. The tea sent to the St. Louis Exhibition was the product of this new process. The cultivation of the plants was also much improved, and the amount of production is fast increasing.

Many improvements have recently been made in other agricultural products, but the above mentioned are the most important. Sugar is the principal product of the Middle and Southern parts; rice and tea of the Northern, Middle, and Southern districts.

Forestry.

Among other industries worthy of notice is forestry. The forests of camphor-trees and cedar (*hinoki*) are the most important: the latter being worth many tens of millions of *yen*, for they contain numerous fine trees such as are rarely found in any other part of the globe.

Mineral products.

The gold mines produce yearly an amount worth 2,000,000 *yen* and promise large expansion in the future.

A great mineral product in the Middle and Southern districts should be petroleum: trial borings are now going on, and should they prove successful as is expected, a new source of wealth will contribute to the prosperity of the island. At present the work is left to private enterprise.

MONOPOLIES

The principal source of revenue in Taiwan at present is the State monopolies, which are three—opium, camphor, and salt. It is thought by many that the first named is inconsistent with latter day ideas; but that is far from being true, for the principle on which the present monopoly is founded, is the gradual prohibition of opium smoking. It is true that, when this measure was made public, there were some in Japan who disapproved of it, believing that such a slow process of prohibition would never attain the proposed end. Nevertheless success is at present fairly in sight. The highest number of opium smokers ever recorded in Taiwan was about 170,000, and after the lapse of ten years this number has fallen to 130,000. The largest yearly sale of opium was nearly 4,000,000 *yen*, and at one time it fell below 3,000,000, but it has now risen to from 3,200,000 to 3,300,000 *yen*. These fluctuations are entirely due to the harvest. A famine for two years in succession produced a marked fall, but a year of abundance which ensued caused an increase in the sale of the drug. It is evident that a general diminution is going on, and there do not seem to be any who newly contract the habit.[1]

Opium monopoly.

A commissioner, who was sent by the United States from the Phillipines to make investigations, instituted various inquiries into the matter, and having heard my explanations he expressed warm admiration for the plan devised and the result attained.

The theory of imperial commercialism has found practical application in Japan in the form of the camphor business, for, by the help of the Government, commercial interests abroad have been permanently established.

Camphor monopoly.

At present the enterprise is carried on by the Government on the principle of modern imperial commercialism. Had it not been for this monopoly our camphor business would have suffered extraordinary loss from over-production of an inferior article, at one time, and from great discredit at another.

---

[1] It may be well to explain that the law prohibits the sale of opium to any but those who had contracted the habit before the new system came into effect, and to them the price fixed is such as to discourage its use.

During the China-Japan War the export of camphor from Formosa almost ceased, and its price rose so high as to reach 80 or 90 *yen* per *picul* or 100 *kin*.[1] This led to excessive manufacture, and then over-production caused a great fall in price, being at one time quoted at 40 *yen* (per 100 *kin*). The loss sustained in consequence was felt not by Taiwan alone, but by the merchants of the whole of Japan. Statistics for the past decade still show great fluctuations in price, the product having been made an object of speculation by merchants. The island having been proved to be the centre from which the world obtains its supplies of this article (and therefore a natural monopoly), it clearly is her business to see that it permanently maintains its commercial standard and value; but in order to attain this end, the supply must be regulated to meet the demand, because the consumption of camphor is limited, the world's demand for it being about five or six million *kin* per year. When the production exceeds this amount, the price falls, and when a smaller quantity is produced, the price rises. Hence a monopoly becomes necessary in order to regulate the amount of supply and maintain the price, and for this reason the Government decided to adopt the monopoly system.

Of late the advance of science has found new uses for camphor, and the demand is consequently increasing, and has reached six or seven million *kin*; so we are now in a position to increase the production,[2] although at the same time it must be mentioned that an artificial camphor is now being manufactured which is endeavouring to compete with the camphor produced in Taiwan. It is probable, however, that in the end the victory will be on the side of natural camphor, as it can hold its ground in point of cost of production, for it is calculated that even if prices were reduced to their lowest rate, there would still remain a profit to the monopoly.[3]

Salt monopoly.   The salt monopoly, as practised in Taiwan, is an instance of the fallibility of the economic doctrine set forth by the followers of the Manchester school. Salt in Taiwan was

[1] A *picul* = 100 *kin*; 1 *kin* = 1322 lb. avoir.

[2] The production of camphor was 3,252,000 *kin*, and of camphor oil 2,986,000 *kin* in 1906.

[3] The value of camphor exported rose from 961,000 *yen* in 1898 to 2,222,000 *yen* in 1906, and 2,619,000 *yen* in 1907.

originally an article of monopoly under the Chinese Government. When Admiral Kabayama became Governor of the island, the monopoly was abolished, in deference to the idea that, salt being an indispensable element in all kinds of food, a good and generous government should not monopolize such an article of necessity. The consequence was the ruin of the salt-fields, and the rise in power of *dohi* in the salt districts, so that salt, which had never previously been imported from other countries, had to be obtained from China. Were the economists of the Manchester school right, the salt business should have thriven, for the Government monopoly was transferred to the free competition of individual enterprise. Such, however, was not the case, for, instead of the people buying salt more cheaply under the new *régime*, they had to pay three times as much as before. The reason is obvious. Salt, under Government monopoly, bore a fixed price. Any man in any district could buy it at the fixed Government price, but once the monopoly was abolished and the sale of the staple made free, merchants could charge any price they pleased. In spite of this, when the producer carried his produce to a salt merchant, the latter would not buy it, pretending that he did not want it, although at the time he may have needed it. When carried to another merchant, it would probably meet with no better reception, until at last the producer would be glad to part with it at any price. Thus the producer found himself in an increasingly worse position and was unable to repair his salt-field, which consequently fell to ruin. Persons thus impoverished often turned *dohi*, or outlaws.

Under the Chinese Government the producers could at any time turn their salt into money at a fixed rate, but even then a large quantity of salt was also imported from China. But when the monopoly was restored under the Japanese Government, not only did the import from China entirely cease, but enough salt was produced to afford an ample supply for the whole island, together with 100,000,000 *kin* sent every year to Japan. Such was the outcome of monopoly. This enforces the conclusion that a theory which condemns monopolies of any kind as detrimental to the development of industry is by no means reliable, but is a conception of economists who are wedded to ' individualism.' A monopoly, when judiciously administered, is far more beneficial to the public than any other system.

Under the present *régime* new occupations, such as the manufacture of straw bags, have been created by the salt business. Lastly, the three monopolies—opium, camphor, and salt—are rendering great service to the finances of Taiwan, the receipts from State properties and monopolies having risen from 8,063,000 *yen* in 1901 to 17,984,000 in 1908.

FINANCE

Finance. The administrative expenditure of the island from its occupation by Japan, up to 1902 were in the aggregate 118,380,000 *yen*. Subtracting from that figure the total revenue, amounting to 71,330,000 *yen*, and public loans amounting to 19,700,000 *yen* (both the principal and interest due by the Government of Taiwan), the amount received as subsidy from the National Treasury up to that date was 27,310,000 *yen* only.

The finances of the island became independent during the financial year 1905–06 ; for not only were the administrative expenditures met with the receipts of the Government of Taiwan without any pecuniary assistance from the Central Government, but it was also found feasible to defray out of the insular revenue the expenses of undertakings which it had been proposed to provide for by means of public loans.

Since then the finances of Taiwan have, notwithstanding changes in the items of revenue, always given satisfactory results on account of a great natural increase of receipts. In the financial year 1907–08 plans were made for the exploitation of hydraulic electricity and construction of waterworks at Taihoku, both of which are to be in working order by the year 1909–10 ; and also plans have been made for commencing in 1908–09 three other undertakings, namely, works for the utilization of water, the building of a harbour at Takao, and the construction of the Taitō Railway. Again, the reform of the coinage system and the condition of business after the

Russian War, especially the expansion of the sugar industry, have greatly increased the volume of trade. Above all, from the working of the Customs Law, the trade with China, a silver-using country, has diminished, while that with the gold-using mother country has increased by leaps and bounds, and the island has come into more intimate relations with the economic world of Japan Proper, to which it is now bound by ties as close as those of mother and child.

The financial year 1908–09 shows an increase on the preceding year of 4,600,000 *yen* (£471,311) in the total revenue and 2,540,000 *yen* (£260,246) in the expenditure. For the purpose of improving the water-utilization works, constructing a harbour at Takao, extraction of camphor, opening for cultivation of land, and developing the timber industry, plans were made for the construction of railways, and after obtaining by means of public loans the sum of 38,990,000 *yen* (£3,994,877), required for the above-mentioned undertakings, it was intended to commence these works in the financial year 1908–09 and complete them by the year 1923–24, the public loans being redeemable within eleven years from the date of completion of the works. But as the present is not a convenient time for raising loans, it is proposed to obtain temporary loans from the Bank of Taiwan according to the provisions of law, and go on with the works as was first planned. As the condition of the sugar industry in the island will not only affect the economy of the agricultural classes, but also have a considerable effect on the finances of the island, the area for the cultivation of improved sugar-cane has been greatly extended; and as the establishment of new companies after the war and the increase of capital of those already existing will from the period 1908–10 enable the island to yield 10,250 tons of sugar, an increase was made (in order to ensure full supply of raw materials) in the subventions granted for the industry, in the grant for the opening of the land in the region of the aborigines, in the subsidies for the navigation between the island and Japan Proper, and in grants for constructions. The sources of revenue for meeting these increased expenditures are to be found in the sugar-excise receipts, increased railway profits, and the revenue surplus from the preceding year.

Increase in subventions.

RAILWAYS

Railways.   A railway, running from Keelung to Shinchiku, existed in
Taiwan under the Chinese Government, but before Japanese
occupation many parts of it had been destroyed.   Under the
Japanese military Government they were repaired to a certain
extent, and traffic was opened over some sections.

Soon afterwards a project was submitted by a railway
company for constructing a north to south line from Keelung
to Takao, but before the scheme was carried into effect General
Kodama became Governor-General and decided to make it a
Government undertaking.   He set out with a plan by which
the whole construction should be finished in ten years, the
expenses to be met by raising a public loan.   With the approval
of the Imperial Diet the work was started in 1899, and when
it had made excellent progress, another proposal was brought
before the Imperial Diet for shortening the term of completion
to five years.   Although it was not expected to be opened until
1909–10, it was finished in April of 1908.   Its length, including
branch lines, is 276 miles.

HARBOUR CONSTRUCTION

Harbour construction is one of the three great enterprises
undertaken by means of public loans, and is divided into three
sections : dredging, building of breakwaters, and making
landing places.

According to the first estimate relating to the Keelung
harbour, an outlay amounting to 10,000,000 *yen* in the aggregate was asked for, of which 2,000,000 *yen* was for dredging,
and the remainder was to be employed on other works.   But
it is now calculated that the whole will involve an outlay
of 13,000,000 *yen*.   The first part of the work has been
completed, it already saves a great deal of expense in landing
the materials for the main work of construction ; the second
portion is well in hand.

The most difficult part of the undertaking is the successful
construction of a breakwater, the maximum depth of water
being no less than ninety feet.   Besides, the spot is exposed to
very heavy seas which often rise to an enormous height, but

the force of wind, tides, and waves, and other factors which influence the work of consideration, have been thoroughly investigated, and everything is now ready for starting.

Of the buildings on land, those for railway warehouses are planned in the most improved and modern style to be met with throughout the East.

LAND SURVEY

The object of this survey is to ascertain the exact extent of the island. Beginning with the trigonometrical method and then filling in the details, a map has already been prepared of sufficient accuracy and minuteness. Some twenty years ago, when the island was yet under the Chinese Government, Liu-Minchuan, Viceroy representing the Emperor of China, took great pains to make an exact land survey for the purpose of establishing a basis of land tax, but the method employed was far from perfect, and the surveyors were stopped in the midst of their undertaking by mob violence, so that the work ended in utter failure, two different results having been obtained in the North and the South; consequently no regular method of taxation could be established.

When the present Government undertook the work, there was some criticism. We were charged with entering upon it too hastily and for the sake of mere ambition, considering that it had been found too difficult for all the power of Liu-Minchuan. But we did not hesitate, for it was our firm belief that a land survey was of the utmost importance for forming a permanent basis of administration. The project was consequently made a part of the work to be undertaken by public loans. It is needless to add that the result of this survey will be of great assistance to the Government in devising a measure for the taxation of land, and in extending full protection to parties holding rights in the same. The survey having been seen to be accurate and clear—quite unlike that of Liu-Minchuan's time—the people have placed confidence in the Government; besides, it has given employment to a number of natives as assistants to the surveyors, whom it is further intended to employ in making registers of deeds. The total number of officials engaged has been nearly a thousand, and the employment of such a number has, from the very outset, taxed our powers of organization to the utmost, but happily all has gone smoothly.

Landholders. In Taiwan there existed a large number of landholders, called *daisokénsha*, who possessed the right of receiving a share of the crops raised by the tenants, and these stood much in the way of carrying out a uniform system of taxation. A bill was therefore brought before the Imperial Diet and passed for buying up their rights by the Government: it is in course of enforcement, so that now the products of the land in Taiwan are shared by four parties—the Government, great proprietors, small holders, and farmers who actually till the soil.

SANITATION

There is much to be said about the sanitary condition of Taiwan. Most people in Japan would consider Taiwan a very unhealthy place and would not dare to go and live there. It is true that, until quite recently, the number of deaths was great, and there were many cases of malaria; but it is now one-fifth of what it was at the date of our occupation, and the number of sick has proportionately decreased, the drainage, water supply, roads and dwellings having been much improved. **Hospital and college of medicine.** With regard to hospitals, there is, in the first place, a large one in Taihoku—the seat of the Taiwan Government—having buildings covering over two and a half acres. The physicians in attendance there are specialists in each branch of the medical art, and are presided over by one who has studied abroad. There is a college of medicine connected with it, in which over one hundred and thirty native students are trained; it has already sent out some graduates, and is showing altogether satisfactory results.

Quarantine establishment. There is also a quarantine establishment on the sea-coast, which was built in the same style as that in the mother country. Ships of various nationalities come for disinfection when cases of contagious diseases have been discovered on board, and it may be confidently said to be one of the best establishments of the kind in the Far East. Besides, there are public physicians who devote themselves to extending benevolence and service to the people at large. In all the principal towns there is a Government hospital, and in the central district there is a sanitary laboratory where drugs are tested, no drugs being allowed to be sold or dealt in which fail to satisfy the laboratory tests.

EDUCATION

As regards education in Formosa, it is as yet a matter of study and consideration what course may be the best to adopt. Opinions are still at variance respecting the biological connection of the Chinese with the Japanese, and it is a question, for instance, what metamorphoses in the mode of life overtake an emigrant stock settled in a foreign land, after the first, second, or third generation, when they have reached the stage of forgetting the mother tongue, or what are the effects upon a people living under a strange sovereignty after the first, second, or third generation, or what moral changes take place in a people by a change of national language, &c. These are subjects of study at present, but it is already decided that, as a lack of understanding between the Japanese and the natives proves an obstacle to all progress, facility of mutual comprehension should be cultivated first of all, so that no interpreters may be required for the ordinary purposes of life.

With this object in view, a National Language School has been established for teaching the Japanese language to native students who seek to become officials or school teachers, as also for teaching the vernacular language to Japanese who desire to be teachers in public schools in Taiwan. *National language school.*

Public schools have also been opened in all districts for the education of the younger generation. These schools number at present nearly one hundred and fifty. Teachers are trained in normal schools. The whole presents a fair prospect for the future. With the object of giving technical education besides language training, courses are now open for trial to students who would engage in railway business, and also to those preparing themselves for the telegraphic and telephonic services. A simple elementary course has also been instituted *Public schools.* *Normal schools.*

Industrial schools.

for the study of agriculture. If these measures should prove satisfactory, it is intended that industrial schools shall be established permanently for those who desire to pursue their studies further after they have completed the general course of education.

COMMUNICATIONS

Post.

The progress and development attained by the postal system in Taiwan is remarkable. The number of letters sent in 1907 was 18,273,000, as against 7,516,000 in 1899.

Telegraphs.

There are two submarine cables, one extending from Keelung to Japan Proper *viâ* Yayéyama, the other from Tamsui to Swasesan in Foochow, China. There are also land telegraph lines running to all parts of the island. In 1907 the length of lines was 413 *ri* and of wire 1573 *ri*, and the messages sent amounted to 935,000.

Telephones.

Until 1897 telephone communication in Taiwan was limited to eight places between Government offices in Taihoku, but since then the number of places has rapidly increased, private individuals having been allowed the privilege of utilizing them. In 1907 the number of offices open was sixty-one, and the length of extensions was 1279 *ri*, and the number of messages sent in the year was 5,116,312.

SHIPPING

The mail service is carried on by the two great shipping companies—the *Ōsaka Shōsén* and the *Nippon Yusén Kaisha*—with subsidies from the Government. The ships placed on the line between Japan Proper and Taiwan are over 2500 tons burden, with a speed of over ten knots, and perfect equipment. These steamers are therefore mostly of the highest classes plying between different ports in the Eastern seas.

CONCLUSION

Conclusion.

Only thirteen years have elapsed since the island of Taiwan was placed under the Imperial Government. But there are already sufficient resources to maintain financial independence, there are industrial monopolies successfully carried out in accordance with the needs of the time, and there are no more *dohi* disturbances, except occasional menaces by some aboriginal tribes. In short, the influence of the Imperial administration now extends throughout the island. It may be anticipated, therefore, that, if such enterprises as those concerning harbours and irrigation, which are not easily within reach of private hands, be carried out in a satisfactory manner, and if the undertakings which have been so zealously promoted by the Government be conducted in such a way as to furnish successful models for private enterprise, not a few individuals will essay various projects requiring capital, and will thus open the greatest and richest treasure-house of the empire.

XXIX

CONCLUSION

Count Shigénobu Ōkuma

In my general introduction to this History of New Japan I outlined the progress of events during the period of fifty years since the country's reopening to foreign intercourse. I also gave a summary of what may be taken to have been the causes that led to those events. In the papers which have followed and which have been contributed by the foremost authorities on each subject, detailed accounts have been given of the trend of affairs in special fields of activity. Historically speaking, therefore, the work may be regarded as fairly complete. But the underlying aim with which it was conceived was to map out a line of action for the nation's future conduct of the state of things which has arisen during the past fifty years, and to call its attention to the imperative need to strive for an even greater advance and higher development, by pointing out its manifold deficiencies. Therefore I deem it my duty, before laying down my pen, to close the work with a chapter proving this.

Impulse of foreign intercourse.

By comparing the Japan of fifty years ago with the Japan of to-day, it will be seen that she has gained considerably in the extent of her territory, as well as in her population, which now numbers nearly fifty millions.[1] Her Government has become constitutional not only in name, but in fact, and her national education has attained to a high degree of excellence. In commerce and industry, the emblems of peace, she has also made rapid strides, until her import and export trades together

[1] At 31st December 1908 it was estimated at 49,319,000 exclusive of Formosa, which was estimated at 3,178,000.

amounted in 1907 to the enormous sum of 926,000,000 *yen* (£94,877,000), an increase of 84,000,000 *yen* (£8,606,000) on the previous year. Her general progress, during the short space of half a century, has been so sudden and swift that it presents a spectacle rare in the history of the world. This leap forward is the result of the stimulus which the country received on coming into contact with the civilization of Europe and America, and may well, in its broad sense, be regarded as a boon conferred by foreign intercourse. Foreign intercourse it was that animated the national consciousness of our people, who under the feudal system lived localized and disunited, and foreign intercourse it is that has enabled Japan to stand up as a world-Power. We possess to-day a powerful army and navy, but it was after Western models that we laid their foundations by establishing a system of conscription, in pursuance of the principle 'all our sons are soldiers,' by promoting military education, and by encouraging the manufacture of arms and the art of ship-building. We have reorganized the systems of central and local administration, and effected reforms in the educational system of the empire. All this is nothing but the result of adopting the superior features of Western institutions. That Japan has been enabled to do so is a boon conferred on her by foreign intercourse, and it may be said that the nation has succeeded in this grand metamorphosis through the promptings and the influence of foreign civilization.

I take it that the Japanese people, as a race, possess the trait of broad-mindedness, little tainted by prejudice against things foreign, and ready to admire, aspire after, and assimilate good points in others. To keep the country's doors wide open and to be abreast of the world's progress is a national principle to which Japan has attached the greatest importance from its earliest days. During the twenty-five centuries of her history, only two and a half centuries found her pursuing a policy of seclusion, and this was therefore a mere incident in her career. It is due to this principle that the moment there came a break in that narrow-minded policy the channel steadily widened for foreign intercourse, and the people, taking advantage of the opportunity to get into touch with

Western civilization in all spheres of activity, cemented a
national union and set out as one entity on the road to progress
and development.

Soon after the Restoration the nation began to feel keenly
the necessity of codifying her laws. For this there were two
reasons. The first arose out of the country's foreign relations.
In other words, the nation had so far advanced in knowledge
that it could no longer bear the humiliation of remaining
tied to the ex-territorial treaties, which had been entered into
with the nations in Europe and America when the Tokugawa
Shōgunate reopened the country to foreign intercourse fifty
years ago, in the days when we had as yet but scant knowledge of international usages. The signing of the treaties
was the result of a misconception on our part, but thereby
the Western Powers secured to themselves the right of ex-
territoriality, and Japan came to be rated on the same level
as China, Turkey, or Persia. It was therefore only natural
that, as we obtained better information and awoke to the
real aspect of affairs, we came to cherish an irrepressible desire
for the revision of the treaties and to have the country placed
in a position of equality. But prior to this being accomplished,
we felt that it was only reasonable that we should prove
that we had attained to a tolerable stage of civilization, and
hence arose the urgent necessity to bring the laws of the land
to a condition of efficiency.

The second reason had its origin in domestic matters.
With the restoration of the *de facto* power of administration
to the Imperial Government, the feudal system fell to pieces,
and the incongruous laws and usages hitherto obtaining in
the various semi-regal fiefs were useless for purposes of general
application; in short, legal uniformity for the whole country
became indispensable. At the same time, with their eyes
opened to the trend of affairs abroad, our statesmen recognized
the value of written codes of law, while their own conception of
legal justice attained to a higher phase of development. Yet
again, after a constitution had been given to the nation, establishing the great principle of government by law, the people
could not be subject any longer to the arbitrary rule of
a few officials. Thus it was only in the order of things that

there should arise a desire to see good and just laws codified, and competent courts established to administer real justice, and to formulate a system whereby the rights and wrongs of the hundred-and-one acts of life should be determined, and everyone (native or foreigner) be brought under the equal control of the same laws. Hence not a day was to be lost in the compilation of codes of law, and consequently steps were at once taken to study the laws of France, Germany, England, and other countries, the result being the enactment of complete codes, comparing not unfavourably with those of the countries senior to us in modern civilization. This done, England, first of all, agreed to the revision of the old treaties, and she was followed by the United States, Germany, France, and others. Thus a thoroughly satisfactory solution of the difficult problems which had vexed the nation for a quarter of a century, from the day of the grand restoration of Imperial administration, was effected. It was a success due to the national awakening, which, in its turn, had arisen out of the stimulus received from foreign civilization, culminating in the replacement of old defective statutes by comparatively perfect codes of law. But it is necessary to acknowledge that foreign intercourse primarily prompted this turn of affairs.

At the same time that these efforts were made to gain a position of equality with Western countries, a system of local autonomy was established, accompanied by efforts to arouse and encourage the spirit of local self-government. This again was an attempt to follow the example of advanced countries, and therefore a result of foreign intercourse. Innumerable, indeed, are the other instances in which our people derived benefit from the introduction from outside of material civilization. Improvements of our armaments is one of them, for it was the acquisition of accurate implements of war, which Western sciences taught us to make and use, that enabled us to face successfully national emergencies and achieve world-wide feats of glory. Although endowed with an intense spirit of patriotism, our people could not have issued victorious from modern warfare had they been without the weapons which Western science had invented. One may recall in this connection the Taiko's Korean expedition of 1592–98. Soldier of rare genius

Local autonomy.

Introduction of the material civilization of the West.

as he was, his weapons of war were not superior to those of his adversaries, and his memorable seven-years' campaign not only failed to accomplish any lasting results, but so exasperated certain critics that they preferred against him the charge of having tarnished the glory of the martial profession. From this it will be seen (and the fact is worthy of more attention than a passing notice) that we of to-day have been thoughtful enough to thoroughly reform our armaments and create an army with systematic training, by drawing liberally on the material progress of Western countries.

Turning to the mental and moral side of national life, the influence exerted by Western civilization is found to have been far deeper and more widespread than that produced on its material side. Indeed, the benefit the nation has thus derived extends to all spheres of activity, and there is not a corner in our social structure but has felt its influence. That this is so is asserted by each and all of the high authorities whose essays form the present compilation.

Old social character istics.

With such radical changes in the national life since the reopening of the country, it may well be asked whether any of the old social conditions remain, and, if so, whether they are destined also to pass away ? I would therefore draw attention to three features which still continue, and which appear peculiarly Japanese when looked at from the Western point of view. The first of these is that the family forms the social unit of the country, a custom altogether different to the strong individualistic tendency prevalent in Europe and America. Each family still has, and must have, its law-appointed head, who is the real governor of its affairs. A universally respected custom exists that at a family council, or a council of relatives, everyone, however distinguished personally he may be, must be subordinate to the head of the house. Any family, once founded, becomes an object to be preserved, and a name to be reverenced, by all its members and their relatives; so it is the general usage to adopt a son or daughter from another house as the lawful successor if a direct lineal descendant is lacking. The second peculiar feature is that sovereignty in Japan is almost infallibly national in its working, so that it can be exercised to promote a public benefit of whatever kind, and when once put into operation it is almost irresistible. The Japanese are like the Greeks and Romans of old in their idea of the State, considering it the height of glory to live and die for it. They have always cherished the idea that man reaches the perfect stage of personal development when he rises to take part in affairs of State. To look up to the State as a sacred institution has always been characteristic of the people, and from the great work of the recent reformation onward there has not been a single event of national consequence which has not originated in this peculiar turn of mind. The third is the circumstance that, as an outcome of the two preceding beliefs, the Japanese people of to-day, besides revering their ancestors and looking up to the State as a sacred institution, have developed the habit of treating all kinds of religion with toleration and respect. Before the Restoration the nation confined its allegiance to *Shintō*, Buddhism, and Confucianism, and re-mained hostile to Christianity. But since then this practice of discrimination has been discontinued, and to-day all stand under the impartial protection of the Constitution. For this reason collisions between Church and State, such as occur in Europe or America, are unknown in Japan. Buddhism and Confucianism in this country are both faiths of foreign origin, and neither of them is so closely related to the State organization as to form an integral and inseparable part of it. In Europe all modern States are ante-dated in their foundation by Christianity, and their history shows that they were brought into existence largely under the guidance of the priestly order. But in Japan the State ante-dates all religions, and it was only by the protection or toleration of the State that they found their way into the country. Consequently there is not a religion represented by any body or in any form that claims in Japan any right or privilege granted by the State. Thus circumstanced, no religion in the land can gather influence strong enough to enable it to act in defiance of the Sovereign or in revolt against the State. It is in truth meritorious, and well deserving of note, that, owing to the large and broad measure of religious liberty enjoyed by the people, no difficulty, administrative or

educational, is now experienced. There being no State religion, and education standing independent of all religions,
the country is absolutely free from the practice of confusing
religion with education and from the evils consequent thereon.
Besides, there arises no occasion for the State to permit or
refuse the interference of a religion or a religious order in matters
of education, marriage, or other civil affairs.

Distinc-
tion of the
classes
erased.

It is a common tendency, when a nation passes through
a sudden social upheaval, which destroys the established
order of things, that the upper class is brought down to the
level of the lower, and that the rise of the commoner to power
and influence tends to lower, instead of elevate, the standard
of national character. Such, however, has not been the
case with Japan. The drastic political changes that came on
the heels of the Restoration demolished the feudal system,
deprived the Court nobles and clan chiefs of their special
privileges, and the *samurai* of their long-established occupations, and resulted in extending the right of equality before
the law even to those classes which had hitherto been regarded
as outside the social pale. What followed was not the disappearance of the better elements of the community, but their
diffusion through every stratum of society in such a way
as to raise the general level of the nation. This was partly
owing to the presence of a wholesome leaven in the national
character of the people at large, and partly to the great success
the nation achieved in its system of popular education.

The
shizoku.

And here it may not be out of place to refer to the part
taken in the development of New Japan by the *shizoku*, who,
as the ancient *samurai*, form the backbone of our middle
class, and are indeed an integral part of the national conscience,
the life of the nation. The political changes incidental to the
Restoration robbed this class of their hereditary occupations,
privileges and pensions, suddenly forcing on them the necessity
of entering into competition with the common people in the
struggle for existence. Such of them as could not shake
off their old ideas and get into touch with the march of affairs
rose in rebellion against the new Government and hurried on
their own destruction. Others, slothful in habit and slow
in mind, were thrust down to the very bottom of society ;

but the large majority, though as it were lost in the wilderness for a time, ultimately succeeded in adapting themselves to the new order of things, the more intelligent of them obtaining posts in the civil or military service under the new Government, or engaging in the work of bringing up the young generation under the new system of education, while the remainder settled down to agricultural, commercial, and industrial pursuits. The result was that the *shizoku*, as a class, not only did not diminish, but even increased in number, keeping pace with the general increase of population : their number, which stood at 1,282,167 in 1872, having risen to 2,168,058 thirty years later. When, in 1872, it was proposed to dismiss the *samurai* from their hereditary profession of arms and to adopt a universal system of conscription, many insisted that the tillers of the soil and the tradespeople were lacking in valour and in the spirit of honour, and that it was a dangerous experiment to entrust the defence of the country to an army of men drafted indiscriminately from all classes of the people. But the complete dissemination of common education and the principle of ' all our sons are soldiers,' when put into practice, served their purpose so well that the country has been enabled to successfully cope with several internal disturbances and to issue victorious from wars with China and Russia. It has thus been proved that to-day our common people compare, in no way unfavourably, with the *shizoku* either in valour or in the sense of honour. An explanation of this is that the qualities necessary to the making of *samurai* have, in course of time, become infused among the common people, and their influence has become nation-wide. After the Restoration, not a small number of the *shizoku* fell far below their class, but at the same time those in the front rank of the common people rose to take their place, and served to uphold the moral and intellectual level of society. This fact furnishes a key to the solution of many difficult problems facing the future of Japan. As stated above, Japan has lately enlarged its territory, while the advance of medical science, the spread of hygienic and sanitary ideas, the re-enactment of laws, the progress of social reforms, and the development of productive industries, have combined to

Advance of the people.

bring about an increase of population as well as to further
the growth of national wealth. Wealth, too, is fortunately
distributed in comparatively favourable proportions, and
though there have been strikes in consequence of the introduction of machinery and of the factory system on a large
scale, no social problem of a dangerous tendency has yet
arisen, as is the case in Western countries. A new phenomenon,
quite unprecedented in the history of the country, is the
way in which the people at large are awaking to the importance
of education. There is not a hamlet, however humble, even
in a remote corner of the empire, where one does not
hear school children learning their lessons. Civilizing influences and agents having thus become thoroughly and widely
extended, the next stage to which the nation may aspire is
comparable to a grand prospect opening to view as a ship sails
out into the ocean after voyaging through a narrow inland sea.
Looked at from every point of view, this country may now be
said to present the appearance of having reached a position
not inferior to that of any nation in the highest, as yet, attain-
able phase of civilization.

To imagine, however, that Japan has reached the goal
can only be the result of very superficial observation. The
least critical inquiry into the character of our civilization in
its present phase will show that the country is disfigured by
many imperfections and failings, which should be pointed out
Imper-
fections specifically and which the nation must strive to correct.
still exis- There can be no doubt that the country has changed marvel-
tent. lously for the better during the past fifty years, as the facts
recorded in the present work attest, and her half-century
history may be regarded as a bright evidence of achievement ;
but the real aim of this book, as already stated, is to impress
as strongly as possible on the mind of the nation that, far
from resting content with the current condition of affairs,
more energy than ever is needed to remain in touch with and
keep abreast of the advance of civilization abroad, and that
there is still much to learn from the nations of the world.
For this reason the remaining pages are devoted to pointing
out the more glaring of our national defects.

The first thing that calls for notice is the primitive

conceptions of the greater part of the people as to their legal National defects: (a) Lack of legal ideas. rights and duties. In other words, the healthy conception of man's rights is but little developed among the larger half of the population. As with individuals so with the nation : its strong points sometimes happen to be also its weak points. The people of this country look up to the State and family with a spirit of reverence and obedience. Having for ages been guided in their actions by a sense of duties to ancestors, rulers, and superiors, the people have as yet made but little progress in consciousness of the rights of the individual, and are not clear in their ideas about personality. With the collapse of the feudal system considerable laxity has overtaken the family institution, accompanied by a change in the ideas pertaining to the State. In consequence of this, a shock has been given to the entire fabric built on the old ideas of duty, while conceptions about personality and the rights of individuals have not yet been fully conceived. Japan is now a law-governed nation with a Constitution guaranteeing every kind of right and liberty, and with codes, civil and commercial, as well as other laws, enacted and brought to a high state of perfection in variety and quality. But man-made laws are essentially non-automatic, and are doomed to remain dead letters when left to themselves : man alone can give them vitality and usefulness. In virtue of the Constitution the Japanese people possess the right of personality, and, in virtue of the self-government system, the right of citizenship as well as a voice in local administration. And yet a majority of them are insufficiently informed to appreciate the *raison d'être* of most of the statute laws, and are deficient in the habit of putting these rights to practical account—a habit that can be acquired only in course of time. It is owing to this circumstance that, living as they do under a constitutional government, they often tolerate and even indulge in unconstitutional antics. The country has in operation a system of local autonomy which should cultivate in the people the spirit of self-government ; but their innocence as to its working not infrequently results in making the system an organ for a small number of men to promote their own private interests. The spirit of blind obedience and involuntary submission that was carefully taught and fostered under the feudal *régime* and by Confucian ethics, no longer finds any trace in the country's laws, but its inherited influence still remains, and injuriously affects the social well-being of the people in ways direct and indirect, intentional and unintentional. Viewed from the standpoint of the completeness with which various statutes have been provided, this country may appear to be behind none of the advanced nations of Europe and America. But judged by the manner in which these laws are utilized, we must confess, to our regret, that we are far from being on the same level with some of those nations. It may be urged that this state of things is inevitable in a transition period such as we are now passing through, but no excuse should be tolerated for making light of the rights of manhood and citizenship. In-

(*b*) Indifference to rights of manhood.

difference in this respect cannot fail to seriously affect the general welfare of the people, and it is for the leading minds of the country to rouse the nation from its lethargy in this respect.

(*c*) Defects in educational system.

And now as regards education : its thorough dissemination cannot be disputed, and it may be claimed that the country yields in no respect to other civilized States in point of the number of schools and students. Completeness exists, however, only in the matter of system and figures. When we look into the actual working of the system, it is seen that the educational administration of the country is unduly encumbered by an excessive centralization of power. The Government schools throughout the country are compelled to conform, in all that relates to their management, to models fixed by the Central Government. With all the completeness of the system as to general organization, but little latitude is allowed for freedom of action by its component parts, and it is a defect of our educational system that no new move can be initiated unless ordered by the central authority. What passes under the name of learning in this country was originally built up on the literature and philosophy of China and India, and subsequently came to include the study of Western science. At present a sufficient advance has been made in the modern direction, so that learning, as such, has digested and absorbed the civilizations of Europe and America manifested in their literature, philosophy, science, and art.　But our scholars are still wanting in breadth and profundity of knowledge, and, while rich in critical acumen, have not yet reached the stage of being able to claim originality and self-enlightenment. Education has indeed ramified, far and wide; but the popular standard of information ranks low, and what the general public looks for in scholars is not the high standard that exists in Europe or America.　Scholars and students are not expected so much to invent as to apply.　A glance over the fields of statecraft, law, economics, physics, chemistry, and other sciences will show that it is very rare to find any original contributions to the stock of the world's knowledge.　Schools for teaching special subjects, scattered over the country, are certainly not few in number ; but what is being done in the lecture-rooms does not, as a rule, go beyond retailing the views and opinions of great men of science and learning in Western countries.　We can as yet hardly point to any of our country-men who have startled the world by their inventions.　This is so not only in the sphere of scientific learning, but also in that of literature and religion, where men great enough to attract world-wide attention are as yet non-existent. This state of affairs can be accounted for by the fact, that since the Restoration there has prevailed a tendency for men of high intellect and natural gifts to be drawn into the civil and military services of the Government, while now the fashion is for this class to become votaries of business activity.　So, too, as regards art and literature : in the days of Old Japan the country attained a high degree of development, but New Japan has produced as yet hardly anything in either branch worthy of being held up to universal esteem.　Here again it may be pleaded that matters are in a transition stage, the old and new civilization being still in the act of commingling and conflicting with each other, while the indigenous and alien elements have not yet succeeded in blending harmoniously.　More noteworthy development may be expected in the future ; but to-day there is nothing in either our art or our literature that deserves attention.

In productive industries and undertakings the country

(*d*) Low standard of education.

(e) Commercial morality.

has doubtless made progress, but in view of the general situation of the world's economics, the present revival of our commerce and industries is a matter of only small significance. The industrial system is still in an initial stage, with business morality undeveloped, as has been pointed out by independent observers, both Japanese and foreign. In statecraft and military affairs the Japanese possess a store of knowledge as well as experience extending over several centuries, and their success in those spheres has been comparatively easy. On the other hand, in the days previous to the Restoration, the national ideas concerning commerce and industry were about of the same nature as those entertained by the Greeks and Romans, for in contrast to the respect in which the tilling of soil was held, all other varieties of labour were looked down upon by the aristocrats, including the *samurai*, and merchants and tradesmen were to them objects of contempt. Thus it happens that, taken as a whole, our people are to a large extent deficient in the necessary training, not having had a sufficient time in which to learn it, so that they are not yet in a position to stand up before the civilized world of to-day and successfully engage in any of the businesses of agriculture, manufacturing industries, mining, commerce, or foreign trade. Hence, what one witnesses to-day is often what would be seen if the people of remote antiquity were called back to life and put to compete with representatives of modern civilization. In foreign trade the experience of our people as yet hardly extends over a third of a century, and it is not unnatural that everything connected with the business should be in an infantile stage. Hence, instances are not infrequent of practices which tend to injure the credit of the nation at large, and which involve the assumption that the commercial morality of our people is rated lower than it really deserves to be. I am in no way pessimistic in my views about business morality in Japan of to-day. Especially do I perceive that a great many long-established commercial and industrial concerns, as well as numerous business men now in their rising careers, are building up a code of wholesome morality which may yet rise above the political morality of the country. None the less, it must be admitted that people in general are still neither over-particular nor profound in their ideas of business morality.[1] As a rule they have not yet acquired the habit of punctuality, nor do they understand how closely and inseparably that habit is interwoven in the growth of credit. That time is money still remains merely an imported saying. Our people should realize that they have yet a long distance to travel before they can rise to the same plane of development in business activity as their *confrères* of the West.

I now come to the question of social manners and customs, about which a comparison with those of other civilized countries cannot but make all honest Japanese feel somewhat abashed. In a word, irregularity is the prevailing feature of our present social situation. If we leave the upper class out of account, the course of events following the Restoration has wrought radical changes in the mode of living and general customs of the middle and lower classes. Many time-honoured usages and precedents have gradually been swept aside, until there no longer exist, with regard to etiquette and personal behaviour, any clearly defined rules commanding the respect of all classes from the highest to the lowest. One may, indeed, go the length of saying that even such serious matters as marriage, funerals, and other important ceremonies are practically left either to the whims of individuals or to different local eccentricities. Some people follow the old formulae of fifty years ago, others local usages, not a few the Western methods, and many no formalities of any kind. *(f)* Social manners and customs.

Of current literature, too, it may be said that, strictly speaking, there exist no definite rules of general acceptance as to grammar and punctuation. Even among the middle classes there is nothing that can be regarded as a typical standard of conversation or writing. Without exaggerating, one may say that there is endless variety everywhere in the

[1] In connection with this, a recent circular addressed by the Japanese Vice-Minister of Agriculture and Commerce to the various chambers of commerce established in the country intimates that, in consequence of the growing intensity of competition, inventions, trade marks, and other industrial rights have been imitated or stolen in Japan, and that foreign trade marks and trade names have also been abused, and the victims have from time to time applied to the authorities for redress ; it adds the hope that 'merchants and manufacturers will endeavour so to engage in their business as to win confidence, which is the fundamental principle of trade, and will try to bring about prosperity by honourable means.'

way people dress, feed, and live. The old religions and old morals are steadily losing their hold, and nothing has yet arisen to take their places. As years go by, the struggle for existence grows fiercer and more exacting, and hard-worked men look about with intense eagerness for means of enjoyment and repose. But the country is as yet only very imperfectly provided with organs for refined amusement to suit the advanced tastes and inclinations of the day. This state of things probably arises from the circumstances that the social changes crowding the past fifty years were too sudden and upsetting at the outset. One looks around, only to be bewildered by a multitude of ideas, sentiments, predilections, demands, and what not, representing different ages. These press for recognition, one by the side of the other, and present a scene of appalling confusion. To old folk, looking superficially, the surroundings may appear to be orderly and systematized, but the new man, who sees with critical eyes, cannot but be sensible of a great lack of things to satisfactorily meet his desires and approval. To summarize the situation, Japan at present may be likened to a sea into which a hundred currents of Oriental and Occidental thoughts—some only conceived, others partially or wholly executed, during the past century or more—have poured in and, not having yet effected a fusion, are raging wildly, tossing, warring, and roaring. To say nothing of those of England, France, Germany, and America, the different civilizations of the other advanced countries of the world are now impressing themselves, in one form or another, on the mind and thought of our people. Thus situated, we may be said to be more than well supplied with all the necessary material from which to select and mould the future civilization of Japan. But, viewed from the standpoint of social orderliness, the spectacle is the acme of jumble and disarrangement. It is not surprising that a certain foreigner, viewing some phases of Japanese life, could not but doubt whether the men he observed belonged to the race that did so well in the Russian campaign. A portion of our people go neither by the old code of ethics and etiquette nor by those of modern days, while they are also disinclined to conform to those of foreign countries, and such persons convey the impression of neither possessing nor being governed by any ideas as to morality, public or private. It is for these reasons that I say we cannot but be abashed as we direct our eyes to foreign countries. There is, however, one consolation. We rise above the nations of Europe and America in being out and out freethinkers in matters of manners and customs. This peculiarity with us does not tend to disturb the peace and order of society ; on the contrary, it powerfully assists the march of general progress and development. Nevertheless I do not hesitate to admit that Japan is still in a preliminary stage, both as to moral and material civilization—a stage of moulding and casting, no complete fusion having yet taken place between the native and foreign elements. Civilization with us has yet immense room for future improvement and progress, and it would be rash to attempt to size up its merits to-day. It behoves the Japanese to recall the golden texts, ' Destroy all low old usages ' and ' Seek knowledge throughout the world,' which occur in the ' Five Articles of the Imperial Oath ' taken in the first year of Méiji, and to accept these as great principles for the guidance of the country in its emergence from the policy of exclusion. In renewed loyalty to these principles, they should resolutely determine to strike for greater national development, and thus bring about a worthy, nay glorious, sequel to the opening of the country. The only way to accomplish this end seems to be to follow the policy of ' move forward and learn,' and to strive always for the absorption of the world's civilization. However high a country may be in its civilization, the moment it begins to rest content with its position, the moment it ceases to profit by stimulus from without and to make unceasing efforts for improvement and reform, from that moment it enters on a career of decline. On the other hand, it may not necessarily be impossible for a country, wide awake to its own shortcomings and eager in the accumulation of knowledge, to arrive sooner or later at the goal of ideal civilization, when its people complete their training and culture, excel in the arts and advance in humane principles, even though its present position does not rank high. This is a point that the Japanese nation should now take to heart more earnestly than ever.

International competition.

I have already dwelt somewhat on the fact that in feudal days our race nourished valour and polished its intellectual qualities in consequence of local rivalry. Feudal times are no more, and the only way whereby our people may be incited to scale the ladder of civilization would appear to be to enter the arena of peaceful international competition. Even as the scale tells the weight of a thing and the tape its dimensions, so intercourse and competition bring to light the merits and demerits of the competitors, and it is only thus that an intelligent comparison may be made. Otherwise there exists no opportunity to appraise and compare differences. As has been already shown, our race possesses the happy trait of being little swayed by any anti-foreign animus, and the gain our country has made since its foundation by learning and adopting the good and excellent points of foreign civilizations has been immeasurably great. If then it is true, as it doubtless is, that fifty years after the reopening of the country its civilization remains defective in many and important respects, one need scarcely urge that redoubled endeavours for higher progress should be made by pursuing the paths indicated above.

Discrimination to be exercised.

But here, however, caution should be exercised. It is all very well to come into contact with a foreign civilization and assimilate its superior features. Equally important is it, however, to discriminate as to those which should be eschewed, and to judge thoughtfully when making a choice, for everything Western is not worthy of admiration or fit for assimilation. In not a few instances Europe and America present objectionable features not yet existing in this country, and unfortunate blunders of selection may bring harm, and harm only. Human laws, which deal with rights as well as duties, may be instanced. Some people, with a smattering of legal knowledge, would insist on standing for rights and rights only, forgetting all about duties; others would build up an individualistic theory of an extreme nature; yet others would essay to transplant into our soil the germs of a socialism of dangerously radical tendencies. I should discourage all such

Socialism.

vagaries. Especially with regard to socialism, it is a problem over which many great statesmen and thinkers of Europe and America are racking their brains. Let it be noted that the most radical of socialists become Nihilists or Anarchists, and these can never constitute a contributory element to the social progress of mankind.　Society is composed of individuals, and everything that tends to facilitate the development of individuals tends also to accelerate the progress of society.　But extreme individualistic freedom can only degenerate into sensuality and lawlessness, which in turn would ultimately lead to upsetting the whole social fabric.　Be it remembered that men are social beings and cannot exist alone or in isolation. It follows that, above all, the common interests of a community should be promoted, even at the expense of individual freedom. To restrict individual freedom may thus be not only a way to ensure the common welfare of society, but also a just step to further the progress and development of individuals themselves.　Such being the case, a well-balanced individualism and sane and sober socialism should co-exist as co-operating principles, and must necessarily, to enable them to prosper, be side by side in mutual harmony, in all ages and in all communities.　Has there ever been a community or an age in which either socialism or individualism dominated alone to the exclusion of the other ?

In the foregoing pages frequent references have been made to the susceptibility of the Japanese to the influences of foreign civilization.　If Japan has been endowed from the earliest days with this peculiarly sensitive faculty, she is gifted also with a strong retentive power which enables her to preserve and retain all that is good in and about herself.　For twenty centuries the nation has drunk freely of the civilizations of Korea, China, and India, being always open to the different influences impressed on her in succession.　Yet we remain to-day politically unaltered under one Imperial House and Sovereign, that has descended in an unbroken line for a length of time absolutely unexampled in the world.　This fact furnishes at least an incontestible proof that the Japanese are not a race of people who, inconstant and capricious, are given to loving all that is new and curious, always running after passing fashions.　They have welcomed Occidental civilization while preserving their old Oriental civilization.　They have attached the greatest importance to *Bushidō*, and at the same time held in the highest

[margin note: Strong points of the Japanese.]

respect the spirit of charity and humanity. They have ever made a point of choosing the middle course in everything, and have aimed at being always well balanced. To keep exclusively in one direction, or to run to extremes, or to look forward only without looking backward, or to remember one side of a thing, forgetting the other, is not a characteristic of our people. We are conservative simultaneously with being progressive ; we are aristocratic and at the same time democratic ; we are in-dividualistic while being also socialistic. In these respects we may be said to somewhat resemble the Anglo-Saxon race. It is not impossible that the future holds some harassing social problems for us to deal with, or some grave international troubles for us to face. However serious the emergency that may arise, however far beyond the range of present conception, I hope, nay it is my firm conviction, that we shall hold steadfastly by the traits handed down to us from our ancestors, and that, nourishing these traits to a still higher stage of development, we shall be well equipped for meeting all difficulties.

Claims to be a great nation.

I come now to the last, but not the least important, point demanding attention. I mean our aspiration to be recognized by the world as a great nation. There is nothing strange in the demand that our people should be accorded the treatment due to their greatness as a Power not merely in the Orient, but in the whole world. I notice one thing which, for the time being, has an important bearing on the realization of this just and fair ambition. It is a phenomenon unexpectedly mani-fested of late among a section of Western peoples, who would exclude our nation on the ground of non-affinity of race. I am well aware that behind this anti-Japanese sentiment there exist various circumstances which deserve consideration. However, in so far as our people are disliked because they are Asiatics, there is nothing reasonable or logical in this hostile feeling. Such a passion or sentiment arises solely from narrow and biased racial prejudice on the one hand, and from miscon-ceptions born of competition among the labouring classes on the other. To reason against and to remove these prejudices and misconceptions is a mutual duty devolving as much on our people as on the Western nations concerned. We have no occasion to be deterred by doubts or to hesitate in pressing for the satisfaction of our just demand. I do not in any way sympathize with the idea that, by sending abroad emigrants who become a cause of domestic trouble in the country of their destination, the rights or honour of a great and civilized Power, such as ours claims to be, will be served. But I contend that, when a treaty Power seeks to enact a law restricting the immigration of our labourers, the terms of such restriction should be analogous and even identical with those applicable to the peoples of other great Powers or civilized countries. As has been stated in these pages, we are a people whose glorious history will bear to be held up to the gaze of Western nations. We have learned a great many things from the West, but there are some instances of our having outstripped our tutors. Take, for instance, the religious freedom that we once learned from the West. To-day it has become our turn to take pride in the working of the principle. In spite of being under one and the same religion, Western countries, because of that very religion, have had to pass through many civil wars and frequent international conflicts. Excepting the United States of America, none of them has been able to extend full freedom to all religions in common, the rest being tied each to its own State creed. With some of them their laws guarantee freedom, but socially they pay allegiance to one sect or another, excluding all other sects and all other religions, and there is not a place where liberty of conscience exists in its entirety. In contrast with this, we have *Shintō* for our indigenous religion and Confucianism and Buddhism as imported faiths, and latterly we have added Christianity to the list. With the promulgation of the Constitution absolute religious freedom has become officially recognized. There is probably no place except Japan where not only is freedom of conscience legally guaranteed, but where socially, and in actual practice, any religion whatsoever may be professed with perfect impunity, provided that it be not subversive of public peace, good order, or morality. To cite another example : in the countries of Europe and America their Constitution cost them many revolutions, often bloodshed. In this country the Constitution, though prefaced by more or less conflict of views between the official and the non-official elements, came to its birth in the midst of a

Freedom of faith.

Promul-
gation of
the Con-
stitution.

general feeling of good will and rejoicing. A claim may thus be fairly asserted that this nation has not only imported all the integral elements of Western civilization, but has also succeeded in making good use of them, and has even effected improvements in some cases. With such a showing to illumine its past, the future of the country points, all the more plainly, to the imperative obligation that, with ever-unswerving determination, our efforts should be continued to seek knowledge far and wide on the earth, and to accumulate the virtues of study and training so as finally to reach an ideal civilization commensurate with our aspirations. I repeat that the development of our country in the past has been solely the result of foreign intercourse which brought us into contact with Western civilization. Such being the case, the nation, with ever-in-

Summary. creasing earnestness, should recognize the necessity that, while endeavouring to mount higher on the steps of progress and to realize high ideals, the Japanese people and State should unite in cultivating foreign intercourse more closely than ever, and, standing in the world's arena of peaceful competition, should come freely into contact with Occidental civilization, so as to choose and adopt its superior features, always looking upward and onward for something higher and nobler. The country has already won a position that entitles it to represent the civilization of the Orient, and now the lot falls to it to introduce the civilization of the Occident to the Orient. This may truly be regarded as Japan's heaven-ordained office, and the Japanese should grow in the belief that on them alone devolves the mission of harmonizing the civilizations of the East and West, so as to lead the world as a whole to a higher plane. Should our people, fully appreciating this their heaven-ordained office, resolve to accomplish the mission, the effect will be far- if not world-reaching. The spirit of international jealousy will gradually disappear ; petty questions of race will no longer find room to exist ; the evils of anti-alienism, which live on misguided traditions or sentiments, will vanish ; international relations, hitherto heterogeneous and militant, will become harmonious and peaceful ; and then, even though enlightenment may not go so far as to make possible the realization of Plato's ideal stage when the statesman should be a philosopher and the philosopher a statesman, it may cease to be a mere dream to look for the day when the nations of the world will federate under one code of international law and form one organic system, creating a new era of fellowship and good will wherein distinctions of native and alien, near and remote, will disappear, and all will be linked together by one uniform bond of harmonious co-operation and coalition to the glory of real civilization. I do not believe that there is another nation on the face of the earth better fitted than the Japanese to achieve this grand mission, for we are a nation which represents the civilization of the Orient and has assimilated the civilization of the Occident.

APPENDIX A

THE CONSTITUTION OF THE EMPIRE OF JAPAN

(*Translation*)

HAVING, by virtue of the glories of Our Ancestors, ascended the Throne of a lineal succession unbroken for ages eternal ; desiring to promote the welfare of, and to give development to, the moral and intellectual faculties of Our beloved subjects, the very same that have been favoured with the benevolent care and affectionate vigilance of Our Ancestors ; and hoping to maintain the prosperity of the State, in concert with Our people and with their support, We hereby promulgate, in pursuance of Our Imperial Rescript of the 14th day of the 10th month of the 14th year of Méiji, a fundamental law of State, to exhibit the principles by which We are to be guided in Our conduct, and to point out to what Our descendants and Our subjects and their descendants are for ever to conform.

The rights of sovereignty of the State We have inherited from Our Ancestors, and We shall bequeath them to Our descendants. Neither We nor they shall in future fail to wield them in accordance with the provisions of the Constitution hereby granted.

We now declare to respect and protect the security of the rights and of the property of Our people, and to secure to them the complete enjoyment of the same, within the extent of the provisions of the present Constitution and of the law.

The Imperial Diet shall first be convoked for the 23rd year of Méiji, and the time of its opening shall be the date when the present Constitution comes into force.

When in the future it may become necessary to amend any of the provisions of the present Constitution, We or Our successors shall assume the initiative right, and submit a project for the same to the Imperial Diet. The Imperial Diet shall pass its vote upon it, according to the conditions imposed by the present Constitution, and in no otherwise shall Our descendants or Our subjects be permitted to attempt any alteration thereof.

Our Ministers of State, on Our behalf, shall be held responsible for the carrying out of the present Constitution, and Our present and future subjects shall for ever assume the duty of allegiance to the present Constitution.

(His Imperial Majesty's Sign-Manual.)

(Privy Seal.)

The 11th day of the 2nd month of the 22nd year of Méiji.

(*Countersigned*)　COUNT KURODA KIYOTAKA,
　　　　　　　　Minister President of State.

COUNT ITO HIROBUMI,
　　President of the Privy Council.

COUNT OKUMA SHIGENOBU,
　　Minister of State for Foreign Affairs.

COUNT SAIGO TSUKUMICHI,
　　Minister of State for the Navy.

COUNT INOUYE KAORU,
　　Minister of State for Agriculture and Commerce.

COUNT YAMADA AKIYOSHI,
　　Minister of State for Justice.

COUNT MATSUGATA MASAYOSHI,
　　Minister of State for Finance, and
　　Minister of State for Home Affairs.

COUNT OYAMA IWAO,
　　Minister of State for War.

VISCOUNT MORI ARINORI,
　　Minister of State for Education.

VISCOUNT ENOMOTO TAKEAKI,
　　Minister of State for Communications.

THE CONSTITUTION OF THE EMPIRE OF JAPAN

CHAPTER I

The Emperor

ARTICLE I

The Empire of Japan shall be reigned over and governed by a line of Emperors unbroken for ages eternal.

ARTICLE II

The Imperial Throne shall be succeeded to by Imperial male descendants, according to the provisions of the Imperial House Law.

ARTICLE III

The Emperor is sacred and inviolable.

ARTICLE IV

The Emperor is the head of the Empire, combining in Himself the rights of sovereignty, and exercises them according to the provisions of the present Constitution.

ARTICLE V

The Emperor exercises the legislative power with the consent of the Imperial Diet.

ARTICLE VI

The Emperor gives sanction to laws, and orders them to be promulgated and executed.

ARTICLE VII

The Emperor convokes the Imperial Diet, opens, closes, and prorogues it, and dissolves the House of Representatives.

ARTICLE VIII

The Emperor, in consequence of an urgent necessity to maintain public safety or to avert public calamities, issues, when the Imperial Diet is not sitting, Imperial Ordinances in the place of law.

Such Imperial Ordinances are to be laid before the Imperial Diet at its next session, and when the Diet does not approve the said Ordinances, the Government shall declare them to be invalid for the future.

ARTICLE IX

The Emperor issues, or causes to be issued, the Ordinances necessary for the carrying out of the laws, or for the maintenance of the public peace and order, and for the promotion of the welfare of the subjects. But no Ordinance shall in any way alter any of the existing laws.

ARTICLE X

The Emperor determines the organization of the different branches of the administration, and the salaries of all civil and military officers, and appoints and dismisses the same. Exceptions, especially provided for in the present Constitution or in other laws, shall be in accordance with the respective provisions bearing thereon.

ARTICLE XI

The Emperor has the supreme command of the Army and Navy.

ARTICLE XII

The Emperor determines the organization and peace standing of the Army and Navy.

ARTICLE XIII

The Emperor declares war, makes peace, and concludes treaties.

ARTICLE XIV

The Emperor proclaims the law of siege.

The conditions and effects of the law of siege shall be determined by law.

ARTICLE XV

The Emperor confers titles of nobility, rank, orders, and other marks of honour.

ARTICLE XVI

The Emperor orders amnesty, pardon, commutation of punishments, and rehabilitation.

ARTICLE XVII

A Regency shall be instituted in conformity with the provisions of the Imperial House Law.

The Regent shall exercise the powers appertaining to the Emperor in His name.

CHAPTER II

Rights and Duties of Subjects

ARTICLE XVIII

The conditions necessary for being a Japanese subject shall be determined by law.

ARTICLE XIX

Japanese subjects may, according to qualifications determined in laws or ordinances, be appointed to civil or military offices equally, and may fill any other public offices.

ARTICLE XX

Japanese subjects are amenable to service in the Army or Navy, according to the provisions of law.

ARTICLE XXI

Japanese subjects are amenable to the duty of paying taxes, according to the provisions of law.

ARTICLE XXII

Japanese subjects shall have the liberty of abode and of changing the same within the limits of law.

ARTICLE XXIII

No Japanese subject shall be arrested, detained, tried, or punished, unless according to law.

ARTICLE XXIV

No Japanese subject shall be deprived of his right of being tried by the judges determined by law.

ARTICLE XXV

Except in the cases provided for in the law, the house of no Japanese subject shall be entered or searched without his consent.

ARTICLE XXVI

Except in the cases mentioned in the law, the secrecy of the letters of every Japanese subject shall remain inviolate.

ARTICLE XXVII

The right of property of every Japanese subject shall remain inviolate.

Measures necessary to be taken for the public benefit shall be provided for by law.

ARTICLE XXVIII

Japanese subjects shall, within limits not prejudicial to peace and order, and not antagonistic to their duties as subjects, enjoy freedom of religious belief.

ARTICLE XXIX

Japanese subjects shall, within the limits of law, enjoy the liberty of speech, writing, publication, public meetings, and associations.

ARTICLE XXX

Japanese subjects may present petitions, by observing the proper forms of respect, and by complying with the rules specially provided for the same.

ARTICLE XXXI

The provisions contained in the present Chapter shall not affect the exercise of the powers appertaining to the Emperor in times of war or in cases of a national emergency.

ARTICLE XXXII

Each and every one of the provisions contained in the preceding Articles of the present Chapter, that are not in conflict with the laws or the rules and discipline of the Army and Navy, shall apply to the officers and men of the Army and of the Navy.

CHAPTER III

The Imperial Diet

ARTICLE XXXIII

The Imperial Diet shall consist of two Houses, a House of Peers and a House of Representatives.

ARTICLE XXXIV

The House of Peers shall, in accordance with the Ordinance concerning the House of Peers, be composed of the members of the Imperial Family, of the orders of nobility, and of those persons who have been nominated thereto by the Emperor.

ARTICLE XXXV

The House of Representatives shall be composed of Members elected by the people, according to the provisions of the Law of Election.

ARTICLE XXXVI

No one can at one and the same time be a Member of both Houses.

ARTICLE XXXVII

Every law requires the consent of the Imperial Diet.

ARTICLE XXXVIII

Both Houses shall vote upon projects of law submitted to it by the Government, and may respectively initiate projects of law.

ARTICLE XXXIX

A Bill, which has been rejected by either the one or the other of the two Houses, shall not be again brought in during the same session.

ARTICLE XL

Both Houses can make representations to the Government, as to laws or upon any other subject. When, however, such representations are not accepted, they cannot be made a second time during the same session.

ARTICLE XLI

The Imperial Diet shall be convoked every year.

ARTICLE XLII

A session of the Imperial Diet shall last during three months. In case of necessity, the duration of a session may be prolonged by Imperial Order.

ARTICLE XLIII

When urgent necessity arises, an extraordinary session may be convoked, in addition to the ordinary one.

The duration of an extraordinary session shall be determined by Imperial Order.

ARTICLE XLIV

The opening, closing, prolongation of session and prorogation of the Imperial Diet shall be effected simultaneously for both Houses.

In case the House of Representatives has been ordered to dissolve, the House of Peers shall at the same time be prorogued.

ARTICLE XLV

When the House of Representatives has been ordered to dissolve, Members shall be caused by Imperial Order to be newly elected, and the new House shall be convoked within five months from the day of dissolution.

ARTICLE XLVI

No debate can be opened and no vote can be taken in either House of the Imperial Diet, unless not less than one-third of the whole number of the Members thereof is present.

ARTICLE XLVII

Votes shall be taken in both Houses by absolute majority. In case of a tie vote, the President shall have the casting vote.

ARTICLE XLVIII

The deliberations of both Houses shall be held in public. The deliberations may, however, upon demand of the Government or by resolution of the House, be held in secret sitting.

ARTICLE XLIX

Both Houses of the Imperial Diet may respectively present address to the Emperor.

ARTICLE L

Both Houses may receive petitions presented by subjects.

ARTICLE LI

Both Houses may enact, besides what is provided for in the present Constitution and in the Law of the Houses, rules necessary for the management of their internal affairs.

ARTICLE LII

No Member of either House shall be held responsible, outside the respective Houses, for any opinion uttered or for any vote given in the House. When, however, a Member himself has given publicity to his opinions by public speech, by documents in print or in writing, or by any other similar means, he shall, in the matter, be amenable to the general law.

ARTICLE LIII

The Members of both Houses shall, during the session, be free from arrest, unless with the consent of the House, except in cases of flagrant delicts, or of offences connected with a state of internal commotion or with a foreign trouble.

ARTICLE LIV

The Ministers of State and the Delegates of the Government may, at any time, take seats and speak in either House.

CHAPTER IV

The Ministers of State and the Privy Council

ARTICLE LV

The respective Ministers of State shall give their advice to the Emperor, and be responsible for it. All Laws, Imperial Ordinances, and Imperial Rescripts of whatever kind, that relate to the affairs of the State, require the countersignature of a Minister of State.

ARTICLE LVI

The Privy Council shall, in accordance with the provisions for the organization of the Privy Council, deliberate upon important matters of State, when they have been consulted by the Emperor.

CHAPTER V

The Judicature

ARTICLE LVII

The Judicature shall be exercised by the Courts of Law according to law, in the name of the Emperor.

The organization of the Courts of Law shall be determined by law.

ARTICLE LVIII

The judges shall be appointed from among those who possess proper qualifications according to law.

No judge shall be deprived of his position, unless by way of criminal sentence or disciplinary punishment.

Rules for disciplinary punishment shall be determined by law.

ARTICLE LIX

Trials and judgments of a Court shall be conducted publicly. When, however, there exists any fear that such publicity may be prejudicial to peace and order, or to the maintenance of public morality, the public trial may be suspended by provision of law or by the decision of the Court of Law.

ARTICLE LX

All matters that fall within the competency of a special Court shall be specially provided by law.

ARTICLE LXI

No suit at law which relates to rights alleged to have been infringed by the illegal measures of the executive authorities, and which shall come within the competency of the Court of Administrative Litigation specially established by law, shall be taken cognizance of by a Court of Law.

CHAPTER VI

Finance

ARTICLE LXII

The imposition of a new tax or the modification of the rates of an existing one shall be determined by law.

However, all such administrative fees or other revenue having the nature of compensation shall not fall within the category of the above clause.

The raising of national loans and the contracting of other liabilities to the charge of the National Treasury, except those that are provided for in the Budget, shall require the consent of the Imperial Diet.

ARTICLE LXIII

The taxes levied at present shall, in so far as they are not remodelled by new law, be collected according to the old system.

ARTICLE LXIV

The expenditure and revenue of the State require the consent of the Imperial Diet by means of an annual Budget.

Any and all expenditures overpassing the appropriations set forth in the Titles and Paragraphs of the Budget, or that are not provided for in the Budget, shall subsequently require the approbation of the Imperial Diet.

ARTICLE LXV

The Budget shall be first laid before the House of Representatives.

ARTICLE LXVI

The expenditures of the Imperial House shall be defrayed every year out of the National Treasury, according to the present fixed amount for the same, and shall not require the consent thereto of the Imperial Diet, except in case an increase thereof should be found necessary.

ARTICLE LXVII

Those already fixed expenditures based by the Constitution upon the powers appertaining to the Emperor, and such expenditures as may have arisen by the effect of law, or that appertain to the legal obligations of the Government, shall be neither rejected nor reduced by the Imperial Diet without the concurrence of the Government.

ARTICLE LXVIII

In order to meet special requirements, the Government may ask the consent of the Imperial Diet to a certain amount as a Continuing Expenditure Fund for a previously fixed number of years.

ARTICLE LXIX

In order to supply deficiencies which are unavoidable in the Budget, and to meet requirements unprovided for in the same, a Reserve Fund shall be provided in the Budget.

ARTICLE LXX

When the Imperial Diet cannot be convoked, owing to the external or internal condition of the country, in case of urgent need for the maintenance of public safety, the Government may take all necessary financial measures by means of an Imperial Ordinance.

In the case mentioned in the preceding clause, the matter shall be submitted to the Imperial Diet at its next session and its approbation shall be obtained thereto.

ARTICLE LXXI

When the Imperial Diet has not voted on the Budget, or when the Budget has not been brought into actual existence, the Government shall carry out the Budget of the preceding year.

ARTICLE LXXII

The final account of the expenditures and revenue of the State shall be verified and confirmed by the Board of Audit, and it shall be submitted by the Government to the Imperial Diet, together with the report of verification of the said Board.

The organization and competency of the Board of Audit shall be determined by law separately.

CHAPTER VII

Supplementary Rules

ARTICLE LXXIII

When it has become necessary in future to amend the provisions of the present Constitution, a project to that effect shall be submitted to the Imperial Diet by Imperial Order.

In the above case, neither House can open the debate unless not less than two-thirds of the whole number of Members are present, and no amendment can be passed unless a majority of not less than two-thirds of the Members present is obtained.

ARTICLE LXXIV

No modification of the Imperial House Law shall be required to be submitted to the deliberation of the Imperial Diet.

No provision of the present Constitution can be modified by the Imperial House Law.

ARTICLE LXXV

No modification can be introduced into the Constitution, or into the Imperial House Law, during the time of a Regency.

Article LXXVI

Existing legal enactments, such as laws, regulations, Ordinances, or by whatever names they may be called, shall, so far as they do not conflict with the present Constitution, continue in force.

All existing contracts or orders, that entail obligations upon the Government, and that are connected with expenditure, shall come within the scope of Article LXVII.

APPENDIX B

PRÉCIS OF THE TREATY OF PEACE BETWEEN JAPAN AND RUSSIA SIGNED AT PORTSMOUTH, NEW HAMPSHIRE, U.S.A., SEPTEMBER THE FIFTH, 1905

ARTICLE 1.—Stipulates for the re-establishment of peace and friendship between the two countries.

ARTICLE 2.—Russia recognises the preponderant interest, from political, military, and economic points of view, of Japan in the Empire of Korea, and stipulates that Russia will not oppose any measures for its government, protection, or control that Japan will deem necessary to take in Korea in conjunction with the Korean Government, but Russian subjects and Russian enterprises are to enjoy the same status as the subjects and enterprises of other countries.

ARTICLE 3.—Stipulates that the territory of Manchuria is to be simultaneously evacuated by the forces of each country.

ARTICLE 4.—Stipulates that the rights possessed by Russia in conformity with the lease to Russia of Port Arthur and Dalny, together with the lands and waters adjacent, shall pass over entirely to Japan.

ARTICLE 5.—The Russian and Japanese Governments engage themselves reciprocally not to put any obstacles in the way of the general measures, which shall be alike for all nations, that China may take for the development of the commerce and industry of Manchuria.

ARTICLE 6.—The Manchurian Railway shall be worked jointly by the Russians and the Japanese.

590

ARTICLES 7 & 8.—Are of minor importance.

ARTICLE 9.—Russia cedes to Japan the southern part of Sakhalin Island as far north as the 50th degree of north latitude, together with the Island depending thereon. The right of free navigation is assured to Japan in the Bays of La Perouse and Tartary.

ARTICLE 10.—Deals with the situation of Russian subjects in South Sakhalin.

ARTICLE 11.—Gives Japanese subjects rights to fish in Russian territorial waters.

ARTICLE 12.—The two parties engage to renew a commercial treaty.

ARTICLES 13 & 15.—Relate to exchange of prisoners and the ratification of the treaty.

ARTICLE 14.—The treaty is to be drawn up in two languages, French and English, the French text being for the Russian and the English for the Japanese. In case of difficulty of translation the French document to be decisive.

APPENDIX C

PRÉCIS OF A SPEECH DELIVERED BY BARON KOMURA, MINISTER FOR FOREIGN AFFAIRS, IN THE IMPERIAL DIET, FEBRUARY 2, 1909, ON JAPAN'S FOREIGN POLICY

The foreign policy of this empire should have for its objects the maintenance of peace and the development of national resources. As regards Great Britain, various events of far-reaching importance have, since the conclusion of our agreement, presented themselves in the relations of the two countries with other Powers, but happily those events have uniformly contributed to the consolidation of the general peace in Eastern Asia, which forms one of the principal objects of the agreement. The alliance has thus steadily gained in strength and solidity, and to-day it stands upon a perfectly firm and enduring foundation. Our relations of good correspondence with Russia are constantly increasing in intimacy. Not only are the two countries scrupulously observing in spirit as well as in letter the compact concluded the year before last, but the pacific policies of both Governments working harmoniously are already yielding actual and momentous effects, and there is every reason to expect unceasing growth of friendly sentiment between the two countries. Our relations with France and Germany are equally on a most satisfactory footing. The Japanese and French Governments, in mutual confidence, are strictly abiding by the arrangement concluded in 1907, and all indications point to the institution of a close *rapprochement* between the two peoples. The declaration made by Prince Bülow last year in the Reichstag has clearly manifested the frank and friendly attitude of Germany towards Japan and the complete accord between the two Governments in their Far Eastern policies. It is sincerely to be hoped that the good relations between Japan and Germany will continue to grow in cordiality.

Concerning China, it is evident that in view of our important and close relations, both political and economical, with that empire, the two nations should be drawn together by ties of sincere friendship and mutual consideration. It is gratifying to note that some of the long-pending questions between the two Governments have recently been successfully adjusted, while, with regard to others, satisfactory solution should not be altogether impossible if both parties, in appreciation of the general situation, yield to a spirit of conciliation and accommodation. Regarding the internal administration of China, we are naturally watching with keen interest and sympathy the progress of her reform. It is our earnest hope that the statesmen of China will always keep in mind the necessity of maintaining general stability in the empire, and will conduct affairs of State in harmonious co-operation in order to facilitate the important work of reform. We have invariably made it the guiding rule to observe the principle of the open door and equal opportunity, and we are firmly determined to adhere to that principle in future, as in the past, with unswerving loyalty.

The friendship between Japan and the United States of America is of traditional standing, and it is absolutely essential to the common interests of both States not only to maintain unimpaired those sentiments of amity, but to extend and strengthen them by every possible means. Notwithstanding the perfect accord which always existed between the two countries in their aim in the Far East and the Pacific, it appears that doubts have been entertained in some quarters as to the sincerity of their intentions. In order to remove all cause of such misunderstandings, the two Governments have deemed it advisable to exchange Diplomatic Notes in official announcement of their common policy, and they are convinced that this declaration will not only materially conduce to the promotion of lasting friendship between the two nations, but will be also largely instrumental in preserving the general repose in the Orient. As regards the question of measures unfavourable to the Japanese which are now pending in the Californian Legislature, the Imperial Government, relying upon the sense of justice of the American people as well as the friendly disposition of the Federal Government, confidently hopes that such questions will not lead to any international complications.

Without making special reference to each of the other Powers with which we are on no less cordial terms, it will be, after all, admitted that the maintenance of peace, which is one of the principal objects of our foreign policy, has now been practically assured. It is believed that in the face of such a situation we can permit ourselves to devote our endeavours to the development of the national resources. In this connection a few explanatory remarks should be made on the subjects of emigration and of coming treaty revision. The first point which claims our attention in dealing with the problem of emigration is that, in view of the new international position assigned to Japan in consequence of the late war and the corresponding extension of our spheres of peaceful activities, it has become necessary that our people, instead of scattering themselves at random in distant foreign lands, should be concentrated in the region of the Far East so as to secure their united and concordant efforts for carrying on those legitimate activities. The next point to be noticed is that we should studiously avoid all matters likely to obstruct the development of our international commerce and industry, which play by far the most important *rôle* among our economic enterprises in the field of foreign intercourse. These considerations have led the Government to follow their avowed policy in respect of emigrants to Canada and the United States, and to enforce in perfect good faith restrictions of emigration to those regions.

With regard to the question of treaty revision, the Government has decided to give notice next year to the various Powers of the termination of the existing commercial treaties. In accordance with the provision, one year after such notice is given the operation of the treaties is to be arrested. It is the intention of the Government to approach the different Powers severally on the subject of the negotiation of new treaties, unhampered by any unequal engagement, and to conclude suitable compacts based entirely upon the principle of reciprocity with a view to the free development of our international commerce.

APPENDIX D

I

S. Ikéda : Contributions to the Embryology of Amphibia.

N. Yatsu : On the Development of *Lingula anatina*.

Note on Histology of *Lingula anatina*.

K. Kishinouyé : Some New Scyphomedusæ of Japan.

A. Iizuka : Observations on the Japanese Palolo (*Ceratocephale Osawai*, n. sp.).

T. Fujita : On the Formation of the Germinal Layers in Gastropoda.

I. Ikéda : The Gephyrea of Japan.

I. Iijima : On a New Cestode Larva Parasitic in Man.

II

LIST OF PLACES WHERE ZOOLOGICAL STUDIES ARE CARRIED ON

The Zoological Institute of the Science College, Imperial University, under Professors Mitsukuri, Iijima, and Watasé. *Zoological institutes.*

The Zoological Institute of the Agricultural College, Imperial University, under Professors Ishikawa and Sasaki.

The Zoological Laboratory of the First Higher School, under Professor Gotō.

The Zoological Laboratory of the Higher Normal School, Tōkyō, under Professor A. Oka.

The Zoological Laboratory of the Higher Normal School, Hiroshima, under Professor Ikéda.

The Entomological Laboratories of the Sapporo Agricultural College, Hokkaidō, under Professors S. Matsumura and Hatta.

The Nawa Entomological Laboratory of Gifu, under Mr. Y. Nawa.

The Laboratory of the Fishery Bureau, the Department of Agriculture and Commerce, under Dr. Kishinouyé.

III

LIST OF BOTANICAL PAPERS IN THE ' JOURNAL OF THE COLLEGE OF SCIENCE '

S. Ōkubo : On the Plants of Sulphur Island.

S. Hirasé : Études sur la Fécondation et l'Embryogénie du *Ginkgo ciloba*. I–II.

M. Miyoshi : Studien über die Schwefelrasenbildung und die Schwefelbacterien der Thermen von Yumoto bei Nikkō.

S. Ikéno : Untersuchungen über die Entwicklung der Geschlechtsorgane und den Vorgang der Befruchtung bei Cycas Revoluta.

T. Itō and J. Matsumura : Tentamen Floræ Lutchuensis. I.

N. Ono : Über die Wachstumsbeschleunigung einiger Algen und Pilze durch chemische Reize.

K. Shibata : Beitrage zur Wachstumsgeschichte ber Bambusgewachse.

K. Endō : Corallinæ veræ Japonicæ.

Y. Yabé : Revisio Umbelliferarum Japonicarum.

J. Matsumura : Revisio Alni Specierum Japonicarum.

S. Kusano : Transpiration of Evergreen Trees in Winter.

M. Miyoshi : Über die Sporocarpenevacuation und darauf erfolgendes Sporenausstreuen bei einer Flechte.

H. Hattori : Studien über die Einwirkung des Kupfersulfats auf einige Pflanzen.

K. Saitō : Anatomische Studien über wichtige Faserpflanzen Japans mit besonderer Berucksichtigung der Bastzellen.

M. Miyoshi : Untersuchungen über die Schrumpfkrankheit (' Ishukubyō ') der Maulbeerbaumes.

T. Inui : Untersuchungen über die niederen Organismen welche sich bei Zubereitung des alkoholischen Getränkes (' Awamori ') betheiligen.

S. Kusano : Studies on the Parasitism of *Buckleya quadriala* (B. and H.), a Santalaceous Parasite, and on the Structure of its Haustorium.

T. Ichimura : On the Formation of Anthocyan in the Petaloid Calyx of the Red Japanese Hortense.

A. Yasuda : On the Comparative Anatomy of the Cucurbitaceæ (Wild and Cultivated), in Japan.

K. Saitō : Untersuchungen über die atmosphärischen Pilzkeime.

K. Endō : A Study of the Genicula of Corallinæ.

K. Saitō : Über das Vorkommen von Saccharomyces Ansmalus beim Sakebrauen.

Tieghemella Japonica.

B. Hayata : Revisio Euphorbiacearum et Buxacearum Japonicarum.

IV

D. Brauns : Geology of Tōkyō and its Environs (Mem. Tōkyō Univ.).

B. Kotō : Some Occurrences of Piedmontite in Japan.

Y. Kikuchi : On Anorthite from Miyakéjima.

B. Kotō : On the so-called Crystalline Schists of Chichibu (the Sambagawan Series).

M. Yokoyama : Jurassic Plants from Kaga, Hida, and Echizen.

Y. Kikuchi : On Pyroxenic Components in certain Volcanic Rocks from Bonin Island.

On Cordierits as Contact Mineral.

B. Kotō : On the Cause of the Great Earthquake in Central Japan 1891.

The Archean Formation of the Abukuma Plateau.

M. Yokoyama : On some Cretaceous Fossils from Shikoku.

Mesozoic Plants from Kōzuké, Kii, Awa, and Tosa.

K. Nishiwada : On some Organic Remains from the Tertiary Limestone near Sagara, Tōtōmi.

T. Hiki : Notes on the Topaz from Mino.

N. Yamazaki : On the Piedmontite-rhyolite from Shinano.

B. Kotō : On the Geologic Structure of the Malayan Archipelago.

Notes on the Geology of the Dependent Isles of Formosa.

S. Yoshiwara : Geologic Structure of the Ryūkyū (Loochoo) Curve and its Relation to the Northern Part of Formosa.

Notes on the Raised Coral Reefs in the Islands of the Ryūkyū Curve.

S. Yoshiwara and J. Iwasaki : Notes on a New Fossil Mammal.

R. B. Newton and R. Holland : On some Fossils from the Islands of Formosa and Ryūkyū.

S. Yoshiwara : On the Fossil Echinoidea of Japan.

B. Kotō : An Orographic Sketch of Korea.

K. Jimbō : Notes on the Minerals of Japan.

M. Yokoyama : Jurassic Ammonites from Echizen and Nagato.

N. Yabé : Cretaceous Cephalopoda from Hokkaidō. I–II.

M. Yokoyama : Mesozoic Plants from Nagato and Bitchū.

N. Yabé : Mesozoic Plants from Korea.

APPENDIX E

JAPANESE WEIGHTS, MEASURES, AND MONEYS, WITH ENGLISH AND FRENCH EQUIVALENTS

	English.	French.
Ri	2·440 miles.	3·927 kilomètres.
Ri (marine)	1·150 ,,	1·851 ,,
Ri (square)	5·955 ,, (square).	15·428 ,, carrés.
Chō = 10 *zan*	2·450 acres.	99·173 ares.
Tsubo	3·953 sq. yards.	3·305 mètres carrés.
Koku = 10 *to*		
= 100 *sho* (liquid)	39·703 gallons.	1·803 hectolitres.
,, ,, (dry)	4·962 bushels.	—
,, (capacity of vessel)	$\frac{1}{10}$ of a ton.	$\frac{1}{10}$ de tonne.
Kan = 1000 *mommé* {	8·267 lb. (avoir.). 10·047 ,, (troy). }	3·750 kilogrammes.
Kin .. .. {	1·322 lb. (avoir.). 1·607 ,, (troy). }	6·000 hectogrammes.
Mommé .. {	2·116 drams (avoir.). 2·411 dwt. (troy). }	3·750 grammes.
Yen = 100 *sen* ..	2s. 0·582d.	2·5013 francs.
Ryō		

Note as to ryō *and* yen.

Previous to the Méiji era—that is to say in the latter part of the feudal *régime*—a very confusing Double-Standard of Currency was in practice. Various coins of gold and silver were in circulation, and the ratio of the two metals was also indefinite. It is, therefore, extremely hard to find an exact equivalent of *ryō* of those days, in English money. Roughly speaking, however, 4 shillings to 1 *ryō* will give an approximate idea of comparison.

In 1871 a New Law of Currency was framed, and for two or three years a gold standard was maintained, and 1 *yen* of this period approximately corresponded to 4 shillings.

From the above-mentioned time until 1897 Japan was practically a country of silver standard. In order to know, therefore, the accurate value of *yen* of this period, it must be calculated by the market price of silver contained in 1 *yen*. The price of silver was, of course, constantly fluctuating; so the only way of comparison is to consider 1 *yen* of those days as roughly equal to 2 shillings.

In 1897 the currency system was reorganized, and gold standard, pure and simple, was adopted. According to the present system 1 *yen* is equal to 2s. 0·582d. : therefore 2 shillings to 1 *yen* will give a simple but fair idea of comparison.

APPENDIX F

INDUSTRY, COMMERCE, AND AGRICULTURE

TABLE of average daily wages of workmen. From the *Financial Annual*, issued by the Department of Finance, 1908.

Kind of Employment.	1895. Yen.	1900. Yen.	1906. Yen.
Carpenter	0·312	0·535	0·650
Plasterer	0·313	0·540	0·650
Stone-cutter	0·359	0·605	0·730
Sawyer	0·307	0·533	0·640
Shingle-roofer	0·293	0·505	0·630
Tile-roofer	0·325	0·585	0·730
Brickmaker	0·380	0·448	0·530
Bricklayer	—	0·628	0·820
Floor-mat maker	0·297	0·465	0·560
Screen and door maker	0·304	0·505	0·610
Paperhanger	0·283	0·495	0·580
Cabinetmaker	0·296	0·500	0·590
Cooper	0·253	0·430	0·500
Shoemaker	0·315	0·473	0·580
Harness-maker	0·298	0·470	0·630
Cartwright	0·279	0·465	0·520
Tailor (for Japanese dress)	0·252	0·390	0·500
Tailor (for European dress)	0·384	0·558	0·680
Dyer	0·237	0·293	0·370
Blacksmith	0·280	0·475	0·570
Jeweller	0·296	0·420	0·530
Founder	0·307	0·468	0·550
Potter	0·217	0·383	0·540
Lacquerer	0·278	0·465	0·550
Paper-maker	0·186	0·318	0·350
Tobacco-cutter	0·249	0·430	0·540
Confectioner	0·206	0·298	0·330
Compositor	0·239	0·353	0·440
Printer	0·236	0·340	0·390
Shipwright	0·322	0·558	0·700
Gardener	0·291	0·513	0·590
Farm-labourer (Male)	0·185	0·295	0·340
,, (Female)	0·114	0·190	0·210
Sericultural labourer (Male)	0·192	0·308	0·340
,, ,, (Female)	0·125	0·193	0·220
Silk-spinner (Female)	0·135	0·200	0·230
Weaver (Male)	0·182	0·325	0·420
,, (Female)	0·115	0·195	0·210
Fisherman	0·232	0·389	0·400
Day-labourer	0·223	0·365	0·420
Male servant, monthly contract	1·710	2·700	3·300
Female servant ,, ,,	0·930	1·560	2·020
Farm-labourer (Male), yearly contract	21·930	32·120	37·330
Farm-labourer (Female), yearly contract	12·180	17·060	18·670

NOTE.—*Yen* = 2*s.* 0·582*d.*

INDEX